FORM AND SUBSTANCE IN ANGLO-AMERICAN LAW

Form and Substance in Anglo-American Law

A Comparative Study of Legal Reasoning,
Legal Theory, and Legal Institutions

P. S. ATIYAH

AND

ROBERT S. SUMMERS

CLARENDON PRESS · OXFORD
1987

Oxford University Press, Walton Street, Oxford OX2 6DP

Oxford New York Toronto
Delhi Bombay Calcutta Madras Karachi
Petaling Jaya Singapore Hong Kong Tokyo
Nairobi Dar es Salaam Cape Town
Melbourne Auckland

Associated companies in Beirut Berlin Ibadan Nicosia

Oxford is a trade mark of Oxford University Press

Published in the United States
by Oxford University Press, New York

British Library Cataloguing in Publication Data
Atiyah, P. S.
Form and substance in Anglo-American law: a comparative study of legal reasoning, Legal theory, and
Legal institutions.
1. Law—England   2. Law—United States   3. Comparative law
I. Title   II. Summers, Robert S.
344.207   KD660
ISBN 0-19-825577-2

Library of Congress Cataloging-in-Publication Data
Atiyah, P. S.
Form and substance in Anglo-American law.
Bibliography: p.
Includes index.
1. Law—Methodology.   2. Law—Philosophy.
3. Law—Great Britain—History and criticism.
4. Law—United States—History and criticism.
I. Summers, Robert S.
II. Title. K213.A86   1987   340'.2   87-7639
ISBN 0-19-825577-2   342

Printed in Great Britain
at the University Printing House, Oxford
by David Stanford
Printer to the University

Preface

THIS book is a contribution both to legal theory and to comparative studies. Its principal focus is on what we believe to be major differences in the nature of law and the general style of legal reasoning between England and America, which we term 'formal' and 'substantive' respectively. In the process of identifying and explaining these differences, we have found it necessary to construct a fairly elaborate theoretical apparatus about 'formality' as an attribute or property of legal systems, and we hope that this itself constitutes an original contribution to legal theory. If our conclusions about the differences between England and America are correct, we will also have made some contribution to comparative studies. The reader will understand these two systems better, having come to see in general ways what they are, and what they are not, in terms of form and substance.

Our qualifications lie in the fields of law and legal theory, and we have both studied the nature of law and legal reasoning in both countries at first hand for many years. But this book has required us to venture into many broad areas, including some regarded as appropriate fields of study for students of politics, government, sociology and other social sciences. In writing of such matters we have been aware that we ourselves lack some of the expertise of some social scientists, and so (for instance) we have not attempted any sophisticated statistical analyses of comparative data in the two countries we have been studying. But we believe that the differences we analyse in this book are primarily of a qualitative rather than a quantitative character anyway. So although our comparisons often take the form of suggesting that English law and legal reasoning are 'more formal' and the American 'more substantive', we do not purport to measure these differences, or indeed, suggest that they involve quantifiable attributes.

We must also add that there are more assertions in this book which are backed largely by our own judgment than we would have wished. Although in fact we cite here an immense range of literature, writings not hitherto so brought together, some of our assertions about the two legal systems and their different 'styles' depend simply on our own judgment, backed by our own experience. So it is appropriate to say here that each of us has had wide experience, not only of his own legal system but also of the other. Professor Summers has spent three full sabbatical years at Oxford, and has over a period of some 10 years taught at Oregon and Stanford on the west coast of America, at Cornell on the East Coast for twenty years, and at Michigan and Indiana in the heartland for brief periods. Professor Atiyah has over many years taught at Harvard, Yale, Duke and the University of Texas at Austin, as well as at Oxford and other English universities.

This book has throughout been written jointly. Each of us has had a hand in writing and rewriting (often several times) every chapter.

February 1987   P.S.A.
                                                                                 R.S.S.

Acknowledgements

MY first debt is to my son Simon (now an assistant solicitor with Linklaters & Paines) who, while preparing for his final examinations in 1982, asked me about American Realism, and so set me thinking that nobody had ever attempted to explain the relationship between Realism and various institutional aspects of the American legal system—and thus led me to the view that here was a major project worth undertaking.

My academic debts are so great that I now have difficulty in identifying all those who helped me over the last five years. I must mention in particular the participants in a series of seminars I gave in 1982–83 at Harvard, Columbia, Yale, Virginia, and Duke, many of whom put me on the track of materials I would never have otherwise located. Among individuals who took much trouble with early drafts of parts of the book, I owe especial thanks to George Christie, Martin Golding and Robert Stevens. I am grateful to the Dean and Faculty at Cornell for their hospitality to me on several visits, and especially in the Fall of 1986 when I and my co-author spent two intensive weeks finalising the text. Dorothy Summers, too, deserves my warmest thanks for putting up with so much of my presence and her husband's absence on that occasion. I join also my co-author in extending our particular thanks to the many members of the Cornell Law School who gave unstintingly of their time in reading and commenting on successive drafts of this book, and to his research assistants, not forgetting Betsy Summers, who provided invaluable help. Last, but never least, I express my eternal debt to Christine for her never failing encouragement and inspiration.

St. John's College,   P.S.A.
Oxford.

My first debt is also to Simon Atiyah whose questions ultimately led his father and me to undertake this venture, one of the most rewarding of my academic career.

My indebtedness to colleagues and others is too great to acknowledge in full. I must first record my gratitude to the following members of the Cornell Law School faculty (regular and visiting) who commented on one or more chapters of the book in the course of its five drafts: Kevin M. Clermont, Roger C. Cramton, Herbert Hausmaninger, James A. Henderson, Robert A. Hillman, Robert Kent, Geoffrey Marshall, Dale A. Oesterle, Marie Provine, Faust F. Rossi, and Charles Wolfram. I am also indebted for comments and suggestions to lecture audiences and seminar participants at Harvard Law School, Cornell Law School, the University of Western Ontario, University of Tübingen, University of Rotterdam, University of Jerusalem, and the Institute of State and Law of the Academy of Sciences of the U.S.S.R. Finally, I wish to thank my several research assistants at Cornell Law School over the last several years, especially Charles Eberhardt, Class of 1987 and Sterling Harwood, Class of 1984, for their valuable contributions. My daughter, Elizabeth Anne Summers provided much valuable assistance in preparing the final manuscript for publication, and I am most grateful to her.

Cornell Law School   R.S.S.

Contents

A Note on Terminology

IN the title we refer to 'Anglo-American law', and in the body of this book, we refer to England and English law, because England (or more strictly, England and Wales) is an independent legal jurisdiction, and English law differs from Scots law. Our concern is with England and English law, but England has no separate political institutions, (as distinct from legal institutions) and it would be distinctly odd to refer to the 'English Parliament' or the 'English Cabinet'. We therefore refer as appropriate to British political institutions, though strictly speaking it would be more correct to refer to these institutions as those of the United Kingdom as a whole. But this usage is common, and we have adopted it in the interests of simplicity.

We add a few notes on a number of legal terms that are in use in both England and America, but which have different meanings in the two countries:

'Brief' in American parlance is a document setting out in full the legal arguments which a party to a lawsuit, or an appeal, submits for the consideration of the court. In England a 'brief' is a set of written instructions given by a solicitor to a barrister. We hope that our usage of the term is clear from the context.

'Costs' in England includes legal expenses and fees payable to a lawyer, and an order for costs is an order that one party pay the other party's reasonable expenses and fees. In America, 'costs' usually refers only to court costs and excludes legal fees. Again, we think our usage is clear from the context.

'Faculty' in relation to universities in America, means the academic staff; in England, it means the institution itself. Thus English academics would refer to a 'law faculty' where Americans would refer to a 'law school'. We have followed the American usage here.

'High Court' is a term sometimes used in America to refer to the United States Supreme Court; in England it refers to the only court of first instance with unlimited jurisdiction.

'Opinion', in relation to legal cases is the American term for what would be referred to in England as the judgment of a court or judge (or, in the House of Lords, the speech). We have followed American usage.

'Professor' is used in American law schools to refer to most members of the academic staff, whereas in England it is confined to the senior academics. Again, we have followed American usage.

Table of U.K. Cases

Table of U.S. Cases

1

Introduction

1. AIMS

Our aims are to discuss a number of important and interrelated questions about legal reasoning, legal theory, legal institutions, and legal systems, and to use a comparative methodology to advance our understanding of these questions. It is our primary thesis that the American and the English legal systems, for all their superficial similarities, differ profoundly: the English legal system is highly 'formal' and the American highly 'substantive'. The precise meanings we attribute to these concepts will be summarised below and dealt with at length in the next section. Here we will simply make two assertions. First, substantive *reasoning* is used far more widely than formal reasoning in the American system when decisions have to be made or other legal actions taken, while in the English system, the reverse is true. Secondly, this difference in methods of reasoning reflects a deep difference in legal style, legal culture, and, more generally, the *visions* of law which prevail in the two countries. In the course of developing and defending our primary thesis we will suggest a number of explanations for these differences, which are mostly drawn from institutional, historical, and cultural differences between the two countries. We believe that the truth of our thesis is something that many observers have long sensed, or felt in their bones. If we have made a contribution in this book, its form may simply be that we have found a meaningful and credible way to articulate and explain this truth.

In sum:

First, we will show that it is possible and useful to distinguish between two types of legal reasoning, which we shall refer to as substantive and formal reasoning.[1] A substantive reason is a moral, economic, political, institutional, or other social consideration.[2] Thus the fact that D has intentionally harmed P is a reason of substance for deciding that D ought to be required by law to pay damages to P. If the law has not yet invoked

---

[1] See generally P. S. Atiyah, 'Form and Substance in Contract Law', in P. S. Atiyah, *Essays on Contract* (Clarendon Press, Oxford, 1986); R. S. Summers, 'Working Conceptions of the Law', in *Law, Morality and Rights*, 3 (M. A. Stewart, ed., D. Reidel, Dordrecht, 1983) reprinted in 1 *Law and Philosophy* 263 (1982).

[2] See R. S. Summers, 'Two Types of Substantive Reasons: The Core of a Theory of Common-Law Justification', 63 *Cornell L. Rev.* 707 (1978).

such substantive reasoning in this particular way, its incorporation into a legal rule (or other form of law) will create a new source of formal reasoning. A formal reason is a different kind of reason from a substantive reason that has not yet been incorporated in the law at hand.[3] A formal reason is a legally authoritative reason on which judges and others are empowered or required to base a decision or action, and such a reason usually excludes from consideration, overrides, or at least diminishes the weight of, any countervailing substantive reason arising at the point of decision or action. For example, it is a formal reason for making a decision that *there is a valid legal rule that*, in the given circumstances, D ought to be made to pay damages to P. Unlike a substantive reason, a formal reason necessarily presupposes a valid law or other valid legal phenomenon, such as a contract or a verdict. Indeed, the very existence of this law or other legal phenomenon, as interpreted, is a formal reason, or generates a formal reason for deciding an issue. Thus, authoritativeness is an essential attribute of a formal reason. A formal reason is also ordinarily in some degree mandatory, that is, it normally prevails over any contrary substantive reasons in the application of the law. If the existence of a rule, for instance, is treated as a formal reason for deciding the case in the way which the rule prescribes, the existence of the rule is normally a formal reason for making no inquiry into any contrary substantive reasons arising at the point of application. We do not say that there is never any case for inquiring into such reasons, but only that a formal reason usually operates as a sort of barrier which insulates the decision-making process from the reasons of substance not incorporated in the rule, either explicitly or implicitly.

A formal reason usually incorporates or reflects substantive reasoning. Thus it is an admixture of certain formal attributes on the one hand, and substantive reasoning on the other. What we here call formal legal reasons are sometimes called 'authoritative' reasons by others, though authoritative reasons may really be only a subspecies of formal reasons. In section 2 of this chapter we will enlarge on the distinction between substantive and formal reasoning, and we will provide a more detailed account of the various attributes of formal legal reasoning.

Secondly, we will argue that reasons of substance and reasons of form are both widely used in the two legal systems with which we propose to deal, and that it is hardly possible to imagine a legal system which does

---

[3] See J. Raz, 'Reasons for Action, Decisions and Norms', 84 *Mind* 481 (1975); *Practical Reason and Norms*, especially at 35–48 and 58–62 (Hutchinson, London, 1975); J. Raz, *The Authority of Law*, at chs. 1–3 (Clarendon Press, Oxford, 1979); J. Raz, 'Authority and Justification', 14 *Philosophy and Public Affairs* 3 (1985) See also H. L. A. Hart, *Essays on Bentham*, 243–68 (Clarendon Press, Oxford, 1982), and R. S. Summers, *supra*, n. 2, at 724–5 (in which such reasons are called 'authority reasons').

not in practice require both sorts of reasoning; indeed both are inherent in any viable conception of law. But, more importantly, we shall offer detailed support for our primary thesis that the English legal system inclines to the greater use of formal reasons, while the American legal system inclines to the greater use of reasons of substance. Thus, we shall suggest not only that the English legal system tends systematically to decide cases according to what the rules require, but also that it relies on formal reasons in a wide variety of other circumstances in which the American system invokes reasons of substance. Though there are some counter-examples to our thesis, we claim that it holds generally and overwhelmingly.

Thirdly, we shall suggest that legal theories, as well as legal systems, divide according as they incline towards the more formal or the more substantive. Thus at one extreme, we can identify highly positivistic theories which insist that 'the law is the law'—that what is authoritatively laid down is virtually always decisive—and that the prime function of legal theory is to account for such valid law and the formal reasons it generates in terms of rules identifiable by reference merely to formal sources—as precepts 'laid down' by authorized officials. We think that literal methods of interpretation are also part and parcel of such theories. At the other extreme are legal theories which concentrate heavily on the substantive and instrumental content of valid law, stressing, among other things, content-oriented, in addition to source-oriented, criteria for identifying valid law, and the substantive reasons incorporated in or lying behind rules, rather than their mere wording, in determining their meaning. We do not claim that actual legal theories can be simplified in this way; all we claim is that many legal theories, like legal systems, have a tendency, an inclination, a leaning, towards one side or the other of the formal–substantive divide. Again, in our view, English legal theory is, and has long been, in general and relative terms, formal and positivistic, while American theory has been and remains influenced by a variety of more substantive theories, some of the natural law or 'rights' variety, and others of a more instrumental nature.

Fourthly, we claim that the tendency of a legal system to incline to the more formal or to the more substantive forms of legal reasoning is likely to be closely correlated with a large number of historical, cultural, and institutional factors, including, for instance, the prevailing legal theories, the constitutional relationship between courts and legislatures, the political role of the legislature and the executive governments, the customs or practices followed with regard to the selection and tenure of the judiciary, and the nature of a country's legal culture and legal education. In particular, we shall suggest that, in the case of England and the United States, these factors correlate very closely with the degree to which the two systems incline, on the one hand, to the more formal, and on the other, to the more substantive, type of reasoning. We do not offer any simple causal explanations of these relationships; it is unlikely that such explanations are to be found. On the contrary, it seems to us likely that basic differences in the styles of reasoning reflect the sort of legal theory implicitly held, however vaguely and inarticulately, by the community and especially by the judges and lawyers in that community; and that, conversely, the institutional and historical factors which we hope to identify in some detail will also be found to reflect differences in styles of reasoning. At the same time, it seems to us very probable that the nature of legal theories that flourish in a society will have something to do with a country's institutions and history. In addition, we shall suggest that different traditions of official trust and distrust have affected styles of legal reasoning in the two countries, as have also differences in the degree to which the two countries reflect an elitist approach to the enforcement of the law.

We think it is clear that causal influences in these respects do not run solely in one direction. We are confident that all the factors which we intend to discuss have, over the years, influenced other factors and been influenced by them. In the result, we see our work as resembling the putting together of an intricate mosaic pattern—or rather two such patterns—in which all of the pieces in each pattern fit readily together, but could not be fitted readily or at all into the other pattern. Furthermore, although the two patterns bear undeniable resemblances to each other, many of the individual pieces do not.

Fifthly, we shall suggest that a different 'vision' of law prevails in the two countries—a more formal vision in England and a more substantive vision in America. Some of the differences which we identify between the English and the American legal systems seem to us plainly to conform to the formal–substantive divide and yet are not truly instances of legal (or any type of) reasoning. To take just one example here (many more are given later), the fact that most civil actions in America are still tried by juries, while in England they are decided by judges, is not the direct result of any particular styles of reasoning, but it does nevertheless seem to us to conform (for reasons we discuss in chapter 6) to the tendency of the English system to be more formal than the American. A great many other institutional aspects of the two legal systems also seem to be of this character, as we attempt to demonstrate in detail in chapter 15. We refer to differences of this kind as differences in the 'vision' of law held in the two countries, though some could also be said to be differences in legal style or legal culture. By a 'vision' of law we mean, roughly, the inarticulate and perhaps unconscious beliefs held to some degree by the public at large, and more especially by judges and lawyers, as to the nature and functions of law, and as to how and by whom it should be made, interpreted, applied, and enforced. It seems to us plausible that in countries like England and America—with long traditions of democratic government—there will be a close fit (over periods of time) between methods of legal reasoning, prevailing legal theories, and the vision of law which the public and lawyers hold and to which institutional arrangements tend to conform.

Indeed, it is possible (we acknowledge) that what we have said about 'visions' of law simply follows from our approach to legal theories and legal institutions. A 'vision' might be viewed as an inarticulate or implicit legal theory; and certainly there can be no doubt that the English and American visions of law which we identify in this book are closely related to the dominant legal theories in the two countries. And, insofar as we deduce the vision of law which a society holds from its institutional arrangements, we are in danger of double counting the factors on which we base our main thesis. But for some purposes the concept of a 'vision' of law seems a useful one. For instance, some scepticism may be felt at the idea that a legal theory can be found embedded in a community's culture, in such a way as to influence its laws and institutional arrangements. But we see no difficulty in supposing that a community may have a 'vision' of law. One society may, for instance, have a vision of law as 'a system of rules'; another society may lean towards a vision of law as, for instance, 'an outward expression of the community's sense of right or justice'. Indeed, it is our thesis that the former of these is the English vision of what law is, while the latter expresses a strong (and possibly dominant) theme in American legal culture, although we do not deny that the former is also represented in American thinking.

2. FORM AND SUBSTANCE IN LEGAL REASONING

We now proceed to enlarge on our distinction between formal and substantive legal reasoning. We will begin with substantive reasons which, for our purposes, are conceptually less problematic. Substantive reasons serve as the primary ingredients of most constitutions, statutes, precedents, and other legally recognized phenomena (including contracts, verdicts, and the like) which give rise to formal reasoning. It follows, too, that they have primacy when new law is made. They also inform the content of the very standards of criticism and evaluation brought to bear on existing law.

A substantive reason may be defined as a moral, economic, political, institutional, or other social consideration. Two basic types of substantive reasons are 'goal' reasons and 'rightness' reasons. A good goal reason derives its justificatory force from the fact that, at the time it is given, the decision (or rule) it supports can be predicted to have effects that serve a good social goal, such as the promotion of general safety, the reinforcement of the family, or the facilitation of democracy.[4] A good rightness reason does not derive its distinctive justificatory force from such expected consequences as such, but from the way in which the decision (or rule) adopted accords with a socio-moral norm of rightness, as applied to a party's past actions, or to a state of affairs resulting from those actions. Norms of rightness bring into play concepts of equity, fairness, good faith, justified reliance, and other similar ideas. The applicability of rightness norms cannot be determined without reference to how the case for decision *came about*.[5] Thus rightness reasons are distinctively past-regarding (or backward-looking) in character, while goal reasons are consequentialist and hence forward looking. Many examples of both basic types of substantive reasons are already widely incorporated in Anglo-American law. Often both will be relevant in the same decisional context.

Substantive reasons inform the content of constitutions, statutes, precedents, and other legally recognized phenomena such as contracts, verdicts, and the like. Such reasons also lead a more independent life of their own, outside and in relation to the law. As already noted, they are brought to bear in evaluating and criticizing the law; they also serve as raw material for the making of wholly new statutes and may play a role in filling gaps in statutes and even in elaborating statutory fragments. In the common law, they are one of the principal bases upon which cases of first impression are decided, and are also often invoked when choices have to be made between conflicting precedents.[6] They may also emerge in the application of the law and compel modifications in the common law. In sum, substantive reasons are to be found both 'in the law' and 'outside the law', so to speak, although we do not think that a substantive reason can be 'in the law' without acquiring a minimal formal element, as we explain later. When particular substantive reasons are not already in the law at hand, they may be usefully thought of as potentially available for incorporation. But although they may exist 'outside the law', they may be influenced by the law; just as they shape the law, so it shapes them.[7]

---

[4] Summers, *supra*, n. 2, at 735–52.

[5] *Ibid.*, at 752–74.

[6] For a detailed discussion of the ways in which common law courts justify such decisions without engaging in close assessments of conflicting substantive reasons, see Summers, 'On Why Courts in Cases not Governed by Binding Law Seldom Need to Assess Closely the Relative Justificatory Force of Conflicting Substantive Reasons' (forthcoming) (1987).

[7] See Summers, 'Some Considerations which May Lead Lawmakers to Modify a Policy when Adopting it As Law', 141 *Zeitschrift für die gesamte Staatswissenschaft* 41 (1985).

When incorporated in a rule (or other legal phenomenon), substantive reasons combine with one or more formal attributes and thereby give rise to one kind—the most common kind—of formal reason. This kind of formal reason is therefore an admixture of particular substantive reasoning and specific formal attributes.

Formal reasons are different in that they frequently do not bring substantive reasons directly into play, even when substantive reasons are explicitly incorporated into the law at hand. A rule, for instance, may incorporate substantive reasons and yet operate as an independent reason for action even when the substantive reasons do not apply, or even when those reasons may point to a contrary conclusion. A formal reason can be a *good* reason for a legal decision or other actions. Thus, contrary to frequent American practice, we do not use the term 'formal' pejoratively. Indeed, one of our principal purposes is to rehabilitate formal legal reasoning, because we are convinced that formal reasons are central to law, and that their proper analysis is one of the most neglected topics in the history of modern legal theory. We have found some work on this topic to be highly suggestive, notably that of Professor Joseph Raz,[8] but we depart from his views in many major respects, and amplify them in many other respects. What we now present on this subject is not merely essential to the clarification of our primary thesis, but is also offered in the hope that it will contribute to jurisprudential understanding of formal reasons as such.

In one common paradigm case, a formal reason is a legally recognized (valid) requirement for writing, or sealing, or perhaps for registration or attestation of some kind. When a document fails to comply with stipulated forms, the law may declare the document to be legally ineffective. A contract, for instance, or a will, required to be in writing, may be declared void or unenforceable for the formal reason that the requirement of writing or a seal, or the like, was not observed. A substantive reason (or reasons) is, of course, reflected in such a requirement, for example, that of ensuring that contract rights and the like have a reliable evidentiary foundation. But the reasoning arising under such a requirement is formal in two important respects. First of all, it is authoritatively formal. It derives from or is generated by a valid legal rule or other legal phenomenon. Second, it is mandatorily formal, that is, it generally overrides or excludes any competing substantive reason. Thus we do not stop in general (though there may be exceptions) to ask whether the failure to comply with a legal requirement for a valid will or contract is outweighed by some other substantive reason in favour of giving legal force to the will or contract. Once the legal rule of

---

[8] See *supra*, n. 3.

ineffectiveness for lack of writing or the like is clearly established, the application of that rule usually shuts out from consideration particular substantive arguments in favour of validity or enforcement, however weighty.

Formal reasons are often *identified* with writing and similar requirements. But this is a mistake. Formal reasons are to be found everywhere in the law, even though not normally referred to as such. Countless statutes give rise to reasons that are highly formal not only in the sense that they are authoritative (legally valid) but also in the sense that they are categorically mandatory. Let us suppose such a statute, one that prohibits the driving of vehicles in a park, and John drives through the park because he is taking a short cut in order to avoid being late for an important meeting. In these circumstances John has a substantive reason for driving through the park. But a judge has no cause to take account of such a substantive reason when it emerges in the particular context with which he has to deal. Ordinarily, the application of a statutory provision simply excludes from consideration such arguments even though they would be relevant in the absence of the statute. Unless there is room for argument about the constitutionality of the statute, or about its interpretation, it is ordinarily pointless to adduce arguments to suggest that the statute leads to unfair results, or odd results, or anomalous results. Still less is it permissible to argue that, whatever may have been the position when the statute was first passed, conditions have so changed, or even the composition of the legislature has so changed, that to give effect to the Act would be to decide contrary to present day social or moral views, or contrary to the views of the majority in the present legislative assembly.[9] In all ordinary cases the statute is, and is intended to be, a formal source of law in the sense that it is intended to exclude from consideration countervailing arguments against the result which the statute dictates. The statute is not just one additional reason to be taken account of by the judge, a reason which may tip the scales in one direction or be overridden by contrary substantive arguments. The statute shuts out contrary arguments.

If a valid statute could be disregarded by a judge whenever he felt that it led to a result which he would not have reached in the absence of the statute, then a statute would cease to be a formal reason for deciding a case in the sense in which we are using the term. It would even cease to be a formal reason for making a decision if the substantive reasons enshrined in the statute were simply treated as additional arguments to be considered along with all the other reasons of substance bearing on

---

[9] But see G. Calabresi, *A Common Law for the Age of Statutes* (Harvard U. Press, Cambridge, 1982).

the case, with the reasons so enshrined having no primacy over other reasons. This does not mean that the strength of formal statutory reasoning does not vary; on the contrary, it is part of our thesis that there are major differences between the extent to which statutes are taken to generate formal reasons in England and America, a topic to which we will return in chapter 4. Here, it is enough to stress that in both countries statutes generate countless formal reasons for decision.

We also take the system of precedent to be a source of formal reasoning. According to the theory of the common law, some precedents are binding on some courts in the sense that the judges in a subsequent case are bound or obliged to follow the principle of the first case even though the substantive reasoning on which it rests may be weak and the countervailing substantive considerations may be strong. In our terminology, such binding precedents generate formal reasons for decisions.

Here, however, the degree of formality is lower than it is with regard to statutes. Not everything that is said in a case is regarded as part of the *ratio decidendi* binding on subsequent judges. Sometimes a subsequent court will have power to alter or depart from a precedent. Further, a subsequent court may be able to distinguish the earlier case; and in any event, there are often rules and practices about the relative hierarchy of courts which mean that superior courts are not bound by the decisions of inferior courts. Again, practice on these matters varies from country to country, time to time, and even judge to judge; and we do not underestimate the significance of these variations in practice. Indeed, it will be part of our thesis that the variations between England and America are very substantial. Moreover, precedent may sometimes be treated merely as an additional reason for deciding in a certain way, rather than as a different kind of reason which shuts out of consideration later contrary substantive reasons. But still, at the end of the day, wherever the common law operates, there must, we think, be many cases where a court feels obliged to follow a precedent of a higher court, solely and simply because that precedent is regarded as a formal reason for making a decision, excluding from consideration all contrary reasons of substance. Even in America, with its much looser doctrine of *stare decisis* than exists in England, inferior courts often have to bow before higher court decisions without any real possibility of evading them or narrowly construing them or distinguishing them away.

If we turn away from the effect of precedents on lower courts and consider their effect on other officials, or even on the citizens at large, it seems still more clear that precedents are treated as normatively formal sources of law binding on everyone, unless and until other courts pronounce on the issues.

It is important to be clear that formal reasoning is nearly always subject to limitations. At some point in determining the bearing of even the most formal reason, it may become appropriate to examine substantive reasons and even to allow substantive reasons to outweigh the formal reasons. Thus to apply the words of a statute literally is an example of formal reasoning, and if the statute is perfectly clear and raises no constitutional issue, then on a formal view there is no room for an inquiry into its underlying substantive reasons at all. But beyond a certain point, even in systems which take such a formal view, this will no longer be so; for instance, if the statute seems to lead to absurd or outrageous results, substantive reasons may outweigh the formal reasoning involved in literal application. We will return to the question of the limits of formal reasoning in a variety of contexts. However, it must be stressed that the very concept of a formal reason, as we use the term, entails that there are *some* circumstances in which countervailing reasons of substance cannot be used to outweigh the formal reason. A statute or binding precedent gives rise to a formal reason because it *sometimes* must be applied even though there are reasons of substance which would—absent the statute or precedent—dictate a contrary result.

It is tempting to identify formal reasons exclusively with rules, but this is too narrow. There are very many recognized legal phenomena which figure in formal reasoning, some of which we will consider at greater length in the course of this book. Many of these phenomena can only be subsumed under the category of rules by a process of definition. Here we simply offer a list of some typical varieties of reasons which are often highly formal, annotated only to the extent necessary to show why we understand them to generate formal reasoning:

1. *Rules* clearly give rise to formal reasons, though (as we shall see later) some rules are much more formal than others: we discuss rules more fully in chapter 3.

2. *Judgments and verdicts*, once final, are formal reasons for determining what are the rights and liabilities of parties bound by them. Issues finally determined by a judgment are (within limits) conclusive. A final judgment that finds the plaintiff to have a certain right cannot generally be attacked with substantive reasons which tend to show that he should not have that right.

3. *Procedural law*, such as statutes of limitation, jurisdictional rules, and so on, often dramatically require decisions to be made without examination of substantive reasons which would favour a different decision.

4. *Matters of status*, such as marital or citizenship status, may be

formal reasons for recognition of certain rights or duties. Thus an obligation may be imposed on a man to maintain his wife (or former wife) just because she is (or was) his wife; reasons of substance favouring a contrary result may be irrelevant (although, of course, that is a matter of actual law, and today may only be so within narrow limits). Similarly, a person's birth in a particular country may, without consideration of reasons of substance at all, give him the right of citizenship in that country. Contrary reasons of substance (for example, that his family came from a different country, that he does not speak the language, and that he has not lived there for twenty years) may simply be legally irrelevant to the conclusion. Similar to matters of status law are laws governing legal personality which also often operate in a highly formal way, shutting out from consideration, for example, the fact that corporations are artificial legal persons and that real persons may own or manage the business of the corporation.

5. *Arbitrary norms as to time, place, or quantity* are often formal in the various respects. Many such norms are, of course, to be found in rules; but some of them are constitutive of institutions rather than rules as such, for instance, the requirement that there should be twelve members for a jury and perhaps also that there should be two witnesses to a will. Such requirements are also to a high degree formal in their selection of these particular numbers. This means that it is rarely possible to invoke reasons of substance in a particular case to justify departure from the requisite number.

6. *Rules crystallizing rights or duties out of many variables* may also be formal, as in the case of status rules referred to above. It is also arguable that contractual liability often rests ultimately on a similar formal idea, namely, that a party who makes a promise for consideration is to be treated as (almost) conclusively acknowledging that the consideration justifies the imposition on him of the particular duties which he includes in his promise.[10] Less controversially, perhaps, it seems clear that in practice a signature is often treated as a formal reason for holding a party bound by the contents of a written contract, even though he has not read it.

3. DIFFERENT TYPES OF FORMALITY IN LEGAL REASONING

Formal reasons may be more or less formal in a variety of different ways. Here we discuss four different kinds of formality which characterize the degree of formality of legal reasoning.

[10] See Atiyah, *supra*, n. 1.

Authoritative formality

Rules or other phenomena (such as contracts or verdicts) which generate reasons must be recognized as legally authoritative. This kind of formality is a matter of degree, and may be divided into 'high' and 'low' along two different continua. First, a formal reason may have what we will call high or low 'validity formality'. (By 'validity' we mean roughly 'recognized as legally authoritative'.) Some legal standards by which the validity of legal phenomena is determined are solely 'source-oriented' and thus purely formal. A standard that says, 'A duly enacted statute is law', is an example, for it requires inquiry not into substance, but solely into the mode of origin to determine validity.

It is also possible for a reason to have *no* validity formality at all, as where a decision-maker resorts entirely to reasons of substance not previously recognized in the law. But once such substantive reasons are incorporated *in the law*, they necessarily acquire some element of validity formality, though the degree may initially be low. For example, a moral reason (not already incorporated in the law) which is relied upon in a common law case of first impression will have no validity formality at all until used as the basis for the decision. Once so used, it will have some validity formality, the degree of which will depend on the status of the court, the extent to which the reason has been relied upon in the court's opinion, and various other factors.

There is thus a spectrum, extending from purely source-based reasoning at one end—highest validity formality—to purely substantive reasoning at the other end—no validity formality. The latter end of the spectrum falls (just) outside the boundaries of the law, but the remainder of the spectrum covers the entire range of legal authoritativeness. Within this range, legal validity may be (as we have said) solely source-based or it may depend on some mix of source- and content-oriented reasoning. To the extent that validity is solely a matter of source, the formal reasoning generated by the resulting rule or other legally recognized phenomena has, in our terms, high 'validity formality'. To the extent that validity is also a matter of satisfying content-oriented tests, the reasoning it generates may be said to be more substantive, and thus to have lower 'validity formality'.

Authoritative formality is also a function of what we call 'rank' formality. A formal reason may have high or low rank formality. In a well-ordered legal system, all formal reasons have a rank in light of rules of priority. But no mere substantive reason (not incorporated in the law) has any degree of rank formality. Thus, in Anglo-American law, constitutional provision displaces contrary statute, statute displaces contrary contract, contract displaces contrary custom, and so on. The formal reasons involved have a higher or lower rank and thus a higher or lower formality not only in relation to each other, but also in relation to mere substantive reasons not incorporated in the law, for the latter have no formal rank at all. Hence substantive reasons drawn from outside the law, for instance from the writings of law professors, can only be ranked by whatever justificatory force they have. (Rules of rank formality may themselves be applied with high or low mandatory formality, which we deal with further below. In England, for instance, this tends to be high. But in America judges often determine issues of hierarchical priority in major part by reference to substantive reasons arising out of the context.)

These two factors of authoritative formality do not necessarily 'track' each other, that is to say, a given formal reason may have high validity formality (its validity may derive solely from source) and yet have low rank formality (it may stem from a low-level source).

Content formality

The particular content of a legal rule (or other authoritative phenomenon), and so the content of the formal reasons it generates, may be shaped by an element of the arbitrary or by relevant reasons of substance, or both. Two factors determine the degree of content formality: the extent to which the rule (or other phenomenon) is shaped by fiat and the extent to which it is under-inclusive or over-inclusive in relation to its objectives, that is, the extent to which cases which the purposes of the rule would embrace are omitted from the rule's coverage, and cases which the purposes of the rule do not embrace are in fact covered by the rule.

If the rule is shaped largely by fiat, it may be said to have high content formality; if shaped largely by particular reasons of substance, it has low content formality. The rule of the road, for instance ('Keep right (or left)'), is an example of a formal reason with high content formality. The choice of one side or the other is largely, perhaps entirely, a matter of fiat. Similarly, to the extent that rules are under-inclusive or over-inclusive, they generate formal reasons that are largely arbitrary, and so have higher content formality. Requirements of form, such as a rule requiring a will to be signed by two witnesses, are often significantly over-inclusive (they invalidate wills even where there is ample evidence from other sources that the will does represent the testator's true desires) and to that extent have higher content formality.

The law often contains different rules, some with high and some with low content formality, covering very much the same terrain. Road traffic laws may, for instance, prohibit driving 'without due care' (low content formality) or driving in excess of a specified speed limit (high content formality), or driving while drunk (low content formality) or driving with a blood alcohol level in excess of a specified figure (high content formality). Even such a simple matter as the laws governing traffic lights can be geared to higher content formality (no right—or left—turn at red lights)—the English rule, or lower content formality (right turn permitted if the motorist reasonably judges it safe in the circumstances)—the rule of many American states.

It is not always easy to measure the extent to which rules have high content formality, partly because the purposes behind the rules are not always clear, or are ambiguous in certain respects. But it is evident that legal rules vary greatly in their degree of content formality. Many rules of the common law are largely substantive in content in both countries, such as the basic rules of tort law concerning damage done by one person to another. A rule which requires a person to avoid causing injury by the failure to take reasonable care is directly oriented to the substantive merits of a class of disputes, and is thus a rule of minimal content formality. Statutory rules, however, are in fixed verbal form, whereas it is very exceptional for common law rules even to approximate to a fixed verbal form. Naturally, rules in such a form tend to be more over-inclusive and under-inclusive. Moreover, statutory rules tend to have more arbitrary content, at least in the sense that there will be many more or less arbitrary provisions as to time, place, and amount in statutes dealing (for instance) with taxation or social security. As we shall see further in chapter 4, these comments all bear on our primary thesis. The same rules of the common law tend to have less content formality in America than in England; statute law tends to be more precisely drafted in England, and to that extent has more of the arbitrary and thus higher content formality than in America; and statute law is itself generally a more important form of law in England than in America.

Where rules have minimum content formality, like many rules of the common law, it may seem somewhat paradoxical to refer to them overall as 'formal' or as generating formal reasons. Yet we know of no better term for our purposes. In any event, when a rule is highly substantive and thus has low content formality, the reasons it generates may still be highly formal in other respects, that is, in authoritative source, as well as in mandatory formality and in interpretive formality (which we have yet to deal with). In these cases it remains appropriate to refer to such reasons as in some degree formal in one or more of these respects, even where the rule or other phenomenon has low content formality.

Interpretive formality

Any species of valid law generating a formal reason may require some interpretation, but precisely what is (or should be) involved in such interpretation is a highly controversial question. We do not profess here to offer anything in the nature of a general theory of interpretation, but merely to identify one key element in any such theory—the degree of formality involved in the interpretive process.

Interpretative methods may be more or less formal, and may thus shape the resulting formal legal reason. An interpretation is highly formal if it merely focuses on literal meanings of words, or on the narrow confines of normative conduct or other phenomena to be interpreted. Interpretation may be less formal and more substantive, in one of two ways. Interpretation may be substantive to the extent that the interpreter searches for and gives effect to underlying purposes and rationales which are implicit in the text or which can be ascertained from other sources (such as legislative history). Sometimes no such purposes or rationales can be identified, but interpretation can still be susbtantive to the extent that the decision-maker then relies on substantive reasons drawn from other, non-legal sources—for example, where a judge draws on his own background political morality,[11] or on a political morality which he attributes to the legislature or to the public. Both these methods of interpretation are substantive and thus differ from more formal interpretive reasoning.

The first of these two substantive methods or styles requires a search for the substantive reasoning underlying a rule (or other phenomenon). But merely because a rule may incorporate or derive from a substantive reason (or several such reasons) it does not follow that the rule does so plainly or clearly. The substantive reason for a rule may not appear very obviously on the face of the rule.[12] Moreover, the literal language of the rule not infrequently forecloses a possible interpretation that may really be more faithful to the underlying substantive reasons which influenced the lawmakers. Legal systems vary greatly in the degree to which they permit interpreters to go behind the verbal expression of the law and thus engage in reasoning that is more substantive than formal in deciding what the law itself *is* in the first place.

Not all types of law or other legal phenomena are equally susceptible of a high degree of interpretive formality. Statutes and other kinds of law in fixed verbal form are most susceptible to this kind of formality. Case law is incapable of the same high degree of interpretive formality as statute law.

It will be seen that interpretation in the light of the substantive purposes and reasons behind the words—low interpretive formality—

---

[11] See Dworkin, '"Natural" Law Revisited', 34 *U. Fla. L. Rev.* 165, 173 (1982).

[12] Llewellyn once wrote that 'The best of [rules] are relatively clear as to whether and when they apply; the best of them are shrewdly tailored to significant types of problem-situation; the best of them carry, also, their reason on their face'. *The Common Law Tradition: Deciding Appeals*, 335 (Little Brown, Boston, 1960).

may operate to reduce one kind of content formality, that is, arbitrariness in the form of under- or over-inclusion.

Mandatory formality

We have said that a formal reason typically has the attribute to some degree of overriding, or excluding from consideration, or diminishing the weight of, at least some contrary substantive reasons. This is what we call mandatory formality. We can distinguish between the prima-facie mandatory formality of rules and other legal phenomena which generate reasons, on the one hand, and the ultimate degree of mandatory formality that remains after defences and collateral doctrines have been taken into account. Prima-facie mandatory formality can be high or low. For instance, a rule prohibiting the playing of musical instruments in the park in unqualified terms is at least prima facie of high mandatory formality; on the other hand, a rule prohibiting the playing of *unreasonably noisy* musical instruments is clearly of lower prima-facie mandatory formality. The first rule prima facie excludes from consideration a wider range of substantive reasons than the second.

But mandatory formality can also be profoundly affected by what happens at the point of application or enforcement of rules. Rules (or other phenomena) of any degree of prima-facie mandatory formality can be cut down at the point of application by the extent to which countervailing considerations are accorded legal effect. Such countervailing considerations often operate by virtue of defences or of collateral doctrines explicitly adopted in the law. They can operate to cut down rules (or other phenomena) of high or low prima-facie mandatory formality. Such operative defensive or collateral doctrines can be of various types. The high prima-facie mandatory formality of a statute prohibiting vehicles in the park may, for example, be:

(1) explicitly or implicitly qualified (for example, 'unless the park police in their discretion waive the prohibition');
(2) defeasible (for example, a driver in the park is not guilty if he can prove duress, entrapment, or the like);[13]
(3) subject to overriding public welfare or other exceptions (for example, emergency driving of an ambulance through the park);
(4) limited in scope (for example, the statute simply does not apply to a park employee emptying the trash cans into his truck);[14]

---

[13] On duress, entrapment, and the like see chapter 6.

[14] This may also be thought of as a special kind of interpretation problem, see Easterbrook, 'Statutes' Domains', 50 *U. Ch. L. Rev.* 533 (1983); Scott, 'The Judicial Power to Apply Statutes to Subjects to Which They Were not Intended to be Applied', 14 *Temp. L. Q.* 318 (1940).

(5) subject to discretionary non-enforcement or minimal sanctioning;
(6) weak in authoritative force;[15]
(7) or subject to being disregarded because of absurdity or manifest injustice.

Mandatory formality, like other varieties of formal reasoning, is thus a matter of degree. A formal reason not only has some prima-facie mandatory formality, but, after defences and collateral doctrines have been taken into account, a formal reason typically continues to exclude, or override, or assign diminished weight to (at least) some countervailing considerations arising at the point of application. The extent to which otherwise relevant substantive considerations are thus overridden, excluded, or diminished in weight—either prima facie or at the point of application—determines the ultimate degree of mandatory formality of the reason. Clearly, not all formal reasons are of maximal mandatory formality: in fact they distribute themselves at various points along a continuum.[16]

There is one other respect in which mandatory formality can be said to be higher or lower. The mandatory formality of a formal reason may be more or less drastic in terms of the nature of the substantive analysis that is overridden or excluded or diminished in weight. It is one thing to preclude a weighing of substantive reasons against a formal reason where the former merely emerges at the point of application; it is far more drastic for a formal reason to operate so as to preclude any inquiry into the substantive, and therefore legally recognized, merits of the case at hand. Yet even the latter may happen with reasons of high mandatory formality, for instance, under certain rules of jurisdiction, or under statutes of limitation.

Varieties of formality

We have now identified the four key attributes of formal reasoning embodied in the law (authoritative or validity formality, mandatory formality, content formality, and interpretive formality) and one additional type of formality (rank formality) which is directly linked to the first of these four.

But there are also other varieties of formality, which are not so much attributes of formal reasoning, as general features of the style or vision of

---

[15] For example, the case may be procedurally borderline, may be lacking in overall substantive justification, etc.

[16] Here in particular we depart from Raz, Hart, and others who see mandatory formality as categorical or 'on–off' rather than as a matter of degree. See Raz and Hart, works cited in n. 3. Raz would presumably also call this attribute of formality 'exclusionary', but we prefer the word 'mandatory' because it more felicitously encompasses both the affirmative requirements and the exclusionary operation of this attribute of formality.

a legal system. For instance, we have suggested that legal theories may be more or less formal, and we return to deal with this in chapters 8 and 9. We have also referred to differing 'visions' of law, a matter we revert to from time to time and summarise in chapter 15. In addition, we have referred to 'rule of law formality', a kind of formality we do not deal with in any detail, but which is easily identifiable as a set of general formal reasons which often override, exclude, or diminish the weight of substantive considerations in the interests of certainty, predictability, and the control of official power.

Later we shall also identify and deal more fully with two other varieties of formality—'truth formality' and 'enforcement formality'. The first of these concerns the degree to which a legal system identifies the 'true facts' to which legal rules and other phenomena relate. A legal system may be said to be more formal to the extent to which it successfully identifies the 'true facts' and applies its rules and other norms to those facts. We return to this in chapter 6. 'Enforcement formality' concerns a related matter. Even assuming true facts are ascertained, how far are legal rules and other norms actually translated into practice? A legal system may be said to be more formal to the extent to which it strives to ensure a high degree of obedience and enforcement of the law. We deal more fully with this in chapter 7.

Both 'truth' and 'enforcement' formality are clearly linked with the other kinds of formality which we have identified. Plainly, the four key varieties of formality presuppose a high degree of 'truth' and 'enforcement' formality, and it would be surprising if a legal system made extensive use of reasoning of high formality while being indifferent to 'truth' and 'enforcement' formality. In fact (we argue later) the English system is, in various respects, more devoted to both truth and enforcement formality than the American.

It is possible that still other varieties of formality can be identified. We think we have identified the most important, but our treatment is not necessarily exhaustive in these respects.

Relationships between the different types of formality

The four key attributes of formal reasoning may all be reflected in the same formal reason at high levels of formality. Assume, for example, that a statute prohibits vehicles in the park between 6 a.m. and 6 p.m., and that the employer of an ambulance driver is charged under this statute because his employee drove an ambulance through the park at 6.05 a.m. If the statute is used to justify convicting the employer in such a case, it may provide a reason of high formality in all four dimensions: (1) high authoritative formality (the statute may be treated as valid law solely by virtue of its formal source); (2) high content formality (in that the precise time limits are arbitrary, and the statute may be both over-inclusive and under-inclusive); (3) high interpretive formality (if, for instance, a search for the rationale of the statute would show that the legislature only intended to penalize actual *drivers* and not employers); and (4) high mandatory formality excluding as irrelevant any substantive reasons arising from the emergency which demanded the presence of the ambulance in the park, and also meaning that the statute is probably not qualified or defeasible or limited by reference to such substantive considerations. On the other hand, a given formal reason may be of high formality in one dimension, and of lower formality in other dimensions. No one type of formality necessarily follows in the footsteps of another type of formality.

Not all the various formal attributes of a reason are essential to its status as a formal reason. It must have some authoritative and some degree of mandatory formality, but it is not essential that a formal reason have any degree of content formality (arbitrariness).[17] Nor is it necessary that a formal reason have any degree of interpretive formality—the interpreter may, for instance, consider fully the substantive considerations shaping a statutory rule, but the rule, when so interpreted, may still be a rule of high content and mandatory formality.

Although we have said that the formal attributes do not necessarily track each other, it is possible for all the key formal attributes to exist to a very high degree—as in our example above—and conversely it is also possible for the substantive side of formal reasons to be overwhelmingly predominant. There is, however, an asymmetry here which is implicit in what we have already said. A reason for decision in law *can be* entirely formal in all four key ways we have identified. But a *purely* substantive reason cannot (as we have already explained) exist *in the law*. If it is truly incorporated in the law, it must have at least the formal attributes of authoritative and mandatory formality to some degree. And although the substantive side may be overwhelmingly predominant, a legal reason can never be drawn exclusively from substantive considerations. But because important legal agencies—especially courts—are empowered to incorporate substantive reasons into the law and then, in the same proceedings, may at once proceed to apply the formal legal norms thereby recognized or created, this point may be of little practical significance.

The subtle ways in which the four key kinds of formality interrelate can be seen by looking at one particular problem to which we have so far adverted in only general terms. We have said above that there are nearly

---

[17] For a different view, see Fuller, 'Reason and Fiat in Case Law', 59 *Harv. L. Rev.* 376 (1946).

always limits to the use of formal reasoning in the law. At some point, formal reasons may produce results which are so obnoxious to all substantive considerations that the decision-maker will reject the mandatory formality of the formal reason and treat the substantive reasons underlying the formal rule as outweighed by newly emerging substantive considerations. But the precise point at which this becomes permissible will itself have to be determined by further criteria, which may themselves be more or less formal in any one of the relevant senses of the term. So (for example) the point at which a court may be entitled to reject the authority of a precedent may itself be determined by criteria with high content formality, high authoritative and rank formality, and so on. Thus if more or less precise rules exist—have been laid down by higher courts—for determining what parts of a precedent are binding (how to select the *ratio decidendi*), if more or less precise rules have also been laid down for deciding when a higher court decision may be discarded as not binding, and so on, the resulting process is one with high formality. The ultimate result may be one of mandatory formality, in that once the court reaches the decision that the precedent is binding, contrary reasons of substance are excluded from consideration; but on the way to that conclusion, other types of formality—authoritative (and rank) formality and content formality—may well be involved. If, on the other hand, the circumstances in which a court is entitled to reject the authority of a higher court decision are less precise, tend not to have been laid down in any authoritative manner, and so on, the mandatory effect of the precedent as a source of formal reasoning is greatly weakened by the ad hoc use of imprecise criteria from case to case in this way.

The same goes for statutes. In a more formal system of law, we should expect to find more or less precise *rules* prescribing when, and to what extent, it is permissible to set aside the literal words of the statute and search for the underlying reasons of substance. In a system of law less inclined to formal reasoning, we should expect to find that the point at which literal interpretation has to give way to more substantive considerations will itself be determined by vaguer criteria, that is, by reasons with lower content formality, and very likely also by criteria which owe little to authoritative or rank formality.

The presence or absence of formal attributes in the typical formal reason is thus a matter of degree and reflects the particular admixture of form and substance involved. When formality is high overall, the substantive side will be low; when formality is low, the substantive side of the reason will be high. The justificatory force of the resulting reasoning is then largely traceable to some combination of the justificatory force of the particular substantive reasons informing the rule or other phenomena involved, and some more general substantive reasons—second-level reasons—which may be said to justify the practice of formal reasoning. It is to these second-level reasons or rationales that we now turn.

4. SECOND LEVEL SUBSTANTIVE REASONS

A second-level substantive reason is a type of reason that may justify a general practice of relying on first level substantive reasoning or on first-level formal reasoning.

Substantive reasoning

It seems hardly necessary to attempt to explain what are the general second level rationales for the widespread practice of incorporating particular lower level substantive reasons into the law. Indeed, the justification for the particular substantive reasons incorporated into the law (and thus given authoritative status) must be the same as the justification for the general substantive considerations themselves. Clearly, this hardly needs explanation or justification. A body of law totally devoid of substantive reasons is scarcely imaginable. No legal system could exist, let alone flourish, on pure arbitrariness, pure fiat; further, the under-inclusion or over-inclusion of rules is scarcely intelligible except in relation to substantive aims. We believe, therefore, that substantive reasoning necessarily informs the content of a very large part of the law. Consider, for example, legal rules protecting the inviolability of the person, rules protecting property, and rules for the enforcement of contracts. The content of all these rules is informed by substantive reasoning, and no modern legal system could be viable without rules having such content. Indeed, we may wonder whether a legal system without a very large content of substantive reasoning could qualify, conceptually, as a legal system at all.[18] There may well be, indeed, almost necessarily will be, limits within which even reasons of substance can be considered, because there will be further, more remote, formal reasons determining *that* question in almost any imaginable situation. Still, within whatever limits, reasons of substance must have their place.

For present purposes, the more interesting aspect of the rationale of substantive reasoning is its relationship to formal reasoning. Clearly, second level reasons of substance often explain the degree to which lower level reasons of substance may be resorted, even when formal reasons are under consideration. First, and most obviously, reasons of substance

---

[18] See generally H. L. A. Hart, *The Concept of Law*, 189–95 (Clarendon Press, Oxford, 1961) on the minimum substantive content of rules necessary for a viable legal system.

must be used when rules are being formulated. If there is no existing rule to cover a problem, or if a legislature is debating the making of a new rule, then, usually, the nature of that rule will be largely determined by appropriate reasons of substance. Similarly, reasons of substance must be examined whenever any other kind of formal reason is being recognized or established. But secondly, and equally important, formal reasons are rarely, if ever, absolute. The prima-facie mandatory force of a formal reason is subject to being cut down by various collateral doctrines, such as those we have identified above, which draw their force from substantive considerations. Furthermore, a rule (as we have said) is a formal reason for a decision, but rules have to be interpreted and applied. The interpreter may be entitled to 'stretch' the rule, or give it some benign construction in order to achieve goals which are felt to be substantively desirable. If he does that, he will be considering reasons of substance, and placing some limits on the formal reason supplied by the rule itself.

Let us reflect on some examples. The effect of a final judgment of a disputed piece of litigation must be, in any mature legal system, to bring to an end some part at least of the dispute which has been determined. The judgment in future will regulate the rights and duties of the parties without further examination of the underlying position. Yet all this is only true within limits. The judgment may be appealed, or set aside for fraud; it may be held not to dispose of collateral issues, or to bind third parties. These limits will all involve, or may all involve, considerations of substance.

Similarly, jurisdictional rules are often very formal. If a judge simply has no jurisdiction to hear a case, it is useless to press him with reasons of substance addressed to the merits of the case; indeed, where there is any serious contest over jurisdiction, a judge will often hear the argument on that point and make his decision before proceeding (if ever) to hear the case on its merits. But a jurisdictional claim is rarely quite so simple that reasons of substance are totally irrelevant. An English judge, for instance, reviewing the legality of the action of some administrative body, has, in theory, no power, no jurisdiction, to enter into the merits of the decision made, unless some error of law has been perpetrated. He is only concerned with the legality of the decision, and with ensuring that proper procedures have been observed. But in reality, the line between the one and the other may be very thin. A judge who feels that the decision of the administrative body is very bad, as a matter of substance, may strive to find that the decision was also unlawful. Furthermore, within limits, this may be perfectly acceptable: a very bad decision approaches the point at which a decision *ought* to be regarded as without a basis in law. But it is easy to see that there is room for two approaches here: on the one hand, a more formal approach which stresses procedures and ignores the actual decision and the reasons of substance for it, and on the other hand, a more substantive approach in which reasons of substance are given greater weight. The justification for one approach rather than another must lie with second-level substantive reasons.

Formal reasoning

We now turn to the second-level substantive rationales for the practice of recognizing formal reasons within a legal system. At the outset we are faced with a genuine dilemma. Rules even of the highest content formality—very arbitrary rules, or rules of high over- and under-inclusiveness—are themselves justified in ultimate terms by reference to substantive reasoning at a second-level. General substantive reasoning in the name of 'rule of law' values (including the desirability of having some checks on official power) and in the name of efficiency, or for institutional reasons, can usually be given to justify the whole practice of acting on formal reasons. For example, acting on formal reasons may operate more certainly and more predictably (and they may be more efficiently self-applied) than always acting for substantive considerations. This is why detailed and precise rules with high content formality are often found preferable to broad rules of very low content formality. Statutory codes governing the safety of industrial workplaces, for example (such as exist widely in England), often lay down in minute detail such matters as the precise dimensions of safety features like scaffolding widths, safety barriers, and the like. Employers clearly must find most of these easier to understand and to comply with than the common law rules of reasonable care, and breach of them is also more easily provable.

Now, because of the possibility of such second-level substantive justification, it might be argued that the over-inclusion and under-inclusion or other arbitrariness of rules is neither necessarily nor commonly arbitrary in ultimate terms; hence (it may be urged) reasoning arising from such rules has no real content formality or arbitrariness after all. Such an argument proves too much. If the first level distinction between particular fiat or arbitrariness, on the one hand, and particular substantive reasoning, on the other, is collapsed on the basis of such second-level substantive reasoning so as to jettison the concept of content formality, the concepts of authoritative formality as well as mandatory formality and interpretive formality must be similarly jettisoned, for the same kind of argument applies to these too. Yet the first-level contrasts between form and substance represented by means of these concepts remain perfectly intelligible and useful.

Despite the apparent paradox that formal reasoning sometimes seems to require (as Bentham once said of the system of precedent[19]) 'acting without reason, to the declared exclusion of reason and thereby in opposition to reason', it is not difficult to find *reasons* to justify resort to such reasoning in a legal system. Indeed, if we take valid law seriously, we *must* treat its rules and other norms as formal reasons for action and for decision. A system whose laws were generally regarded merely as giving rise to prima-facie reasons no weightier than the substantive considerations underlying them simply could not be a viable legal system. It would not have law with sufficient authoritativeness or formal mandatoriness, and therefore could not be governed by the rule of law at all. Such a system could not, therefore, adequately serve values characteristically associated with the rule of law, such as uniformity, predictability, freedom from official arbitrariness in the administration of the law, and the like.[20]

But beyond these more or less obvious justifications for formal reasons, we wish to stress several more functional and pragmatic justifications for the widespread resort to formal reasoning in the law, justifications we think sufficient to convince even the most hardened sceptic. The first, and by far the most important, pragmatic justification for the use of formal reasoning in the law is the only one to which we need devote any extended treatment. It seems clear to us that the need for formal reasons in a legal system arises out of the necessities of decision making. One of the principal purposes of a legal system is to provide for the *making of decisions* that have some *finality*. All political and legal activity requires that proper procedures exist for the making of decisions in an orderly manner, whether in the settlement of disputes or the arrangement of affairs concerning the citizen and the state, whether by legislation, administration, or adjudication. But to do things in an orderly manner requires that proper procedures should exist for regulating how disputes should be determined and how public affairs should be organized. Efficient procedures for such matters require that there should be a proper time and place in which issues can be raised, appropriate procedures for raising issues, and proper officials before whom they can be raised. That means that when a matter is brought before an official for a decision to be made—whether the issue is a litigated case before a judge or a bill brought before a legislative assembly—there must exist rules whereby certain matters can be raised, and certain matters cannot be raised. Matters which are out of order

---

[19] See Collected Works of Jeremy Bentham, *Constitutional Code*, vol. 1, 434 (F. Rosen and J. H. Burns, edd., Clarendon Press, Oxford, 1983).

[20] See Summers, 'Working Conceptions of the Law', in *Law, Morality and Rights*, 20–2 (*supra*, n. 1) reprinted in 1 *Law and Philosophy* 263, 280–2; see also Summers, *supra*, n. 7.

cannot be raised *now*, before *this* assembly or judge, on *this* occasion, by *this* procedure. This makes it highly desirable (to say the least) that rules should be treated as giving rise to formal reasons for decisions. Treating rules in this way prevents countervailing substantive reasons being brought up whenever a rule is invoked, and thus provides a powerful reason for ruling matters out of order in a discussion.

In the absence of such formal reasons, there would always be pressure, whenever one party to a dispute relied on a rule, to permit the other party to argue that the rule was a bad rule which ought to be changed because (for instance) the reasons of substance bearing on what would be desirable had not been adequately canvassed when the rule was being formulated. The exploration of reasons of substance—in legislative assemblies or in courts—would be in danger of going all the way back to the roots of political theory and philosophical analysis. No doubt, other contrary reasons of substance (such as cost considerations) would intervene long before that stage was reached, but formal reasoning not only operates to prevent such absurdities, it also operates in a much more precise and efficient manner than purely substantive reasons could ever do in controlling and limiting agendas.

It is only because there are formal reasons for decisions which exclude from debate here and now some of the underlying reasons of substance, that it become possible to manage our affairs, decide legal disputes, deliberate in legislative assemblies in an orderly manner, and so on. Formal reasons enable us to say: this issue is to be debated within certain limits, other matters are not upon the agenda today; or, this case is to be decided as a dispute between these parties on certain assumptions which are not open for discussion here and now. It is reasoning of this kind which enables a judge to decide a case in accordance with a rule, just because the rule mandates the result, even though (were the matter to be fully ventilated) it might be thought that the rule ought to be changed, or that it ought not to apply to these parties, or that it ought not to be applied to the subject matter of the dispute, or even that it ought to be repealed altogether. One of the main purposes of treating the rule as a formal reason is to leave for another day, another procedure, another person, the ventilation of these other issues.

We now turn to deal with some of the other rationales for the use of formal reasons in the legal system, but we can deal with these relatively shortly. The next second-level rationale, which is closely associated with the first, concerns the question of cost. Formal reasoning is extremely cost-effective, though of course it has a price. To take a simple example, if the interpretation of a statute is in question, formal reasoning requires the interpreter to confine himself to the text of the statute; substantive reasoning would open up all sorts of additional questions, including (but not solely) the possibility of searching for legislative intent outside the text of the statute. This may get substantively better results, but it may be very costly. Similarly, the enforcement of contracts may be thought to rest upon a species of formal reasoning.[21] It is much cheaper to decide a dispute by using the parties' own agreement to resolve matters between them than it would be if the question were left at large for the judge to decide, for instance, on what would be a fair price for services rendered, or whether any reliance on a promise had been justifiable.

A third functional and pragmatic rationale for formal reasoning is that its use may minimize the risk of error. When writing is required for a will, for instance, this minimizes the danger that we will incorrectly give effect to what we think are the intentions of the testator, although of course it does so at the price of excluding from consideration cases where there is very good ground for thinking we know the testator's real intentions, even though they were not written down. If, however, we are willing to look at all cases in which we think there is such good ground, we are more likely to go wrong than if we exclude all such cases from consideration. This is an empirical proposition, of course, which may be false; but if it is false then we think the use of the formal reason in this particular situation would be unjustified. Thus when we say that the use of formal reasoning may be justified by assumptions of this character, it must be appreciated that we mean that it is justifiable in principle. If the empirical assumptions are unsoundly based, then the formal reason will be inappropriate.

Fourthly, formal reasons may be justified by value judgments about the appropriate persons to make decisions, as in the case of contracts once again, where one of the reasons for not going behind the agreement of the parties in the usual case is the value judgment that individual freedom of choice should be respected.

Fifthly, there is the value of repose and security and peace in human affairs, which is why statutes of limitation may operate to bar actions without examination of the underlying equities, and why judgments must be treated as finally disposing of many issues. Many of these reasons, of course, will overlap in various circumstances.

Last but by no means least, it seems to us clear that, generally, appropriate formal reasoning is likely to make the law more certain and predictable. That this is likely to be the result of formal reasoning can be seen by looking at each of the four facets of formality which we have identified. It is surely obvious that laws which can be identified solely by reference to their source or origin are in general easier to discover than those which must also pass some content-oriented standards of validity.

---

[21] See Atiyah, *supra*, n. 1.

Indeed, given that such content-oriented standards will probably depend on diverse and changing moral ideals, it is not surprising if much disagreement occurs among those charged with identifying these standards, and that such disagreements make much American law exceptionally uncertain and unpredictable, compared with that of England. Moreover, rules (and other legal phenomena) with higher content formality are easier to apply than those with lower content formality; indeed, one of the chief justifications for some obvious rules of high content formality (for example, speed limits on the roads) is precisely to make the law easier to follow, both for those who wish to comply with and for those who wish to enforce the law. Further (although this is more controversial) we think it is at least plausible that (given the appropriate institutional and other background conditions) interpretive formality also tends to lead to more predictability, a matter we develop more fully in chapter 4. Finally, mandatory formality also tends in the same direction. When rules (or other legal phenomena) are not easily displaced by contrary equitable or discretionary or other substantive considerations emergent at the point of application, the application of these rules will tend to make the law more certain and predictable.

We stress here that the factors mentioned above only 'tend' to make more formal legal reasoning more certain and predictable in outcome. They do not alone determine these results, but, in the two countries which are the focus of our study, there are many other factors which also tend in the same direction. In the result, we are in no doubt that, on most matters, English law is markedly more certain and predictable than American law. Because in this chapter we are only concerned to discuss the relationship between formal reasoning and legal certainty, we postpone to a later point fuller discussion of a number of other issues relating to this question of certainty. In particular, we shall there address the strain of American scepticism about the possibility that law can ever be certain, or (perhaps) very certain.

So far we have been discussing general justifications of the whole practice of formal reasoning. We now add a few words to account for the justificatory force of particular formal reasons in a particular context. This requires consideration of both first- and second-level reasoning. First level reasoning within the law seldom consists of purely formal reasons. Far more often, it consists of a robust admixture of particular substantive reasoning and varying degrees of the four key attributes of formality: authoritative formality, content formality, interpretive formality, and mandatory formality. The overall justificatory force of the resulting reasoning is then largely traceable to some *combination* of the justificatory force of the particular substantive reasons informing the rule or other pheneomena involved (first-level) and the justificatory force of applicable second-level substantive reasoning in the name of the rule of law, efficiency, or the like.

5. FORMAL AND FORMALISTIC, SUBSTANTIVE AND 'SUBSTANTIVISTIC' REASONING

We now wish to introduce a pair of important distinctions. First, we shall distinguish between formal and formalistic reasoning, and secondly, between substantive and 'substantivistic' reasoning. So far, and throughout this book, we generally use the terms formal and substantive reasons or reasoning in evaluatively neutral terms. No particular formal reason is inherently good, a reason with sufficient justificatory force. But in our scheme of thought there is nothing inherently bad about such a reason either. As we have shown in the last section, there are strong rationales supporting the general practice of resorting to formal reasons in the law, and whether the adoption of a particular formal reason is justifiable must be decided by looking to these general rationales.

Of course a particular formal reason may be bad, may lack justificatory force, on a number of grounds. It may rest on law that is not really valid law; or it may misconstrue that law, or it may go beyond that law as properly interpreted and applied.[22] It may also incorporate bad substantive reasons. These are distinct kinds of bad formal reasons, but we do not call them formalistic. Nonetheless, there is a connection of the following general character between formal reasoning and formalistic reasoning. Most, if not all, varieties of formalistic reasoning can be represented as degenerate species of one or more of the basic attributes of formal reasoning.

Thus, authoritative formality degenerates into formalistic reasoning when, for example, a judge ignores gaps in the law, or refuses to acknowledge the nascent and fragmentary chracter of a piece of pre-existing valid law, and so over-extends that law as if it truly generated formal reasons governing the issue at hand. Another example occurs when a judge relies on a distinguishable precedent, or fails to see that he is confronted with a genuine case of first impression where it would be more appropriate to invoke substantive reasoning relevant to the merits of the dispute. Content formality degenerates into formalistic reasoning when, for example, judges refuse to recognize the excessive arbitrariness of a common law rule, and therefore adhere to that rule where this would not be justifiable by reference to second level reasoning either. Interpretive formality degenerates into formalistic reasoning when, for instance, a judge adopts a conceptualistic interpretation of statutory

---

[22] For other examples, see Summers, *Instrumentalism and American Legal Theory* 136–59 (Cornell U. Press, Ithaca, 1982).

language—an interpretation that ignores the elemental fact that the language has been incorporated into a statute to achieve a purpose plain on the face of the statute. Mandatory formality likewise can degenerate into formalistic reasoning when, for example, a judge allows an existing common law rule to exclude or override substantive considerations arising at the point of application even in a case where the judge should plainly overrule the precedent (or create an exception to it) and thus allow the newly emerging substantive reasons to carry the day.

We are not unaware, of course, that the term 'formalism' is today often used in American and, to a lesser extent, in English legal writing and legal theory, to refer to such vices as conceptualism, over-emphasis on the inherent logic of legal concepts, the over-generalization of case-law, and the like. Some of the vices associated with 'formalism' have nothing to do with formal reasoning as we use that term, and are therefore not our concern. But there is clearly some overlap between the American use of the term 'formalism' and our own use of the concept of formalistic reasoning, and where both terms are used pejoratively, our usage of the one is in part an attempt to be more precise about what is wrong with 'formalism'.

We think that there may also be some examples of reasoning which we would call, non-pejoratively, formal, where others might apply the pejorative term formalistic. For example, a relatively literal case of statutory interpretation might be seen by us as an appropriate use of formal reasoning, where others might condemn the reasoning as formalistic. However, many, probably most, instances of divergence of this kind can probably be resolved if one important point is remembered. We have suggested above that formalistic reasoning involves a failure to take substantive considerations into account *when they ought to be taken into account*. But we now must stress that it is not possible to decide when such substantive considerations *ought* to be taken into account without reference to other norms of the legal system in question. One legal system may contain norms which—for very good reasons of a second-level character—dictate that substantive considerations should not be taken into account in a certain situation, that the problem must be resolved solely by reference to formal reasoning. Another legal system may take a different view, also for perfectly good reasons of a second-level character. For example, a complex problem arising from an obscure statute could easily be handled by an English court in a rather formal way where an American court would rely more heavily on substantive reasoning.[23] Both approaches may be justified by the context in which

[23] Compare e.g. *Cartledge* v. *Jopling & Son Ltd.* [1963] AC 758 and *Urie* v. *Thompson* 337 US 163 (1949) (effect of Limitation Acts on insidious disease whose early symptoms were not detectable).

the courts operate: in England, there may be good ground to think the problem will receive fuller attention from law reform agencies and from Parliament than it can receive within the confines of a single piece of litigation, while in America, it may be almost certain that the problem must be solved by the courts without legislative assistance.[24] Where such differences exist between two legal systems, the very same second order substantive reasons may suggest that use of formal reasoning in one system is perfectly correct and justifiable, while its use in the second legal system would be inappropriate and hence would be formalistic. It is thus necessary to be extremely careful in using the term 'formalistic' in a pejorative sense, when one is describing a legal system with which one may not be wholly familiar.

The distinction we have drawn between formal and formalistic reasoning can be paralleled by a distinction between substantive reasoning and what might be called—to coin an ugly word—'substantivistic' reasoning. As with formal reasoning, we generally use the term 'substantive reason' in an evaluatively neutral way; no particular substantive reason is necessarily good or bad. A particular substantive reason, like a particular formal reason, may of course be bad, may lack justificatory force on a number of grounds (many of which one of the present authors has canvassed at length elsewhere[25]). For example, such a reason may be bad because it rests on faulty factual premisses or because it relies on an inappropriate or unsound value. These may be bad reasons but they are not what we have called 'substantivistic'. That term we use pejoratively to designate first-level substantive reasons beyond their appropriate scope or range. Just as we have demonstrated that there is a connection of a general character between formal and formalistic reasoning, so it could equally be shown that there is a similar kind of connection between substantive and 'substantivistic' reasoning. Thus there are degenerate forms of substantive reasoning where judges use reasons of substance inappropriately, corresponding to the degener-

---

[24] In England the decision in *Cartledge* v. *Jopling & Son Ltd.* (though indefensibly hard on the individual plaintiff) was dealt with by the Limitation Act 1963, following the report of the Committee on Limitation of Actions in Personal Injury Cases (Cmnd. 1829, HMSO, London, 1962), which was already available at the time of the House of Lords' decision; the Act sorted out a number of consequential problems. (See now Limitation Act 1980, ss. 11(4) and 14.) In America, *Urie* v. *Thompson* left many difficulties in its train, some of which have still not been sorted out, concerning the relationship betweeen limitation rules and the liability of insurers, see Note, 'Adjudicating Asbestos Insurance Liability', 97 *Harv. L. Rev.* 739 (1984). We are indebted on this point to an Oxford D.Phil. thesis on 'Compensation for Diseases' (1984), by Jane Stapleton, which deals with the point more fully than her *Disease and the Compensation Debate*, 26–32 (Clarendon Press, Oxford, 1986).

[25] See Summers, *supra*, n. 2, at 743–9, 759–63 (on how goal reasons and rightness reasons may break down, respectively).

ate species of formal reasons illustrated above. For instance, a judge who, in interpreting a statute, goes behind the statute to the extent of relying on manufactured evidence of legislative purpose deliberately planted by a legislator in the records of the legislative proceedings is improperly relying on substantive reasoning[26]—assuming, that is, that the legal system in question does not generally tolerate such procedures. Similarly, a judge who treats the existence of a truly binding precedent merely as one reason to be weighed along with other substantive reasons emergent in the context is, without more, over-relying on substantive reasoning, and thus being 'substantivistic'.

In suggesting that the terms 'formalistic' and 'substantivistic' should only be used pejoratively where they involve inappropriate reasoning, *according to the criteria properly employed by the legal system in question*, it may seem that we are abdicating the right to criticize the whole style of reasoning of a legal system. An American may, for instance, wish to criticize the whole style of legal reasoning in England as 'formalistic' even though such reasoning is properly employed in accordance with recognized criteria in England itself. Of course we do not deny anyone the right to make such criticisms, nor do we dictate the meanings to be attributed to words as others may use them. But we do think that when terms like 'formalistic' are used in this pejorative way to describe reasoning which is perfectly proper according to the (second level substantive) criteria employed in the legal system itself, it behoves the critic to explain very carefully what precisely is wrong with that kind of reasoning as it is used *in that kind of legal system*. On the whole it seems to us to make for clarity if pejorative words like 'formalistic' are only used in the way we suggest; it then becomes perfectly intelligible to suggest that the English legal system as a whole is a highly formal system and the American a much less formal system, which is, of course, exactly what we claim, without *necessarily* implying any criticism of the two systems. Criticisms should then be directed either at apparent inconsistencies, or at the way the systems work as a whole; and the latter can only be properly done, we suggest, when they are looked at as a whole—which is one of the things this book tries to do.

Nevertheless, we do not deny that, given the more formal nature of the English legal system, formalistic reasoning is more likely to be found in England than in America; but conversely, we shall suggest that, given the more substantive nature of legal reasoning in America, 'substantivistic' reasoning is also more likely to be found in that country than in England.

---

[26] Justice Jackson once remarked that some American judges seek to make the interpretation of statutes fit not their texts, but their legislative histories! *Schwegmann Bros.* v. *Calvert Distillers Corp.* 341 US 384, 396 (1951).

6. ANGLO-AMERICAN DIFFERENCES

Our primary thesis is that the English approach to law is more formal and the American more substantive. As will have been apparent from our insistence that all legal systems rely heavily on both formal and substantive reasons, we are anxious to avoid exaggeration or caricature. The English legal system is not nearly as formal as many American lawyers think, and the American system relies far more on formal reasoning than many English lawyers believe. But there is a widespread, and we think well-founded, view that the English legal system is more formal than the American, and much of this book will be devoted to detailed differences between the two systems which illustrate this profoundly important fact.

In chapter 2 we take up standards for determining the authoritativeness of rules and other legal phenomena giving rise to formal reasoning, and we show how the two systems differ in the degree to which they rely on source-oriented and content-oriented standards of validity. We also demonstrate how the American system leads to many more situations of conflict between otherwise valid laws, and how these conflicts tend to be resolved in a more substantive fashion than in England, where the general approach is to invoke relatively formal rules of hierarchical priority.

In chapter 3 we begin with rules and their relative place in the two systems, and we shall attempt to show that there is a deep divergence between the English and the American traditions with regard to the formality of rules. In the English system, rules tend to have, in our terminology, higher content formality, higher interpretive formality, and higher mandatory formality than in the American system.

We turn in chapter 4 to differences in statute law. We argue that statute law is inherently more formal than case law and that the English system relies relatively more heavily on statute law than the American system. English methods of statutory interpretation are also more formal than American. In chapter 5, we compare the English and American approaches to precedent. We explain how the principle of *stare decisis* generates formal reasons, and we demonstrate that there are major limits on the operation of this principle in the American system, limits that either do not exist in England or exist only to a lesser degree. Throughout this chapter we identify major differences between the American and English legal and social systems which make the former less hospitable to full scale operation of the principle of *stare decisis*.

The trial process is the topic of chapter 6, and we shall there suggest that the much more extensive use of civil juries in America is symptomatic of the more substantive tendencies of American law and gives rise to many examples of 'rule nullification', usually on substantive grounds. In chapter 7 we treat the judicial enforcement of the law. We shall argue that the American system has a tendency to allow substantive reasons not incorporated in the law to influence findings of fact and the administration of the law, and in this respect to have lower 'truth formality' than the English system. We also claim that that the greater speed, efficiency, and finality of English court decisions combine to make that system more formally effective than the American and thus to have a higher degree of 'enforcement formality'.

These, then, are the main differences between the English and the American systems which we think bear out our thesis that the former inclines to the formal and the latter to the substantive. There may well be other realms of comparison, and certainly many more illustrations of the distinctions we draw will occur to our readers than we have attempted to document.[27] But we think we have done enough to substantiate our thesis in all essentials. Before we turn to outline what we intend to say about possible explanations for these differences, we wish to stress three caveats.

First, the differences we have described in chapters 2 through 7 are all matters of degree. Both English and American scholars have for too long bemused themselves with extreme examples from each other's systems of, on the one hand, formal reasoning in England, such as wooden interpretation of statutes and extreme unwillingness to develop the common law by judicial activism; and on the other hand, of free-wheeling substantive reasoning in America, such as liberal statutory interpretation which seems sometimes to ignore the text of a statute altogether, and of judicial activism of such a high level that it sometimes seems to substitute government by judiciary for government by the people's elected representatives. Such extreme examples can be found, but they are not typical. The differences we detail in chapters 2 through 7 are mostly less dramatic than this, though we do not doubt they are important differences for all that. Furthermore, their effect is cumulative, and this is all the more significant because, in most cases, the differences point in the same direction.

Our second caveat is that our generalizations about the English legal system can, in the nature of the case, be firmer and less qualified than our generalizations about the American system. The English legal system is much more centralized, much more homogeneous, and much more monolithic in character than the American legal system. Thus when we speak of a typical English judge, or a typical English appeal court, or a

---

[27] Examples which have occurred to us, but which we have not examined in detail, include the treatment of taxation laws and the effect of the incorporation of companies.

typical English barrister, there is little difficulty in identifying the characteristics we have in mind. The American legal and political system, on the other hand, is far more diverse, so that generalizations are much more difficult. A typical American judge is impossible to identify, as compared with a typical English judge. A federal appeal court judge from the north-eastern part of the country, for instance, may be a very different sort of person (and a very different sort of lawyer) from a state trial judge in the south-western part of the country. The same is true of practising lawyers, of law schools, and of almost all features of the legal systems. Thus, making comparisons between England and America is often difficult, and the comparisons we do make must be understood in light of this fact. The spectrum of variations in the American legal system often approaches English views and practices at one end. There are some American courts in which activism is frowned on almost as much as it was in the House of Lords over which Lord Simonds presided in the 1950s.[28] There are American judges who think formally that 'the law is the law' in much the same way and almost to the same degree as many English judges. There are many American attorneys who will look up the law of their own state for a client with almost as little uncertainty as an English lawyer doing the same for an English client. It would be quite wrong to overlook these aspects of the American legal system. But equally, it would be misleading not to recognise that, at the other end of the spectrum, things in America may be very different indeed from the general position in England. And this other end of the spectrum tends to include the pace-setting judges, and therefore often to be more important. Law and legal systems tend not to stand still; so conservative judges and courts tend not to be the most influential in the long run. It is, of course, impossible to quantify the degree to which one part of the American spectrum is more representative than another and we will not attempt to do so. But if, as may be the case, there is a tendency for the greater part of the system to cluster somewhere around the mean, then the differences between the two systems are profound indeed.

Our third caveat is this: while we must of necessity in this book discuss each aspect of the English and the American systems in isolation from the rest of the system to which it belongs, each aspect must in the end be viewed as part of a larger whole, and not judged in isolation. When viewed on its own, a given aspect may seem peculiar or unjustified, but when fitted into a larger whole it may be seen to make more sense, especially if, as we believe to be the case, there are usually quite

---

[28] For Lord Simonds's conservatism in the House of Lords, see Robert Stevens, *Law and Politics*, 341–54 (U. of North Carolina Press, Chapel Hill, 1978).

understandable reasons why each system as a whole has evolved in the way it has.

7. THE BACKGROUND TO THE DIFFERENCES

In chapters 8 through 14 we treat various theoretical, cultural, historical, and institutional factors relevant to the two systems. Some of these factors help to account for the differences which we have outlined in the last section, and which we describe in detail in chapters 2 through 7. But it would be wrong to think of these factors, and we do not offer them, as *explanations* for the differences between the systems. In many instances, causal influences have clearly run in both directions, and in some of these it would be difficult to say in which direction the influences have run more strongly. But although the factors we deal with in chapters 8 through 14 are not just explanatory of the differences between the two systems, we do not doubt that there are strong relationships between them. For example, we cannot say whether the differing traditions of the two countries with respect to prevailing legal theories (chapters 8 and 9) have *influenced* the English to develop a more formal, and the Americans to develop a more substantive, legal system; but what we can and do say is that there is a strong correlation between the degree of formality in the two systems and the degree to which lawyers and theorists in those systems adhere to more, or less, formal theories of law. Further, it seems highly probable that the various factors we identify have been mutually reinforcing in producing a more formal legal system in England, and a more substantive one in America.

In chapters 8 and 9 we identify some of the leading characteristics of various legal theories which have been influential in England and America during the past two hundred years, and attempt to locate them on a formal–substantive spectrum; positivism (not surprisingly) turns out to be a highly formal legal theory, while natural law and instrumentalist theories are more substantive in their orientation. In these two chapters we adopt a historical presentation, and substantiate our claim that, during the past two centuries, positivism has prevailed in England, and natural law and instrumentalist theory in America.

In chapter 10 on the role of appellate courts in the two countries, chapter 11 on the content, drafting, and enactment of legislation, chapter 12 on the judges, chapter 13 on the legal profession, and chapter 14 on law schools, legal education, and legal literature, we draw together a number of important factors that are also closely related to the fact that the English take a more formal approach to law, and the Americans a more substantive. Again, we do not simply call these explanatory factors, because they are to some extent the result of, as well as causes of, the very distinct formal and substantive approaches of the two countries. But beyond these factors there is one fundamental and complex factor that links most of the other institutional factors, and this one is so deep-rooted and traditional that it seems appropriate to introduce it here, so we close this introductory chapter with some treatment of this linking factor.

The widespread use of formal reasons seems to us to *presuppose* that relevant substantive reasons will be, or have been, or at least could be or could have been, more appropriately and more satisfactorily dealt with at some other time, at some other place, before some other body, by some other procedure, or whatever. When we bar an action under a statute of limitation, for example, we do so in the belief that the action could and should have been brought within the proper time limit, and then adjudicated upon on its merits. If that assumption is unfounded, for example, because the statute of limitations may bar an action even before the plaintiff could have been aware that he had a cause of action, then something is very wrong indeed. Thus it is not surprising that when it appeared that this might be the result of statutes of limitation, steps were taken in both countries to avoid this result, characteristically, in England by legislation[29] and in America by decisions of the courts.[30]

Or again, when an action is dismissed for want of jurisdiction, there is a possibility that some other court or body may have jurisdiction; indeed, in America, this is highly probable. But even if this is not the case so that there is no legal remedy in the present law, automatic dismissal for want of jurisdiction at least presupposes that the matter could receive the attention of the legislature. But here too, if the question at issue could not be considered by any other court, and if there were reasons for supposing that the legislature would never deal with the matter, the formal jurisdictional reason for a decision would come to look unpersuasive and eventually perhaps quite unacceptable. This is generally thought to be one of the main reasons that led the United States Supreme Court eventually to intervene in a wide range of matters in which it became evident that federal or state legislatures would not act. We do not here pass judgment on these specific interventions, but merely note that they illustrate *perceived* limits on formal reasoning in the American system.

Or again, literal, that is, formal, interpretation of a statute, ignoring the result, and perhaps even the legislative intention (save so far as it appears from the text itself), is more likely to be justifiable if it can be assumed, first, that statutes are drafted and enacted with care, so that

---

[29] See the Limitation Act 1980, ss. 11 (4) and 14. See n. 24.
[30] *Urie* v. *Thompson* 337 US 163 (1949). See n. 24.

there is a strong presumption that the literal meaning correctly represents the intention of the legislature; secondly, that the administrative or executive or judicial authorities responsible for applying or enforcing the law will (without overtly departing from the formal use of the statute) nevertheless take account of some of the substantive reasons which appear to have been overlooked by the legislature and apply the statute in a sensible manner; and thirdly, that the legislature is likely to act reasonably promptly to remedy any deficiencies in the law caused by such a decision. If the drafting of statutes is constantly done with ineptitude and obscurity, and if the result of this is that those responsible for applying or using the statutes constantly arrive at absurd or unreasonable decisions, and if the legislature refuses to do anything to remedy this state of affairs, then it is to be expected that the courts will be less inclined to interpret statutes in a formal and literal manner.

Similarly again, the principle of finality of judgments, still adhered to pretty rigidly in England, but rather less so in America, is justifiable only if we can generally assume that trials are held with due process, that judgments are carefully considered, and rendered with competence and integrity, and that opportunities for appeal are available. If these conditions do not obtain, if, for instance, federal courts cannot always trust state courts to observe federal law with reasonable competence and integrity, then it is not surprising that the finality of judgments comes to be somewhat weakened or undermined.

To make a decision by reference to formal reasons, after all, is to refuse to consider reasons of substance arising in the circumstances of the case which bear on the issue. This requires a degree of confidence in the decision-maker that the rest of the system is working properly, so that he can exercise some self-discipline and refuse to deal with it himself, here and now. But if these reasons of substance are never to be considered at all, still more, if there never has been any opportunity to consider them, then to make the decision by purely formal reasoning shuts out the possibility of that decision ever being based on the factors most directly relevant to it. Rational institutions and a rational legal system demand that we do not do this if we can avoid it at reasonable cost. Now it seems to us that one of the underlying threads which links the variety of institutional factors distinguishing the English and the American legal systems is that the assumptions which are made in the two countries about the workings of the rest of the legal and political system are fundamentally different. On the one hand, it seems clear that English judges generally have a high degree of confidence in the proper functioning of the rest of the machinery of government and of its officials. In America, this degree of confidence is often lacking, and (it must be said) not without some justification. In America, it is true that appellate courts (especially federal courts) cannot always trust lower courts (especially state courts) to observe the law properly—hence the system of collateral attack on state court judgments; it is true that legislative processes do not usually work as well or as efficiently as in England—hence different methods of interpretation and different levels of judicial activism; it is true that the competence of trial attorneys and trial judges is sometimes lower than it is in England—a factor that, along with others, explains jury powers to use substantive reasons rather than formal ones. And so on.

On the other hand, it seems to us equally clear that English judges are much less inclined to trust the people at large, or the jury, which is the people's representative. There are strong elitist traditions in England which influence the way in which formal and substantive reasoning is used. For instance, English judges have throughout history shown anxiety lest the effect of legal prohibitions should be weakened by equitable modifications designed to show mercy or compassion (or even justice) to those who committed prohibited acts in exceptional situations of stress or ignorance or lack of cognitive understanding.[31] This elitism betrays a lack of trust of the public itself, and often also of the jury. It also leads to the greater use of formal rules of high mandatory formality. The public, in other words, must not be given grounds to believe that the law will take account of substantive reasons arising in the particular circumstances of the case: formal rules ought to be observed by the populace without question, but the elite may sometimes stretch out the hand of mercy. This mercy will not lead to the incorporation of these substantive reasons in the rules themselves, but it may be available by way of discretion in sentencing, or by extensive use of the power of pardon, or in other ways.

The American tradition seems to us to reject these elitist assumptions. Law, to the American, is not something imposed or laid down from above, by a sovereign. It comes from grass-roots origins—from the people. If formal legal rules ought to be modified because of substantive considerations in some exceptional situations, the person in that exceptional situation, in the front line, as it were, must be trusted, at least in the first instance, to make his own decision as to whether to observe the formal rule or depart from it. Of course, he does this at his peril, because his conduct will subsequently be scrutinized by his peers; but if they agree that he acted properly he may be granted an acquittal. The elitism implicit in the English view is also unacceptable in American ideology. It is no ground for refusing to introduce equitable modifica-

---

[31] The elitist position as to the defence of necessity in the criminal law, for example, was clearly put by Sir James Stephen in his *A History of the Criminal Law of England*, vol. 2, 110 (Macmillan & Co., London, 1883).

tions to a formal rule that it may tend to weaken the general deterrent force of a criminal prohibition because the people can see perfectly well that there are many reasons why formal laws are not always enforced to the letter anyhow. It is not possible (or even desirable) to fool the people into thinking that criminal prohibitions are more absolute than they really are.

Thus we have this major difference between the English and the American milieu. English judges tend to trust the rest of the legal–political 'establishment'—governments, legislatures, officials, police—and, in elitist fashion, to distrust the public at large and their representative, the jury. American judges, by contrast, distrust the 'establishment' and trust the people and the jury. We believe this difference leads to—or anyhow is related to—other major differences. English judges are more likely to use formal reasoning in many sorts of cases where this means the substantive issues are left to others in the legal–political 'establishment'. American judges, on the other hand, are more likely to use formal reasoning where they are laying down rules of conduct for other officials whom they do not trust, such as the police.

Many illustrations of these two situations will appear in the course of this book, but at this point one contrasting pair of cases will suffice. We think there can be no doubt that American courts use more substantive (and less formal) reasoning than English courts when making many ordinary common law decisions—decisions which can hardly be seriously regarded as laying down rules of conduct for the general public, but are perhaps more often addressed to other judges. On the other hand, it also seems clear that American decisions relating to the powers of the police often impose on the police themselves more formal requirements as to the exercise of their powers than corresponding decisions in England. And there can be no real doubt that a major reason for this distinction is that American judges do not trust American police to behave properly, or to be called to account by other political or disciplinary processes, whereas English judges do trust English police to behave properly or to be called to account by other means. Again, it seems clear that English judges are less willing to leave substantive considerations justifying the modification of criminal prohibitions, in exceptional circumstances, to the populace or to juries; they prefer to leave these substantive reasons to other members of the elitist or ruling groups where, in America, they would be left to the public and to juries.

In saying that certain assumptions which are regularly made in England about the workings of the rest of the legal system are less well founded in America, it does not follow that we are making any criticism of the American legal system. What we are saying is that the resort to formal reasoning can be justified on these assumptions; and if they cannot be made, then formal reasoning probably has less place in a legal system. The system may be none the worse for that, although we think it is likely to be a more uncertain and a more costly system to operate, because (as we have suggested) formal reasoning is, on the whole, a great deal more certain and cost-effective than using reasons of substance. But this greater uncertainty and cost cannot be treated as a criticism of American law without challenging some of the funda-mental bases of the American legal–political system, because there is a sense in which America has almost deliberately chosen to incur this uncertainty and these additional costs. This is partly because its political and legal system declines to make the assumptions about the proper working of the rest of the legal and political machine which we suggest are foundations for the more extensive use of formal reasons. For whereas the English legal and political machine is a well integrated machine in which the various constituent parts operate with a high degree of trust for each other's functions and role, the American legal and political machine is to a large extent based on a contrary principle, a principle of *distrust* for other constituent parts.

It could, indeed, be said that the American system of government has even institutionalized its distrust to a considerable degree.[32] The people distrust all government,[33] so the powers of government are limited, divided, checked, and balanced. The state governments, from the beginnings of the revolutionary period, have distrusted powerful centralized government, and the federal authorities in turn often distrust the state authorities. Further, each of the distinct branches of govern-ment (both at the federal and at the state level) tends to distrust the other branches. Jurors are sometimes encouraged to distrust the judge, and perhaps the rest of 'the system' as well. So, whether the distrust is always

---

[32] 'But the great security against a gradual concentration of the several powers in the same department, consists in giving to those who administer each department, the necessary constitutional means, and personal motives, to resist encroachments of the others. The provision for defence must in this, as in all other cases, be made commensurate to the danger of attack.' *The Federalist Papers*, No. 51 at 321–22 (John Madison) (Arlington House, New Rochelle, NY, 1966); '[C]onstitutional law appropriately exists for those situations where representative government cannot be trusted, not those where we know it can.' J. H. Ely, *Democracy and Distrust*, 183 (Harvard U. Press, Cambridge, 1980).

[33] A striking example from Michigan confirms that this general distrust of all government is still sometimes found. In 1980, when the state was facing a fiscal crisis, a tax reform package was put on the ballot, jointly sponsored by the Republican governor and the Democratic legislative leadership; it was supported by local government leaders, labour and business leaders. It was rejected by the voters by almost three to one. P. Kobrak, 'Michigan', 99, 106, in *The Political Life of the American States* (A. Rosenthal and Maureen Moakley, edd., Praegar, NY, co-published with the Eagleton Institute of Politics, 1984).

justified or not, one of the chief assumptions which we believe it is necessary to make if formal reasons are to be as widely used as one might expect in the legal and political system is often ruled out in America by the very nature of the country's traditions and institutions.

2

Standards for Determining the Authoritativeness of Law

1. INTRODUCTION

We have seen that authoritativeness is one essential formal attribute of genuinely formal reasoning. In fact this attribute is derivative in nature. A genuinely formal reason derives its authoritative formality from the authoritativeness of a rule or other valid legal phenomena. Issues as to the authoritativeness of statutory and case-law rules and still other phenomena (such as contracts, judgments, and verdicts) which generate formal reasons frequently arise in the English and American legal systems. Courts may resolve these issues by reference (1) to standards of validity having some degree of 'validity formality'; (2) to rules of hierarchical priority, that is, what we have called 'rank formality'; (3) to other forms of law; and (4) to substantive reasons.

In this chapter we will identify two fundamental respects in which English standards for determining authoritativeness are more formal and the American more substantive. First, in England it is usually enough for a rule (or other legal phenomenon such as a contract or judgment[1]) to satisfy a source-oriented standard of validity, for example: 'Does the rule originate from a duly authorized lawgiver?' In America, on the other hand, one also encounters many content-oriented standards of validity,[2] for example: 'Does the statute incorporate an unduly arbitrary classification, and thus violate the equal protection clause of the federal Constitution?' Mere source-oriented standards generate what we call 'high validity formality'. They do not call for inquiry into substantive content. On the other hand, content-oriented standards of validity tend to low 'validity formality',[3] for they make issues of validity depend partly on the substantive content of the law in question. The

---

[1] For an example of the latter, see chapter 7 where we point out that habeas corpus cannot be used in England to challenge the validity of the *grounds* of detention of a convicted prisoner, if the detention order issues from a superior court.

[2] On standards of validity in general, see H. L. A. Hart, *The Concept of Law*, ch. 9 (Clarendon Press, Oxford, 1961); R. S. Summers, *Instrumentalism and American Legal Theory*, chs. 4, 5, 7 (Cornell U. Press, Ithaca, NY, 1982); R. S. Summers, 'Toward a Better General Theory of Legal Validity', 16 *Rechtstheorie* 65 (Duncker & Humblot, Berlin, 1985); R. S. Summers, *Lon L. Fuller*, ch. 4 (Stanford U. Press, Stanford and Edward Arnold, London, 1984).

[3] Or even (arguably) none at all, see *supra*, p. 12.

ubiquity of content-oriented standards in the American system, and their relative absence in the English, represents a profound difference between the two systems.

Second, conflicts between otherwise valid rules and other forms of law arise both in England and in the United States. However, because of basic differences in the structure of the two systems, such conflicts arise far less often in England, and when they do arise, they tend to be resolved solely by reference to formal rules of hierarchical priority without reference to substantive reasoning (for example, statute law prevails over case-law). That is, the English system simply assigns to the forms of law involved different degrees of 'rank formality', with the higher prevailing over the lower. The American system also relies to some extent on rules of rank, but, as we shall demonstrate, that system at the same time relies heavily on substantive analysis (often *ad hoc*) to resolve conflicts of this kind.

2. CONTENT-ORIENTED STANDARDS OF VALIDITY

Standards for determining the validity of rules (and other legal phenomena) are themselves an important variety of law. The standards of validity in a given system may be embodied in written constitutions, in statutes, in common law, or even, in some cases, in lower levels of law such as (in America) administrative regulations or (in England) delegated legislation. In most legal systems, judges have wide responsibility for the authoritative interpretation and application of such standards, though America is unique in the extent to which these standards authorize the judges to override legislation.

So far as America is concerned, we start with the basic fact that it is frequently not enough that a duly constituted state legislature, or the federal Congress, has duly enacted a statute, following all the proper procedures for passing an Act. A state statute may still be challenged as invalid under the state or federal Constitution as having substantive content inconsistent with those bodies of law. A federal statute, similarly, may be challenged under the federal Constitution as having substantive content inconsistent with that body of law. The issues in such cases are issues of *validity* and every year hundreds of such issues are litigated in American courts. Among the most familiar of content-oriented standards of validity to be found in provisions of the American federal Constitution are the following:

(1) The 'due process' clauses which, among other things, and along with other parts of the Constitution, have been invoked not merely to

invalidate statutes failing to provide for fair procedures, but also to invalidate statutes infringing upon substantive rights, such as the right to privacy.[4]

(2) The equal protection clause which, among other things, has been invoked to invalidate certain racial distinctions and other unjustified substantive provisions of statutes.[5]

(3) Clauses on religion which operate to invalidate certain statutes abridging freedom of religion, or giving one religion a degree of state support denied to others.[6]

(4) Clauses on freedom of expression which have been applied to invalidate statutes restricting freedom of expression.[7]

(5) Clauses securing certain privileges and immunities of citizenship which, among other things, have been interpreted to invalidate statutes restricting freedom of movement.[8]

(6) The clause prohibiting cruel and unusual punishment which has been invoked to invalidate certain statutes under which objectionable forms of punishment have been imposed.[9]

(7) A variety of other clauses (which we need not refer to in detail) have also been extensively used for imposing substantive requirements on the content of laws.[10]

It needs to be said that it is possible to see even the most content-oriented standard of validity in highly formal terms. Despite the extreme vagueness and breadth of some of the resounding phrases of the United States Constitution (for example, the guarantee that no person shall be deprived of life, liberty, or property without 'due process of law'), it was at one time argued that challenges to the constitutional validity of legislation could be, and had to be, tested, in a highly formal manner, merely by laying the text of the impugned legislation alongside the Constitution and seeing whether the one squared with the other. Such

---

[4] US Const. amend. V and amend. XIV, § 1. See, e.g., *Roe* v. *Wade*, 410 US 113 (1973) (privacy); *Goldberg* v. *Kelly*, 397 US 254 (1970) (termination of AFDC benefits without prior notice or hearing). In all the examples given in the text, other forms of official action besides legislation can also be invalidated.

[5] US Const. amend. XIV, § 1. See, e.g., *Hunter* v. *Erickson*, 393 US 385 (1969) (race); *Craig* v. *Borden*, 429 US 190 (1976) (sex); *Reynolds* v. *Simms*, 377 US 533 (1964) (legislative apportionment).

[6] US Const. amend. I. See, e.g., *Lemon* v. *Kurtzman*, 403 US 602 (1971) (establishment); *Wisconsin* v. *Yoder*, 406 US 205 (1972) (free exercise).

[7] US Const. amend. I. See, e.g., *Cohen* v. *California*, 403 US 15 (1971) (opposition to draft); *Miller* v. *California*, 413 US 15 (1973) (obscenity).

[8] US Const. art. IV, § 2, cl. 1, and amend. XIV, § 1. See, e.g., *Edwards* v. *California*, 314 US 160 (1941).

[9] US Const. amend. VIII. See, e.g., *Coker* v. *Georgia*, 433 US 584 (1977) (death penalty is disproportionate punishment for rape).

[10] See generally on substantive due process Tribe, *American Constitutional Law*, 886–990 (Foundation Press, Mineola, NY, 1978).

arguments go back to the origins of judicial review, the opinion of John Marshall in *Marbury* v. *Madison*,[11] and they were repeated as recently as 1936 by Justice Roberts in a well-known passage:[12] 'The judicial branch of the government has only one duty—to lay the article of the Constitution which is involved beside the the statute which is challenged and to decide whether the latter squares with the former.' On such an approach, the court applies, in a mechanical and formal way, a rule of hierarchical priority ('rank formality') to the effect that the Constitution prevails over a contrary statute. But this textual literalism is not acceptable to most American constitutional lawyers today,[13] though the argument is still sometimes invoked in defence of the courts against public criticisms that they are overstepping the judicial role. Textual literalism is criticized partly because the vagueness of the constitutional texts concerned is such that in nearly all difficult cases the impugned legislation is not really being tested for consistency with the literal words of the Constitution, but for consistency with certain substantive moral ideals for which the Constitution is believed to stand.[14] Moreover, these moral ideals may have little determinate content in any absolute or ultimate sense. They are sometimes even summed up 'in the words "natural law"', as Judge Richard Posner has recently written.[15] In some cases, the position might not be substantially different if the Constitution simply declared that 'All Unjust Laws shall be Void'. No doubt, even then there would be literalists and positivists who would be prepared to assert that the only function of the judges was to test impugned statutes against the text of the Constitution, but it would hardly be possible to take such an argument seriously.

This, of course, is not to say that formal source-oriented criteria of validity play no role in constitutional adjudication in America today. Obviously, most species of putative laws in America will usually have to satisfy source-oriented criteria of validity as well as content-oriented

---

[11] 5 US (1 Cranch) 137 (1803).

[12] *United States* v. *Butler* 297 US 1, 62 (1936).

[13] See, for example A. Bickel, *The Least Dangerous Branch* (Bobbs-Merrill, Indianapolis, 1962); J. H. Ely, *Democracy and Distrust* (Harvard U. Press, Cambridge, 1980); Philip Bobbitt, *Constitutional Fate* (Oxford U. Press, NY, 1982) for a sample of the large literature.

[14] Justice Hugo Black was a famous critic of this development, and his opinions, particularly those concerning the Bill of Rights, are monuments to a literalist interpretation, see, e.g., *Griswold* v. *Connecticut*, 381 US 479, 507 (1965) and *Katz* v. *United States*, 389 US 347, 366 (1967); see also H. Black, *A Constitutional Faith*, 45 (Knopf, NY, 1969).

[15] See R. A. Posner, *The Federal Courts: Crisis and Reform*, 193 (Harvard U. Press, Cambridge, 1985), citing Corwin, 'The Supreme Court and the Fourteenth Amendment', 7 *Mich. L. Rev.* 643 (1909).

criteria. Statute law, for example, must always satisfy such criteria.[16] Moreover, the federal Constitution is now so overlaid with interpretive case-law that the task of applying constitutional standards of validity requires that putative doctrines be traced to prior precedents laid down by the United States Supreme Court.

In England the orthodox view is that the content of laws is never a matter relevant to their validity, except in the case of subordinate legislation (administrative regulations), where it is settled law that the content must fall within the powers conferred by Parliament. But apart from this, the validity of all laws is entirely determined by reference to their sources.[17] Statutes duly made are law, and must be interpreted according to the proper canons of construction, whatever the result may be; cases are binding in accordance with the doctrine of precedent, however obnoxious the results may seem to later judges. Subordinate legislation can only be declared *ultra vires* if it exceeds the powers delegated by Parliament which means that content can be looked at only to determine whether it falls outside those powers, and for no other purpose.

Now, we do not ourselves wholly accept this extreme view of the true English position. For example, when the content of subordinate legislation is looked at to determine whether it is within the parliamentary delegation of power, the courts will certainly pay attention to the degree to which the content of the putative law may be offensive to fundamental notions of justice.[18] And even in the case of statutes, we take the view that the true construction of a statute will often be influenced by the effects which it is claimed to have. True this is, in England, always done under the guise of interpretation, and of having regard to what Parliament must be 'taken to have intended', but, to put the matter at the lowest, it could not be seriously suggested that the fact that a particular reading of a statute leads to very unjust results carries no weight with the judges in deciding whether that is the true construction of the statute. Of course English courts cannot set aside the words of a clear statutory provision, as American courts can do. All that we say is that, in England, as in America, the content of putative laws

---

[16] There are, however, some rare cases in which the principles contained in an invalid statute have been applied by courts as valid norms of common law, thus demonstrating that it is possible for a statute to meet substantive criteria of validity even where it fails to meet the formal criteria. See, e.g., *Clinkscales* v. *Carver* 22 Cal. 2d 72, 136 P. 2d 777 (1943).

[17] See generally H. L. A. Hart, *The Concept of Law*, ch. 6 (Clarendon Press, Oxford, 1961).

[18] See *Raymond* v. *Honey* [1982] 1 All ER 756 (Prison Rules held *ultra vires* insofar as they restricted prisoner's access to the courts, because this was a fundamental right not to be taken away without clear statutory authority).

does sometimes have a bearing on their interpretation and legal effect. It may be said that this is a different matter from saying that content may affect *validity*, but the difference seems to us largely verbal. If an unjust interpretation of a statute is *for that reason* rejected by a court, then the court has determined that the statute so construed has not validly (that is, with legal effect) created that unjust norm. And certainly, so far as case law is concerned, it could not be contended that even in England the binding effect of precedents is not, at the outer extreme, weakened, if not entirely undermined, when a precedent seems to stand for a quite unacceptable, because monstrously unjust, principle or rule.

Thus the differences between England and America respecting the application of content-oriented standards of validity to legislation may be said to be matters of degree. Nevertheless, it is a part of our central thesis that these differences in degree are very great and very important. Indeed, the very fact that what we have said above concerning the incidence of content-oriented standards even in England would be considered controversial, and perhaps wrong, by many orthodox English lawyers is an indication of the great gulf between English and American law on this topic. Many English lawyers (let alone legal theorists) would insist, contrary to our own view, that the validity of legislation never depends upon its content, except with regard to subordinate legislation.

American common law is also widely subject to content-oriented standards of its own—far more so than English case law. First of all, and as a general matter, it is not enough merely that a court has 'laid down' the common law, an elemental source-oriented requirement. A precedent must usually also pass a minimum threshold test of content before it can become *settled* law. If it does not become settled law, it will not be valid law. And if it is not 'good law', it is unlikely to become settled law.[19] Lon Fuller once alluded to the prevalence of content-oriented standards of validity when he referred to the United States as:[20] 'a nation where both law and good law are regarded as collaborative human achievements in need of constant renewal, and where lawyers are still at least as interested in asking, "What is good law?" as they are in asking, "What is law?"' In this connection it is interesting to note the different meaning attributed to the phrase 'good law' by English lawyers, for whom the words generally signify law which has been clearly and authoritatively laid down, without any implications whatever as to its ethical content.

The American common law provides countless examples of new

[19] See H. M. Hart, 'Holmes' Positivism: An Addendum', 64 *Harv. L. Rev.* 929, esp. at 936 n. 21 (1951).
[20] 'Positivism and Fidelity to Law: A Reply to Professor Hart', 71 *Harv. L. Rev.* 630, 648 (1958).

decisions that later failed subsequent, content-oriented reappraisal, and consequently did not become valid, settled law. A recent products liability case aptly illustrates this phenomenon. In *Beshada* v. *Johns-Manville Products Corp.*,[21] the Supreme Court of New Jersey in 1982 considered whether manufacturers and distributors of asbestos products containing no warnings should be held strictly liable for asbestos-related illness where the asbestos was manufactured before such products were known to be dangerous. The plaintiffs were workers and the survivors of deceased workers exposed to asbestos from the 1930s on. The defendants invoked a 'state of the art defence' that they had no duty to warn because medical science did not recognize the hazards from asbestos products until the 1960s.

Both plaintiffs and defendants relied on the earlier decision of *Freund* v. *Cellofilm Products, Inc.*[22] for support. The *Beshada* court concluded that while *Freund* did not directly address the 'state of the art' defence, its principle (that knowledge of dangerousness is imputed to the defendant in strict liability) supported the plaintiffs' position. The heart of the *Beshada* opinion, however, was the court's inquiry into 'whether imposition of liability for failure to warn of dangers which were undiscoverable at the time of manufacture will advance the goals and policies sought to be achieved by our strict products liability rules'.[23] Such liability, the court said, did further the three goals of risk spreading, accident avoidance, and simplification of the fact-finding process. Hence the state of the art defence failed.

The *Beshada* decision was roundly criticized in the legal literature as an inappropriate application of strict liability principles.[24] Without expressly rejecting the court's normative premiss that spreading the cost of injuries to those who produce, distribute, and purchase products is preferable to imposing it on innocent victims, several commentators focused on the probable undesirable consequences of the *Beshada* rule: inefficient over-investment in safety research, the withholding of safe new products from the market leading to technological stagnation, investment in additional insurance instead of in accident avoidance, bankruptcies of companies unable to procure additional liability

---

[21] 90 N J 191, 447 A. 2d 539 (1982).

[22] 87 N J 229, 432 A. 2d 925 (1981).

[23] 90 N J 205, 447 A. 2d at 547.

[24] Page, 'Generic Product Risks: The Case Against Comment K and for Strict Tort Liability', 58 *NYUL Rev.* 853, 877–82 (1983); Schwartz, 'The Post-Sale Duty to Warn: Two Unfortunate Forks in the Road to Reasonable Doctrine', 58 *NYUL Rev.* 892, 901–5 (1983); Comment, 'Requiring Omniscience: The Duty to Warn of Scientifically Undiscoverable Product Defects', 71 *Geo. L. J.* 1635 (1983); Comment, 'Beshada v. Johns Manville Product Corp.: Adding Uncertainty to Injury', 35 *Rutgers L. Rev.* 982, 1008–15 (1983); Note, 'Products Liability—Strict Liability in Tort—State-of-the-Art-Defense Inapplicable in Design Defect Cases', 13 *Seton Hall L. Rev.* 625 (1983).

insurance, and disproportionate increases in the prices of new products to make up for the fact that the prices of products manufactured decades ago did not reflect unknowable risks. At least one writer warned specifically of the 'chilling' effect *Beshada* could have on the pharmaceutical industry.[25]

It was to be expected that the Supreme Court of New Jersey would itself subject *Beshada* to further content-oriented evaluation before relying on it as valid, settled law. In fact the first time the case was cited for its holding on the 'state of the art' defence in *O'Brien* v. *Muskin Corp.*,[26] a defective design case, its rule was phrased narrowly by the majority,[27] and was described as 'intolerably extreme' and 'exotic' by a concurring justice.[28] Then in the second case in which *Beshada*'s 'state of the art' defence rule was considered, *Feldman* v. *Lederle Laboratories*,[29] which came before the court only two years after *Beshada*, a unanimous Supreme Court of New Jersey noted the controversy surrounding the earlier decision, and restricted it 'to the circumstances giving rise to its holding'.[30] The court reinstated the requirement that in design defect cases the manufacturer is only liable for hazards known or knowable at the time of manufacture.

As Llewellyn once put it, confining a case to its facts is a common method of killing it off entirely.[31] Thus within the short span of two years, the *Beshada* decision failed to pass the general content-oriented test of validity operative in this branch of the common law, and failed to become settled, valid law. Plainly, such content-oriented standards of validity are necessarily substantive, and highly so. And the failure of a precedent to pass them in American common law is revealed by many judicial techniques besides that of 'confining a case to its facts'. Such techniques include, for instance, specious distinguishing, creation of 'exceptions' that in truth swallow the rule, *sub silentio* overruling, and others.

Now, many of these techniques are found in England as well—indeed, many of them probably originated in England. But it would be wrong to conclude therefore that there is no difference between England and America in this respect. For a start, some of these techniques such as *deliberate sub silentio* overruling would be regarded as illegimate in England today, though of course this may occasionally happen inadvertently. And the other techniques are more dependent on formal criteria

---

[25] See last cited Note in n. 24, *supra*, at 638–41.
[26] 94 N. J. 169, 463 A. 2d 298 (1983).
[27] *Ibid.*, at 183–4, 463 A. 2d at 305.
[28] *Ibid.*, at 189, 463 A. 2d at 308 (Clifford J. concurring).
[29] 97 N. J. 429, 479 A. 2d 374 (1984).
[30] *Ibid.*, at 455, 479 A. 2d at 388.
[31] K. N. Llewellyn, *The Common Law Tradition*, 87 (Little Brown, Boston, 1960).

in England. For example, confining a decision to its facts or distinguishing it on specious grounds would often be found legitimate only if done by a court of high status, and perhaps of co-ordinate status with the court which originally made the decision concerned. Moreover, a *Beshada*-type story is itself very unlikely to occur in England for other reasons. First, English courts rarely pay any heed to academic commentary and criticism of their decisions, which are indeed rarely cited to them;[32] secondly, because most English courts still profess generally not to be concerned with 'policy',[33] the kinds of substantive criticism of the decision made of *Beshada* would, even if cited, carry little weight with a subsequent court which would tend to say that such matters were for the legislature; and third, a decision of the highest court—the House of Lords—and especially a decision only two years old, would almost never be reconsidered in this way.[34]

The role of content-oriented standards in America is not limited to newly decided case-law. There is also a long and respected tradition in the United States of ultimate judicial modification and displacement ('overruling') of long-settled and unquestionably valid law. Such modification is generally justified by one or more of three content-oriented theories, or a combination of them: the rule was really wrong from the beginning (original error); the rule is no longer appropriate in light of changed circumstances (rule obsolescence); or, the rule should be changed because we would today say that it is unduly harsh or unjust (growing moral enlightenment). As we shall see more fully when we return to this topic as part of our treatment of *stare decisis* in chapter 5, English courts are much more hesitant about overturning long-established law, and when they do indulge in this, they tend to rely on the first of these three justifications. The second and third, though invoked in a few major decisions in recent years, generally involve too overt a recognition of the legislative role of the courts for English tastes.

The use of content-oriented analysis does not, of course, necessarily lead to the overturning of long-settled common law doctrine; it not uncommonly results in reaffirmation of long-standing doctrine. For instance, in *Pashinian* v. *Haritonoff*,[35] the Illinois court conducted a

---

[32] See *post*, p. 403.

[33] See *post*, ch. 10.

[34] See *post*, pp. 139–140. Since we first wrote this passage, *R.* v. *Shivpuri* [1986] 2 All ER 334 has provided a unique instance of something close to the *Beshada* story in England (House of Lords overruling very recent decision on construction of statute, partly in response to academic criticism); but even this decision was based largely on the ground that the earlier case simply failed to give effect to the parliamentary intent, rather than on directly substantive grounds. The case is certainly no warrant for thinking that a single precedent of high authority does not usually settle the law in England.

[35] 81 Ill. 2d 377, 410 NE 2d 21 (1980).

content-oriented re-examination of the tort principles governing the liability of the occupiers of premises. The court considered adopting a uniform standard of ordinary care in place of the common law rules, but was 'not persuaded that conditions have so changed as to require a change in the law'.[36] The court did not, however, doubt its power to effect such a change,[37] which has indeed recently been implemented to varying degrees by other American state courts.[38] By comparison, the English position with regard to such common law doctrines is that, while they can be modified, they cannot be uprooted by the courts themselves. But in the result, the distinction between invitees and licensees was abolished in England by the Occupiers Liability Act 1957.

We have already seen how in America numerous content-oriented standards of validity embodied in constitutions are applicable to statutes, and we have now seen how many content-oriented standards are widely applicable within the common law. Private contract, the largest body of governing norms in the American system, is also subject to wide-ranging content-oriented standards of validity. Among the most important of these are the 'fine print' doctrine, the general obligation of good faith and fair dealing, substantive unconscionability, public policy restrictions on exculpatory clauses, the rule against penalty clauses, and certain implied warranties of habitability and merchantability.[39]

Once again—as with legislation and case-law—the English position is comparable in some respects, but differs profoundly in other respects. The English view is that the courts have no general common law power to subject contracts to content-oriented standards of validity, either by striking down clauses, or by reading clauses in.[40] Apart from a few established (and limited) doctrines, such as the public policy rules, and those governing penalty clauses, English courts have denied that they can strike down exculpatory clauses (which are not thought to be within the scope of public policy). There are no recognized substantive doctrines of good faith in English contract law, and the implication of terms is also said to be subject to a most stringent test of 'necessity'.[41]

Some English commentators (including the first named author) have

---

[36] *Ibid.*, at 380, 410 NE 2d at 22.

[37] *Ibid.*, at 381, 410 NE 2d at 22.

[38] For an example of a state decision which has overturned the common law rules, see *Basso* v. *Miller*, 40 NY 2d 233, 352 NE 2d 868, 386 NYS 2d 564 (1976).

[39] Nearly all of the above are fully discussed in E. A. Farnsworth, *Contracts* (Little Brown, Boston, 1982).

[40] See *Photo Production Ltd.* v. *Securicor Transport Ltd.* [1980] AC 827, 843, 851; *National Westminster Bank* v. *Morgan* [1985] AC 686, 708.

[41] See *Liverpool CC* v. *Irwin* [1977] AC 239, 254, 256; *Tai Hing Cotton Mill Ltd.* v. *Liu Chong Hing Bank Ltd.* [1985] 2 All ER 947, 955.

argued that there is a residual power to strike down unconscionable contracts or clauses, and also that many content-oriented standards are in practice relied upon under the guise of interpretation and implication of terms.[42] But the very fact that legislation has had to be adopted in the form of the Unfair Contract Terms Act 1977 to deal with exculpatory clauses is an indication of the much more limited English common law position. It is true that, once enacted, a statute like the Unfair Contract Terms Act does import content-oriented standards into English contract law, but then that statute has to be interpreted and applied by English courts, using the more formal techniques that we have already adverted to, and to which we will return in the next chapter. The result, therefore, is that in all three areas we have looked at here—statute law, common law, and contract—the American legal system makes much more extensive use of content-oriented standards of validity than the English.

The significance of all this for the more substantive style of the American legal system is profound. In the first place, the nature of issues of validity is such that American judges are thrust into the forefront of those whose business it is to resolve fundamental value-conflicts in society. Second, many content-oriented issues of validity arise in cases in which private parties assert that the law (or some official action under it) infringes their own individual rights, and is therefore invalid. As Professor Dworkin has observed,[43] this imputes a distinctive 'individual rights' flavour to the rule of law in the United States that is much less evident in Britain. Third, we believe that the nature of the standards of validity operating within a system of law can, over time, play a part in subtly shaping the entire system in many ways. If these standards are not exclusively source-oriented, but are also significantly content-oriented, they may promote a general vision of law in which law is less likely to be equated with formal authority, but tends to be equated instead with reason and justice and morality.

The American use of content-oriented standards of validity in these ways, and to this extent, encourages the view that the force of an argument in court depends less on its prior official sponsorship or endorsement, and more on its substantive merits. This tends to bring in its train some fairly obvious advantages and disadvantages. On the positive side, such a legal system tends to be more resistant to the excesses of formalism to which the English approach to validity is more likely to be prone. The 'law is law' mentality—that is, the attitude that laws must be identified and enforced regardless of content—is less likely

---

[42] See P. S. Atiyah, 'Contract and Fair Exchange', XXXV *U. Tor. L. J.* 1 (1985), reprinted in P. S. Atiyah, *Essays on Contract* 329 (Clarendon Press, Oxford, 1986).
[43] Ronald Dworkin, 'Political Judges and the Rule of Law', LXIV *Proc. Brit. Acad.* 259, 286 (Oxford U. Press, London, 1978).

to flourish in the American context. Further, the use of content-oriented standards of validity operates not just negatively, to invalidate laws after they have been passed, but also positively, to encourage public and private makers of law to adopt statutes, precedents, and contractual law which meet these standards. Again, in a legal system in which substantive criteria of validity count for as much as source-oriented standards, it is likely (as happens in America) that judges will respond more robustly and in a creative spirit to novel issues, rather than resorting to mere considerations of consistency, coherence, and the like.[44]

On the other hand, there is a price to be paid for all this. Substantive standards of validity are usually much more difficult to agree upon and apply than formal standards. Naturally, a legal system which relies so heavily upon content-oriented standards as the American is likely to suffer more from problems of uncertainty in the law, as compared with a system which relies far more on source-oriented standards.

3. CONFLICTS BETWEEN OTHERWISE VALID LAWS

If laws are to be identified solely by formal criteria, that is, if they are to be treated as valid law just because they have been laid down by persons or bodies authorized to make law, without examination into their substantive purposes, underlying policies, or rationales, then it seems to follow that conflicts between the authorized sources of law should be reduced to a minimum, and that very clear formal criteria should exist for the resolution of such conflicts as remain. We submit that this is the situation in England.

It is elementary that the number of authoritative sources of law in England is far more limited than the number in the United States. Until recently it would have been true to say that there were basically only three such sources—enacted statutes, delegated legislation made under statutory authority (what in America would be called administrative rules and regulations), and judicial decisions.[45] Two minor complications relate to Scotland and the Royal Prerogative. Scotland is a different jurisdiction, with its own courts (though sharing with England the House of Lords as a final appeal court in civil cases), but conflicts of jurisdiction between England and Scotland are rare. A large part of the statute law, with minor variations, is common to both jurisdictions. Even in

---

[44] R. S. Summers, *Instrumentalism and American Legal Theory*, chs. 4, 6, 7 (Cornell U. Press, Ithaca, NY, 1982).
[45] See generally C. K. Allen, *Law in the Making* (7th edn., Clarendon Press, Oxford, 1964).

common law matters, large areas of the law are today identical whether the case arises north or south of the border.

The Royal Prerogative has not been regarded as a strict source of law in the formal sense since 1689. The Crown does, it is true, retain certain residual prerogative powers which could theoretically be used to the prejudice of citizens' rights, even though the Crown cannot actually make law. For instance, the Crown still retains certain powers relating to the seizure of private property for defence purposes in time of war,[46] but in modern times these powers are almost invariably superseded by detailed statutory provisions. The only part of the prerogative which remains of much legal importance today concerns the conduct of foreign affairs; but it is elementary law that a treaty entered into by the Crown cannot affect English law unless enacted by due parliamentary authority.

Since 1973, of course, the above simple picture has been profoundly affected by Britain's membership of the EEC, which was given parliamentary sanction by the European Communities Act 1972. On one view, the only effect of this Act has been to give legislative recognition to the Treaty and to give delegated authority to the organs of the EEC to enact legislation which will be a formal part of English law. This is, however, a somewhat unreal version of what is now happening, having regard to the character and volume of this new legislation, to the fact that it is ultimately supervised and interpreted by the organs of the EEC, including the European Court of Justice, to which English courts are bound to defer, and to the fact that Parliament does not exercise over it the kind of supervisory control which it normally exercises over ordinary delegated legislation. Moreover, there remains the as yet unsettled question of enormous jurisprudential interest (and potentially perhaps of enormous practical importance too), namely, whether Community law will be held by English courts to take precedence over subsequently enacted English legislation. If this should ever happen, it will certainly be necessary to recognize that English law has acquired a new formal source of law.

But, important as these questions are, they remain, for the moment, of limited scope. The great mass of English law remains unaffected by the EEC complication, and it still continues to be true for most practical purposes that there are only three formal sources of law, if delegated legislation is counted as a distinct source; or perhaps more simply, two such sources, treating delegated legislation as a species of legislation, though legislation of inferior authority, and subject to some degree of judicial control.

---

[46] The requisitioning of civilian vessels for the Falklands campaign was done under the Prerogative, see the Requisitioning of Ships Order 1982.

Furthermore, the possibility of conflict between these sources of law does not often raise serious practical difficulty. Statutes are of paramount authority, and any conflict between a statute and a judicial decision must be decided in favour of the statute. There can, of course, occasionally be difficulty in deciding whether a statute does conflict with, and, therefore, override, a case, but this too is relatively unusual for reasons we discuss below when we deal further with legislation as a source of rules. It is elementary that no question of constitutional validity arises with regard to duly enacted statutes. More difficulty can occur with delegated legislation where issues of *ultra vires* can arise, and courts can declare such legislation invalid, in whole or in part, on the ground that it goes beyond the power delegated by the authorizing statute. No doubt this principle remains important for certain purposes in modern administrative law, but there are also reasons—again to be discussed below—why in practice such excesses of power occur only rarely in modern England.

By comparison with the English position, the United States has a veritable profusion of formal sources of law. To some degree it is a matter of taste what is to be counted as a separate formal source of law in the American context, but a reasonable count includes *at least* nine sources in the US legal system, namely:

The federal Constitution
Federal legislation
Federal administrative rules and regulations
Treaties duly entered into by the President and ratified by the US
    Senate
Federal judicial decisions
State constitutions
State legislation
State administrative rules and regulations
State judicial decisions

Among other candidates for inclusion in this list are state laws adopted by popular initiatives or referenda which have legal recognition under some state constitutions.[47]

With all these sources, the potential for conflict between otherwise valid law in the American system is very great indeed, and this potential is indeed realized in a great many cases. We will now list the most common kinds of conflicts that do in fact arise so that a decision must be made, by a court or otherwise, as to which law in conflict ultimately prevails. Such decisions themselves have to be made in accord with the

[47] See, e.g., the California Constitution, art. II, § 8, art. IV, § 1, Cal. Elec. Code §§ 3500–5353 (West, 1977 & Supp. 1987).

law, and it is our thesis not only that such conflicts are far more common in the American system, but also that they tend to be resolved by reference to bodies of law and methods of analysis that are often highly substantive, including reasoning of low interpretive and mandatory formality. The most common types of conflict are these:

— Conflicts between the federal Constitution and all other law, including federal and state statutes;
— Conflicts between federal statutes (and regulations, etc.) and state statutes (and regulations, etc.);
— Conflicts between federal common law and state law of all kinds;
— Conflicts between federal rules of procedure and state law;
— Conflicts between federal statutes and regulations and rulings of federal administrative agencies; and conflicts between state statutes and regulations and rulings of state administrative agencies;
— Conflicts between different federal statutes, and between different statutes of the same state;
— Conflicts between regulations and rulings of different federal administrative agencies, and similar conflicts of regulations and rulings of different agencies within a state;
— Conflicts between precedents in the federal courts, and between precedents from the same state;
— Conflicts between laws of different states applicable to the same multi-state transaction or occurrence.

The American system, like the English, has certain formal-seeming rules of hierarchical priority for the resolution of some of the above conflicts. These rules appear on the surface to resolve such conflicts by reference to the differing degrees of 'rank formality' of the competing laws. Thus the federal Constitution is supreme and takes precedence over all forms of law to the contrary; valid federal statutes take priority over contrary federal case-law and contrary state law generally, and so on. But the formulation, interpretation, and application of these seemingly formal hierarchical doctrines generates a great deal of litigation in the American system that is resolved largely by reference to forms of law and methods of analysis which are highly substantive in character. This situation does not really parallel anything in the English legal system.

We will now proceed to review in a general way how some of these types of conflict are approached in the American legal system, but it is unnecessary to restate our earlier treatment in the first section of this chapter of how conflicts between the federal Constitution and contrary federal and state law are resolved. As we have already seen, federal constitutional issues of validity are regularly resolved in accord with modes of analysis in which substantive reasoning is openly and frontally considered, weighed, and balanced. The same applies to issues arising under state constitutional provisions.

Conflicts between federal and state legislation

Conflicts between federal statutes (or administrative regulations or rulings), on the one hand, and state statutes (or regulations or rulings), on the other, are not at all uncommon in the American legal system. The formal rule is that valid federal statutes take priority, a rule itself set out in the broadest terms in the so-called Supremacy Clause of the United States Constitution, which provides:[48]

This Constitution and the Laws of the United States which shall be made in Pursuance thereof; and all Treaties made, or which shall be made, under the Authority of the United States, shall be the supreme Law of the Land; and the Judges in every State shall be bound thereby, any Thing in the Constitution or Laws of any State to the Contrary notwithstanding.

Under this clause it has been held that no state:[49]

may . . . enact legislation in conflict with the statutes of Congress passed for the regulation of the subject, and if it does, to the extent that the state law interferes with or frustrates the operation of the acts of Congress, its provisions must yield to the superior power given to Congress by the Constitution.

This kind of formal rule of priority is analogous to English hierarchical rules for resolving conflicts. Such a rule operates most clearly where the two enactments are flatly contradictory on their faces. For example, federal Treasury regulations (and, if valid, they are for this purpose equivalent to an Act of Congress) which provide that a co-owned bond will pass on the death of one co-owner to the surviving co-owner will override a state system of community property which allows devise of the deceased co-owner's undivided half interest in the bond.[50]

But American courts have also held that a state law need not be contradictory on its face to be in 'actual conflict' with federal law. The court looks at whether the state law 'stands as an obstacle to the accomplishment and execution of the full purposes and objectives of Congress'.[51] On this approach, for example, a state law denying unemployment benefits to any applicant who had filed charges of unfair labour practices with the National Labor Relations Board was overridden because it conflicted with an *underlying* objective of federal

---

[48] US Const. art. VI, cl. 2.
[49] *McDermott* v. *Wisconsin*, 228 US 115, 132 (1913).
[50] *Free* v. *Bland*, 369 US 663 (1962).
[51] *Hines* v. *Davidowitz*, 312 US 52, 67 (1941).

legislation.[52] The Supremacy Clause really says nothing about this in so many words. Courts go behind the language and invoke substantive considerations underlying the theory of federal supremacy, as these shape up at the point of application. The entire mode of analysis involves low degrees of interpretive and mandatory formality.

Further, when Congress, either expressly or implicitly, evinces a clear intent to 'occupy the field'—either with a regulatory scheme of its own or with a vacuum of no regulation at all—any state action or legislation within that field is invalid.[53] Such pre-emption by Congress can occur in many substantive areas, under any of Congress's enumerated powers. Under Article I § 8 of the federal Constitution, Congress is empowered (among other things) to impose taxes and pay debts, to regulate commerce with foreign nations and among the several states, to promote the progress of science and the arts, to constitute inferior tribunals to the Supreme Court, to declare war and provide for defence and the armed forces, to exercise exclusive legislative power over the District of Columbia, and, generally, to make all laws necessary and proper for carrying into execution the specifically enumerated powers.[54] But again, the 'intent to occupy the field' doctrine is not expressed in so many words in the Supremacy Clause; and in this respect also, the clause is treated with low interpretive formality.

Conflicts between federal and state common law

Another important kind of conflict is that between common law made by state courts and common law made by federal courts. Because of the Supremacy Clause in the federal Constitution, it is often assumed, especially by foreign observers, that common law made by federal courts always prevails over conflicting common law made by state courts, at least where the proceedings are brought in a federal court. However, according to the famous 1938 case of *Erie Railroad* v. *Tompkins*[55] (overruling *Swift* v. *Tyson*),[56] the federal courts have no power to create a general federal common law. Indeed, this is so even when the subject matter falls within the law-making powers of Congress, unless Congress specifically authorizes the courts to make such law. Thus federal courts must follow state law, including state common law, 'except where the constitution or treaties of the United States or Acts of Congress otherwise require or provide'.[57] This general *Erie* doctrine is of great

---

[52] *Nash* v. *Florida Industrial Commission*, 389 US 235, 239 (1967).
[53] *Florida Lime and Avocado Growers* v. *Paul*, 373 US 132 (1963).
[54] On the enumerated powers, see generally L. Tribe, *supra*, n. 10 at p. 44.
[55] 304 US 64 (1938).
[56] 41 US (16 Pet.) 1 (1842).
[57] Rules of Decision Act, 28 USC § 1652 (1982).

importance in so-called diversity of citizenship cases in the federal courts—cases in which the parties are citizens of different states. According to *Erie*, the federal constitutional grant of diversity jurisdiction to federal courts does not imply that the federal courts have power to make common law for such cases. As Justice Brandeis put it, 'There is no federal general common law'.[58] Instead the federal court must apply the applicable state common law, or any other valid state law. The federal courts are thus not to create (for example) a general federal common law of torts or contracts.

This may seem a relatively straightforward formal rule of priority, and in regard to ordinary substantive doctrines of tort or contract or the like, the rule causes little difficulty. Indeed, it avoids what could otherwise be serious problems. It is easy enough to see that having two different bodies of tort or contract law applicable to the same diversity case, depending on whether it is brought in a federal court or in a state court, would result in uncertain and inequitable administration of the laws, and would undesirably encourage 'forum shopping'. These and other concerns of federalism and the rule of law were uppermost in the minds of the *Erie* court.

What happens when the federal court sitting in a diversity case finds (as it not infrequently does) that the state has no law on the subject? One common answer, illustrating a highly substantive approach, is given in the following passage from a federal opinion in which the court was required to apply the law of Vermont:[59]

[T]here seems to be neither statute nor judicial precedent in Vermont bearing on the problem. And the problem presented has been variously decided in various jurisdictions. Confronted with this dilemma our task is not to surmise which line of judicial precedent a Vermont court would follow if presented with the case, but rather, by looking to the same sources which a Vermont court would presumably consult and by weighing the comparative reasoning of learned authors and conflicting judicial decisions for their intrinsic soundness, to define the pertinent law which when thus ascertained is presumably the law of Vermont even though as yet unannounced by a Vermont court.

Another problem which often gives rise to some concern as a result of the *Erie* decision is whether particular federal rules of civil procedure may be invalid in a federal court diversity case, at least where their application would produce an outcome different from that in a state court applying state procedural rules. On one view, *Erie* does not itself provide the test of validity here. Rather that test is laid down in the

---

[58] *Erie RR* v. *Tompkins*, 304 US 64, 78 (1938).
[59] *Socony-Vacuum Oil Co.* v. *Continental Casualty Co.*, 219 F. 2d 645, 647 (2d Cir. 1955).

federal Rules Enabling Act.[60] But according to that Act, a rule of procedure must not 'abridge, enlarge or modify any substantive right'. The problem, of course, is to discover what 'substantive' means in the Act, a problem with which the federal courts have been struggling ever since *Erie* was decided in 1938. Given the very language of the Rules Enabling Act, this struggle is itself necessarily highly substantive.

There are, however, some narrow situations where the federal courts will apply, and if necessary create, federal common law which takes priority over state law. For instance, federal common law usually applies where Congress has constitutionally vested jurisdiction in the federal courts and given them the power to create governing rules of law.[61] Thus a statutory grant by Congress to the federal courts of jurisdiction over suits involving breach of contract betwen employers and labour unions in interstate commerce was held to empower the courts to create and apply federal common law in such suits.[62] Similarly, federal courts apply federal common law in the areas of admiralty jurisdiction,[63] and in suits involving foreign relations.[64]

It is also recognized that, when there is a compelling interest in federal law governing, federal courts can apply federal common law. Examples are areas such as federal commercial paper,[65] apportionment of water from interstate streams,[66] and suits in which the United States is a party and which involve government contracts.[67] But state law may be incorporated as federal law where there is no need for national uniformity.[68]

Still, despite the areas of valid federal common law, there are many areas, much larger in scope, in which the federal courts have no power to make or apply federal common law under the *Erie* doctrine. But the process of choosing between state or federal common law involves case-by-case, issue-by-issue analysis with obvious implications for deciding with any degree of certainty the *general* validity of a rule of law. It is sometimes impossible to label a given rule as valid or invalid, except with respect to the particular case at hand. It is unnecessary to stress how this militates against a formal analysis of law, in which the validity of

---

[60] Rules Enabling Act, 28 USC § 2072 (1982). The Act grants the Supreme Court power to make rules of procedure for federal district and appeals courts.

[61] See *D'Oench, Duhme & Co.* v. *FDIC*, 315 US 447, 465–72 (1942) (Jackson J. concurring).

[62] *Textile Workers Union of America* v. *Lincoln Mills of Alabama*, 353 US 448 (1957).

[63] *Edmonds* v. *Compagnie Générale Transatlantique*, 443 US 256 (1979).

[64] *Banco Nationale de Cuba* v. *Sabbatino*, 376 US 398 (1964).

[65] *Clearfield Trust Co.* v. *United States*, 318 US 363 (1943).

[66] *Hinderlider* v. *La Plata River and Cherry Creek Ditch Co.*, 304 US 92, 110 (1938).

[67] *United States* v. *Seckinger*, 397 US 203 (1970).

[68] *US* v. *Kimbell Foods*, 440 US 715 (1979).

laws can be simply determined by looking to their source, and to formal hierarchical rules of priority.

Conflicts between administrative action and authorizing powers

A major kind of conflict between laws in the American system arises when an administrative agency makes a regulation or adopts a ruling which is in conflict with a statutory grant of authority to the agency. Such conflicts arise in the federal system when a federal administrative agency acts beyond its powers and, in a state system, when a state agency does likewise. Two different bodies of law govern these conflicts: federal law applies within the federal system, and state law in a state system. Here we will only offer a brief summary of how most such conflicts are resolved at the federal level. It will be seen at once that the simplistic formal rule of priority, to the effect that federal agency regulations and rulings in conflict with the relevant statutory grant of authority must be held invalid, is another of those 'general propositions that do not decide concrete cases' of which Justice Holmes reminded Americans.[69]

There are comparable problems in England, of course, but their resolution is more formal;[70] even though here also there is sometimes scepticism over whether such problems can truly be resolved just by looking to see whether the impugned actions or regulations exceed the powers granted by Parliament, this remains the orthodox position. Moreover, in one major (and possibly crucial) respect this formal approach leads to a fundamental difference between the position in the two countries.[71] In England, administrative actions can usually be set aside only for excess of jurisdiction, procedural impropriety, error of law, or complete perversity—the test of which is so stringent that this last is hardly ever found.[72] In America, on the other hand, the scope for judicial review or control is much wider.

In the American federal system, the federal courts are ultimately called

---

[69] *Lochner* v. *NY*, 198 US 45, 76 (1905).

[70] See generally J. Beatson, 'The Scope of Judicial Review for Error of Law', 4 *Ox. J. Leg. St.* 22 (1984); De Smith's *Judicial Review of Administrative Action*, esp. at 32–3 (J. M. Evans, ed., 4th edn., Stevens, London, 1980). American writers who have looked at English administrative law have found it very rigid and technical, probably because they find it too formal for their tastes, see, e.g., Davis, 'The Future of Judge-Made Public Law in England', 61 *Col. L. Rev.* 201 (1961) and Davis, 'English Administrative Law: An American View', [1962] *Public Law* 139; Jaffe is somewhat less critical, see 'English Administrative Law—A Reply to Professor Davis', [1962] *Public Law* 407; 'Research and Reform in English Administrative Law', [1968] *Public Law* 119.

[71] See, e.g., *Re Racal Communications* [1981] AC 374.

[72] It is misleadingly said that administrative actions can be set aside if they are 'unreasonable', but it is well settled in English law that this has the special meaning of 'so unreasonable that no reasonable administrator could have made this decision'—a very stringent test, see, e.g., *Secretary of State* v. *Tameside Metropolitan Borough Council* [1977] AC 1014, 1051, 1054, 1064, 1070.

upon to resolve such conflicts between administrative actions and the statutes pursuant to which they are taken, and they do this in accordance with a body of rules called 'scope of review of questions of law', a body with low content formality, low interpretive formality, and relatively low mandatory formality. In short, the analysis is highly substantive. The basic point of departure is section 706 of the Administrative Procedure Act,[73] under which administrative actions may be set aside for excess of jurisdiction, capriciousness, arbitrariness, abuse of discretion, or if 'otherwise not in accordance with the law'. Most of these grounds of review have analogous or comparable heads in English administrative law, though they might be differently classified. It is also true that there are cases predating the Administrative Procedure Act in which a rather formal analysis seems to resolve the question of validity,[74] but more often the American courts engage in a much more substantive analysis which goes beyond anything that can be done in English law.

In theory, American courts will inquire whether the agency action has a 'rational legal basis' and, if the court so determines, the action will be upheld, even though the court would not have arrived at that decision itself, if it had been charged with making the original decision itself. All this is, on the face of it, much the same as the comparable approach of English law, but we now come to the crucial difference. On the pretext that decisions lack a 'rational legal basis', American courts frequently do go on to substitute their own judgment for that of the agency in many large categories of cases, and this practice is vigorously defended by Professor K. C. Davis, a renowned and influential scholar of the subject. Davis has written:[75]

Substitution of judicial for administrative judgment is often rather clearly desirable, especially when the statutory purpose is unclear, in many large categories of cases, including those involving problems which (1) transcend the single field of the particular agency, (2) call for interpretation of the common law, (3) are primarily problems of ethics or fairness of a common-law type, (4) are affected substantially by constitutional considerations, whether or not a constitutional issue is directly presented, (5) require analysis of legislative history, especially when political conflict is the essence and not legislative inquiry into technical understanding within the agency's field of specialization, (6) bring into question judge-made law previously developed in the course of statutory interpretation, and (7) impel the reviewing court to make a discretionary choice for any reason, explained or unexplained, to create or mold law as a guide for the agency and for affected parties.

---

[73] Administrative Procedure Act, Scope of Review, 5 USC § 706 (1982).

[74] See, e.g., *Morrill* v. *Jones*, 106 US 466 (1883). But see *NLRB* v. *Hearst*, 322 US 111, 131 (1944) (courts are supposed to inquire whether the agency's factual findings have 'warrant in the record' and whether its legal conclusions have a 'reasonable basis in law').

[75] *Administrative Law Treatise* § 30.07 at 232–33, West, St. Paul, 1958).

Professor Davis's reasoning is reinforced by the fact that a great many federal statutes conferring power on agencies do so in very broad terms. Indeed, many statutes delegate law-making powers to federal agencies without *any* explicit accompanying legal standards for the exercise of these powers. Much the same is true in many state systems. It seems clear, then, that here, as so often elsewhere, the American methodology is highly substantive—far more so than the English.

Contradictory statutes

Another basic type of conflict arises in the American legal system when a court is confronted with two contradictory statutes from the same legislative body. Again, the problem is not unique to America, but such conflicts arise far more often in America than in England, for reasons which will become clear in chapter 11. Courts in both countries often appear to resolve such conflicts by reference to relatively formal rules of statutory construction, supplemented by hierarchical rules such as that the most recent statute prevails over earlier ones. But we believe that American courts are much more likely than English courts to treat these formal rules as rebuttable presumptions or as general principles subject to exceptions in the light of other substantive reasons. Many American courts are much concerned with enforcing what they perceive to be the true legislative intent or purpose underlying statutes, even where that purpose is not evident from the legislative text itself, and also with applying statutes in the light of substantive reasoning which is quite extrinsic to the legislative intent or underlying purpose.

Conflicts between statutes of the same legislative body often involve the question whether a subsequent Act impliedly repeals an earlier one. In England, such conflicts occur relatively rarely because of the greater technical proficiency of the drafting process (see chapter 11) and, when they do occur, are nearly always settled by invoking formal criteria, such as the 'presumption' that a subsequent general statutory provision is not intended to repeal a prior particular provision.[76] In America a different approach is often found. The Georgia case of *Curtis* v. *Ashworth*[77] illustrates how American state courts often resolve such conflicts by substantive reasoning.

In *Curtis*, the defendant's wife, while driving her own automobile, injured the plaintiff. The plaintiff brought an action for damages against the defendant, without joining the defendant's wife, alleging negligence on the wife's part. The common law rule that a man is liable for his wife's torts had been codified by a Georgia statute in 1863, but in 1866 Georgia

---

[76] F.A.R. Bennion, *Statutory Interpretation*, 433–35 (Butterworths, London, 1984).
[77] 165 Ga. 782, 142 SE 111 (1928).

adopted its Married Women's Property Act, later incorporated in the state constitution. Later the tort liability rule was repeatedly re-enacted as part of a general codification of some statutory rules of tort law. The court held that the Married Women's Property Act had completely undercut the common law rule that a man was liable for his wife's torts by removing its underlying rationale that the civil existence of the wife is merged in that of the husband. The court then held the tort rule inapplicable, reasoning that '[t]he reason for the liability having ceased ... the rule imposing liability should likewise cease.'[78] (We may note in passing, that the identical point was differently decided in England.[79]) It might seem that the common law rule should have been given effect because of its re-enactment by a later statute having priority over the earlier one; but the court avoided this formal, hierarchical analysis. Instead it treated the common law rule's re-enactment as a purely technical matter, with no legal effect.

The federal courts similarly resort to substantive reasoning in resolving conflicts between federal statutes. In *Associated General Contractors, Cal.* v. *Secretary of Commerce, U.S.*,[80] private contractors and four associations of contractors and subcontractors challenged a provision of the Public Works Employment Act of 1977 that required 10% of the amount of each federal grant applied for under the Act to be expended for minority business enterprises. A federal district court concluded that the Act violated the equal protection aspect of the Fifth Amendment's Due Process clause, but also held the law invalid because it was inconsistent with Title VI of the Civil Rights Act of 1964, prohibiting various forms of discrimination under programmes receiving federal assistance. According to traditional rules of statutory construction, however, there would have been a presumption that the more specific 1977 statute should have prevailed over the general 1964 Act. The court acknowledged this as 'hornbook law' but went on to say:[81]

But the court is compelled to go beyond the hornbook and must ascertain the purposes underlying any such conflicting enactments, and may not dispose of the problem by using such mechanical judicial slide-rules. The two hornbook principles are not to be applied when the results are 'extraordinary', or when the results do not reflect the true 'presumed intention of the law making body.' It follows that when an overriding public interest is demonstrably clear, in that the general statute sets forth the true Congressional mandate, and the later specific statute is less conducive to the public welfare, then the public good controls and

---

[78] 165 Ga. 787, 142 SE 113 (1928).
[79] *Edwards* v. *Porter* [1925] AC 1.
[80] 441 F. Supp. 955 (1977), *vacated*, 438 US 909 (1978). The Supreme Court remanded to consider the question of mootness, see 459 F. Supp. 766 (1978).
[81] 441 F. Supp. at 968.

the general statute will invalidate the specific statute. So also will the prior invalidate the subsequent.

The court justified its position that the 1964 Act and not the 1977 Act expressed the 'true' intention of Congress by reference to the legislative histories of the two statutes. The voluminous history of Title VI of the 1964 Act plainly stated the Congressional mandate and unequivocally declared the law to be national policy, while the provisions of the 1977 Act, on the other hand, had absolutely no credible legislative history. Translated into more blunt language, perhaps, what this means is that Title VI was passed in a blaze of publicity, and had continued to receive a great deal of publicity since it was passed, whereas the 1977 provision had slipped through Congress, almost unawares, as the result of an amendment first introduced on the floor of the House at the Report stage of the bill. It is quite plain that such a result could never have been arrived at by an English court, especially given that the more particular statute was the later one, so that the court's decision meant that the 1976 provision was void from the outset.

Irreconcilable conflicts between statutory provisions enacted during the same legislative session pose even greater problems of validity, because of the presumptions that statutes are intended to have effect together,[82] and that implied repeals are not to be expected.[83] Here many American courts bypass formal rules of priority altogether and make direct inquiries into 'legislative intent'. An Arkansas case, *Horn* v. *White*,[84] is illustrative. In *Horn*, the losing candidate in the race for the office of Montgomery County Judge contested the election results. The winner moved to dismiss the complaint because his rival had filed his certificate of nomination only 20 days before the general election. Although this was within the time required under an old statute, a subsequent statute of 1953 (Act 211) required filing 45 days before the election, and Act 241, also passed in 1953 (at almost exactly the same time), required filing at least 30 days before the election. The court first rejected the plaintiff's argument that the inconsistent 1953 statutes cancelled each other out, leaving the original Act standing. It then went on to refuse to follow the normal rule that the later of two inconsistent enactments should prevail. While acknowledging that this was the normal rule of construction, the court went on: 'But this "last passed" rule is admitted to be merely a rule of statutory construction and must and does yield when it is clear that the legislature intended the earlier

---

[82] J. G. Sutherland, *Statutory Construction* § 23. 17 (Sands, 4th edn., Callaghan, Willmotte, Ill., 1972); Bennion, *supra*, n. 76, 434–5.

[83] Sutherland, *ibid.*, § 23. 17; Bennion, *ibid.*

[84] 225 Ark. 540, 284 SW 2d 122 (1955).

Act passed at the same session to be the governing Act.'[85] In this case the first of the new Acts (211) contained a complex timetable for electoral procedures, while the second only amended one provision of the earlier law, and would have been almost unworkable with other provisions of Act 211, which were not directly affected by it. The court therefore concluded that it was the intent of the legislature to fix a timetable for elections and that the 45-day rule was most consistent with that intent:[86]

It would be putting form above substance and the letter above the spirit of the law to hold that Act 241 [the subsequent 30-day Act] changed Act 211. We therefore find and declare that the *legislative intent* was that Act 211 be the governing Act; and we so declare and hold Act 241 to be nullified by Act 211.

No English court could possibly have reasoned in the same way, but it is worth noting (at the expense of anticipating chapter 11) that this case illustrates not only the less formal approach of American courts to such conflicts between laws, but also one of the reasons why a less formal approach is necessary. The way in which statutes are today prepared and enacted in the two countries makes the sort of grotesque legislative error involved in *Horn* much more likely to occur in America than in England.

Conflicts in case law

Federal case law below the level of the United States Supreme Court is often conflicting, and the same is true in the lower state courts. The United States is such a large country, and the federal courts must cover such a wide geographical spread, that uniformity of decisions on many matters of federal law cannot always be expected below the level of the highest appellate court. For most federal suits, the federal courts of appeals are in practice the courts of last resort, and they not infrequently reach conflicting decisions on matters of federal or constitutional law. Sometimes the Supreme Court of the United States will wait a considerable time before attempting a definitive resolution of such conflicts. While this process is taking place, large 'repeat-litigators' including federal agencies and government departments can in practice go 'forum shopping', that is, they can pick and choose where to test or litigate particular issues. Here then is another source of conflicts of legal norms in the American legal system which has no real parallel in England, because (as we shall see in chapter 5) conflicting appeal court decisions in England would almost invariably lead to (and be felt to demand) immediate resolution by the House of Lords. Attempts have been made to discourage this sort of forum shopping in America by

---

[85] *Ibid.*, at 545, 284 SW 2d at 126.
[86] *Ibid.*, at 547, 284 SW 2d at 126–7.

introducing provisions for the transfer of cases from one Circuit to another where they can more appropriately be dealt with by the latter. But this has raised yet another problem: ought a case so transferred be dealt with by application of 'the law' adhered to by the transferor court or by the transferee court?[87] Further uncertainty while this issue is tossed around seems the only certainty, other than that the issue is certain to be resolved in the light of substantive reasoning.

In this connection it should be noted that while these conflicts remain unresolved—and they may remain unresolved far more often and for more prolonged periods in America—anyone who needs to act with reference to the law will have no way of resolving the conflict in a formal manner, and may therefore be forced to do so according to his own substantive reasoning. A citizen may thus decide to act on his own (or his lawyer's) view of which of the conflicting precedents is substantively correct, and government agencies may be inclined to do the same. It is by no means unknown for federal government agencies to refuse to abide by decisions of a federal appeals court, even within the area of that court, because there are conflicting decisions of other appeals courts which the government believes to be substantively more correct.[88]

Conflicts of laws in the traditional sense

In the American multi-jurisdictional legal system, consisting of fifty states and a federal system as well, numerous cases arise every year posing 'conflict of laws' problems, that is, problems arising from the possible application of law from more than one jurisdiction. Of course, such 'choice of law' problems can and do arise in England also, but far less commonly, because England is a single jurisdiction, and such conflicts can only arise where one or more parties has some contact with other jurisdictions.

Within each American jurisdiction, such conflicts of laws are resolved by reference to the common law rules dealing with 'choice of law'.[89] This body of law has become progressively less formal in America, and in

---

[87] J. C. Wallace, 'The Nature and Extent of Intercircuit Conflicts: A Solution Needed for a Mountain or a Molehill', 71 *Calif. L. Rev.* 913 (1983); Marcus, 'Conflicts among Circuits and Transfers within the Federal Judicial System', 93 *Yale L. J.* 677 (1984).

[88] For the failure of agencies to acquiesce in court rulings (on substantive grounds) see generally Note, 'Administrative Agency Intracircuit Nonacquiescence', 85 *Col. L. Rev.* 582 (1985); Note, '"Respectful Disagreement": Nonacquiescence by Federal Administrative Agencies in US Courts of Appeals Precedents', 18 *Col. J. of Law and Soc. Probs.* 463 (1985).

[89] See generally E. Scoles and P. Hay, *Conflict of Laws* (West, St. Paul, 1984).

most states today is characterized as an 'approach' (or approaches) rather than a set of rules.[90] The approach has been formulated in a variety of terms, usually providing that a court should apply that state's substantive law which most accords with a weighing and balancing of a number of factors. In some formulations, one of these factors is simply: whichever state law is 'the better rule of law'.[91] Section 6 of the new *Restatement (Second) of Conflict of Laws*[92] is sometimes said to favour the law of the state having the 'most significant relationship' to the matter involved. This section does not incorporate the 'better rule of law' factor in so many words, but it does require the court to weigh and balance a variety of 'policies', and in practice this may come to much the same thing, despite protestations by the Restaters to the contrary. Within particular substantive areas such as tort and contract, the new Restatement usually provides a further (and non-exhaustive) enumeration of substantive factors for the deciding court to take into account. It is difficult to imagine a more substantive overall approach to choice of law than that outlined above. Formal rules such as those requiring application of 'the law of the state where a tort occurred', or 'the law of the state where the contract was made', have been abandoned in most American states, though a minority of states retain a more formal approach based on the traditional 'vested rights' theory.

The famous 1973 Minnesota case of *Milkovich* v. *Saari*[93] aptly illustrates how far in the direction of a totally substantive analysis the modern approach may be carried. In this case, the plaintiff was a guest in a car driven by the defendant. Both plaintiff and defendant were residents of Ontario, Canada, but the accident occurred in Minnesota. The Ontario and Minnesota substantive laws potentially applicable to the case were in conflict: Minnesota law only required the plaintiff to prove negligence on the part of the defendant, but Ontario law was governed by a 'guest-statute' requiring the plaintiff to prove gross negligence. The Minnesota Supreme Court decided that Minnesota law should be applied largely because the Minnesota common law rule requiring only proof of ordinary negligence was thought to be 'the better rule of law', and was more consistent with Minnesota's 'concept of fairness and equity'.

By contrast, the English conflict of laws continues to be more formal, and the leading English text on the subject is formulated like a Code in

---

[90] See Reese, 'Choice of Law: Rules or Approach', 57 *Cornell L. Rev.* 315 (1972).

[91] See R. Leflar, *American Conflicts Law*, sec. 107 (3rd edn., Bobbs-Merrill, Indianapolis, 1977); see also W. C. Powers, 'Formalism and Non Formalism in Choice of Law Methodology', 52 *Wash. L. Rev.* 27 (1976).

[92] See E. Scoles and P. Hay, *supra*, n. 89, at 36.

[93] 295 Minn. 155, 203 N.W. 2d 408 (1973).

terms of 'Rules'.[94] It is true that, in some areas, the rules are so flexible that they may appear more like discretions, allowing a highly substantive approach, for instance with regard to contract cases, where the general rule is that the applicable law is that 'with which the contract has the closest connection'.[95] And it is also true that some academic commentators have become sceptical about the firmness with which conflicts 'rules' appear to be applied, detecting an element of 'result-orientation' in the case-law which indicates a more substantive approach.[96] But there is still a very large gap between the English and American approaches. Perhaps this subject is in its nature less suited to a highly formal approach, which would explain why English law is more substantive here than in other fields; but then one has to note that American law shifts still further to the substantive approach, thus preserving the gulf between the two systems.

[94] A. V. Dicey and J. H. C. Morris, *The Conflict of Laws* (10th edn., Stevens, 1980).
[95] See P. S. Atiyah, *From Principles to Pragmatism*, 13 (Clarendon Press, Oxford, 1978) reprinted in 65 *Iowa L. Rev.* 1249, 1257 (1980).
[96] See Fawcett, 'Result Selection in Domicile Cases', 5 *Ox. J. Leg. St.* 378 (1985).

3

Rules and Other Varieties of Law

1. INTRODUCTION

Law without rules and the regular following of rules would not be a system of law as we know it. It would be an *ad hoc* 'system' of discretionary decision making. Logic does not exclude the possibility that such a system could exist in some sense. But for such a system to work, the society would have to be very different from modern industrial societies. And such a system would at least require rules (however implicit) which enable persons to determine who the decision-makers of the society are, and which of their activities are to count as decision making.

Furthermore, a legal system as we know it requires that many of its rules be treated as generating formal reasons for decisions, and not simply as additional factors to be weighed or balanced against reasons of substance, or treated as merely a summing up of the normal balance of such reasons, liable to be displaced whenever a decision-maker has to probe more deeply into the grounds of decision. It may be helpful to recall that in our scheme of analysis, two extreme polarities are possible. At one extreme what is authoritatively laid down is always decisive. In effect, 'the law is the law' or 'a rule is a rule'. *All* contrary substantive reasons arising at the point of application are disregarded (high mandatory formality). Substantive reasons underlying the rules, or other substantive reasons in light of which the rules could be differently interpreted, are also irrelevant in determining the effect of those rules (high interpretive formality). Even a desire for consistency may be brushed aside if firm rules dictate result X in this case and result Z in a relevantly identical case, but one which the rules say is to be treated differently. At the other extreme is the view which never treats any rule as itself generating a formal reason, but invariably invokes underlying or additional reasons, principles, and policies, and also readily takes into account contrary substantive reasons emerging in the context. Indeed, at this extreme it is hard to see how there can be any genuine rules at all, except perhaps rules for identifying who the officials are and what are to count as their decisions.

We doubt whether any legal system, or any court, could consistently operate at one of these polarities. The extreme formal position inevitably leads to mechanical rule-application, to inconsistency and anomaly, and to a failure to articulate clearly what in fact a court does when it fills gaps in the law; it must also lead, very often and obviously, to bad rules. But the substantive extreme is also one which has its problems. The most devoted American instrumentalist must acknowledge *some* fixed datum points, some firm rules, if every decision is not to open up all political theory and philosophy for discussion, indeed, if there is to be a rule of law at all. No judge is in the position of being able to redesign the universe; every search for a principle or policy must take for granted certain assumptions which are not, in this case, and on this occasion, up for discussion. The rule of law requires that these limits on substantive reasons should take the form of firm rules, and not merely further substantive reasons which would tend to be vague and less precise.

2. THE NATURE AND ROLE OF RULES

A rule may be defined (at a high enough level of abstraction to embrace English and American usage) as a norm which applies to a class of cases. Thus a rule must be general in some respect, and this generality can relate to classes of persons, objects, events, and circumstances, or some combination of these.

As we saw in the last chapter some rules have the highest degree of formality. Such rules derive from constitution makers or legislative bodies and are valid solely by virtue of their source (high authoritative formality), are shaped largely by fiat (high content formality), are categorically dispositive (total mandatory formality), and foreclose nearly all inquiry outside the text into substantive rationales for the purpose of interpretation (strict interpretive formality). In this chapter such rules will be called 'hard and fast rules', and they bind somewhat like fetters bind. In a modern legal system we also have rules at the other end of the spectrum with correspondingly low degrees of formality. Most rules of this kind grant discretion with or without standards for its exercise, or incorporate vague concepts such as 'reasonableness'. These rules typically lack significant degrees of mandatory or interpretive formality. They are not hard and fast; we will call them 'flexible rules'.

Hard and fast rules have a strong tendency to generate formal reasoning, but even the most flexible rules must have some formal attributes, in the sense that they will at least require that a judge or given official make a decision, or that a given factor be taken into account, or the like, so that they involve some degree of authoritative formality and at least minimal mandatory formality. In between hard and fast rules and the most flexible rules there are many intermediate varieties.

Rules are not the only kind of normative phenomena in a legal system.

Orders, broad principles, rulings, maxims, and still other normative phenomena are to be found. But hard and fast rules, highly flexible rules, and rules falling somewhere between these two make up the great proportion of the normative phenomena operative in modern legal systems. Leading legal theorists as diverse as H. L. A. Hart and Lon Fuller have even claimed that a legal system is essentially or in large measure *a system of rules*.[1] Certainly, both the English and the American legal systems rely heavily on hard and fast rules, on highly flexible rules, and on rules in between. This necessarily means that there is a good deal of formal reasoning in those systems. Indeed, a significant proportion of the rules to be found in both the English and American systems tend to be of the more hard and fast variety, and thus relatively formal.

Rules as such are a necessity if we are to have centralized government. Governments are *constituted* by rules.[2] Rules are needed to define roles and procedures to be followed in the required organization and division of legal labour. Who is to make law, and by what steps? Who is to administer it, and by what procedures? How is it to be enforced and by whom? The necessity for rules addressed to these matters derives not merely from the need for an elaborate, complex, and consistently administered division of legal labour. It also arises from the fact that the judges and other officials involved could not, over time, command legitimacy in the absence of a rule-defined structure, for there could not be sufficiently defined governmental institutions to serve as the *object* of this legitimacy. Moreover, it seems to us clear that core rules of this kind, relating to the basic structure of government, are likely to be heavily formal. That the Constitution of the United States *is* the existing Constitution, and not some other Constitution, signifies that its *basic structure* is a matter of high mandatory formality. It does not admit of basic exceptions, qualifications, or departures based on reasons of substance. Of course, this high formality is somewhat tempered by the fact that many particular norms of constitutional law are not themselves nearly so formal, but this does not alter the fact that the basic and fundamental constitutional structures are almost by necessity highly formal. Similarly, in Britain, the sovereignty of Parliament is a matter of the highest formality. Although there are today one or two uncertainties surrounding this sovereignty,[3] in almost all areas the rule that what Parliament enacts is law is literally absolute.

---

[1] H. L. A. Hart, *The Concept of Law*, 77–96 (Clarendon Press, Oxford, 1961); Lon L. Fuller, *The Morality of Law* (revised edn., Yale U. Press, New Haven, 1969).

[2] R. S. Summers, 'Working Conceptions of the Law', 1 *Law and Philosophy* 263, 281 (1982).

[3] See, for a simple explanation of these doubts, P. S. Atiyah, *Law and Modern Society*, 60–3 (Oxford U. Press, Oxford, 1983).

Without a large core component of rules and rule observance, the values most commonly associated with the rule of law could not be sufficiently realized in a modern society of any complexity. The more formal the rules are, the more they restrict the scope for official arbitrariness, help secure that like cases (as marked out by law) are treated alike, bring regularity and predictability to social and commercial life, and facilitate 'self-governance' by citizens acting on their own.[4]

Another virtue of the rule of law, suggested by Professor Fuller, is also essentially dependent upon formal rules and the following of rules. When judges and other officials proceed by a known rule laid down in advance, they necessarily afford those subject to the rules a fair opportunity to adapt their conduct to the requirements of the law, thereby avoiding any adverse legal consequences that may flow from non-observance.[5] This is a basic form of fairness in the relations between governor and governed, which may also be readily classified as a distinctive 'rule of law' value.[6] And although Fuller did not use our distinctions between high and low mandatory formality, and between high and low interpretive formality, his point is much stronger in relation to rules of high rather than low formality. A person who is seriously worried about the consequences of breaking the rules will be more anxious to know what precisely is expected of him than to know the underlying reasons or policies behind the rules. And he cannot know precisely what is expected of him if the rules are readily modifiable in the light of substantive reasons which may be relevant when they come to be applied to his case. He may, to be sure, want to see those reasons and policies available for debate and reform in a process to which he has some access; but in the meantime, he will prefer to know what the rules are with some certainty, something which (we suggest) is generally much easier when the rules are of a more formal character. The demand for formal rules—and especially for clarity and proper enforcement of the rules—is thus more likely to come from the ruled themselves than from officials who wish to wield power.

We are not unaware that the position sketched out above is a value-loaded one.[7] The desire to know in advance what rules will be applied is of special value to those best equipped to conform their conduct to those rules and thus to take advantage of them. It is of somewhat less value to those who are too ignorant, weak, or foolish to do so. These members of

[4] Lon L. Fuller, *supra*, n. 1, ch. 2.

[5] *Ibid.*, see also R. S. Summers, *Lon L. Fuller*, 37–8 (Stanford U. Press, Stanford and Edward Arnold, London, 1984).

[6] This also entails 'rule of law *formality*' in the sense that the fairness of the process is independent of the substantive merits of the law itself.

[7] See generally Kennedy, 'Form and Substance in Private Law Adjudication', 89 *Harv. L. Rev.* 1685 (1976).

a community, who are almost by definition the less articulate, might be better off if they had a system of less formal rules under which substantive reasons were more often relied upon by judges and officials; and if they were articulate enough to make their wishes felt, they might indicate that they actually preferred such a system. But we do not wish to become involved in this particular debate. It is enough for us to recognize that, as things now stand, this value choice has already been made to a significant degree by England and America, and that the choice entails the proper use of formal rules in many ways. But it also seems that the precise extent to which formal rules are used is a matter of 'fine tuning' on which different societies may differ considerably. And it is this aspect of the nature of formal rules which is our main focus here.

Another reason for the proliferation of formal rules in modern legal systems is that the satisfactory realization of many substantive public policy goals would be impossible without resort to formal rules. These goals today include public welfare, public health, environmental control, public education, social security, as well as more traditional goals such as the common defence, the provision of a postal service, and the like. Pursuit of broad public goals of this kind requires use of formal rules for at least three reasons. First, the effective implementation of complex and widely ramifying goals such as these generally calls for sophisticated forms of social organization, and these forms are not possible without rules to institutionalize the required structure, processes, and functions.[8] Second, the predictability, uniformity, and publicity of rules and their administration is required to secure the public confidence and co-operation necessary for the realization of goals of this kind, particularly those involving substantial expenditures of public funds and extensive redistributive schemes of public benefit. Imagine, for example, the difficulties of trying to run a modern welfare state, including such complex matters as the tax system and the social security system, without any resort to rules! Third, these rules clearly must be at the formal end of the spectrum. At least one reason for this is that they must be administered by relatively minor officials, and the public is less tolerant of rules of low mandatory formality (granting broad discretions, for instance) where those rules are to be applied by a host of minor administrative officials rather than, for example, by highly visible judges.

If it is true, then, that both the English and the American systems rely heavily on rules, including hard and fast rules, it might seems at first sight that there are no significant differences between the two systems

---

[8] See further R. S. Summers and C. G. Howard, *Law: Its Nature, Functions and Limits*, ch. 4 (Prentice Hall, Englewood Cliffs, NJ, 1972); Summers, 'The Technique Element in Law', 59 *Calif. L.Rev.* 733 (1971).

with regard to rules. In fact we believe that there is much here to support our thesis that the English system is more formal and the American more substantive, as we shall now attempt to demonstrate.

3. THE FLEXIBILITY OF RULES

Although we know of no way to do a systematic count, we believe that the proportion of flexible rules to hard and fast rules is much higher in the American system than in the English. This means that substantive reasons at the point of application are more often determinative in America. It also means that substantive reasoning plays a larger role in the interpretation of rules in America. Conversely, the English system, with its higher proportion of hard and fast rules, is more formal in its law and in its reasoning. In defence of our position, we will cite examples from public law generally, and from two basic fields of private law—tort and contract.

Constitutional law

To begin with, the American system includes large bodies of federal and state constitutional law which have little by way of genuine counterpart in the English system. Of course, in terms of authoritative formality, American constitutional law may be said to be highly formal. The rules are rules of the highest origin, and they override all other conflicting legal rules. But in relevant comparative terms the same is true of England. The sovereignty of Parliament ensures that the rules created by legislation are invested with the highest authoritative formality and override all contrary rules.

Most rules of American constitutional law, however, are not hard and fast, but flexible, often, indeed, highly flexible. Typically, they have low degrees of content, interpretive, and mandatory formality. Many American constitutional provisions merely state broad substantive principles, and judges and others are thus not only permitted to take account of substantive reasons arising at the point of application,[9] but may also go behind the authoritative wording of these rules into their substantive underpinnings, or otherwise read them in light of substantive reasons when interpreting and applying such rules.[10] The pressure for low mandatory and interpretive formality arises from a variety of

[9] On the legitimacy of judicial review, compare Learned Hand, *The Bill of Rights*, ch. 1 (Harvard U. Press, Cambridge, 1958), and Wechsler, 'Towards Neutral Principles of Constitutional Law', 73 *Harv. L. Rev.* 1 (1959). Concerning the interpretivist theory of judicial review, see J. H. Ely, *Democracy and Distrust: A Theory of Judicial Review*, ch. 1 (Harvard U. Press, Cambridge, 1980).

[10] See, e.g, *Griswold* v. *Connecticut*, 381 US 479 (1965); see also P. Bobbitt, *Constitutional Fate: Theory of the Constitution* (Oxford U. Press, NY, 1982).

sources, of which we will note only two. First, the Constitution's makers could hardly have foreseen the immense social and economic changes which have accompanied the industrialization and settlement of the United States. Secondly, for special reasons, the federal Constitution is not easily subject to formal amendment, so that change in American constitutional law has to take place through some form of interpretation. Both of these factors exert continuous pressure for relatively low interpretive and mandatory formality.

Other public law

What about non-constitutional rules of public law? As already conceded, important bodies of both English and American public law include many hard and fast rules, and this is especially true of statutory rules. Most of the rules governing social security benefits and the taxation of private persons are aptly illustrative. Even here, we believe that non-constitutional American public law includes relatively more flexible rules in comparison with England.[11] Much American regulatory law, for instance, is actually drafted in highly flexible terms. Indeed, important branches of the law even verge on the vacuous. A famous example is the Communications Act of 1934 which provides that the FCC may regulate the activities of radio and television stations 'as public convenience, interest or necessity' requires.[12] Another more recent regulatory statute simply granted the President the power to 'regulate prices' in the entire economy.[13] Under various recent federal regulatory statutes, administrators have discretion to create exceptions to the operation of entire regulatory programmes.[14] These, of course, are extreme examples, but much American public law is to be found towards this end of the spectrum.

It would be difficult to find comparably extreme examples in English law, at any rate in time of peace: at least we know of none. In wartime, it is certainly not unknown for vast statutory powers to be delegated to the

---

[11] For the view that in the taxation field American courts have pursued substantive reasoning (not always very successfully) see Isenbergh, 'Musings on Form and Substance in Taxation', 49 *U. Chi. L. Rev.* 859 (1982) (book review). In England, the House of Lords has recently begun to see some virtue in this substantive approach in some limited tax avoidance cases, see *W. T. Ramsay Ltd.* v. *IRC* [1982] AC 300; *Furniss* v. *Dawson* [1984] AC 474. But the very fact that these cases have been perceived as revolutionary in the English context is itself highly suggestive. See, e.g., Note, [1984] *British Tax Rev.* 201, 202: '[T]he House of Lords has undermined one of the cornerstones of commercial life in this country.'

[12] Communications Act of 1934, ch. 652, § 303, 48 Stat. 1082 (current version at 47 USC § 303 (1982)).

[13] Economic Stabilization Act of 1970, § 202, 84 Stat. 799–800.

[14] See K. C. Davis, *Administrative Law Treatise*, vol. 2, §§ 8:1–8:12 (2nd edn., West, St. Paul, 1979). See also *post,* p. 133, n. 42.

executive in the broadest of language, but in peace time this kind of thing would not generally be tolerated by Parliament, despite the degree to which Parliament is normally subservient to the wishes of the executive.

That American public law includes highly flexible rules filled with open-ended concepts and broad grants of discretion (with, and sometimes without, standards for the exercise of that discretion) is hardly surprising and not of itself a basis for criticism. No modern system could get by on hard and fast rules alone. As Professor K. C. Davis said in his well-known book, *Discretionary Justice*:[15]

No legal system in world history has been without discretionary power. None can be. Discretion is indispensable for individualized justice, for creative justice, for new programs in which no one yet knows how to formulate rules, and for old programs in which some aspects cannot be reduced to rules. Eliminating discretionary power would paralyze governmental processes and would stifle individualized justice. Those who would forbid governmental coercion except on the basis of rules previously announced seem to me to have misunderstood the elements of law and government.

One of the present authors has recently demonstrated that even in England there is an important trend in public law (and beyond) away from hard and fast rules, and towards more flexible rules incorporating wide discretionary power.[16] Indeed, there are some areas that are governed less by hard and fast rules in England than in America, as we shall see below. Nevertheless, we adhere to the proposition supporting our general thesis, that American public law includes proportionately more flexible statutory rules, as drafted, than hard and fast rules, as compared with the English system.

But even if English and American statutory rules of public law were not significantly different *on their face* in terms of relative flexibility, we have no doubt that most American rules are more flexible than English ones *as applied*. In America, what seems hard and fast when drafted frequently becomes highly flexible in application, a tendency that is nothing like so pervasive or so strong in England. Countless examples could be cited, but it will suffice here to refer to one of the best known, the Sherman Anti-Trust Act. This Act declared all contracts in restraint of trade to be illegal, but the courts interpreted this as applying only to 'unreasonable' restraints, which, of course, introduced an element of

[15] *Discretionary Justice: A Preliminary Inquiry*, 216–17 (Louisiana State Univ. Press, Baton Rouge, 1969).
[16] P. S. Atiyah, *From Principles to Pragmatism* (Clarendon Press, Oxford, 1978, reprinted in 65 *Iowa L. Rev.* 1249 (1980)).

extreme flexibility into the operation of the rule.[17] As we shall see more fully in the next chapter, there is overall much less interpretive formality in the American system, and this tends to transform apparently hard and fast rules into rather more flexible ones. Judges and other officials in America feel much freer to go behind (or beyond) the language of public law statutes to determine their authoritative meaning. Furthermore, American judges and officials generally accord less mandatory formality to statutes than do English judges and officials. This too tends to transform rules which appear hard and fast on their face into rules which are subject to discretionary modification at the point of application, in the light of contrary substantive reasons relevant there. Both of these factors are, in turn, influenced in America by a distinctively substantive conception of what constitutes a rule in the first place, a matter to which we will return later in this chapter.

Apart from these variations in the flexibility of apparently formal rules, we believe that flexible rules explicitly providing for discretion also tend in the English system to be more formal in operation than their American counterparts. Indeed, even if there are actually more flexible rules explicitly providing for discretions in England (as there probably are in certain fields), we think it is still the case that England is overall more formal in its rule adherence and application than America. In fact English law increasingly includes examples of overt judicial discretion conferred by statute. This may be precisely because English law overall is tighter and more constrained by formal rule application in the ordinary way than American law. In America the element of discretion often exists, submerged in institutional or other factors, even when it is not explicitly conferred. On the other hand, when it is *not* overtly recognised in England, the courts may find themselves unable to make adequate use of substantive reasoning to enable the system to strike a proper balance between formal rule application and individualized justice. Hence the pressure for some overt legislative grant of such discretions may become overwhelming; this is, we believe, what has happened in England during the past thirty or forty years.

As we have stressed, the lack of a formal grant of a discretion does not signify that no discretion exists. In America, many areas nominally governed by rules are in reality the subject of considerable discretionary judgment. This is true not only with respect to specific legal issues in particular fields of law; it is true also in wider ranging terms of any system of law which relies, as does the American legal system, on the jury

---

[17] See *Standard Oil Co.* v. *US* 221 US 1 (1911), *US* v. *American Tobacco Co.* 221 US 106 (1911). See generally E. Hodges, *The Antitrust Act and the Supreme Court* (West, St. Paul, 1941).

to find facts and to return general verdicts with only the lightest touch of judicial supervision. Thus it is particularly relevant that the civil jury is still widely used in American whereas it has been little used in England for over 50 years. One illustration will suffice at this point to indicate how covert jury discretion operating in the American system is much less subject to formal control than the overt judicial discretion that is its English counterpart. In England the common law contributory negligence rule was replaced by a comparative negligence rule by statute in 1945.[18] This Act gives the trial judge the power to reduce the plaintiff's damages to such extent as appears just and equitable, having regard to the plaintiff's share of the responsibility for what happened. Nothing could appear more discretionary and less rule-governed than a power of this kind. By contrast, most American states retained the common law rule until comparatively recent times, and some still do so today.[19] However, it has been widely acknowledged by lawyers that, despite the apparent all-or-nothing nature of the common law rule, American juries in practice often compromised by awarding a plaintiff reduced damages.[20] Yet we would confidently suggest that the open and avowed statutory discretion conferred on English judges operates in a more structured and predictable fashion than the *de facto* jury modification of apparently firm rule that occurs in America. The reasons for this are fairly clear. Judges give reasons for their decisions, even discretionary ones, juries do not; and judges share a corpus of professional opinions and ideas (far more so in England than in America, of which more later) which ensure a greater uniformity of outlook than is likely with juries.

The extent to which a system remains loyal to formal, as opposed to substantive, reasons, in its use and control of discretion, appears to us to depend on a number of factors other than the bare conferral of discretion. Discretion embedded within a tight structure of formal legal rules is a very different thing from discretion added to a system already much less dependent on formal rules. Discretion in English law tends to be surrounded by the constraints of a system of formal rules. We suggest that the following are the most important factors to be considered in deciding how far grants of discretion actually weaken the general formal approach of a legal system to the application of rules:

(1) The degree to which discretionary grants are themselves enclosed

---

[18] Law Reform (Contributory Negligence) Act 1945.

[19] See Prosser and Keeton on *Torts*, 453, 468–9 (5th edn., West, St. Paul, 1984).

[20] See Professor (now Judge) Robert E. Keeton, 'Comments on *Maki* v. *Frelk*—Comparative v. Contributory Negligence: Should the Court or Legislature Decide?' 21 *Vand. L. Rev.* 889, 916 (1968), noting that jury modification of the contributory negligence rule operated in 'unpoliced, irregular, and unreasonably discriminatory fashion'.

within a well-defined area so that they are clearly marked off from the area within which surrounding rules govern;

(2) The breadth of choice which the grants of discretion confer, and the extent to which they are dispositive of the main issues in the types of case involved;

(3) The extent to which the legal criteria that are to influence the exercise of discretion can be readily identified and applied in light of the evidence in the particular case;

(4) The degree of uniformity attainable in the exercise of discretion (which in turn is largely dependent on the homogeneity of outlook of the decision-makers and the availability of appellate procedures capable of imposing some uniformity on lower court decisions);

(5) The degree to which predictability is possible in the actual exercise of discretion, which is itself no doubt largely determined by factors (1) to (4) above.

Even if there are more instances of open grants of discretionary powers to courts in England than America (and in some areas there probably are), the former system is still, we think, more formal in its approach when account is taken of the above factors. Of these factors, we believe it is in general accurate to say that discretion in English law is usually found within a carefully structured framework of formal rules; that the principal factors relevant to its exercise can usually be identified without great difficulty and, indeed, are today often laid down as 'guidelines' by appellate courts or even statutes;[21] that the homogeneity of outlook of English judges leads to high levels of uniformity in the exercise of discretion; and that the totality of these factors does not seriously impair predictability of result, even in comparison with the use of formal rules. The one source of doubt concerns factor (2) listed above. There are certainly some circumstances today in which very broad discretion exists in English law, some of which confers quite dramatic new powers on the judiciary, such as (for instance) the power to order 'reasonable' provision to be made out of the estate of a deceased person to some one who was wholly or partly dependent upon him, and for whom the deceased has made no or inadequate provision.[22] When powers of this nature are first conferred, the legal system would seem *pro tanto* to have abandoned rule for blanket discretion, and there are enough instances of this kind in English law to raise anxieties, as one of the present authors has previously argued elsewhere.[23] But even in cases

---

[21] See, e.g., Unfair Contract Terms Act 1977, Sched. 2; Matrimonial Proceedings and Property Act 1970, s. 5; and for judicial statements of guidelines as to the exercise of a judicial discretion, see *Jefford* v. *Gee* [1970] 2 QB 130; *Cookson* v. *Knowles* [1979] AC 556.

[22] See Inheritance (Provision for Family and Dependants) Act 1975.

[23] P. S. Atiyah, *supra*, n. 16.

of this extreme nature there is a tendency, as cases multiply, for the discretion to become much more closely circumscribed. Guidelines for its exercise may be laid down, and even other exercises of the discretion, though not strictly binding as precedents, may have a persuasive influence on a homogeneous judiciary where uniformity and predictability of result are highly prized, and where deference to colleagues is widely practised.

Many students of English social and political practice have observed that there sometimes appears to be a noticeable lack of rules in fields which are instead governed by customary norms, or even by an apparent lack of norms altogether. In comparable social and political fields in America, rules are, by contrast, found in profusion. We will cite two examples, and consider how they bear on our primary thesis.

The first example which comes to mind concerns the way in which decisions were made about the use of kidney machines when the supply was plainly inadequate to the need. In *Tragic Choices*[24] Guido Calabresi and Philip Bobbitt noted the tendency for American solutions to be rule-structured, while they appear to have been somewhat shocked by the British response which largely took the form of leaving the decision in the uncontrolled hands of medical personnel. Inevitably, the British response meant that whatever criteria were in fact used by the medical personnel were never explicitly formulated, nor available for public discussion, nor could any serious attempt be made to ensure uniformity or enlightened application throughout the country.

A second example of an area in which rules are found in America while England seems to manage with informal understandings and customs is more directly related to the legal process itself. Formal rules relating to the circumstances in which a judge should recuse himself on grounds of interest are almost totally unknown in England. Motions that a judge should recuse himself are equally unheard of in England. Such formal rules as do exist all arise out of *ex post* determinations relating to the conduct of inferior tribunals or courts. Not for over a hundred years has a decision of one of the superior courts in England been set aside on the ground that the judge should not have sat due to interest. But the reason for the absence of formal rules about these matters is that the higher judiciary is of such integrity that rules are felt to be unnecessary. No English judge would ever sit in a case in which he felt any real doubt about the propriety of his doing so. There are instances of judges informing counsel that they have some very remote and indirect interest, and offering to withdraw if counsel should desire it. The almost invariable reaction of counsel is to decline such an offer.[25]

[24] G. Calabresi and P. Bobbitt, *Tragic Choices* (Norton, NY, 1978).
[25] For instance, in *Bromley London BC* v. *Greater London Council* [1982] 1 All ER 129,

By contrast, rules on reversal or disqualification exist in profusion in the United States,[26] and motions and decisions on disqualification are commonplace.[27] Informal guidelines were prepared by the American Bar Association as far back as 1924, and recently superseded by the Code of Judicial Conduct in 1972. This code was substantially adopted for the federal judiciary by the Judicial Conference of the United States in the following year. Congress legislated in this area as early as 1792,[28] and more recently passed the Judicial Disqualification Act of Dec. 5, 1974.[29] We do not see how to reconcile these examples with the thesis that the English legal system is more formal than the American. It can hardly be suggested that the English approach is actually more formal than the American if England deals with a problem without rules at all (or so it seems) while America has rules aplenty. These examples do therefore run counter to our thesis, and no doubt there are others of a like kind.

These counter-examples, however, seem to be confined to areas of activity that are regulated by law in America, while remaining largely unregulated by law in England. At first sight it may seem surprising that there should be any such activities if we are right in our principal thesis, that the American legal system is generally less formal than the English. We think that a number of special features explain why such counter-examples exist. First, these are areas of activity in which the values at stake (life itself, in the kidney machine example, and judicial integrity, in the second example) are of exceptional importance. Secondly, they are areas of activity in which there exists (or may exist) in England, what is markedly lacking in America, a corpus of customary norms arising from the greater homogeneity of the British people, and the greater homogene-

---

131–2, in which the legality of a rate precept (local property tax) was challenged, Lord Denning informed counsel in the CA that he was a ratepayer in the Greater London Council, and offered to withdraw. The offer was declined.

[26] For literature concerning judicial recusal in America, see J. van Schaick and K. Sampson, *Selected Literature on Judicial Conduct and Disability: An Annotated Bibliography* (American Judicature Society, Chicago, 1983); C. A. Wright, A. Miller, and E. Cooper, *Federal Practice and Procedure,* vol. 13A, §§ 3541–53 (West, St. Paul, 1984); see also Levy, 'Judicial Recusals', 2 *Pace L. Rev.* 35 (1982); Markey, 'The Delicate Dichotomies of Judicial Ethics', 101 FRD 373, 377–84 (1980). For a remarkable modern example of judicial insensitivity to the ethics of recusal, see Stolz, *Judging Judges,* 368–88 (Free Press, NY, Collier Macmillan, London, 1981).

[27] See generally F. Tilewick, *Decisions Construing the Judicial Disqualification Statute* (Federal Judicial Center, Washington, 1977); Wright, Miller, and Cooper, *supra,* n. 26.

[28] For a historical review of canons and codes governing the ethics of judicial conduct, see Comment, 'Disqualification for Interest of Lower Federal Court Judges: 28 USC § 455', 71 *Mich. L. Rev.* 538, 538–41 (1973).

[29] 28 USC § 455; Public Law 93–512; 88 Stat. 1609 (1982).

ity of the English judiciary. Conversely, these are areas of activity in which, in the absence of formal reasoning and formal rules, substantive reasoning in America might be found to lead (and indeed, in perhaps both these examples, did lead) to unacceptable degrees of disharmony, disagreement, and unpredictability.

The result is that, despite the fact that in these areas English law is, exceptionally, less formal than American, the position in England may in practice resemble the formal approach, even though the normal attributes of formal reasoning are absent. England may succeed in these areas—even at the price of suppressing debate about very important public issues (in the kidney machine example)—in achieving the same results that formal reasoning is designed to achieve, especially uniformity and predictability, without the apparatus of formal rules. By contrast, the American position, though concededly more formal in legal terms than the English in these instances, is affected by the generally low level of formality which rules so often have in the American legal system. The position overall thus comes close to that in which overt discretions exist in English law, while the position in America is apparently governed by rules: we have already suggested that in many such cases the English legal system is in operation more formal than the American. We cannot go quite so far as this in dealing with these counter-examples because, in the absence of formal rules, the English position lacks authoritative formality altogether, but at the same time we do not regard these counter-examples as significantly weakening our principal thesis.

Private law

We now turn to private law, and in particular to the rules of contract and tort. Again, we have no doubt that the American common law of contract and tort includes a relatively higher proportion of flexible rules than hard and fast ones compared to English law. For several decades now, the American legal system has been substituting explicitly discretionary law in place of relatively hard and fast rules, and the developments are particularly striking in regard to the basic theories of obligation operative in the contractual field. Thus, in the Restatements and in the case-law, the underlying principles governing justified reliance,[30] restitutionary claims,[31] and claims based on 'past consideration'[32] are all formulated today in terms which include specific reference to the words 'justice' or 'injustice', and to the need to avoid injustice. For example, the remedy available for claims based on justified reliance is to

[30] Restatement (Second) of Contract, § 90 (1979).
[31] Restatement (Second) of Contract, § 372 (1) (*a*) (1979); and the word 'justice' appears also in § 371.
[32] Restatement (Second) of Contracts, § 86 (1979).

be limited as justice requires. This may have originally been designed to ensure that only reliance damages are awardable in claims based on promissory estoppel, but in modern times many American courts have used this sort of principle to justify limiting damages where it seems just to do so even in breach of contract claims. Indeed, there are signs that the whole law of damages in American contract law is slowly becoming discretionary, with the courts coming to award the sort of damages which seem to them appropriate according to the substantive reasons emerging at the point of application in the particular case.

Similar developments have been taking place in America with regard to good faith, unconscionability, excuses for non-performance and general equitable principles. The entire subject of excuses for non-performance in contract, and the related subject of justified termination of contractual relations, are shaped by increasingly flexible or discretionary notions. Even the most important body of American statute law applicable to contract—the Sales Article of the Uniform Commercial Code—includes numerous discretionary provisions and 'safety valve' concepts.[33] The trend is now widely recognized and accepted. It is also reinforced and extended by the general tendency of many judges in the American system to transform rules that are less flexible on their face into something relatively more flexible at the point of application, as well as by the practice of jury trial which often transforms the rules involved, as we shall see later.

In the English law of contract, there have been some similar developments, but the position overall remains far more formal than in America. For example, the English law of contractual damages continues to be treated by judges and writers as governed by highly formal rules.[34] Even with respect to problems which are inherently difficult to force into a framework of formal rules—such as the foreseeability principle of *Hadley* v. *Baxendale*[35]—English courts still try to formulate the law in terms of specific formal rules,[36] and most English judges try (if, as some may think, rather futilely) to apply these rules formally.[37]

Again, there is an interesting contrast between the English and American approaches to the law of consideration. In America, Corbin

[33] See generally, J. White and R. S. Summers, *Handbook of the Law under the Uniform Commercial Code* (2nd edn., West, St. Paul, 1980). This overall trend toward open-ended rules was stressed by Grant Gilmore in his celebrated book, *The Death of Contract* (Ohio State U. Press, Columbus, 1974) and was underscored recently by Burnett Harvey: 'Discretionary Justice under the Restatement (Second) of Contracts', 67 *Cornell L. Rev.* 666 (1982).

[34] For a highly formal approach to the English law of damages, see G. H. Treitel, *Law of Contract*, ch. 21 (6th edn., Stevens, London, 1983).

[35] (1854) 9 Ex. 341.

[36] See *Koufos* v. *C. Czarnikow Ltd. (The Heron II)* [1969] 1 AC 350.

[37] See, e.g., *H. Parsons (Livestock)* v. *Uttley, Ingham & Co. Ltd.*, [1978] QB 791.

popularized the notion that consideration is a *reason* for the enforcement of a promise,[38] thus introducing a highly substantive approach into what had hitherto been a rather formal area of the law even in America. Since then, a much more flexible approach to the problem of consideration has become evident in America, as judges strive to look for the substantive reasons which may justify the enforcement of a promise, rather than merely to a set of formal rules. But in England, the law of consideration continues to be perceived as a 'doctrine', full of technical, formal, and hard and fast rules.[39] When the first named author of the present book wrote an article some fifteen years ago, under the influence of Corbin's work, and tried to introduce his ideas into England,[40] the immediate reaction of England's leading orthodox contract scholar was hostile on the very ground that to treat consideration as a *reason* for the enforcement of a promise was to throw away the rule book.[41] And there is no sign even now that English judges are willing to adopt a similar approach to Corbin's.[42]

Similar differences in the two legal systems can be observed in relation to that perennial problem of modern contract law, the exculpatory, or exemption, clause. Many American courts, looking underneath the formal indications of assent in standard form contracts, rightly concluded that many exculpatory clauses are not read, understood, or in any real sense agreed to, by consumers, and they have accordingly rejected them on various grounds, such as unconscionability or for reasons of public policy.[43] English courts, however, floundered about with the problem for many years, unwilling to enforce such clauses in many circumstances, but also unable to depart from the formal effect of apparent agreement. They accordingly resorted widely to strained methods of construction (as indeed, had earlier generations of American judges) until they were rescued by the Unfair Contract Terms Act 1977. This Act strikes down some types of exemption clauses, and gives the court overt discretion as to other types, this being a prime example of that kind of explicit statutory discretion referred to above. While the discretion appears broad and unfettered, in practice, it is likely that,

---

[38] See Corbin on *Contract*, vol. 1, §§ 109–11 (revised edn., West, St. Paul, 1963).

[39] See Treitel, *supra*, n. 34, at 51–78.

[40] P. S. Atiyah, *Consideration in Contract: A Fundamental Restatement* (Australian National U. Press, Canberra, 1971), and see now the revised version in P. S. Atiyah, *Essays on Contract* (Clarendon Press, Oxford, 1986).

[41] Treitel, 'Professor Atiyah's Fundamental Restatement: A Critical Analysis', 50 *Aus. L J* 439 (1976); Treitel, *supra*, n. 34, at 54.

[42] For a modern example of a very formal analysis of consideration see *Centrovincial Estates PLC* v. *Merchant Investors Assurance* (1983) Com. LR 158.

[43] See, e.g., *Henningsen* v. *Bloomfield Motors* 32 NJ 358, 161 A. 2d 69 (1960); *Weaver* v. *American Oil Co.* 257 Ind. 458, 276 NE 2d 144 (1971).

after a few more cases have been decided under it, lawyers will be able to predict how the discretion will be exercised in most circumstances.

Much the same general contrast can be found when we turn to the law of tort. Modern American tort law is shot through with flexible rules and principles, while English law remains in general loyal to the idea of law as a set of formal rules. But perhaps the greater contrast here arises from the mode of trial, rather than the rules of liability, though the former has a great influence on the latter. Because so many tort actions are tried by juries in America and by judges in England, formal rules have developed in England with reference to many matters, such as the computation of damages in personal injury cases, which in America remain a matter for the jury. How to discount lost future earnings, for instance, is almost entirely a matter for jury discretion in America, while it is the subject of fairly precise rules and practices in England.[44] Again, the effect of tax liability on damages for lost earnings is subject to firm rule in England (the amount of tax is deducted from the damages),[45] while in America, although in theory many courts adopt the opposite rule, in practice the matter is usually left in the hands of the jury. Indeed, some American courts have actually decided to inform the jury of the tax position, without telling the jury what they ought to do with this information—by English standards, an astonishing emasculation of formal rules.[46] Similarly, the permissibility of awards of exemplary damages in tort cases is much restrained by formal rules in English law,[47] while in America the tendency of recent years has increasingly been to leave such questions to the jury with only the vaguest directions as to when such an award is appropriate.[48]

Both English and American tort law make extensive use of the concept of 'reasonableness', but once again, since decisions on such questions are made in England by judges, and of course by English judges who are generally more formal in their approach, it is not surprising to find that they take the concept seriously, and give fully reasoned decisions for

---

[44] See, e.g., P. S. Atiyah, *Accidents, Compensation and the Law*, ch. 7 (4th edn., P. Cane, ed., Weidenfeld & Nicolson, London, 1987).

[45] See *British Transport Commission* v. *Gourley* [1956] AC 185.

[46] Thus in *Burlington Northern Inc.* v. *Boxberger* 529 F. 2d 284 (1976) the Court of Appeals for the Ninth Circuit held that the jury must be informed in federal tort claims that the damages will not be subject to income tax, though they did not go on to require that the jury be instructed to award damages on the basis of net income. But see now *Norfolk & Western Railroad* v. *Liepelt* 444 US 490 (1980) which does seem to require such instruction.

[47] See *Rookes* v. *Barnard* [1964] AC 1129; *Cassell & Co. Ltd.* v. *Broome* [1972] AC 1027.

[48] See, e.g., Mallor and Roberts, 'Punitive Damages: Towards a Principled Approach', 31 *Hast. LJ* 639 (1980); Owen, 'Punitive Damages in Products Liability Litigation', 74 *Mich. L. Rev.* 1257 (1976); Ellis, 'Fairness and Efficiency in the Law of Punitive Damages', 56 *So. Cal. L. Rev.* 1 (1982).

finding that there has (or has not) been negligence. In America, on the other hand, the modern trend has been increasingly to leave issues of negligence to juries, and their findings are nowadays less challengeable on appeal. Thus it is unclear to what extent the apparent rules of negligence (flexible though these already are) tend to be observed in practice in America.

Other concepts which are used in the law of torts in both systems also illustrate how much more flexible American law is in its approach to rules. For example, the concept of 'intention', which is obviously central to certain torts, has been stretched in America to such a degree that (for example) many malpractice actions are held to be intentional torts because the patient's consent was obtained without fully informing him of the risks involved;[49] in England, this development has been rejected, and such actions are treated as claims in negligence.[50] So too the standards used by American courts to decide when to impose strict products liability are unclear, to say the least.[51]

One area in which the American trend towards flexibility has so far been staved off is worth noting, even though here English and American law are similar. In both legal systems, a general rule of a fairly formal ('brightline') nature has held sway for many years, to the effect that a plaintiff cannot obtain damages for economic loss resulting from negligent damage to property in which he has no proprietary or possessory interest.[52] This rule has been under increasing attack in both countries, as negligence liability has expanded, but in general the attacks have so far been fended off in England[53] and in the American federal courts.[54] It will be seen that if the formal rule here is once breached in general terms, there will be no rule at all with which to replace it—what plaintiffs are to be entitled to recover for what economic losses will have

[49] See, e.g., *Canterbury* v. *Spence* 464 F. 2d 772 (D.C. Cir. 1972). See also Prosser and Keeton, *supra*, n. 19, who note (at 33–34) that, even though the American Law Institute drafted both the Restatement (Second) of Torts and the Model Penal Code, their respective definitions of intent read differently.

[50] *Sidaway* v. *Bethlem Royal Hospital* [1985] 1 All ER 643.

[51] See Brown, 'Comment on Calabresi and Klevorick's Four Tests for Liability in Torts', XIV *J. Leg. St.* 629, 631–2 (1986): 'Courts seem to have a vast array of legal rules from which to choose. Their criteria for choice are totally unclear.'

[52] See *Robins Dry Dock* v. *Flint* 275 US 303 (1927) and *Cattle* v. *Stockton Waterworks* (1875) LR 10 QB 453; *Candlewood Navigation Ltd.* v. *Mitsui OSK Lines* [1985] 3 WLR 381.

[53] *Spartan Steel and Alloys Ltd.* v. *Martin & Co. (Contractors) Ltd.* [1973] QB 27; *Candlewood Navigation Ltd.* v. *Mitsui OSK Lines, supra*, n. 52; *Muirhead* v. *Industrial Tank Specialities*. [1985] 3 All ER 705, but cf. *Junior Books Ltd.* v. *Veitchi Co. Ltd*. [1983] AC 520.

[54] See *State of Louisiana* v. *M/V Testbank* 752 F. 2d 1019 (CA 5th Cir., 1985); *Barber Lines* v. *M/V Donau Maru* 764 F. 2d 50 (CA 3d Cir., 1985). See Atiyah, Note, 'Economic Loss in the United States', 5 *Ox. J. Leg. St.* 485 (1985).

to be worked out on a case-by-case basis over many years of litigation, with the courts necessarily resorting to substantive reasoning in the process. Although (as we have said) most American courts have drawn back so far from this potentially immense expansion of the flexible area of liability for negligence, several American judges in recent federal cases have shown a willingness to face this possible development without flinching.[55]

4. TWO CONCEPTIONS OF RULES

We believe that English and American judges and lawyers have different conceptions of what a rule is, and this difference also helps account for the greater formality of the English legal system in regard to rules and other norms. Many American judges have a very non-formal or substantive conception of what counts as a true rule. As Roscoe Pound (a former judge as well as jurist) once put it:

[The American judge] conceives of the legal rule as a general guide to the judge, leading him to the just result, but insists that within wide limits he should be free to deal with the individual case, so as to meet the demands of justice between the parties and accord with the general reason of the ordinary man.[56]

Pound's conception of a rule as a 'mere guideline' is thus one that tolerates low formality in at least two major dimensions: mandatoriness and interpretation. A rule conceived as no more than a mere 'guide' may, for example, allow contrary substantive reasons arising out of the context to override it, even if these reasons are only slightly weightier. And such a rule invites interpreters to go behind it to determine its meaning almost without limit. In Llewellyn's words, 'the rule follows where its reason leads; where the reason stops, there stops the rule.'[57] There is widespread evidence that a great many American judges and theorists have held to, and continue to hold to, a conception of a rule as a mere guideline.

By contrast, we believe that nearly all English lawyers and judges adhere to a narrower and more formal conception of what a rule is. Indeed, we believe that one reason why English judges seldom regard principles (as distinct from rules) as forms of law is that they tend to

---

[55] See the dissenting opinions in the *Testbank* case, *supra*, n. 54, discussed in Atiyah, Note, *supra*, n. 54 and see also *J'Aire* v. *Gregory, Inc.*, 598 P. 2d 60 (1979).

[56] Pound, 'The Scope and Purpose of Sociological Jurisprudence', 25 *Harv. L. Rev.* 489, 515 (1912).

[57] K. Llewellyn, *The Bramble Bush*, 189 (Oceana Publications, NY, 1960). Taken literally, this view of the relationship between a rule and its purposes would nearly exclude all content and interpretive formality.

think that only rules (preferably hard and fast rules) can be *real* law.[58] They think of a rule as a norm which attaches detailed legal consequences to specific and well-defined states of fact. They thus have a conception of a rule in which the rule is highly mandatory and in which the rationales, principles, and policies underlying or involved in the rule are viewed as something distinct from the rule itself, except insofar as these are more or less explicitly incorporated into the language of the rule. A striking, and not unsophisticated, expression of this viewpoint comes from an opinion of Maule J. in 1842 in a case concerning the exclusion of the testimony of spouses of parties under the common law rule then in force:

The textbooks generally give, as the reason for the rule as to excluding the testimony of husband or wife, the necessity of preserving the confidence of the conjugal relation; and that may be so. But it by no means follows that the rule is co-extensive with the reason given in support of it; and indeed it would be very inconvenient if it were so; as the question would frequently be raised as to whether or not some particular communication or fact occurring between husband and wife was of a confidential character; which would give rise to endless embarrassment and distrust. A rule may be a very good rule, though the reason on which it is founded may not be applicable to every case which is governed by the rule.[59]

The difference between the English and the American approaches in this respect is brought out by the much greater importance attached in America to Coke CJ's old maxim, *Cessante ratione, cessat ipsa lex*. A 'stunning' example of an innovative use of the *cessante ratione* maxim in recent American case-law is to be found in *Abele* v. *Markle*.[60] Newman DJ here was prepared to hold a Connecticut anti-abortion statute void, not because it *per se* infringed the Constitution, but because the reasons underlying the legislative purpose (protection of the mother's health) had been shown to be unsound (because childbirth in fact poses a greater risk than abortion).

American courts often rely explicitly or implicitly on the *cessante ratione* maxim.[61] It is also enshrined in some statutes, for example, the California Civil Code, § 3510 of which enacts that, 'When the reason of a rule ceases, so should the rule itself.' This Code is treated by the California courts as though it were a 'common law' code.

---

[58] As to principles, see section 5 of this chapter, *post*, p. 93.

[59] *O'Connor* v. *Marjoribanks* (1842) 4 M. & G. 435, 445, 134 ER 179, 183.

[60] 342 F. Supp. 800 (1972). The adjective 'stunning' is Calabresi's, see his *A Common Law for the Age of Statutes*, 22 (Harvard U. Press, Cambridge, 1982). Calabresi canvasses but rejects the possibility of a rule permitting general nullification of statutes if the original basis of the statute has ceased to apply. *Ibid.*, 23.

[61] For just one example, see *Kennedy* v. *Parrott*, 243 NC 355, 90 SE 2d 754 (1956) (adopting new rule for unauthorized extension of surgery).

By contrast, the English view is that the *cessante ratione* maxim is of quite limited scope. First, it is firmly subject to the doctrine of *stare decisis*, so that an English court bound by a prior decision is not entitled to reject the authority of that decision by praying in aid the maxim.[62] This, it will be seen, is an emphatic affirmation of the mandatory formality of the doctrine of *stare decisis*, and a rejection of the notion that substantive considerations at the point of application can restrict that formality. Second, in any event, even in the case of courts not strictly bound by prior decisions, the mandatory formality of old and often-repeated judicial holdings tends to become so great that the courts will not discard the precedents merely because the reasons for them are no longer applicable. The precedents lay down law, and the law (in the view of English courts) can only be changed by Parliament, except in minor details.

For example, in *Ex parte Good, Re Armitage*[63] it was sought to limit the extent of the rule that the release of one joint debtor necessarily releases the others. While holding that the rule did not apply to the case in hand, Sir George Jessel MR nevertheless refused to go into the purposes or origin of the rule, and added for good measure: 'It is very dangerous for modern judges to endeavour to find modern reasons for these old rules.'[64] The implication, presumably, is that judges should apply rules strictly without worrying about the reasons for them. Similarly, in *Admiralty Commissioners* v. *SS Amerika*,[65] an attempt was made to persuade the House of Lords to depart from, or limit the effect of, the old common rule that death could not give rise to a cause of action in tort. Lord Sumner's answer to this was that 'an established rule does not become questionable merely because different conjectural justifications of it have been offered, or because none is forthcoming that is not fanciful'.[66] These are extreme and rather dated examples of this approach, and we do not say that they would necessarily reflect the viewpoint of modern English judges; but even modern judges are often reluctant to regard themselves as entitled to create exceptions to a 'firm' rule laid down in a somewhat dogmatic manner by a higher court.[67]

---

[62] See the House of Lords decision in *Miliangos* v. *George Frank (Textiles) Ltd.* [1976] AC 443.

[63] (1877) 5 Ch. D. 46.

[64] At 57.

[65] [1917] AC 38.

[66] At 56.

[67] For a striking example of a modern rule being applied with high mandatory formality, see *A/S Awilco* v. *Fulvia SpA di Navigazione (The Chikuma)* [1981] 1 WLR 314 (owner of chartered ship held entitled to terminate charter because of technical and trivial delay in payment of charter rent on due date). See criticisms of F. A. Mann in Note, 'Uncertain Certainty', 97 *Law Q. Rev.* 379 (1981). Cf., for a much more substantive decision, *Holwell*

Some American lawyers are sceptical about the English tendency to think that adherence to rule can be pursued relatively neutrally, without regard to policies and reasons underlying or otherwise relevant to the rule. The purported neutral application of rules is, they argue, a sham: whatever English judges may say, they are always making implicit decisions about the purposes of legal rules and legal concepts when they apply rules, at any rate if the rules contain references to legal concepts. Certainly, the more substantive method of legal reasoning characteristic of modern American law tends to break up the unity of legal concepts and this necessitates a greater willingness to look to the underlying purposes behind rules. But we do not think that it is impossible to apply rules and concepts relatively neutrally, in the more formal manner which the English approach requires.

Of course there is no doubt that blind, mechanical rule application without any reference to policies or purposes can easily lead to absurdity and to formalistic reasoning, as distinct from formal reasoning. But open modification of the rule to allow purposes or policies to be taken into account is, anyhow, only one way of dealing with the problem. We think this is the most characteristic way of meeting the problem in America. Other methods involve the use of equitable modification, the use of fictions, and the use of discretions affecting the way in which the law is enforced, rather than affecting legal liability in formal terms. These methods have been, we think, more characteristic of the English legal system, though today equitable modification is itself a way of reducing the legal effect of the rule.

We will illustrate this contrast between the English and American approaches to rules by discussing an example which we have already used, and which was originally given by Lon Fuller in a reply[68] to H. L. A. Hart's Holmes Lecture on the separation of law and morals.[69] The example illustrates the differing degrees of mandatory and interpretive formality in the two systems. Suppose that a penal statute provides that 'no vehicles shall be taken into public parks'. No specific rationales or purposes are explicitly written into this statute, but it is clear (let us say from its legislative history) that the substantive purpose of the statute was to secure quiet and safety in the park. Now suppose further that a war veteran mounts a World War II jeep (in running order, let us say, but

---

Securities Ltd. v. *Hughes* [1974] 1 WLR 155 ('postal' rule as to contractual acceptance not applicable where result would be absurd).

[68] 'Positivism and Fidelity to Law: A Reply to Professor Hart', 71 *Harv. L. Rev.* 630, 663 (1958).

[69] 'Positivism and the Separation of Law and Morals', 71 *Harv. L. Rev.* 593 (1958).

without a battery) on a concrete slab in the park as a war memorial. Did the defendant take the vehicle into the park in violation of the statute?

We believe most American judges would say, 'No'. They would hold to a broad teleological conception of a rule in which its purposes are part of the rule or, at least, must be taken into account when interpreting it. Accordingly, the defendant would be held not guilty because what he did had no adverse effect on park quiet and safety.

On the other hand, we think that most English judges would incline to say that the defendant had violated the statute, because they would lean toward holding that the statute just consists of what is more or less expressed in the language of the enactment, in the light of ordinary conventional word meanings. The jeep just is 'a vehicle'. Thus they would deploy a narrow and formal conception of a rule, one that does not include or take account of the rationales or purposes of the statute, except insofar as the specific language of the statute may incorporate them. So in this example, English judges would be inclined to apply the rule literally, even though such an interpretation might in no way further the objects of the statute. But it does not follow that matters would remain there. Many English judges, while thinking that a conviction is strictly correct in such circumstances, might add that the authorities would be well advised not to bring a charge in such a case, or that, if it is brought, the accused should be given an 'absolute discharge'.[70]

Indeed, this is exactly what happened in the case of *Smedleys Ltd.* v. *Breed*[71] in 1974. The defendants were a well-known company engaged in the production of foodstuffs; they were prosecuted under the Food and Drugs Act 1955 for selling a tin of peas which contained a small caterpillar. Despite the defendants' apparently very elaborate screening system of mechanical devices and human inspection, this caterpillar escaped detection because it was almost the same size and colour as a pea. It was proved that in 1971 the defendants had produced some $3\frac{1}{2}$ million tins of peas only four of which had given rise to any complaint, and this particular case was evidently not regarded by the House of Lords as one of much gravity. As Lord Hailsham pointed out in his speech, the caterpillar was entirely harmless and could have been consumed by the buyer without injury 'and even, perhaps, with benefit'. Yet the House of Lords nevertheless construed the statutory provisions as providing no defence in these circumstances even though there were two provisions in the relevant Act which could, with some benevolence, have been construed so as to enable the defendants to escape liability.

---

[70] The 'absolute discharge' is itself an interesting illustration of the need to which a more formal system of law may give rise, of having some way of mitigating the letter of the law in special circumstances without apparent modification of the nature of the prohibited act.

[71] [1974] AC 839.

But having thus decided that the defendants were technically in breach of the Act, the House of Lords unanimously went on to say that the authorities had no duty to prosecute in cases of this kind where a prosecution would serve no useful purpose, and if a charge was brought the magistrates would be fully justified in granting an absolute discharge.

The deep divergence in the prevailing conceptions of what counts as a rule is part and parcel of a deep divergence in jurisprudential tradition. The wider and looser conception prevalent in America correlates with the instrumentalist tradition in legal theory which has been so influential there in the present century.[72] If rules are conceived essentially as instruments—as means to sound goals—then it is hardly surprising that interpreters will be ready to engage in wide-ranging inquiry behind the rules to satisfy themselves as to what the goals are. And these goals are, of course, the very substantive reasons and rationales of the rules. Similarly, if the application of a rule in a particular case would turn out not to be a very satisfactory means to its goals, or to conflict with other important goals, small wonder that many judges shrink from applying the rule, and may be ready to modify it accordingly.

All this is reinforced by another feature of the American jurisprudential tradition. One tenet of the legal realist wing of the American instrumentalist movement is what has been called 'rule scepticism'. Most rule sceptics writing in the 1920s and 1930s did not deny the very existence of rules, although such an extreme posture has often been attributed to them by their English critics. But what a number of them did deny was that rules are the heavily operative factor in the decision-making process. They stressed the existence of 'leeways' and 'freedom of decision'.[73] It is hardly surprising that in this atmosphere, which remains influential today, there should have emerged a conception of what a rule is that was relatively devoid of high mandatory formality. It remains only to add that a similar instrumentalist revolution in legal thought has never taken place in England, and England has never had influential 'rule sceptics' in its midst. We will return to these matters in chapters 8 and 9.

5. LEGAL PRINCIPLES

Many particular reasons of substance of the 'rightness variety' can be reformulated generically as principles. For example, the particular

---

[72] R. S. Summers, *Instrumentalism and American Legal Theory*, ch. 6 (Cornell U. Press, Ithaca, NY, 1982).
[73] *Ibid.*

reason for a decision might be, 'The plaintiff loses because he should not be allowed to profit from his own wrong,' a reason that could be reformulated generically as the principle that 'No person should profit from his own wrong'. Societies recognize many such particular substantive reasons with their corresponding generic principles. Among these principles, for example, are the following: 'Always act honestly and in good faith'; 'make due provision for one's relatives and dependants before being generous to others'; 'accord others their just deserts'. Principles of this nature might be called 'daily life' moral principles.[74]

Such daily life moral principles generate highly substantive reasons ('rightness reasons') upon which private persons may act in the conduct of their ordinary affairs. But it is also possible for lawmakers, judges, and other officials in a legal system to act on such reasons too, and thereby invoke the corresponding principles. In this way the legal system may be said to recognize such principles *as law*. Indeed, a constitutional assembly or a legislature may even adopt such a principle explicitly as a statutory provision.[75] Once some form of legal recognition is accorded such a principle, it may then be said to become a form of valid law and, as such, a formal reason or the source of formal reasons for decision. A strong case can even be made that such principles can impose legal obligations without the aid of rules or other valid legal norms.[76] Yet such principles and the reasons they generate are, in our scheme of analysis, of minimal formality, and a legal system that regularly resorts to such principles in this way as discrete forms of valid law would be far more substantive than a system which refused to do so. Such principles lack formal content—indeed, they are made up exclusively of substantive considerations. They command little or no interpretive formality, because (given their generality) those who deploy them can hardly do so faithfully without exploring their underpinnings and the bearings those underpinnings have on the context at hand. They also lack significant mandatory formality, because as used in the law they are commonly subject to being overridden by competing principles arising at the point of application.

In our view, there can be little doubt that lawmakers, judges, and other officials in the American system resort far more often to such principles, directly and indirectly, as *forms of valid law*, than is true in the English system. They are to be encountered in American constitutional law,

---

[74] On principles of 'common morality', see R. S. Summers, *supra*, n. 72, at 53, 251–2; see also R. S. Summers, 'Two Types of Substantive Reasons: The Core of a Theory of Common-Law Justification', 63 *Cornell L. Rev.* 707, 718–22, 752–74 (1978).

[75] See, e.g., Cal. Civil Code §§ 3509–99 (West, 1970).

[76] Dworkin, 'The Model of Rules', 35 *U. Chi. L. Rev.* 14, 22–32 (1967).

common law, and sometimes even in statute law. In England, principles can only be invoked in case-law, and even there, resort to principles, as opposed to rules, is relatively unusual. These principles are highly substantive, so we may say, then, that here too the English system remains more formal than the American, though this is by default—a failure to resort more directly and more often to moral principles as a form of law.

4

Statute Law

In this chapter we shall argue that the English legal system is more formal than the American in three further respects. First, statute law plays a larger role than case-law and other non-enacted law in England than in America, and statute law is (we shall suggest) in its nature a more formal kind of law. Secondly, the English system is more formal in its methods of statutory interpretation, still adhering generally to a 'plain meaning' or literal approach in which the interpreter less often goes directly into policies and rationales, whereas in America a much more substantive approach is followed. And thirdly, we shall suggest that statute law in America tends anyhow to have lower mandatory formality than is true of English statute law. Sometimes, as we shall see, it is even *expressly* qualified by substantive equitable considerations arising at the point of application.

1. THE INHERENT FORMALITY OF STATUTE LAW

In both the English and the American legal systems, statute law is, in several different respects, an inherently more formal type of law. First, statute law has a very high level of 'rank formality': thus it takes priority over all conflicting law (other than constitutional law) including especially judge made law.

Secondly, statutes generally have a higher degree of what we have called 'content-formality' than non-enacted law. That is, an element of the arbitrary more often informs the content of statute law than that of case-law. If there is to be a flat rule of a somewhat arbitrary kind, legislators are generally more willing than judges to adopt such a rule, and such rules are more commonly found in statutes than in case-law.[1] There are a number of possible reasons for this. One is that arbitrary lines appear to smack more of expediency or policy than of principle, and it seems more acceptable that such considerations should be handled by legislators than courts.[2] Another reason is that arbitrary lines are more acceptable if they are easily discoverable and known to all, and this

---

[1] E. Freund, *Legislative Regulation*, 5–10 (Commonwealth Fund, NY, 1932).

[2] This appears to be an interesting example of a point made by Professor Dworkin, see *Taking Rights Seriously*, ch. 4 (New Impression, Harvard U. Press, Cambridge, and Duckworth, London, 1978).

is more likely to be achieved if they are embodied in the publicly available textual form of a statute. Thus it is no accident that (for example) we have 'statutes of limitation' and not 'precedents of limitation'. Case law is not generally such a clear vehicle for expressing sharp lines. Moreover, the very nature of case-law as a body of reasoned precedent means that it must necessarily incorporate a fabric of substantive principle with much less in the way of mere fiat.[3]

Statutes also commonly state general rules in fixed verbal form, and such rules are usually over-inclusive or under-inclusive, in relation to underlying substantive reasons, to a much greater degree than case-law. Case law rules can be more readily modified at the point of application (if judges so wish) so as to minimize the gap between the rules themselves and their substantive rationales and purposes. Indeed, certain accepted techniques of case-law reasoning may be said to demand as much, within limits (which differ in the two countries). For example, when courts construe a precedent 'in light of the facts before the prior court' they frequently adjust the scope of the precedent in light of the substantive reasons generated by those very facts. Statutes, on the other hand, are not similarly construed 'in light of the facts'. Indeed, the usual statute is devoid of any relevant facts. For this reason also, then, statute law will tend to have higher content formality, for under and over-inclusion are in their own way arbitrary, though the arbitrariness can be reduced by techniques of purposive interpretation.

Thirdly, statutes have inherently greater mandatory formality than case-law. That is, statutes often operate categorically, through the formal reasons they generate, to exclude contrary substantive reasons newly arising at the point of application. With case-law the position is different. When such considerations emerge, they will often signal that the precedent may properly be considered 'distinguishable' in its entirety, so that the court may disregard it altogether. But statutes cannot be so disregarded, and it is no accident that the very notion of 'distinguishing a statute' is not a part of our received techniques.

Fourth, as we have said, statute law is embodied in a fixed form of words—in canonical form—and it is those very words which constitute law. It is thus the paradigmatic type of formal law. Enacted law is law just because it has been enacted in those very words, and is thus susceptible of much higher degrees of interpretive formality than case-law. Although it would be possible for a legal system to accord no particular respect to the verbal form in which legislative texts are cast, treating statutes simply as cases are treated in the common law system,

[3] See generally H. M. Hart, 'Comment on Courts and Lawmaking in Legal Institutions Today and Tomorrow' in *Government Under Law*, 139 (A. Sutherland ed., Harvard U. Press, Cambridge, 1956).

this is not in fact the position in either England or America. But case-law simply *could not* be treated with the same interpretive formality as statute law is treated in these two systems because it is not issued in canonical form. It can thus only be meaningfully applied in the light of the facts, the issues, the rulings, and the reasoning in the case as a whole.[4] Of course there are limits, recognized in both systems, to interpretive formality.

Thus statute law is more formal in all of the four key respects which we have identified as characteristic of formal reasoning. But we can perhaps add a fifth point, which cuts across some of these. Because statute law is a better source of rules than case-law, and because many rules are susceptible of highly formal treatment, this also tends to make statute law a more formal kind of law. Case law can be extremely *ad hoc*—simply a method of deciding disputes without providing much, if any, guidance for the future. Indeed, in some cases the courts appear exclusively concerned with the past, with clearing up a mess after the fact. The usual statute is not like this at all: it is prospective, and operates through rules, many of which are hard and fast rules.

In general it seems clear that a detailed and well-drafted piece of enacted law will embody rules and specify the circumstances in which they are applicable more meaningfully than less detailed enactments, or case-law. This assertion must be taken with common sense. An over-elaboration of detail may actually be self-defeating, making a statute more complex and difficult to interpret and apply, and thus encouraging use of substantive reasoning and an unwillingness to take the text too seriously. But we think it cannot reasonably be disputed that an enactment which strikes a balance between over-vagueness and generality on the one hand, and a profusion of detail on the other, is more likely to provide a clear source of detailed rules than is any mass of case-law, however orderly. We are not asserting that this necessarily makes for a better legal system. What we do assert, with Bentham, is that enacted law can have, and often does have, intelligibility and accessibility, characteristics which case law probably cannot have and certainly does not usually have to the same degree.

Having thus demonstrated that statute law is inherently more formal than case-law , we now suggest that the English system relies far more heavily, in its living law, on statute law than on case-law, and so overall has a much more formal system. It is not possible to support our position with precise quantitative data. For one thing, there are no settled criteria by which to individuate a statutory scheme as embodying one statute

---

[4] For a vivid presentation of this point as to case-law, see K. Llewellyn, *The Bramble Bush*, 47 (Oceana Publications, NY, 1960).

rather than two or more.[5] But we believe there are some pointers which strongly confirm our generalization. To begin with, the American system is dominated in many fields by the federal and state constitutions, and, although these are of course in fixed textual form somewhat like statutes, their broad and vague language means that constitutional law is in large part a case-law subject in modern America. Lawyers working in this field spend only a small fraction of their time reading the constitutional texts, and not much more in reading statutes. Rather, they immerse themselves in the constitutional case-law, and often proceed very much as if they were working in a common law field. There is, of course, nothing comparable to this in England.

Secondly, there is non-constitutional public law, which may also appear to be largely statutory, and in England is certainly so, except for the rules governing judicial review. But many branches of American public law are only superficially drawn predominantly from statute law. Often American public law statutes merely block out broad spheres over which legislative policies are to range, or merely grant power and set procedure for its exercise, or merely set broad limits on official power. When this occurs, administrative and judicial adjudication generate vast bodies of case-law that, within limits, become primary sources of law in the fields involved.[6] Thus even when an area of law is nominally statutory, the nature of the questions posed may be such that the application of the law to particular cases has to be performed in a common law manner, that is by case-by-case analysis of the policies and principles involved. Judge Richard Posner, in an interesting and arresting analysis, has recently suggested that a large number of American cases of statutory origin can nevertheless be classified as 'common law cases' in the functional sense.[7]

In England, on the other hand, a much higher proportion of the primary sources of modern public law is statutory, and the statutes concerned (with their subordinate legislation) tend to be very detailed, and to leave little scope for judicial gloss or intervention in the case law fashion. Interpretation of particular statutory provisions is, of course, often required, but this is a much more *ad hoc* exercise, and is quite different from case-law activity. It must be conceded that the English public law system also sometimes works by entrusting the detailed decision making to other bodies (elected or non-elected) without any

---

[5] On this complex problem, see J. Raz, *The Concept of a Legal System*, ch. 4 (2nd edn., Clarendon Press, Oxford, 1980).

[6] See Davis, 'The Future of Judge-made Public Law in England: A Problem of Practical Jurisprudence', 61 *Col. L. Rev.* 201 (1961).

[7] Posner, *The Federal Courts: Crisis and Reform*, especially at 314 (Harvard U. Press, Cambridge, 1985).

appeal to the courts, so that the detailed application of a statutory scheme is treated as raising political issues and not legal questions at all.

Even in private law there is plenty of evidence that statute law plays a more significant role in England than in America, because of the long tradition of legislative rather than judicial reform in England. A great many of the reforms of private law in recent times—often similar sorts of reforms in the two countries—have been carried out by statute in England, and by courts in America. We shall return to the subject of judicial reform of the law in chapter 5 where we illustrate this major difference with various examples.

2. STATUTORY INTERPRETATION

Few matters affect the style of a legal system in a modern state more than the methods used to interpret statutes. As with most of the questions discussed in this book, it is possible to discern two extreme polarities relating to statutory interpretation. At one polarity, the statutory wording is treated as having a single 'plain' or 'true meaning', which is to be ascertained by literal methods of construction without regard to the intentions of the lawgiver (save insofar as they appear from the text itself) or to the result, the underlying rationale of the statute, or other substantive considerations which may seem relevant to the statutory scheme. Statutory reasoning in such a system has what we call high interpretive formality. At the other polarity, the statutory wording is treated as of relatively little importance in itself, the statute being treated largely as an authoritative source of certain purposes or rationales, or as a mere vehicle for the implementation of certain substantive policies which become even more important than the words. Here courts range freely and widely outside the wording to determine relevant purposes and rationales. Statutes are therefore interpreted in a much more substantive fashion, and the reasoning they generate has relatively low interpretive formality. Between these two polarities there are numerous variations, and of course the two approaches may sometimes merge to some extent, as in a case in which substantive purposes are entirely evident from the statute's own plain meaning, and are invoked to cast light on the rest of the statute.

Of course every judge interpreting an enactment must usually give some weight to the statutory language, and it is difficult to believe that there are judges who *never* look to the underlying substantive purposes of the legislature.[8] But it is our belief that English judges tend to adopt a

---

[8] But we think it is entirely possible that other officials who have to apply statutes may try to interpret them without any regard at all to their purposes.

more textual, literal approach,[9] while American courts tend to take a more purposive and, therefore, substantive, approach.[10] It is difficult to document these differing approaches without a meticulous analysis of the texts of a wide range of judicial opinions in the two countries. This would require much more space than would be warranted by the results, especially as there is fairly wide general agreement on the nature and extent of the differing approaches in the two systems. We will therefore largely content ourselves with assertion rather than illustration, though we have already seen some examples of differences of approach in the last chapter.

In specific terms, three things seem to us beyond doubt. First, English judges generally emphasize the overall primacy of the ordinary meaning of words used in the statute far more than do most American judges. An English lawyer would be amazed to hear it said (as it has recently been said by an American judge) that a judge 'rarely starts his inquiry with the words of the statute, and often if the truth be told, he does not look at the words at all'.[11] Second, the accepted doctrine of English law is that courts are not entitled to consider the statutory purpose unless the words used in the statute have no determinate ordinary meaning, and are thus unclear on their face in some way.[12] Although it has recently been questioned whether this is correct,[13] and there are certainly some cases where the English courts do depart even from a very clear literal meaning,[14] we believe that, subject to one qualification, this still does represent the general practice of English judges. The qualification is that there are cases where the literal meaning has to be supplemented by other background pieces of law; it has not perhaps been sufficiently recognised in analysis of statute law that no statute is a piece of law unto itself alone. A statute which states that 'any person' who does such-and-

[9] See, e.g., Lord Reid in *Beswick* v. *Beswick* [1968] AC 58, 73–4; Lord Diplock in *Duport Steels* v. *Sirs* [1980] 1 WLR 142, 157; Lord Simon in *Maunsell* v. *Olins* [1975] AC 373, 395. See generally Lord Evershed, 'The Impact of Statute on the Law of England', XLII *Proc. Brit. Acad.* 248, 260 (1956). For striking examples of literal interpretation, see *IRC* v. *Hinchy* [1960] AC 748; *Fisher* v. *Bell* [1961] 1 QB 394; *Attorney-General* v. *Prince of Hanover* [1957] AC 436.

[10] See, e.g., *Johnson* v. *Southern Pacific Co.*, 196 US 1 (1904) and *US* v. *American Trucking Ass'ns., Inc.*, 310 US 534 (1940). Many other examples of a full-blooded purposive approach are cited in Wald, 'Some Observations on the Use of Legislative History in the 1981 Supreme Court Term', 68 *Iowa L. Rev.* 195, 198–9 (1983). See also R. Dickerson, *The Interpretation and Application of Statutes* (Little Brown, Boston, 1975) and the many references therein to American practice.

[11] See Posner, 'Statutory Interpretation—In the Classroom and in the Courtroom', 50 *U. Ch. L. Rev.* 800, 807–8 (1983).

[12] See, e.g., *R.* v. *Oakes* [1959] 2 QB 350, 354; *Jones* v. *DPP* [1962] AC 635, 658.

[13] See F. A. R. Bennion, *Statutory Interpretation*, 199–222 (Butterworths, London, 1984); see also Glanville Williams, 'The Meaning of Literal Interpretation', 131 *New LJ* 1128 and 1149 (1981).

[14] See Bennion, *supra*, n. 13, at 214–15.

such is guilty of an offence, for instance, is not to be taken as overriding principles of law to the effect that persons under the age of criminal responsibility cannot be convicted of an offence. Yet clearly this is to disregard the literal meaning of the words. So we can hardly doubt that there must be principles of statute law enabling us to supplement the literal words in various ways and for various purposes;[15] but, subject to this, it seems to be established that the English theory requires the court to try to interpret statutory provisions in accord with the literal or plain meaning, and without regard to policies or rationales, *unless the statute itself is first determined to be unclear.*[16] Most American judges, on the other hand, are willing to consider evidence of purpose in deciding whether the words are unclear in the first place.[17]

Third, when English judges do consider evidence of purpose, they almost invariably limit themselves to the words of the statute itself, other parts of the same statute, antecedent common law or statute law, and little else. On the other hand, most American federal court judges, and also (where the relevant materials are available) most American state court judges, go deeply into any legislative history for evidence of any actual legislative intent not evident on the face of the statute, and also into other purposes and policies whether or not evidence of any legislative intent is forthcoming. As elsewhere, we must stress that these differences express a generalization which is not necessarily and always true of individual courts and judges. We would be surprised if cases could not be found in which *some* American judges have adopted literal, textual constructions of a kind which would be rejected by *some* English judges,[18] but we have no doubt of the overall correctness of our generalization. It is difficult to cite evidence for this, or, more strictly speaking, it is difficult to evaluate or weigh up the evidence which could be cited in abundance, but our own combined experience confirms this belief which is widely shared in Anglo-American legal circles.[19]

---

[15] See Atiyah, 'Common Law and Statute Law', 48 *Mod. L. Rev.* 1 (1985).

[16] See, e.g., Lord Reid in *Westminster Bank Ltd.* v. *Zang* [1966] AC 182, 222; Halsbury, *Laws of England*, vol. 44, para. 856 (4th edn., Butterworths, London, 1983).

[17] Posner, *supra*, n. 11. See, e.g., *United States* v. *Madison D. Locke*, 471 US 84 (1985), where the Supreme Court considered the effect of a requirement that a document be registered 'prior to December 31'—words which to an English lawyer could only have one meaning. In the result, the Supreme Court also adopted a literal construction though three judges dissented.

[18] See, e.g., Murphy, 'Old Maxims Never Die: The "Plain Meaning Rule" and Statutory Interpretation in the Modern Federal Courts', 75 *Col. L. Rev.* 1299 (1975).

[19] See, for example, the Report of the Law Commission and the Scottish Law Commission, *The Interpretation of Statutes* (Law Com. No. 21, HMSO, London, 1969). See also references in H. M. Hart and A. M. Sacks, *The Legal Process: Basic Problems in the Making and Application of Law*, 1148–58 and 1410–17 (unpublished teaching materials, 1958); Kernochan, 'Statutory Interpretation: An Outline of Method', 3 *Dalhousie LJ* 333,

This general difference of approach parallels or tracks another fundamental difference that we dealt with at the end of chapter 3: most English judges have a much narrower conception of what constitutes a legal rule than many American judges do. As we have seen, English judges typically think of a legal rule as not including values, purposes, rationales, except insofar as these are (more or less) *explicitly* incorporated in the rule. Many American judges, on the other hand, believe that a rule encompasses these matters regardless of whether they are explicitly incorporated in the text of the rule. Naturally, therefore, Americans find it congenial to interpret rules by reference to their purposes and rationales, because these are, on this approach, already *part* of the rules. The American approach is encouraged by the fact that many American legislative texts explicitly incorporate preambles, comments, and other explanatory material, while modern English legislative texts almost never do so.[20]

We do not here consider which basic approach to statutory interpretation is actually 'better' (in the short or the long run—which may be different, of course), or which is more 'rational' or more philosophically defensible. Such a discussion seems to us relatively unprofitable unless it is conducted in the context of a legal system as a whole. Some legal systems evolve one method of statutory construction and some another; prima facie it seems likely that each system evolves a method which fits the other features of that system, and we believe this is the case with regard to England and America. This seems to us so obvious that we can only wonder why differences in the overall legislative contexts in the two countries have received so little attention from theorists of statutory interpretation in the past.[21] Neglect of differences of context has led

---

339 (1976); Lord Hailsham, 'Addressing the Statute Law', [1985] *Statute L. Rev.* 4 (expressing belief that the 'literalists' are still dominant in English statutory interpretation). For some contrary views, see Lord Renton, 'The Interpretation of Statutes', 9 *J. of Legislation* 252, 258–9 (1982) (claiming that the English system has become more purposive); Note, 'Intent, Clear Statements and the Common Law: Statutory Interpretation in the Supreme Court', 95 *Harv. L. Rev.* 892 (1982) (claiming that the US Supreme Court has recently adopted more literal or 'plain meaning' approach). This latter conclusion is disputed by Wald, *supra*, n. 10.

[20] English statutory instruments (a species of delegated or subordinate legislation) do include a brief explanatory note, but this is always declared *not* to be part of the instrument itself. English legislative draftsmen take the view that explanatory material either leads to the same result as the legislative text, in which case it is superfluous, or to a different result, in which case it is mischievous. This highly formal approach simply excludes the legislative purpose as an irrelevancy.

[21] The point is touched on but not developed in Judge Breitel's Cardozo lecture, *The Lawmakers*, 36 (Association of the Bar of the City of New York, 1965). Fuller also refers to

many discussions of statutory interpretation to take the form of caricature. It is common for American lawyers to poke fun at seemingly formalistic and wooden decisions by English judges, and at their apparently simplistic faith in the belief that statutes have a simple or plain meaning which can be arrived at by methods of literal interpretation.[22] Conversely, English lawyers are easily shocked by what they see as the free-wheeling and sometimes 'substantivistic' methods of American judges which seem on occasion to pay scant regard to the wording of the legislative text at all. Criticisms of this character seem to us unfruitful. When seen in the light of basic differences of context, the divergent approaches to interpretation in the two countries are much more understandable and not irrational, although that does not mean they are above criticism.

Although in this book we generally postpone until later chapters the task of discussing the institutional background to the two legal systems, we will digress slightly here to identify some institutional factors which, in our view, have led English courts to incline towards one polarity, while American courts incline in the other direction, in this matter of statutory interpretation. We think it possible to list at least six reasons which English lawyers would rely on to explain why English courts are so strongly inclined to follow a 'plain meaning', literalist style of interpretation.

First, if the drafting of statutes is done well and with technical proficiency, as it generally is in England, the 'plain meaning' of the words used will tend to correspond with the legislative purpose rather closely, or at least with the intent of those responsible for the production of the text which the legislature has approved.

Secondly, an incorrect or unsatisfactory statutory construction can today, and in England probably will, be readily put right by legislative amendment, or, alternatively, its defects will be mitigated because other persons and bodies in the legal system (such as lawyers, prosecutors, magistrates, or administrators) can be trusted to behave sensibly.

Thirdly, English lawyers tend to believe that the 'plain meaning' approach is in general more certain in its results, and that, while there are, of course, difficult and obscure enactments, the great majority of enactments can be sensibly interpreted and applied by giving effect to

---

it in *The Morality of Law*, 91 (Yale U. Press, New Haven, 1964), but from a somewhat different perspective from ourselves.

[22] See, e.g., Hart and Sacks, *supra*, n. 19, at 1148–58, discussing *Whiteley* v. *Chappell* (1868) LR 4 QB 147, an admittedly extreme example of mechanical interpretation which probably few English judges would defend today.

their plain meaning. Conversely, the search for legislative intent, purposes, or policies, except through the medium of the legislative text itself (and that much is permitted by English judges), is thought by English lawyers to require access to unreliable material (whose intent is to count anyway?) and to open up much more controversy. For these reasons also, therefore, the search for legislative intent outside the text is thought to lead to greater uncertainty.

Fourth, the citizen is entitled to rely on the written text which is the only formal part of the law to which the legislature has given its blessing. As an English judge has put it:

[T]he court is not solely concerned with what the citizens, through their parliamentary representatives meant to say; it is also concerned with the reasonable expectation of those citizens who are affected by the statute, and whose understanding of the meaning of what was said is therefore relevant.[23]

Fifth, English lawyers would argue that more substantive methods of statutory interpretation are politically wrong, because they involve the danger that the courts will encroach on controversial political issues which are properly the business of the legislature.

And sixth, if interpretation extends the search for 'legislative intent' beyond the legislative text, additional and unnecessary expense will be incurred.

To American lawyers, the validity of some of these arguments is highly controversial. But we believe that the general approach we adopt in this book, which stresses the differences between the English and American context, should defuse much of the controversy. We can perhaps dispose quickly of the first and second arguments, (that literal interpretation is more defensible when statutes are drafted with precision, and when legislative correction of errors is relatively easy), because these are quite plainly contingent on the context. Many American lawyers would accept these arguments in principle, though they would rapidly qualify their agreement by insisting that the conditions do not obtain in America. We agree that the required conditions do not obtain in America. But Americans may also be sceptical as to whether the conditions do in fact obtain in England to the degree to which English lawyers may think, or to the degree necessary to support the arguments. This, however, is a matter of empirical fact, as to which we only claim that English conditions certainly *tend* in this direction more than American conditions.

Some English critics may be as sceptical as Americans with regard to the ready availability of legislative reversal of judicial decisions on

[23] See Lord Simon in *Black-Clawson International Ltd.* v. *Papierwerke* [1975] AC 591, 645.

statutory interpretation, and we do not pretend that such legislative correction is always instantly to hand in England. But what we do claim is that legislative correction is far more readily available in modern times in England than in America. Because English lawyers are probably unaware of the practical limits on the powers of Congress in this respect, it may be useful here to cite the recent comment of Judge Richard Posner that 'Congress's practical ability to overrule a judicial decision misconstruing one of its statutes... is less today then ever before, and probably was never very great.'[24] And we doubt if the position in most states is very different from this. We shall show in detail in chapter 5 how legislative reform of the law is more easily obtained in England, and, in chapter 11, how the drafting of legislation differs in the two countries.

American lawyers might add two other objections to the first and second arguments: they might say that, even if these arguments are sound, and even if the facts justify them, there will still be many occasions on which, no matter how skilful the draftsman, the statute fails to give effect to the legislative intent or to pay due regard to relevant substantive considerations (argument one); and again, that there will be many occasions on which the legislature does not respond quickly enough to the need to correct a misconstruction of a statute or other persons do not respond so as to alleviate or mitigate the defects of an unsatisfactory situation (argument two) and that this will result in injustice. The English lawyer cannot deny that injustice will occasionally ensue in this way, but he would suggest that his own arguments are based on an appreciation of the best way of minimizing the risk of error. True, technical proficiency by the draftsman will not avoid every problem. But to assume that the draftsman has been less than fully competent as a starting-point, and that there generally is less than good reason to believe that the legislative words mean what they say, seems, to English lawyers, to be likely to lead, in the long run, to more error.

It may, however, be true that English courts are sometimes too inclined to rely on the ready availability of statutory amendment, and to shirk what would more reasonably be their responsibility to reach the proper result in the case at hand. Just as the American system of judicial review may sometimes render legislatures irresponsible,[25] so also the

[24] See Posner, *supra*, n. 11, at 816.
[25] See Robert Stevens, *Law and Politics*, 192–3 (U. of North Carolina Press, Chapel Hill, 1978), where this is referred to as 'a reverse Thayerian effect' because J. B. Thayer seems to have been the first American author to call attention to the fact that judicial review may lead to legislative irresponsibility; see Thayer, 'The Origin and Scope of the American Doctrine of Constitutional Law', 7 *Harv. L. Rev.* 129 (1893). For more modern discussions of this question, see A. M. Bickel, *The Least Dangerous Branch*, 24 (Bobbs-Merrill,

English system may make courts a little too ready to pass the buck for some statutory error to Parliament.[26] Occasionally, English judges just seem to waste parliamentary time by insisting in a formalistic way on some pedantic, narrow construction of an Act which will inevitably lead to amendment. Still, the fact is that the amending process is there, and in modern times can usually be relied upon; and it is this which distinguishes the American situation where the amending process cannot be relied upon to the same degree.[27] Thus we conclude that arguments one and two do have more force in the English context, and less in the American.

The third argument (the claimed superior certainty of the 'plain meaning' approach and the unreliability and inaccessibility of extra statutory sources of purpose and rationales) is, perhaps, more difficult, though here, too, we suggest that our contextual emphasis is not irrelevant. Obviously, if statutes are badly drafted, a 'plain meaning' approach may well lead to great uncertainty, because the results may be so absurd that nobody can be quite sure if the courts really will stick to the 'plain meaning' interpretation; further, with badly drafted statutes, there will often be several alternative constructions, none of which more obviously fits the plain meaning. Another contextual argument, which remains to be more fully developed in chapter 5, is also relevant at this point. American lawyers are often sceptical about English claims that the law can be made more certain by the 'plain meaning' method of interpretation. Uncertainty, they claim, is inherent in language, and in statutory texts; and the use of a 'plain meaning' approach may be merely a covert way of importing values without discussion or analysis; furthermore, such importation of values decreases rather than increases certainty, because values differ and thus generate conflicting substantive purposes and reasoning. Undoubtedly this argument has force; but it has less force to the extent that the value systems of those operating as

---

Indianapolis, 1962); Posner, *supra*, n. 11; but compare J. Skelly Wright, 'Professor Bickel, the Scholarly Tradition and the Supreme Court', 84 *Harv. L. Rev.* 769 (1971); Eugene V. Rostow, 'The Democratic Character of Judicial Review', 66 *Harv. L. Rev.* 193 (1952).

[26] For a well-known, though trivial, example, see *Fisher* v. *Bell* [1961] 1 QB 394 (display of flick-knife in shop window not an 'offer' to sell, and so not within statutory prohibition, reversed by Restriction of Offensive Weapons Act 1961.)

[27] See generally Friendly, 'The Gap in Lawmaking: Judges who Can't and Legislators who Won't', 63 *Col. L. Rev.* 787 (1963); G. Calabresi, *A Common Law for the Age of Statutes* (Harvard U. Press, Cambridge, 1982); Note, 'Congressional Reversal of Supreme Court Decisions 1945–57', 71 *Harv. L. Rev.* 1324 (surmising that Supreme Court decisions are usually reversed by Congress only when they arouse the unanimous hostility of virtually all interest groups).

interpreters are more homogeneous. If lawyers and judges tend to have similar values over a wide range of areas, then the inarticulate major premises from which they start will more often be the same, and the fact that they arrive at similar results through a 'plain meaning' approach will not be as bogus or unreal as it may seem. In many respects which we develop later (see chapters 12 and 13) the English legal profession and the English judiciary are much more homogeneous than the American legal profession and judiciary.

But it is anyhow open to question whether the 'plain meaning' approach does always involve covert use of judicial values. There is indeed evidence that English judges are so afraid of trespassing on sensitive political terrain (for instance, in controversial labour law cases) that they do in fact adopt a 'neutral' approach to statutory interpretation,[28] however bad the results may be—leaving it to the legislature to react, as react it often will. For this purpose the 'plain meaning' approach is actually more suitable than a more purposive approach, which tends to require more open examination of policy considerations. Once it is agreed (as it is agreed in England, though not of course in America) that judges should avoid controversial policy decisions as much as possible, this result becomes more intelligible.

Despite American scepticism about the greater certainty derivable from English methods of interpretation, we can hardly doubt that more literal methods of interpretation in the English context will more readily yield up clear rules (if not always the most sensible or appropriate rules) than full-blown purposive interpretation in the American. At any rate, we do not think this is open to doubt so long as the drafting and enacting processes of legislation are relatively efficient, and understood by the judges, as they are in England. Perhaps this result would be less certain in America, where this proviso is not so clearly met. But the very language in which the protagonists of these two modes of interpretation have conducted their debate seems to us to show that most lawyers at least assume that literal or 'plain meaning' interpretation will lead to more certainty or predictability in the law, despite all their scepticism about the degree of the certainty or predictability that can be arrived at. Thus it does seem to be widely assumed that cases of a clear literal meaning but doubtful underlying purpose are more common than cases of an obscure statutory text with a clear legislative purpose. Advocates of the purposive style of interpretation are generally willing to concede that this approach leads to more controversy and uncertainty in the law. But they suggest (1) that the additional uncertainty has been exaggerated by

---

[28] Gareth Jones, 'Should Judges be Politicians? The English Experience', 57 *Ind. LJ* 211 (1982).

advocates of the literal approach, and (2) that anyhow any additional uncertainty of the law is a price worth paying for the greater rationality or justice (or other benefits, more or less identified) thereby gained.[29]

We now turn to the fourth argument, which is that the citizen is entitled to rely on the plain meaning of the text the legislature has passed, because this is indubitably the law which the legislature has enacted, and the citizen does not have satisfactory access (even with the aid of his lawyer) to other sources of information as to the legislative intent, or the policies he feels the courts are likely to regard as being pursued by the Act. This depends to some degree on the other factors, and is perhaps parasitic on them. Where statutes are well drafted and the courts habitually use the 'plain meaning' approach, citizens obviously ought to be able to do the same, with the aid of legal advice as appropriate. But if statutes are not infrequently badly prepared and ill thought out, so that the plain meaning often leads to objectionable or even absurd results, courts are more likely to look for a different approach, and where courts regularly do that, the citizen is given due warning that he cannot rely on the 'plain meaning' approach either. Still, the difference between these approaches clearly involves a value judgment between the more formal and the more substantive vision of law. The English approach which involves an attempt to protect reliance is less concerned with the substantive justice of that reliance. The less literal method of interpretation places less weight on the protection of the citizen's reliance, and more weight on the force of substantive reasoning as it shapes up in the particular case.

The fifth argument concerns the appropriate division of responsibility between the judges and the legislature. The English view is that most policy issues (and especially very controversial policy issues) raise substantive questions which are for the legislature to settle. Literal interpretation is thought to be one way in which the judges can steer clear of these substantive issues. The usual[30] American response to this is that policy issues, even of a controversial character, are inherent in the judicial and interpretive function, and that the judges must (where necessary) import their own political morality to resolve interpretive questions when the legislative intent is doubtful or (sometimes, and within limits) even when the legislative intent is just substantively bad. Of course this difference in outlook reflects differences between the two

---

[29] Fuller, 'Forms and Limits of Adjudication', 92 *Harv. L. Rev.* 353, 372–81 (1978); Fuller, 'Positivism and Fidelity to Law: A Reply to Professor Hart', 71 *Harv. L. Rev.* 630, 661–9 (1958).

[30] Of course (we reiterate) not *all* American judges take this view—indeed there is now (1986) some evidence of a return to more literalist methods, especially among judges who are opposed to the recent traditions of judicial 'activism'.

countries with respect to the whole nature of the relationship between judges and legislatures, and the political role of the judges. As we shall see in later chapters (especially chapters 11 and 12) these differences are now so great in the two countries that arguments about the proper judicial function in interpreting statutes can no longer intelligibly proceed without taking account of the entire interlocking system in which the judges operate.

The sixth argument concerns the extra costs of the search for legislative intent beyond the legislative text. There is no doubt that purposive interpretation, as understood in America, has great practical problems which add significantly to the cost of applying statute law. As is well known, a wide range of sources may be consulted by American courts in their search for legislative intent.[31] These include Congressional (or state legislative) debates; reports of committees; statements of those sponsoring the legislation; comments and views of legislators, officials, and other parties at legislative hearings, and other similar material. Much of this material is not only unhelpful in ascertaining 'legislative intention' but deliberately distorting[32]—such as speeches inserted in the *Congressional Record*, but never actually delivered, or statements made with the deliberate aim of influencing judicial interpretation, even though they do not represent a general view in the Congress. And in many states there is anyhow no recorded legislative history.[33] We do not, of course, suggest that such sources are always consulted whenever a statute has to be interpreted by American lawyers or courts. Doubtless, in some cases the 'plain meaning' of the words turns out in the end to be so plain that even an American court will look no further. Conversely, of course, cases occur in England where the 'plain meaning' of the words is so absurd that even an English court will look for some evidence of underlying purpose, though usually only within the four corners of the enactment itself, supplemented by the court's knowledge of the prior law. Again the differences we observe are matters of degree.

We have so far discussed the arguments which English lawyers make

---

[31] Dickerson, 'Statutory Interpretation: Dipping into Legislative History', 11 *Hofstra L. Rev.* 1125 (1983); Mangum, 'Legislative History in the Interpetation of Law: An Illustrative Case Study', 1983 *BYUL Rev.* 281.

[32] For the comments of Justice Jackson on the efforts of certain American lawyers and judges to make the text of a statute fit its legislative history, see p. 31, n. 26. For a modern example of distortion of legislative history, see the opinion of Marshall J. in *Patsy* v. *Board of Regents* 457 US 496 (1982) (relying on expressed *fears* of Congressman to infer legislative *purpose*.)

[33] See M. Cohen and R. Berring, *Finding the Law*, 327 (West, St. Paul, 1984); see generally for what *is* available M. Fisher, *Guide to State Legislative Materials* (F. B. Rothman pub. for the American Assoc'n. of Law Libraries, Littleton, Colo., 1983).

to justify the formal interpretive approach in England, and in so doing we have already conveyed much of the flavour of the American approach which is also rooted in its own context. Many American lawyers and judges assume that the ultimate function of statutory interpretation is to give effect to the legislative intention, but that the legislative text often does not express that intention very well. In addition, it is contended that there are many problems of statutory interpretation where no legislative intent existed at all, in which case it is thought to be necessary for the court to decide almost as it would a common law case, though starting from the general premises of the statute rather than with some common law principle. Thus the function of the court in such a case has been said to be one of 'imaginative reconstruction' rather than interpretation.[34]

Such an approach involves very low degrees of interpretive (and mandatory) formality. The justification and the explanations for such an approach encompass all the factors about the American legal system—the relationship of courts to legislatures, the system of drafting, and so on—to which we have already alluded, and which we detail more fully in later chapters. But we can perhaps conclude this discussion by adding a reference to one further and rather special factor which may help explain why American courts find it easier to go behind a legislative text. This factor derives ultimately from the very wide effect given by American courts to constitutional guarantees. If these guarantees are to be treated seriously, then courts must be prepared to deal with ingenious and devious methods of evasion. Legislatures in America have in fact sometimes passed statutes apparently innocuous on their face, but which have the hidden purpose of subverting constitutional guarantees.[35] American courts then are called upon to look behind the statutes in constitutional cases. We believe that this encourages them to adopt a more purposive and thus substantive approach to statutory interpretation in general.

This willingness to look behind or beyond the wording of a statute has led to much recent discussion of the problem of obsolete statutes. If statutes were formerly passed to deal with problems which have long since disappeared, or are based on values long since abandoned, and if legislatures fail to repeal or update them, the courts may have to struggle with them as best they can, or they may strive to interpret them into harmlessness, or strike them down on constitutional grounds. But

---

[34] Posner, *supra*, n. 11, at 817.

[35] So it has long been held that legislation may be unconstitutional not only if it is bad on its face, but also if it is intended to be operated in an unconstitutional manner: see *Yick Wo* v. *Hopkins* 118 US 356 (1886) and, for a more modern illustration, *Hunt* v. *Washington Apple Advertising Commission* 432 US 333 (1977).

proposals have recently been made in America for the courts to take on themselves the wider power of actually refusing to enforce obsolete statutes unless the legislature renews them.[36] Such an approach, it will be seen, would require the courts to pay still more attention to the policies and purposes behind an Act because only in this way would it be possible to determine whether a statute is truly obsolete or not.[37] Needless to say, the very idea that a court could deal with obsolete statutes in such a way would seem utterly unacceptable to English lawyers.

3. THE MANDATORY FORMALITY OF STATUTES

Modern statutes sometimes have express provisions which reduce their mandatory formality by enabling a court to take account of substantive equitable considerations which emerge at the point of application. Provisions of this kind can be found in both English and American statutes, but they seem to be more widespread and more dramatic in their effect in America. Perhaps the most striking example of a vast body of statute law, the whole of which is made subject to such substantive equitable considerations, is the American Uniform Commercial Code.[38] This Code has been enacted virtually in its entirety in all American states but one. It governs transactions in goods, commercial paper and banking transactions, letters of credit, bills of lading and warehouse receipts, investment securities, and secured transactions in personalty.

This great body of law includes an explicit provision, Section § 1-103, that not infrequently reduces the prima-facie mandatory formality of the several hundred specific provisions in the Code.[39] This explicit provision is derived from, and is in similar language to, comparable English provisions traditional in nineteenth-century codifying statutes. It preserves the 'principles of law and equity' relating to the law merchant, contractual capacity, principal and agent, fraud, misrepresentation and duress, and various other specified branches of the law. In England such provisions have never been interpreted as giving the courts power to apply broad 'equitable' considerations. Indeed, it is even unclear how far *technical* equitable rules survive such codifications, except insofar as they are incorporated in them, because (it has been argued) the value of codification would be much reduced if alongside the codified rules there

---

[36] See G. Calabresi, *supra*, n. 27.

[37] See, e.g., the opinion of Newman in *Abele* v. *Markle* 342 F. Supp. 800, 805 (D. Conn. 1972).

[38] On the UCC, see generally J. J. White and R. S. Summers, *The Uniform Commercial Code* (2nd edn., West, St. Paul, 1980).

[39] See generally Summers, 'General Equitable Principles under Section § 1-103 of the Uniform Commercial Code', 72 *Northwestern L. Rev.* 906 (1978).

continued to exist equitable rules inconsistent with them.[40] This argument (it will be seen) derives from the belief that it is desirable that such statutes should have high mandatory formality. But in America, Section § 1-103 of the UCC permits substantive equitable considerations (in the broad and non technical sense) to be considered at the point of application, if the section has not been displaced.[41]

This provision is by no means an isolated phenomenon in the sea of American statute law. A good many other American statutes explicitly provide that equitable considerations arising at the point of application override the effect of otherwise applicable statutory language. This is even true in public law fields. Indeed, in recent times, whole regulatory programmes have been adopted which explicitly provide that administrators at the point of application have general power, on equitable and other substantive grounds emergent in the circumstances, to create exceptions to the scope of a part or even the whole of a programme.[42] Then, too, various American public law statutes of a distributive rather than a regulatory character sometimes give overriding effect to emergent equitable considerations. For example, the federal statutes on eligibility for public welfare benefits include a general provision entitling a non-eligible person who has received and relied on an overpayment, or a payment to which he is not otherwise entitled, to retain the payment so far as it would be against 'equity and good conscience' to make him refund it.[43]

In England, there is nothing comparable to these extensive provisions enabling whole statutes or programmes to be overridden or modified by substantive considerations at the point of application. There are, however, a considerable number of modern statutes which lay down a rule, and then give the court a discretionary power to depart from it in exceptional circumstances. One important example, which is the result of many years of legislative experimentation on the subject, is section 33 of the Limitation Act 1980, which gives the court a discretion to override the usual three years' limitation period in personal injury cases. These discretions, which, as we have previously noted, are now very common in English statute law, reduce the extremely high mandatory formality of nearly all English statutory rules; but, as we have also previously observed, discretions of this kind have to be understood in the context of the English legal system. Given the fact that these discretions tend to

---

[40] See *Re Wait* [1927] 1 Ch. 606, especially the judgment of Atkin LJ.

[41] See Summers, *supra*, n. 39 for examples of this phenomenon.

[42] See generally Aman, 'Administrative Equity: An Analysis of Exceptions to Administrative Rules', 1982 *Duke LJ* 277; Note, 'Regulatory Values and the Exceptions Process', 93 *Yale LJ* 938 (1984).

[43] 42 USC § 404 (*b*) (1982).

operate within an overall framework of tight rules with high mandatory formality, and given that the system of precedent may still have force even in the case of discretions,[44] it is clear that use of such discretions in the English legal system does not amount to complete rejection of mandatory formality.

Moreover, some threshold will often have to be passed—for example the circumstances must be shown to be exceptional—before the equitable or discretionary modification will prevail over the usual statutory provision. And in the English discretions there are often specific factors to which the court must have regard. So statutes which contain provisions of this kind may retain a considerable degree of mandatory formality, and we believe that this will usually be higher in England than in America for many of the same reasons that affect interpretation and common law methodology. Furthermore, in the case of public programmes administered by relatively minor officials (such as the social security legislation) English law seems to rely much less on discretion than comparable American law. Thus the provisions in English social security law as to the recovery of overpayments (comparable to those cited above) confer no overt discretion on the administrators, but require repayment unless 'due care and diligence' have been shown by the beneficiary.[45]

In chapter 11 we shall return to differences between English and American statute law which arise from differences in the role and working methods of the legislatures in the two countries. We shall then see that there are many other ways in which statute law tends to be a more substantive source of law in America than in England.

---

[44] But see Atiyah, *supra*, n. 15, at 4–5 (1985), where some anxiety is expressed at the proliferation of non-appealable discretions.

[45] See Ogus and Barendt, *The Law of Social Security*, 576 (2nd edn., Butterworths, London, 1982).

5

The Common Law

1. INTRODUCTION

The system of precedent means that the judges make law in the course of resolving disputes between litigants in common law litigation, and—though it is not our main concern in this chapter—precedents can also be made on points of constitutional and statutory interpretation. A given precedent may be 'binding' on subsequent judges, or it may be only 'persuasive' authority, to use the terminology of common lawyers. Judges are obligated to follow binding precedents, but not merely persuasive ones. An example of a persuasive precedent is a case decided in another common law jurisdiction, or (in America) another state. To the extent that subsequent judges regard precedents as binding and follow them, they observe the principle of *stare decisis*.

If a decided case is to qualify as a legal precedent and thus as a formal reason for deciding a later case, then it must first of all be taken as authoritative by appropriate classes of subsequent judges, for example by judges of lower courts. It must thus have what we call authoritative formality. If subsequent judges follow the earlier decision *merely* because they are persuaded by the strength of the substantive reasoning supporting that decision, then they are not treating that case as authoritatively binding on themselves. Lord Devlin once put this in blunt terms: 'The principle of stare decisis does not apply only to good decisions; if it did, it would have neither value nor meaning. It is only if a [prior] decision is doubtful that the principle has to be invoked'.[1] But as we shall see shortly, legal systems can differ significantly in *how* doubtful a precedent may be in substantive terms and still remain authoritative.

Further, if a prior case is to qualify as a source of formal reasoning, it is also necessary that the subsequent judges for whom it is authoritatively binding accord it some degree of mandatory formality. That is, the subsequent judges must treat the earlier decision as excluding or overriding or diminishing the weight of countervailing substantive reasons arising out of the circumstances of the later case. *Stare decisis*, then, generates formal reasons out of precedents which later courts invoke *because they are the law*. But the principle of *stare decisis* has its

---

[1] *Jones* v. *DPP* [1962] AC 635, 711.

own general justifications, and these of course are substantive in nature, reasons of a second-level kind. As we saw in chapter 1, there is no paradox in saying that a general legal practice—following precedent—that generates formal reasons nevertheless itself rests on general substantive reasons of a different level or order. The general justifying reasons behind a practice need not be of the same kind as the particular reasons generated by the practice. What then are the general substantive reasons behind the practice of *stare decisis*?[2] Numerous reasons may be suggested. For example, (1) the practice secures equality before the law at least in the sense that like cases are treated alike; (2) it limits the scope for bias, arbitrariness, and the like; (3) it facilitates planning and reliance on the part of private parties by providing a reasonably predictable and stable legal framework within which to make decisions; (4) it helps secure legal compliance on the part of losing parties, for they are more likely to see that decisions are not made against them personally, but apply to a class falling under a rule; (5) it serves efficiency by saving resources that would go into examining each case afresh, and by discouraging potential litigants from bringing lawsuits or appealing; (6) it brings home to the judges their responsibilities by forcing them when deciding entirely new issues to consider the various possibilities more carefully.[3]

Given these arguments (and more could be offered) it is hardly surprising that the English and the American legal systems have adopted the principle of *stare decisis*, and that they both therefore have large and complex bodies of binding common law precedents.[4] However, we find that the principle of *stare decisis* operates in the two countries in a markedly different way, and that these differences, too, bear out our general thesis that the English legal system is the more formal in many important respects.

There is probably little—perhaps suprisingly little—difference in *perceptions* of the judicial role on the part of English and American

---

[2] For general treatment of the substantive rationales behind the practice of *stare decisis*, see Goodhart, 'Case Law in England and America', 15 *Cornell L. Rev.* 173 (1930); Oliphant, 'A Return to Stare Decisis', 14 *ABAJ* 71 (1928); Von Moschzisker, 'Stare Decisis in Courts of Last Resort', 37 *Harv. L. Rev.* 409 (1924); Sprecher, 'The Development of the Doctrine of Stare Decisis, and the Extent to Which it Should be Applied', 31 *ABAJ* 501 (1945).

[3] K. N. Llewellyn, *The Common Law Tradition*, 26 (Little Brown, Boston, 1960); see also Greenawalt, 'The Enduring Significance of Neutral Principles', 78 *Col. L. Rev.* 982 (1978).

[4] See generally on the English system Sir Rupert Cross, *Precedent in English Law* (3rd edn., Clarendon Press, Oxford, 1977); C. K. Allen, *Law in the Making* (7th edn., Clarendon Press, Oxford, 1964). For America, see generally Wise, 'The Doctrine of Stare Decisis', 21 *Wayne Law Rev.* 1043 (1975); Hardisty, 'Reflections on Stare Decisis', 55 *Ind. LJ* 41 (1979).

judges, when they are taken as a whole, although there is much more deviation from the mean in America. In both countries, most judges probably perceive their primary role to be that of loyalty to the law, and to the principle of *stare decisis*. Most judges in England and America (or, at least, those on courts of last resort) acknowledge a secondary but more active role, which may be seen as one of 'keeping the law up to date', or of 'interstitial legislation', or simply as that of being a 'lawmaker'. In both countries, there are different views as to the relative importance of the two roles. In England the House of Lords usually includes some judges who see their role as being primarily that of law interpreters or law declarers, and others who see greater scope for judicial activism.[5] In America, the United States Supreme Court almost always has a similar mix of 'strict constructionists' and activists. State supreme courts, although in recent decades generally less activist than the US Supreme Court,[6] appear to have particular traditions of their own, some being more activist and some more restrained, although they, too, certainly have judges with a mix of views. Studies have revealed wide disparities between levels of activism on state supreme courts.[7]

It also seems to be true that judges in both countries continue to describe themselves as law interpreters in utterances designed for public consumption. In England, there is considerable evidence that even the judges who themselves favour an active role for the judiciary prefer to down play their law-making activities when addressing the public, or when giving judgment in cases which are expected to receive widespread publicity.[8] Even in the United States, where it might have been thought that half a century of realist critique would by now have made it pointless, or hopeless, to attempt such a strategy, it is still not uncommon to find similar assertions.[9]

[5] See Alan Paterson, *The Law Lords* (Macmillan, London, 1982); John Bell, *Policy Arguments in Judicial Decisions* 269–70 (Clarendon Press, Oxford, 1983) suggests after a careful analysis of several areas of law that English judges perform the role of 'interstitial legislators'.

[6] See, for example, Barr, 'Judicial Activism in State Courts: The Inherent Powers Doctrine', in *State Supreme Courts*, 129 (M. C. Porter and G. A. Tarr, edd., Greenwood Press, Westport, Conn., 1982).

[7] See, e.g., Baum and Canon, 'State Supreme Courts as Activists: New Doctrines in the Law of Torts', *ibid.*, at 83, which discusses disparities in the level of innovation that state supreme courts have undertaken in tort law.

[8] See, e.g., Atiyah, 'Judges and Policy', 15 *Israel Law Rev.* 346 (1980); but cf. Paterson, *supra*, n. 5.

[9] For example: 'Perhaps no characteristic of an organized and cohesive society is more fundamental than its erection and enforcement of a system of rules defining the various rights and duties of its members, enabling them to govern their affairs and definitely settle their differences in an orderly, predictable manner.' *Boddie* v. *Conn.* 401 US 371 (1971). But in a survey of judges of four state supreme courts, only 34.6% said that 'non-legal factors' were of no importance in judicial decisions. H. R. Glick, *Supreme Courts in State Politics*, 83 (Basic Books, NY, 1971).

Notwithstanding this appearance of transatlantic uniformity of views, our study of observable behaviour by courts of last resort will present rather a different picture, one that reveals American courts of last resort to be in general far more activist than English courts, and also far less technically rule-bound or formal in their approach to *stare decisis*, as well as to other forms of law such as statutes and judgments.[10] Further, the functions that the courts, and especially courts of last resort, play in the two countries differ in very significant ways, ways that contribute to the conclusion that English courts are more formal in their approach than their American counterparts. In this chapter we shall attempt to explore a number of factors which explain why this is so, while deferring until chapter 10 more detailed consideration of the differing roles of courts of last resort in the two countries.

2. STARE DECISIS: DIFFERENCES

In the history of the common law, two different versions of the principle of *stare decisis* have prevailed at different times and in different places. In the very strict version which prevailed in England in the first half of the twentieth century all courts were regarded as bound to follow their own previous decisions, and lower courts were also bound to follow the decisions of higher courts. Further, these requirements were strictly interpreted. In the looser version which prevailed in England until the twentieth century, and which largely prevails in America today, courts of last resort are not bound to follow their own previous decisions, though they will in practice do so in most ordinary circumstances. Lower courts are regarded as bound to follow decisions of higher courts, but the degree of freedom which they have to escape even these shackles may be considerable. But some obligation on lower courts to observe higher court rulings is regarded as almost a necessity in common law countries. Other things being equal, it is generally assumed that even higher courts are likely to follow their own previous decisions, so it seems a logical corollary of appeal processes that lower courts should be bound to follow higher court precedents. But in the looser version of the doctrine as it operates in America, the lower courts themselves are not bound to follow their own decisions, even though they will often do so in practice, probably more often than not.

More to the point, perhaps, is that in this looser version of the doctrine, the authority of a court's own prior decisions depends largely on the persuasiveness of the reasoning of the earlier courts. Indeed, it is said that in this version of *stare decisis* a court will follow its own

[10] See, e.g., Atiyah, *supra*, n. 8 as to England, and H. R. Glick, *supra*, n. 9 as to state supreme courts.

previous decision unless it feels the prior case to have been wrongly decided; this, however, seems almost to deny the force of precedent altogether as a formal reason for decision. This is because the judge of the correctness of the earlier decision must be the later court, and if the later court is entitled to disregard its own earlier case whenever it feels that case to have been wrongly decided, the earlier case has no authority *as a precedent* at all. Its only power, or tendency to persuade later courts to follow it, will lie in the correctness or persuasiveness of its substantive reasoning. If and insofar as this represents the practice of some American courts, therefore, it suggests that they have departed from the position of regarding their own precedents as truly formal reasons for decision.

The version of *stare decisis* which prevails in England today is somewhat less strict than the version which operated earlier in this century, but is still very strict by modern American standards. The actual rules (if they are rules[11]) governing which courts are strictly bound to follow precedents of which other courts are not on the face of it very different in the two countries, but the differences in practical operation of *stare decisis* are nevertheless very great. Thus it seems that the difference between the two versions of *stare decisis* lies not so much in any formal rules as in the general attitude of the judges to a number of key issues. This difference of attitude could also be seen as a difference in the general 'vision' of law to which the judges adhere. Judges who adhere to their own earlier precedents even though their reasoning was demonstrably faulty, or due to a misunderstanding of history, or the like, are thus demonstrating their belief that the precedent is binding law because of its authoritativeness. They are demonstrating their belief in the high authoritative and mandatory formality of the principle of *stare decisis*. Judges who are more concerned with the substantive reasoning of the earlier courts reject this high formality, and adhere to a different vision of the nature of law itself. Law, in their view, is not just something 'laid down', but must also, to be binding, have a certain substantive persuasiveness.

It should by now be apparent that the more limited or restricted is the

---

[11] There has been some theoretical controversy over whether the 'rules' are rules of law or merely rules of practice, see, e.g., Rickett, 'Precedent in the Court of Appeal', 43 *Mod. L. Rev.* 136 (1980); Aldridge, 'Precedent in the Court of Appeal—Another View', 47 *Mod. L. Rev.* 187 (1984); Evans, 'The Status of Rules of Precedent', [1982] 41 *Cambridge LJ* 162. The questions said to turn on this distinction are (1) whether decisions on the application of the doctrine of precedent should themselves be citable as authority, and (2) whether the courts can change the rules of precedent of their own accord. See Aldridge, 195–8. An American lawyer (and some English lawyers) would not see why these issues should turn on the distinction between a rule of practice and a rule of law, which some would regard as artificial and unreal.

operation of the principle of *stare decisis*, the less formal a legal system will be. As we will now show, the principle of *stare decisis* operates in many respects in a more limited and restricted fashion in America than in England, so that this is another major respect in which the English system is the more formal of the two. American limits on *stare decisis* not only reflect different policy choices, but also reflect differences in general legal and social conditions. As we shall explain later, conditions in America are simply not congenial to full scale operation of the principle of *stare decisis*.

The power to disregard otherwise binding precedents

The first major difference in the operation of the principle of *stare decisis* in the two countries is that in America subsequent judges at all levels have more extensive (lawful) power to disregard an otherwise binding precedent. (This power should not be confused with the power to overrule, which is available to a narrow range of courts, though often exercised on similar grounds.) There are several important types of cases in which American judges may legitimately disregard otherwise binding precedent, when English judges may not. First, in most branches of the common law in the American legal system, it is not always enough, in order that a decided case constitute a precedent, that it has merely been laid down by the highest (or a higher) court. Whenever the substantive reasoning in a case seems at all dubious, the case must go through a period of evaluative trial before it can be regarded as settled and therefore valid law. That is, it must be, at least in minimal terms, 'good' law. Lower court judges, as well as the deciding court, participate in this process of evaluation, and if a case is found fundamentally wanting, judges may appropriately disregard it, even though the American theory of precedent does not fully acknowledge the practice in so many words. A lower court so deciding is, of course, subject to reversal, but that only demonstrates that such a court may fail to exercise its power to disregard properly, not that it does not have such a power. Whenever a lower court's disregard of a new case that is dubious on substantive grounds is upheld, it is appropriate to say that the case never really became binding law. It simply failed to pass a threshold test—a content-oriented test—of legal validity.[12]

In England, on the other hand, no such general threshold content-oriented test of legal validity is operative. A single decision of a higher court is enough to qualify that decision as a binding precedent which may not be disregarded on substantive grounds by a lower court.

Secondly, there are cases in which the prior decision is marked by

---

[12] See our detailed discussion, ch. 2 at pp. 47–49.

various institutional weaknesses. For example, several different opinions may have been given in the prior case, but cases can only be treated as binding sources of law if a clear *ratio decidendi* or, in America, a clear statement of substantive reasons can be extracted from them. This is only possible of appellate opinions where they are unanimous, or where a clear majority view can be found. Where there is no such unanimity or majority, the decision is referred to in American terminology as a 'plurality opinion', and American judges often feel free to disregard such opinions even if they would otherwise be binding.[13]

English judges are not nearly so free to disregard precedents on grounds of this kind. For example, a subsequent court faced with a plurality opinion will strive to extract from it a *ratio decidendi* which it must follow; sometimes this can only be done by applying somewhat arbitrary rules, such as the rule that the narrowest holding is taken to be the *ratio decidendi*.[14] There are, it is true, certain recognized exceptions to the principle of *stare decisis* in England. For example, the Court of Appeal may depart from an earlier decision of its own if there is another decision of that court in conflict with it, or if it is inconsistent with a decision of the House of Lords.[15] But these exceptions to the principle of *stare decisis* are limited and tend themselves to be of a formal nature. They are, moreover, often the subject of legal argument and judicial decision in English courts in highly formal terms, implying that the whole matter is one of fixed rules with high mandatory formality.[16]

There is a third type of case in which an American judge may consider himself free to disregard otherwise binding precedents, and that is where the subsequent judge thinks that the prior case will probably be overruled by a higher court if it is taken to that court on appeal. So, for instance, a federal appeals court may disregard a precedent of the Supreme Court if it thinks that the Supreme Court is itself likely to overrule that precedent.[17] Disregarding such a precedent is referred to in

---

[13] See, e.g., *State* v. *Baker*, 15 Md. App. 73 (1971) cert. den. 411 US 951 (1973) in which a Maryland court concluded that because the plurality decision (4:2:3) of *United States* v. *Jorn*, 400 US 470 (1971), contained no 'opinion of the court', its various opinions were of persuasive value only. The Maryland court then adopted the dissent's analysis and dismissed the defendant's double jeopardy claim. See generally Note, 'The Precedential Value of Supreme Court Plurality Decisions', 80 *Col. L. Rev.* 756 (1980); Note, 'Plurality Decisions and Judicial Decisionmaking', 94 *Harv. L. Rev.* 1127 (1981).

[14] See Cross, *supra*, n. 4, 90, 96–9. On one occasion the English CA adopted the same approach as that in *State* v. *Baker* (*supra*, n. 13), only to be rebuked by the House of Lords. *Ibid.*, 98–9.

[15] See *Young* v. *Bristol Aeroplane Co.* [1944] KB 718; *Morelle Ltd* v. *Wakeling* [1955] 2 QB 389; Cross, *supra*, n. 4, ch. 4.

[16] *Ibid.* See also *Davis* v. *Johnson* [1978] 1 All ER 841 (illustrating mixture of formal and substantive reasoning being used to justify rejection of earlier precedent).

[17] Kniffin, 'Overruling Supreme Court Precedents: Anticipatory Action by United States

American terminology as 'anticipatory overruling', but this is somewhat misleading because plainly the lower court does not itself actually have power to overrule the higher court's decision.

A recent article addresses this problem and concludes that federal appellate courts 'anticipatorily overrule' Supreme Court precedents for a number of reasons. The author's list includes: belief that the precedent has been eroded by later Supreme Court cases; a perceived trend in Supreme Court decisions; belief that the Supreme Court is awaiting an appropriate case to adopt the new rule; a sense that a change in court personnel will lead to a new rule; and the possibility that the Supreme Court made a mistake of law in the earlier case and will alter its position.[18] No doubt another major factor is simply that the lower court judge disagrees substantively with the higher court's position and hopes that his innovation will carry the day. It hardly needs to be stressed that any serious growth of the practice (and legitimacy) of anticipatory overruling (especially on the basis of a mere substantive disagreement) will greatly erode the doctrine of *stare decisis*. If a lower federal court (how low?) can disregard a decision of the United States Supreme Court because the judge thinks the court erred, what is left of *stare decisis*? There have been famous examples of successful predictions by a lower court of changes in the attitude of the Supreme Court, but other less successful predictions have probably been more common.[19] In England, this sort of behaviour by lower courts has occurred once or twice in recent years, but the judge concerned has been Lord Denning, and his attempts to anticipate changes of doctrine by the House of Lords have been denounced as improper by the law lords themselves in no uncertain terms.[20] Some American state supreme courts have similarly reprimanded lower courts,[21] so the practice of 'anticipatory overruling' is not followed everywhere in America.

Courts of Appeals', 51 *Fordham L. Rev.* 53, 57 (1982); Comment, 'Stare Decisis in the Lower Courts: Predicting the Demise of Supreme Court Precedent', 60 *Wash. L. Rev.* 87 (1984).

[18] Kniffin, *supra*, n. 17, at 53–4.

[19] See *Barnette* v. *West Virginia*, 47 F. Supp. 251 (1942), aff'd. 319 US 624 (1943). See also Murphy, 'Lower Court Checks on Supreme Court Power', 53 *Am. Pol. Sc. Rev.* 1017, 1027 (1959).

[20] See the saga of *Cassell & Co.* v. *Broome* [1972] AC 1072 where the English CA indulged in something close to anticipatory overruling, only to be severely rebuked by the House of Lords.

[21] See *Hoffman* v. *Jones* 280 So. 2d 431 (1973) where the Florida Supreme Court was highly critical of a lower court attempt to introduce a comparative negligence rule into Florida. Of course, even by American standards, this was an extraordinarily bold decision for a lower court to make.

The power to overrule precedents

The second major difference in the operation of *stare decisis* in the two countries relates to the power to *overrule* prior precedents. This power, as already noted, can usually only be exercised by a narrower range of courts than the power to *disregard* otherwise binding precedents. Courts, especially American courts, can sometimes disregard higher court precedents where they have no power to overrule them. The power to overrule requires that the overruling court have authoritative status over the court which made the original decision, being either superior to that court in its hierarchy, or at least equal to that court in authority. Thus all American state supreme courts (the major makers of common law) as well as the Supreme Court of the United States (which makes some common law) have a general power to overrule the decisions of their lower courts and also their own past common law decisions,[22] and even American intermediate appellate courts not infrequently overrule their own decisions. These courts often overrule precedents on highly substantive grounds, such as, for example, obsolescence,[23] poor reasoning in the prior case,[24] failure of the prior court to understand the precedents,[25] or inconsistency with newly found moral and social insight or enlightenment.[26]

We do not suggest that American appellate courts will overrule whenever they think a precedent substantively wrong or mistaken, so there is still some scope for the operation of *stare decisis* in the more formal sense. But still, the position differs dramatically from that in England, where until 1966 even the ultimate court of last resort (the House of Lords) disclaimed the power to overrule its own decisions,[27] and since then has exercised the power very sparingly by American standards.[28] The English Court of Appeal, the major intermediate

[22] See generally Douglas, 'Stare Decisis', 49 *Col. L. Rev.* 735 (1949); Baum and Canon, *supra*, n. 7, 83. For other citations and illustrations see *post*, this chapter and notes.

[23] *Hundley* v. *Martinez* 151 W. Va. 977, 158 SE 2d 159 (1967), *post* p. 135.

[24] See, e.g., *Shroades* v. *Rental Homes Inc.*, 68 Ohio St. 2d 20, 427 NE 2d 774 (1981) (overruling an Ohio decision of 15 months earlier concerning landlord's liability for injuries caused by failure to maintain the leasehold in accordance with Ohio statute).

[25] See generally, Llewellyn, *supra*, n. 3, at 62–87, 'Precedent Techniques', numbers 43 and 46. On the English notion of decisions *per incuriam*, see *Morelle Ltd.* v. *Wakeling* [1955] 2 QB 379, 406.

[26] *Monge* v. *Beebe Rubber Co.* 114 NH 130, 316 A. 2d 549 (1974), see *post*, p. 135.

[27] *Beamish* v. *Beamish* (1861) 9 HLC 274, 338, 11 ER 735, 761; *London Tramways* v. *LCC* [1898] AC 375. It has been suggested that the doctrine of the first of these cases reflects Austinian notions of law as a rule *laid down* by authority: Wise, *supra*, n. 4, at 1048.

[28] See Practice Statement [1966] 1 WLR 1234; Cross, *supra*, n. 4, ch. III; Leach, 'Revisionism in the House of Lords: The Bastion of Rigid Stare Decisis Falls', 80 *Harv. L. Rev.* 797 (1967). As to the limited use made of this new power, see Alan Paterson, *supra*, n. 5, 156, 162 (1982); *Fitzleet Estates Ltd.* v. *Cherry* [1977] 3 All ER 996, 999. It is an open secret that Lord Denning tried unsuccessfully to persuade the CA judges to adopt a similar practice while he was Master of the Rolls (President of the CA).

appellate court in England, has little power freely to depart from its own precedents.[29] We return to this in section 4, below.

The evasion of precedents

A third difference between the two systems appears to be that American courts are more willing to use various techniques for escaping the effect of an otherwise binding precedent, some of which may be legitimate (such as perfectly genuine 'distinguishing') while others appear less legitimate (such as specious distinguishing, confining a case 'to its facts', and so on).[30] However, it is difficult to be sure that there is much difference between the two systems here, especially since English judges are often quite adept at the art of 'distinguishing',[31] though certainly some techniques (such as knowingly ignoring a precedent) appear to be used in America which would not (we think) be used by English judges.

The determination of the ratio decidendi *(or holding)*

Fourth, English judges also generally take a more formal approach to determining which part of a decision counts as the *ratio decidendi*, as English lawyers call it (the 'holding' in American terms), which is binding on later courts. In England, this subject is itself discussed in cases and a substantial legal literature[32] (which has no real counterpart in America)[33] in such a way as to suggest that it is also capable of being formulated in precise rules of high mandatory formality.[34] And although nobody has yet been very successful in formulating the appropriate rules in such a way as to command general assent,[35] there is wide agreement that the *ratio* must take the form of a relatively narrow rule, the boundaries of which are largely fixed by the precise issues before the

---

[29] *Young* v. *Bristol Aeroplane Co.* [1944] KB 718; *Davis* v. *Johnson* [1979] AC 264; R. Cross, *supra*, n. 4.

[30] Llewellyn, *supra*, n. 3, 84–7.

[31] See generally, Glanville Williams, *Learning the Law*, 73–8 (9th edn., Stevens, London, 1973).

[32] See, for a sample of a very voluminous literature, Cross, *supra*, n. 4, chapters II, III and IV; Goodhart, 'Determining the Ratio Decidendi of a Case', in A. L. Goodhart, *Essays in Jurisprudence and the Common Law*, 1 (Cambridge U. Press, 1931); Stone, 'The *Ratio* of the *Ratio Decidendi*', 22 *Mod. L. Rev.* 597 (1959). For judicial discussion of the distinction between *ratio* and *dicta* see *Jacobs* v. *London County Council* [1950] AC 361.

[33] Though there are occasional articles, see, e.g., those by Wise and Hardisty, *supra*, n. 4; and see also Posner, *The Federal Courts: Crisis and Reform*, 252–8 (Harvard U. Press, Cambridge, 1985) for an extensive discussion of the distinction between *ratio* and *dictum*.

[34] A. L. Goodhart's (admittedly highly controversial) formulation of the *ratio decidendi* of a case does in fact ignore the reasons for the decision. 'The principle of a case is not to be found in the reasons given in the opinion.' Instead, it is to be found by taking account of the facts treated by the judge as material, and his decision based on those facts. A. L. Goodhart, *supra*, n. 32, at 25. Compare R. Cross, *supra*, n. 4, at ch. II.

[35] D. N. MacCormick, *Legal Reasoning and Legal Theory*, 82 (Clarendon Press, Oxford, 1978).

prior court and the facts of the case which it considered to be 'material'. The late Professor Rupert Cross once commented that this approach 'greatly curtail[s] the influence that can be exercised on legal development by means of the *reasons* which a particular judge gives'.[36]

The American approach to determining the holding of a prior case often seems, by contrast, so substantive in character that it is not clear how much is left of the principle of *stare decisis* as a true source of formal reasoning. Many American scholars and theorists urge judges and lawyers to apply precedent in light of the substantive reasons that underlie the previous decision.[37] We have already noted Llewellyn's suggestion that a rule should only go so far as the reasons for it,[38] a view which drastically limits the content formality and also the mandatory and interpretive formality of rules. Many American judges do, in fact, appear to treat the effect of precedents in this way.[39] They often seem to be less interested in identifying some relatively narrow rule in a precedent than in deriving some general substantive reasoning or general principle from the case in question. Of course, sometimes the English and the American approaches will produce the same results, but they often diverge significantly, as Cross and others have noted.[40]

The synthesizing of precedents

A fifth difference in approach manifests itself when a series of precedents is involved. English courts then often try to formulate some kind of a 'synthesized' *ratio decidendi*,[41] and, indeed, the text of earlier opinions is sometimes subjected to almost the same kind of minute verbal analysis which English judges customarily adopt when interpreting statutes.[42] Again, American judges proceed differently. Sometimes, indeed, they merely list the authorities cited to the court by counsel and then go immediately into the substantive reasons for which they are

---

[36] R. Cross, *supra*, n. 4, at 42.

[37] K. N. Llewellyn, *The Bramble Bush*, 187–8 (Oceana Publications, NY, 1960); see also Dawson, 'The Functions of the Judge', in *Talks on American Law*, 19, 27 (Berman, ed., 2nd edn., Random House, NY, 1971); Llewellyn, *supra*, n. 3, at 75–87 (1960), especially 'Precedent Techniques' numbers 13, 17, 18, 20, 26, and 47.

[38] See *supra*, p. 88.

[39] See generally Summers, 'Two Types of Substantive Reasons: The Core of a Theory of Common-Law Justification', 63 *Cornell L. Rev.* 707 (1978). For specific cases, see, e.g., *Comunale* v. *Traders & General Ins. Co.* 321 P. 2d 768 (1958); *McKenna* v. *Ortho Pharamceutical Corp.* 622 F. 2d 657 (3d Cir. 1980).

[40] R. Cross, *supra*, n. 4, at 17, 25; Tunc, 'The not so Common Law of England and the United States', 47 *Mod. L. Rev.* 150 (1984).

[41] R. Cross, *supra*, n. 4, at 16.

[42] Thus the central paragraph of the opinion of Willes J. in *Indermaur* v. *Dames* (1866) LR 1 CP 274, 288 (dealing with occupier's liability) was for long treated almost as a statutory enactment, but the practice was deplored by most of the law lords in *London Graving Dock* v. *Horton* [1951] AC 737.

thought to stand. Occasionally, it even appears, as a leading French observer recently put it, that the American judge becomes 'fed up' with the precedents,[43] and refuses even to attempt a synthesis!

The authoritative weight of precedents

Sixth, even if a precedent is valid and not impeachable on any available ground, and even if it is binding on the court involved, and there is no available way round it, its overall authoritative force or weight is generally not so great in America as in England. Put another way, precedents have lower mandatory formality in America than in England. The distinction between binding and persuasive precedents is thus less sharp in the American legal system, and some scholars go so far as to suggest that precedents really are little more than 'guides'[44] or 'something to go on'.[45] Indeed, extreme statements can be found to the effect that *stare decisis* was already dead in America in 1930,[46] and we think this is largely true of courts of last resort if *stare decisis* is taken to mean that precedents must be followed simply because they are *binding*—because they generate formal reasons as such.

But this is not true of American lower courts, nor is it true of *stare decisis* in a looser sense, that is, in the sense that courts look to earlier decisions for the substantive reasons which may guide them to a decision. In this sense *stare decisis* is not by any means dead in American law. As Cardozo said, *'Stare decisis* is at least the everyday working rule of our law.'[47] Even the United States Supreme Court still *tends* to follow its own decisions in important classes of cases.[48] Courts also generally follow prior decisions on the interpretation of statutes. And, of course, precedent is generally treated as binding in those cases where there has been a clear prior decision by a court to which an appeal lies in the instant case.[49] The highest courts in each state still tend to follow their

[43] Tunc, *supra*, n. 40, at 153.

[44] See *supra*, p. 88, for the views of Roscoe Pound.

[45] Grant Gilmore once drew parallels between the study of precedent, history, and chess, rejecting the notion that we can predict the future from the past: 'Law, Anarchy and History', vol. 14, no. 2, *The University of Chicago Law School Record* 6 (1966).

[46] Thus Max Radin wrote in 1933, that 'As applied in the United States, the rule of stare decisis is a matter of technique. In whatever way courts reach their conclusion, they are expected to place the situation they are judging within the generalized class of some existing decisions.' 'Case Law and Stare Decisis: Concerning *Prajudizien Recht in Amerika*', 33 *Col. L. Rev.* 199, 212 (1933).

[47] *The Nature of the Judicial Process*, 20 (Yale U. Press, 1921). Some would say that much has changed since 1921, however.

[48] See generally Maltz, 'Some Thoughts on the Death of Stare Decisis in Constitutional Law', 1980 *Wisc. L. Rev.* 467.

[49] Hanna, 'The Role of Precedent in Judicial Decisions', 2 *Vill. L. Rev.* 367 (1957). But there have been some remarkably heroic decisions by lower courts such as that of the Michigan judge who eliminated the defence of charitable immunity in tort law: see *Parker v. Port Huron Hospital* 361 Mich. 1, 105 NW 2d 1 (1960) affirming his decision.

own decisions, but with much greater freedom to overrule and renovate than in England.[50] It is difficult to generalize about federal appeals courts.[51] Frequently, different panels of a large appeals court feel no obligation to follow decisions of another panel, although, if the point recurs frequently or is of great importance, the court as a whole may try to resolve the issue with an *en banc* hearing before all the judges of the court and this is then binding on all the court's judges.

It would be equally wrong to think that English practice is always as rigid and formal as we may have made it appear, even though one can find extreme statements like that of Lord Wright who once wrote that a binding precedent is to be treated 'as if part of an Act of Parliament, and is as little affected by criticism or in need of justification'.[52] Even in England, the authority of a badly reasoned precedent is not as good as that of a well-reasoned precedent; even in England, there are ways of distinguishing unpopular precedents, and there are precedents which get pushed aside or discarded because they are universally regarded as unsatisfactory. So also the rules about what is to count as *ratio decidendi* and what *obiter dictum* can sometimes be applied with a good deal of fluidity. Thus the differences are matters of degree, though they are profound differences for all that.

Persuasive decisions

Finally, there are also differences as regards non-binding decisions. English judges are much more willing (it seems to us) to follow decisions with which they personally do not agree, even where they are not bound to so so. This willingness to defer to colleagues, especially to numerous and senior colleagues,[53] is one of the most striking differences between the daily practice of appellate courts in England and some (though not all) American courts, a difference which also contributes to the generally stricter operation of stare decisis. Judge Richard Posner has recently commented on the large number of cases in which American appellate judges insist on delivering dissents or separate opinions in which they express minor reservations about majority opinions.[54]

3. SOME EXPLANATIONS FOR THE DIFFERENCES

We have identified important differences between English and American

[50] See, e.g., R. Keeton, *Venturing to Do Justice* (Harvard U. Press, Cambridge, 1969).

[51] See Note, 'Securing Uniformity in National Law: A Proposal for National Stare Decisis in the Courts of Appeals', 87 *Yale LJ* 1219 (1978). See also Marcus, 'Conflicts among Circuits and Transfers within the Federal Judicial System', 93 *Yale LJ* 677 (1984).

[52] Wright, 'Precedents', 8 *Camb. LJ* 118, 126 (1943).

[53] For a well-known example, see the opinion of Lord Blackburn in *Foakes* v. *Beer* (1884) 9 App. Cas. 605, which is in substance a dissenting opinion, and yet, in the end, Lord Blackburn deferred to his colleagues and agreed with the decision.

[54] See Posner, *supra*, n. 33, 227–47.

practice with respect to *stare decisis,* and we proceed to offer some explanations for these differences. In chapters 10 through 14 we shall explore important social and institutional factors which may partly account for these differences. Here we will confine comment to three factors which more directly affect the working of a case-law system: the volume of case-law, the proportion of dissenting opinions, and the incidence of 'plurality' opinions.

The volume of case-law

Many of the differences we have outlined above stem from the immense growth in the volume of reported American cases which now number over three million.[55] This alone creates serious problems of accessibility. The American lawyer is frequently unsure whether he has covered all relevant cases, even those binding on the court concerned.[56] American lawyers are not unaware of the extent to which a system of precedent depends on a manageable number of available precedents. Indeed, as Gilmore once suggested,[57] it may well be that the establishment of West's National Reporter system in the 1870s was one of the causes of the collapse of the older stricter system of precedent; and perhaps today even the looser system of precedent presently followed in America is being threatened by the deluge of reported cases.

Of course, the American lawyer need not always consult the huge bulk of American case-law. Each of the fifty states has its own separate body of precedents, which is all that the lawyer need refer to in many cases. In this light, the vast bulk of American case-law becomes more manageable. Indeed, where state law alone governs, the American lawyer may occasionally have less case law to review than his counterpart in England; and where this is the situation, cases may still tend to be treated in a stricter way, as binding authoritative sources of law, without regard to substance.[58] But the fact that American judges get used to handling cases in a different manner because, in so many situations, a very large number of cases from different jurisdictions has to be canvassed probably has a spillover effect, so that even within a single state system,

---

[55] M. L. Cohen and R. C. Berring, *Finding the Law*, 99 (West, St. Paul, 1984).

[56] Gilmore, 'Legal Realism: Its Cause and Cure', 70 *Yale LJ* 1037, 1041 (1961).

[57] *Ibid.*, at 1041. This problem explains moves by federal circuit courts to promulgate rules giving themselves power to issue decisions which are not published or citable as precedents. See Reynolds and Richman, 'The Non-Citable Precedent: Limited Publication and No Citation Rules in the United States Courts of Appeals', 78 *Col. L. Rev.* 1167 (1978). But see Wise, *supra*, n. 4, at 1056, for the proposition that American case law is reasonably retrievable, and will become more so with computer assistance.

[58] See Wise, *supra*, n. 4, who suggests (at 1056) that many American cases are argued and decided purely in terms of local law according to notions of *stare decisis* which would be acceptable to English judges.

cases are less likely to be treated as authoritative to the same degree as in England. But we certainly do not suggest that this never happens.

In addition, as we saw in chapter 2, a large number of basic conflicts between otherwise valid laws occurs in the American system,[59] and some of these conflicts can persist for many years. Many of these are conflicts between precedents on both sides of a faint line. The conflict may even involve the Constitution. If the law in State A and the law in State B differ because federal appeals courts take a different view of the law, and the United States Supreme Court refuses to grant *certiorari* to review the conflict, it must just be accepted that—perhaps for years—the Constitution of the United States is taken to mean different things in different parts of the country. It is not easy to reconcile such basic facts as these with highly formal notions derived from the idea that 'the law is the law'. It is thus not surprising if an over-abundance of precedents leads to many conflicting precedents, and if this in turn leads to individual precedents being accorded less authoritativeness.

Indeed, there are so many cases from so many jurisdictions in America today that it is almost literally true, and not just a cynical comment, that one can find authority for any legal proposition at all. On most seriously controverted legal issues, it is today possible to cite a considerable mass of authorities on both sides of any line that can be drawn. When this happens in England, and needless to say it happens far less often, the courts still usually strive to reconcile all or most of the cases cited to them, and explain why some are binding and will be followed, while the others are distinguishable and need not be followed, or, just occasionally, are wrong and ought to be overruled. Even in England, this sort of exercise sometimes looks artificial and strained, but in America it would often be regarded as absurd. It would today be widely agreed among American lawyers that, faced with many conflicting precedents, a court should select, on non-legal substantive grounds—on policy or value grounds—some premises from which it can draw a rule to apply. This was one of the fundamental lessons of the realists,[60] and there has been, to some extent, a self-fulfilling element about their teachings. As more judges have absorbed the lessons of realism they have come to assert openly that they have to choose between conflicting principles or precedents on substantive policy or value grounds, and they often do so.

One other result of the huge mass of American reported cases has been perhaps less obvious, but is nevertheless of profound importance. The volume of cases from such a variety of jurisdictions has perforce turned

---

[59] See *supra*, 55–69.
[60] See Gilmore, *supra*, n. 56.

Americans to some degree into comparative lawyers.[61] Among other things, they have learned that the same problem can be dealt with in one state through use of one conceptual apparatus, and in another state through use of an entirely different apparatus. Thus the same conduct will be treated as (say) contributory negligence in one jurisdiction and assumption of risk in another. It becomes apparent that both of these conceptualizations may be workable even though they may produce different (or the same) results. It would be impossible to assert, as English judges are still wont to assert, that there is only one 'true' or correct conceptual way of approaching or classifying a particular problem. This also tends to make the American system more substantive, because where more than one basic conceptualization is possible and appropriate, no one of them can have the significance that the substantive reasons have which underlie them all. Substantive reasoning may still require the use of legal concepts, but they will be used as tools, with less suggestion that they have some kind of objective reality.

Dissenting opinions

Another difference of some significance for our theme relates to the very different traditions governing the behaviour of judges in appellate courts in the two countries. In particular, dissent seems rarer in England, though this is an assertion to be taken with some caution. It may well be (as we shall see in more detail in chapter 10) that there is not a great deal of difference between *average* dissent rates in the two countries, but there is certainly more deviation from the mean in America. Some American courts have dissent rates far higher than anything encountered in England, and as these courts often include some of the most important courts in the country, their influence may be greater than that of other courts with lower dissent rates.

Clearly, a dissent, especially in a final appeal court which regularly overturns its own decisions, must weaken the precedential value of a decision as a source of clear and dependable rules. As Hughes CJ once said: 'A dissent in a court of last resort is an appeal to the brooding spirit of the law, to the intelligence of a future day when a later decision may possibly correct the error into which the dissenting judge believes the court has been betrayed'.[62] Scarcely any English judges would concur in this vision of the function of a dissenting opinion which would seem akin to an invitation to mutiny proffered to future generations.[63] When

---

[61] Although it must be conceded that some American academic lawyers are somewhat parochial as regards the comparative study of American with non-American law. Most English academic lawyers probably know much more about American law than vice versa.

[62] Hughes, *The Supreme Court of the United States* 68 (Columbia U. Press, NY, 1928).

[63] Alan Paterson, *supra*, n. 5, at 101, records one law lord who thought that dissent in the

it is remembered that today over 50% of Supreme Court opinions are customarily affected by dissent, it will be appreciated how far this understanding of the role of a dissent weakens the precedential force of a judicial decision. But the difference between the English and the American tradition must not be exaggerated. As we have repeatedly stressed, the American judicial tradition covers a wide spectrum of opinion and behaviour; at one end, the tradition is close to that of England, at the other end it is very different. Even in America there are some who would favour the view that dissents are, for instance, a 'menace to law and order', and that they impair predictability.[64] These views are more likely to be held by those who incline to the English view of the judicial role, but they do seem to be those of a minority in America today.[65]

Plurality opinions

We have already seen that American courts today often decline to accord much (if any) precedential value to plurality opinions where there is no clear majority for any one ground of decision. So one reason for the declining authority of the principle of *stare decisis* may be the recent growth of plurality opinions. This is particularly marked in the United States Supreme Court. Between 1800 and 1956 the Supreme Court issued only 45 plurality opinions. In the 36 years between 1955 and 1981, the court issued 130 such opinions, 88 of them in the last 12 years of this period.[66] There is some evidence that plurality opinions are also becoming more common in state supreme courts. Faced with such ambivalent holdings, some lower courts have chosen to accord plurality opinions no precedential value.[67] Hence they can, of course, generate no formal reasons.

On the other hand, the authority of a precedent and the ability of future lawyers to extract a clear ruling from it is not necessarily enhanced if a majority is made up of judges of differing views who concur in a single opinion. In this situation, bargaining may take place between the

---

House of Lords might be addressed to a future House reconsidering the instant case. See also L. Blom-Cooper and G. Drewry, *Final Appeal*, 88 (Clarendon Press, Oxford, 1972); Lord Diplock in *Carter* v. *Bradbeer* [1975] 1 WLR 1204, 1206–7 (no point in dissenting law lord giving reasons when case turns on narrow point of statutory interpretation).

[64] Lee, 'Dissenting Opinions', 2 *John Marshall LQ* 404, 405–6 (1937).

[65] See Friedman, Kagan, Cartwright, and Wheeler, 'State Supreme Courts: A Century of Style and Citation', 33 *Stan. L. Rev.* 773, 785 (1981); we deal in more detail with dissent rates in chapter 10.

[66] Note, 'Plurality Decisions and Judicial Decisionmaking', 94 *Harv. L. Rev.* 1127 n. 1.

[67] *Supra*, n. 13.

judges,[68] much as happens in American legislatures, to produce a majority. Such bargaining naturally tends to produce less clear cut rulings. Although some form of bargaining of this kind is probably not unknown among English judges, it seems more limited in scope and frequency.[69]

Plurality opinions are not unknown in the House of Lords. But they are rare, and when they do occur, what commonly happens is that a further case is very soon taken on appeal to clarify the law thus left doubtful.[70] It seems that English lawyers are seriously perturbed (perhaps reflecting their clients' perturbation) when a confusing plurality opinion is handed down by the House of Lords, and they usually take steps to clear up the ensuing confusion as soon as possible. The judges themselves seem acutely conscious of the need to clear up doubts and confusions created by their own plurality or otherwise confusing decisions; and it is not unknown for a clear and unanimous opinion to be delivered when a second case is thus taken on appeal after confusion in an earlier one.[71] American lawyers seem more accustomed to living with a legal system which does not provide clear answers to many problems. Unanimity in result may, of course, still create difficulties for those seeking to extract a rule from the decision where the judges give separate opinions and differ widely in their reasoning. And it is true that it is still very common for English judges to give separate opinions even where there is no substantial disagreement between them in result or reasoning (although this is no longer the standard practice in the House of Lords). Usually, each judge simply puts the same thing in different words. Most American courts would regard this as a waste of resources, and separate opinions there usually connote at least some difference in reasoning. But the multiplication of separate opinions in England must not mislead; such separate opinions do not necessarily indicate that there is no unanimity or clear majority view. Significant differences of view do seem more common in America, especially in the higher appellate courts.

[68] The extent to which such 'political' trading takes place among American judges is not easy to verify, but for one (somewhat discredited) view of the Supreme Court justices, see B. Woodward and S. Armstrong, *The Brethren* (Simon and Schuster, NY, 1979). A more reliable account of the Warren Court, however, confirms that some political trading does occur: Bernard Schwartz, *Super Chief* (New York U. Press, NY, 1983).

[69] Alan Paterson, *supra*, n. 5, at 109.

[70] For one example, see *British Railways Board* v. *Herrington* [1972] AC 877 where the failure of the House of Lords to provide a clear ruling was rapidly followed by the case of *Pannett* v. *McGuinness & Co. Ltd.* [1972] 2 QB 599.

[71] See, e.g., *Johnson* v. *Agnew* [1980] AC 367 where the House of Lords was plainly determined to clear up a mess left by a series of CA decisions.

Stare decisis *and predictability*

As we have seen, English judges tend to see their practices with regard to *stare decisis*, dissent, and the desirability of unanimity as contributing significantly to the predictability of decisions and certainty in the law generally. Although it is no part of our purpose to defend English theory, we need to confront here the probable reaction to this claim of some American lawyers (including academics) because we believe that these lawyers do not understand the conditions which make this claim plausible in the English context. Because the doctrine of precedent at one time appeared to be almost as strict in America as it is in England, and because the rules by which precedents were held to be strictly binding eventually came to be so weak that they were easily evaded and ultimately largely discarded, some American lawyers are sceptical that *stare decisis* can produce much certainty or predictability in the English legal system. Some have noted, too, that a judge like Lord Denning, while professing to operate within the general parameters of the English system of precedent, was nevertheless able to discard cases almost at will; and they have suggested that English law could in fact be revolutionized by a few more judges like Lord Denning without actually overruling any cases.[72] This is a mistake.

Although it may be true that several Lord Dennings operating simultaneously could drastically reform the law without overruling many decisions (simply by distinguishing or explaining them away), what this fails to allow for is that it is virtually inconceivable that there could be several Lord Dennings sitting on the bench. As can be seen from the number of cases in which Lord Denning dissented (or provoked dissent) and from the many opinions of other judges in such cases, most English judges thought that Lord Denning simply did not operate according to the rules which they felt to be binding upon them, and that this was inappropriate behaviour in a judge. Certainly it is hard to imagine a Lord Chancellor recommending the appointment of several judges whom he expects to behave in the same fashion as Lord Denning. As we shall suggest later in this book (see chapter 12) the rules and conventions governing the selection of judges, the kind of people they are, the way they are expected to behave, the norms they tacitly accept, and their critical reflective attitudes are all just as important in understanding a legal system as the nominal rules of law. Anyone who thinks that English law could survive as substantially the same system of law if it had a whole benchful of Lord Dennings is failing to pay adequate attention to these considerations.

---

[72] An opinion expressed in a letter to the first-named author by Professor Duncan Kennedy of the Harvard Law School.

4. THE METHODOLOGY OF LEGAL CHANGE

So far in this chapter we have identified and explained major differences between England and America with respect to the principle of *stare decisis*. In this section we shall deal more fully with the way in which the law (and not merely the common law) is changed in the two countries, and with the implications of these differences for other aspects of our thesis. In brief, it will be our argument here that far more legal change comes from the courts in America, by comparison with England, where such change is overwhelmingly the work of the legislature. We shall then offer some explanations for this difference in practice, and finally we will comment on the light which this sheds on the different visions of law which appear to be held in the two countries.

Judicial law making

We shall start by comparing English and American practice with regard to the explicit overruling of old case-law as a major method of legal reform. This is, of course, only one mode of legal change, and we shall not here deal with all the other modes such as implicit overruling, the creation of exceptions, the gradual extension of doctrine, and so forth.

We will open with the American position in its leading common law courts—the courts that create the great bulk of American common law, namely the fifty state supreme courts (some of them known by different names). These courts frequently overrule precedents in open and explicit fashion on at least three major and often independently significant grounds: (1) circumstances have so changed since the precedent was created that it has become substantively obsolete; (2) growing moral and social enlightenment indicates that the substantive values underlying the precedent are no longer acceptable; and (3) the precedent was substantively erroneous or badly conceived from the beginning. Countless examples could be cited in each of these categories, and we will discuss a few to lend concreteness and flavour to our thesis, and to enable the reader to compare the methodology of change in England and America.

In *Lemle* v. *Breeden*[73] the Supreme Court of Hawaii explicitly relied on a change in circumstances when it re-examined and discarded the common law rule of *caveat emptor* for residential tenancies, replacing it with an implied warranty of habitability and fitness. The court acknowledged the common law rule that there was normally no such implied warranty in a lease, and then proceeded:

The rule of *caveat emptor* in lease transactions at one time may have had some basis in social practice as well as in historical doctrine. At common law leases were customarily lengthy documents embodying the full expectations of the

[73] 51 Hawaii 426, 462 P. 2d 470 (1969).

parties. There was generally equal knowledge of the condition of the land by both landlord and tenant. The land itself would often yield the rents and the buildings were constructed simply, without modern conveniences like wiring or plumbing. Yet in urban society where the vast majority of tenants do not reap the rent directly from the land but bargain primarily for the right to enjoy the premises for living purposes, often signing standardized leases as in this case, common law conceptions of a lease and the tenant's liability for rent are no longer viable.[74]

The court also resorted to 'moral enlightenment' reasoning, arguing that the implied warranty of habitability and fitness was 'a just and necessary implication' from the nature of a lease, as in the case of sales of goods.[75]

A second representative example of a court departing from a common law rule because of changed circumstances is provided by the West Virginia case of *Hundley* v. *Martinez*.[76] This was a malpractice action in which the Supreme Court of Appeals reconsidered the old 'locality' rule to the effect that expert evidence was required as to the standard of care prevailing in the community where the defendant practised. The court decided that this rule needed modification because in modern times doctors in rural areas have available to them most of the same facilities as practitioners in the city, and generally speaking the same standard of care prevails throughout the country.

The general movement towards implying covenants of good faith and fair dealing in all contracts affords numerous examples of cases in which courts have departed from long-settled law because of growing 'moral enlightenment'. The New Hampshire case of *Monge* v. *Beebe Rubber Company*[77] is aptly illustrative. In this case the plaintiff won a jury verdict for damages for breach of an oral employment contract, having claimed that she was harassed and ultimately fired for refusing to 'date' her foreman. On appeal, the court reconsidered the well-settled (American[78]) common law rule that an employment contract for an indefinite period of time is presumed to be 'at will' and terminable at any time by either party. The court noted that the laws governing the workplace have evolved to reflect changing social relations and it insisted that 'the courts cannot ignore the new climate prevailing generally in the relationship of employer and employee'.[79] The court went on to hold that a bad faith or malicious termination of the employment contract would be regarded as a breach of the contract,[80]

---

[74] *Ibid.*, at 430, 462 P. 2d at 472–3.
[75] *Ibid.*, at 433, 462 P. 2d at 474.
[76] 151 W. Va. 977, 158 SE 2d 159 (1967).
[77] 114 NH 130, 316 A. 2d 549 (1974).
[78] The English common law rule is slightly different: an indefinite contract of employment is only terminable on reasonable notice.
[79] *Supra*, n. 77, at 133, 316 A. 2d at 551.
[80] *Ibid.*, at 134, 316 A. 2d at 552.

and concluded that there was sufficient evidence for the jury to find that the plaintiff was in fact discharged in bad faith.

These cases provide a flavour of detail that illustrates the general willingness of the courts to overrule what they perceive to be outmoded or unenlightened precedent. Another way to convey this attitude is to review some of the major changes made in the last two decades in American tort and contract law through judicial overruling and substitution of new law. In the law of torts the list includes: recognition of a new theory of strict products liability;[81] replacement of the common law contributory negligence rule by an apportionment principle based on comparative fault;[82] abrogation of governmental,[83] charitable,[84] and parental[85] immunity to liability; revision of the duty of an occupier to those entering on his premises;[86] modification of a host driver's duty to guest passengers;[87] recognition of a wife's right to damages for loss of consortium;[88] expansion of liability for causing mental suffering;[89] and modification of the assumption of risk defence.[90]

The change from the original common law rule of contributory negligence to the apportionment principle of comparative negligence affords a particularly striking illustration of the reach of American judicial law making, because the earliest attempts to persuade the courts to change the rule were defeated. In 1968 in *Maki* v. *Frelk*[91] an Illinois appellate court had decided to adopt the principle of comparative negligence, but this decision was reversed by the state supreme court (by a 5:2 vote) on the ground that such a change should be made only by legislation. The *Vanderbilt Law Review* published a series of academic comments on this case,[92] most of which were adverse to the supreme court's decision. Fleming James perhaps summed up the general academic opinion when he wrote that, 'The proposition that changing the law is properly and exclusively the function of the legislature runs

---

[81] *Henningsen* v. *Bloomfield Motors, Inc.*, 32 NJ 358, 161 A. 2d 69 (1970), 75 ALR 2d 1 (1960).

[82] See, e.g., *Alvis* v. *Ribar* 85 Ill. 2d 1, 421 NE 2d 886.

[83] See, e.g., *Muskopf* v. *Corning Hospital District* 55 Cal. 2d 211, 11 Cal. Rptr. 89, 359 P. 2d 457 (1961).

[84] See, e.g., *Bing* v. *Thunig*, 2 NY 2d 656, 143 NE 2d 3, 163 NYS 2d 3 (1957).

[85] See, e.g., *Briere* v. *Briere*, 224 A. 2d 588 (NH 1966).

[86] See, e.g., *Rowland* v. *Christian* 69 Cal. 2d 108, 443 P. 2d 561, 70 Cal. Rptr. 97 (1968).

[87] See, e.g., *McConville* v. *State Farm Mutual Auto Ins. Co.* 15 Wis. 2d 374, 113 NW 2d 14 (1962).

[88] See, e.g., *Diaz* v. *Eli Lilly & Co.*, 302 NE 2d 555 (Mass. 1973).

[89] See, e.g., *Dillon* v. *Legg* 68 Cal. 2d 728, 69 Cal. Rptr. 72, 441 P. 2d 912 (1968).

[90] See, e.g., *Williamson* v. *Smith* 83 NM 336, 491 P. 2d 1147 (1972).

[91] 85 Ill. App. 2d 439, 229 NE 2d 284 (1967), reversed, 40 Ill. App. 2d 193, 239 NE 2d 445 (1968).

[92] 21 *Vand. L. Rev.* 889–948 (1968).

counter to Anglo-American tradition.'[93] In due course this weight of academic opinion bore fruit, and by 1975 the California Supreme Court was prepared to make the change on its own responsibility.[94] Since then a further nine states (including Illinois itself[95]) have made the change by judicial decision, but a much greater number has done so by legislation.

In the law of contract it is possible to draw up a similar list of major new decisions in which old cases have been overruled and new law laid down. Thus we have witnessed relatively recently the growth of liability for promises grounded in the past;[96] a growth in liability for reliance reasonably incurred;[97] a willingness to provide remedies despite indefiniteness of agreement;[98] the striking down of exculpatory clauses in contracts which have been signed without being read;[99] enlargement of the defence of duress;[100] abolition of the pre-existing duty rule in the law of consideration;[101] extension of relief for unilateral mistake;[102] expansion of excuses for impossibility and frustration;[103] relaxation of the requirement that damage be shown with certainty;[104] and greater availability of punitive damages.[105]

Nearly all these changes were introduced by state supreme courts, though some were initiated by intermediate appellate courts, which exist in 32 states and which, in some of these states, have power to overrule or at least modify prior state supreme court precedents, subject of course to the ultimate control of the supreme court.[106] The existence of such a power at the intermediate court level (in extreme cases extending to the power of 'anticipatory overruling' as we have noted earlier[107]) is itself an additional factor leading to the greater use of the overruling power, because these courts hear many more cases than courts of last resort.

---

[93] Comment, *ibid.*, at 892. Insofar as James included the English tradition in his comments, and insofar as he may have implied that the change in question was the kind of change made by courts in modern times, he was certainly wrong.

[94] *Li* v. *Yellow Cab Co. of California* 13 Cal. 3d 804, 532 P. 2d 1226 (1975).

[95] See *Alvis* v. *Ribar, supra,* n. 82.

[96] See, e.g., *In re Gerke's Estate* 271 Wis. 297, 73 NW 2d 506 (1955).

[97] See, e.g., *Hoffman* v. *Red Owl Stores*, 26 Wis. 2d 683, 133 NW 2d 267 (1965).

[98] See, e.g., *Wheeler* v. *White*, 398 SW 2d 92 (Tex. 1965).

[99] See, e.g., *Weaver* v. *American Oil Co.* 257 Ind. 458, 276 NE 2d 144 (1972).

[100] See, e.g., *Eckstein* v. *Eckstein*, 38 Md. App. 506, 379 A. 2d 757 (1978).

[101] See, e.g., *Winter Wolff & Co.* v. *Co-op Lead & Chem. Co.*, 261 Minn. 199, 111 NW 2d 461 (1961).

[102] See, e.g., *Elsinore Union Elementary School Dist.* v. *Kastorff*, 54 Cal. 2d 380, 353 P. 2d 713 (1960).

[103] See, for an extreme example of this trend, *Aluminium Co. of America* v. *Essex Group*, 499 F. Supp. 53 (WD Pa. 1980) (purporting to apply state law).

[104] See, e.g., *Rombola* v. *Cosindas*, 351 Mass. 382, 220 NE 2d 919 (1966).

[105] See, e.g., *Vernon Fire & Cas. Ins. Co.* v. *Sharp*, 264 Ind. 599, 349 NE 2d 173 (1976).

[106] See generally Summers, *supra,* n. 39, at 724.

[107] See Kniffin, *supra,* n. 17.

Of course it is not possible to quantify meaningfully the number of cases annually overruled by state supreme courts, but many of them average two or three such decisions every year. Naturally, this cuts down the authoritative and mandatory formality of common law reasoning, and after overruling the old law, the court will also go on to justify the new law which it lays down in substantive terms.

So far we have said nothing about the influence and example of the United States Supreme Court and the federal courts of appeals. They do not, of course, play a very large role today in ordinary areas of common law. But there is a vast body of American constitutional law of which these courts are the custodians, and much of this constitutional law takes the form of case-law interpreting the federal Constitution. If the United States Supreme Court takes the view—which it does—that federal constitutional case-law is not at all sacrosanct, but that it may, in a proper case, be overruled, it is hardly surprising if state supreme courts should follow suit with respect to the common law of which they are the chief custodians.

One reason why the Supreme Court responds thus to constitutional cases is that it can hardly defer to the formal processes for amending the Constitution. To do so would be a meaningless gesture, because historically very little reform has come from this source; indeed, only twenty-six amendments have been passed in a period of nearly 200 years. The Supreme Court has overruled constitutional cases on a variety of grounds. Some cases have been overruled on the ground that they were wrong from the start. Perhaps the most famous example is the doctrine of *Swift* v. *Tyson*,[108] decided in 1842, according to which a federal court sitting in a 'diversity of citizenship' case was originally thought to have power to create general federal common law. This was overruled in the *Erie* case[109] in 1938 which we have already noted in chapter 2. *Erie* had far-reaching ramifications throughout the American legal system. At one fell swoop it wiped out huge branches of federal common law (and also recently published multi-volume treatises expounding that law!).

More recently, of course, there have been the famous cases arising from the greater moral enlightenment of the times, as a result of which the Supreme Court finally overruled *Plessy* v. *Ferguson*[110] in the great case of *Brown* v. *Board of Education*[111] in 1954. This decision also had wide ramifications, this time on the public school system in America

---

[108] 41 US (16 Pet.) 1 (1842).
[109] 304 US 64 (1938); see chapter 2, *supra* p. 58.
[110] 163 US 537 (1896).
[111] 347 US 483 (1954).

and, indeed, more widely on the general problem of racial discrimination. Overrulings at the Supreme Court level have also occurred for reasons of obsolescence and change of circumstances.[112]

The total number of major Supreme Court decisions overruled in constitutional matters is disputed. Some scholars put the number for the period 1810 to 1980 at 170.[113] Between 1966, the date of the House of Lords' Practice statement, and 1980, the Supreme Court, according to one view, expressly overruled 55 of its own decisions.[114] In the same period the House of Lords overruled 8.[115] If we assume conservatively that each state supreme court in the same period overruled only one case per year, this would give a total of 50 cases per year for 14 years, that is, over 700 cases. Even leaving aside federal appeal courts and state intermediate courts, the score would thus show: America 755, England 8. We hasten to add that this does not indicate a 'victory' to either 'side', but these numbers do seem to demonstrate how radically different is the operation of *stare decisis* in the English and American legal systems.

We now turn to consider the general position with respect to these matters in England. The contrast is striking. First, we consider the power of the courts to change the law by overruling old precedents. Only the House of Lords has a general power to overrule and its normal practice is to leave reform to Parliament. When it does overrule, it does so on limited grounds, and has repeatedly insisted that the power to overrule its own decisions is to be sparingly exercised. It has refused to overrule previous decisions on general substantive grounds, or, for instance, on the ground that an earlier decision had been much criticized as an infringement of the principle of legality in the criminal law (that is, the principle that criminal prohibitions must be clearly laid down in advance).[116] It has made minor modifications to tort doctrine, as previously laid down by earlier decisions of its own, for instance as to the liability of an occupier to trespassers,[117] but to such a limited degree that further reform by statute was still needed.[118] Its most dramatic use of its new power to overrule old cases is to be found in the *Miliangos* case in 1976.

---

[112] See, e.g., *Baker* v. *Carr*, 369 US 186 (1962); see generally, L. Tribe, *American Constitutional Law*, 738–41 (Foundation Press, Mineola, NY, 1978).

[113] *The Constitution of the United States of America: Analysis and Interpretation*, 1789–97 (L. Jayson and J. Killian edd., US Gov't Print Office, Washington, 1973) and 332–3 (Supp. 1982).

[114] *Ibid.*

[115] See Alan Paterson, *supra*, n. 5, at 163.

[116] See *Knuller* v. *DPP* [1973] AC 435.

[117] See *British Railways Board* v. *Herrington*, supra, n. 70.

[118] See Occupiers Liability Act 1984.

The case involved the ability of an English court to give judgment for a debt in German marks, rather than in devalued British pounds. It would be difficult to find a rule of English law of greater authority, antiquity, and uniformity than the rule that judgment could only be given in an English court in pounds sterling. The rule was at least 300 years old, and had been reaffirmed only a few years earlier by the House of Lords itself in *In re United Railways of Havana*,[119] in which even the great iconoclast, Lord Denning, had concurred. However, in the *Miliangos* case[120] the House of Lords overruled the *Havana* case, and decided that, in appropriate circumstances, English courts could now give judgments in a foreign currency. But, as though to give warning that this did not indicate that the bonds of precedent should now be regarded as undone, the House of Lords also said that the majority of the Court of Appeal had been wrong in refusing to follow the *Havana* decision. According to standard English practice, the Court of Appeal is bound by decisions of the House of Lords, and the House rejected the idea that the force of an otherwise binding precedent could be overcome by invoking the maxim *cessante ratione lex cessat ipsa lex*. The maxim is not, insisted the House, 'a licence to courts to change the law if it appears to them that the circumstances in which it was framed have changed'.[121] The maxim, in other words, can only be applied subject to the doctrine of *stare decisis*, and anticipatory overruling is completely impermissible.

This was by far the most dramatic use of the new power to overrule, and there has been nothing else like it since 1966.[122] We have also noted above that the English Court of Appeal does not claim the freedom to overrule its own decisions, though there are some strictly limited exceptions to the principle that it is absolutely bound by its own decisions. The general position thus appears to be radically different from that prevailing in America.

However, we must now go on to note that legislative reform of the common law is, in modern times, frequent in England, and certainly much easier to obtain than in most American states. If, for instance, we look at the cases and doctrines cited above as illustrations of the powers of American courts to change the common law, we shall find that many of them can be matched by English legislation. Indeed, in some cases the English legislation antedates by many years the comparable judicial decisions in America. Thus (to illustrate) England has statutes importing implied warranties of habitability and fitness in various forms of

---

[119] [1961] AC 1007.
[120] *Miliangos* v. *George Frank (Textiles) Ltd.*, [1976] AC 443.
[121] *Ibid.*, at 476 (Lord Simon).
[122] But see *R.* v. *Shivpuri* [1986] 2 All ER 334, *supra*, ch. 2 n. 34.

residential leases,[123] bad faith or malicious discharge of employees is compensatable by Industrial Tribunals as 'unfair dismissal',[124] the common law contributory negligence rule was replaced by a comparative negligence statute in 1945,[125] governmental immunity in tort was abolished by statute in 1947,[126] spousal immunity to suit went in 1962,[127] and the law relating to the liability of occupiers was reformed by the Occupiers Liability Act 1957. Some of the changes achieved in America have also been introduced in England by cases (such as the abolition of charitable immunity in tort),[128] but these were never so firmly established in English law as in America. The list of changes in contract doctrine could largely be matched by a similar list from England, though this has been done without major overrulings of authoritative cases. Statute has, however, contributed here also as with the implied warranties noted above, the introduction of the concept of 'unfair dismissal', the control of exculpatory or exemption clauses by the Unfair Contract Terms Act, and the modification of remedies available on frustration by the Law Reform (Frustrated Contract) Act 1943.

The overall picture, therefore, does not suggest a greater legal conservatism in England, but merely a basic difference in the methodology of law reform. We will now go on to say something about the reasons for this difference, though we must defer to later chapters an account of the broad-ranging cultural and institutional influences which we believe to underlie it.

Influences on the courts

Obviously the most important matter is the nature of the relationship between the legislature and the courts. Since English courts, unlike American courts, can often assume that reform will be forthcoming from the legislature if necessary, the courts themselves are often unwilling to make the changes which seem desirable. This is partly because judges are used to deferring to the legislature in England, but partly also because they believe legislative methods of law reform are superior. And in the

---

[123] See Housing Acts 1957, sections 4 and 6 (implied warranty of habitability in low rental housing—figures badly need updating); Housing Act 1961, section 32 (implied covenant to repair in short term leases). But there is no general warranty of habitability in English law.

[124] First introduced in the Industrial Relations Act 1971, and now in the Employment Protection (Consolidation) Act 1978, as subsequently amended.

[125] Law Reform (Contributory Negligence) Act 1945.

[126] Crown Proceedings Act 1947.

[127] Law Reform (Husband and Wife) Act 1962.

[128] See *Gold* v. *Essex CC* [1942] 2 KB 293 explaining away the decision in *Hillyer* v. *St Bartholomew's Hospital* [1909] 2 KB 820 which may have been influenced by the desire to shelter charitable hospitals from tort liability; but apart from this case, English law never explicitly recognized a doctrine of charitable immunity in tort.

English context, this is generally true, because legislation is usually preceded by careful study of the position, sometimes by government departments, but often by specially appointed committees, who are able to obtain a wider range of information and canvass a wider group of interested parties, before making proposals for change.

A second factor, not unrelated to the first, is the fear that judicial law reform will lead to uncertainty. The reason for this is not a fear of legal change *per se*, because the courts often invite and welcome legislative law reform. It is due to a belief that a change in the law has to be carefully dovetailed into the existing fabric of the law, so that the precise extent and ramifications of the change are thought through and implemented in advance. Although some American judges evince concern about these matters, they seem to weigh far more heavily with English judges.[129]

In those rare English cases where major upheavals in case law are caused by an exceptionally creative decision, the opinions of English judges are today likely to be lengthy and detailed. Conflicting case-law will probably be exhaustively reviewed (something which remains possible in a single jurisdiction, like England, with a manageable body of law reports), and inconsistent decisions will usually be expressly overruled, or declared to remain as anomalies or exceptions, notwithstanding the present decision. Inevitably, some loose ends may remain. Some previous cases may be overlooked, the full implications of the instant decision on other, remoter bodies of law may not at first be appreciated, and further developments of the law may eventually lead to the overturning of authorities at first thought to be consistent with the new decision. But uncertainties of this kind are marginal or fringe matters, and in any event, major decisions of this kind are rare indeed in England. Probably only a few House of Lords' decisions could reasonably be said to fall into this category since the end of the Second World War, for example, the *Hedley Byrne* case,[130] the *Miliangos* case,[131] and perhaps one or two others.

We think English judges are right in believing that legal change, and especially major legal change, through judicial decisions, is apt to create much uncertainty in the legal system. Such change frequently creates uncertainty because it tends to leave many loose ends to be tidied up at a later date. Legislative changes may also create uncertainty, but careful planning and drafting of legislative change can greatly reduce the uncertainty.

We do not argue that uncertainty is, *per se*, a bad thing, though most

---

[129] See, e.g., Lord Simon in the *Miliangos* case [1976] AC at 487 (suggesting Parliament better placed to deal with implications and ramifications of legal change).
[130] [1964] AC 465.
[131] [1976] AC 443.

English lawyers and perhaps many American lawyers would agree that it is. We accept that uncertainty is an inherent part of a legal system, and that it can never be eliminated, so that its mere existence proves nothing. But we have already given reasons for believing that, other things being equal, more formal legal systems are likely to be more certain and more predictable than systems which rely more heavily on substantive reasons. Certainty and predictability in a legal system are very much matters of degree, and these depend on the nature of the legal system taken as a whole. A system which entrusts as much power of change to its courts as the American system does, inevitably, we think, invites a much higher degree of uncertainty than a system which does not.

We now turn to some of the ways in which using the courts to introduce major legal changes in America has led to uncertainties of a kind which are not encountered in England (or most other legal systems) and which have tended to break down the view that law can be seen as a system of rules, generating formal reasons for decisions.

We look first at a set of complications concerning conflicts of authority in case-law in the American legal system which have no real parallel in England. Major changes of legal doctrine at the constitutional level often have a considerable impact on a complex network of state law, including common law. For example, when the Supreme Court in *Brown* v. *Board of Education*[132] first rejected the doctrine of 'separate but equal' with regard to school segregation, it was clear that much state case-law and statute law was thereby rendered unconstitutional and void. But (even leaving aside the problem of state recalcitrance in giving effect to the Supreme Court decisions, which we deal with in chapter 10) it was inevitably a difficult and doubtful matter to work out the precise impact of such decisions on the numerous branches of state law that might be affected. Whether or not a particular body of state case-law or statute law was inconsistent with the new Supreme Court ruling was thus a matter which often required further judicial elucidation, much of which was long drawn out and bitterly fought.[133] In the interim, the problem of deciding what was 'the law' in any particular area or what was 'the rule' that governed a particular situation was often incapable of a clear answer. Moreover, in some areas it was bound to be many years before a clear answer could be given.

The problem discussed above is by no means confined to the kind of far-reaching constitutional change typified by the *Brown* decision and its aftermath. It is 25 years since the Supreme Court decision in *New York*

---

[132] 347 US 483 (1954).
[133] See generally, J. Peltason, *Fifty-eight Lonely Men: Southern Federal Judges and School Desegregation* (U. of Illinois Press, Urbana, Ill., revised edn., 1971).

Times v. *Sullivan*[134] revolutionized the American (common) law of defamation, but numerous uncertainties in the law still remain unresolved.[135]

A similar problem can sometimes arise out of shifting personnel and attitudes in the US Supreme Court. Many state constitutions contain Bills of Rights with language modelled on that of the federal Constitution. These state Bills of Rights cannot validly confer lesser rights on the citizen than the federal Constitution, but they can confer more extensive rights. When the Supreme Court of the United States gives very wide interpretations to the provisions of the Bill of Rights in the federal Constitution, state supreme court judges will often find it unnecessary to decide what effect ought to be given to the Bills of Rights in their own state constitutions. But if the US Supreme Court should then backtrack and hand down a decision which cuts down on the citizen's rights, it at once becomes necessary for the state courts to decide what their own constitutional rights are to be, before it can be said what the law of each state is. The state supreme courts often follow the US Supreme Court, but they are under no obligation to so in this regard, and frequently do not. Given the fact that many of the most sensitive issues involve political questions of current controversy, it is hardly surprising if some state courts refuse to follow changes of mind on the US Supreme Court resulting from changes of personnel or attitudes on that court. But of course, this kind of thing adds to the uncertainty of law in the whole American system.[136]

A similar situation is sometimes thrown up in America by another aspect of the relationship between courts and legislatures. The constitutional process sometimes requires courts and state legislatures to arrive at a certain type of result, but it may be left to the state to decide by which organ it will initiate the required change. For example, the reapportionment cases[137] left the states with the responsibility of complying with the Supreme Court mandate, but within each state the courts could legitimately give the legislature time to 'put its own house in order' before moving itself. It is clear that legal decisions of this nature are hard to make on principled grounds, and it is equally hard to identify the legal 'rules' governing the electoral process in the interim stages of the changeover.

More generally, it often happens that American constitutional decisions cannot be immediately implemented without the co-operation of

---

[134] 376 US 254, 84 S. Ct. 710, 11 L. Ed. 2d 686 (1964).

[135] For example, the account given in Harper, James, and Gray, *The Law of Torts*, vol. 2 (2nd edn., Gray, ed., Little Brown, Boston, 1986) mentions numerous points of uncertainty in page after page.

[136] See Porter, in Porter and Tarr, edd., *supra*, n. 6.

[137] *Baker* v. *Carr*, 369 US 186 (1962).

state executives or even legislatures, and where the decision is likely to produce major reversals of previous social policies, time must be allowed for implementation. The best-known illustration of this in modern times was the second school desegregation case in which the Supreme Court required implementation of its first decision 'with all deliberate speed'.[138] But the full significance of this cryptic expression was never spelled out by the Supreme Court, which left lower federal courts to implement it. Now, the speed at which a state or local community is required to change its social policies is itself such an obviously policy issue as virtually to defy principled application. And pending full implementation of the new law it would, once again, be difficult to cast the law in traditional 'rule' terms. What was the applicable 'rule' immediately after the decision in *Brown* v. *Board of Education*?[139] Or six months later? Or five years later? When courts make decisions like the first *Brown* decision they are retreating from the arena of rules. It is impossible for them to work out the implications of decisions of this character in any formal manner, by asking 'what the law is' and applying it. There is no 'rule' which can be treated as a formal reason for decision, excluding most or all substantive reasons from consideration. The detailed implementation of legal change in this way can only be resolved through substantive means-end reasoning tailored to the particular administrative problem at hand.

Episodes of this character tend to illustrate that, when major constitutional decisions of this kind are being made, the American courts are not dealing in 'rules' at all, but either in legal principles at a much higher level of abstraction and generality, or in particular administrative adjustment of substantive means–end relations. Principles, whether these are truly Dworkinian principles or not,[140] cannot be applied formally in the way that rules can be applied. Rather, they translate directly into reasons of substance. Similarly, managerial administration can seldom be a matter of following a rule.

There are no real parallels in English law to the sort of situation created by decisions of this kind, where the courts are willing to allow time for social adjustment to the new rulings. The nearest parallel, perhaps, might be a nuisance injunction whose operation might be suspended in some cases in order to give the defendant an opportunity to comply. But this is really no parallel at all, because time for *social*

---

[138] *Brown* v. *Board of Education* 349 US 294 (1955).
[139] *Brown* v. *Board of Education* 347 US 483 (1954).
[140] See Ronald Dworkin, 'The Model of Rules I', in *Taking Rights Seriously*, 14 (Harvard U. Press, Cambridge, 1978); R. Dworkin, 'A Reply', in *Ronald Dworkin and Contemporary Jurisprudence*, 263–68 (Marshall Cohen., ed., Rowman & Allanheld, Totowa, NJ, 1983).

adjustment would simply not be permitted by an English court. Compliance with an injunction at the earliest practicable date would be required and expected, on pain of the direst penalties by a modern Equity court. Where physical works need to be undertaken, for instance, to deal with a pollution-nuisance, time may be allowed the defendant to have the work done; but that is all that will normally be permitted.[141]

Prospective overruling

We turn now to another factor which accounts for the reluctance of English courts to exercise the sort of powers of changing the law which American courts use. The traditional declaratory theory of law led English common law courts to assume that precedents could only be overruled with full retrospective effect. If courts never 'make' law but only 'declare' it, then it follows that an overruled decision must have been wrong from the beginning, and the new decision must have been 'law' all along, and must therefore be given full retroactive affect. Of course, in practice this is liable to upset reasonable expectations and reliance deriving from the earlier decisions. The solution appears to be to overrule only prospectively.[142] Rather than disappoint reasonable reliance on prior law by applying the new law retroactively, a court could decide to change the law only for future cases, applying the old law to the present controversy, and to all other cases that have arisen but not yet been decided. This would protect reliance on the old law, and yet give future litigants the benefit of the new law. But into this balance must be thrown a third consideration: should the old law, which is now acknowledged to be bad law, be applied to the detriment of the party against whom it works in the instant case? If litigants who persuade a court to overrule a bad precedent are not themselves accorded the benefit of the new law, would they have sufficient incentive to litigate such cases so that bad law is not perpetuated?

Balancing these three considerations, many American courts have adopted a flexible approach.[143] In cases where reliance plays its heaviest role, such as property, contract, or tax cases, courts have tended to give prospective effect to a decision overruling an earlier case.[144] In other

---

[141] See, e.g., *Pride of Derbyshire Angling Assocn. Ltd.* v. *British Celanese Ltd.* [1953] Ch. 149, where the Birmingham Corporation was required to alleviate river pollution by a massive and immediate expenditure on sewage disposal facilities.

[142] See Keeton, *supra*, n. 50.

[143] For some further complications, see Calabresi, *A Common Law for the Age of Statutes*, 280–2 (Harvard U. Press, Cambridge, 1982).

[144] See *Gelpcke* v. *City of Dubuque* 68 US (1 Wall) 175 (1863). See also Munzer, 'Theory of Retroactive Legislation', 61 *Tex. L. Rev.* 425 (1982).

cases, including many tort cases, courts have in recent decades given prospective effect to a decision overruling a prior precedent, except that the particular litigant who has obtained the new ruling is permitted to take the benefit of it.[145] This is a very pragmatic approach which often seems to do substantial justice, but it will be observed how hard it is to see the overall result in terms of formal rule-application. It is difficult to say, as a result of decisions like this, what was 'the law' governing a particular incident. Indeed, what is happening is that the courts are deciding, first to change the law, and second, the 'effective' date of that law. Both such decisions are made by use of substantive reasoning since there are no rules with any real mandatory formality determining when they should be made.

English courts have never asserted the power to overrule prior case-law prospectively, still less the power to do this with an exception for the litigant in the instant case. We think there are two main reasons why this has not been done in England. First, it involves openly acknowledging the law-making function of the judges in a more 'official' way than they have ever been willing to do. Although it must always have been obvious enough to judges that in some sense at least their decisions 'make' law, it has long been the accepted approach to gloss over this fact. Arguments in court almost invariably proceed on the basis that the function of the court is to ascertain what the law 'is', even where it is clear that there is no established law on the point, or even where the court is being invited to overrule a discredited authority. After the decision has been made, an element of realism creeps in, and some lawyers then begin to talk of the case as having decided the law, or even as having changed the law, but at the time the case is being argued this is not the way English lawyers talk.[146]

A second reason why prospective overruling has never been adopted by English courts is, we feel, that English judges, with their greater inclination to formal law application than American judges, would be troubled by using a technique which makes it so hard to state what is 'the law' or 'the rule' which is being applied. When a court is empowered to determine the law and then decide whether that law is to be applied to certain litigants or not, it is much more difficult to think in terms of

---

[145] See, e.g., *Molitor* v. *Kaneland Community Unit. Dist. No. 302* 18 Ill. 2d 11, 163 NE 2d 89 (1959). See also *Great Northern Ry. Co.* v. *Sunburst Oil & Refining Co.*, 91 Mont. 216, 7 P. 2d 927, aff'd., 287 US 358 (1932); *Hare* v. *General Contract Purchasing Corp.*, 220 Ark. 601, 249 SW 2d 973 (1952); Traynor, 'Quo Vadis, Prospective Overruling: A Question of Judicial Responsibility', 28 *Hast. LJ* 533 (1977) (discussion of these and other cases, providing an excellent summary of the law).

[146] Sir Henry Sumner Maine, *Ancient Law*, 31–2 (London, John Murray, 1861, 4th ed., 1891).

concepts like 'the law of the land'; and formalism of 'the law is the law' kind becomes less viable.[147]

Modes of change and legal theory

In chapters 8 and 9 we shall suggest that there is a close relationship between the greater formality of English law and the long positivist tradition in English legal theory; and on the other hand, an equally close relationship between the greater substantive nature of American law and dominant American legal theories, from natural law and rights theories to instrumentalism and realist emphasis on 'policy'. Here we wish to suggest one respect in which the process of changing the law by judicial decision tends to be inconsistent with the positivist approach to law, whereas the process of statutory change, especially as now operated in England, tends on the contrary to be derived from and to reinforce the positivist tradition.[148] Because courts (even some American courts) in general eschew the overtly legislative role and because it is not infrequently hard to distinguish between a truly novel judicial decision and the mere application or extension of an already existing principle or rule of law, it is much more difficult to distinguish the 'is' and the 'ought' in a case-law system, whether it be English or American. Common law judges often find it unnecessary to draw a clear line between what ought to be and what is. On the one hand, change is glossed over, if not obscured altogether, by the judicial tendency (which exists even in America, though to a lesser degree than in England) to claim that a new decision does not really amount to a change at all. On the other hand, the judges may advance reasons of substance for what the law ought to be, and then render a decision stating that the law already *is* what it ought to be. The result is that it is often unclear whether the judges are spelling out the reasons of substance embedded in the formal law involved, or truly changing the law.

Of course this tendency exists in England as well as in America; it was, after all, the practice of the English courts in failing to distinguish the 'is' and the 'ought' which aroused the wrath of Bentham who insisted that this distinction was the beginning of all wisdom for the legal critic or reformer (or 'censor' in Bentham's own language). But today it is the American legal system which relies far more heavily on the courts for legal change. And the result is that there is a powerful tendency in

[147] Lord Simon in *Jones* v. *Sec. of State* [1972] AC 944, 1026; see also Nicol, 'Prospective Overruling: A New Device for English Courts?' 39 *Mod. L. Rev.* 542 (1976).

[148] For the view that the strict system of precedent is difficult to reconcile with Dworkinian anti-positivist theories of law, see Pannick, 'A Note on Dworkin and Precedent', 43 *Mod. L. Rev.* 36 (1980). This Note seems to us to suggest that precedent is based on formal reasoning, while Dworkinian theory relies largely on (substantive) principles.

America for the law, and more especially the common law, to be perceived as a continuous stream, a dynamic force, never at rest, a process in which the 'ought' is constantly becoming the 'is'.

We have pointed out how much legal change in America today comes from the courts, but the courts themselves have to get their ideas from some source. In the absence of the English system of government, law reform agencies, and so forth, many of the ideas which American courts incorporate into the common law are the result of a slow process of distillation. Ideas are put forward and developed, for example by law professors in legal journals, they are discussed at conferences and symposiums and meetings of the American Law Institute; they may be put into legislative bills and, even though most of these will not be passed, issues may be ventilated at legislative committee hearings. These proposals for change have, of course, no authoritativeness behind them, no formal validity; they compete in the market-place of ideas, entirely on the strength of their substantive reasoning. Some of them will be so criticised that they will perish. Others may gather greater support. Eventually some of these ideas may be picked up, in some shape or form, and used by the judges to develop the common law. This slow distillation process again emphasizes substantive reasons, and again blurs the line between the 'is' and the 'ought' in various ways. This may also affect the style of those who produce the ideas on which the courts draw. For example, a law professor writing an article on the common law in an American journal may choose not to emphasize the difference between what he perceives the law *to be*, and what he thinks it *ought to be*. He will often simply suggest ways in which the common law could be improved by following a different line of reasoning, and he does this in the knowledge (and with the hope) that some day some court may actually adopt his 'oughts' as 'the law'.[149]

By contrast, in modern times, the process of law reform, or legal change, in England is typically conceptualized in terms of sharp breaks with the past. It is thus truly Benthamite in its methodology and, therefore, in its theoretical underpinnings. The modern technique for legal change in England is overwhelmingly legislative; furthermore, it is a very widely followed practice today for British governments (or departments of State, or semi-independent agencies like the Law Commissions) to prepare and publish papers setting out their proposals for change before these are introduced into Parliament. These papers will usually (and always in the case of the Law Commissions) set out in

---

[149] As we have seen in chapter 4 (and will illustrate further in chapter 11), because much American legislation takes the form of broad enactments of principle, the filling in of such legislation is also often done in a similar way, that is by courts, themselves frequently drawing ideas from academic writings.

some detail what the law is currently understood to be, what are perceived to be the deficiencies in that law as thus set out, and what changes it is proposed to make to correct those deficiencies. The process of legislative change as thus operated emphasizes the discontinuity in the law, the breaks being made by the legislature with the past, the distinction between the 'is' and the 'ought'. Further, committee reports, especially when they come from major bodies of some importance or standing (such as Royal Commissions), are often—provided they are accepted in principle by the government—treated as themselves providing virtually formal reasons for settling the precise details of any subsequent legislation.

As a matter of plain historical fact, it seems clear that this kind of procedure was one of the products of Bentham's influence in early nineteenth-century England. What perhaps has not been appreciated in the past is that this kind of procedure is based on a theory of the nature of law; and given the source of the procedure, it is hardly surprising that that theory should turn out to be a positivist theory of law. Nor has it perhaps been appreciated that, if a legal system tends to use a methodology which is based on a positivist theory of law, this is likely to reinforce the tendency of those who live and work in that system to adhere to a positivist conception of law. We readily acknowledge that Benthamites (of a kind) are often at work in America too. But they are less dominant there, especially in regard to the common law.

5. PUBLIC LAW LITIGATION

We now turn to another major realm of judicial law making and administration in America, which has no parallel at all in England. The school desegregation cases are but one example of a major new type of litigation in the United States, mainly in the lower federal courts. Other cases of this type concern the administration of hospitals, prisons, and police forces. Professor Chayes has called this major new development 'public law litigation'.[150] Mostly it involves the use of federal district court decrees to implement public programmes of education, health care, police activities, fair employment, environmental regulation, and the like, consistently with constitutional and statutory law. The litigation is frequently initiated by way of a class action on behalf of a large interest group rather than by individual plaintiffs. The defendants may be either agencies of government (local, state, or national) or private parties. The

---

[150] Chayes, 'The Role of the Judge in Public Law Litigation', 89 *Harv. L. Rev.* 1281 (1976); Chayes, 'The Supreme Court 1981 Term Forward: Public Law Litigation and the Burger Court', 96 *Harv. L. Rev.* 4 (1982); Fiss, 'The Supreme Court 1981 Term Forward: The Forms of Justice', 93 *Harv. L. Rev.* 1 (1979).

plaintiffs often seek lengthy and complex injunctive relief ordering the defendants to take affirmative steps to remedy deficiencies in the functioning of a public or private body. The relief sought is usually intended primarily to regulate the future conduct of the defendant, sometimes by way of imposing 'structural reform', rather than to obtain damages as redress for past injuries. The judicial role here goes far beyond traditional equitable jurisdiction.

The administration of these decrees quite naturally calls for substantial ongoing court involvement, because the court is frequently called upon to resolve disputes over whether the defendants are complying with the decree, or over whether the decree should be modified because of unanticipated practical problems, changed circumstances, and so on. Just as the school desegregation cases have consumed, and continue to consume, much federal court time and effort, so too do court decrees directing detailed changes in the management of hospitals, or the running of prisons, or comprehensive decrees regarding the recruitment, training, and supervision of policemen. Decrees of this kind are bound to be complex, encompassing such questions as space availability, staffing, health, recreation, job training, sanitation, nutritional requirements, and so on. This complexity in turn requires flexible remedies so as to enable the defendants themselves to comply, and to enable the courts to review their decisions in the light of their practical effect. In such cases, the courts are seldom able to confine equitable remedial discretion within the framework of the traditional two-party dispute in which the plaintiff seeks a simple remedy to enforce a straightforward right. This kind of judicial rule-making tends, rather, to merge rules and rights, making it impossible in some cases even for the Supreme Court itself to say what is the rule being applied.[151]

The resulting (often elaborate) decree is unquestionably 'law'. And the law-making process involved is both similar to, and different from, the creation of ordinary common law. First, it is similar in that the law is at least nominally judge made, insofar as the actual decrees themselves are concerned. The decrees presuppose, of course, constitutional or statutory duties that the defendants are required to carry out, but these duties are usually very general, a fact that partly explains the need for a more detailed implementing decree. Secondly, the decrees are immediately binding on the parties to the litigation, as with an ordinary common law judgment, and in this respect the decrees may be said to generate formal reasons for defendants to act. But the mandatory formality of such decrees is rather lower than that of ordinary common law rulings,

---

[151] See, e.g., *Rhodes* v. *Chapman*, 452 US 337 (1981) (court unwilling to say that deterioration in prisoner's mental and physical health was 'cruel and unusual punishment'); see also Chayes, *supra*, n. 150, 96 *Harv. L. Rev.* at 45–60.

because these decrees may be modified on a wide range of substantive grounds. Third, there is a basic similarity between the ingredients that inform the law-making process in a common law case of first impression, and those involved here. Both are highly substantive in the sense that the judges entertain substantive reasoning from both sides in deciding what decree to enter, or to approve, if (as often happens) the parties agree to a resolution of their controversy and then embody it in a decree.[152]

Of course public law litigation cannot be fully conducted by resort to formal reasoning. The very nature of this kind of litigation is highly substantive and instrumental. Judges are being asked how best to ensure that very general constitutional and statutory goals are achieved. In devising ways and means judges are driven to consider reasons of substance at every stage of the proceedings. What reasons support holding that the constitutional or statutory right is X rather than Y in the first place? What measures will best protect this right? What further measures will best ensure that violations of the decree can be properly sanctioned? And so on. There is almost no question here of identifying a specific rule and treating it as a formal reason for action, irrespective of underlying or countervailing reasons of substance. Nearly the whole case will be about reasons of substance. As one commentator has noted, the American legal system is here 'an unusually fluid and indeterminate system of procedural forms and legal rules, hospitable to accommodating an array of purposes'.[153]

One major respect in which this kind of litigation differs from that of the ordinary common law is that the principle of *stare decisis* has little application to these decrees. Past decrees rarely generate formal reasons for judges to act on when they are asked to formulate decrees in future cases, a fact that is not difficult to explain. Public programmes vary from locale to locale. Resources vary greatly. Personnel vary greatly. Defendants vary greatly. Variations of this sort preclude the use of such decrees as binding precedents.

American public law litigation over the design and content of these implementive decrees is thus highly substantive. It has no real counterpart in England. Indeed, an English judge would recoil from the managerial powers assumed by American judges over schools, prisons,

---

[152] See 89 *Harv. L. Rev.* 1281, 1309 (1976) (*supra*, n. 150). But Fiss thinks that Chayes exaggerates the negotiated element in the process: 93 *Harv. L. Rev.* 1, 54 (*supra*, n. 150).

[153] Horowitz, 'Decreeing Organizational Change: Judicial Supervision of Public Institutions', *Duke LJ* 1265, 1269 (1983). Horowitz notes that in 'a more hidebound, formalistic system' (and a footnote suggests he is thinking of England) 'it is quite possible that the requisite changes would not have taken place'. *Ibid.* But the thrust of our argument is that they would not have taken place because they would not have been necessary, and that is what justifies the use of a more 'hidebound formal' system (though not a formalistic one: see *supra*, p. 28 for the distinction we draw between formal and formalistic reasoning).

and mental hospitals. The nearest parallel, perhaps, to these American procedures would be a nuisance injunction whose requirements might be spelled out in some detail. For instance, in one recent case of nuisance by noise caused by a club running water speedway events, the court specified in its decree the number of permissible events per annum, and the times when practice and other events could be conducted.[154] But one only has to look at this case (which is itself almost unprecedented in England) to see that the American cases involve a degree of managerial detail in their decrees totally different in character from anything in the English case.

Why does there seem to be a need for this type of litigation in the United States but not in England? Obviously we cannot fully answer this question here, but we will offer a few suggestions. One explanation goes deep and implicates the central thesis of this book. The special need in America for these particularized judicial decrees stems partly from the low mandatory formality of many constitutional and statutory rules. Given such open-ended law, *some* official institution must be responsible for considering the detailed practical issues which arise when these laws come to be implemented, and must thus reconcile the conflicting substantive reasons which arise at that point, and embody the result in concretely meaningful decrees. Another explanation of the need for public law litigation may be that traditional legal remedies are too often unavailing to ensure an adequate level of rule-observance. Certainly America has large (public and private) bureaucracies at all levels in which the norms of due observance of law are simply not well established. Consequently, a traditional remedy, say a tort action against a deviant police officer, to take an example suggested by Professor Fiss,[155] may have little impact on the behaviour of other members of that police force.[156]

Without, we hope, bestowing undue praise on the political–legal system in England, it seems to us manifest that the demand for this sort of public law litigation has not arisen there because adequate (and perhaps better) alternative procedures exist to deal with the problems —which in any event are much less acute. Consider again Professor Fiss's example of the tort action against the policeman and its relative ineffectiveness in preventing further police misbehaviour, as compared with structural reform of the recruitment, training, and supervision of policemen, pursuant to an elaborate court decree. This argument assumes that there is such a widespread violation of established norms

[154] See, e.g., *Kennaway* v. *Thompson* [1981] QB 88.

[155] 93 *Harv. L. Rev.* at 21–2.

[156] See A. E. Bent, R. A. Rossum, *Police, Criminal Justice and the Community*, 69 (Harper & Row, NY, 1976).

that the ordinary tort action will have little significant impact. This assumption may be valid in America in some fields. In the case of the police, the jury system sometimes operates to shelter the police from many consequences of illegality, and is a further factor creating the conditions in which public law litigation and structural reform may be needed.[157]

We doubt if the assumption of widespread failures of norm observance in particular areas is true of many English institutions or bureaucracies, though some people think it is true of the police. But even if the assumption is valid for some particular institutions, a well-publicized tort action would almost certainly lead to demands for inquiry and action. In 1982 an action for assault and wrongful imprisonment by a husband and wife against some police officers led to an award of £20,000 exemplary damages to each,[158] something which is almost unprecedented in modern times. The judge's decision was widely reported in the press, and questions were asked in Parliament on the same day. It is certain that some official investigation would have been immediately instigated into the incident. Had the inquiry revealed a *pattern* of systematic and repeated behaviour of a similar character, it is almost certain that there would have been debates in Parliament and further demands for a more wide-ranging public inquiry. Such an inquiry might well have been followed by further civil or criminal proceedings of a conventional character. In the end, if structural reform were needed, it would have been introduced through legislation. Indeed, there has for many years been constant parliamentary interest in the procedures for enabling the public to make complaints against the police, and the methods by which these complaints are inquired into; and although no wholly satisfactory solution to this problem may yet have been arrived at, the issue is plainly upon the parliamentary agenda, and will remain there so long as there is public dissatisfaction with the present position.[159]

All this is not to say that systematic and serious illegalities never occur in English bureaucracies, nor to contend that such illegalities can invariably be flushed out and dealt with promptly by ordinary legal

[157] See Newman, 'Suing the Lawbreakers', 87 *Yale LJ* 447 (1978) (arguing that ethnic minority plaintiffs do not easily secure verdicts against police); Project, 'Suing the Police in Federal Court', 88 *Yale LJ* 781 (1979) (review of empirical study showing defendants successful in 20 out of 28 such cases, with plaintiffs obtaining low damages in other cases).

[158] See *White* v. *Metropolitan Police C'ssr.*, The Times, 24 Apr. 1982, pp. 1, 6; and for another similar case, see *Connor* v. *Chief Constable of Cambridgeshire*, The Times, 10 Apr. 1984, p. 3. By English standards these damage awards are very high for non-physical injuries.

[159] The latest legislative experiment in this field is Part IX of the Police and Criminal Evidence Act 1984 which establishes an independent Police Complaints Authority to investigate public complaints against the police.

actions, publicity, and parliamentary reaction.[160] But it does suggest to us that the need for these new procedures in America arises from factors not always to be found in countries such as England, including patterns of officially accepted non-compliance with established law in particular areas, and an unwillingnes on the part of legislative bodies to devote energy to the problems, or to vote the funds necessary for reform.

The traditional role of courts as law-enforcers depends on the assumption that most people will observe most of the law most of the time, without threats of compulsion or sanctions. That assumption seems far more true of England than of the United States. It will also be seen how closely this fits in with our suggestion in chapter 1 that formal reasoning in the law is based partly on the assumption that other parts of the legal and political system are working well and performing their proper functions in the proper manner. Where this is manifestly not the case, more drastic measures are needed, and these may involve the rejection of formal reasoning, and direct resort to reasons of substance. In the area of police malpractice, for example, a widespread pattern of officially accepted non-compliance with the law may be a sign that the system is not functioning properly elsewhere, so that the courts cannot rest content with formal reasons for decisions. But, as also suggested in chapter 1, the lack of trust which courts feel for administrators guilty of widespread violation of constitutional or statutory norms leads the courts to impose formal rules on those very same administrators, while *themselves* using the broadest of substantive reasoning.

Similarly, a failure by juries to protect citizens against serious police malpractices (when such failure occurs) may reflect the malfunctioning of another part of the system. Even if we accept that, in the American legal system, juries may properly invoke broad and equitable standards of justice, rather than strict and technical formal rules, juries sometimes decide on the basis of bias and prejudice. Furthermore, if it appears that such malpractices cannot be or will not be addressed by legislatures, the pressures on the courts to respond may prove irresistible. As has been noted by Professor Horowitz, 'The civil rights filibuster was a parent of the desegregation cases.'[161] These failures of other parts of the system to work properly, then, also help to explain why courts depart from formal reasoning in public law litigation. In England, despite signs of unease and anxiety, there is still a fundamental faith that other parts of the political system work properly, and that the courts can therefore largely confine themselves to formal application of legal rules.

Still another factor may help explain the need for public law litigation

[160] One institutional reason why this may be more difficult in England than in America stems from the much greater stringency of English defamation laws.
[161] Horowitz, *supra*, n. 153, at 1282.

in America. Although the disregard of legal norms may well have been the origin of much public law litigation, once this kind of legal remedy has become an established mechanism, there seems to be a temptation for other institutions—state executive and legislative bodies in particular—to shirk their responsibilities in the knowledge that the courts will not shirk theirs. The odium of voting taxes for unpopular purposes (to reform jails or mental hospitals, for instance) is thus apparently avoided by bodies responsive to electoral pressures, and becomes instead, at least indirectly, a matter for the courts. This is another facet of a problem referred to in chapter 1, that, under the division of power in the American system of government, executive and legislative officials do not feel the same sense of responsibility for dealing with social problems as corresponding bodies do in England. Not surprisingly, therefore, the American courts feel it incumbent on them to act in ways in which English courts do not.

6

The Trial Process

1. INTRODUCTION

In chapters 4 and 5 we concentrated on the relative formality of statutory and common law reasoning in England and the United States. Now, the formal legal reasoning arising under statutes and common law, in the name of which rights are conferred, duties imposed, and sanctions and remedies authorized, comes into play only in relation to particular states of facts in the real world. To put this perhaps more simply, every form of law, and the formal reasoning arising under it, contemplates a state of fact and is applicable only when the facts so contemplated are present.

The applicability of a statute or precedent may then be disputed on the ground that the facts to which the law properly applies do not exist, and such disputes are, we think, more common than disputes over the meaning of law in the face of agreement on facts. This is not difficult to explain. Even when all plausible grounds of dispute over the meaning of a statute or precedent are judicially or otherwise laid to rest (and the possible number of these under an ordinary legal rule will certainly be relatively discrete), there will still remain scope—continuous scope through time—for disputes over the facts in almost any episode that takes place to which the legal rule might be applicable. The sources of such disputes are legion. The parties may differ in their recollection of relevant events, or over the credibility of a key witness, or over the qualifications of an expert witness, or over the inferences which may reasonably be drawn as to events which were not directly perceived by any witness, or over many other similar matters. Moreover, where parties differ in recollection, the differences may arise because they perceived the relevant events differently in the first place, or because they have drawn different inferences from the raw events, or because of their own subsequent emotional involvement which may colour their recollections and interpretations of what happened.[1]

Mechanisms for the effective ascertainment of the truth are plainly important for all legal systems, whether they are more formal or more substantive. If courts do not seek the truth, they can not consistently implement rules of law embodying substantive social policies of any

---

[1] See generally Summers, 'Law, Adjudicative Processes, and Civil Justice', in *Law, Reason and Justice*, 172–3 (G. Hughes, ed., New York U. Press, NY, 1969).

kind.[2] Many rules of law are means to external ends of social policy, and simply cannot be effective if the true facts are not discovered.

Truth is important for another basic reason. When a rule is authoritatively applied to an authoritatively determined state of facts (relevant under the law), general propositions of law come into contact with concrete reality. If that reality is true reality, the judge can test the soundness of the general proposition against the concrete facts, and, if the generality is found wanting, the judge may, at least in common law fields, have power to abandon the generality or to modify it in some way, not only in the case at hand, but also for the future. Judges are not mere rule appliers, even in England. They may to some extent renovate the law, but if they are to discharge this task properly, they must renovate in light of the true facts. If they proceed upon the basis of a reality which is untrue, then their formulations will not be soundly based.[3]

Now, it is only if a factual dispute is resolved in accord with the true facts that it is possible to assert that a statute or precedent and the formal reasoning it generates really apply to support a given legal conclusion. The authoritative resolution of a dispute over facts is one thing, the resolution of such a dispute in a fashion that coincides with the true facts is another thing. If the true facts are found, and if the law and the formal reasoning it generates are then applicable and are so applied, we have a state of affairs in which the 'law in books' may be said to translate into the 'law in action'. In this chapter we call such a state of affairs 'formal'. We distinguish this kind of formality from the four key types of formality discussed at length in chapter 1, by calling it legally relevant 'truth formality', but there is plainly a relationship between this kind of 'formality' and the others. It is clear that formal reasoning would be quite subverted if applied to 'untrue' facts—whether this is attributable to mistaken fact finding, or fictitious suppositions about the facts, or the like.[4] Moreover, where formal reasoning is subverted in this way, the result will usually be traceable to external influences of a substantive kind. For example, a jury may be moved by their view of the substantive merits of a case to find 'facts' that are not really facts in order to acquit the accused, or in order to award damages to a plaintiff.

[2] Summers, Comment, 'On the Adversary System and Justice', in *Philosophical Law*, 122–3 (R. Bronaugh ed., Greenwood Press, Westport, Conn., 1978).

[3] Lawyers who remain preoccupied with 'law in books' when it really does not represent 'law in action' may also be accused of taking an excessively 'formal' view, in a rather different sense. Of course, a divergence between the law in books and the law in action does not necesssarily signify that the law in action in that instance should be taken to be the valid law. The question is more complicated, and is discussed in R. Summers, *Instrumentalism and American Legal Theory*, 112–15 (Cornell U. Press, Ithaca, NY, 1982).

[4] See Hart, 'Comment', in *Government under Law*, 139 (A. Sutherland, ed., Harvard U. Press, Cambridge, 1956).

A more formal legal system must therefore need better mechanisms for ascertaining the truth than a more substantive system. In addition, we think a more formal system is likely to be more effective in inducing voluntary out-of-court settlements of disputes. All legal systems, whether more or less formal, must rely heavily on encouraging such settlements because their court systems will otherwise be in danger of being overwhelmed with trial work.[5] But such settlements are less likely to be made where the alternative of authoritative coercive resolution in court is not itself highly truth-oriented. Certainly, parties who have little or no confidence in the truth-finding capacity of the courts could not so easily be persuaded to settle their claims (or defences) on the basis of the facts as they actually are. Some settlements would doubtless still be made, but they would tend to reflect bargaining power to a much greater degree, and the actual rules of law to a much lesser degree, than where the parties do have confidence that courts are likely to find the facts correctly.

It is therefore apparent that the role of fact finding in the resolution of disputes is not as simple a matter as it may seem. Indeed, we suggest that the traditional view of fact finding is in reality linked to more formal theories of law. There are, in principle, two ways of resolving a dispute in a legal system by a trial process. The first, which is the more formal, is for some tribunal such as a judge or an arbitrator to (1) find the facts, (2) ascertain the relevant law, and (3) apply that law to the facts. This is such a standard way of stating the function of a court in modern times that it is perhaps difficult to accept that it is by no means the only way in which a court can function. It is perfectly possible for courts or tribunals to operate in a second manner which is a great deal less formal than the first. This is for the tribunal to attempt to resolve a dispute by doing justice or equity in a broad way without necessarily finding all the relevant facts, ascertaining the law, or applying the law to the facts. The standard formal way of resolving disputes by finding facts and applying the law to those facts tends to resolve a dispute by first polarizing the position of the parties. But in other ages and other traditions, different methods may be more highly regarded whereby (for example) mediation or the like is treated as the main aim of dispute-solving. Where that is the case, a tribunal may prefer to try to resolve a dispute without so much stress on finding the facts and the law. In practice, these two methods tend to shade into each other for a number of reasons.

First, the very process of finding facts is itself not entirely separable from rules of law, and hence from the influence of values and policies embodied in those rules. Fact finding has to be done at a particular time

---

[5] See generally Mnookin and Kornhauser, 'Bargaining in the Shadow of the Law: The Case of Divorce', 88 *Yale LJ* 950 (1979).

and place, and in accord with rules of procedure and of evidence that are not wholly truth oriented.[6] These needs may prevent the true facts from being ascertained, and the decision will then have to proceed on a false version of the facts, or on assumed facts. The result may be justice of a kind, but it is not justice achieved by a formal application of the law to the real facts contemplated by that law.

Secondly, a less truth-oriented approach has sometimes been bolstered in modern times by sociological or philosophical theories which may deny that there are real, objective 'facts' waiting to be discovered by a tribunal. Facts, it may be suggested, vary according to the eye of the beholder, especially when these same facts concern issues such as states of mind or complex social facts whose mere statement requires a rich classificatory and linguistic apparatus. For example, statements that a person had a fraudulent state of mind, or that a policeman had reasonable cause to believe that another had committed an offence, or even that a man and woman are married, or that a company owns a piece of property are all statements of fact in a sense, and all would probably be treated by most legal systems as statements of fact in appropriate contexts. Yet none of these facts are raw or brute facts in the sense that they are immediately accessible to the senses.[7]

We do not propose to discuss these philosophical questions. It is enough for us to note that the legal system does often deal in raw or brute facts as well as more complex facts. Many criminal cases turn upon such simple questions as whether the accused actually and physically struck a victim, or whether he actually and physically took certain property from a victim; many civil cases turn upon similar issues arising out of the causation of physical injuries by one person to another. Moreover, even with more complex issues, it is possible for the legal system to treat these as closely as it can to raw or brute facts. Of course, it is easy enough to see that a less formal approach to fact finding may be appealing with respect to issues of this character. No doubt, less precise and broader feelings of justice or equity underlie many decisions in which complex social facts have to be found.

The judicial fact-finding process can, therefore, never be solely truth-oriented, nor can it be said that the finding of facts is a straight-forward value-free exercise. It naturally follows that less formal rule-application is required when such cases have to be decided.

---

[6] Other values (such as efficiency) may have to be served besides truth, and these may sometimes conflict. See generally Hart and McNaughton, 'Some Aspects of Evidence and Inference', in *Evidence and Inference in Law* (D. Lerner, ed., The Free Press of Glencoe, Chicago, 1958). On the conflict between truth and finality, see p. 168.

[7] See generally Mandelbaum, 'Societal Facts', *Br. J. of Sociology* (1955) reprinted in *Theories of History*, 476 (P. Gardiner, ed., 1959); see also Anscombe, 'On Brute Facts', 18 *Analysis*, No. 3, (1958).

Nevertheless, it does need to be insisted that this is not always the case, and that there are many legal disputes in which facts can be found straightforwardly. A legal system which encourages the broad or less formal way of deciding issues of fact when they are complex and highly disputed may find that its tribunals carry over this methodology into simpler cases where it may seem less justifiable. But whether it is less justifiable or not must depend, in the ultimate analysis, at least partly on the vision or theory of law to which the legal system adheres. A legal system which *claims* to believe in the rule of law, and in the objective ascertainment of facts and the application of the law to those facts, in as neutral a way as possible, is being false to its own theory if it actually tends to decide factual disputes in a broader and perhaps more equitable way. Perhaps this is also the case where a legal system relies on substantive reasoning (for instance the desire to protect the litigant's rights) to prevent the full facts being laid before the tribunal responsible for the decision.

A third factor is that the ascertainment of the law and the application of the law to the facts is a much more complex process than it may seem. Even the distinction between 'law' and 'fact' is often very complex.[8] If the law to be applied consists of or includes standards, principles, and discretions, then certainly the application of the law to the facts will require an exercise of judgment; and of course, this leaves out of account the difficulties in ascertaining what the law actually is in any particular case.

As we have indicated, both the English and the American legal systems are *relatively* formal in their approach to fact finding, but as between the two, we believe that fact-finding processes in civil and criminal cases in England tend to be much more truth-oriented than in the United States. As a result there is less divergence between the 'law in books' and the 'law in action' in England than in the United States. In England, the formal reasoning derived from statutes and precedents—the 'law in books'—is more often translated into the law in action when the factual premises of that reasoning are disputed. This is therefore another major respect in which the English system is more formal then the American: it has greater 'truth formality'.

2. THE TRIAL AS A FORMAL FACT-FINDING PROCESS

We cannot prove that the English trial actually leads to more accurate

---

[8] For an exceptionally penetrating discussion, see L. Jaffe, *Judicial Control of Administrative Action*, 546–9, 550–5 (Little Brown, Boston, 1965). On the essentially constitutive nature of fact finding, see Kelsen, 'Sovereign Equality of States,' 53 *Yale LJ* 207, 218 (1944).

fact finding than the American trial, but we can identify a number of features of the English legal system which suggest that it is more truth-oriented than the American, and which, taken together, make it probable that the English system resolves disputed factual issues in accord with the truth more often than the American.

Both systems of fact finding are adversarial ones in which the lawyers are the prime movers, and the theory is that, from the clash between them, the 'truth will out'.[9] A number of characteristics of English trial lawyers, their role, their professional ethical code, and their general manner of functioning, appear to play a part in making English trials more seriously concerned with ascertaining the truth, as compared with American trials. The fact that, in England, High Court (and most other important) litigation is all conducted by barristers, and that barristers have a special professional status, is commented on in more detail in chapters 12 and 13. Here we only draw attention to the implications for the fact-finding process of having a small body of trial lawyers who are (in effect) certified as having the necessary qualifications to conduct trials.

It is exceptionally difficult to generalize about such matters as professional standards of competence and skill, and impossible to offer any evidence of comparative skills and competence, other than general impressions. Nevertheless, we will assert that there are differences in professional standards in the two countries. Most members of the English bar are of high ability, and most have to acquire extensive courtroom experience, if they are to remain in the profession at all.[10] Although today some would say that there is a greater number of less competent barristers in England than there has ever been before, few of these less competent barristers would ever be entrusted with important litigation.

In the United States, the position is rather different. While there are many first-class trial lawyers, there are many others with lesser qualifications and skill. And even non-trial lawyers do occasionally conduct quite important cases in America, sometimes before the highest courts, although manifestly unfitted to do so. Yet the trial lawyer's arts are professional arts, and there is therefore great scope for different levels of ability. These variations are often to be seen in the American courtroom, and have been the object of a good deal of criticism in recent

---

[9] See Fuller, 'The Adversary System', in *Talks on American Law* 34 (2nd edn., H. J. Berman, ed., Vintage Books, NY, 1971); see also, 'Professional Responsibility: Report of the Joint Conference', 44 *ABAJ* 1159 (1958).

[10] See generally R. E. Megarry, *Lawyer and Litigant in England* (Stevens, London, 1962); *The Bar on Trial* (R. Hazell, ed., Quartet Books, London, 1978).

years.[11] When a civil case is being tried in which an inadequately trained or insufficiently experienced lawyer appears on each side, there cannot be the same confidence that the true facts will be found as in an English case conducted by almost any experienced barristers. There are also cases in the American courts in which the opposing lawyers are strikingly mismatched, with similar probable results so far as accurate fact finding is concerned. Such gross mismatches rarely occur in England.

There is also a number of specific rules and practices in England which we think are more likely to lead English courts to a true finding of the facts. For example, there are rules of practice and professional ethics which regulate the contacts which lawyers may have with witnesses prior to trial, and which in our view make it more likely that the truth will be found in an English court. In both countries, of course, lawyers have some professional responsibility for not actually telling witnesses what they should say to a court; but the rules are very different in the two countries, and we suspect that the American rules, lax as they are by comparison with the English rules, are also less stringently enforced. American lawyers are generally free to 'prepare' and 'coach' witnesses in advance of trial[12] in ways and to an extent which would be regarded as a breach of professional ethics in England. Indeed, an English barrister does not normally talk to the witnesses at all prior to the trial, except for his own client and any expert witnesses. A distinguished English barrister once explained to an American lawyer friend that witnesses were interviewed only by solicitors in English trial practice, and that the barrister was not allowed to see them.

This mystified my correspondent even more [wrote the barrister]. He had never heard of such an idea. Whose fault was it, he asked, if a witness 'fell down on the stand' (which, being translated, means: collapsed in cross-examination)? I replied that it was nobody's fault. It happened as often as not that the oral evidence of a witness fell far short of the statements appearing in the proof which had been taken from him by the solicitor, and indeed it was this sort of incident which so often provided the judge with the clue that he needed to ascertain the truth. Mystification was now total. My friend replied: 'But don't you fellows try to *win* your cases?'[13]

---

[11] See, e.g., Burger, 'Conference on Supreme Court Advocacy: Opening Remarks', 33 *Cath. U. L. Rev.* 525 (1984); Burger, 'Some Further Reflections on the Problem of Adequacy of Trial Counsel', 49 *Fordham L. Rev.* 1 (1980); Burger, 'The Special Skills of Advocacy', 3 *J. of Contemp. L.* 163 (1977); Clark, 'The Continuing Challenge of Advocacy', 16 *Washburn L.J* 243 (1977); Clark, 'Incompetency and the Responsibility of Courts and Law Schools', 50 *St. John's L. Rev.* 463 (1976); H. Packer and T. Ehrlich, *New Directions in Legal Education* (McGraw Hill, NY, 1973).

[12] See, e.g., Jerome Frank, *Courts on Trial*, 86 (Princeton U. Press, Princeton, 1949) and see also, Freedman, 'Professional Responsibility of the Civil Practitioner: Teaching Legal Ethics in the Contracts Course', 21 *J. Leg. Ed.* 569, 574 (1969).

[13] C. P. Harvey, *The Advocate's Devil*, 63–6, (Stevens, London, 1958).

The English barrister would probably have been shocked to see a film made by the American Trial Lawyers' Association in co-operation with the University of Michigan Law School which depicts the events in a road traffic case from the time of the accident through the entire trial. When the plaintiff first visits her lawyer in this film, she explains that she does not remember the distances or the speed of various vehicles involved in the accident. Her lawyer then tells her that she will *have* to remember if she wishes to recover any damages. He explains to her the basic elements of the law of negligence, and makes it clear that, if she is to win a verdict, she will have to establish negligence on the part of the other driver. He is shown saying to the client, 'You are going to have to try to remember. Whether you like it or not, you are going to have to recall distances and speed.'[14]

Comment seems almost superfluous. An English lawyer would probably think that the American lawyer is inviting his client to invent a recollection which she has already told him she does not have. The American lawyer would deny this implication, and might suggest that it is important that witnesses should be aware of the probable consequences of inability to remember details. American lawyers might concede that their system involves greater risk that 'coached' testimony will affect outcomes, yet argue that overall they are permitted to become much better prepared on the facts than English barristers, with the result that American trials more nearly approximate the truth, all things considered. We consider this point below. Here we go on to suggest that there are other structural differences between the two legal systems which seem to us to offset any advantages the American system may have in this respect. We proceed to mention a few of the most obvious.

We find it hard to believe that the fact-finding processes of a civil trial are not influenced by the competence and trial experience of the judge. Here again there are major differences between the two countries. It cannot be doubted that in England the judge brings on average a higher level of competence to the entire trial process.[15] The judge is invariably a former barrister of many years' experience and high standing at the bar, and thus brings all of his training and experience to the fact finding process. In America, again, the situation is much more variable. A good many judges were formerly first-class trial lawyers, but many American judges have had little or no trial experience, and although many of these turn out to be good trial judges nonetheless,[16] some unfortunately do not.

Of course in America judges do not generally act as fact finders

---

[14] See J. O'Connell, *The Injury Industry and the Remedy of No-Fault Insurance*, 11 (Commerce Clearing House, NY, 1971).

[15] On the judges, see chapter 12.

[16] *Ibid.*

anyhow, but in England they do. The civil jury is all but dead in England today.[17] Civil cases are tried by judges who not only find the facts but also assess damages. In America, in personal injury and in other important classes of litigation, the facts are found by lay juries functioning under the supervision of trial judges.[18] There is a vast literature on how good juries are at finding facts and otherwise discharging their responsibilities, and we return to this literature in section 3 of this chapter. Here we want to stress a number of features of English and American practice which we think demonstrate the greater truth-orientation of the English legal system. Perhaps the most obvious point is that, even in simple seeming cases, fact finding is a complex matter, and the professional fact finder—the experienced barrister turned judge—is simply better qualified to analyse, sift, and evaluate evidence than a group of lay jurors.

Second, the English judge in ordinary civil trials is today free of most of the restrictions on evidence contained in the hearsay rule,[19] which operates to exclude much relevant evidence in the American jury trial. This rule existed at common law, of course, for the very reason that it was assumed that lay fact finders would be unable to evaluate such evidence. Similarly, there are many more examples of 'privilege' in modern American law than in English law, and these also exclude much relevant evidence from the jury.[20]

Third, an English judge typically takes careful longhand notes of the testimony (something jurors generally cannot do), stops the witnesses from time to time to have the testimony repeated (again something jurors can rarely do), asks questions different from or in addition to those put by the barristers, to clear up doubts or ambiguities in the witness's evidence (again something which jurors cannot do), and so on.[21] Fourthly, an English judge is expected to give reasons for his findings of fact where the facts have been seriously controverted, and this itself is a salutary discipline which restrains any tendency to sloppy fact finding, or any temptation to do substantive justice or equity between the parties by fudging the fact-finding process.

[17] See Kaplan and Clermont, 'England and the United States', in XVI *International Encyclopaedia of Comparative Law*, ch. 6, 6-45 (1982).

[18] *Ibid.*, at 6-54; and see *post*, 169.

[19] See the Civil Evidence Act 1968 which substantially modifies the hearsay rule in civil cases.

[20] For American law, see generally *McCormick on Evidence*, title 5 (E. Cleary, ed., 3rd edn., 1984) (Privilege: Common Law and Statutory); *ibid.*, title 6 (Privilege: Constitutional). For English law, see Sir Rupert Cross and C. Tapper, *Cross on Evidence*, ch. XII (6th edn., C. Tapper, ed., Butterworths, London, 1985).

[21] Kaplan and Clermont, *supra*, n. 17, 6-48 to 6-49 and 6-58. See also Kaplan, 'An American Lawyer in the Queen's Courts: Impressions of English Civil Procedure', 69 *Mich. L. Rev.* 821, 830–5 (1971).

We suspect that some American lawyers, especially perhaps trial lawyers, would dispute the suggestion that judges are necessarily better triers of fact than jurors, and in the American context—where judges are not necessarily experienced trial lawyers—this may well be true. But it is very hard to believe that an able and experienced trial judge is not in general likely to be more efficient and accurate at fact finding than a lay jury, and in England the gradual decline in use of the civil jury over the last 50 years is itself partly due to the fact that barristers actually prefer trial by judges to trial by jurors in civil cases. And this in turn is due to the fact that barristers prefer more rational, and less emotional, fact-finding procedures, and have greater confidence in the fact-finding ability of judges. This difference in the preference of trial lawyers in the two countries may also suggest that English barristers subscribe to a more formal vision of law than American trial lawyers.

The English system of appellate review is, we think, also more truth-oriented, at least when taken together with the central features of the English civil trial. For one thing, the English appellate court is reviewing a trial judge's findings of fact and conclusions of law, and the reasons for the judge's findings are all laid out in the transcript which will be before the appeal court. That court will know just what the trial judge has found as facts and why, and will generally be able to evaluate those findings in the light of the evidence, and either affirm or reverse his findings accordingly. Although findings of primary fact, especially where these turn to some degree on the credibility of the witnesses, are not easily upset on appeal in modern English practice, other findings of fact which depend on inference or the evaluation of evidence—such as findings of negligence—can be fully reviewed by an appellate court[22] in a way not normally possible in jury trials where a general verdict has been rendered.

In America, appellate review of jury fact finding is severely restricted, wherever the trial judge enters judgment on a 'general verdict', as commonly happens. Here the jury has a dual role, that of finding the facts and of applying the law to the facts, and the resulting verdict may simply be, in effect, a finding that the plaintiff loses, or the plaintiff is awarded the sum of $— in damages. Such an outcome can be reviewed for some errors in fact finding, but the appellate court is hampered by its lack of information as to why the jury reached its verdict. Some errors may be evident by comparing evidence in the record with the general verdict to see if there is sufficient support for the verdict in the record, but other errors will not be evident. For example, even so egregious an error as finding the plaintiff guilty of contributory negligence, but then going on to compromise by giving the plaintiff some damages

---

[22] See *Benmax* v. *Austin Motor Co.* [1955] AC 370, 373.

because of the defendant's negligence (contrary to the common law rule of contributory negligence, which is still operative in some states) is an error that will not necessarily appear from the record or the general verdict. Such an error is not therefore open to correction on appeal.

We pause here to consider two counter-arguments which may suggest that, at least in some respects, the English legal system is less truth oriented than the American. First, English law does not provide for as much pre-trial investigation of the facts as does the law in the United States; one example of this is that pre-trial discovery in England is far more restricted than in America, and another example is that (as we have noted) English barristers do not interview most witnesses before trial. It may be suggested that even English barristers cannot respond adequately to unexpected testimony,[23] and, given also that English judges are unlikely to adjourn a trial just because the witnesses say unexpected things, this may make it more difficult to ascertain the whole truth. In America, pre-trial discovery makes this sort of thing less common.[24] We doubt that this argument is as strong as it may seem. Surprise and untruth are not the same thing. Coaching of witnesses and pre-trial discovery may eliminate the element of unexpected testimony, but in the process may also help to eliminate the very factors which assist the trier of fact to ascertain the truth. And extremely thorough (if often last-minute) preparation for a trial is an essential professional responsibility of the English barrister who knows that once the trial starts, adjournments will rarely be granted merely because of unexpected testimony. It may be that American trial lawyers come to court better prepared than English barristers as a result of their pre-trial contact with witnesses. But what they are—perhaps—better prepared to do is to present a case, not necessarily to assist the court in a search for the truth. As indicated in the quotation above, the lack of coaching of witnesses is often the very thing which helps an English judge to find the truth.

A second possible counter-argument to our thesis derives from the fact that many American rules of court are more generous in allowing concluded cases to be reopened so that further evidence can be taken,[25]

---

[23] See Kaplan, *supra*, n. 21, at 830–3.

[24] On the extensiveness of pre-trial discovery in America as compared to England, see generally, J. B. Levine, *Discovery: A Comparison between English and American Civil Discovery Law with Reform Proposals* (Oxford U. Press, Oxford, 1982); but for the view that some of these differences are explicable by the absence of jury trial in England, see Zuckerman, 'Can an Enlarged Law of Discovery Make Civil Trials Redundant?' 4 *Ox. J. Leg. St.* 250 (1984).

[25] See, e.g., Fed. R. Civ. P. 59, 'New Trials: Amendments of Judgments'. Under this Rule, it is the duty of a federal trial judge to order a new trial 'if he deems it in the interests of justice to do so'. C. A. Wright and A. R. Miller, *Federal Practice and Procedure*, § 2803

and this does in fact occur from time to time,[26] certainly more often than in England, where the rules governing the reopening of cases for admission of new evidence are very stringent.[27] Moreover, American rules of procedure are generally applied more laxly than in England, precisely because (it seems) rigid adherence to rules may sometimes prevent one of the parties from adducing relevant evidence, or making a relevant argument.

These factors might seem to be contrary to our thesis. Because the finding of facts must itself be done in accordance with rules of procedure and evidence, a strict and formal adherence to those rules may sometimes lead to false facts being found or assumed. By contrast, a legal system which is less formal in its adherence to rules might actually find the facts more accurately, and if this is regarded as necessary to do substantive justice between the parties, the less formal system may incline to do just this. We refer in chapter 7 to the *Ampthill Peerage* case[28] in which one of England's most perceptive judges commented that the conclusiveness of a final judgment might be said to mean that the courts preferred justice to truth. Thus formal adherence to legal rules such as the rules relating to *res judicata* may prevent the courts giving effect to the real facts; and the same is of course true of rules of evidence, rules of pleading, and other rules of procedure. In these respects, then, it may seem, at any rate at first sight, that the English legal system, for all its greater adherence to formal rule application, is actually less devoted to the search after truth than the American legal system, which is much less formal in its rule application. We think this conclusion would be mistaken.

When a court refuses to reopen a final judgment to allow new facts to be proved, it does so in the belief that, *in the long run*, courts are more

---

(West, St. Paul, 1973). Under Fed. R. Civ. P. 60(*b*), a court may reopen a judgment because of newly discovered evidence at any time up to a year after judgment was entered. See generally Wright and Miller, *ibid.*, § 2859. But Wright says that '[T]he courts have exercised their discretion under the rule with a scrupulous regard for the aims of finality.' C. A. Wright, *Law of Federal Courts*, 662 (4th edn., West, St. Paul, 1983).

[26] But not very frequently in practice, see generally Wright, *ibid.*, at 662; M. D. Green, *Basic Civil Procedure*, 216–17 (Foundation Press, Mineola, NY, 1979).

[27] English trial courts have no general authority to reopen judgments on the ground of new evidence, but such evidence may be a ground for appeal, see *de Lasala* v. *de Lasala* [1980] AC 546. But new evidence will only be admissible on appeal if (1) it could not have been discovered with reasonable diligence before the trial and (2) it is of sufficient cogency to have an important influence on the result: *Ladd* v. *Marshall* [1954] 1 WLR 1489; *Skone* v. *Skone* [1971] 1 WLR 812.

[28] [1977] AC 547, see *post*, 211–12.

likely to arrive at the correct solution if this is not done. Perhaps, on this occasion, the facts were found incorrectly the first time; but English judges would contend that this is more, and not less, likely to happen in future if litigants, lawyers, and judges know that trials are not final, and that judgments can readily be reopened whenever new evidence is discovered. If lawyers and litigants think that they can, at a later date, easily introduce newly discovered evidence, it is plausible to suppose that they will devote less effort in the first place to a comprehensive search for all the relevant evidence. Similarly, with most other rules of procedure and evidence, although in some cases the exclusion of evidence may shut out knowledge of the real facts, English lawyers would justify adherence to most of these formal rules by arguing that, on the whole, and in the long run, following formal rules of procedure and evidence is more likely to lead to the discovery of the real facts. Of course, we cannot say whether these empirical assumptions are well founded. If they are incorrect, then the more formal approach is open to the objection that it seems, at any rate in these respects, to be less concerned with truth than the more substantive approach to legal rules. But these empirical assumptions are somewhat akin to the belief that fewer people will miss trains if they leave punctually than if the train-driver occasionally delays to allow late comers to clamber on board. While the truth of such assumptions may be difficult to prove, we find them intuitively plausible.

We conclude this section by suggesting that there may well be many other factors—some of which particularly affect the criminal process (for example, plea bargaining)—which also tend to make the American trial less truth-oriented than the English. But many of these raise highly controversial issues, and involve factors which are difficult to evaluate, so it would require very extensive research to substantiate our thesis in relation to these other factors. We therefore leave them aside.[29]

3. THE JURY

We return to the problem of the jury. In both countries the jury is still used for serious criminal trials; in the United States, indeed, there is a constitutional right to jury trial in all criminal cases and many civil cases,[30] though the right may be waived.[31] The major difference between the two countries concerns civil trials which in America are still held

---

[29] See generally Hughes, 'English Criminal Justice: Is it Better than Ours?' 26 *Ariz. L. Rev.* 507 (1984).

[30] US Constitution, Sixth and Seventh Amendments; C. A. Wright, *supra*, n. 25, at 605 ff.

[31] P. DiPerna, *Juries on Trial*, 67–9 (Dembner Books, W. W. Norton Co., NY, 1984).

before juries in much ordinary common law litigation, though not in equitable suits, nor in certain cases dealt with by federal courts, such as suits against the federal government. In England, trial by jury has almost disappeared from civil litigation except where a person's reputation is at stake (for example, where he sues for libel, or where he is accused of fraud) in which case there is a normal right to ask for a jury,[32] which, however, is often not exercised even in these cases.

The use of juries in trials raises two questions relevant to the present work. The first assumes that jurors try honestly and conscientiously to fulfil the role which formal law assumes they will perform, that is, find the facts and apply to them the law given to them by the judge. The question then is: how reliable are jurors in this role? The second question arises because it is widely believed that in certain classes of cases the jurors do not try to find the facts and apply the law to them as directed by the court, but attempt some broad equitable decision according to the merits as they see them in some overall sense.

Plainly, truth formality declines insofar as juries resort to their subjective views of the substantive merits, or are otherwise relatively unreliable fact finders. At the same time we must note the paradox that deference to the jury's decisions (precluding examination of the substantive grounds of their decision) is itself an example of source-based reasoning. The jury's verdict is (largely) treated as conclusive because it has authoritative formality. But in this particular instance, the relatively high mandatory formality attaching to a jury verdict (which can only be set aside on relatively narrow grounds) actually enhances the overall substantive element injected into the legal process by juries.

The first question, then, concerns the reliability or accuracy of jurors as fact finders. This question raises all sorts of difficulties since we can rarely know whether the jurors have found the facts correctly. Research in both countries (in England, largely confined to criminal cases) has tended to take the form of trying to discover to what extent other participants in the trial (and particularly the judge) actually agreed with the jury's verdict.[33] This method fails to separate out those cases in

[32] Supreme Court Act 1981, s. 69.

[33] For America, see H. Kalven Jr. and H. Zeisel, *The American Jury* (U. of Chi. Press, Chicago, 1971); R. J. Simon, ed., *The Jury: Its Role in American Society* (Lexington Books, Lexington, Mass., 1980); Green, 'Juries and Justice: The Jury's Role in Personal Injury Cases', *U. Ill. L. F.* 152 (1962); *Selected Readings: The Jury* (G. R. Winters, ed., American Judicature Society, 1971); Erlanger, 'Jury Research in America', 4 *Law and Soc. Rev.* 345 (1970); Kalven, 'The Dignity of the Civil Jury', 50 *Va. L. Rev.* 1055 (1964); Levene, 'The Legislative Role of Juries', *ABFRJ* 605 (1984). For England, see J. Baldwin and M. McConville, *Jury Trials* (Oxford U. Press, Oxford, 1979); *The British Jury System* (N. Walker, ed., U. of Cambridge, Institute of Criminology, Cambridge, 1975).

which jurors have actually tried to do what the judge has directed them to do, but done it badly (or at least, in the judge's opinion, done it badly); and cases in which the jurors have made no real effort to do this at all, but have rendered a verdict in accordance with their sense of the equities. This means that there are great difficulties in trying to assess jury accuracy as fact finders by this particular method.

These difficulties are reflected in the literature.[34] Jury trial gives rise to vehement controversy in both England and in America, but it may well be that the controversies stem more from the ideological stance of the participants than from anything else. Even in England, the controversies are closely related to the very politically charged 'law and order' question. In part they stem from the allegations of the former Commissioner of the London Metropolitan Police, which received widespread publicity some years ago, that juries acquitted far too many guilty persons.[35] The ideological divide about juries is probably different in America. Those who dislike jury trial in America are often technocrats, including many lawyers (other than trial lawyers) who find juries unreliable and slow. The more conservative Americans who, like their English counterparts, are concerned about the 'law and order' question, are not necessarily so averse to jury trial, because many of them have the traditional confidence in the American jury as a quasi-democratic institution.[36]

There are some who regard jurors as utterly unreliable as fact finders as compared with judges, largely on a priori grounds.[37] It is widely assumed by these writers that judges are less likely to be swayed by emotion or prejudice, and that they have more experience in sifting and weighing evidence. Even Jerome Frank, whose attacks on the unreliability and unpredictability of fact-finding decisions[38] have been regarded by

---

[34] See the excellent bibliography in Baldwin and McConville, *supra*, n. 33, at 135–43.

[35] Sir Robert Mark, 'Minority Verdict', BBC Dimbleby Lecture for 1973; Zander, 'Are Too Many Professional Criminals Avoiding Conviction?' 37 *Mod. L. Rev.* 28 (1974); Baldwin and McConville, 'The Acquittal Rate of Professional Criminals: A Critical Note', *ibid.*, 439; Zander, *ibid.*, 'The Acquittal Rate of Professional Criminals: A Reply', 444; Mack, 'Full Time Major Criminals and the Courts', 39 *Mod. L. Rev.* 241 (1976); A. Sanders, 'Does Professional Crime Pay? A Critical Comment on Mack', 40 *Mod. L. Rev.* 553 (1977).

[36] A Gallup survey conducted in America in 1982 revealed that senior executives and businessmen were significantly more hostile than the general public to the power of jurors to determine the amount of damages in civil litigation. See *Attitudes Towards the Liability and Litigation System: A Survey of the General Public and Business Executives*, conducted for the Insurance Information Institute by the Gallup Organization (Gallup Organization, Princeton, NJ, 1982).

[37] See, e.g., Glanville Williams, *The Proof of Guilt*, ch. 10 (3rd edn., Stevens, London, 1963).

[38] See in particular his *Law and the Modern Mind* (Brentano's, NY, 1930) and *Courts on Trial* (Princeton U. Press, Princeton, 1949).

many commentators as grossly exaggerated,[39] thought that judges were better fact finders than juries.[40] We note also that manuals for American practitioners on how to select a jury often give advice on the 'excessively' rational type of juror who is to be avoided if the lawyer's client seeks to rely on emotional appeal.[41] These manuals also contain much advice on how to make such emotional appeals.[42]

There is also a certain amount of information about the ability of jurors to understand what they are told by judges about the law, and more generally, their ability to understand the evidence in complex cases of fraud, antitrust, and the like.[43] It has been suggested that psychological evidence presents a picture of litigation as 'influenced and often controlled by factors that are irrelevant to a rational, fair trial outcome'.[44]

On the other hand, the massive study of the civil jury by Kalven and Zeisel[45] found that judges and juries agreed in about 80% of the cases, and that the remaining 20% divided roughly evenly between cases in

[39] For example, Wyzanski says that jury verdicts are indeed only too predictable: 'A Trial Judge's Freedom and Responsibility', 65 *Harv. L. Rev.* 1281, 1286–7 (1952).

[40] See *Courts on Trial, supra,* n. 12, at 145.

[41] For instance Fahringer, 'In the Teeth of the Blind: A Primer on Jury Selection in a Criminal Case', 43 *Law and Contemp. Prob.* 116, 133 (1980), cites a manual stating: 'Engineers, scientists, accountants and bookkeepers are, for the most part unemotional. They are trained to be objective and reach conclusions based on facts. They would be unsuitable in a case where the defence rests upon a heavy emotional appeal.' See also E. H. Sutherland and D. R. Cressey, *Principles of Criminology,* 442 (7th edn., Lippincott, Philadelphia, 1966), citing Darrow as having once said, 'I don't want a Scandinavian for he has too strong a respect for law as law.'

[42] See generally J. Frank, *Law and the Modern Mind, supra,* n. 12. American legal literature contains much practical advice to trial lawyers about how to appeal to a jury's emotions, see, e.g., Cone, 'Techniques for Developing Jury Empathy', 19 *Trial* 54 (July 1983); Bieder, 'How to Grab the Jury's Attention in a Medical Malpractice Case', 1982 *Personal Injury Deskbook* 296 (1982); Reaves, 'Feelings: Communicating with a Jury', 70 *ABAJ* 37 (Feb. 1984).

[43] For example, Rosenberg points to the fact that in the 1930s to 1950s lawyers often used special verdicts and served interrogatories on jurors asking them how they had arrived at their verdicts. The result was that the 'jury's odd responses stood starkly revealed as inconsistent or absurd or both. Often their answers to specific interrogatories were at odds with their general verdicts. Often their special verdicts were inconsistent with one another, or incomplete or impossible.' See 'Contemporary Litigation in the United States', in *Legal Institutions Today: English and American Approaches Compared,* 179–80 (H. W. Jones, ed., American Bar Association, 1977). For psychological evidence about jury understanding of judicial instructions, etc., see Charrow and Charrow, 'Making Legal Language Understandable: A Psycholinguistic Study of Jury Instructions', 79 *Col. L. Rev.* 1306 (1979); *The Psychology of the Courtroom* (N. L. Kerr and R. M. Bray, edd., Academic Press, NY, 1982). See also Bane, 'Uses of English Legal History in America', 2 *Ox. J. Leg. St.* 297 (1982) noting response of a jury foreman to a complex antitrust case.

[44] O'Connell and Carpenter, 'Psychology and Trials: Some Disturbing Insights', 48 *Mo. L. Rev.* 299, 310–11 (1983) a review of *The Psychology of the Courtroom, supra,* n. 43. See also O'Connell's more general attack on jury trial in personal injury cases in his *The Lawsuit Lottery,* 89–94 (Free Press, NY, 1975).

[45] *Supra,* n. 33.

which the jury found for the plaintiff while the judge would have found for the defendant, and cases where the jury found for the defendant and the judge would have found for the plaintiff. These findings were claimed to constitute a stunning refutation of the idea that juries fail to understand the issues, or to decide rationally; the extent of the disagreements between judges and juries showed no systematic pro-plaintiff bias (as some have suspected) and were said to constitute a reasonable level of disagreement in close cases. These findings, however, have not stilled the controversies; Kalven and Zeisel's methodology has been severely criticised,[46] and the arguments continue to rage.

There is also much controversy over the extent of the jury's power to render a broadly equitable verdict in disregard of the law,[47] or, putting the matter less tendentiously, whether the jury has the right to decide what the law ought to require on the facts of the case. Everyone agrees that the jury does have the *power* to do this, because there is no way of overturning a verdict within the range of reasonableness that the courts allow juries, and, in criminal cases, a verdict of acquittal cannot usually be impeached at all, either in England or in America. But there has been a good deal of controversy over whether juries should be told that they have this power, and whether the power includes a right. During much of the colonial period, and well into the nineteenth century, American juries were thought to have this right,[48] though it was ultimately denied by the United States Supreme Court in 1895,[49] and by most state supreme courts since then.[50] But whether or not juries are told of their powers by the judge, there is little doubt that many jurors do know of their power and do exercise it to a considerable degree in criminal cases, and perhaps to a lesser degree (though no one really knows) in civil cases. Reference has already been made, for instance, to the widely held view that in those American jurisdictions in which the contributory negli-

---

[46] See, e.g., Walsh, 'The American Jury: A Reassessment', 79 *Yale LJ* 142 (1969); Bottoms and Walker, 'The American Jury: A Critique', 67 *J. of Amer. Stat. Assocn.* 773 (1972).

[47] See Scheflin and Van Dyke, 'Jury Nullification: The Contours of a Controversy', 43 *Law and Contemp. Prob.* 51 (1980). The question whether the jury has a right as opposed to a power to disregard the law has received little attention in England since the eighteenth-century controversies surrounding the *Dean of St. Asaph's case* (1784) 9 Doug. 73, 99 ER 774, though it is discussed in Lord Devlin, *The Judge*, ch. 5 (Clarendon Press, Oxford, 1979). Since the eighteenth century, juries have been so much more strictly controlled by judges that it is hard to imagine a modern English court acknowledging the jury's right to render a verdict contrary to the judge's rulings on the law.

[48] See Howe, 'Juries as Judges of Criminal Law', 52 *Harv. L. Rev.* 582 (1939).

[49] *Sparf and Hanson* v. *United States* 156 US 51 (1895).

[50] See cases cited by Scheflin and Van Dyke, *supra*, n. 47. The great majority of the modern cases seem to be against any direction to the jury to remind them of their power to return a verdict against the judge's directions.

gence rules hold, or held, sway, juries often compromise (or used to compromise) over their verdicts so that they do, in effect, use a comparative negligence standard, whatever the theory of the law may be. Similarly, a study of Chicago personal injury verdicts has suggested that 'jurors tend to ignore relevant legal rules, and rely more heavily on their perceptions of the plaintiff's family situation'.[51]

The above is the barest sketch of a substantial and controversial literature. It is impossible to try to resolve the issues raised by this literature here, and anyhow it is unnecessary. We are not primarily concerned with the question whether the jury is a competent decision-making body, or whether it uses broad community standards of equity and mercy to temper the law in a satisfactory or an unsatisfactory way. We are concerned with a narrower question, namely to what extent the use of the jury affects the truth formality of the system. The answer to this question is, surely, scarcely amenable to doubt.

Whether the jury is a 'better' instrument of the trial process than a judge must depend upon what a trial is for. In the classical and more formal version of the function of the trial, it is (as we have already seen) the accepted view that the object is to ascertain the facts in dispute, if any, and then to find and apply the law to those facts. If this really is the sole function of the trial process, it is hard to believe that there could be any serious argument that in general terms a professional judge would do a better job than a jury. Where facts are complex and in dispute, nobody outside a courtroom (or, we should add, the political process[52]) would think of consulting a random selection of laymen for the answer. If we want to know what caused an explosion, or an accident, or a plane crash, or the malfunctioning of a piece of electronic apparatus—outside the courtroom—we consult experts; we give them the necessary facilities for their investigation, and we let *them* ask the questions. Similarly, if the sole object of a trial is to apply and enforce rules of law laid down by authorities whose agents the courts are, then the jury would in most cases be an aberration. If, however, law is conceived in a less clear-cut way, not as something laid down by authority, imposed from on high on the people down below, as it were, but as comprising norms and standards of

---

[51] Broeder, 'Plaintiff's Family Status as Affecting Jury Behavior: Some Tentative Insights', 14 *J. Pub. Law* 131 (1965). See also Hammitt, Carroll, and Relles, 'Tort Standards and Jury Decisions', XIV *J. Leg. St.* 751 (1985) (finding that jurors systematically take account of factors in the assessment of damages which are legally irrelevant).

[52] Control of juries was much diminished in America during the nineteenth-century movements to a more democratic society, by withholding the power to comment on the evidence and, in some cases, requiring the judge to give his charge before counsels' final addresses: James, 'Sufficiency of the Evidence and Jury-Control Devices Available before Verdict', 47 *Va. L. Rev.* 218 (1961).

behaviour arising in specific contexts, and emanating from the people —with all their prejudices, ideals, and limitations—then jury trial becomes more intelligible.

This is surely borne out by the fact that one of the most widely used justifications of the jury system is that the jury can inject into the legal process an element of non-rule justice, itself almost necessarily substantive rather than formal.[53] This does not mean that, even in America, the average trial is a complete sham, that facts are constantly found in defiance of the evidence and of all reason, that the enforcement of the laws is rendered completely nugatory by the jury. As we have repeatedly stressed, the comparisons we are drawing concern matters of degree. Many American trials will be conducted by judges and juries performing, no doubt in different fashions, the same basic functions as are performed in an English civil trial by a judge alone, or, in a criminal trial, by an English judge and jury. In a large proportion of the cases the results would probably be the same. But still—and we choose our words carefully—in a significant proportion of cases the results are likely to be very different.

We can illustrate this by looking at one very important area of the law in which the differences are indeed striking, that is, in the law relating to personal injuries, and the assessment of damages for personal injuries. Legal doctrine in England and America does not differ greatly in most such cases. There are more rules of strict liability in America than in England, but in practice these do not seem to make a great deal of difference to results. Far more significant than differences in legal rules are differences in the mode of trial. Because these cases are tried by a judge alone in England, and damages are assessed by judges, with full and detailed reasons given, the calculation of damages has become much more regularized.[54] Discount rates for future earnings, pre-judgment interest rates, and even the fixing of damages for non-pecuniary loss ('pain and suffering') are much more systematic and uniform in England than in America. Nobody can pretend, of course, that damages for pain and suffering can be objectively quantified according to any utilitarian scale, but the English system does at least permit a high degree of consistency within the system. If plaintiff A receives £20,000 for (the non-pecuniary consequences of) loss of a leg, it is certain that plaintiff B, other things being equal, will receive more for loss of two legs, and that

---

[53] See, e.g., Zeisel, 'The American Jury', in Final Report of the Annual Chief Justice Earl Warren Conference on Advocacy in the United States, *The American Jury System*, 65, 69–70 (Roscoe-Pound-American Trial Lawyers' Foundation, 1977).

[54] See P. S. Atiyah, *Accidents, Compensation and the Law*, ch. 7 for details of the assessment of damages in personal injury cases in England (4th edn. by P. Cane, Weidenfeld & Nicolson, London, 1987).

plaintiff C, with the same qualification, will receive substantially less for loss of a foot.

In America such results would not be certain at all. The range of awards for pain and suffering in similar cases is very much larger in the American system of trial, almost entirely as a result of the use of juries, and as a result of variation in local sentiment on such questions. One consequence of this seems to be that the levels of English awards are more predictable and this may be one explanation of why a much higher proportion of English claims are settled without trial. The ability of the parties to settle a personal injury suit depends largely on their ability to predict whether liability is likely to be found by a court, and if so, what the probable range of damages will be. English figures suggest that the settlement rate for personal injury claims is about 99%;[55] but the massive DOT study in 1970 of 220,000 suits arising out of road accidents in 1968 found the American settlement rate to be as low as 93%.[56] If this figure is accurate, the proportion of cases which remain unsettled, and therefore go to judgment, is seven times higher in America than it is in England. It may well be that the system of jury trial in America is one factor which causes more of these cases to go to trial, and that this is one of the major causes of congested courts. Although this is speculative, it is surely very plausible. The findings and awards of American juries are much less predictable than those of English judges, and unpredictability leads to uncertainty which naturally encourages more litigation and more appeals.[57]

Once again we do not suggest that one procedure is *overall* superior to another. America is a much bigger country than England, and contains many distinct regions and distinct communities within those regions. It is perhaps, also, a less egalitarian-minded country than England. There is no a priori reason why it should be thought necessarily better that damage levels in all these places should be on the same scale, though some will certainly think the American system neglects values such as equal treatment of like cases, uniformity, and fairness. At the same time, it will be seen how the difference reflects a different vision of what law is. In England, the procedure reflects a vision of law as a set of rules laid

[55] See Report of Pearson Royal Commission on Civil Liability and Compensation for Personal Injury, vol. 2, Table 11 (showing 215,000 tort payments made p.a.) and vol. 2, Table 122 (showing 2,203 cases tried in 1974, assumed to be typical year) (Cmnd. 7504, HMSO, London, 1978).

[56] DOT Study, *Automobile Accident Litigation*, 8 (1970). D. Trubek *et al.*, The Civil Litigation Research Project, *Final Report* (1983) found that as many as 9% of road accident claims went to judgment.

[57] See, e.g., R. A. Posner, *The Federal Courts: Crisis and Reform*, 77–92 (Harvard U. Press, Cambridge, 1985), where a careful statistical analysis supports the conclusion that the dramatic increase in federal appeal cases since 1960 is due to increased uncertainty of the law.

down by courts and Parliament, which it is the duty of the judges and the legal profession to observe and implement. In America, the result reflects a vision of law as an instrument of local justice, assessed and enforced by a section of the local community.

As always, we wish to guard against overstatement of our thesis. Some recent decisions of the United States Supreme Court concerning the exclusion from juries in capital cases of anyone holding conscientious objections to the death penalty may be thought to show that here at least the American courts have come down on the formal side.[58] At issue in these cases has been the right of the accused to a jury representing a true cross section of the community, on the one hand, and the unacceptability of jurors who are unable conscientiously to try the case according to law, on the other hand. In one recent case[59] the majority of the Supreme Court held that a juror could properly be excluded where his views would substantially impair the performance of his duties in accordance with his oath. This decision thus does show the Supreme Court adhering to a moderately formal position on the role of the jury in criminal trials.[60] It is, however, noteworthy that in the opinion of Brennan J., dissenting, there remains considerable stress on the right of the accused to a representative jury, almost as a quasi-democratic body, rather than as a pure fact-finding or rule-applying body, and to that extent there is still a minority view which approves a less formal approach to the function of the jury. The majority opinion confirms that at the time of writing (1986) the balance in the United States Supreme Court has, on this issue, swung back towards a slightly more formal vision of law than had previously prevailed.

We have focused here on substantive reasons directly affecting the outcome of a trial which may (in a more substantive legal system) be thought to justify the use of juries. But there are also a number of other substantive considerations of a broader kind which are sometimes invoked to justify the system. For example, there is the 'democracy' argument, that jury trial is valuable because it enables ordinary people to rule directly on issues which might otherwise be reserved to non-accountable professionals. And there is also the related argument that jury-service provides a valuable educational experience in civic responsibility. Both these arguments are, of course, highly substantive in their orientation and quite independent of truth formality.

---

[58] *Witherspoon* v. *Illinois* 391 US 510 (1968); *Adams* v. *Texas* 448 US 38 (1980); *Wainwright* v. *Witt* 105 S. Ct. 844 (1985).

[59] *Wainwright* v. *Witt, supra*, n. 58.

[60] Note the very formal way of putting the role of the jury in the remarks of Rehnquist J., for the majority: '[T]he quest is for jurors who will conscientiously apply the law and find the facts.' *Wainwright* v. *Witt, supra*, n. 58, at 852.

4. SUBSTANTIVE NULLIFICATION OF FORMAL LAW

It has often been observed that the most fundamental characteristics of a legal system are usually revealed in distinctive fashion in the workings of that system's criminal process. We believe that the more substantive vision of law in America is distinctively revealed in the American criminal process, especially in the lower degree of mandatory formality of duty-imposing rules which allow substantive considerations arising out of the context to be taken into account more readily than in England.

In some cases, this result hinges upon the power of a criminal jury to disregard the facts or the law as laid down by the judge, and to return a verdict of acquittal from which no appeal lies.[61] When this happens, the jury is in effect taking the law into its own hands, and it almost certainly does this on *substantive* grounds not recognized by the law itself. The result is that criminal liability is, for that case, nullified. It follows that the mandatory formality of the criminal prohibition is nullified as well. This can occur in England as well as in America, but we believe that it happens less often in England, partly because English juries are probably more deferential to judges, and partly because English judges keep a much tighter control over the whole trial process, commenting on the evidence and forbidding counsel from raising issues with the jury which he has ruled out as unsupported by any evidence fit for the jury's consideration.[62] Although there have been some celebrated cases of an English jury defying the judge,[63] we can only record our belief (which is also consistent with many newspaper reports of criminal cases in the two countries) that these are relatively rare events in England as compared with America.

In other cases, of course, the prima-facie mandatory formality of criminal prohibitions is cut down by substantive considerations arising at the point of application which are themselves embodied in the law,

[61] For 'jury nullification' in America, see 2 LaFave and Israel, *Criminal Procedure*, § 21. 1 (*g*) (West, St. Paul, 1984); Levene, *loc. cit.*, *supra*, n. 33. For English practice, see Lord Devlin, *supra*, n. 47, ch. 5, and Glanville Williams, *The Proof of Guilt* (3rd edn., Stevens, London, 1963).

[62] See Kaplan, *supra*, n. 23, at 835, pointing out that the English judge, unlike the American, 'can steer the jury away from the shoals of sentimental foolishness... by "commenting" on the evidence' and thereby influencing the jury's verdict. And for further comparison of the degree to which English and American judges retain control over a criminal trial, see Smith, 'The Personnel of the Criminal Law in England and the United States', *Camb. L. J.* 80 (1955).

[63] The best recent example is the acquittal of Mr Clive Ponting in February 1985 for alleged violations of the Official Secrets Act (which consisted in his sending to a Member of Parliament some documents which were said to show that a government minister had misled the House of Commons). But this prosecution was a particularly egregious piece of folly, and the result highly predictable. Such cases are rare in England. For the Ponting case, see McCormick, 'The Interest of the State and the Rule of Law', in *Essays in Memory of F. H. Lawson*, P. Wallington and R. Merkin edd. (Butterworths, London, 1986).

and are available as ordinary defences in a criminal case. Examples are lack of criminal intent, incapacity, insanity, and the like, but these defences go directly to issues of guilt. In still other cases in America, the prima-facie mandatory formality of criminal prohibitions is drastically cut down by substantive considerations of policy arising at the point of application which do not qualify as traditional defences, and have little or nothing to do with issues of guilt. These are sometimes called defences and some of them (like necessity) arise by way of excuse. But others (such as the effect of the exclusionary rule, or discriminatory prosecutions) do not even reach the level of an excuse, and yet they may operate to nullify the mandatory formality of even the most serious kinds of crime. In this way the American legal system gives effect to substantive reasoning—independent social policies—and thereby reduces the formality of the criminal law. We will now illustrate this with examples from several areas of the law.

In America, it is for the moment a settled part of constitutional doctrine that a person cannot generally be lawfully convicted of a crime on evidence obtained in violation of the accused's constitutional rights. Thus, for example, under the 'exclusionary rule' of *Mapp* v. *Ohio*,[64] any evidence obtained in violation of the Fourth Amendment which prohibits 'unreasonable searches and seizures' is constitutionally impermissible, and any conviction obtained with the aid of such evidence may be set aside by the courts.[65]

The effect of this constitutional doctrine is that a person cannot be convicted of violating a criminal prohibition even though it is possible to prove, and even though it has been proved, by evidence in an ordinary criminal trial, that he did in fact violate that prohibition. English law rejects this doctrine,[66] subject to one long standing and traditional exception concerning confessions or admissions of guilt.[67] Such confessions must be proved to have been made 'voluntarily', and there is much case-law as to what justifies the exclusion of a confession on this ground.[68]

It is not our purpose here to discuss the policy issues lying behind these divergent legal approaches, but rather to draw attention to the way

[64] 367 US 643 (1961).

[65] In fact the exclusionary rule has been cut down by recent cases holding that a full and fair hearing of the constitutional issue in the state courts precludes collateral attack unless the defendant has been substantially denied a fair trial: see, for example, *Stone* v. *Powell* 428 US 465 (1976) but cf. *Jackson* v. *Virginia* 443 US 307 (1979) and *Rose* v. *Mitchell* 443 US 545 (1979).

[66] See Sir Rupert Cross and C. Tapper, *supra*, n. 20, at 427; Glanville Williams, 'Evidence Obtained by Illegal Means', [1955] *Cr. L. Rev.* 339.

[67] See for instance *Commissioners of Customs and Excise* v. *Harz* [1967] 1 AC 760.

[68] The law on confessions has now been slightly amended and restated by s. 76 of the Police and Criminal Evidence Act 1984.

in which they illustrate some of the themes of this book. In the first place, it will be seen that the English doctrine approaches the requirements of a fair trial more formally than the American doctrine. English judges look *at the trial itself* to see if the accused has had a fair trial. It is, of course, the overriding duty of an English judge (as no doubt it is of an American judge) to see that the accused has a fair trial; but English judges do not generally look *behind* the trial to see what went on before the case was presented to the court. If the evidence is presented, and if it shows that the accused did violate the criminal law, that is sufficient to constitute a trial with due process of law, according to the English doctrine. By contrast, the American doctrine insists on looking behind the trial to see what happened before the case was presented to the court. Thus, just as with the approach to sources of law, like legislation, and precedents, the American approach to the problem requires judges to look behind some formal process to underlying facts and rationales.[69]

It will also be seen how, once again, the more formal English approach requires that the trial process should be conducted on the assumption that other actors in the legal and political machine are doing their job properly. If the police are in fact guilty of regular violations of the law relating to proper police interrogation methods, then, according to the English view, there are other ways of dealing with these violations.[70]

The more substantively open character of the American criminal process as a result of which prima-facie criminal liability can be nullified in particular cases is also revealed in other important ways. For example, the doctrine of 'entrapment' can be seen as another instance of 'rule nullification' in American law. Roughly put, a person who actually committed a criminal act, violated a criminal prohibition, is, in American law, entitled to be acquitted if it is shown that he would not have committed the criminal act had he not been persuaded, against his will, to do so by law enforcement officers.[71] The doctrine is justified in a number of different ways by American lawyers, but the justifications are all of a substantive character.[72]

English law, however, rejects the defence, though once again there are qualifications which need to be made to this statement.[73] Entrapment is

---

[69] The contrast can be most tellingly seen by comparing the language used in *Mapp* v. *Ohio* 367 US 643 (1961) with that of *R.* v. *Sang* [1980] AC 402, 432.

[70] *R.* v. *Sang* [1980] AC 402, 433 (Lord Diplock), 451 (Lord Scarman); *Fox* v. *Chief Constable of Gwent* [1985] 3 All ER 392, 397. Many English lawyers would be dissatisfied with these answers; but that is irrelevant to our theme.

[71] *Sorrells* v. *US* 287 US 435 (1932); Barlow, 'Entrapment in the Common Law', 41 *Mod. L. Rev.* 266 (1978).

[72] See, e.g., Rehnquist J. in *US* v. *Russell* 411 US 423 (1973) (doctrine rests on implied statutory intent). Compare the minority view in *Sorrells* v. *US*, *supra*, and *Sherman* v. *US* 356 US 369 (1958) (doctrine based on inherent requirements of fair procedure).

[73] *R.* v. *Sang* [1980] AC 402.

not a defence in English law, but it is a mitigating factor to be taken account of in sentencing; and it may also be a disciplinary offence for the law enforcement officers guilty of it, to which the judge may draw attention at the trial.

Another instance of what might be seen by some as contrasting attitudes to the possibility of 'rule nullification' arises out of the defence of necessity in the criminal law. On substantive reasoning, it would today be widely agreed that a person who commits what would otherwise be a crime under some overwhelming necessity ought to be treated as less culpable or even excused altogether. Two famous cases illustrate the possible application of a defence of necessity in extreme circumstances, even to a charge of murder. In *US* v. *Holmes*[74] (where some passengers were thrown out of an overloaded lifeboat at sea) an American court seems to have been prepared to uphold the defence of necessity on straightforward utilitarian grounds, namely, that it was better that some should be killed and others saved than that all should perish.

On the other hand, a different view was taken in the famous English case of *R.* v. *Dudley and Stephens*[75] sometimes known as the case of the *Mignonette*, after the name of the ill-fated vessel in that case. The accused in this case were shipwrecked sailors who, in their dire distress, had actually killed and eaten the flesh of one of their number. The background to this case has now been fully explored by Professor Simpson in his fascinating book, *Cannibalism and the Common Law*,[76] from which it is apparent that, right from the start, the authorities formed 'a determination to secure a conviction for murder, combined with a humane and slightly inconsistent desire to see that Dudley and Stephens did not suffer unduly in consequence'.[77] The outcome was what the authorities wanted. The accused were convicted of murder, and the message went forth from the judges that sailors had no licence to kill even in the direst extremity; but mercy was also served out to the accused whose sentence was commuted to six months' imprisonment.

The result of the *Mignonette* case seems so typical of the English approach to such problem cases that it is worth a moment's reflection to ask why it should seem appropriate to the authorities to seek a conviction for murder in circumstances in which no one would expect or want the punishment for murder to be carried out. It seems clear to us that the answer lies partly in the more formal approach the English

---

[74] 1 Wallace Jur. 1, 26 Fed. Cas. 360 (1842).

[75] (1884) 14 QBD 273. Much interesting material on differing attitudes to such issues is to be found in Fuller, 'The Case of the Speluncean Explorers', 62 *Harv. L. Rev.* 616 (1949).

[76] U. Chicago Press, Chicago and London, 1984.

[77] At 79. See also Gardner, 'Instrumentalism and Necessity', 6 *Ox. J. Leg. St.* 431 (arguing that the case hinged upon the distinction between excuse and justification).

judges take to law. They believe in law having a high degree of mandatory formality, and are especially unwilling to carve out substantively grounded exceptions to general liability in what appear to be marginal cases. We also point to the elitism[78] implicit in this case, which we have previously suggested to be a characteristic of the English legal system,[79] and which often leads to or reinforces the sort of formal approach to law which we are contrasting with the American tradition.

Elitist judges are worried about the effect which famous cases may have on the general public; they believe, rightly or wrongly, that people will misinterpret the results of such cases if they show a wavering from the strict application of formal law.[80] If the *Mignonette* case had been decided otherwise, the judges (and the Home Secretary) seem to have thought that common sailors would see the verdict as a licence to kill and commit cannibalism in extreme distress, while the commutation of the sentence as an act of mercy would not be so seen.

One other example of 'rule nullification' in American law has no counterpart in English law. There is a considerable body of authority which holds discriminatory prosecutions to be constitutionally impermissible.[81] Thus, an accused, though unquestionably guilty of a straightforward violation of the simplest of statutory prohibitions (such as failing to register as required by draft legislation), may escape conviction if he can show that he has been singled out by the prosecution authorities on constitutionally impermissible grounds. A prosecution in these circumstances violates the constitutional guarantee of equal protection of the laws. Of course, prosecutors still have some discretion in deciding whether to bring a prosecution, and may prosecute some of those believed to have been guilty of a criminal act while not prosecuting others involved in the same act. But prosecutors may not select sacrificial victims on constitutionally impermissible grounds. For instance, if the selection was based on racial grounds, this would clearly

---

[78] J. Auerbach, *Unequal Justice*, esp. at 83–6 (Oxford U. Press, NY, 1976) suggests that elitism in the law may lead to a *less* formal approach to rules; and he believes that the elitism of leading American law schools is one of the causes of the modern trend away from the formal use of rules in the law. This may be correct, but there is clearly a difference betwen the elite talking among themselves or instructing the potential elite (which is what Auerbach sees in American law schools), and the elite instructing the non-elite (which is how we have suggested English judges view their role.)

[79] See chapter 1, at p. 38. And see now *R. v. Howe*, [1987] 1 All ER 771.

[80] That this tradition persists in England may be seen from a recent prosecution (and conviction) of a social worker who helped a blind and helpless woman of 84 to commit suicide. The judge, in passing a sentence of nine months' imprisonment, said, 'What you did, you did with the highest morals . . . I have no desire to punish you, but I must consider public policy and deter others, less altruistic than yourself, who might be tempted to accelerate death under different circumstances.' See *The Times*, 15 Dec. 1984, p. 3.

[81] See, e.g., *Bodenkircher* v. *Hayes* 434 US 357, 364 (1978); *United States* v. *Batchelder* 442 US 114, 125 (1979).

violate the constitutional requirement of equal protection. But the doctrine of discriminatory prosecution does not stop there. It extends into more controversial areas, as for example, when it prohibits the selection of one out of a large number of persons (such as draft resisters) on the ground that this person was a ringleader or more vocal in urging others to join in the commission of the offence. In this much more difficult area, the Constitution may protect the defendant if he can show that his prosecution has a discriminatory effect and was motivated by a discriminatory purpose. In *Wayte* v. *United States*[82] the Supreme Court held that it was not unconstitutional to select for prosecution for failure to register for the draft only those who had vocally and actively failed to register; in these circumstances selective prosecution was justified because there was no intent to discriminate. But the decision casts no doubt on the general unconstitutionality of discriminatory prosecutions.

There is nothing whatever to parallel this doctrine in English law. The decision to launch a criminal prosecution remains almost entirely beyond the reach of judicial control or supervision. And it is difficult to see how English judges could, consistently with their whole approach to law, follow the American courts into these waters. If a person is brought before a court, and evidence is available to show that he was guilty of an offence, it simply would not avail a defendant to argue that the prosecution has unfairly selected him for prosecution. It would be said, and with some justification, that such unfair selection does not in any way affect the guilt of the accused. If he has broken the law, he cannot complain that he is charged and convicted merely on the grounds that others, equally, or even more guilty, have not been charged. Again, of course, qualifications would have to be made. In a serious case of discriminatory prosecution it is to be expected that inquiries would be made of the prosecuting authorities; that parliamentary questions and complaints would abound; that some steps would be taken to investigate and control any abuses by some internal processes. All this, once again, presupposes confidence in the other organs of the administration of justice and the political process; and it is possible that the confidence is sometimes misplaced or exaggerated. But it would nevertheless be insisted by English lawyers that questions of guilt cannot be affected by impermissible behaviour by prosecuting authorities.

It is possible to reconcile these instances of 'rule nullification' with a formal vision of law. It might be said that the exclusionary rule and the entrapment doctrine are *part* of the law, and that the law itself is simply according priority to these doctrines. Thus (it may be urged) the criminal prohibitions are not thereby nullified, they are simply overridden by

---

[82] 105 S. Ct. 1524 (1985).

rules of higher rank formality. This is a possible viewpoint, but to us it is fundamentally unsatisfying. We prefer the general analysis offered by Mortimer R. Kadish and Sanford R. Kadish in their book *Discretion to Disobey*,[83] in which they suggest that American law manifests its more substantive orientation by according legal status to independent social policies which are then allowed to nullify fundamental criminal prohibitions. The upshot is that American law itself recognizes a much wider range of substantive considerations that, in the view of American courts and legislators, *ought* to nullify criminal liability or immunize individuals from its consequences.

Many examples are given in *Discretion to Disobey* which clearly demonstrate the enormous pressures generated in the American criminal justice system to refuse to treat rules of the criminal law with high mandatory and interpretive formality, but to rely instead on reasons of substance. Apart from the role of the jury, which we discussed earlier in this chapter, similar factors often affect the police, prosecutors, and judges. The police, for instance, often exercise a broad power of choice in deciding whether to arrest: sometimes this is done, as the Kadishes say, 'because of the police perception that the legislative purpose in making certain conduct criminal would not be served by arresting all persons who engage in the prohibited conduct'.[84] They illustrate this by reference to the deliberate non-enforcement of gambling laws against social gamblers, even though the formal law does prohibit social gambling, and by similar non-enforcement of legislation prohibiting extra-marital and other deviant sexual behaviour between consenting adults, on the ground that 'the laws do not really reflect a community judgment that this conduct should be criminally punished'.[85] In short the police must often take account of substantive considerations which reduce the mandatory formality of the criminal prohibitions.

Similar pressures affect prosecutors and even judges. In the 1960s Michigan judges and prosecutors were faced with a narcotics law which imposed a mandatory 20-year jail sentence for anyone convicted of selling drugs, including cannabis. The judges, abetted by the prosecutors, simply refused to enforce the law literally, routinely downgrading 'selling' charges to 'illegal possession' charges where the defendant was not a real dealer in drugs.[86] One judge justified this procedure (in private) by saying: 'This is ridiculous law, passed in the heat of passion

---

[83] *Discretion to Disobey: A Study of Lawful Departures from Legal Rules* (Stanford U. Press, Stanford, 1973).

[84] *Ibid.*, 73.

[85] *Ibid.*, 73–4.

[86] D. Newman, *Conviction: The Determination of Guilt or Innocence without Trial*, 178 (Little Brown, Boston, 1966).

without any thought of its real consequences. I absolutely refuse to send to prison for twenty years a young boy who has done nothing more than sell a single marijuana cigarette to a buddy. The law was not intended for such a case.'[87] This seems to be an example of a fairly widespread phenomenon. In some states it seems that routine charge reduction is used 'to bypass legislatively fixed mandatory sentences' as a way of responding to 'bad law'.[88]

Although there are sometimes similar pressures in England on officials to take action (or no action) in such a way as to cut down the mandatory formality of statutes—for example, the police or prosecutors may decline to proceed in trivial cases—the English position tends to differ from the American in two respects. First, in England, these examples of practical non-enforcement of the law tend to be confined to instances of a marginal character, and relatively trivial crimes, whereas it seems clear that American non-enforcement practices often extend to large tracts of the criminal law, and can also affect very serious crimes (as we saw in dealing with entrapment and the like). And secondly, the American position is significantly influenced by the existence of ill-conceived, badly drafted, and obsolete legislation which it is very difficult to reform by legislative means. This is much less of a problem in England, for reasons we develop in chapter 11.

[87] *Ibid.*
[88] *Ibid.*, 174.

7

The Judicial Enforcement of Law

1. INTRODUCTION

In a formal system of law statutes, precedents and other 'law in books' and the formal reasoning which arises under them translate into the 'law in action' at least in those cases in which one party seeks compulsory application of the law in books. In such cases due legal remedies or sanctions are brought to bear on particular defendants, and the goals of the law in books are thereby vindicated in particular cases. This at the same time encourages the observance of law in books throughout the system, though it is by no means the only factor which operates to secure higher levels of compliance. Certain other factors also come from the law, and include various forms of administrative (rather than judicial) enforcement in particular cases. Then there are factors of a non-legal character, among which various sociological influences may be of high importance, such as traditions of due obedience to law. Our concern here, however, will be solely with judicial enforcement of the law in particular cases, the classic paradigm most relevant to our thesis.

In the more formal vision of law it is simply taken for granted that, other things being equal, the more compliance there is with the dictates of formal legal reasoning, the better. And it follows from this that judicial enforcement procedures and mechanisms ought to be devoted to securing as much compliance with the formal law as possible, compatibly with other policies and goals. An alternative vision or perception of the proper role of enforcement procedures and mechanisms has (we think) never been thought through or articulated, but it does seem clear that such an alternative vision is implicit in a less formal approach to law, such as we have suggested is widely evident in America. For if the function of law itself is taken to be in large measure a matter of enforcing what is right or just according to a community's sense of values, and if (as we saw at the end of the last chapter) the law even goes so far as to provide occasionally for its own 'nullification' in certain circumstances, it must surely follow that there will be circumstances in which actual enforcement of formal law in the books will be found undesirable. Indeed, there is a sense in which jury trial and its potential for nullification of the formal rules of law is itself an instance of the legal system making provision for the non-enforcement of its own norms. We could, therefore, just as well have dealt with jury trial here.

186

In this chapter we continue with the general theme of how formal law fails of implementation when the law in action diverges from the law in books. In the last chapter we concentrated mainly on how the law in action diverges from the law in books when disputes are not judicially resolved in accord with the true facts. But there are many other reasons why the law in action may diverge from the formal law in books. Such divergences may occur because one of the parties to a controversy has no, or inadequate, access to court machinery in the first place, or because the courts are congested, or because court proceedings are slow and inefficient, or because judicial remedies and sanctions are inadequate, or because final judgments are not easily enforceable, or for still other reasons. We will now consider a number of basic contrasts between the English and the American legal systems in regard to matters of this kind, but the nature of this book precludes any attempt at exhaustive treatment.

The kind of formality we identify in this chapter will be called 'enforcement formality'. Low enforcement formality exists when the law in books does not translate into law in action because courts are inaccessible to one or both parties, court proceedings are delayed or otherwise inefficient, judgments lack finality, and so on. Such factors may, of course, also explain why the true facts of a dispute are not found. 'Truth formality', dealt with in the last chapter, might even be viewed merely as a facet of enforcement formality, but here we separate the two, and confine enforcement formality to the various factors considered in this chapter. Not only may these factors (along with others considered in the previous chapter) subvert truth formality, they may even account for instances in which no effort is made to bring formal law into play at all, as well as other instances in which, although the true facts are found, the governing law is not properly applied or, if properly applied, not enforced. Naturally, a high level of enforcement formality in these terms has its effects outside as well as inside the courts.

Enforcement formality and our concept of mandatory formality are not unrelated. For example, enforcement rules which themselves have low mandatory formality cut down overall enforcement formality by allowing substantive and other considerations emergent in the process to interfere with the translation of law in books into law in action. Even if enforcement rules were all of high mandatory formality, the process might still lack significant enforcement formality if the rules are not well designed in other ways to secure due observance of law in books.

2. THE ACCESSIBILITY OF THE COURTS

When courts are inaccessible—for whatever reason—and when people are unwilling to comply with legal norms without some pressure from the courts, then there will *pro tanto* be less rule observance. Disputes will have to be decided outside the courts where the legal norms *may* continue to have some effect, but not so much as they would have in the courts themselves. The less effect the legal norms have on such forms of dispute resolution, the less formally will the legal system be working; though whether this is evidence of adherence to a less formal vision of law may well depend on the extent to which this result is generally desired or tolerated, and to what extent it is perceived as an unsatisfactory situation.

In the sense in which we use the term, 'accessibility' applies as much to a defendant as it does to a plaintiff or a prosecutor. If a valid defence is not put before a court because (for example) the defendant cannot afford a lawyer and the case goes against him by default, then the legal norms are not being observed, and the real dispute is in effect resolved outside the court.

Courts may be inaccessible for different reasons. The two most usual are cost, on the one hand, and overloaded lists or dockets on the other. As to the first, we doubt if it is possible or profitable to attempt any comparisons between England and America here. While there can be no doubt that litigation (and legal services generally) are much more costly in America, we have no real means of judging the extent to which this makes the courts inaccessible (in the broad sense ascribed above) to plaintiffs, defendants, or those accused of crime. Both countries have procedures for giving legal assistance to those accused of serious crime,[1] and in both machinery of a kind exists for poor civil litigants (primarily, legal aid in England, the contingent fee in America).[2] But any attempt to make serious comparisons here would take us too far from our main theme. We will content ourselves at the outset with two points which ideally would demand further exploration, but which would be very difficult to develop without further data than is presently available. What we say here is offered largely to rebut possible counter-arguments to our thesis rather than provide affirmative support for it.

The first point is that we should beware of too readily assuming that the vastly greater volume of civil litigation (and criminal trials and appeals) in America can by itself be taken as evidence of the greater

---

[1] See generally W. LaFave and J. Israel, 2 *Criminal Procedure*, 1–11. 2 (West, St. Paul, 1984) (US); Legal Aid Act 1974 (England); R. M. Jackson, *The Machinery of Justice in England*, 235–51 (7th edn., Cambridge U. Press, Cambridge, 1977) (England).

[2] See generally on the contingent fee ch. 13, pp. 381–2, and on legal aid in England, R. M. Jackson, *supra*, n. 1, at 435–54; *Legal Aid Handbook 1984* (The Law Society, London, 1984).

accessibility of the courts, still less of a higher degree of enforcement formality. A wide variety of institutional and cultural factors contribute to this greater volume. Institutional factors include the precipitous increase in the government's regulatory functions,[3] the growth of novel causes of action occasioned by legislation or (more usually) judicial activism,[4] increases in the size of damage awards in tort actions,[5] and the breakdown of traditional procedural barriers.[6] The cultural roots of American litigiousness are more difficult to pin-point, but some writers view it as an expression of American individualism,[7] competetiveness,[8] or moralism.[9] Law in America has also been described as a substitute for bonds of community in a mobile, immigrant society.[10] In light of such factors, the bare fact of voluminous litigation tells us little about the accessibility of the courts to those with limited means.[11]

Our second point here is based on little more than an intuitive feel about the relationship between English law in books and law in action, and it may call for some qualifications to our thesis. There is some evidence that many legal rights are not in practice enforced in England because of limited means or understanding on the part of those concerned. For example, there is evidence that many of those who suffer personal injury could obtain damages if they pursued claims which are at

---

[3] See Van Dusen, 'Comments on the Volume of Litigation in the Federal Courts', 8 *Del. J. Corp. L.* 435, 437–9 (1983) (quoting US Attorney-General William French Smith).

[4] See M. A. Marks, *The Suing of America*, 5 (Seaview Books, NY, 1981); J. K. Lieberman, *The Litigious Society*, 18 (Basic Books, NY, 1981).

[5] See generally Friedman, 'The Six Million Dollar Man: Litigation and Rights Consciousness in Modern America', 39 *Md. L. Rev.* 661 (1980); Meador, 'The Federal Judiciary: Inflation, Malfunction and a Proposed Course of Action', *BYUL Rev.* 617, 620 (1981).

[6] For example, the liberalization of pleading requirements, when combined with liberal pre-trial discovery procedures, permits the bringing of a lawsuit on little more than speculation.

[7] See generally J. K. Lieberman, *supra*, n. 4.

[8] See M. A. Marks, *supra*, n. 4, at 12.

[9] *Ibid.*, at 4–5.

[10] See generally J. K. Lieberman, *supra*, n. 4.

[11] Doubts have been expressed as to whether America really does have more litigation than other comparable countries, see, e.g., J. K. Lieberman, *supra*, n. 4; Galanter, 'Reading the Landscapes of Disputes: What We Know and Don't Know (and Think We Know) About Our Allegedly Contentious and Litigious Society', 31 *UCLA L Rev.* 4 (1983). But both Lieberman and Galanter seem to have erred in using English statistics of writs and summonses issued as evidence of the volume of *litigation*; in fact most writs and more specially summonses are mere debt-collecting instruments and lead to no litigation at all. Further, the relative sizes of the judiciary and legal profession (as to which see chapters 12 and 13) are out of all proportion to population differences, as Galanter acknowledges. If all these American judges are not hearing cases, as Lieberman and Galanter imply, what are they doing? In addition, there can be no serious doubt that there is vastly more tort litigation in America arising out of malpractice and product defects, because the evidence of insurance premium disparities here speaks for itself.

present not pursued.[12] And it is also widely believed that many of those who are currently denied welfare benefits could appeal successfully if they had the knowledge of how to do so, or the means to employ lawyers to do it for them.[13] Yet there seems a massive indifference to these failures of the law to work in accordance with its own norms. Is this then evidence that the enforcement formality of English law is not as high as we have suggested?

A partial answer to this question is that these examples of the failure of the system to work in accordance with its professed norms are largely imperceptible to practising lawyers. They come to light as a result of academic research, but in England few practising lawyers read academic research of this kind; and when they do, they are often very sceptical about the methodologies and the results. Actual cases illustrating such problems, almost by definition, rarely come the way of legal practitioners or judges. When they do, the practitioners and judges may think they are aberrational and rare examples of the failure of the system for which they feel little sense of responsibility since, *ex hypothesi*, the failures occur outside the courts and in one sense outside the legal system as a whole.

If cases of this kind were frequently brought home to the attention of the practising profession and the judges, it may be that they would begin to react differently. Some evidence for this is provided by the recent history of criminal legal aid in England. Legal aid for defendants in criminal cases is available at the discretion of the local magistrates,[14] and some years ago the higher judiciary were taking the complacent attitude that all defendants charged with serious crimes could confidently expect to obtain legal aid from the magistrates. In fact academic research brought to light the fact that magistrates were exercising their discretion on very different criteria in different parts of the country, and that many defendants charged with very serious offences for which substantial jail terms could be expected were being refused legal aid by magistrates in certain areas. When these facts were brought to light, the judges acted with commendable vigour and began to tell the magistrates in no uncertain terms that such defendants must be granted legal aid.[15]

This evidence is of course very sketchy, and there may exist other areas in which legal norms are widely flouted in practice in England, and yet in which the judges and practising lawyers and even the public seem indifferent to the situation. To the extent that this might be shown to be

[12] See B. Abel-Smith, M. Zander, and R. Brooke, *Legal Problems and the Citizen*, 169–78, 183–5 (Heinemann, London, 1973).

[13] See, e.g., Harris, 'The Reform of the Supplementary Benefit Appeals System', *J. Social Welfare L.* 212, 222 (1983).

[14] Legal Aid Act 1974, Part II, as subsequently amended by a variety of statutes.

[15] See Zander, 'Promoting Change in the Legal System', 42 *Mod. L. Rev.* 489, 497–8 (1979).

the case, it will have to be conceded that qualifications will need to be made to our basic thesis. Much further study and research is plainly needed at this point. But what matters for the purposes of this study is the comparative position in the two countries; and—though data again is lacking in any satisfactory form—it seems to us probable that instances of massive divergence between legal norms and the actual operation of the legal system will more readily be found in America than in England. Such divergence is evident in American constitutional,[16] civil,[17] and criminal[18] law. Plea bargaining practice, for instance, is a widely acknowledged example of the considerable extent to which criminal law in books does not translate into law in action in America. Furthermore, there is strong evidence (some of which we referred to in chapter 6) that discretionary prosecution and sentencing practice undermine formal law where harsh penalties do not accord with public or judicial notions of substantive justice, as in the enforcement of severe speeding, drunk driving, and drug possession laws.[19]

In addition, we think American judges in general are more likely than English judges to turn a blind eye to statutes and binding precedents when they think that strict application of the formal law will result in serious injustice. Such misapplication of the law does not necessarily create valid new law or change the existing law—it amounts simply to an evasion or 'nullification' of the formal law. Obviously this practice cannot be quantified, but it may help to explain why there are often many conflicting precedents within one American jurisdiction, and why American judges will sometimes just ignore seemingly contrary decisions where an English judge would feel obliged to attempt to reconcile them. It also helps explain why American judges sometimes take great liberties with statutes.

Although it is perhaps more likely that such instances of divergence between law in books and law in action will be brought to light by research in America, the chances of overt statutory reform are less for reasons which will be apparent from our discussion of the obstacles to such reform in chapter 11. Furthermore, the American system of

[16] See, e.g., K. M. Dolbeare and P. E. Hammond, *The School Prayer Decisions: From Court Policy to Local Practice* (U. of Chicago Press, Chicago, 1971).

[17] For example, the American rule as to 'costs' means that plaintiffs with small claims are unable to pursue them in practice, see Mause, 'Winner Takes All: A Reexamination of the Indemnity System', 55 *Iowa L. Rev.* 26, 33 (1969). But the problem of enforcing small claims is also serious in England, where the indemnity rule has actually been abolished for such claims with a view to making them *easier* to enforce. See County Court Rules, Order 19, rule 2(3) and (6); Langan and Henderson, *Civil Procedure*, 356–7 (3rd edn., 1983).

[18] See generally H. L. Ross, 'The Neutralization of Severe Penalties: Some Traffic Law Studies', 10 *Law and Soc. Rev.* 403 (1976); J. Q. Wilson, *Thinking About Crime* (Basic Books, NY, 1975); K. C. Davis, *Discretionary Justice* (U. of Illinois Press, Urbana, 1971).

[19] See Ross, *supra*, n. 18, and see also ch. 6 at 184–5.

government, with its lack of any centralized Cabinet responsible for a general oversight of the legal system, means that, even when such instances are brought to light, nobody may feel an immediate responsibility for doing anything about it. The courts may respond to it (as in the examples of public law litigation discussed in chapter 5), but court-inspired change is more patchy and difficult to administer than sweeping legislative change of the kind so much more readily obtained in England.

We turn now to the question of inaccessibility of the courts through congestion, overloaded lists or dockets, on which there is a good deal more data. Such congestion may be a major obstacle to accessibility in any legal system; in general terms it is much more serious in the United States than in England. As so often with our comparisons between the two countries, it may well be that there is not a great difference in *average* delays in getting cases to trial or appeal, but the variations from the mean appear much wider in America. There certainly appear to be many places in America where court delays reach levels which would be regarded as unacceptable in England. The pace of litigation (or prosecution) even in England is not exactly hurried, but most of the delays are due to the need for preparation of a claim, or of a defence or prosecution, as well as to allow time for events to take their natural course (for example, for a medical condition to stabilize in a personal injury case). Once the parties are ready to proceed, a civil case can normally be heard within six to twelve months in the High Court, and even civil appeals are often disposed of within a few months of the trial, especially where they involve urgency.[20] In the County Courts, where much litigation takes place in smaller cases, delays are not much of a problem as a general rule, though bottlenecks and congestion occur from time to time in particular areas. In criminal cases, the courts tend to move faster, and there are strong pressures to introduce in England the Scots rule of criminal procedure under which an accused has a statutory right to be freed on bail unless he is brought to trial within 110 days of his arrest. (A right to be freed on bail in this sense would be more potent than a corresponding right in America since bail costs nothing in England.) The position concerning court congestion in England tends to vary a good deal, regularly moving through cycles every few years. But once a serious build up occurs, committees are appointed, inquiries held, and steps taken to reduce the congestion and delays. It is virtually unthinkable in modern times that England would allow an almost

---

[20] In 1985–6 the average waiting time for hearing before the Court of Appeal varied from only 3 to 4 weeks for child custody cases to about 13 to 18 months for the most difficult Chancery appeals. Sir John Donaldson, *Review of the Legal Year, 1985–86*, 136 *New LJ* 989 (1986).

permanent state of serious court congestion to remain unremedied for many years. The relatively low volume of litigation and criminal trials in England means that congestion can usually be remedied by the appointment of a handful of extra judges at little cost.

In America, as is well known, congested courts are almost everywhere the norm in large urban centres. Even if some courts process civil litigation as fast as English courts do, it is nothing out of the ordinary for cases to have to wait upwards of three or four years for trial; and appellate dockets are also correspondingly swollen.[21] Commenting in 1971 on the comparison between delays in England and America, Professor (later Judge) Kaplan noted that the average waiting time for trial was then 9 months in London and $5\frac{1}{2}$ months elsewhere in England, but 35 to 42 months in Middlesex County, Massachusetts, Kaplan's own county.[22] By 1973, the delay from answer to trial for civil jury trials cases in Middlesex County averaged 51 months and the national average for personal injury cases tried by a jury was 22 months.[23] Of course, figures like these vary from time to time and place to place, but there is little doubt about the overall picture. Court delays are today often far worse in the United States than in England.

Inevitably, considerations of cost and of court delays lead to great pressure for out-of-court settlements, and we do not think it can be doubted that this pressure is usually greater in America than in England. Now the mere fact that parties make an out-of-court settlement does not by itself show that the outcome is not in accordance with the applicable legal rules or other norms. Where the settlement process is itself part of a

---

[21] The problem of congestion and delay has been much studied but there are few hard data on actual or 'average' delays, partly because of lack of any satisfactory measure of 'delay', but mostly for sheer lack of information. The latest study (of 21 metropolitan courts across the US) shows median 'trial list disposition time' from filing complaint to closure of trial record of 357 days in New Orleans to 980 days in Bronx County, New York. Thomas Church Jr., and Others, *Justice Delayed: The Pace of Litigation in Urban Trial Courts* (National Center for State Courts, Williamsburg, Va., 1978). See also Sipes, 'The Journey toward Delay Reduction in Trial Courts: A Traveler's Report', 6 *State Court Journal*, No. 2, 5, and Trotter and Cooper, 'State Trial Court Delay: Efforts at Reform', 31 *American Univ. Law Rev.* 213 (1982). As to appeal court delays, see Weisberger, 'Appellate Courts: The Challenge of Inundation', *ibid.*, 237. Most state appellate courts take at least 9 months from filing notice of appeal to render a decision, and 9 courts averaged 18 months. J. Martin and E. Prescott, *Appellate Court Delay: Structural Responses to the Problems of Volume and Delay* (National Center for State Courts, Williamsburg, Va., 1981).

[22] 'An American Lawyer in the Queen's Courts: Impressions of English Civil Procedure', 69 *Mich. L. Rev.* 821, 840 (1971). The English figures given by Kaplan come from the *Report* of the Royal Commission on Assizes and Quarter Sessions, Appendix 8, 165 (Cmnd. 4153, HMSO, London, 1969).

[23] 1974 Institute of Judicial Administration Calendar Status Study ii, 7. The national figures are based on data from 81 jurisdictions in 45 states, and relate to personal injury cases tried by juries in state trial courts of general jurisdiction.

careful rule-structured system, where it operates as a genuine alternative to court processes so that the parties bargain their way to a settlement fully 'in the shadow of the law' (as the phrase goes), the settlement results may approximate those which the rules require. Furthermore, clarity of rules, high truth formality and predictability of results facilitates such settlements, and these factors, we believe, operate to produce this result more powerfully in England than in the United States. We have already referred to figures suggesting that the settlement rate for personal injury cases, for instance, is far higher in England than in America.[24] Of course, even in England, bargaining and compromises will mean that any resulting settlement only approximates to the result which the trial process would have produced; and almost always one party will be under greater pressure to settle more quickly and less favourably, so that his bargaining position will be weaker, and the result less close to that which the rules would otherwise suggest. All these factors, we doubt not, operate in England as in America; but there are many reasons for thinking that settlements follow the formal legal rules more closely in England than in America.

For one thing, English lawyers advising their clients as to settlements appear to take the legal rules more seriously. For instance, it is quite common for a single test case to be brought to trial in order to obtain a judicial ruling which will affect a large number of other cases, which can then be settled by the parties with the aid of their lawyers, in accordance with the general principles laid down by the judge. This happened recently, for example, where a very large number of actions were brought claiming damages against employers for negligently subjecting their employees to the risk of industrial deafness.[25] Because the sort of issues which arose in these cases were largely issues of fact (as classified in Anglo-American law) they would have had to be resolved by juries in America. But jury findings in one case do not constitute precedents for other cases, so a settlement process of this kind would be unlikely to occur in America. Class actions are sometimes possible in American civil procedure in such mass cases, and settlements can be negotiated in such class actions, but the more aggressive tactics of American trial lawyers, combined with knowledge that such cases would be tried by juries if they went to court, means that the bargaining to a settlement in America appears to take place in a much rawer and more competitive

---

[24] *Supra*, at 176.
[25] *Thompson* v. *Smiths Shiprepairers Ltd.* [1984] 1 All ER 881. There were over 20,000 such claims, and lawyers acting for these parties agreed that a small number of them should be brought to trial with a view 'to establishing a set of criteria which would be applicable to the broad majority of claims'. *Ibid.*, at 884.

market-place, so that the outcomes probably differ rather more in America from those prescribed by formal rules of liability.[26]

Then again, the high legal costs and choked court dockets in America almost inevitably skew the result against the party under the greater pressure. In personal injury cases, the total result led the authors of the Michigan automobile accident study to say:

The statistics confirm what every lawyer and adjuster knows—that questions about negligence, proof, defendant's ability to pay, and the client's desire for an end of litigation, lead to compromises of claims at levels which correspond to no theory of legal right.[27]

So great is the pressure produced by court congestion and related factors in America that some courts have recently been experimenting with pre-trial conferences and other techniques which are in novel ways partly or mainly designed to encourage the parties to settle. Indeed some judges regularly seek first to bring about a settlement and may go to great lengths to do so, all without much (or any) knowledge of the facts or the relevant legal issues. Once again, it is evident that results so reached will often involve significant departure from the rules which govern the rights of the parties according to the letter of the law.[28]

3. SPEED AND EFFICIENCY OF THE JUDICIAL PROCESS

Court procedures may operate in a fashion that is inefficient, costly, and time consuming. Even if a formal legal right is ultimately vindicated at the end of legal proceedings, the formal right will mean less to the winner if it has only been obtained at inordinate cost and after great delay. Moreover, such inefficiencies in the actual operation of the judicial process may discourage plaintiffs or defendants from bringing claims or raising defences in the first place, and thus lead to serious divergence between law in books and law in action. In addition, these inefficiencies may also reflect a divergence between *procedural* law in books and law in action, and thus indicate that the system is less formal in this respect also.

The point made above about the importance of speed in certain types of proceedings can be shown by taking as a simple illustration a

[26] See Fiss, 'Against Settlement', 93 *Yale LJ* 1073 (1984); Eisenberg, 'Private Ordering through Negotiation: Dispute Settlement and Rulemaking', 89 *Harv. L. Rev.* 637 (1976); Mnookin and Kornhauser, 'Bargaining in the Shadow of the Law: The Case of Divorce', 88 *Yale LJ* 950 (1979). For some recent examples of class action settlements, see Sugarman, 'Doing Away with Tort Law', 73 *Calif. L. Rev.* 555, 596–603 (1985).

[27] A. F. Conard and Others, *Automobile Accident Costs and Payments*, 318 (U. of Michigan Press, Ann Arbor, 1964).

[28] Professor Fiss, *supra*, n. 26, at 1085 is critical of these pressures because they tend to ignore the values in litigated resolutions.

straightforward contract for the sale of a house, followed by default by the vendor without any genuine legal justification. According to the legal rules, in both England and the United States, the answer is in principle clear: the buyer ought to be able to get a decree of specific performance to compel the vendor to convey. But it is far from clear whether the reality matches the rules in the United States, though in this instance it certainly does so in England. A writ claiming specific performance, together with an affidavit setting out the essential facts and also the plaintiff's belief that there is no reasonable defence to the action, can usually be expected to produce a decree of specific performance in the Chancery Division of the High Court within a few weeks. Furthermore, appeals or delaying tactics after the decree is granted will usually be impossible, if there is really no legal ground for them, if only because counsel would refuse to take the necessary steps if he thought his client was just abusing the system. The purchaser will therefore get his house and his legal rights will be vindicated.[29]

But in many American state courts, the delays in getting such a case even to a hearing are so great that the whole point of the exercise is lost. One important explanation for such delays is that lawyers in America can more readily raise arguable defences given the more substantive orientation of the American legal system as a whole. But in a simple case of this kind, unless the purchaser can get his decree of specific performance within a short time, he is likely to abandon his claim (except perhaps to damages) and find an alternative house. As this example shows, the force of some rules is undermined by delays so that their whole point is lost when speedy compliance is not assured. Here enforcement formality is very low.

Once again, we enter the caveat that delays are by no means unknown in England in certain kinds of cases, and in special circumstances speedy hearings can be secured in the United States. But we believe the fore-going example does not misrepresent the general picture. Furthermore, as we shall elaborate later, we believe that the differences between the two countries in these respects are not just fortuitous, but do reflect some of the deeper differences in judicial style which are linked to the underlying vision of law adhered to in the two countries. In England, by and large, there is a strong belief that legal rules ought to be strictly

---

[29] See Rules of the Supreme Court, Order 86, and notes thereto in the *Supreme Court Practice 1985* at 1199 ff. (Specially speedy provisions are available for the disposal of simple commercial cases, see Order 72 of the Rules of the Supreme Court, and *Supreme Court Practice 1985* at 1059 ff; see also Practice Statement [1967] 1 WLR 1545 and Practice Direction [1981] 3 All ER 864.) We do not claim that English lawyers will never assist their clients in purely dilatory tactics, but barristers are less likely to go along with them, and there are definite limits beyond which no English lawyer is likely to go. For instance, it is one thing to defend a claim, another to launch an appeal.

complied with, and that legal procedures ought, as far as possible, to be fashioned to enable such rules to be enforced. In America, it seems to us, the stress on due process, on the right to have claims tried or defended before a jury, on the right to one's day in court, and, perhaps more generally, the belief that rules themselves are not always right or just, means that the enforcement of the primary legal norms themselves often takes second place.

Those who have some knowledge of the workings of English and American law would probably agree that English judges retain a greater degree of control than their American counterparts over court procedures at all stages, pre-trial, trial, and post-trial, and use this control to minimize opportunities for exploitation of delaying and harassing tactics. But it is unwise to rest on personal impressions unsupported by evidence, and we therefore lay more stress on a number of specific rules of procedure and practice in which the English position differs markedly from the American.

The first is unquestionably the practice of awarding 'costs' to a winning party in civil litigation (in the English sense, which includes legal professional fees and other reasonably necessary expenses of litigation). It is well known that this is the almost universal practice in English civil litigation, and this practice extends to both the trial stage and appellate stages of litigation.[30] A party who ultimately wins on appeal will usually be entitled to an order for costs covering the original trial and all subsequent stages in the litigation; furthermore, the order will cover pre-trial costs as well as those actually incurred at the trial and on appeal. The losing party will thus have the double burden of paying his own attorney's fees plus those of his opponent. But the award of costs is discretionary, and it is one of the most potent weapons by which English judges are able to discipline lawyers (and therefore their clients) into due observance of the procedural rules. Hence there are circumstances in which even a winning party may be 'deprived of his costs' (usually in part only) where the conduct of the case has imposed unnecessary costs on the other party. For instance, a party who requests a last minute adjournment on some flimsy or inadequate ground (even if the request is granted which it often will not be) will nearly always be required to pay the costs of the other party in connection with the abortive hearing, whatever the ultimate outcome of the case. This is a very potent instrument, especially because it will be obvious to the client who has to pay these costs that they were attributable to his own lawyer's request for the adjournment, which the lawyer may in consequence have

---

[30] See A. L. Goodhart, 'Costs', 38 *Yale LJ* 849 (1929). See today the voluminous notes to the Rules of the Supreme Court, Order 62 in the *Supreme Court Practice 1985*.

to explain or justify to his client. The result is that a request for an adjournment on flimsy grounds would rarely be made in England.

The winning party does not, however, usually recover all his costs, but only those 'reasonably necessary'; this is usually thought to be about two-thirds of the total, so that even a plaintiff who is confident of ultimately winning still has an incentive not to incur wasteful expenditure in the preparation of his case. These rules about costs do not always apply in full today to personal injury and other actions in which one of the parties has legal aid, because the law has to protect the legally aided party against the possibility of an order for costs, if the purposes of legal aid are to be met. Thus there are severe limits to the extent to which an order for costs can be made against a legally aided party; but even then there are other means by which unreasonable or delaying tactics can be discouraged or prevented. For example, there is an elaborate system of rules, very often used in personal injury cases, under which a defendant can 'pay into a court' a certain sum (chosen by him) in satisfaction of the plaintiff's claim. If the plaintiff refuses to accept this sum, but proceeds with his action and is subsequently awarded lower damages than were paid into court, the defendant (and not the plaintiff) will be entitled to an order for costs from the date of the payment in.[31]

It is, of course, well known that the general practice in America is not to award costs in the English sense—attorney's fees—to the winning party in civil litigation. There are some exceptions, and it is also widely believed that, in personal injury actions, jury awards of damages are often based on the assumption that part of the award will be used to pay the lawyer's fees. Since this is usually part of the contractual arrangement between the client and the attorney, and this fact is pretty well known to jurors, an award of damages in this kind of case quite closely resembles an English award of damages and costs.

The result is that it often happens that a winning plaintiff gets most of his legal costs paid by the defendant in both countries; but the costs system in England has important disciplinary effects on the conduct of litigation and the practices of lawyers which are largely absent in the United States.[32] In England, a defendant who knows that he has no real defence to an action, but who simply wishes to prevaricate or spin out the legal process as long as possible, will often find this an expensive procedure, even if he can find lawyers who are prepared to act for him in this way (on which more later), and even if the courts are prepared to

---

[31] See Rules of the Supreme Court, Order 22, *Supreme Court Practice 1985* at 364 ff.

[32] '[F]ee awards to deter and compensate for the costs imposed by dilatory and harassing litigation tactics seem underused in [the US].' T. D. Rowe, 'The Legal Theory of Attorney Fee Shifting: A Critical Overview', *Duke LJ* 651, 661 (1982). See also Comment, 'Court Awarded Attorney's Fees and Equal Access to the Courts', 122 *U. Pa. L. Rev.* 636 (1974).

tolerate such tactics. In America, on the other hand, there has been great reluctance to use the award of costs as a disciplining measure to secure compliance with procedural rules.[33]

A still more potent weapon, though one reserved for rather serious cases, is the English rule that a solicitor may be personally ordered by the court to pay any costs which have been needlessly incurred through some professional malpractice or failure to comply with court rules and procedures.[34] This jurisdiction of the English courts is quite severe in operation, and has been used to order solicitors personally to pay 'costs' (in the English sense) even for cases of relatively mild negligence,[35] where the costs have been incurred improperly or without reasonable cause. A comparable provision under a statute of 1813 (28 US § 1927) has existed in American federal procedure, but until recently was little used. The statute was, however, amended in 1980[36] to make it possible to order an attorney not only to pay costs in the American sense, but also to pay 'costs' in the English sense, that is, attorney's fees, to the other party, where he has been guilty of multiplying the proceedings 'unreasonably and vexatiously'. There are some signs that the federal courts may be more willing to use this sanction against attorneys who file patently frivolous suits, or who fail to exhaust administrative remedies.[37] There are also other modern changes in the Federal Rules of Civil Procedure—rules copied in most states—which now contain severe sanctions against attorneys who engage in harassing and delaying tactics,[38] though Judge Posner has complained that federal courts are still too reluctant to impose sanctions on lawyers who file frivolous appeals.[39] It is still too early to tell whether such sanctions will make a

[33] See 'Sanctions Imposable for Violation of the Federal Rules of Civil Procedure', A Report to the Federal Judicial Center by R. E. Rodes, Jr., K. F. Ripple, and C. Mooney (The Center, Washington, DC, 1981), especially the Conclusion (at 85) where present practices are criticized for leading to 'considerable laxity in the day-to-day application of the rules'. See also Advisory Committee Note to 1983 Amendments of the Federal Rules of Civil Procedure, 97 FRD 165, at 198, 220.

[34] See *Myers* v. *Elman* [1940] AC 282.

[35] See, e.g., *Davy-Chiesman* v. *Davy-Chiesman* [1984] 1 All ER 321 (solicitor acted on advice of counsel but failed to appreciate effect of changed circumstances).

[36] Act of July 22, 1813, ch. 14, § 3, 3 St. 21 (current version at 28 USC § 1927 (1982)).

[37] See McKirdy, '28 USC § 1927: Counselor Beware', 71 *Ill. Bar J.* 708, 710–12 (1983). See also *Roadway Express Inc.* v. *Piper* 447 US 725, 766 (1980) (assessment of attorney's fees against counsel who wilfully abuses judicial process).

[38] See, e.g., Fed. R. Civ. P. 11, 26; Advisory Committee Note to 1983 Amendments, *supra*, n. 33, 198, 216. For application of the rule by federal courts, see C. A. Wright, A. R. Miller and M. K. Kane, 5 *Federal Practice and Procedure*, §§ 1331–5 (West, St. Paul, Supp. 1985). There are differences of opinion as to whether Fed. R. Civ. P. 11 is working well in restraining abusive and harassing tactics. See *New York Times*, 2 Oct. 1986, 25, 31, citing Professor A. R. Miller (who thinks it is) and Judge Jack B. Weinstein (who thinks the rule is itself being used as a further weapon of abuse and harassment).

[39] See Posner, *The Federal Courts: Crisis and Reform*, 244 (1985).

significant difference to court congestion, settlement rates, and litigation strategies—and hence to the relatively lower enforcement formality of American law.

The discipline of costs is reinforced in England by the very extensive use made in modern times of the power to award a succesful plaintiff pre-judgment interest on his damages.[40] It is now almost taken for granted that a plaintiff who has been 'kept out of his money', as English lawyers put it, is entitled to a proper rate of interest on that money for the whole period during which he has been deprived of its use. The rate of interest awarded is in the discretion of the court but, especially in straightforward commercial claims, it nowadays approximates to ordinary commercial interest rates.

Here again, American practice differs.[41] Traditionally, the award of interest has not been favoured by American courts, and pre-judgment interest has generally been available only in actions for liquidated debts.[42] Prejudgment interest awards usually rest on statutory powers, and are limited in various ways even in those states with such statutes.[43] Many jurisdictions still limit pre-judgment interest to liquidated claims, and most still have low statutory interest rates even when interest is awarded at all. The theory behind the strict limits on which pre-judgment interest is awarded is that such interest is semi-punitive, and hence not justifiable when a defendant has merely exercised his 'right' to defend a lawsuit.[44] But there are some signs of a trend away from this approach in federal jurisdiction, and also in some states, for instance in Texas and Alaska. This change of opinion (though still only a minority view) is based on the argument long since accepted in England, that pre-judgment interest is needed to compensate the plaintiff properly and is not in any event punitive since the defendant may be presumed to have benefited from having the money in his possession from the commencement of the cause of action. But another argument, and one more directly relevant to our thesis, is that restrictions on the award of pre-

---

[40] See Administration of Justice Act 1982, s. 15, replacing provisions first enacted in 1934. For details as to the law and practice of the courts under these provisions, see Rules of the Supreme Court, Order 62 and notes thereto in *The Supreme Court Practice 1985* at 859 ff.

[41] See generally Rothschild, 'Prejudgment Interest: Survey and Suggestion', 77 *N.W.U. L. Rev.* 192 (1982), on which we have freely drawn. The Note recommends substantial adoption of the English approach, at 221. See also Note, 'Prejudgment Interest: Too Little, Too Much or Both?' 10 *UCLA-Alaska L. Rev.* 192 (1981); Note, 'Prejudgment Interest: An Element of Damages not to be Overlooked', 8 *Cum. L. Rev.* 521 (1971).

[42] C. T. McCormick, *Damages*, § 51 (West, St. Paul, 1935).

[43] See Rothschild, *supra*, n. 41.

[44] *Kespohl* v. *Northern Trust Co.* 131 Ill. App. 2d 188, 266 NE 2d 371 (1970); *Guls* v. *G. C. Murphy Co.* 629 F. 2d 248 (3rd Cir.) *cert. denied*, 449 US 949 (1980), vacated on other grounds, 451 US 935 (1981).

judgment interest discourage defendants from settling and put a premium on delay.[45] In an inflationary economy the delay premium is all the greater. At least one state supreme court has recently specifically recognized the importance of pre-judgment interest in reducing incentives for defendants to delay litigation.[46]

In addition to these financial controls, English courts make extensive and effective use of summary procedures to dispose of frivolous or delaying claims or defences. Under Order 14 of the Rules of the Supreme Court, a plaintiff may, on issuing his writ, swear an affidavit asserting his belief that there is no reasonable defence to his claim, and asking for summary judgment. The onus is then on the defendant to show that he has a reasonably arguable defence,[47] and the courts are quick to distinguish cases in which the defendant is just seeking delay from those where a genuine defence may exist.[48] In doubtful cases, the defendant may be required to give security, or pay part or even all of the amount claimed into court, as a condition of being given leave to defend the action.[49] Although a defendant cannot obtain summary judgment in precisely the same way, procedures exist which enable the defendant to have a claim struck out without trial if it discloses no arguable cause of action.[50] These summary procedures are heard, in the first instance, before a Master of the Supreme Court[51] (with appeal to the judge), but they are held in chambers (in private), not in open court, so (for instance) a wildly speculative claim will be struck out before it attracts any publicity. A plaintiff who launches such a claim will, therefore, get little joy from it: rapid and summary dismissal with an order for 'costs' (in the English sense), and no publicity, is the likely outcome.

American summary procedures are not directly comparable with the English ones. In America, legally invalid claims may be challenged in pre-answer motions to dismiss for failure to state a claim or in motions for judgment on the pleadings.[52] Because most modern rules are quite liberal as to the legal sufficiency of a complaint, however, such motions

---

[45] There is much controversy over the degree to which court delays would be reduced by greater use of pre-judgment interest awards, see, e.g., Longdrigan and Smith, 'Is there Profit in Court Delay?' 23 *Judges' Journal* 12 (1984).

[46] *State* v. *Phillips* 470 P. 2d 266 (Alaska, 1970).

[47] Rules of the Supreme Court, Order 14. See generally on summary judgment Langan and Henderson, *Civil Procedure*, ch. 4 (3rd edn., 1983).

[48] See, e.g., *European Asian Bank* v. *Punjab and Sind Bank* [1983] 2 All ER 508.

[49] See, e.g., *M.V. Yorke Motors* v. *Edwards* [1982] 1 All ER 1024.

[50] See Langan and Henderson, *supra*, n. 47, at 123–30.

[51] On the use of Masters in English legal procedure, see Zavatt, 'The Use of Masters in Aid of the Court in Interlocutory Proceedings', 22 FRD 283 (1985). Zavatt concludes that Masters simplify issues, help the parties to define the issues more narrowly, and increase the pressure to settle—the first two at least being aids to formal decision making.

[52] See, e.g., Fed. R. Civ. P. 12 (*b*) (6) and 12 (*c*). Haber, 'Speeding Along Justice: Model Rules of Summary Civil Procedure', 21 *Harv. J. of Legis.* 173, 175, n. 7 (1984).

are seldom granted.[53] Summary judgment, strictly so-called, is a method of disposing of claims 'sufficient in law on their face'[54] but raising no genuine issue of material fact.[55] Summary judgment can be rendered in favour of either party. A major difference between English and American procedure is that in America the party moving for summary judgment has the onus of proving that no genuine issue of fact remains to prevent judgment being entered in his favour. In both countries summary procedures are most frequently used in actions on bills of exchange, promissory notes, and liquidated debt claims,[56] and are difficult (or impossible) to invoke in cases of negligence where the standard of the reasonable man makes it almost impossible to determine in advance of a full trial that one party is entitled to a verdict as a matter of law.[57]

Although it is not easy to compare the degree to which these varying sets of provisions are actually used in the two countries so as to control or restrain dilatory and frivolous use of legal procedures, our general impression is that the English courts make much greater use of these procedures. Certainly, it is apparent from the daily press reports of court activities that American lawyers still seem to find it worthwhile to launch claims or file motions which must stand very little chance of success, and which would in England be immediately struck out as disclosing no arguable claim or defence. There is also evidence that some American judges have been particularly noted for their reluctance to use Federal Rule 56 (on Summary Judgment), which may be partly explicable by their deference to the jury.[58] Clearly, if judges really believe that a jury is *entitled* to set the rules of law at naught, summary procedures deny the litigant the right to test the willingness of a jury to exercise that right in his favour. The logical conclusion of this would be to refuse the use of summary procedures altogether, but American jurisdictions do not go that far.

In one important area, indeed, summary proceedings are extensively used in America, and in this area, their summariness exceeds that of any comparable English proceedings. This is the American summary ejectment procedure, which developed in response to the demand for a

[53] See for federal practice C. A. Wright, *Law of Federal Courts*, 432 (4th edn., West, St. Paul, 1983).

[54] *Weather-Rite Sportswear Co.* v. *United States*, 298 F. Supp. 510 (Cust. Ct. 1969).

[55] Fed. R. Civ. P. 56.

[56] C. Wright, *supra*, n. 53, at 665.

[57] *Ibid.*, at 665; Forkosch, 'Summary Judgment in Automobile Negligence Cases: A Procedural Analysis and Suggestions', 53 *Cornell L. Rev.* 814, 815 (1968).

[58] Jerome Frank was noted as one such judge, see, e.g., *Arnstein* v. *Poerter* 154 F. 2d 464 (2d Cir., 1946), noted 55 *Yale LJ* 810 (1946).

more effective alternative to slow and expensive ejectment suits.[59] The result, achieved by limiting remedies and defences available, has been characterized as a judicial 'mill'.[60] As one writer has put it:

There is nothing quite so depressing for one's sense of the majesty of the law than to sit through a morning session of an American metropolitan landlord–tenant court and watch the judge issue seventy-five judgments in as many minutes. Summonses for summary proceedings are generally returnable within a week or ten days. The defenses which may be raised in the proceedings are frequently limited to a denial that rent is owing, and frequently no set-offs or counterclaims are allowed.[61]

Under such procedures a landlord may be able to secure eviction of a tenant in little more than two weeks from filing a complaint.[62] Such extreme remedies may well sacrifice truth formality for the sake of efficiency, but in any event they seem very untypical of American legal procedures taken as a whole. Lengthy delay, not excessive speed, is the norm in American litigation.

Indeed, a few American lawyers seem almost to have perfected the art of delay in civil litigation. It is not uncommon for civil cases to take years before a matter is finally resolved. Before trial even begins, there is a vast array of delaying devices available to the American lawyer, perhaps the most effective of which are the discovery rules.[63] Through discovery (which bears little resemblance to its English equivalent), the parties in a civil suit narrow the issues before trial, gather important evidentiary material for use at trial, and learn of the opposition's evidence which may later be used at trial.[64] The purpose underlying the American discovery rules is to allow broad inquiry into the opposing party's evidence and theories, comporting generally with the policy behind liberal notice pleading. As the Supreme Court has noted, '[The rules of discovery] together with pretrial procedures make a trial less a game of blindman's buff [*sic*] and more a fair contest with the basic issues and facts disclosed to the fullest practicable extent.'[65] The rules

[59] See generally Donahue, 'Change in the American Law of Landlord and Tenant', 37 *Mod. L. Rev.* 242 (1974).

[60] Gibbons, 'Residential Landlord-Tenant Law: A Survey of Modern Problems with Reference to the Proposed Model Code', 21 *Hast. L. J.* 369, 372 (1970).

[61] Donahue, *supra*, n. 59, at 244–5.

[62] C. Donahue, T. Kauper, and P. Martin, *Cases and Materials on Property*, 856 (2nd edn., West, St. Paul, 1983).

[63] For comparison of American and English discovery rules, see generally Levine, *supra*, 167 n. 24; Epstein, English and American Discovery: A Comparative View', 7 *National LJ* 15 (26 Nov. 1984); Note, 'Discovery in Great Britain: The Evidence (Proceedings in Other Jurisdictions) Act', 11 *Cornell Inter. LJ* 323 (1978).

[64] C. A. Wright and A. R. Miller, 8 *Federal Practice and Procedure*, §§ 2001 (West, St. Paul, 1970).

[65] *United States* v. *Procter & Gamble Co.* 356 US 677, 682 (1958).

have, however, facilitated abuse by delay both in the discovery process and in avoidance of discovery.[66]

A party in a civil suit may take depositions of potential witnesses and parties,[67] serve written interrogatories on opposing parties,[68] request the production or inspection of documents,[69] or in some cases move the court to order physical examinations.[70] Complex litigation gives rise to the most widespread use of discovery for purposes of delay.[71] Judge Becker has lamented:

With the advent of automatic typewriters, and availability of verbose lengthy forms of written interrogatories and of descriptions of documents, there has arisen a substantial abuse of discovery by submission of voluminous, unnecessary, and undesirable written interrogatories and requests for production of documents addressed to an adverse party.[72]

To compound the difficulties, parties are generally unwilling to disclose damaging evidence easily, and thus the most important documents sought to be discovered may be hidden amidst thousands of irrelevant documents, requiring a long and thorough search through the submitted materials.

The Federal Rules of Civil Procedure also specifically declare that it is no ground for objection that the information sought will be inadmissible at trial if the information appears reasonably calculated to lead to the discovery of admissible evidence,[73] thus inviting practices that would be condemned in England as 'fishing expeditions'.[74] Discovery has, not surprisingly, been one of the primary targets of the current procedure reform movement in America. The 1983 amendments to the Federal Rules were explicitly designed to prevent discovery being used to coerce litigants, and to enable sanctions to be imposed on attornies who abuse the rules.[75] Even so, three Supreme Court judges thought the amendments did not go far enough.[76]

---

[66] See generally Sherman and Kinnard, 'Federal Court Discovery in the 80's: Making the Rules Work', 95 FRD 245 (1982).

[67] Fed. R. Civ. P. 30 (*a*), 31.

[68] Fed. R. Civ. P. 33.

[69] Fed. R. Civ. P. 34.

[70] Fed. R. Civ. P. 35.

[71] See Levy, 'Discovery: Use, Abuse, Myth and Reality', 17 *Forum* (ABA) 465, 468 (1981) for a list of common discovery abuses. For discussion of some of the causes of such abuse, see generally Shapiro, 'Some Problems of Discovery in an Adversary System', 63 *Minn. L. Rev.* 1055 (1979); Note, 'Discovery Abuse under the Federal Rules: Causes and Cures', 92 *Yale LJ* 352 (1982).

[72] Becker, 'Modern Discovery', 78 FRD 267, 277 (1978).

[73] Fed. R. Civ. P. 26 (*b*) (1).

[74] Epstein, *supra*, n. 63, at 15.

[75] See the Advisory Committee Note to the 1983 amendments, *supra*, n. 33, at 218, 220.

[76] 446 US 997 (1980) (Powell, Stewart, and Rehnquist, dissenting).

Besides discovery, American lawyers have other means to delay the adjudicative process. Delay has become so commonplace in America that in many places it is frequently taken to be a matter of professional discourtesy to refuse an opponent's request for a continuance (*anglice*, adjournment). Once the pleadings are submitted to the court it may be asked to rule on a variety of motions, including a motion to dismiss for either lack of jurisdiction or failure to state a claim. Assuming the plaintiff survives these motions, and the matter is finally tried, either party may request the judge to stay the judgment, or to refuse to render judgment after the verdict, for an intrinsic matter appearing in the record which would render the judgment, if given, erroneous or reversible. Thus many matters which would in England be grounds for appeal only, can in American procedure, be raised, first by way of motion before the trial judge after the jury's verdict, and then again, by way of appeal afterwards. And once judgment is given, that is only the beginning of a new process—but we will defer until the next section consideration of questions relating to the finality of judgments.

In English legal procedure, by comparison, the combined result of the differing practices as to costs and interest and the use of summary procedures undoubtedly makes it generally impossible or at least unattractive for a plaintiff to launch wild or speculative litigation, or for a defendant to indulge in delaying tactics. No doubt defendants do still sometimes indulge in delaying tactics even in England, but a defendant will often find it cheaper to borrow money to pay a claim at the outset, rather than to run the risk of a heavy bill for costs and interest at the end of the day. All this tends to give real teeth to rules of substantive liability, as well as rules of procedure. As we have reiterated, English judges are insistent and emphatic in their belief that the law must be complied with and, if necessary, enforced.

As compared with England, American legal processes seem to be based more on an 'open courthouse' philosophy, which encourages parties who can afford it to come to court—or to defend suits brought against them—even though their claims or defences may be rather unfounded.[77] There is a real ideological basis to this concept of the 'open courthouse', which is partly compounded of faith in the jury system (thus no claim or defence should be said to be ill founded until a jury so pronounces it), and also partly of a democratic desire to see, through the contingent fee and legal aid, that the poor have access to litigation—or the right to defend a lawsuit—as much as the rich. But laudable as these ideals may be, to the English observer, American law has, until quite

---

[77] M. Rosenberg, 'Contemporary Litigation in the United States', in *Legal Institutions Today: English and American Approaches Compared*, 152, 163 (H. W. Jones, ed., American Bar Association, 1977).

recently, seemed to tolerate abuse of litigation tactics by both plaintiffs and defendants. While the recent amendments of the Federal Rules give the judges the power to control some abuses, it is still doubtful whether they will dramatically change the way American lawyers conduct lawsuits. The following extract from a Note published some 30 years ago paints a picture which still accords with general impressions today, though systematic evidence is not easy to come by:

Despite centuries of exasperation and ever-increasing calendar congestion, the courts still find themselves beset by the nagging problem of the bad-faith litigant. Strike suits and spite suits, harassment with multiple actions, baseless petitions for injunctions brought against business competitors, small claims brought in courts of superior jurisdiction—these are but some of the tactics devised by parties plaintiff for purposes of vexation. As for defendants, there is the credit man's bête noir, the debtor who withholds payments until threatened with suit and then proposes settlement for 85% or less, blandly pointing out that litigation is bound to cost the creditor at least as much as the discount thus extorted [Citation omitted]. Likewise, some corporations, especially common carriers, withhold payment of small claims in the hope that the claimant will drop the matter entirely rather than go to the trouble and expense of a lawsuit.

Finally, there are those who, whether plaintiff or defendant, systematically badger their adversaries by the sedulous perversion of procedural devices. Harassed by a barrage of sham pleadings, frivolous demurrers, refusals to answer interrogatories, sham affidavits, constant requests for continuances and dilatory or otherwise frivolous appeals a litigant with a bona fide claim or defence may well wish that he had never asserted it in the first place. If he does dig in and stubbornly fight it out, the chances are that even though he emerges victorious, he will carry away with him an undying contempt for the law and its practitioners.[78]

It may be that the recent American reforms referred to above will gradually bring some of the worst excesses under control, and there are also other means of deterring some of these abuses (such as increasing

---

[78] Note, 53 *Col. L. Rev.* 78 (1953). Many instances could be cited of the exploitation of the law's potentiality for delay. See, for one example, K. M. Dolbeare, *Trial Courts in Urban Politics*, at 7 (Wiley & Sons, NY, 1967), discussing a case 'in which a single individual, supported by a local citizens' association, managed to delay for a fifth year the construction of a multi-million dollar incinerator by a government representing over a quarter of a million people...by means of adroit use of litigation...and there was no assurance that another five years of delay might not be in the offing'. Although the exploitation of litigation for the purposes of delay is not unknown in England, we do not believe that delays of this magnitude (or anything approaching it) could in practice be achieved. See also D. M. Provine, *Case Selection in the United States Supreme Court*, at 20 (U. of Chicago Press, Chicago, 1980) noting a memo sent by Frankfurter J. to his fellow justices in 1951 protesting at the use of a *certiorari* petition as an 'easy instrument for the purposes of delay', and suggesting the use of some fee (costs) sanctions.

recognition that bad faith litigation is itself a tort,[79] and greater willingness to award punitive damages against insurers for vexatious refusal to settle claims[80]). But there are also still plenty of signs that the picture painted by the above Note is far from obsolete. Naturally, procedural abuses and the failure to sanction harassing or dilatory tactics affect the credibility of legal rules and lead to a low level of what we have called 'enforcement formality'. As the late Arthur Leff once put it, 'Under the American law of contracts, after the other party has fully performed his obligations, it is absolutely irrational for you to fully perform yours.'[81] The thought behind this, as the above cited Note suggests, is that it is almost always cheaper for the other party to accept some lesser performance of what he is owed than for him to incur the costs of suing to enforce full performance. Leff's point may be an exaggeration, because (as indeed he concedes) it overlooks extra-curial sanctions for non-performance of a contractual duty, and the rational desire of one party to maintain a working contractual relation with the other, not to mention the desire to avoid being blacklisted by credit agencies or commercial directories. But such motivations do not by any means always operate, and even when they do, they do not necessarily restore the credibility of the rules as *legal* rules.

By contrast English lawyers generally believe that most litigation is the result of uncertainty either in the facts or in the legal rules. When the facts are not disputed, or are reasonably clear and easily proved, and when the law is also clear, the parties to a dispute are likely to receive advice from their lawyers which puts heavy pressure on the party believed to have the weaker case to settle out of court or to abandon his claim. And such settlements will strongly tend to track the rights of the parties.

In this connection it is worth adding a word about the position of the English barrister, which differs significantly from that of an American attorney because of the division of the English legal profession into two distinct sections.[82] This division means that it is only the solicitor who normally has continuous and perhaps long-standing contact with his client, from whom further work may be expected in the future. Lawyers

---

[79] Thus most American states now treat bad faith litigation as tortious, even in the absence of proof of special damage (contrary to the English rule, which assumes that recovery of costs is an adequate compensation for the successful litigant); see Restatement of Torts (Second) §§ 674, 681 (*b*), and (by way of illustration) *O'Toole* v. *Franklin* 279 Or. 513, 569 P. 2d 561 (1977).

[80] Couch on *Insurance*, § 58: 1 (2nd rev. edn., Lawyers Co-op, Rochester, 1983); R. E. Keeton, *Insurance Law*, 508–21 (West, St. Paul, 1971).

[81] 'Injury, Ignorance and Spite: The Dynamics of Coercive Collection', 80 *Yale LJ* 1, 5 (1970).

[82] See *post*, p. 360, for further discussion of the role of the English barrister.

who deal thus with clients are likely to associate themselves readily with their clients' interests, and indeed may do so to such a degree that they become unable to proffer truly disinterested advice about the likely outcome of possible litigation. The English barrister whose opinion is sought on a possible claim or defence arising out of some dispute is not in the same position. He will usually have seen nothing of the parties before, and cannot assume that he will have the conduct of the litigation if he advises that it should be undertaken. He is in an altogether more detached position, and the tradition of the English bar requires him to try to preserve this detachment. Hence an English barrister feels no qualms about advising that a claim which his client wishes to pursue is likely to prove hopeless, or that there is no serious defence to an action being brought against his client, who should accordingly accept liability or try to settle for as low a figure as possible, or that there are no grounds for appeal against a judgment already rendered.[83] In short, the detached position of the English barrister assists in maintaining high levels of enforcement formality, not only in court, but also out of court.

We conclude, then, that law in books in England does indeed translate more often and more speedily into law in action than is true in America. The speed and efficiency of the English judicial process generally exceeds that of the American, a factor that would also indicate that settlements in England probably approximate the legal rights of the parties more closely.

4. THE FINALITY AND ENFORCEMENT OF JUDGMENTS

Another piece of this intricate mosaic concerns the finality of judgments. When a matter has finally been fully investigated by duly established courts, and when a decision has finally been given by judge or jury, the more formal approach of English lawyers leads to the view that the issue should now be regarded as finally settled, subject only to the possibility of appeals, and perhaps other very rare cases in which judgments can be set aside for fraud or on some other similar ground. But apart from these possibilities, the English view is that final judicial decisions should be promptly entered as judgments and then promptly enforced by appropriate means. This is what we call high enforcement formality. Furthermore, English appeal courts today are very reluctant to order new trials because of the costs and delays involved, and, wherever possible, they prefer to enter a final judgment themselves, even where this involves some variation of the original judgment. American appellate courts, by contrast, often order retrials, especially where the original trial was by

[83] See, e.g., Mr Peter (now Mr Justice) Webster, 'The Bar of England and Wales: Past, Present and Future', in *Legal Institutions Today, supra*, n. 77, 84 at 97–8.

jury, because in such a case the appeal court may not be entitled to enter a final judgment on its own. Even in non-jury cases, American appeal courts sometimes remand cases to the trial judge several times[84]—something which would never happen in England today.

There are very few cases in which an English trial judge has power to alter a judgment already entered. A clerical mistake such as an accidental slip or omission may be corrected at any time under what is known as 'the slip rule',[85] and default judgments too can be set aside fairly easily,[86] but other challenges to a judgment must generally be made by way of appeal.[87] Furthermore, as we have already noted, the rules under which new evidence can be admitted on appeal (or a case sent back for retrial in the light of new evidence) are very strictly applied by English courts.[88]

In America, a judge has similar powers to correct clerical errors, and to set aside default judgments.[89] But he also has power to vacate or alter a judgment entered with prejudicial error in the record, obtained by fraud, unconscionable conduct, or in the event of newly discovered evidence.[90] The result is that motions for a new trial or for judgment *non obstante veredicto* are everyday matters at the conclusion of an American trial.[91] They are, today, almost unknown in England, having been largely replaced by appeal procedures. And though appeals can be sought for dilatory purposes in England, no less than America, counsel have to draft and sign a notice of appeal which sets out some arguable grounds of appeal; and that, according to the traditions of the English bar, is not a formality.[92] The Federal Rules of Civil Procedure impose no comparable

---

[84] Thus Judge Posner protests at the readiness of American federal appeals courts to remand cases time and again to the trial court: *supra*, n. 39, at 244.

[85] See Rules of the Supreme Court, Order 20, rule 11, *Supreme Court Practice 1985*, 351.

[86] But even a default judgment will only be set aside if there is some irregularity or alternatively if some defence on the merits can be shown. See notes to Rules of the Supreme Court, Order 13, rule 9 in the *Supreme Court Practice 1985*, 127.

[87] See, e.g., *de Lasala* v. *de Lasala* [1980] AC 546 (even consent orders can only be set aside for mistake or fraud by way of appeal or fresh action, and not by way of motion).

[88] *Supra*, at 168.

[89] See generally M. D. Green, *Basic Civil Procedure*, 224–7 (Foundation Press, Mineola, NY, 1979). As in England, some defence on the merits has to be shown: C. A. Wright, *supra*, n. 53, at 661.

[90] See M. D. Green, *supra*, n. 89, at 224–5.

[91] Denial of such motions cannot themselves be appealed against but appeal may of course lie against the judgment when entered. Thus such motions add an additional (and it might be thought wholly unnecessary) level of procedure, unknown in England. See C. A. Wright, *supra*, n. 53, at 636–7.

[92] Indeed, in criminal cases the courts specifically require that counsel should not draft grounds of appeal unless 'he considers that the proposed appeal is properly arguable'. Practice Note, [1980] 1 All ER 555. It should be stressed that such directions are expected to be observed in England, and that a barrister who disregarded them might well be charged with a disciplinary offence.

requirement on attorneys filing notices of appeal.[93] In any event, the more open nature of the American legal system, and the greater uncertainty that results from its more substantive orientation, make it far easier to find an arguable point or arguable ground of appeal in America.

Moreover, a motion after trial and before judgment is more dilatory than an appeal, because such a motion delays the actual entry of judgment by the trial court, while an appeal does not automatically stay the effect of the trial court's judgment.[94] In England, a stay must be applied for, and is by no means automatically granted,[95] especially where the application is thought to be a purely dilatory tactic. In some cases, however, a stay is necessary almost as a matter of course, if the appeal is to serve any useful purpose at all, for example, where the owner of a house obtains a possession order against a tenant whose lease has expired, or who is claimed to be in breach of his lease for some reason. Even in England, therefore, an appeal has been regarded in such cases as a simple way of postponing the effect of the trial court's judgment, although at the price of extra costs in the end. But it is symptomatic of the English approach to such questions that the Court of Appeal now provides expedited hearing dates for appeals in such cases where delay seems to be the main object of the appeal.[96]

American courts are also, in theory at least, anxious to avoid granting a stay of execution purely as a dilatory tactic. Thus a stay pending a post-judgment motion before the trial court is discretionary and is rarely granted.[97] But pending the outcome of an appeal, a defendant can get an automatic stay, under the Federal Rules of Procedure, by posting a bond as security for ultimate payment.[98] English procedure seems a little more stringent, though in practice the plaintiff would probably agree to accept an adequate bond if offered.

Another difference between English and American appellate practice is that in American courts there is often a prescribed period between the date when the court's decision is handed down and the earliest date at which judgment can be entered; and during this period, it is not uncommon for the losing party to petition the court for a

[93] See Fed. R. App. 3(*a*) and (*c*). But the appellant may be required to post a bond. Fed. R. App. P. 7.

[94] See Rules of the Supreme Court, Order 59, rule 13 and notes thereto in the *Supreme Court Practice 1985*, 842–4.

[95] Thus even an order for payment of damages must normally be complied with pending appeal, unless there is a real risk that the money may be irrecoverable if the defendant wins the appeal. *Ibid.*

[96] See the statement of Sir John Donaldson, Master of the Rolls, reported in *The Times*, 5 Oct. 1983, p. 10.

[97] See C. A. Wright and A. R. Miller, *supra*, n. 64, vol. 11, § 2904, esp. at p. 316.

[98] *Ibid.*, at § 2905, p. 326.

rehearing. Such a petition is in effect just an invitation to the court to change its mind, and would be unthinkable in England. It is true that, even in America, such petitions are rarely granted, and they often seem to be presented to let off steam, rather than with serious hope of success. But successful petitions are by no means unknown.[99] In England judgments are expected to be entered as soon as possible after a decision has been rendered, often in a few days, and the judges have recently taken steps to minimize delay at this stage.[100] Petitions for rehearing are completely unknown.

Of course the classic doctrine dealing with finality in the law is the doctrine of *res judicata*. Once a final judgment has been entered and appeals disposed of, the matter is regarded as having been finally and immutably determined by that judgment, at least between the parties to it and their successors.[101] This is a highly formal legal doctrine in our sense; if the doctrine applies, the rights and duties of any parties bound by it are regulated by the judgment, however wrong or unjust the judgment may have been. There is no room for going behind the judgment, for looking at the underlying reasons of substance for the judgment, or anything of that kind. Of course, both in England and in the United States the doctrine of *res judicata* is recognized by all courts. But there may well be differences in the degree to which this doctrine is today applied in the two countries. In England, the doctrine is still adhered to very firmly, and its scope has recently been extended.[102] Lord Wilberforce in a recent decision has re-emphasized the values of finality in civil proceedings as follows:[103]

English law, and it is safe to say, all comparable legal systems, place high in the category of essential principles that which requires that limits be placed upon the

[99] Even the Supreme Court of the US has occasionally granted a rehearing and there are at least some instances of reversal on rehearing: D. Karlen, *Appellate Courts in the United States and England*, 76–8 (New York U. Press, NY, 1963). There have also been some spectacular changes of mind by the California Supreme Court, see, e.g., *People* v. *Tanner* 596 P. 2d 328 (1979); *Cooper* v. *Bray* 582 P. 2d 604 (1978) (which involved *two* changes of mind); *American Bank & Trust Co.* v. *Community Hospital* 683 P. 2d. 670 (1984) (constitutionality of an important Act sustained after first being struck down). In *McCrae* v. *Wainwright*, 422 So. 2d 824 (1982) the Supreme Court of Florida, by a 4:3 majority, first set aside a death sentence and later (after the state Governor had publicly criticised the decision) reinstated it.

[100] See 124 *Solicitors Journal* 432 (1980).

[101] See Restatement (Second) of Judgments § 17, whose rule is stated in a form which is probably applicable in both countries.

[102] See, e.g., *Ampthill Peerage Case* [1977] AC 547 (legitimacy declaration final even though changes in law would have rendered new evidence admissible, and possible blood tests could have settled doubts conclusively); *Hunter* v. *Chief Constable of West Midlands* [1982] AC 529 (civil action may not be used as collateral attack on final decision of criminal court even of side issues, namely, whether confessions extracted by police by improper means.)

[103] *Ampthill Peerage Case* [1977] AC at 569.

right of citizens to open or reopen disputes...Any determination of disputable fact may, the law recognises, be imperfect: the law aims at providing the best and safest solution compatible with human fallibility and having reached that solution it closes the book. The law knows, and we all know, that sometimes fresh material may be found, which perhaps might lead to a different result, but, in the interests of peace, certainty and security it prevents further inquiry. It is said that in doing this, the law is preferring justice to truth. That may be so: these values cannot always coincide. The law does its best to reduce the gap. But there are cases where the certainty of justice prevails over the possibility of truth...and there are cases where the law insists on finality. For a policy of closure to be compatible with justice, it must be attended with safeguards; so the law allows appeals: so the law, exceptionally, allows appeals out of time: so the law still more exceptionally allows judgments to be attacked on the ground of fraud: so limitation periods may, exceptionally, be extended. But these are exceptions to a general rule of high public importance, and as all the cases show, they are reserved for rare and limited cases, where the facts justifying them can be strictly proved.

The doctrine of *res judicata* is, of course, adhered to in general terms by all American courts, as well as English courts, and in some respects there has actually been a tightening up of the American doctrine in recent years.[104] It is true that occasionally American judges have protested against allowing a judgment to stand as a final determination of issues on the grounds of 'simple justice'[105] (that is, substantive justice), though the more formal approach was firmly restated by the United States Supreme Court in an opinion of Rehnquist J. in 1981.[106] But there are nonetheless more exceptions recognized to the doctrine in American practice, for example,[107] where there was no opportunity for appellate review of the original decision, or where the issue was one of law and there has been a change in the legal context,[108] or where a new determination of the issues is justified by differences in the quality or extensiveness of the procedure followed in the two courts. None of these would be allowed to overcome the effect of *res judicata* in England.[109]

In some areas there also seems to have been some relaxation in America of the central rules relating to *res judicata*, although this proposition needs to be taken with some caution for present purposes. Certainly it has been said that there has recently been a remarkable

---

[104] C. A. Wright, *supra*, n. 53, at 679.
[105] *Ibid.*
[106] *Federated Dept. Stores Inc.* v. *Moitie* 452 US 394 (1981).
[107] See C. A. Wright, *supra*, n. 53, at 683.
[108] This was specifically rejected in the *Ampthill Peerage case*, *supra*, n. 103.
[109] Thus there is no hint of any such exceptions to the *res judicata* doctrine in the discussion of exceptions in Halsbury, *Laws of England*, vol. 16, paras. 1552–64 (4th edn., Butterworths, London, 1976).

transformation in the doctrine in the United States.[110] Instead of consisting of a series of specific and mandatory rules, which were clearly rules of law, they now seem to consist of a series of guidelines which leave considerable room for discretion.[111] At first sight this looks like further clear support for our main thesis: firm rules of law in America are giving way to discretionary guidelines which enable the courts to look behind the rules for reasons and underlying policies; in England, by contrast, there is no sign of any such change. But this American development needs to be carefully interpreted before it can be clearly said to constitute support for our thesis. It may simply be that what has happened in the United States is that the doctrine of *res judicata* is now being applied to a much wider range of circumstances than it was formerly, and once the courts expand the scope of the doctrine, for instance to hold non-parties bound by a previous decision, some fluidity and flexibility may well be essential. It is not clear whether this involves a spillover effect, weakening the doctrine at its core and replacing firm rule by discretionary guidelines even in those central cases. It would certainly not be surprising if this did happen, because there seems no doubt that, in related fields, American law is more flexible and fluid than English law.

One of those related fields concerns the impeachability of jury verdicts for irregularity. In general the courts of both countries share a desire to avoid hearing evidence of what went on in the jury room, even where evidence is available suggesting that some irregularities have occurred there.[112] But English courts seem more inclined to apply this rule absolutely than American courts. For example, in *R.* v. *Thompson*[113] the Court of Appeal refused to admit evidence showing that the jury had agreed on an acquittal until the foreman of the jury had produced a list of the accused's previous convictions in the jury room. In the very similar American federal case of *US* v. *Howard*[114] a different result was arrived at.

One other recent development in American law needs to be noted here. Since the decision of the Third Circuit Court of Appeals in *Finsberg* v. *Sullivan*[115] it has been increasingly held that constitutional

---

[110] See Holland, 'Modernizing Res Judicata: Reflections on the Parklane Doctrine', 55 *Ind. LJ* 615 (1980); and C. A. Wright and A. R. Miller, *supra*, n. 64, vol. 5, §§ 4401 and 4403.

[111] See Holland, *supra*, n. 110, at 616–17.

[112] As to England, see *Boston* v. *W. S. Bagshaw & Sons* [1967] 2 All ER 87; as to America, see Federal Rules of Evidence, Rule 606 (*b*), and C. A. Wright and A. R. Miller, *supra*, n. 64, vol. 5 at 264–72.

[113] [1962] 1 All ER 65; see also *Ellis* v. *Deheer* [1922] 2 KB 113; *Nanan* v. *The State* [1986] 3 All ER 248.

[114] 506 F. 2d 865, 868 (1975).

[115] 634 F. 2d 50 (1980).

requirements of due process may in certain circumstances impose requirements for some kind of a hearing before judgments can be enforced. Thus, if a creditor obtains a judgment for money damages, and attempts to garnish money due to the judgment debtor, the debtor is entitled to a 'hearing' in order (for example) to show that the debt due to him was not garnishable by law. The precise extent to which the courts may take this new doctrine have still to be worked out, but it will be seen how this opens the door to yet one more delaying tactic which can weaken the force of a court judgment. And although this may not, in a technical sense, affect the doctrine of *res judicata*, it clearly involves potentially weakening the formal status of the finality of judgments. If, at the subsequent enforcement stage, courts are going to start reopening issues thought to be closed by the judgment, then they will be treating the judgment as a more substantive and less formal reason for decision.

We proceed to add a few comments on some other differences between England and America with respect to the enforcement of civil judgments. In both countries, the enforcement of civil judgments is the responsibility of the winning party: it is up to him to take the necessary legal steps, such as trying to attach the defendant's property or garnish debts due to him, to obtain actual payment of a money judgment. There is no doubt that in both countries a debtor who wishes to evade payment of a judgment debt can give the creditor a good deal of additional trouble at this stage of the proceedings; though the fact that in England the debtor will have to pay the costs of enforcement of the judgment against him is still a deterrent against frivolous and vexatious dilatoriness.

But there are a number of peculiarities about the position in America which can make the enforcement of judgments even more troublesome than it is in England. First, the federal system means that the defendant may simply move himself and his assets to another state, in which case the creditor may have to bring a second action in the second state before he can enforce the judgment he has already obtained. While the second state is generally bound to enforce the out-of-state judgment,[116] the defendant may attack it by challenging the competency of the first court, for example on the ground that it did not have personal jurisdiction over the defendant.[117] Because England is a unitary jurisdiction there are, of course, no exactly comparable problems, though there can be difficulties in enforcing judgments obtained in other countries. But legislation is

---

[116] US Const. art. IV, § 1, cl. 1.

[117] See R. H. Field, B. Kaplan and K. M. Clermont, *Materials for a Basic Course in Civil Procedure*, at 796–7 (Foundation Press, Mineola, NY, 1978). The Supreme Court of Colorado has gone so far as to hold that a judgment enforcing a contract contrary to public policy is subject to collateral attack: *People ex. rel. Arkansas Valley Sugar Beet & Irrigated Land Co.* v. *Burke* 72 Colo. 486, 212 P. 2d 837 (1923).

currently making it easier to enforce judgments of courts in other EEC countries, in order to restrict the defences which may be raised against such judgments.[118]

Further differences between England and America concern the assets a creditor may levy execution upon in order to enforce his judgment. All states exempt from execution assets that they consider to be essential for the maintenance of the debtor and his family. Exempted items often include one house,[119] one car,[120] and farm equipment,[121] besides less controversial items like clothing. Some states have very generous exemptions for particular items, for instance Illinois has a life insurance exemption without limit.[122] By English standards these exemptions are generous indeed. In England the corresponding exemptions from seizure are limited to the clothing and bedding of the debtor and his family, to a value not exceeding £100—about $160[123] (in 1987).

Taken individually, many of these American doctrines or decisions may seem perfectly justifiable and not to require any theoretical explanation. But taken altogether, it seems to us clear that the effect is to weaken the credibility of rules of liability, and that this both stems from and leads to the erosion of the formal status of rules of law as conclusive reasons for decisions. When legal procedures can be drawn out, seemingly for years, when cases, and even interim decisions, can be taken to appeal, or subjected to collateral attack time after time, when lower court orders are routinely suspended pending appeal, when even the enforcement of a judgment may entail further 'due process' requirements, when the finality of a judgment can be challenged by erosion of the doctrine of *res judicata*, the threat of legal liability must surely be seriously weakened, and the very reality of the rules on which those threats are based may come to seem questionable. Legal *liability*, of course, is not destroyed by these practices. Defendants are still regularly held liable and compelled to pay damages in the United States. But the mandatory formality of legal *rules* of liability is certainly not as

---

[118] See Civil Jurisdiction and Judgments Act 1982.

[119] See, e.g., Ill. Rev. Stat. ch. 52, § 1–12 (West, St. Paul, 1975); ($10,000 value limit); Tex. Prop. Code Ann. § 41.001 (Vernon, West, St. Paul, 1984) (no dollar limit, but only one acre per family if city, town, or village land, or 200 acres per family if rural land).

[120] See, e.g., Ohio Rev. Code s. 2329.66A(A) (2) (Page Supp., Anderson, Cincinnati, 1986) ($1,000 value limit).

[121] See, e.g., Tex. Prop. Code Ann. vol. 2, § 42.002(3)(A).

[122] Insurance Code of 1937, 238, Ill. Rev. stat. ch. 73, 850 (West, St. Paul, 1975).

[123] See Protection from Execution (Prescribed Value) Order 1980 made under the Administration of Justice Act 1956, s. 37. Different provisions apply to the value of goods which a *bankrupt* debtor may retain. See Insolvency Act 1985, s. 130 (only items 'necessary for satisfying the basic domestic needs' of the bankrupt and his family exempt from bankruptcy).

high in the American legal system. And the overall result is a rather lower level of 'enforcement formality'.

5. FINALITY IN CRIMINAL PROCEDURE

One further serious example of the erosion of the finality of judicial decisions in the United States, and therefore of enforcement formality, deserves discussion on its own, partly because of its inherent importance, but partly also because in this instance a clear contrast with the practice and even values of English judges can be demonstrated from the case-law.

As is well known to American lawyers, the combined availability of appeals and habeas corpus procedure or similar means of collaterally attacking criminal convictions in state and federal courts makes it possible to return to the courts time after time, often for years, after an initial trial and determination of guilt.[124] It is entirely possible for a defendant convicted in a state court to have his case reheard on the merits, or on the request for a rehearing, numerous times before his conviction is final. A state prisoner, for example, may petition the trial court for a new trial, take an appeal as of right to the state's intermediate appellate court, and, if unsuccessful there, can still appeal to the state court of last resort. If defeated there, he can petition the United States Supreme Court for *certiorari* review—that is (in English terms) for leave to appeal from the state court of last resort to the United States Supreme Court. If *certiorari* is denied, the prisoner can then 'collaterally attack' his conviction by the writ of habeas corpus, claiming that his constitutional rights were violated in some way by the state court conviction. He can pursue this collateral attack through the state appellate courts in the usual way. Having exhausted his opportunities for direct and collateral attack in the state courts, the prisoner can then petition for habeas corpus review in the federal district court, claiming again that his conviction was unconstitutional, usually on grounds of lack of due process. As with the state collateral remedies, the prisoner can appeal from a federal district court denial of relief, first to the United States Court of Appeals, and then (if *certiorari* is granted) to the United States Supreme Court. By the end of the process (which can be repeated partially for different issues) the prisoner might have presented his case for review on ten different occasions. In addition to the habeas corpus procedure, convicted criminal defendants can sometimes employ other post-conviction procedures to delay the taking effect of the sentence. For example, in *Ostrer* v. *United States*[125] a convicted defendant used two

---

[124] See generally, W. LaFave and J. Israel, *supra*, n. 1, at 3, §§ 27. 1–27. 11.
[125] 584 F. 2d 594 (2d Cir., 1978).

trial motions, appeals, bail requests, and habeas corpus petitions to delay his incarceration for five years after his conviction.

Although the availability of these post-conviction remedies clearly reduces the finality of criminal determinations of guilt in the United States, two countervailing considerations merit attention. First, recent Supreme Court decisions have somewhat curtailed the availability of federal habeas corpus review of state court decisions, when the defendant fails to raise his claim at trial, or the state provides the prisoner with a full and fair opportunity to argue the constitutional claim.[126] However, this attempt to shut the door against frivolous habeas corpus applications has not been very successful, because if the accused's attorney has failed to raise the point in time in the state courts, it may now be argued that the accused has not had the 'effective representation' of counsel to which he is constitutionally entitled.[127]

Secondly, there is one respect in which the lack of finality may actually enhance the determinacy of American law, and therefore may in the long run tend to make the formal criminal law more effective. The availability of federal habeas corpus review allows federal supervision of state court treatment of constitutional matters. This promotes both uniform interpretation of constitutional rights and compliance with those rights. A threat of reversal on federal habeas corpus review undoubtedly prompts state court judges to heed the dictates of the Supreme Court's interpretation of the Constitution.

The whole concept of collateral attack is utterly alien to English lawyers, and indeed seems to them to be subversive of the authority of judicial decisions. An English lawyer regards an appeal as the proper way to attack a criminal conviction (or indeed any other judicial determination), and if appeals have failed, or not been pursued, the decision is, and should be treated as, final. Only in the very special case of fraud can a judgment be attacked collaterally in English law, and such cases are almost unknown in modern times. Furthermore, because a judgment is treated as a formal reason for decision, and it is not possible to go behind it, it is impossible to use the writ of habeas corpus to challenge a criminal conviction in English law. If a writ of habeas corpus were issued to the prison governor (as the person detaining the prisoner), the governor would simply respond to the writ by producing to the court a certified copy of the order of the trial court sentencing the prisoner to jail. That would demonstrate that the prisoner was being lawfully held, and there

---

[126] See, e.g., *Wainwright* v. *Sykes*, 453 US 72 (1977); *Stone* v. *Powell*, 428 US 465 (1976).

[127] See *Evitts and Armstrong* v. *Lucey* 469 US 387 (1985).

would be nothing further that the court could do on the hearing of the writ of habeas corpus.[128]

Because England has no written constitution of the American kind, English courts have never had themselves to address the question whether collateral attack ought to be permitted in the American style as a way of vindicating constitutional rights. But a very striking rejection of the American view is to be found in a recent Privy Council appeal from Trinidad and Tobago which does have a written constitution incorporating, *inter alia*, a guarantee against deprivation of liberty without 'due process of law'. In *Chokolingo* v. *Attorney General of Trinidad and Tobago*[129] it was held that a person duly convicted by a court of competent jurisdiction could not attack his conviction collaterally on the ground that he had been deprived of his liberty without due process of law. The English (and Scots) law lords, sitting in the Privy Council, denounced the idea of collateral attack as 'quite irrational and subversive of the rule of law'.[130] A person who had been properly tried (and this had to be assumed in the absence of a successful appeal) had been convicted by 'due process of law' and that was the end of the matter.

This is an apt illustration of the more formal treatment of judgments by English judges, as compared with American judges. The judgment of a competent court becomes, to an English lawyer, a conclusive determination. In some cases, the American judge, by contrast, seems to see the search for real, substantive justice, even in the individual case, as (almost) one without end. Justice is not what a particular court has decided—for its decision may be wrong and unjust; even the failure to appeal does not prove that the original decision was right and just. Injustice must always be rooted out, no matter how endless the process seems. Of course, like all else discussed in this book, everything hangs together in the end. The doctrine of collateral attack in America was designed largely to deal with the inadequacies of certain state courts and the injustices perpetrated by them. Collateral attack makes more sense in a system in which there is a fundamental lack of confidence in the trial courts of some states, and appeal procedures are possibly inadequate. In England, judges do not feel this lack of confidence, and so find collateral attack quite irrational.[131] Unfortunately, English judges sitting in the

---

[128] See *Carus Wilson's Case* (1845) 7 QB 984. According to R. S. Sharpe, *The Law of Habeas Corpus*, 47–50, 141–2 (Clarendon Press, Oxford, 1976) there was historically no inherent reason why habeas corpus could not have been used to challenge a conviction on indictment, but the English judicial belief in finality led to this result.

[129] [1981] 1 All ER 244.

[130] *Ibid.* at 249.

[131] One American judge who did completely accept the right of state courts to make their own decisions—Holmes J.—seems to have been much closer to English judges than to

Privy Council rarely investigate local conditions to see whether attitudes bred in England are altogether appropriate in other places.

6. DUE PROCESS: A POSSIBLE COUNTER-EXAMPLE?

We need now to add a few words about a possible counter-example to our thesis which may come readily to the reader's mind. In recent years American law has become especially concerned with 'due process', especially in matters of criminal procedure. Some might argue that modern American law is highly technical and rule-oriented as regards matters of procedure and, in these respects, has become less concerned with reasons of substance, and hence more formal, than English law which, on the whole, seems less concerned with procedural regularity as such. We are not sure whether the premiss itself is sound over the whole field of law, though it may well be correct in some areas, such as the administration of the criminal law. As we have seen in chapter 6, modern American constitutional law often leads to the reversal of state criminal convictions on grounds of violation of constitutional rights in circumstances which many observers would regard as extremely technical; English courts seem far more inclined to disregard police irregularities and other procedural flaws in the criminal process, and to dismiss appeals on the ground that 'no substantial miscarriage of justice has occurred', to use the language of the relevant statutory provision.[132]

However, on closer examination, we do not think that this sort of difference really represents a counter-example to our thesis. Because the American judiciary generally emphasizes procedural propriety much more than the English, it does not follow that the American system is, in this respect, more *formal* than the English. We need to inquire further into the reasons for this emphasis on due process. There are at least three reasons which can be identified, all of which reflect the American orientation to substantive reasoning. First, in the American system, procedure is seen as a distinct realm within which independent substantive policies may be pursued. For example, judicial allegiance to procedural propriety at the pre-trial stage is seen as one way of controlling the police. If this means that that the criminal sometimes goes free because the police have violated procedural norms, then this is

---

contemporary American judges on this question. His refusal to grant a stay in the *Sacco-Vanzetti* case clearly proceeded on the basis that collateral attack presupposed a lack of confidence in state courts which he did not feel *entitled* to entertain. See O. K. Fraenkel, *The Sacco-Vanzetti Case*, 180–1 (Russell & Russell, NY, 1969).

[132] Criminal Appeal Act 1968, s. 2(1), proviso.

seen (if too substantively) as part of the price to be paid for better quality police behaviour. Second, procedural propriety is seen also to secure (or at least to contribute to securing) the realization of such 'process values' as fair participation of the accused in a trial and overall trial legitimacy. These, too, are substantive values, though they can only be realized in the course of the workings of a process. And third, procedural propriety also, of course, helps to secure the ascertainment of the substantive legal and factual merits of particular disputes.

When an American court insists on procedural propriety on one or more of these three grounds (and these are the usual grounds), this displays a substantive orientation, rather than a 'law is law' formality, or a merely arbitrary, and in this sense formal, preoccupation with procedural proprieties.

Conversely, the English position is in practice more formal and, indeed, even formalistic than it appears on the surface. Although English courts appear in this context to pursue substance more than process, what they strive after is not substantive justice *as such*, but justice *according to law*. In this sense it remains true to say that English courts display a greater adherence to formal reasoning even though they devote less attention to procedure than American courts may do.

This is particularly well illustrated by the workings of English criminal appeal courts which in recent years have demonstrably and lamentably failed to identify and quash convictions which, though impeccably arrived at by procedural means, have later been found to be utterly unfounded in fact. A number of recent and well-publicized cases have thrown an unprecedented burden on the Home Secretary (who is called upon to recommend pardons in such cases) when the appeal courts have simply failed to penetrate the barrier of due process. Demands for some kind of further appeal or non-court advisory process were made, but were rejected by the government. Instead, in an almost unique (and arguably improper) manner, the Home Secretary and the Lord Chief Justice had a 'quiet chat' as a result of which the latter assured the former that the courts would in future be rather more ready to exercise their appellate powers to admit new evidence or order new trials when the facts seemed unsatisfactory.[133] The matter for the moment rests there. This episode seems to illustrate the fact that English courts are quite truly faithful to the ideal of justice according to law; however unhappy they may be about jury verdicts reached in a properly conducted trial, they have traditionally been extremely reluctant to interfere even where there is very strong evidence to suggest that the verdict was un-

---

[133] See Justice, 26th. *Annual Report*, 10–11 (London, 1983).

founded.[134] Many will find this an unhappy illustration of a formalistic approach, in which truth formality is sacrificed.

[134] For example, in the notorious 'Luton murder case', the Court of Appeal three times refused to set aside convictions for murder even where grave doubts must have existed in the mind of any reasonable person as to the (substantive) correctness of the convictions. Eventually, the two accused were released from prison by executive action, though without the pardons usual in such cases. *Ibid.*, 11.

8

Legal Theories in England and America: 1776

1. ENGLISH LEGAL THEORY IN 1776

In this and the following chapter we shall say something about the legal theories which have been most widely held in England and America during the past two centuries. Our purpose is to show how even explicit legal theories, of the kind which might be thought (especially perhaps by English lawyers) to be totally divorced from the practical world of law and politics, in fact tend to partake of the formal/substantive divide which we have discussed in the first seven chapters. We shall, in short, demonstrate how English legal theory has been, and continues to be, much more formal, and American legal theory more substantive. We do this, not primarily to suggest that the formality of a legal theory may help explain the formality of legal reasoning in a given system, but rather to show how, in these two systems at least, theory and practice are 'all of a piece'.

Although we do not propose to give a detailed historical account of legal theory in the two countries since 1776—this book is not intended as a historical work—we cannot resist the temptation to start with 1776. That year saw a series of events which encapsulate much of the theme of this book: in America, the Declaration of Independence, with its explicit use of substantive principles of natural law, and in England, the publication of Bentham's *Fragment on Government* which can perhaps be taken as the beginning of the long positivist tradition which Bentham inaugurated in England.[1] In addition, it is now known that Bentham was largely the author of a pamphlet published in the name of his friend John Lind, in the same year, in which the natural law basis of the Declaration of Independence was remorselessly criticised; it was (declared Bentham) 'a hodgepodge of confusion and absurdity, in which the thing to be proved is all along taken for granted'.[2]

We will begin with Bentham and his imperative theory of law. It is not

---

[1] Of course the positivist tradition has long roots, extending back at least to Hobbes, but it is enough for us to start with Bentham.

[2] *An Answer to the Declaration of Independence of the American Congress* (1776). See generally H. L. A. Hart, *Essays on Bentham*, 63–5 (Clarendon Press, Oxford, 1982) (hereafter cited as Hart, *Essays*). (The quoted words do not in fact come from the 1776 pamphlet but from a much later date, see Hart, *Essays*, 65 n. 43).

our purpose to provide a detailed examination or critique of English positivism. The subject has received extensive comment and analysis from many distinguished writers[3] to which we have no need to add, though we will address a few remarks later to the characteristics of this positivist tradition, and the degree to which it can truly be fathered on Bentham and John Austin. Our present concern is not so much with the theory itself (or the variants of it, for of course, there were variants) as with the relationship between the theory and a formal approach to law.

We start with Bentham's attempt to identify the very nature of law as a command of a political superior to a political inferior.[4] In this command or imperative theory of law, the law emerges from a sovereign whose will is translated into law by express or implied commands. A command is, in essence, an expression of will, backed by a threat of a sanction. On this view it becomes possible to state law in normatively neutral and indeed factual terms. If a sovereign can be identified in a political society, in accordance with Bentham's definitions, and if the sovereign issues a wish, making it clear that, if the wish is not complied with, something unpleasant will be done to the persons addressed, then this wish can be termed a command; and the result is a law. We have here the beginnings of the notion of law as something *posited* by an authority. The existence of valid law is always a matter of form—of satisfying only source-oriented standards of validity and not also content-oriented standards.

The second characteristic of Bentham's positivism was his insistence that law is essentially a body of *rules* laid down by the sovereign. Although Bentham wrote from time to time of law as if it took the form of commands, it is plain from his writings that what is commanded really consists of rules, at least in the usual case. At the same time, Bentham stressed that ideally law should take the form of *statutory* rules. All his life he urged the benefits of legislation and statutory codification of the common law. He vigorously opposed judge-made law. Here, then, we have an early source of the prevalent contemporary English view of the proper division of legal labour with respect to law making: most of the law, and nearly all of the reform of the law, is to come from the legislature, not the courts.

A third and related characteristic of Bentham's positivism was, of course, his insistence on the separation of law and morals. As is well known, Bentham took vehement exception to Blackstone's habit of stating legal rules as though they carried their own moral (or other)

---

[3] See H. L. A. Hart, *The Concept of Law*, chs. II–VI (Clarendon Press, Oxford, 1961).

[4] *A Fragment on Government*, ch. 1, para. 12, n. o, p. 49 in the Collected Works edition, *A Comment on the Commentaries and A Fragment on Government* (J. H. Burns and H. L. A. Hart, edd., U. of London, Athlone Press, London, 1977). Bentham later elaborated the notion of a command, see Hart, *Essays*, 245.

justification with them. Bentham found this expository technique exasperating for the legal critic or law reformer, because the target always seemed to be moving: at one moment, it was the law as laid down; at another, it was the reasons being offered in justification of the law. So one of Bentham's most strongly expressed convictions was the necessity of separating out the role of expositor of the law from the role of critic or censor.[5] In order to evaluate, or to reform, the law, it is absolutely necessary to clear the mind of the confusion which arises when exposition and justification are run together in the Blackstonian fashion. So to Bentham, the very first step when setting out to reform the law is to ascertain *what the law is*; the next stage—which of course does require focus on the substantive justifications of the law—is to ascertain what are its defects, and how they can be remedied.

The fourth aspect of Bentham's positivism was his resounding rejection of natural law, natural rights, and all pre-existing rights of property. All rights, insisted Bentham, come from positive law. A right without law, or without political society, is therefore simply nonsense; and thus out of the window went the Lockean idea that the chief function of society was to protect pre-existing rights of property. Talk of moral rights was equally nonsensical, though Bentham did later in life come to acknowledge that one could intelligibly use the phrase 'moral right' to signify a right which it was expedient to recognize in accordance with the principle of utility.[6]

Clearly we have here the germs of many kinds of formal reasoning, and of the rejection of many kinds of reasons of substance. All reasons of substance about 'rights' (except reasons based on the principle of utility) are thus rejected as not genuine reasons at all, mere mystification, mere sounds to dispute about. So also, the insistence that rights are granted *by* the law, and are not the source of legal rules, was in a sense a blow against the use of reasons of substance, especially when taken with other aspects of Bentham's theories. The reason for this may not at first appear obvious because Bentham could, of course, have fallen back on the principle of utility as the source of reasons of substance: he did not necessarily have to stress law as 'fiat' rather than as something based on reason. But (it seems) Bentham was not anxious to use the utility principle as a direct source of rights in this way, because it interfered with his notion of law as a command. Commands created duties, and

---

[5] See Bentham's *Fragment*, Preface, at 397–8 of the Collected Works edition, and Hart, *Essays*, 1–2, 12, 41, 137. Cf. Postema, 'The Expositor, The Censor and Common Law', 9 *Can. J. of Phil.* 643 (1979).

[6] See Hart, *Essays*, 88–9. This idea led Bentham into difficulties and he did not much like it, see *ibid.*, 86–7.

rights were merely the correlatives of duties, rather than the direct creation of the principle of utility.[7]

These four characteristics of Bentham's theories plainly fit very well the formal vision of law which we have suggested was implicit in the workings of English legal and political institutions. The idea that all law is posited or laid down by a duly authorized source, that law has no necessary connection with morality, that judges are not to make or reform the law and that all rights, including property rights, actually derive from the law, all fit a formal vision and are inconsistent with, or anyhow less hospitable to, a more substantive vision of law. But at the same time these theories were surely not uninfluenced by the facts of the British political and constitutional system. The characterization of law in the language of commands fitted well with the newly established role of Parliament in the British political system. Since the Revolution of 1688 the supreme legal authority of Parliament had become increasingly recognised, despite the fact that, in Bentham's time, Parliament represented only a fraction of the populace. Moreover, most of the general (or public[8]) law enacted by Parliament at this time took the form of criminal statutes, which of course is the type of law closest to a command.[9] All this confirms our identification of the formal vision of law with the central tenets of English positivism, because obedience to a command is surely the archetypal formal reason for action.

One other aspect of the command theory of law—though much less noticed—also fitted English political institutions and has perhaps continued to do so. A command carries connotations of superiority, and indeed, Bentham used the language of political superior and political inferior in the elaboration of his theory. At the time that Bentham wrote, and for many years thereafter, Britain was far from being a democracy. Even in the nineteenth century, the vote remained much more confined in England than it became in America during the years of Jacksonian democracy. Moreover, Parliament was very much under the control of the aristocratic classes in 1776, and for many years afterwards; even after the Reform Act of 1832, the aristocracy continued to share power with the middle classes, and their political dominance was not finally broken until very late in the nineteenth century, or, indeed, perhaps the early twentieth. And even today, there are some respects in which Britain remains a much more elitist country than the United States. Without attempting to penetrate the full meaning of an elitist society, it

---

[7] *Ibid.*

[8] Bentham does not seem to have noticed that most parliamentary legislation at this period consisted of *Private* Acts whose function was property adjustment, rather than prohibition.

[9] Except perhaps for an executive order which actually *is* a command.

does seem clear to us that English people still think of law as something imposed from above, rather like a command. Although political power may be as diffused in Britain as it is in other democracies, it seems to us that, in the English vision of law, neither law itself nor political sovereignty is conceived of as something that comes from the people. In England, 'the government' governs, though the people can turn it out and replace it with another. That also was how Bentham saw the democratic ideal,[10] which he came to embrace in his later years.[11] To Bentham, and to pretty well everybody today, democracy in England may be government of the people, and it may be government for the people, but it is not government *by* the people.[12]

Although much of Bentham's work and thought was anti-elitist in tendency, there is another respect in which one can see a link between Bentham's theories and English elitism. As we suggested in chapter 6, English law has been reluctant to permit defences to criminal prohibitions, even in extreme circumstances on such grounds as necessity, entrapment, unfair prosecution practices, and the like. As a result the prima-facie mandatory formality of English criminal law remains higher than that of American law. We have suggested that this might have something to do with the fear of the elite, or governing classes, that the people to whom laws are addressed might question their application in circumstances somewhat less extreme perhaps than those in which some equitable or other substantive adjustment to the law would generally be agreed to be desirable. Elitism here takes the form of reserving to the elite themselves the prerogative of mercy, or equitable modification of the law, and attempting to persuade the people that the laws are really rather more severe than they are. Now this sort of attitude is also associated with a formal vision of law, because it requires that rules be applied even though there may be substantive reasons warranting the displacement of the rule. Equitable or other substantive modification at the point of application may sometimes still take place, but it takes place outside the rule, as, for example, by the use of prosecutorial discretion, or the grant of an absolute discharge on conviction.

The link between this aspect of English elitism and the positivist tradition can be seen by looking at one feature of utilitarian thought with which positivism had close connections. The debate which has taken place in modern times over the rival merits of rule utilitarianism and act

---

[10] See Hart, *Essays*, 68, citing unpublished Bentham MSS.

[11] See Dinwiddy, 'Bentham's Transition to Radicalism', 36 *J. Hist. Ideas* 683 (1975); Hart, *Essays*, 70–1.

[12] See Searing, 'Rules of the Game in Britain: Can the Politicians be Trusted?' 76 *Am. Pol. Sc. Rev.* 239, 251 (1982).

utilitarianism is relevant here.[13] Act utilitarianism presupposes that each individual utilitarian has to weigh the pros and cons of every proposed piece of conduct, displacing even firm rules if he thinks there are adequate grounds for doing so, though naturally paying attention to the dangers of unconscious bias in making such decisions. The rule utilitarian, on the other hand, treats rules in a more formal way, insisting that the rule must be observed, even if there may appear to be some reasons for displacing it in the special circumstances of the case. These special circumstances are not to be evaluated by those to whom the rules are addressed—'theirs not to reason why'—but may be examined by those who are responsible for making or changing the rules. Rule utilitarianism then may be interpreted as a more elitist theory,[14] and although we are not aware that Bentham himself ever addressed this question, there is certainly some evidence that his disciple John Austin did so, and that he favoured the rule utilitarian version of the theory.[15]

The growing ascendancy of Parliament in the British political scene also goes far to explain why Bentham's theories fitted so well in other respects with the legal–political system of the country. In particular, the notion of any moral law of a higher law character than Parliament's own laws was becoming difficult to sustain in the late eighteenth century. With the defeat of the claims of the Crown, Parliament was left with only one possible rival for ultimate legal supremacy—namely, the common law. But there were many reasons why this potential never developed into a reality. For one thing, Parliament and the common lawyers had been allies in the seventeenth-century struggles against the Crown; they did not see themselves as rivals. For another thing, the judges themselves came from the small class of Whig parliamentarians, and were throughout the eighteenth century very much members of the establishment—the ruling elite—who identified themselves with other parts of the elite. They had no separate political constituency which could have been a rival power base to the authority of Parliament.

Even so, it must be added that Parliament's legal supremacy—though acknowledged by Bentham himself, as by all other lawyers at the time he wrote—was not perhaps perceived as quite so absolute in Bentham's day as it became subsequently. It was possible, even for lawyers in eighteenth-century England, to condemn parliamentary legislation as

---

[13] See, e.g., J. Rawls, 'Two Concepts of Rules', 64 *Phil. Rev.* 1 (1955); D. Lyons, *Forms and Limits of Utilitarianism* (Clarendon Press, Oxford, 1965).

[14] D. Lyons, *supra*, n. 13, at 130–1, 149; Kerner, 'The Immorality of Rule Utilitarianism', 21 *Phil. Q.* 36 (1971).

[15] See John Austin, *The Province of Jurisprudence Determined*, especially Lecture III (Library of Ideas, H. L. A. Hart, ed., Weidenfeld & Nicolson, 1955). See further, P. S. Atiyah, *The Rise and Fall of Freedom of Contract*, 651–5 (Clarendon Press, Oxford, 1979).

wrong and contrary to law in some higher sense;[16] proposals to change the fundamental common law of England would have been thought by many not only to be improper or wrong as a matter of policy, but, in some sense, also to be illegal or unconstitutional. Probably, people who spoke or thought thus were using the term 'law' or 'illegal' in a special sense; certainly, there is very little sign that in Bentham's day the lawyers had any doubts that the courts would unhesitatingly enforce whatever laws Parliament chose to pass. There were, of course, those famous, if rather vague flourishes of Blackstone,[17] in which he had repeated the similar assertions of Coke in *Bonham's Case*[18] that the courts might be able to declare an Act of Parliament to be void. But Blackstone's remarks do not seem to have been taken seriously in England, as they were in America, and as for Coke's dictum in *Bonham's Case*, it was unrealistic not to recognize that this was uttered during the struggles for constitutional supremacy which were largely settled in 1688. The outcome of the Glorious Revolution was not merely the defeat of the pretensions of the Crown, but also the establishment of the ascendancy of Parliament over the common lawyers. After that, the idea that the judges could refuse to enforce an Act of Parliament seems to have become pretty well obsolete.

However, there is an element of reading history backwards in suggesting that Bentham's theories fitted the British political system, though it is difficult to be sure how much. For it was partly as a result of Bentham's own influence that Parliament began to be the great reforming instrument of nineteenth-century England, and partly as a result of that very process of history that it became possible to assert more dogmatically than ever before that Parliament's legislative authority was supreme and untrammelled. It may be noted that the passing of the great Reform Act of 1832, which ushered in this era of parliamentary activity, coincided almost exactly with the end of Bentham's long life.

As we have previously seen,[19] the method of law reform which became traditional in England in the nineteenth century was highly Benthamite. The process of inquiry into what the law is, of ascertaining its defects, and of recommending change to overcome those defects came to be more and more regularly used as Britain's institutions were slowly overhauled during the nineteenth century. And conversely, the more that

---

[16] See, e.g., the words of Lord Camden in the debates on the Declaratory Bill, asserting that the bill was 'illegal, absolutely illegal, contrary to the fundamental laws of this constitution'. 16 *Parliamentary History* 178 (1766), cited by Corwin, 'The "Higher Law" Background of American Constitutional Law', 42 *Harv. L. Rev.* 149, 365, at 404 (1928). Lord Camden was Chief Justice of the Common Pleas 1761-6, and Lord Chancellor 1766-70.

[17] Bl. Com. I, 91.

[18] Co. Rep. 118a (1610).

[19] See *supra*, 149.

Parliament exerted its legislative authority, the more did the judges retreat from the realms of high policy into matters of technical doctrine, what came increasingly to be called 'lawyer's law', as though it were a matter of interest only to lawyers. Both these developments would have been highly approved of by Bentham. Both of them fitted nicely with his theories about the nature of law as commands, about the separation of law and morals, and about the best way of reforming the law. It is, of course, impossible to be sure to what extent the developments were themselves due to the influence of Bentham's work, and to what extent his genius enabled him to identify the trends of the future long before most of his fellow countrymen had done so. But whatever the truth on this point, it is, in retrospect, blindingly clear that Bentham's positivist theory of law fitted supremely well the British legal and political system which was coming to be settled in the late eighteenth century and which has largely continued to the present day with only immaterial changes. It is also, we think, entirely clear that Benthamite positivism was highly congenial to a formal vision of law, and that the prevalence of positivist theories in England helps explain, and is itself explained by, the widespread reception of a formal vision of law in England.

2. AMERICAN LEGAL THEORY IN 1776

When we turn to consider the position in America in and around 1776, the picture could hardly be more different. America did not produce any legal theorists of Bentham's stature in the eighteenth century, but it did have its share of lawyers who thought deeply about many of the issues relevant to the distinction between form and substance in the law. For some years even before 1776, the dominant version of legal theory was heavily influenced by strains of natural law. America in the late eighteenth century was, at least in these respects, more plainly identifiable as a land of the Enlightenment than England. And the Enlightenment brought with it the same distrust of mystification in law which had caused Bentham to hurl his invectives at Blackstone. But the anti-mystification ideal in America led in a different direction. It led to a belief in substantive reason, to the natural law texts, to the belief in a 'higher law' and in self-evident truths, to the belief that means could be rationally derived from ends, to the ideal that all laws must ultimately be justifed by their purposes, and that these purposes were the government of political society for the good of mankind. Much has been written about this,[20] but for present purposes it will suffice to refer to the thought and work of a few leading American lawyers of the revolutionary period.

[20] See Corwin, *supra*, n. 16; Morton White, *The Philosophy of the American Revolution* (Oxford U. Press, NY, 1978).

We may start with a few words concerning Thomas Jefferson who, as the draftsman of the Declaration of Independence, has received perhaps more than his fair share of scholarly attention. Jefferson was himself no philosopher, but there is no doubt that he drew heavily on the thought of many philosophers, from Locke to Burlamaqui.[21] Although the final version of the Declaration of Independence refers only to 'self-evident truths', it seems clear that Jefferson espoused both a rationalist version of natural law and a theory of moral sense. Both reason and feelings could thus be prayed in aid of natural law. In 1793 Jefferson wrote that, for the reality of the principles of natural law, he appealed to 'the true fountains of evidence, the head and heart of every rational and honest man. It is there nature has written her moral laws, and where every man may read them for himself.'[22]

What did these natural law principles have to say for Jefferson? In the first place, of course, they told him that the purpose of all law was to protect the pre-existing natural rights of man. The 'right to life, liberty and the pursuit of happiness', as the Declaration of Independence worded it, and the right to property which Jefferson and the other revolutionaries would certainly have included in these rights, were to him plainly natural rights, rights which it was the prime purpose of law to protect. Furthermore, these rights were inalienable, again in the words of the Declaration, by which (it seems) the revolutionaries meant that the rights could not be sold or voluntarily conveyed away, not that the State could never justifiably intrude upon them.[23] It is needless to labour the well-known respects in which the Americans had elevated 'taxation without representation' into one of their principal grievances. Enough to point out that the theoretical basis for this complaint was that it involved the deprivation by Britain of the property of Americans, and that this deprivation was without their consent. It was, at this time, standard natural law doctrine that property rights could only be taken away with the consent of the holder: either by contract in the market-place, or by taxation by an assembly containing representatives for whom he could have voted, or by whom at least he could be deemed to have been represented. Since the British Parliament was not such a body, it followed that what it laid down could not be law for Americans.

We can see here several other respects in which American positions in 1776 were inconsistent with a formal vision of law, and we can also see why this was so. In the first place, the assertion of the right of rebellion involves the use—*in extremis*—of what might be called the ultimate reason of substance. It involves the repudiation of loyalty to the

---

[21] See Morton White, *supra*, n. 20, *passim*.
[22] *Ibid.*, p. 116.
[23] *Ibid.*

existing constitutional regime by reference to the failure of that regime to perform its functions properly. Here therefore is a total negation of 'the law is the law' formality. If even the constitution itself can be overthrown—and *rightfully* overthrown—because its functions are not being properly performed, its substantive purposes are not being properly served, then it is hardly surprising if the reasons behind ordinary laws come to be regarded as open to question and examination as a matter of course, so that law generally may come to have rather low levels of mandatory formality. In a sense, of course, all rebellions involve a rejection of positivism, a refusal to accept the existing regime, just because it is the established law; what is unusual about the American Revolution was not so much the rejection of positivism *per se*, but the articulation of the reasons and the justification for what was being done. Moreover, because of the symbolic significance of the Declaration of Independence, and the fact that it soon took its place as a great historical document in the annals of the new republic, the anti-formal sentiments which underlay it came themselves to play a significant role in the creation of a new tradition about the nature and purposes of law.[24]

Jefferson himself espoused the revolutionary mentality—at least on occasions—to a degree reminiscent of modern Marxists who believe in the continuing revolution. On one occasion he even asserted the desirability of rebellion every twenty years as a means of bringing men back to first principles![25] This itself is an indication of a strongly anti-formalist tendency in his thinking, for to go back to first principles is to penetrate the barrier of formal reasons and search for the original reasons of substance lying behind them. To do this repeatedly comes close to weakening if not destroying the value of formal reasoning altogether. Other signs of deep impatience with formal reasoning are to be found in some of his remarks, with which even modern Americans might be uncomfortable, to the effect that national officials must be willing, when necessary, to risk going beyond the strict law when the public preservation requires it.[26] Jefferson was also, of course, one of the chief progenitors of the Bill of Rights, and although he may have seen this primarily as an instrument for controlling the powers of the federal government in the interests of the states, many of the provisions of the Bill of Rights were clearly rooted in natural law thinking.

[24] These factors help explain why the British Revolution of 1688 did not lead to the same anti-formal tradition in England as the American Revolution did in America. In 1689 everyone in England was at great pains to minimize the change that had been made and to gloss over the discontinuity in the legal basis of the new regime, whereas in post-revolutionary America the situation demanded magnification of the discontinuity.

[25] Beitzinger, 'The Philosophy of Law of Four American Founding Fathers', 21 *Am. J. Juris.* 1, 11 (1976).

[26] *Ibid.*

One other respect, less obvious, but in our view of great significance, in which Jefferson favoured a tradition which led easily to an anti-formal vision of law was in his espousal of populism. Jefferson was no elitist. When he talked of self-evident truths he seems to have thought that these truths were self-evident to everyone, or at least that most people could be trained to see their self-evidence.[27] In this respect Jefferson turned the new republic away from the initial course set by Washington and John Adams, and when he became President in 1801 he adopted an informality of manner and attire which greatly impressed foreign diplomats, who may not all have approved of it, as well as Bentham who very much did.[28] As we have noted above, elitism tends to be adopted by those who distrust the mass of the people, and who prefer that they should be taught to observe and obey the law unquestioningly. Elitism is therefore congenial to a formal approach to law, in which mercy and equitable modifications or adjustments to the law may be made, but are preferably made by methods which do not actually appear to weaken the general prohibitions (or commands) of the law. But populism easily leads to a different route. Those leaders or governors who trust the people and are confident that they will choose wisely cannot require them to obey laws unquestioningly, when they themselves are ready to question those laws. And the link between Jefferson's populism and the anti-formal approach to law was historically a very clear one: for Jeffersonian populism led by direct descent to Jacksonian democracy, to the election of judges, and the greater enthronement of juries.[29] And as we observed in chapter 6, the American jury is one of the most significant factors which institutionalizes the belief in reasons of substance as opposed to reasons of authority or formal reasons.

Another obvious way in which the American situation at the time of the Revolution differed from the English and supported the theoretical ideals of natural law was, of course, the fact that the property which the revolutionaries regarded as belonging to them by natural right had largely been extracted from the soil within recent memory. It is hardly surprising that Americans found it in some sense 'natural' that the wealth they had extracted as the fruits of their own labour should belong to them by some natural right. But in this respect, the ideals and theoretical bases of the Revolution were anyhow not fundamentally different from those which prevailed in England. The Lockean tradition

[27] Morton White, *supra*, n. 20, at 136–41.

[28] Hart, *Essays*, 72.

[29] Though as regards the election of judges, there is some evidence that this was not so much due to populism, as to a desire to wrest the nomination of judges from the hands of corrupt executives. See Hall, 'Progressive Reform and the Decline of Democratic Accountability: The Popular Election of State Supreme Court Judges 1850–1920', *ABFRJ* 345 (1984).

concerning rights of property and labour was still powerful at the time of the American Revolution, though Bentham had attacked this tradition with great vigour. As noted above, Bentham was largely the author of a pamphlet published in answer to the American Declaration of Independence in the name of his friend John Lind. In this pamphlet Bentham criticised the concept of property rights as pre-existing by natural law. All property rights derive from the State and the law, insisted Bentham, so that the arguments of Americans that they could not be deprived of their property without their consent (by contract or by representative taxation) was so much hot air. According to Bentham, taxation was merely the redrawing of the boundaries of property rights which were anyhow the creature of the law and could not therefore be in any way dependent on the consent of the governed.[30]

We turn now to say something of John Adams, first Vice-President and second President of the United States. Though eclipsed in fame, at least in modern times, by Jefferson, Adams may well have had a greater influence in institutionalizing the natural law tradition in America. For Adams played a larger role than Jefferson in the Continental Congresses and in the drafting of the Constitution of the United States.[31] He was the author of the first draft of the first constitution of the independent Commonwealth of Massachusetts, and his model of what a state constitution ought to look like, and what it ought to contain, was widely copied by the other states. He was also one of those responsible for popularizing the use in American legal discourse of the phrase 'A Government of Laws and not of Men', and it was he who first produced a draft constitution with the system of checks and balances which subsequently became the standard pattern of American constitutions. Although Adams was not one of those who favoured a federal Bill of Rights, he included in his draft of the Massachusetts constitution a Declaration of the Rights of the Inhabitants which formed one of the sources of the federal Bill of Rights.

John Adams was a natural lawyer. He read widely among the European natural lawyers, including Grotius, Locke, Puffendorf, Burlamaqui, and Vattel, and we can see the influence of this natural law thinking in Adams's writings and activities from long before the American Revolution. As early as 1765 we find Adams writing in his *Diary* of the purposive nature of the interpretation of documents (and citing Vattel):[32]

[30] Hart, *Essays*, 57.

[31] Porter and Farnell, 'John Adams and American Constitutionalism', 21 *Am. J. Juris.* 20 (1976).

[32] *Diary and Autobiography of John Adams*, vol. 1, *Diary*, 278 (27 Dec. 1765) (L. H. Butterfield ed., 1962).

In unforeseen Cases, i.e. when the State of things is found such as the Author of the Disposition has not foreseen, and could not have thought of, we should rather follow his Intention than his Words, and interpret the Act as he himself would have interpreted it...If a Case be presented, in which one cannot absolutely apply the well known Reason of a Law or a Promise, this Case ought to be excepted...Every interpretation that leads to an absurdity ought to be rejected...

Early in the next year, Adams made some Notes arguing that it was an 'infallible' rule that strict interpretation of the words of a document should not be adhered to when it would be 'unlawful, i.e. repugnant to the Laws of God and Nature'.[33]

In 1771 Adams had supported the right of a jury to give a valid general verdict contrary to the judge's instructions on the law, and we suggest that this shows a leaning towards reasons of substance as a very justification of the institution of the jury.[34] In his record of the Continental Congress of 1765 Adams noted a number of speeches which supported the invocation by the Congress of natural law (with which he agreed, and some of which may indeed have been his own),[35] one of which seems especially apposite, whether it was one of Adams's own speeches or not: 'The Colonies adopt the common law, not as The Common Law, but as the highest Reason.'[36]

Over and over again in his writings and work, Adams recurs to the purposive nature of law, to the necessity that laws should fit their purposes, to the idea that the end of all law is justice, which is reflected in general rational rules, rooted in human nature, and equally applied to all,[37] and that men have a right to alter or abolish government which is destructive of its proper ends.[38] Drawing on Coke's famous dictum in *Bonham's Case*,[39] Adams argued that 'An Act [of Parliament] against the Constitution is void; an Act against Natural Equity is void...'.[40] In 1765 an article had appeared in the *London Evening Post* dismissing American arguments against the invalidity of the Stamp Act with the simple assertion that Parliament was a supreme legislative body which could at any time set aside colonial charters by legislation. John Adams wrote in reply:

You tell us that a Resolution of the B[ritish] Parliament can at any time annull all the Charters of all our Monarchs. But would such an Act of Parliament do no

---

[33] *Ibid.*, 289 (9 Jan. 1766).
[34] *Ibid.*, vol. 2, *Diary*, 3–4.
[35] Corwin, *supra*, n. 16, at 400–1.
[36] John Adams, *Diary* (*supra*, n. 32), vol. 2, 128–9 (1774).
[37] Beitzinger, *supra*, n. 25.
[38] Morton White, *supra*, n. 20, at 234–6.
[39] 8 Co. Rep. 118*a* (1610).
[40] Corwin, *supra*, n. 16, at 398.

wrong? Would it be obeyed?[41]...The gallant struggle in America is founded in Principles so indisputable, in the moral Law, in the revealed law of God, in the true Constitution of Great Britain, and in the most apparent Welfare of the Nation as well as the People in America that I must confess it rejoices my very soul.[42]

Later in the same year, when Adams served as legal counsel in order to petition Governor Hutchinson to reopen the courts of Massachusetts (which had been closed because nobody would comply with the Stamp Act), he boldly argued that the Act was void because it had not been consented to by the Americans.[43]

One of the most interesting aspects of the theoretical justifications for their actions which the Americans offered was that they nearly all claimed to be acting in the true spirit of the British constitution, and in accordance with the principles of the common law. Until the Declaration of Independence, they were, after all, British citizens, subjects of the Crown and entitled to the protection of the law. They claimed that it was indeed the British constitution and the common law of England which recognized the rights they asserted. Today, after two centuries of positivism and nearly three centuries of pretty well undisputed parliamentary supremacy, it may be difficult for an English lawyer to accept that in the 1770s it was possible to make quite a respectable legal argument of a substantive nature against the validity of British attempts to legislate for the colonies. As we have mentioned above, Adams made just such an argument before Governor Hutchinson, though the details of his argument are now lost. But many of these arguments were made in published pamphlets, and one fully developed example of such an argument survives in the *Considerations on the Nature and Extent of the Legislative Authority of the British Parliament* by James Wilson, published in 1774.[44]

Wilson, though today much less known than Jefferson or Adams, was a lawyer who took a prominent part in the American struggle for independence, and in the framing of the Constitution of 1788; he was appointed by Washington to the new Supreme Court of the United States, and also found time to be a professor of law in Philadelphia between 1790 and 1792, during which time he gave courses of lectures

---

[41] John Adams, *Diary* (*supra*, n. 32), vol. 1, 272–5 (1765).

[42] *Ibid.*, 275.

[43] *Ibid.*, 276–7.

[44] See *Works of James Wilson*, vol. 2 (J. D. Andrews, ed., 1896). There were, in addition, any number of pamphlets attacking the political or moral right of the British Parliament to legislate for the colonies, and many of these relied on varieties of natural law. For a sample of such pamphlets, see Charles S. Hyneman and Donald S. Lutz, *American Political Writing During the Founding Era, 1760–1805*, especially in vol. 1 (Liberty Press, Indianapolis, 1983).

on (among other things) the law of nature, some of which were later published.[45]

In this pamphlet Wilson set out to make a legal argument for the invalidity of British legislation purporting to tax the colonies who were unrepresented in the British Parliament. The argument is no mean one. Wilson cited cases decided in the reign of Richard III (and subsequently) holding that British parliamentary legislation did not extend to Ireland.[46] It was true, he admitted, that the judges added that the result would be different if Ireland was expressly named in the Act, but he rejected these remarks as dicta of no great weight. The substantive reason given by the judges for the decision, says Wilson, was that Ireland was not represented in the British Parliament, and that remained the case whether or not Ireland was expressly declared to be subject to the Act. Here is a splendid example of the way in which a formal reason could be rejected for a reason of substance by someone, like Wilson, who was thoroughly steeped in the works of the eighteenth-century natural lawyers. What Parliament actually *said* about the application of its enactments to overseas colonies or territories might have been more important to English positivists; but the substantive reason for the judges' refusal to apply such legislation was more important to Wilson in constructing his legal argument. He goes on to ask how the British Parliament ever acquired a natural right to make laws binding on the Americans. In the absence of a right by conquest, their title to make laws for America could only be grounded on the consent of the Americans; but in the absence of parliamentary representatives, there was no consent. And so the familiar arguments rolled on.

These illustrations from the work and thought of three American founding fathers are enough to give us a real flavour of natural law and related substantive thinking which was widespread in pre-revolutionary America. Of course there were varieties of natural law thought on many issues, and it cannot be said that everyone agreed with particular natural law tenets. But we can say in general terms that American natural law thinking in the colonial period embraced a number of central ideas. First, natural law was widely relied upon to provide a body of substantive ideals and principles for the evaluation and criticism of positive law. These ideals and principles varied both in content and in support; most were moral or political in nature, and could be (and were) readily expressed in the language of rights. Some were procedural rather than substantive. Few had any connection with religious doctrine. Examples include the moral right not to be deprived

---

[45] *Ibid.*, vol. 1, ch. 3.
[46] See *Calvin's case*, 7 Co. Rep. 1a, 22b, 77 ER 377, 404.

of liberty or property except by due process of law; the moral right to be secure in one's own person and home, not only from unreasonable interference by other citizens, but also by governments; and the moral right, within appropriate limits, to the fruits of one's own labour.

Secondly, whatever may have been the position of classical natural law theorists such as Aristotle and Aquinas, many American natural law thinkers did believe in a 'higher law' version of natural law, according to which positive law contrary to natural law was simply invalid as law or, even if valid, imposed no duty of obedience; indeed, in extreme cases, government action contrary to natural law gave rise to the right of rebellion or revolution.

Thirdly, many of these natural law theorists brought to their thinking about positive law a general preconception of the very nature of positive law, namely that it is not something that merely bears the imprimatur of state authority. Law must also have substantive content which is not contrary to reason or natural law, though this is not to say that reason or natural law dictates all the twists and turns of legal doctrine. Thus positive law is not merely something laid down; typically and almost necessarily it embodies a reasoned reconciliation of conflicting considerations. Of course tyrants might rule by sheer fiat, but then this would not be a form of *government under and by law*.

Fourth, law was not conceived of as something merely *made* by an official or body at a given moment of time. Much law was not thus wholly 'made up'. Rather, law was to some extent already 'there', to be discovered through reasoned reflection on the needs and dictates of the human condition. Indeed, on this view, the appropriate legal norms were not infrequently to be found arising from, or implicit in, recurrent social situations or contexts, as well as in institutional structures and forms. Sometimes natural law notions of this kind were presented as self-evident insights, or as matters of moral intuition, when it might have been better merely to say that the basic factual assumptions involved were not disputable (for example, that all persons are susceptible to injury at the hands of others) and that the weight of reason is often heavily on one side (for example, that there ought to be rules protecting persons and property).

And fifth, there are (as we have seen) signs of the theory that statutes and other documents should not be interpreted literally, but in light of their purposes and reason, or, as we would say, in light of moral, policy, and other substantive considerations informing the content and wording of the law.

It is clear enough that these aspects of natural law thinking fit well with a substantive vision, and do not fit at all with a formal vision of law. In their belief in the role of substantive reasoning, in a 'higher law' which could override positive law, and in substantive rather than formal or literal methods of interpretation, and in many other respects which we have lightly touched upon, eighteenth-century Americans were demonstrating their vision of law to be very different from that which was beginning to be so firmly held in England.

We have also suggested above that there was a close fit between Benthamite positivism, on the one hand, and British political institutions and practice in Bentham's time, on the other hand. It only remains now for us to indicate how the American espousal of natural law ideas (which we have identified in the thought of Jefferson, Adams, and Wilson) similarly harmonized with the newly created political institutions of the United States.

First, under the new Constitution, there was no sovereign with unlimited legal powers. The whole concept of limitless sovereignty could only be reconciled with the new Constitution by shifting sovereignty to the people. But this shift was highly antithetical to Benthamite positivism, because most laws manifestly emanated from legislatures and judges, and not from the people. It is true that many American thinkers later tried to reconcile the federal Constitution with positivist conceptions of sovereignty, but the attempt was doomed, and has now been abandoned by virtually all. In retrospect, it seems clear that the Constitution was based on ideas quite incompatible with English positivistic theories of sovereignty.

Then again, the new Constitution plainly reflected the natural law idea that the people have pre-existing moral rights—above all, the right to life, liberty, and the pursuit of happiness—which it was the function of governments and laws to protect. The Constitution rejected Bentham's idea—which was indeed one of the main reasons that he criticized the Constitution—that rights of all kinds must come from the law itself.

Further, the power of judicial review which soon established itself under the new Constitution involved to some degree a reliance on a higher form of law than mere positive law. Together with the Bill of Rights, it also involved the rejection of merely source-oriented criteria for the identification of valid law, and required gradually increased recognition of content-oriented criteria of validity.

Again, highly purposive interpretation of written law generally—and so of low interpretive formality—existed from the very beginning of the new republic, and was rendered a practical necessity by the vague and broad language of the Constitution itself.

And finally, the great powers entrusted to judges under the new Constitution, and the restricted powers conferred on the legislatures, meant that the Constitution created a system of government in which legislation could never play the overwhelmingly dominant role for which it was cast by positivism and which it actually played in England. At the same time, such a system by its very nature invited a larger law-making role for courts in non-constitutional matters as well, an invitation soon accepted.

With such an ancestry to legal theory as this, it is hardly surprising that English positivism did not flourish in America. Indeed, what is surprising is that a version of positivism did make headway during the nineteenth century in America. However, as we have said, we do not intend to trace in detail the history of legal theory in England and the United States throughout these last two centuries, and in the next chapter we shall therefore, after a few comments on English and American jurisprudence in the nineteenth century, proceed straight to the twentieth century.

9

Legal Theories in England and America: The Nineteenth and Twentieth Centuries

1. ENGLISH LEGAL THEORY IN THE NINETEENTH CENTURY

In this and the next section we shall briefly survey developments in the nineteenth century. Our treatment in no way professes to be a full discussion of nineteenth-century legal thought: our main concern is rather with the 'fit' between English legal theory and the formal character of the English legal system. It is therefore enough to note here that in England the Benthamite positivist tradition took hold and waxed most vigorous. Because much of Bentham's work was wrapped in obscurities and jargon of his own invention, and because indeed so much of it remained (and still remains) unpublished, it was through the work of his disciple John Austin, rather than through Bentham's own work, that his views were propagated. But although Austinian positivism did differ in a number of respects from the Benthamite version, it was solidly cast in the same mould.

From the time of Bentham and Austin, English lawyers and jurists increasingly subscribed implicitly, if not explicitly, to many of their leading tenets. Precisely what those tenets were, and what some thinkers later took them to be, may well have become somewhat different things over the years. One of us has previously noted that some discussions of positivism often attribute views to Bentham and Austin which they did not hold and, indeed, in some cases, vigorously repudiated.[1] Nevertheless, positivism of a broadly Benthamite character dominated English legal theory and the English legal system. Whether everything that was attributed to Bentham or Austin can truly be fathered on them is not, for this purpose, wholly material. Certainly, *some* of the central tenets of positivist thought must be attributed to them. In particular, the command or imperative theory of the nature of law took a firm hold, and this, as we have suggested, involved use of a purely formal standard for identifying (valid) law itself. What *was* law could only be identified by asking if it was something which had been commanded by the sovereign; what he commanded, and only what he commanded, was law. Law was not, therefore, something to be identified by reference to its substantive

[1] R. S. Summers, 'The *New* Analytical Jurists', 41 *NYUL Rev.* 861 (1966).

content, let alone the dictates of reason, or appeals to the law of nature or the law of God.

Judges also began to lay down rules about the extent to which judicial decisions were binding. In mid-century the House of Lords, in *Beamish* v. *Beamish*,[2] first began to assert that the House was bound by its own decisions no less than other courts, because these decisions had *laid down* the law. Later, the increasingly hierarchical nature of the judicial system enabled more precise rules to be laid down as to which decisions of which courts bound other courts. And there developed also more refinement about the distinction betwen *ratio decidendi* and *obiter dictum* (where again Austin had anticipated the courts[3]), though most of these subtleties did not reach their peak until the present century. These developments reflected a formal approach consistent with a theory of legal validity as purely a matter of authoritative source.

A second basic tenet of the reigning positivism was that the essential and overwhelmingly predominant form of law consisted of rules, preferably, in the views of Bentham and Austin, statutory rules. Though Bentham and Austin frequently wrote of 'commands' of the sovereign, it is clear on analysis that they usually meant rules adopted by the legislature, expressly or tacitly.

Third, the positivist methodology also seems to have resulted in more formal methods of statutory interpretation (though this went hand in hand with increasingly professionalized methods of statutory drafting). For here again, if the sole function of a court applying the law was to find the sovereign's commands, the underlying reasons behind those commands could arguably be said to be immaterial. Both Bentham and Austin (with modest qualifications) approved of the literal method of statutory interpretation which became part of the English legal tradition.[4]

Fourth, the English positivist tradition was historically followed by, and may well have influenced, a new methodology of law reform. This methodology depended on legislation as opposed to judicial decisions, and stressed the desirability of maintaining a firm separation between law and morals. Bentham sharply distinguished between 'expository jurisprudence', concerned with describing the law 'as it is' with clarity and precision, and 'censorial jurisprudence', which was concerned with

---

[2] (1861) 9 HLC 274, 338, 11 ER 735, 761.
[3] W. L. Morison, *John Austin*, 102 (Stanford U. Press, Stanford, 1982).
[4] As to Bentham see J. Bentham, *A General View of a Complete Code of Laws*, ch. XXXIV, reprinted in *Complete Works of Jeremy Bentham* (J. Bowring, ed., 1853); J. Bentham, *Of Laws in General*, ch. XIV, in *Collected Works of Jeremy Bentham* (J. H. Burns and H. L. A. Hart, edd., University of London, Athlone Press, 1970). As to Austin, see W. L. Morison, *supra*, n. 3, at 105; John Austin, *Lectures on Jurisprudence*, vol. 2, ch. XXXVII (James Cockcroft & Co., NY, 1875).

setting forth the law 'as it ought to be', in particular for purposes of legislative law reform.[5] As Austin put it, 'the existence of law is one thing, its merit or demerit is another'.[6] Bentham and Austin both insisted that this sharp separation between law and morals was the only way to ensure that laws could be rationally evaluated, criticised, and, above all, reformed. Bentham, indeed, quite explicitly drew from his own theoretical premisses the blueprints of the new methodology of law reform: that the existing law should first be ascertained, that the social conditions in which the law operated should be examined in detail, that the deficiencies in the law should then be specifically identified, and finally that legislation should be enacted to correct those deficiencies. All this naturally contributed to the ultimately dominant view in England that 'law' was for the courts and 'morals' (and other substantive policy matters) for the legislature, so that judges should not generally engage in law reform. Law reform was the legislature's province. Bentham certainly held this view of the judicial role, though Austin was more tolerant of judicial law making.

We believe that this sharp separation between law and morals also sometimes had the effect of eliminating substantive moral notions (especially non-utilitarian ideas of rightness) from the law. So, for example, signs of legal rules which openly acknowledged some obeisance to principles of morality were expunged from the law, such as the famous 'moral obligation' doctrine in the law of consideration.[7] So too, Equity went into a decline in nineteenth century England from which it never wholly recovered, as a source of some kind of 'higher law' closely associated with the moral law. Equity became more and more technical, more and more like an ordinary part of the law, and was eventually merged with the common law through statutory reforms culminating in the Judicature Acts of 1873–5.[8]

The separation of law from morals extended also to the separation of law from other 'non-legal' or 'extra-legal' factors. English jurists concentrated on neutral or formal analysis of legal phenomena and legal concepts; the context in which legal concepts were used and the purposes for which they were used seemed immaterial in this kind of formal analysis.[9] And while explicit legal theory moved increasingly in the

---

[5] J. Bentham, *An Introduction to the Principles of Morals and Legislation*, 294 (J. H. Burns and H. L. A. Hart, edd., Methuen, London, 1982)

[6] J. Austin, *The Province of Jurisprudence Determined*, 184 (Library of Ideas, H. L. A. Hart, ed., Weidenfeld & Nicolson, London, 1955).

[7] *Eastwood.* v. *Kenyon* (1840) 11 A. & E. 438, 113 ER 482; see P. S. Atiyah, *The Rise and Fall of Freedom of Contract*, 491–3 (Clarendon Press, Oxford, 1979).

[8] P. S. Atiyah, *supra*, n. 7, at 392–7, 671–80.

[9] See, e.g., the methods of analysis used for concepts like 'right' in Markby, *Elements of Law*, 49–54 (Clarendon Press, Oxford, 1871); T. E. Holland, *Elements of Jurisprudence*, ch.

formal direction, so also did the legal world itself. Policy came to be increasingly treated as something of a non-legal character, something for the legislature and not for judges to meddle in.[10] When A. V. Dicey published his celebrated lectures on *The Law of the Constitution* in 1909, he drew a sharp line between constitutional law and political conventions[11] which has also established itself as part of English legal orthodoxy.

This tendency for positivism to become still more formal, and sometimes perhaps even formalistic, as time went on, may have been related to the fact that the theory of value which underpinned it in Bentham's and Austin's own work gradually lost its sway in England during the nineteenth century. Bentham and Austin were, of course, both utilitarians. Austin's books on legal theory included many pages on utilitarianism, and it is difficult to believe that he did not think of this as an integral part of his legal theory, as indeed has recently been argued.[12] But by 1900, it seems that utilitarianism was no longer the influence it once had been among theorists and philosophers, despite the great practical successes that it had had as a political and reforming ideology. Certainly among legal theorists utilitarianism and, indeed, all theories of value were largely ignored by 1900. This development greatly strengthened the tendency of positivism to lend support to formal reasoning because the general theory of law became increasingly divorced from the ingredients of substantive value relevant to the content of positive law.

In all these respects, the fit between English legal theory, on the one hand, and the more formal approach of the English legal and political system, on the other, became tighter as the nineteenth century drew to its close, but we certainly do not suggest that all this was due to the influence of Bentham and Austin and what they were thought to have said.[13] As we have repeatedly stressed, theory and practice influenced each other. Indeed, one of the reasons why so many opinions have been fathered on Bentham and Austin which they would not have accepted may well have been the tendency to attribute to them support for various features of the

---

VII (Clarendon Press, Oxford, 1880); J. Salmond, *Jurisprudence*, 219–24 (Sweet & Maxwell, London, 1902); or the concept of 'possession' in F. Pollock and R. S. Wright, *Possession in the Common Law* (Clarendon Press, Oxford, 1888).

[10] P. S. Atiyah, *supra*, n. 7, at 660–71; R. B. Stevens, *Law and Politics* (U. of North Carolina Press, Chapel Hill, 1978).

[11] First published 1885; 10th edn., ch. XIV (Macmillan, London, 1959).

[12] W. E. Rumble, *The Thought of John Austin: Jurisprudence, Colonial Reform, and the British Constitution* (Athlone Press, NH/London, 1985).

[13] We think W. L. Morison *supra*, n. 3, at 133–41, errs in failing to see the extent to which the positivist analysis was itself modelled on British legal and political institutions.

actual British constitutional and political system. Only in two respects did the Benthamite legacy run into trouble. The first was a very curious development, for which a full explanation remains to be given, a task we shall not attempt here. While Bentham's positivism was, *par excellence*, an instrument for law reform, devised by the greatest law reformer the world has ever known, English positivism in the nineteenth and twentieth centuries became a theory which gave great comfort to legal conservatives. The idea that the duty of the judges was simply to 'follow the law', to which positivism readily contributed, easily became a conservative instrument. Judges who assumed that 'the law' was always something previously 'laid down' which they had no power themselves to make or develop (even where it plainly had *not* been previously 'laid down') could easily disclaim responsibility for the state of the law, and pass the buck to Parliament. And though Parliament did indeed assume the responsibility for reforming and remoulding all the country's legal and political institutions, the fact was that it had neither the time nor the expertise to do everything at once.

The second respect in which the Benthamite legacy ran into trouble is also rather odd, and it is indeed only as a result of the work of H. L. A. Hart in very recent times that we now know how far English nineteenth-century positivism had departed from Bentham's own ideas.[14] Paradoxically, it was from Blackstone, rather than Bentham, that English positivists obtained one of their leading ideas about the nature of the sovereign who was the source of all law. It was Blackstone who had insisted that 'There is and must be in all [governments] a supreme, irresistible, absolute, uncontrolled authority, in which the *jura summi imperii*, or the rights of sovereignty, reside.'[15] It is now clear that Bentham himself had a great deal of trouble with this simplistic notion, partly because he knew perfectly well that there had been historical examples of political societies in which such supreme and unlimited legal authority had never existed in any one source. And even before the Constitution of the United States was adopted in 1788 Bentham actually envisaged the possibility that a political society might exist in which the courts could declare legislation void.[16] But the notion of limited sovereignty gave Bentham trouble because of his insistence that law was the command of a sovereign, and he naturally had great difficulty in explaining the possibility of *legal* limitations on the power of a sovereign from whom all laws sprang. He struggled with the theoretical implica-

---

[14] H. L. A. Hart, *Essays on Bentham*, 58–60, and ch. IV (Clarendon Press, Oxford, 1982).

[15] Bl. Com., I, 49 (1765).

[16] Hart, *supra*, n. 14, at 58–60.

tions of these difficulties for many years, and never reached a wholly satisfactory conclusion.

John Austin's version of the positivist theory grappled even less successfully with these difficulties. Like Blackstone, Austin thought that legal sovereignty was in its nature unlimited and illimitable. And like Blackstone, Austin thought that the British constitution exemplified this doctrine: Parliament was a supreme legislative body with unlimited legislative powers. Austin was not, of course, any more than Bentham, ignorant of the United States Constitution, but his attempt to apply his theory of sovereignty to that Constitution was little more than grotesque: he argued that the federal government was the delegate of the governments of the United States.[17] Interestingly enough, James Wilson, the natural lawyer referred to in the preceding chapter, wrote in 1803 one of the leading opinions in the United States Supreme Court in *Chisholm* v. *Georgia*[18] which established that the United States was a sovereign nation, and not just a confederacy of independent states.

But it was, at least on this point, Austin's version of positivism which became the dominant tradition in England and so thoroughly influenced English lawyers and judges that it became almost literally inconceivable that the judges could ever have power to question the authority of Acts of Parliament. For years, nobody even noticed that the Act of Union with Scotland in 1707 had actually put an end to the Parliaments of England and Scotland and established a new Parliament of Great Britain which, according to the very wording of the two Acts of Union, was not to have unlimited power as regards Scotland.[19] Even today, this fact is rarely given much attention in discussions of the nature of parliamentary sovereignty. English jurists were very slow to wake to the realization that the unlimited nature of Parliament's legislative powers was not a necessary truth, derived from the inherent nature of a sovereign legislature, and that the United States Constitution illustrated a political society in which the law itself defined and limited the authority of law-making and law-applying bodies. At any rate, it is once again clear that the dominant legal theory of nineteenth and twentieth-century England closely meshed with English political and legal reality.

2. AMERICAN LEGAL THEORY IN THE NINETEENTH CENTURY

As we have already mentioned, it is rather remarkable that, given the

---

[17] Austin, *supra*, n. 6, at lecture 6; Morison, *supra*, n. 3, at 83.
[18] 2 Dallas 419 (1792).
[19] MacCormick, 'Does the UK have a Constitution?' 29 *Northern Ireland Law Q.* 1 (1978).

natural law background to the American Revolution, legal positivism should ever have made the very considerable headway in late nineteenth-century America that it did. It is even stranger that this should have happened after the reception of the Constitution of 1788, for (as we argued in the last chapter) the Constitution institutionalized many facets of the natural law tradition. The positivist conception of unlimited sovereignty, and the concept of law as commands or rules laid down by the sovereign, were clearly incompatible with fundamental aspects of the United States Constitution. Certainly, nobody could have argued—especially after *Marbury* v. *Madison*[20]—that any American legislature had unlimited sovereign powers. However, American legal theory had an answer to this problem which nicely fitted the new populism: sovereignty resided in the people, not in the legislatures. Even John Adams, who was not himself a populist, adopted this solution to the dilemma presented by the Blackstonian imperatives.[21]

But positivism of a kind did make substantial headway in America during the later part of the nineteenth century. At the same time there was an increased tendency to formal and formalistic reasoning. Although formal reasoning need not give way to formalistic excesses,[22] it did do so in late nineteenth-century America. This, in due course, provoked the twentieth-century instrumentalist revolution in American legal theory, with its realist offshoots.

By the turn of the century Oliver Wendell Holmes, Jr., and John Chipman Gray, to cite but two prominent examples, subscribed to at least two major positivist tenets: (1) law is essentially something laid down by officials, and therefore valid solely in virtue of its authoritative source, and not even partly in virtue of its content (a doctrine that was actually at odds with the federal Constitution);[23] and (2) law and morals must be sharply separated.[24] At the same time, Holmes, Gray, and others became, in positivist spirit, sharply critical of natural law theorizing. A number of other American thinkers subscribed to further positivist tenets. For example, Christopher Columbus Langdell thought that law essentially took the form of rules and that legal study was really a form of scientific study.[25] We shall see later how Langdell's positivism also

---

[20] 1 Cranch 137 (1803).
[21] See M. White, *The Philosophy of the American Revolution*, 192 (Oxford U. Press, NY, 1978).
[22] See *supra*, ch. 1, 28–30 for the distinction between formal and formalistic reasoning.
[23] Holmes, 'The Path of the Law', 10 *Harv. L. Rev.* 457, 459 (1897); John Chipman Gray, *The Nature and Sources of the Law*, ch. 4 (Columbia, NY, 1909). As to the influence of the English utilitarians and positivists on Holmes, see H. L. Pohlman, *Justice Oliver Wendell Holmes and Utilitarian Jurisprudence* (Harvard U. Press, Cambridge, 1984).
[24] See Holmes, *supra*, n. 23 and Gray, *supra*, n. 23 p. 94.
[25] See generally Gray, 'Langdell's Orthodoxy', 45 *U. Pitt. L. Rev.* 1 (1983).

helped to account for his formalistic approach to law, whereas the positivism of Holmes and Gray did not prevent them being vigorously anti-formalist.

Given our argument that, over time, a close fit can usually be expected between a country's legal theories and the political and legal institutions actually operating in that country, it is incumbent on us to offer some explanation of why—for about half a century—positivism thus took hold in America, despite the very anti-positivist elements which we have already identified in the federal Constitution. Because we do not profess to survey in detail the history of American nineteenth-century legal thought, we can do little more here than offer some possible explanations for this development.

First, of course, any authoritative legal order to *some extent* invites a positivistic account of legal validity. Despite the many powerful strains of natural law ideology embodied in the federal Constitution, the American legal order—like all others known to us—recognized the concept of authoritative legal validity. Naturally, even the American system used (and still uses) a conception of rules whose validity can at least in part be traced to an authoritative source. This, of course, Holmes and Gray saw without difficulty, though they did not use the language of validity. What they seem to have missed, and what the natural law theory informing the Constitution should have taught them, was that merely source-oriented standards of validity are not necessarily the whole story.

One reason why Holmes himself seems to have been attracted to positivism was his complete antipathy to natural law. In this respect Holmes was a Benthamite in spirit. He rejected all talk of morals and morality, except insofar as morality could be identified with a purely utilitarian calculus. His deep moral scepticism, not to say cynicism, pervaded his thought and his work, and the immense influence of Holmes—as well perhaps as the growth of secularism in American thought—must have been an important factor in the declining importance of natural law thinking in the first 30 or 40 years of the twentieth century.

The second reason for the rise of positivism in mid and late nineteenth-century America may have simply been that most American lawyers were little interested in theory during the nineteenth century: they were engrossed in the very practical business of establishing the law across the new continent. This led to some pressing needs, one of which was for a high degree of uniformity and concentration of legal authority. The decision of the United States Supreme Court in *Swift* v. *Tyson*[26] that

---

[26] 16 Peters 1 (US, 1842).

the federal courts had power to declare 'the common law' across the whole United States was an important response to these needs. Although Holmes later denounced the doctrine of *Swift* v. *Tyson* on the very ground that it conflicted with the notion that law was the command of some sovereign or quasi-sovereign,[27] it is in fact not difficult to see the decision as itself dictated by a more positivist conception of law. If there was only one common law throughout the United States, and if the Supreme Court had the authority to lay down what that law was, the Supreme Court could easily be seen as at least the delegate, the articulate voice, of the sovereign. Paradoxically, the ultimate rejection of *Swift* v. *Tyson* by the Supreme Court in *Erie Railroad* v. *Tompkins*[28] can also be explained as a product of the positivist approach. By 1938 the court was concerned about the implications of *Swift* v. *Tyson*: in particular, that case tolerated the idea that more than one sovereign could be issuing commands with regard to the same subject-matter, thereby violating the positivistic canon that there must be only one final and ultimately authoritative legal voice. The court in *Erie* was, of course, also concerned about other related consequences of having multiple sovereigns: inequality before the law, unpredictability of the law, and forum shopping.

Other factors which may explain the reception of positivistic tenets in nineteenth century America may have been the growing separation of law and politics, and the need for lawyers to maintain a low public profile. As to the first point, the natural law heritage and positivist doctrines did not at this time significantly diverge: both led to the view that law was and in some sense had to be 'neutral', and in this sense differed profoundly from politics, which depended upon diverse political ideologies. As to the second point, the waves of Jacksonian democracy and the general distrust of professionalism which permeated nineteenth century America may well have led many judges and lawyers to shelter themselves behind rules and reasoning from rules. Formal reasoning seems to be a way of disclaiming responsibility: if 'the law is the law' then anything that is wrong with the law is not the responsibility of the interpreter or the judge, but of the lawgiver or the legislature.

Furthermore, the extraordinary political power available to the judges when interpreting or applying the federal Constitution may well have tended to encourage a more rule-centred style of reasoning at a time when the people had perhaps still not become accustomed to the notion that their Constitution had entrusted such extensive political power to the judges. Thus towards the end of the nineteenth century a predomi-

[27] *Southern Pacific Co.* v. *Jensen*, 244 US 205, 222 (1917).
[28] 304 US 64 (1938).

nantly conservative judiciary was able to justify both a general refusal to reform the law, and also the striking down of regulatory and welfare legislation by use of formal (if not formalistic) reasoning.

A related factor may have been the necessity for judges and lawyers to cope with the 'peculiar institution' of slavery. Even at the time of the Declaration of Independence, and still more at the drafting of the Constitution of 1788, slavery was something of an embarrassment to those who proclaimed the natural equality and the natural rights of man. It must have been still more of an embarrassment to judges who had to decide legal disputes about slaves as chattels—as items of property which were being bought and sold and pledged. Understandably, judges who had to deal with such cases may have eschewed substantive reasoning and especially the language of morality in their opinions. Better, perhaps, to retreat into positivistic legal rules and formal reasoning altogether, and thus avoid the language of moral rights, when such a peculiar institution, held to be utterly immoral in a large part of the civilized world, gave rise to legal disputes.[29]

There are doubtless other, perhaps deeper, explanations for the reception of positivism in American law during the latter part of the nineteenth century, of which we will mention only one. Scientific positivism seems to have helped to pave the way. Legal positivism reflected an empiricist ethos—valid law just is a verifiable and social fact. To determine the existence of valid law, on the positivist approach, judges needed only to apply source-oriented standards of validity to the *brute facts* of prior legislative or judicial decision making. At the same time, merely source-oriented standards of legal validity also promised high levels of certainty and predictability in the determination of law—values especially appealing to positivists. Such standards do not invite, and indeed allow relatively little room for, substantive argument, with all its uncertainties. Scientific positivism may also have been congenial to positivism by virtue of its influence on the *study* of law. Some came to think that law should be studied as if it were some kind of social fact devoid of all context and substantive purpose. They proclaimed, indeed, that law was itself a science.

3. AMERICAN LEGAL THEORY 1900–1950

As we saw in the last section, important features of English positivist theory had become influential in America at the turn of the century, particularly the doctrine that valid law is merely something laid down by officials—a source oriented standard—and the view that law and

---

[29] Compare Nelson, 'The Impact of the Anti-slavery Movement upon Styles of Judicial Reasoning in Nineteenth Century America', 87 *Harv. L. Rev.* 513 (1974).

morality must be sharply separated. At the same time, the content and working of the legal system became infested with what is often today called formalism. We have previously suggested that formalism is to some degree identifiable with what we have called formalistic reasoning, but it is also sometimes used to describe attributes of a legal system which may have nothing to do with formalistic reasoning. We have also tried to distinguish between the appropriate use of formal reasoning and its inappropriate use which can be called formalistic, a variety of formalism.

Formalism never reached the status of being a legal theory as such,[30] but it clearly had associations with an extreme formal vision of law and often revealed itself in formalistic reasoning. Among its chief characteristics in America at the turn of the century, we may identify the following beliefs, most of which had some implications for the style of reasoning:

(1) Belief that a legal system is something essentially complete and comprehensive, and thus contains pre-existing answers to virtually all questions that arise.

(2) Belief that the doctrine of the separation of powers is an inherent and necessary attribute of a legal system, and that one consequence of that doctrine is that only legislatures and not courts can make law.

(3) Belief that, when a legislature makes new law, it must give heavy if not overriding weight to how the proposed new forms of law harmonize with existing law.

(4) Belief that 'the true law' consists of the rules of law in books, regardless of the nature and extent of divergences between law in books and law in action.

(5) Belief that high generality and abstractness are virtues of law, and are thus to be preferred to concrete formulations in terms of particular fact patterns.

(6) Belief in resort to the inner logic of legal concepts appearing in rules as the primary tool of legal reasoning ('conceptualism').

(7) Belief that judicial decisions must be justified by subsuming their outcome under general concepts embodied in the relevant legal rules.

(8) Belief in certainty and predictability as the highest legal ideals.

No American legal theorist explicitly subscribed to this entire set of beliefs. But these beliefs had, by the turn of the century, become evident in some degree in many judicial decisions, and in other aspects of the working of the American legal system.[31] It was because of this that Karl

---

[30] For a more extended account of the various facets of formalism treated here, see R. S. Summers, *Instrumentalism and American Legal Theory*, ch. 6 (Cornell U. Press, Ithaca, 1982).
[31] *Ibid.*

Llewellyn once referred to this period as 'the least happy days of our legal system'.[32]

Extreme postures and beliefs of this kind generally lead to reactions and this was no exception. Discontent with formalism became increasingly evident during the last decade of the nineteenth century. A group of theorists—we call them instrumentalists—became highly critical of formalism. The leaders of this group were Oliver Wendell Holmes, Jr., then a judge on the Massachusetts Supreme Judicial Court, Roscoe Pound, (who became Dean of Harvard Law School in 1915), John Dewey (who was probably the most influential American philosopher of any era, and who took a strong interest in the law and legal theory), and John Chipman Gray (also at Harvard). Indeed, it was at the turn of the century that the 'instrumentalist revolution' in American legal theory, which was in large part a reaction to the formalism of the preceding period, took shape. Later in the 1920s and 1930s a younger group of writers and theorists carried things a stage further. Some members of this younger group, who constituted a sort of 'left wing' (among whom may be counted Llewellyn), will be referred to here as 'realists', although this term is sometimes used more broadly.

These American theorists were very critical not only of formalism, but of formal reasoning as well. They pursued highly substantive reasoning of the kinds we identified in the first seven chapters. Perhaps because of their hostility to formal reasoning, these theorists failed to note the important distinction between the appropriate use of formal reasoning, on the one hand, and formalistic reasoning or formalism, on the other.

We begin with an essay by Holmes which has probably been the most widely read single essay in the entire history of American legal theory. Called 'The Path of the Law',[33] and published in the *Harvard Law Review* in 1897, this essay includes (not without inconsistency) nearly all the major ideas involved in the instrumentalist revolution. In attacking formalism, Holmes emphasized that the law is not a comprehensive and complete 'system of reason', nor a deduction from 'admitted axioms'.[34] Rather the law is 'what the courts will do in fact'.[35] And referring to judicial opinions which were frequently cast in logical form, Holmes asserted that:[36] 'Behind the logical form lies a judgment as to the relative worth and importance of competing legislative grounds, often an inarticulate and unconscious judgment, it is true, and yet the very root and nerve of the whole proceeding.'

[32] *The Bramble Bush*, 158 (Oceana Publications, NY, 1960).
[33] 10 *Harv. L. Rev.* 457 (1897).
[34] *Ibid.*, at 460.
[35] *Ibid.*, at 461.
[36] *Ibid.*, at 466.

In this way Holmes stressed the primacy of underlying substantive considerations over the mere logical form in which so many opinions and justificatory arguments were written. He also emphasized not generality, nor abstractness, but the particularity of the circumstances of cases, for it is from these that substantive arguments arise. It was this which he had in mind in his famous remark that 'General propositions do not decide concrete cases'.[37] Two years after 'The Path of the Law' appeared, he put his general position in these terms:[38]

We must think things not words, or at least we must constantly translate our words into the facts for which they stand, if we are to keep to the real and the true. I sometimes tell students that the law schools pursue an inspirational combined with a logical method, that is the postulates are taken for granted upon authority without inquiry into their worth, and then logic is used as the only tool to develop the results. It is a necessary method for teaching dogma. But inasmuch as the real justification of a rule of law, if there be one, is that it helps to bring about a social end which we desire, it is no less necessary that those who make and develop the law should have those ends articulately in their minds.

Here we have both a broadside against formalism and an articulation of the two leading tenets of the instrumentalist's overall affirmative position: that any law must 'serve the social ends we desire'—a utilitarian theory of value, which the law is to try to realize, and an instrumentalist conception of law itself. These two themes are highly complex in their own ways, and we cannot pursue them here; suffice it to say that they recur in various parts of 'The Path of the Law' as well. Indeed, in that famous essay, Holmes said that the lawyer must be essentially concerned to 'consider the ends which the . . . rules seek to accomplish, the reasons why the ends are desired, what is given up to gain them, and whether they are worth the price'.[39] Elsewhere, Holmes frequently insisted that he had 'no criterion [sc., of right and wrong] except what the crowd wants'.[40] In all this, he displayed great faith in calculation, for utilitarian and other purposes, proclaiming that 'for the the rational study of the law the black-letter man may be the man of the present, but the man of the future is the man of statistics and the master of economics'.[41] In the face of conflicting desires, he prescribed the highly Benthamite proposal that we must simply measure their intensity and choose the 'greater'.[42] Holmes and other instrumentalists em-

---

[37] *Lochner* v. *New York* 198 US 45, 76 (1905) (one of Holmes J.'s most famous dissents).
[38] 'Law in Science and Science in Law', 12 *Harv. L. Rev.* 443, 460 (1899).
[39] 10 *Harv. L. Rev.* at 476.
[40] See *Pollock–Holmes Letters* (published in America as *Holmes–Pollock Letters*), vol. 1, 163 (M. DeWolfe Howe, ed., Harvard U. Press, Cambridge, 1941).
[41] 10 *Harv. L. Rev.* at 469.
[42] 12 *Harv. L. Rev.* at 456.

phasized the importance of determining the effects of legal rules to ascertain whether they were serving their ends, also an essential feature of utilitarian consequentialism.[43]

We come now to the all important division of labour in the creation of law. Here we must leave Holmes generally and 'The Path of the Law' in particular, because neither sounded the dominant note in instrumentalist theory on these issues. Indeed, Holmes held that courts do not, and ought not to, make much law. They could only make law 'interstitially', so to speak.[44] Most other leading instrumentalists took a very different view.

For example, in his influential book, *The Nature and Sources of The Law*, published in 1909, John Chipman Gray demonstrated in detail that judges had made law for centuries. Indeed, he argued that only the judges can be the true lawmakers, for they always have the last word, even as to the meaning of statutes.[45] Thus for him, legislation was a mere 'source of law'. Only when the judge speaks is there real law. Gray went on to argue that judges *ought* to make law, too, lots of it.

Others did not adopt Gray's view that *only* judges make the law, but nevertheless insisted that judges do make much law (not merely interstitially), and that they ought to do so as well. For example, Pound stressed that the courts have a major responsibility for the substantive quality of the common law and for the quality of decisions interpreting statutes and constitutions.[46] Pound even saw judges as 'social engineers', a term that soon caught on.[47] The later instrumentalists, writing in the 1930s, some of whom were members of the realist wing of this movement, were even more emphatic than Gray and Pound about the essential law-making role of judges, and they regularly criticized courts for failing to be more open about how much freedom of decision they really had and exercised.[48] Indeed, it is safe to say that American theorists in the twentieth century became preoccupied with the judicial process as such.

In this instrumental revolution Pound was even more prominent then Holmes. Pound's writings powerfully expressed an instrumentalist viewpoint and were immensely influential, as many later thinkers acknowledged.[49] Among some of his more important contributions to

---

[43] 10 *Harv. L. Rev.* 457, *passim*.

[44] *Southern Pacific Co.* v. *Jensen* 244 US 205, 221 (1916).

[45] Gray, *supra*, n. 23, at ch. V.

[46] Roscoe Pound, 'Common Law and Legislation', 21 *Harv. L. Rev.* 383 (1908).

[47] *Ibid.,* and see Roscoe Pound, *An Introduction to the Philosophy of Law*, 47 (Yale U. Press, New Haven, 1922).

[48] K. N. Llewellyn, *supra*, n. 32, *passim*.

[49] See, e.g., Llewellyn, Book Review, 28 *U. Chi. L. Rev.* 174 (1960); see also the assessment by Dean Griswold, 'Roscoe Pound', 78 *Harv. L. Rev.* 4 (1964).

instrumentalist thought, which are of particular relevance to our theme, are these. He demonstrated that judges and lawyers usually do rely on general theories of law, whether or not they admit this, and that such general theories should be made more explicit.[50] In formulating his own theory of value for legal ordering, Pound developed an elaborate substantive 'theory of interests' which greatly influenced legal education and legal practice.[51] In filling out his instrumentalist conception of law as a means to an end, he sought to explore the resources of law that could be brought to bear to secure various interests.[52] He was one of the first to see how the law in books can systematically diverge from the law in action, but he believed that this was not always something to be deplored,[53] thereby demonstrating his distrust of high enforcement formality, at any rate in some contexts. He emphasized the need for social science studies essential to the discovery of 'policy facts' on which lawmakers could base new laws.[54] He also enriched our understanding of the relationship between law and morality.[55] And he stressed that much law takes the form, not of hard and fast rules, but of flexible rules incorporating standards, principles, and 'general clauses'.[56]

The realist wing of the instrumentalist movement (Llewellyn, Cook, Frank, and others) deserves to be singled out for comment, because it has, we think, contributed distinctively to the American developments. It is true that, in some of their characteristic writings, the realists merely carried certain instrumentalist ideas further. For example, Llewellyn attacked conceptualism by characterizing it as 'lump concept' thinking[57] that fails sufficiently to differentiate the variety of problems often masked under a single concept or generalization.[58] Some of the realists, following Holmes, also attacked the search for certainty in the law which they thought to be an illusion.[59] But in two respects members of the realist wing struck out more on their own. First, some asserted that *all* law was highly indeterminate; indeed some even came to be called 'rule sceptics'.[60] Jerome Frank also wrote at length on what he called 'fact

---

[50] 'The Philosophy of Law in America', 7 *Archiv für Rechts und Wirtschaftsphilosophie* 214 (1913).

[51] See, for example, Pound, 'Interests of Personality', 28 *Harv. L. Rev.* 343 (1915).

[52] *Ibid.*

[53] 'The Law in Books and the Law in Action', 44 *Am. L. Rev.* 12 (1910).

[54] 'The Scope and Purposes of Sociological Jurisprudence', 25 *Harv. L. Rev.* 140, 489 (1912).

[55] See especially *Law and Morals* (U. of North Carolina Press, Chapel Hill, 1924).

[56] 'Justice According to Law', 14 *Col. L. Rev.* 1 and 103 (1914).

[57] *Cases and Materials on Sales*, 565 (Callaghan & Co., Chicago, 1930).

[58] *Ibid.*

[59] Holmes for instance thought certainty an illusion: 'The Path of the Law', 10 *Harv. L. Rev.* 457, 466 (1897).

[60] See in particular the Preface to, J. Frank, *Law and the Modern Mind* (Anchor Books, 1963 edn.).

scepticism'. In his view, and that of those who followed him, the finding of facts by jurors was so unreliable that it undermined all attempts to state the law in any realistic sense.[61]

Many features of instrumentalist theory, then, are not only inconsistent with specific elements of a formal vision of law, but profoundly at odds with its general spirit as well. On the other hand, mainstream American instrumentalist theory was (and remains) highly congenial to a robust substantive vision of law, in particular in its emphasis on a general value theory for law, on the substantive purposes of law, on the importance of policy in case-law decisions, on the role of reasons of substance behind decisions in applying precedent, on purposive methods of statutory interpretation, and on judicial law making generally. The realist wing of instrumentalism was, if anything, still more hostile to formal reasoning and a formal vision of law.

The close fit which we identified in the last chapter between eighteenth-century natural law ideology and the Constitution of 1788 is paralleled by the equally close fit between many of the tenets of instrumentalism and realism, on the one hand, and the political–legal reality of the twentieth century, on the other.

First, the idea that rules were generally not hard and fast, but were mere guidelines, was not simply a matter of theory. It mirrored the way American courts were increasingly tending to treat rules. Secondly, the belief that precedents should be treated as less binding formal sources of reasoning was also a reflection of what was happening in the courts, deluged as they now were under the weight of the West Reporter system.

Thirdly, the great emphasis placed by the instrumentalist and realist thinkers on judicial law making was also closely related to the realities of the American legal system. In the twentieth century it became increasingly clear that many legal changes in America could be more easily secured from the courts than from the state legislatures, or even the Congress. It was this (among other things) which explained, for instance, the new stress on 'policy facts' as a necessary basis for judicial law making.[62]

Fourthly, the rejection of the older belief in literal methods of

---

Llewellyn himself did not deny the existence of rules, but he did deny that they were the 'heavily operative factor' in most decisions: 'Some Realism about Realism', 44 *Harv. L. Rev.* 1222, 1237 (1931).

[61] J. Frank, *supra*, n. 60.

[62] By comparison, 'policy facts' in England had long since been treated as a matter solely for the legislature, and in the post-Benthamite world the British Parliament was bombarded with an endless supply of policy facts in the famous series of parliamentary papers, or 'blue books'. See G. M. Young, *Portrait of an Age* 33 (2nd ed., OUP, London, 1953).

statutory interpretation is often attributed to a greater appreciation on the part of the instrumentalists of the nature of the judicial task in handling statutes. But it seems equally plausible to suggest that these thinkers were also now more aware of the kind of statutory material they were working with—much of which (as we show in detail in chapter 11) was and is very different from that confronting English judges.

A fifth important strain in the work of the new American theorists which seems to have had a great deal to do with the American legal scene was the new scepticism about the alleged certainty of law. Both rule- and fact-scepticism plainly owed a great deal to increasing awareness that the American legal system was often extremely uncertain in its actual operation. As we have previously pointed out, the pursuit of substantive reasoning in all the different forms we have identified increases uncertainty in American law to very high levels.

More generally, it seems clear in retrospect that the American instrumentalists did not themselves appreciate the extent to which their theories applied to or reflected their own legal and political institutions, but would have been inappropriate transplanted into a different institutional environment like that of England. In this respect they were no different from English positivists who likewise failed to see how deeply rooted positivism was in English legal and political institutions, and who often criticised American instrumentalists in terms suggesting that they understood very little of the American legal context.

In closing this section we need to explain another apparent paradox. If positivism in England proved to be highly congenial to a formal style of reasoning and the institutionalization of that style in England, then why did the same thing not occur in the United States? After all, America by the end of the nineteenth century had a relatively formal (even formalistic) system, and the instrumentalists who came on the scene at this time were (as we have seen) also positivists in at least two major respects. Yet, as we know, the positivism of the American instrumentalists did not in any way inhibit their assault on formalism and formalistic reasoning.

The paradox can be easily resolved. Positivism in American during the late ninteenth and early twentieth centuries was accompanied by an instrumentalist conception of law as a means of social improvement and also by a reformist theory of value—utilitarianism. American positivism at the turn of the century, accompanied as it was by instrumentalism and utilitarianism, tended to foster a much more substantive style than did English positivism at this time. Indeed, as we have seen, utilitarianism all but dropped out of English legal theory in the latter part of the nineteenth century, and instrumentalism never did have much place in English positivism. Moreover, American positivism was less full-blooded to begin with. It was never linked, in the English fashion, with the twin notions of a highly dominant legislature and a relatively inert judiciary concerned only to 'follow the law'. Nor did the positivist notion that the basic form of law consists of a body of hard and fast rules take hold among many American instrumentalists.

4. ENGLISH LEGAL THEORY 1900–1950

English legal theory between 1900 and 1950 need not detain us long, because while the instrumentalist revolution in legal thought was taking place across the Atlantic, English legal theory hardly moved at all. Throughout the whole of this period, legal theory in England remained dominated by the Austinian positivist tradition. Although there were criticisms of Austin's theories in this or that corner, he remained the figure in whose shadow all legal theorists contained to dwell and to write. In 1954 H. L. A. Hart wrote that 'Austin's influence on the development [of legal theory] in England has been greater than that of any other writer,'[63] and as late as 1964, Sir Carleton Allen was still able to write that Austin's general theory is the 'characteristic jurisprudence of England'.[64] We may add, too, that English practising lawyers and judges who have no express views on jurisprudence or legal theory frequently absorb Austinian positivism as part of their general legal training. Furthermore, given (as we have shown) the close fit between Austinian positivism and the actual legal–political system of England since the early nineteenth century, all this is hardly suprising.

We have already identified the close affinities between positivism and a formal approach to law. While Austin himself would not necessarily have adopted the extreme formal approach at all points (for example, he was not wholly resistant to the idea that judges should reform the law[65]), his views are undoubtedly closer to the formal than to the substantive approach, nearly all the way along the line.

5. CONTEMPORARY LEGAL THEORY

To try to separate currents or trends in contemporary legal theory in England and the United States is a difficult enterprise, especially as legal theory has become so closely associated with legal philosophy, and legal philosophy has itself (at least in England and America) come increas-

---

[63] See Hart's Introduction to J. Austin, *The Province of Jurisprudence Determined*, xvi, *supra*, n. 6.

[64] *Law in the Making*, 7 (7th edn., Clarendon Press, 1964). This is also the view of Rumble, 'The Legal Positivism of John Austin and the Realist Movement in American Jurisprudence', 66 *Cornell L. Rev.* 986 (1981).

[65] *Ibid.*, Rumble at 1017–21.

ingly to wear the appearance of being a completely international or trans-cultural subject. But we think it is nevertheless possible to identify distinct trends in the two countries, and to see, even now, that positivist theories in England are attuned to the more formal legal and political system there, while the neo-natural law and instrumentalist theories in America are attuned to the more substantive American system.

In England itself, it really can hardly be doubted that positivism still reigns supreme, despite the recent rebirth of interest in natural law theories,[66] as well as increased interest in theories of law of a more sociological nature.[67] If Benthamite and Austinian positivism had become stale by mid-century, the work of Professor H. L. A. Hart since he became Professor of Jurisprudence at Oxford in 1953 has greatly revivified the strength of English positivism,[68] and there is every sign that the tradition will be continued in the work of one of Hart's most distinguished Oxford disciples and successors, Professor Joseph Raz.[69] In the process, many of the weaknesses of the early positivist theories have been exposed and replaced by the more subtle and flexible version defended by Hart. Among the essential tenets of Hart's version of positivism, the following are readily identifiable.

First, Hart introduced a much more sophisticated, but still positivist, theory for the identification of valid law within particular societies. Hart articulated many of the objections to the command theory,[70] and introduced in its place the concept of a socially accepted fundamental 'rule of recognition', specifying criteria or standards by which valid law could be identified. Although (in one short passage) Hart allowed in his framework for the logical possibility that standards of validity could be content-oriented as well as source-oriented, his emphasis was entirely on the latter—on what one leading contemporary theorist has called 'formal tests of pedigree'.[71] At the same time, Hart recognized that various forms of otherwise valid law could come into conflict, for example, legislation

---

[66] See, e.g., J. Finnis, *Natural Law and Natural Rights* (Clarendon Press, Oxford, 1980).

[67] For some recent examples of writings from a sociological perspective, see A. Hunt, *The Sociological Movement in Law* (Temple U. Press, Philadelphia, 1978); McBarnet, *Conviction, The State and the Construction of Justice* (Macmillan, London, 1981); Podgorecki and Whelan, edd., *Sociological Approaches to Law* (St. Martin's Press, NY, 1981).

[68] See, especially, H. L. A. Hart, *The Concept of Law* (Clarendon Press, Oxford, 1961); H. L. A. Hart, *Essays in Jurisprudence and Philosophy* (Clarendon Press, Oxford, 1983); D. N. MacCormick, *H. L. A. Hart* (Stanford U. Press, Stanford, 1981).

[69] See his *The Concept of A Legal System* (2nd edn., Clarendon Press, Oxford, 1980); *The Authority of Law* (Clarendon Press, Oxford, 1979); *Practical Reason and Norms* (Hutchinson, London, 1975); 'Authority and Justification', 14 *Philosophy and Public Affairs* 3 (1985).

[70] H. L. A. Hart, *The Concept of Law*, supra, n. 68, chs. I–VI.

[71] Ronald Dworkin, 'The Model of Rules', in *Taking Rights Seriously*, ch. 2 (revised edn., Harvard U. Press, 1978).

could conflict with case-law, case-law might conflict with custom, and so on. Here again he adopted a formal approach. Such conflicts are to be resolved by formal rules of hierarchical priority, with no reference whatsoever to substantive reasons arising at the point of conflict.

Secondly, Hart also jettisoned the theory of unlimited sovereignty that had been so prominent in earlier positivist thought. The rule of recognition could itself specify what sort of legislation could be validly enacted, and could thus impose limits on legislative powers. For the first time, English positivists now had a theory which explained how the law makers and the law-making process could themselves be *subject to law*.[72]

Third, Hart saw that his positivist predecessors had, at least in terms, fundamentally misrepresented the basic *form* of law. Law, according to Hart, consists not of sovereign commands, but of a system of *rules*, rules which owe their validity to the rule of recognition.[73] Such a system is also highly comprehensive—the rules rarely run out—and the system is quite determinate—the rules govern nearly all situations.

It is evident that, in our terms, Hart's general jurisprudential emphasis on rules may also be characterized as relatively formal. Most genuine rules are susceptible of high content formality (at least in terms of over- and under-inclusion) and, if taken seriously, they must also have high mandatory formality. Similarly, Hart's stress on the comprehensiveness of existing law is formal. On his view, there is almost always an applicable pre-existing rule. If cases of first impression and the like are rare, there will be little occasion for judges to resort to substantive reasoning. Hart's stress on the determinateness of rules also falls on the formal side of the spectrum. Although he accepts that rules have 'open-texture', he believes (at least he did in his early and middle period) that judges ordinarily do not need to go beyond the 'plain meaning' of the words in which the law is expressed.[74] Thus Hart espouses a formal theory of interpretation.

Hart's position on these issues led him to be especially critical of the extreme scepticism of the realist wing of the American instrumentalist movement. Although he failed to see that some of the causes of their scepticism lay in peculiarities of the American legal system not replicated in England, Hart's own practical experiences as a lawyer in England had probably taught him that this extreme scepticism was much exaggerated in the English context with which he was most familiar. Drawing also on his learning as a philosopher, and on modern philosophical linguistic theories, Hart argued that much of the indeter-

[72] H. L. A. Hart, *supra*, n. 70.
[73] *Ibid.*, at ch. V.
[74] See especially Hart, 'Positivism and the Separation of Law and Morals', 71 *Harv. L. Rev.* 593 (1958). But for the 'later' Hart, see Hart, *supra*, n. 14, at 8.

minacy of the law lay in the open-textured language in which many legal rules were cast; but that this indeterminacy was something which only affected fringe or marginal situations. Central or core cases, falling fair and square within the scope of a rule, give rise to no indeterminacy, and can be dealt with by those whose business it is to apply the law without falling back on any element of discretion. Thus, insisted Hart, rules remain at the centre of a legal system, and law is indeed 'a system of rules':

The life of the law consists to a very large extent in the guidance both of officials and private individuals by determinate rules which, unlike the [discretionary] applications of variable standards, do not require from them a fresh judgment from case to case.[75]

Fourth, Hart continued the positivist tradition of insisting that there is no conceptual link between law and morals. For him, as for Austin, 'The existence of law is one thing; its merit or demerit another.' Unless the positive law *explicitly* incorporates standards of validity requiring that the law have moral content, the certification of law as legally valid implies nothing whatsoever as to the morality of its content. A valid law may be iniquitous. An invalid law may embody the highest morality.[76] One of Hart's reasons for continuing to insist on this separation of law and morals was that (like Bentham) he believed this to be the best way of preserving our ability to criticize and evaluate laws, and of bringing to bear an appropriate focus for purposes of law reform. Again, there is little doubt that Hart's emphasis here is formal rather than substantive in tendency, so far as concerns the daily application and use of law by citizens, officials, and judges. A judge who follows this tradition will think of himself first and foremost as bound to 'follow the law', and will thus be less inclined to take opportunities to improve upon the existing positive law. He will tend to see the job of improving the law as a matter for the legislature.

Finally, and here it must be said that this tenet of Hart's thought is not formal in thrust, Hart advanced upon his predecessors in the positivist tradition when he conceded that a minimum moral content (rules protecting persons, property, and promises) is essential to a viable legal system.[77] In this he repudiated the highly formal views of Kelsen and others to the effect that a system of positive law may have 'just any content' and still be law.

American legal theory today displays a much greater variety of thought than English theory, and it is difficult to encapsulate it within

---

[75] Hart, *supra*, n. 70, at 132.
[76] *Ibid.*, at ch. IX.
[77] *Ibid.*, at 189–95.

any narrow formulation. That there are still strains of positivism is not open to doubt. That instrumentalism and its realist wing have also left enduring legacies in various respects is also not open to doubt. But, in spite of a general reluctance to recognize the fact, it also seems indisputable that the natural law tradition is far from dead. After World War II, Jerome Frank and Karl Llewellyn espoused important tenets of natural law thinking.[78] They both came to stress the primacy of substantive reason in legal ordering, and the extent to which the dictates of reason are not merely creations of the legal mind, but are discoverable in the human condition—in the situations and contexts with which the law must deal.

But it was Lon L. Fuller who became the leading standard bearer of secular natural law in American after World War II.[79] He went beyond the later Frank and the later Llewellyn in several important respects. He attacked the positivist quest for formal, source-oriented standards of validity, and argued that the American system recognized numerous criteria, constitutional and non-constitutional, that make the substantive content of putative law directly relevant to its validity as law.[80] He even argued for a very special version of the ancient doctrine that positive law in conflict with moral law cannot be *valid* law. Thus he held that even a specific rule of highly moral content could not be valid law, 'if it was in fact part of a system... oblivious to the internal morality of law'.[81] The 'internal morality' of law meant for Fuller a variety of norms requiring that law ought to be in the form of rules, ought to be prospective, clear, publicly promulgated, and so on, so that, in the end, citizens would have a fair opportunity to obey. It should be evident that Fuller's doctrine may require, in determining the validity of law, substantive inquiries of large-scale proportions going far beyond merely formal tests of legal validity.

In the same spirit, Fuller generally opposed law having high content formality—law in which fiat was the primary dictate of content. Although in his famous essay on reason and fiat in the common law he argued that an element of both was inevitable in any form of law, he was emphatic that reason should be allowed to 'push' as far as it can.[82] Fuller was also a spirited advocate of purposive interpretation, and thus of low interpretive formality, with respect to both written and unwritten law. He, along with Llewellyn, believed that 'The rule follows where

---

[78] See R. S. Summers, *supra*, n. 30.

[79] See R. S. Summers, *Lon L. Fuller* (Stanford U. Press, Stanford and Edward Arnold, London, 1984).

[80] L. Fuller, *The Law in Quest of Itself* (Northwestern U. Press, 1940).

[81] Summers, *supra*, n. 79, at 71.

[82] Fuller, *supra*, n. 80.

its reason leads; where the reason stops, there stops the rule.' Any such view of the scope of authoritative rules (as we have earlier pointed out) not merely bespeaks low interpretive formality, but at the same time almost eliminates the mandatory formality of rules. In sum, we again see how a general orientation in legal theory, natural law rather than positivist in this instance, can reinforce a vision of law—here the substantive vision.

Fuller had a good deal of influence on American theorists, particularly on Henry M. Hart and Albert Sacks, whose materials on the legal process (though never published) became immensely influential at Harvard and elsewhere in the 1960s and 1970s.[83] Fuller's writings have also become increasingly influential since his death in 1978, despite the fact that he failed to work out his views in a systematic way. Fuller failed to develop, as has American legal theory generally, a synthesis reconciling natural law and positivism, and this helps account for the somewhat schizophrenic appearance which contemporary American legal theory seems to present. Indeed, Professor Hart has suggested, perhaps rather ungenerously, that American legal theory is today divided into a nightmare and a noble dream.[84]

The nightmare is one of the outcomes of instrumentalism and realism which liberated American theorists and judges from an excessive belief in certainty, and from the imaginary and self-created shackles of formalism. Unfortunately, the process of liberation, exhilarating though its immediate effects were, left American theory somewhat rudderless. Mainstream instrumentalism did not evolve into a usable theory of substantive reasoning for the law, and extreme realism served to destroy the previous road, but led nowhere itself.[85] Some facets of realism did fasten on sociological reality, but to a large extent this led to sterile empiricism, ending in 'the deadly bog of behaviorism'.[86] In the 1960s and 1970s a sublime confidence emerged that economics could provide the answers. Hence the growth of interest in the economic analysis of law which, however, has perhaps already begun to wane, at least among lawyers and legal theorists as opposed to economists. More recently the Critical Legal Studies movement has emerged, a movement that has so

---

[83] See H. M. Hart and A. M. Sacks, *The Legal Process* (unpublished teaching materials, 1958). For the influence of these materials, see R. B. Stevens, *Law School*, 271 (U. of North Carolina Press, Chapel Hill, 1983).

[84] 'American Jurisprudence through English Eyes: The Nightmare and the Noble Dream', 11 *Georgia Law Rev.* 969 (1977), reprinted in H. L. A. Hart, *Essays in Jurisprudence and Philosophy*, 123–44 (Clarendon Press, Oxford, 1983).

[85] See Leff, 'Economic Analysis of Law: Some Realism about Nominalism', 60 *Va. L. Rev.* 451 (1974).

[86] To borrow a phrase one of us has used before: R. S. Summers, *supra*, n. 30, at 115.

far generated little constructive theory, but which to many of its critics also has some of the characteristics of a nightmare!

The noble dream, on the other hand, is, according to Professor Hart, the theory of Ronald M. Dworkin, the Professor of Jurisprudence at Oxford University. Dworkin is an American and, in our terms, an advocate of perhaps the most substantively oriented legal theory of all times.[87] Naturally, we do not find it surprising that Dworkin is at the same time a vigorous critic of the positivist tradition, including Hart's work. Though Dworkin was a pupil of Hart's, his legal theory is much more Fullerian than Hartian in spirit.

According to Hart Professor Dworkin's 'noble dream' is that a Herculean judge can find, and ordinary judges ought to try to find, the 'correct' legal answer to almost every case by deciding the case so as to provide the closest 'fit' with existing rules and other forms of law consistent with the best version of the entire body of substantive moral and other justificatory *principles* underlying those rules and other forms of law.[88] Whether or not one thinks this general theory to be unworkable and thus only a kind of 'noble dream', the point we wish to stress is that such a general theory unfolds in a variety of important respects that, in our terms, are highly substantive.

First, Dworkin has enabled us to see more clearly than anyone before him the full meaning of the criticism that traditional positivist theories of legal validity are formal and thus cannot account for the legal status of important varieties of law, especially in the American legal system. Dworkin not only stresses that valid law often depends on the satisfaction of content-oriented standards of validity; he goes well beyond this in showing that that there is an important form of law—capable of generating legal rights—which he calls 'principles'. Such principles cannot be accounted for, according to Dworkin, by source-oriented standards of validity. One of the examples he gives is the principle that 'no person shall profit from his own wrong', and he cites cases in which this principle has been recognized as law, and has actually generated legal rights. The status of such principles cannot (he argues) be explained by reference to formal source-oriented criteria of validity. Such principles may be decisive in some cases, but not in others, depending on their *weight*, a substantive dimension that cannot be captured by source-oriented 'tests of pedigree'.[89]

Second, and implicit in this analysis, Dworkin rejects Hart's theory that law takes the form of *a system of rules*. Of course Dworkin

---

[87] See especially, *Taking Rights Seriously* (revised edn., Harvard U. Press, Cambridge, 1978); *A Matter of Principle* (1984); *Law's Empire* (Harvard U. Press, Cambridge, 1986).
[88] See Dworkin, *Taking Rights Seriously*, *supra*, n. 87, at ch. 4.
[89] *Ibid.*, at ch. 2.

recognizes that a legal system must contain rules, but he places much greater stress than Hart on other forms and ingredients of law, including substantive principles, policies, and so on. He also recognizes that *if* a rule clearly governs (and this is to be determined partly in light of principles—a form of substantive reasoning) then it usually controls even in the face of a conflicting principle, unless that principle is embodied in a form of law entitled to priority. Thus in our terms Dworkin allows for the mandatory formality of rules, but, compared with Hart and many other positivists, Dworkin not only determines the applicability of rules partly in light of substantive considerations, he also sees more situations in which the rules do not clearly govern, or in which it is appropriate for the judge to recast the rules or even depart from them in the name of substantive reasoning to improve the law. In this respect, Dworkin's theories fit the American legal system far more closely than the English.

Dworkin thus has a highly substantive theory of the judicial role. Much of his theory focuses on so-called 'hard cases' where, for example, the rules do not unqualifiedly displace pre-existing principles, the rules 'run out', the rules conflict, or the weight of countervailing principles is so great that the rule (in the case of the common law) should be abandoned and a better one substituted. Here Dworkinian judges are to be sensitive to the very real possibilities of improving and developing the law—indeed, when they properly assess the bearing of applicable principles, they may find that the substantively best law has really been the law all along. The Dworkinian judge is not, in the fashion of the Hartian judge, categorically enjoined to 'stick by the rules', subject only to the scope allowed him by their open texture. In Dworkin's overall scheme, legal rules do not have the relatively high degree of mandatory formality that most English judges accord them.

Dworkin has written a great deal, but it was not until his *Law's Empire*, published in 1986, that he set forth a fully developed general theory of interpretation. Earlier he had frequently argued that the proper scope of a rule is, in our terms, to be determined largely in light of its underlying substantive reasons, a view of low interpretive formality that operates to cut down any under- or over-inclusion of the rule, and thereby also reduce its content formality. In *Law's Empire*, he goes beyond this, and advocates an interpretive attitude to law, with a view of law as 'integrity' in which propositions of law are true if they follow from the principles of justice, fairness, and procedural due process that provide the best constructive interpretation of the community's legal practice, an approach that requires judges to draw on their own convictions about justice and fairness.[90] On this view, many rules should be recast so that they can be understood in their best possible light.

Dworkin has at the same time explicitly and articulately injected a general theory of rights back into legal theory.[91] Such rights derive from rules, principles, and other forms of law, but they also derive from moral principles. If not called a theory of natural rights, and not explicitly based on notions of human nature, Dworkin's theory is surely a first cousin to an old tradition in American law and theory.

The essence of Dworkin's theory on rights seems to lie in the belief that the judicial function, being an undemocratic political function exercised by unelected and unaccountable judges, cannot be supposed to involve the degree of judicial legislation which Hartian positivism and American instrumentalism require.[92] According to Dworkin, judges are not expected to weigh utilitarian goals about the collective welfare when deciding points of unestablished law. Their function is to protect rights, which have a weight to them which cannot be simply overridden by considerations of collective welfare. The most fundamental of these rights (which perhaps embraces all others) is the right to equal treatment and respect.[93]

It would not be difficult to find a considerable body of philosophical and jurisprudential literature in America today which discusses legal issues, and the judicial function, from a somewhat similar perspective.[94] Indeed, there are signs of growing revulsion from the lessons of the instrumentalists among those who espouse the belief that modern legal theories ought to be based on rights, because the instrumentalists were arguably fundamentally utilitarians, and rights theory is anti-utilitarian.[95]

Once again, we find it hardly surprising that these theories seem to fit the legal and political contexts from which they arise. American law is

---

[90] *Law's Empire, supra*, n. 87.

[91] Of course modern rights theory has been detached from natural law, and especially religious natural law, and so faces the accusation that 'it looks too much like an attempt to keep the grin while silently and surreptitiously disposing of the now rather embarrassing cat'. Milton, 47 *Mod. L. Rev.* 751, 758–9 (1984). But as we noted in ch. 8, eighteenth-century natural law in America was already predominantly secular.

[92] A colleague has suggested to us that American rights theory is not truly a *limitation* on instrumentalism, but is in fact complementary to it, because the individual right-holder is the source of all authority in America, being a sort of quasi-sovereign; and, with the rest of the citizenry, the full sovereign.

[93] See, e.g., 'Is there a Right to Pornography?' 1 *Ox. J. Leg. St.* 177 (1981).

[94] For instance, the writings of Charles Fried, see, e.g., *Contract As Promise* (Harvard U. Press, Cambridge, 1982); *Right and Wrong* (Harvard U. Press, Cambridge, 1978); see also the symposium in 13 *Georgia Law Rev.*, 1117ff. (1979).

[95] See, e.g., Moore, 'The Need for a Theory of Legal Theories: Assessing Pragmatic Instrumentalism: A Review Essay of *Instrumentalism and American Legal Theory*, by Robert S. Summers', 69 *Cornell L. Rev.* 988 (1984).

today full of discussion of rights. The United States Supreme Court for the past thirty years, though with some ebbing and flowing of the tide, has been protecting fundamental constitutional rights, and this has sometimes been done with the implication that such rights cannot be outweighed by utilitarian considerations of collective welfare. For instance, as we saw earlier, the Supreme Court's treatment of the exclusionary rule under the Fourth Amendment is sometimes based on the protection of the rights of the accused against wrongful and degrading police activities, irrespective of the fact that a utilitarian weighing of the costs and benefits might suggest that the rule should be waived and a conviction recorded.[96] Similarly, the Supreme Court's use of the entrapment defence to criminal prosecutions has sometimes been based on arguments which, if not actually expressed in the language of rights, appears close to an acceptance of that theory and a rejection of more utilitarian considerations.[97] So also, Congress has recently taken to passing Acts which confer rights, often in the vaguest terms, and with ill-defined standards, which might be thought support for the view that the elaboration and defence of rights in general is an appropriate role for the courts.

We cannot today attempt any assessment of where rights theory is leading in America. Certainly, these developments are not replicated in England, where (as Dworkin himself has noted[98]) the language of political discourse tends still to be strongly utilitarian in character, and even judicial protection of rights is nearly always balanced against considerations of the public welfare or public interest.[99] But what surely can be said is that rights theory has a long and honourable ancestry in the natural law tradition in America, and that it has long been closely associated with less formal and more substantive modes of legal reasoning, which fit the American context for the reasons we have sought to explain. By contrast, natural law theory has had little following in England at least since the time of Bentham, and rights theory today would be found hard to reconcile with the more formal styles of legal reasoning which are generally more appropriate in the English context, as well as with the strongly utilitarian character of English political debate.

---

[96] *Supra*, 179.

[97] *Supra*, 180.

[98] R. Dworkin, 'Political Judges and the Rule of Law', LXIV *Proc. Brit. Acad.* 259, 285–6 (1978).

[99] See, e.g., J. Bell, *Policy Arguments in Judicial Decisions*, especially chapters IV, V, and VI (Clarendon Press, Oxford, 1983).

10

The Courts

1. THE FUNCTION OF COURTS OF LAST RESORT

In the first part of this book we have identified various respects in which the English legal system relies more heavily on legislation and less on appellate courts as engines of reform and change. We have argued that this is one of the factors that makes English law more formal than American law. We now need to look more closely at the courts in the two countries. Appellate courts and, in particular, courts of last resort necessarily have a special place in any legal system, but they do not serve precisely the same function in all legal systems. Differences in their functions naturally reflect upon, and are reflected by, differences in their methods of working. In this chapter we shall explore a variety of factors relating to the courts as institutions, factors which bear on the degree of formality with which they tend to operate. As we shall see, various institutional factors help to explain why English courts are more formal and American more substantive.

We shall begin by looking at courts of last resort, and we shall then turn to other appellate courts and trial courts. There is only one court of last resort in England—the House of Lords (which indeed functions also as the court of last resort for the separate jurisdictions of Scotland and Northern Ireland); in the United States there are many courts of last resort, one for each of the fifty states, those for the territories, and the federal Supreme Court.

In England it is almost universally held that judges should and generally do avoid 'political' decisions. In America, on the other hand, a body of legal opinion holds that all 'judicial opinions are inescapably and rightly political',[1] even those that purport merely to apply law enacted by the legislature. The English position may be criticised as being theoretically incoherent or indefensible; how can it be possible for judges to take account of policy factors in exercising their secondary function of law making (as most English judges now admit must

---

[1] R. Dworkin, 'Political Judges and the Rule of Law', LXIV *Proc. Brit. Acad.* 259, 261 (1978), noting that this is not a unanimous view in America. See also R. A. Posner, *The Federal Courts: Crisis and Reform*, at 18–19 (Harvard U. Press, Cambridge, 1985), noting that 'American law is inherently more political than English'; W. Murphy and C. Pritchett, *Courts, Judges and Politics* 3 (2nd ed., Random House, NY).

sometimes be done[2]), if they are not to be 'political'?[3] Clearly, the two positions are inconsistent unless a narrow meaning can be given to the term 'political' here, and it may be that there are serious difficulties in trying to do this. Since value judgments underlie nearly all policy choices, and since selection of values is the essence of political controversy, it is hard to avoid the conclusion that policy making is a political activity. If the judges could claim that they only chose uncontroversial policies, where the underlying values would be widely or almost universally accepted, it might be argued that judicial policy decisions were 'non-political'; and the somewhat 'positivist' nature of much English contemporary morality may lend support to the belief, or at least the appearance, that judges are not making controversial value judgments when they decide policy questions. On the other hand, detailed examination of a number of areas of case-law suggests that policy decisions in England cannot be explained in this way.[4] But however theoretically weak the position of the judges may be on this question, what matters for present purposes is that the English judges believe that it is possible to make policy decisions (on the occasions when this is necessary—rare occasions, in their view) in a neutral sort of way without seriously impinging on the general, formal, rule-oriented nature of the legal system. These beliefs are important, however ill founded they may be, because they influence the judicial view of the proper function of courts of last resort, and hence also influence the way they decide cases.

It would be a formidable task to attempt to collect direct evidence to support the hypothesis that many American judges in courts of last resort actually perceive their function differently from English judges, and we will not undertake that task here.[5] Instead we will enumerate several factors which support the hypothesis. Specifically we will argue that certain differences between the American and English courts with respect to their constitutional positions, political influence, case selection procedures, and reliance on arguments from the bar tend to make the English judiciary much more cautious in exercising their law-making

---

[2] See, e.g., *McLoughlin* v. *O'Brian* [1983] 1 AC 410, though note the view of Lord Scarman that judges should stick to principle and eschew policy, *ibid.*, at 430. See also Lord Roskill, 'Law Lords, Reactionaries or Reformers', 37 (1984) *Cur. Leg. Prob.* 247, 258 (judges have a 'policy' but not a 'political' role).

[3] See J. Bell, *Policy Arguments in Judicial Decisions*, 4–7 (Clarendon Press, Oxford, 1983). There are signs that Lord Hailsham is more aware than most of his colleagues that policy judgments and politics are inseparable, see *ibid.*, 5.

[4] See the conclusions of Bell's study, *supra*, n. 3, especially ch. IX.

[5] But for the view of one American judge, not (yet) on the court of last resort, see Posner, *supra*, n. 1, at 18–19. *Cf.*, for America perceptions of judicial role among state supreme court judges, H. R. Glick and K. N. Vines, 'Law making in the State Judiciary', 2 *Polity* 142 (Winter 1969).

function. We begin by pointing to the different constitutional positions of the courts of last resort in the two countries.

There are many political issues on which the judges have the last word in the United States, but not in England. In particular, there is the striking phenomenon of judicial review in the United States which is, of course, unknown in England. This has been the subject of so much discussion in the literature of lawyers and political theorists that emphasis on it may perhaps have obscured a number of other equally important points on which we intend to focus.

First, we note one crucial, and indeed symptomatic, difference between the two highest courts. The United States Supreme Court is one collegial court, in which all the judges participate in all the decisions (unless a judge is disqualified from sitting in any particular case). But the House of Lords is not a collegial court; it is composed of about ten judges who are qualified to sit, rather than one single court. In practice the House of Lords sits in two panels, usually of five judges each. This difference is highly significant, because it reflects the English belief that it is largely immaterial which judges hear which appeals; the United States Supreme Court could not possibly sit in panels without a radical change in its functions. It is well known that there are nearly always ideological, if not indeed 'political', divisions of opinion among the judges of the Supreme Court, and given the highly political nature of many of the decisions the court is called upon to make, the composition of a panel would frequently determine the outcome of the appeal. Moreover, given the case selection procedure (which we deal with later in this chapter), the body which selected the cases and allocated them to the different panels would become more important than the Supreme Court itself, clearly an impossible state of affairs.

Second, the judiciary in America also often has the last word with regard to the way statutes are to operate, and to the way in which the common law is to develop. As we saw in chapters 4 and 5, the situation is very different in England. Any House of Lords decision with serious political implications is open to subsequent modification or reversal by Parliament,[6] sometimes even with retrospective effect.[7] And in the British political system, this is no mere ritual phrase on the lips of judges anxious to disclaim ultimate responsibility for the long-term state of the law. It is a reflection of political reality. It may occasionally happen that, for some political reason, the government feels unable to overrule a

---

[6] And this is sometimes done very quickly, see, e.g., the Trade Disputes Act 1965 overturning the decision in *Rookes* v. *Barnard* [1964] AC 1129.

[7] See, e.g., War Damage Act 1965 retrospectively overturning the decision of the House of Lords in *Burmah Oil Co.* v. *Lord Advocate* [1965] AC 75.

judicial decision which it would have preferred to see go the other way, but in the British political system this will be a rare event.[8]

Of course, even in America, judicial interpretation of legislative enactments, and ordinary common law judicial decisions, are in theory subject to legislative change, as in England. But it is often far more difficult to overrule decisions of courts of last resort in America than it is in England. Some of the reasons for this have already been referred to,[9] and others will be touched upon in the next chapter. American executive branches do not control legislatures, party lines are much less strongly observed in practice, legislative procedures often give disproportionate influence to the chairmen of committees and subcommittees, and so on. In short, American legislatures, both at the federal and state level, are far less efficient in *the production of legislation* than is the British system of government. This gives the American appellate courts greater freedom to pursue their own policies and values, even in those cases in which they are in principle subject to legislative reversal. This freedom is exercised vigorously, not only by federal courts, but also by many state courts, which are sometimes even more 'activist' than the federal courts.[10] Indeed, there can be little doubt that one of the principal reasons that American courts make so much law is that (by comparison with the British Parliament) American legislatures make so little.[11]

The fact that American courts are willing to perform many functions which in other countries would fall to the legislature naturally reacts back onto other members of the legal world. Law reformers, lobbyists, political pressure groups, and so on are encouraged to turn to the courts for legal change in America, where in England they would always turn to Parliament, the government bureaucracy, or the political parties. Indeed, it has been suggested that legal change in America is both more speedily[12] and more cheaply[13] obtained through the judicial than

---

[8] Dworkin overlooks this in his British Academy lecture, *supra*, n. 1.

[9] See *supra*, at 156.

[10] See Howard, 'State Courts and Constitutional Rights in the Day of the Burger Court', 62 *Va. L. Rev.* 874 (1976).

[11] One illustration is provided by the way in which some courts introduced comparative negligence by judicial decision after their state legislature had repeatedly failed to enact comparative negligence statutes simply because procedural devices were used to ensure that they never had a chance to vote on them. See the discussion in ch. 11, at 327. See also, on the weaknesses of the state legislative process and the consequent necessity for judicial activism, M. C. Porter, 'State Supreme Courts and the Legacy of the Warren Court: Some Old Inquiries for a New Situation', 3, 8–9, in *State Supreme Courts*, (M. C. Porter and G. A. Tarr, edd., Greenwood Press, Westport, Conn., 1982).

[12] M. Rosenberg, 'Anything Legislatures Can Do, Courts Can Do Better?' 62 *ABAJ* 587 (1976).

[13] R. Neely, *How Courts Govern America*, 30, 71 (Yale U. Press, New Haven, Conn., 1981).

through the legislative process, results which seem astonishing to the English lawyer.

Judicial activism in America is not, however, merely the result of the failure of legislatures to legislate. It is also due to the fact that American legislatures are often unable to perform (or to perform effectively) other functions performed by Parliament in England. For example, Parliament retains certain questioning and inquisitorial functions, such as searching out instances of executive corruption or failures of the democratic system. In America, the federal Congressional committee system can often be a useful weapon for inquisitorial purposes (sometimes more effective than parliamentary questioning), but it is in general much slower to respond to events, and tends to become unwieldy and cumbersome in operation. The result is that the inquisitorial functions of the legislature have to some degree been taken over by the courts,[14] particularly with regard to such matters as executive corruption and the policing of the democratic system itself.

Courts of last resort in the American system thus know that their decisions are not likely to be overruled by the legislature even when they are not immune to such overruling for constitutional reasons. As a result American judges are much more free than their English colleagues to decide cases in accordance with their own personal value systems and predilections, and there is much in the substantively oriented American traditions and institutions to encourage them to do just that.[15]

As we shall see in chapter 12, both the function and the personal backgrounds of judges in America tend to be far more overtly political than those of their English counterparts. We shall comment on this in greater detail below; here we simply note that, almost by definition, politicians tend to be either goal-oriented people or power-ambitious people; such people are more likely to decide questions of law in legal disputes in accord with the results they want to produce in the legal system or in society at large. English judges, who see their role as more professional and less political, and who nowadays rarely have any political background before appointment to the bench, are far less likely to decide cases in accordance with their own political beliefs and desires.

2. SELECTION OF CASES FOR DECISION

The extent to which an appellate court can control the cases it will decide

---

[14] *Ibid.*, ch. 5.

[15] There is a considerable literature attempting to document this in statistical terms. See, for a sample, Glendon Schubert, *The Judicial Mind* (Northwestern U. Press, Evanston, Ill., 1965) and *The Judicial Mind Revisited* (Oxford U. Press, NY, 1974). For one tentative attempt to do a similar job for England, see David Robertson, 'Judicial Ideology in the House of Lords: A Jurimetric Analysis', 12 *Br. J. of Pol. Sc.* 1 (1982).

may not only facilitate but encourage a court to see its role in more substantive terms, as that of carrying out various programmes of judicial innovation and reform, rather than in more formal terms, as that of merely applying rules to correct errors of law committed by lower court judges. A court with a large number of cases to choose from can, in deciding what cases to hear, select those that will afford the most opportunities to advance desired policies (a substantive enterprise) rather than hear those in which formal law may have been misapplied. American courts of last resort have increasingly asserted control over their own dockets or (as they would be called in England) lists.

These courts are today overburdened with appeals and applications for review. Complaints about the crowded United States Supreme Court docket, both from the Chief Justice of that court and others, are too numerous to detail. State supreme courts experience similar burdens. For instance, between 1975 and 1976, the number of cases pending before 37 state courts of last resort increased by 15.6%.[16] The result of these pressures is that since about 1960 most state supreme courts in the larger and medium-sized states have acquired power to choose their own dockets,[17] in the same way as the US Supreme Court. This enables these courts to select those cases that they regard as the most suitable vehicles for making policy pronouncements designed to have a significant legal or social impact. Indeed, it is quite easy for such a court virtually to invite appeals on certain issues, and then to select them for decision when they are presented.[18] Thus one of the traditional restraints on the political powers of courts—that they have no power to *initiate* policy decisions —is today much less operative in many American courts of last resort. That some of these courts do actually use their power of selecting which cases to hear for political purposes—that is, to advance certain policies the judges believe to be important—is indisputable. Indeed, in the case of the US Supreme Court,[19] this seems not only an evident fact, but one

---

[16] State Court Caseload Statistics, *Annual Report* 1976; Kagan, Cartwright, Friedman, and Wheeler, 'The Evolution of State Supreme Courts', 76 *Mich. L. Rev.* 961 (1978). Between 1977 and 1983, the caseload of courts of last resort continued to increase dramatically, by 17% in states with intermediate appellate courts, and by 29% in states without. In four states which created intermediate appellate courts after 1977, the caseload of the highest court fell by 21%. Over a thousand cases were filed in each of the highest courts of 21 states in 1981. Flango and Elsner, 'Advance Report: The Latest State Court Caseload Data', 7 *State Court Journal* 16, 22 (1983).

[17] Kagan, Cartwright, Friedman, and Wheeler, *supra*, n. 16, at 973.

[18] See generally D. M. Provine, *Case Selection in the United States Supreme Court* (U. of Chicago Press, Chicago, 1980).

[19] D. M. Provine, *supra*, n. 18, cites at 34 the statement of one (anonymous) justice who said he would vote not to take a case he thought 'outrageously wrong' if he believed the court would affirm it. 'I'd much prefer bad law to remain the law of the 8th Circuit or the State of Michigan than to have it become the law of the land.'

whose legitimacy is now largely taken for granted.[20] The Supreme Court can be extremely selective in the cases that it chooses to hear and perhaps *use*, in order to make policy decisions. In 1982, for instance, the court agreed to hear only 3% of the cases for which petitions for *certiorari* review were filed.[21]

The Supreme Court's power of discretionary review is not the only doctrine affecting the cases it decides. Doctrines of justiciability, standing, mootness, ripeness, and the like have long enabled the court to *avoid deciding* difficult issues. Yet in some cases, such as *Duke Power Co.* v. *Carolina Environmental Study Group, Inc.*,[22] the court seems to have tortured concepts of justiciability in order to enable it to *decide* a controversial issue. Despite serious questions about the plaintiffs' standing to sue, and the ripeness of their claim, the court in the *Duke Power* case declared that a federal statute limiting the liability of nuclear energy bodies was constitutional. One commentator concluded that '*Duke Power's* extreme departure from traditional articulated standards of justiciability stemmed from the court's desire to affirm the constitutionality of [the federal statute]'.[23] Thus even the limiting doctrine of justiciability may itself be circumvented when the judges wish to advance their policy views.

These changes in the ways in which cases are selected for review by courts of last resort have affected the kinds of cases that they hear. There has, for example, been a vast increase in the number of cases dealing with public law, including constitutional rights and criminal law—cases which generally offer more scope for broader policy making—and a great decrease in the number of private and commercial cases heard by such courts.[24] Many commercial law cases also have other disadvantages for judges who wish to advance their own policy views: they often raise more complex technical issues, as well as being less exciting in human terms.

In the upshot, it seems no exaggeration to conclude that—whatever the judges may say—most (or at least many) courts of last resort in America see their primary function not as that of correcting errors in the lower courts, nor as that of exercising a general oversight of the

[20] See, e.g., the remarks of Vinson CJ in 1949 cited in J. B. Grossman, *Lawyers and Judges: The ABA and the Politics of Judicial Selection*, 12 (Wiley, NY, 1965). It is widely believed that the failure of the Freund Study Group's Report (on reducing the burden of cases on the Supreme Court) to secure general support was due to their lack of appreciation of the importance of case selection to the role of the Supreme Court. (The Study Group proposed the creation of a National Court of Appeals which would have selected most of the cases for the Supreme Court to hear).

[21] *National LJ*, 2 May 1983, p. 1, col. 1.

[22] 438 US 59 (1978).

[23] Varat, 'Variable Justiciability and the *Duke Power* Case', 58 *Tex. L. Rev.* 273, 280 (1980).

[24] Kagan, Cartwright, Friedman, and Wheeler, *supra*, n. 16, at 990.

functioning of the lower courts, but as that of making law for the future. As long ago as 1927, even so moderate a judge as Cardozo expressed the view that the state's highest court existed not for the 'individual litigants, but for the indefinite body of litigants'.[25] Today, though the trend is now under attack,[26] it is very widely accepted that American appellate courts have a broad social function as innovators of desirable change, especially in matters of public law. This attitude on the part of many courts also reflects back on the bar, because counsel seeking to persuade a court to take a case for review will naturally stress the important social implications of the case and invite the court to take the responsibility for a bold and innovative decision.[27]

It has been observed by some American commentators that there is a tendency for other American appellate court judges to emulate the US Supreme Court model (with its almost complete docket control), even though that model is in many ways inappropriate for other appellate courts, whose primary business has traditionally been that of correcting lower court errors, rather than making law.[28] Thus even though litigants have a right of appeal to federal appeals courts, there are signs, which some lawyers find worrying, of a tendency for those courts to grant full hearings only to those cases offering opportunities for innovative decision making. While it is hardly surprising that overburdened courts should act in this way, the result is to facilitate the more active political role which many American judges wish to play, as compared with their English counterparts.

It is scarcely open to doubt that similar motives often influence state supreme courts.[29] Some critics protest that this approach is unfair to litigants who may thus be denied their opportunity for a real scrutiny of the law laid down or applied to their case. But our interest lies in the wider implications for the legal system as a whole. For instance, this approach may influence lower court behaviour (as we shall see later) if judges in those courts have the impression that their decisions may not

---

[25] *Ibid.*, 973.
[26] See, e.g., Rehnquist, 'The Notion of a Living Constitution', 54 *Tex. L. Rev.* 693 (1976).
[27] See Kagan, Cartwright, Friedman, and Wheeler, *supra*, n. 16.
[28] See Paul D. Carrington, 'Ceremony and Realism: Demise of Appellate Procedure', 66 *ABAJ* 860 (1980).
[29] One author notes that supreme courts with discretionary review reverse more frequently, have more frequent dissents, commonly involving constitutional or controversial issues, and produce longer opinions. Project, 'The Effect of Court Structure on State Supreme Court Opinions: A Re-examination', 33 *Stan. L. Rev.* 951 (1981). This may be caused in part by the use of these selected cases as tools to make policy decisions. See also Preble Stolz, *Judging Judges* (The Free Press, NY, London, 1981), esp. at 194–6; Kagan, Cartwright, Friedman, and Wheeler, *supra*, n. 16, at 983, 990, and the same authors' 'State Supreme Courts: A Century of Style and Citation', 33 *Stan. L. Rev.* 773, 806 (1981).

be subject to serious review by higher courts when the issues are not of great social importance. More generally, doing substantive justice from case to case may become more important than securing compliance with the formal rules of law.

In all these respects, the position in England differs quite fundamentally from that in the United States. English courts would certainly reject the idea that courts ought to be initiators of social change. One recent extra-judicial pronouncement on the judicial role in England confirms that the primary function of the courts is still to determine disputes in accord with rules of law, and that though 'the decisions of the courts ought to reflect change which has been taking place', it is not a function of the courts to *initiate* or *prevent* social change.[30] This general view would almost certainly be non-controversial among English judges. What controversy there is concerns the degree to which the courts, as opposed to Parliament, have the responsibility for changing the law to keep pace with existing social change.

As regards case selection, the position in England is that all English appeals to the House of Lords come from the Court of Appeal, and either that court or the House of Lords' appellate committee has to grant leave to appeal.[31] So far as comparisons with the US Supreme Court are concerned, only applications to the House of Lords' appellate committee are relevant, and the total volume of applications for leave to appeal is very low compared with the number of cases heard.[32] There is nothing at all resembling the immense ratio of rejected to granted *certiorari* applications in the US Supreme Court. The grounds on which leave to appeal is granted by the House of Lords' appellate committee[33] are not always apparent, and no doubt vary from case to case.[34] Dissent in the Court of Appeal is usually a sufficient ground. Other cases are taken because of their public importance (for example, tax cases, or cases challenging the validity of some important governmental action), but, given the general nature of the English judicial role and the apolitical background of the judges, it is almost unthinkable (as well as largely

---

[30] Sir Sydney Templeman (now Lord Templeman), 'An English View of the Judicial Function', in *Legal Institutions Today: English and American Approaches Compared*, 6 (H. W. Jones, ed., ABA, 1977).

[31] Administration of Justice (Appeals) Act 1934; see generally L. Blom-Cooper and G. Drewry, *Final Appeal*, ch. VII (Clarendon Press, Oxford, 1972).

[32] For instance in 1982 there were only 110 applications for leave to appeal made to the House of Lords, of which 34 were allowed and 74 refused (two were withdrawn). See *Judicial Statistics 1982* (HMSO, 1983). For earlier years, see Blom-Cooper and Drewry, *supra*, n. 31, at 42–3.

[33] As to applications to the Court of Appeal for leave to appeal from that court to the House of Lords, see Blom-Cooper and Drewry, *supra*, n. 31, at 140.

[34] See generally Blom-Cooper and Drewry, *supra*, n. 31, ch. VII. The grounds for granting leave by the Court of Appeal are more easily discerned. *Ibid.*, 146–8.

pointless) for leave to appeal to be granted by judges with the aim of furthering some policy views of their own. The only policy that seems to be clearly followed is to grant leave to appeal where lower court decisions seem to be aberrational, or to depart from established law. It is also unthinkable for the House of Lords not to hear an appeal where conflicting decisions have been rendered by lower courts of equal authority (which itself rarely happens in England), for this would leave the law in a state of uncertainty unacceptable to the English legal profession. By contrast, it is by no means unknown for the US Supreme Court to refuse to hear a case even though differing decisions raising the identical point have been rendered by different appeals courts.

Thus correcting errors in lower courts remains the major function of the English House of Lords, and is seen to be such by most judges of the House of Lords.[35] Although the broader public importance of their decisions is not irrelevant in the selection of cases for appeal, this public interest is usually seen to lie in clarifying the law, or in eliminating doubts or confusion following from lower court decisions, and thereby providing guidance to judges and, of course, enabling parties and their advisers to plan their affairs. These are formal 'rule of law' values.

One result of these differing criteria for selecting cases to be heard by courts of last resort is that few criminal cases reach the House of Lords, perhaps two or three per annum;[36] by contrast, American courts of last resort hear very large numbers of criminal cases though most of them raise issues of due process rather than substantive law. On the other hand, the House of Lords still hears many contract or commercial cases of great importance to the parties, but of little general significance; indeed, many House of Lords' decisions are of so little general legal interest that they remain unreported.[37] As we have noted, the US Supreme Court hears few such cases, and the proportion in state supreme courts is also declining.[38]

We conclude this section with another reference to the multiplicity of jurisdictions existing in the United States, which often gives parties a choice of several possible courts in which to initiate litigation.[39] This multiplicity not only influences litigant behaviour; it may also influence

[35] Alan Paterson, *The Law Lords*, 10 (Macmillan, London, 1982).
[36] The number has increased recently, see Smith, 'Criminal Appeals in the House of Lords', 47 *Mod. L. Rev.* 133 (1984).
[37] As can be seen by comparing the number of reported House of Lords decisions with the number of appeals heard. Reported cases are only about half the total number of decisions. Blom-Cooper and Drewry, *supra*, n. 31, at 43.
[38] Kagan, Cartwright, Friedman, and Wheeler, 'The Business of State Supreme Courts, 1870–1970', 30 *Stan. L. Rev.* 121, 133 (1977).
[39] See, e.g., C. A. Wright, *Law of Federal Courts*, ch. 1 (4th edn., West, St. Paul, 1983) (choosing between federal and state forums); Schwartz, 'Towards a More Convenient Forum in Conflict of Laws and Long-Arm Statutes', 32 *A.T.L.J.* 100 (1968).

courts themselves. Innovation is encouraged because, given the variety of courts and judges, it is probable that *some* court, *somewhere* in the country will contain more adventurous and less risk averse judges than would be the case in a more centralized, hierarchic judicial system like England's. Naturally, whenever the jurisdictional rules allow a choice of forum (which itself occurs far more often in American than in England), litigants who need adventurous judges to decide in their favour (because their claims are unprecedented, for instance) will gravitate to the courts in which the more adventurous judges are to be found. Once innovative decisions are made by such courts, there is a tendency for other courts to follow suit unless the results have proved manifestly unsatisfactory.[40] This process is not limited to novel issues of constitutional rights or public law. For example, the Supreme Court of California rejected the common law contributory negligence rule and adopted a comparative negligence (apportionment) rule not long ago.[41] Once this bold decision had been made, a number of other states followed suit, including some which had previously decided that the change was too substantial for a court to make.[42]

3. PROCEDURE OF APPELLATE COURTS

Another set of institutional factors may help explain many of the differences between the workings of the English and the American judiciary, though again it is sometimes difficult to disentangle cause from effect. The procedure of appellate courts in the two countries is now very different indeed. In particular, the proceedings in English appellate courts remain almost entirely oral. Legal argument is presented largely in oral form, often at great length; argument before the House of Lords may last for several days. English lawyers do not file appellate briefs on the American model. It is true that in the Court of Appeal counsel are now asked to submit in writing a bare summary of the legal points to be made ('skeleton arguments'), amplifying the formal grounds of appeal which have to be filed when appeal is made, but this is in no way intended to be a full statement of the arguments.[43]

In the House of Lords, a brief summary of the legal arguments which are to be presented have to be included in the formal documents (the 'case') filed by the parties, but this again bears no resemblance to an

---

[40] Robert M. Cover, 'The Uses of Jurisdictional Redundancy: Interest, Ideology and Innovation', 22 *Wm. and Mary L. Rev.* 639, especially at 672ff. (1981).

[41] *Li* v. *Yellow Cab Co.* 13 Cal. 3d 804, 532 P. 2d 1226 (1975).

[42] For example, Illinois (see *Alvis* v. *Ribar* 85 Ill. 2d. 1, 421 NE 2d 886 (1981)) and Michigan (see *Placek* v. *City of Sterling Heights* 405 Mich. 638, 275 NW 2d 511 (1979)).

[43] See Practice Note [1983] 1 WLR 1055.

American brief. In practice most appeal judges will read the papers filed with the court in advance, so that they are familiar with what the case is about when they take their seats. Nevertheless, to hear an argument in court, one might often suppose that the judges knew nothing about it when they first came into the courtroom. Counsel takes them through everything orally in open court, sometimes reading at length from documents, or from opinions in cases, or from the transcript of evidence.

In most American appellate courts, especially the most busy courts, proceedings are never now conducted in such an oral fashion. Legal argument is usually presented to the court in a substantial written 'brief', with citations to cases, though not usually with any long quotations from earlier judicial opinions. The oral argument is often very short indeed. In the US Supreme Court, parties are allowed thirty minutes each, including the time taken up by the judges in putting questions to counsel. The same time is allowed counsel in the New York Court of Appeals,[44] the Supreme Court of California,[45] and in many other states. It is clear that little effective oral argument can be made within this time, and that the oral proceedings are often hardly more than a formality, though they do sometimes enable an effective series of questions to be put by the judges to counsel about the arguments in his brief. In the federal courts of appeals very large numbers of appeals are disposed of summarily without any oral argument at all. For example, in the 1970s only 8% of the appeals to the large Fifth Circuit received the full time normally allocated to a hearing.[46]

We believe this difference in the mode of conduct of the proceedings has had a considerable impact on a variety of matters, many of which interact. For example: because the writing of briefs takes place in an office, the role of counsel as oral advocate has significantly declined in America. Many briefs can be as well written by a law professor as by an attorney. Indeed, they occasionally *are* written by law professors (who usually know the law better than attorneys anyhow). Then again, judges deciding appeal cases have to read the briefs, and perhaps dig up the material cited in the brief if they want to do their work conscientiously. But briefs are not always well researched,[47] and in any event it would be impossible for judges to read all the materials cited in all the briefs submitted to them, so there has grown up the system of law clerks who

[44] McKinney's NY Rules of Court, § 500.8 (*a*) (West, St. Paul, 1984).
[45] Calif. Rules of Ct. Rule 22 (West 1984). Where the death penalty has been imposed, 45 minutes are allowed.
[46] See J. Woodford Howard, Jr., *Courts of Appeals in the Federal Judicial System*, 278 (Princeton U. Press, Princeton, 1981).
[47] Judge Posner has said that, if judges in federal district and appeal courts rely only on the briefs, 'this will mean all too often, dependence on inadequate research by lawyers'. Posner, *supra*, n. 1, at 109–10.

assist the judges in their legal research. We shall say more about law clerks in section 4 below.

When American judges actually come to make their decisions, they make them in their offices, not in open court. They have more time to think of the issues in broader terms, and they can see the case in front of them in a context—the context of the legal system, and especially that part of it in which the case arises. Counsel's written brief will naturally help to put the case in some sort of framework also. All this encourages—we suggest—a tendency to see the law as more important than the facts, a tendency to see points of law in a more theoretical framework, and less as a narrow contest between two parties, confined to specific issues raised in the pleadings by the parties. An appeal judge, studying the briefs in his office (or chambers), may be more likely to ask himself, 'What is the right (substantive) answer to this kind of question?' rather than, 'Which of the formal legal arguments before me is the sounder?' We shall have more to say about this also. Here we shall concentrate on only a few of the more important consequences of the differing modes of procedure in the two countries.

In the first place, English appellate judges, when deciding questions of law, rely more heavily on the arguments of counsel and much less heavily on their own research.[48] In part this is forced on English judges by the lack of any research and even of adequate secretarial assistance (lacks which they share with law professors). English judges have no clerks to do research for them; if they want to research a problem, they must do it themselves. Moreover, little time is available for research, at least given the traditional English view that decisions ought (except in the House of Lords) to be handed down on the conclusion of the argument if that is at all possible. In the English Court of Appeal—which is the final appellate court for the vast majority of cases—most appeals are still decided at the conclusion of the oral argument, and extempore oral opinions are delivered immediately; furthermore, English Court of Appeal judges sit continuously during the legal term so that most research and writing has to be done in the evenings or at weekends.[49] It is true that in the House of Lords, where judgment is never given until the law lords have had a chance to consider the case, there is more time for reflection and research and consultation with colleagues. Nevertheless, there is not in fact a great deal of such research or consultation partly

[48] A majority of counsel who regularly appear before the House of Lords expressed the view that the Lords should 'restrict the propositions of law in their speeches to matters covered by counsel in argument...': Alan Paterson, *supra*, n. 35, at 20–1.

[49] See D. Karlen, *Appellate Courts in the United States and England*, esp. at 152–4 (New York U. Press, NY, 1963). There has been some relaxation of late with a view to providing Court of Appeal judges with more time to write opinions: personal communication with various judges.

because of tradition, and partly because the facilities are scarcely adequate.

It seems clear that the English tradition also encourages the judge to see himself in the role of passive arbitrator whose business it is to decide which of the rival contentions offered by opposing counsel is the better.[50] That does not mean that even English judges will never formulate the law in terms which neither party has suggested, but it does mean that English judges are discouraged from setting off on voyages of discovery of their own, rejecting the views of both parties, and fashioning their own result to match some private vision of the public good or the rights of the parties.

Indeed, most English judges regard it as improper for a judge to rely on precedents or arguments that have not been canvassed by counsel.[51] The proper course for a judge who believes counsel have overlooked some important cases or arguments is to invite counsel to argue these issues (and, if necessary, to relist the case for further hearing), but it is by no means unknown for counsel to decline such an invitation, in which case the court traditionally decides the issues on the arguments presented. This can occasionally lead the court to make a decision whose authority may be largely valueless because an important legal point has not been argued.[52] Plainly, a court would be justified in refusing to hear the appeal on such an artificial basis; but in all ordinary cases, the court will only decide on the issues argued before it. English judges and lawyers would be astonished at the way in which the Supreme Court of the United States, uninvited and without arguments, overruled *Swift* v. *Tyson*[53] in *Erie RR Co.* v. *Tompkins*,[54] or the California Supreme Court similarly introduced the doctrine of strict products liability in tort in *Greenman* v. *Yuba Power Products.*[55]

Of course this more passive role of the judge involves a high degree of reliance on the competence and integrity of the bar. It is only if the judge

---

[50] See Lord Goff, 'The Search for Principle', LXIX *Proc. Brit. Acad.* 169, 182–4 (1983) (commenting on 'fragmented' nature of judge's vision of the law).

[51] See Alan Paterson, *supra*, n. 35, at 46.

[52] See, e.g., *Attorney General* v. *Prince of Hanover* [1957] AC 436, and on this case see Lord Kilbrandon, 'Scots Law Seen from England', 2–3 (the Child & Co. Oxford Lecture, 1980/81). See also *Saif Ali* v. *Sydney Mitchell* [1980] AC 198 where Lord Diplock protested against (though he acquiesced in) the fact that the House of Lords was required to decide how far a barrister should be immune from liability for negligence in the absence of any argument that the immunity should be abolished altogether. For tactical reasons it suited both parties to argue for a limited immunity rather than none at all.

[53] 16 Peters 1 (US, 1842).

[54] 304 US 64 (1938). To be fair, probably many American lawyers were astonished at this too, though the same thing happened in *Mapp* v. *Ohio* 367 US 643 (1961). But we do not suggest that this kind of thing is an everyday event in American courts.

[55] 59 Cal. 2d 57, 27 Cal. Rptr. 697, 377 P. 2d 897 (1963). See Note, 'Manufacturers' Warranties and the Sales Act', 15 *Stan. L. Rev.* 381, 388, n. 27 (1963).

can rely on counsel to present all the relevant arguments and authorities that a judge can justify or even perceive his role as that of merely 'following the rules'. Judges who habitually felt that counsel were overlooking important arguments would probably be driven to a more active role—which may be one reason for American developments here.[56] Indeed, it has been suggested by some distinguished American academics that 'A professional staff to help research and write might be more reliable than litigants' lawyers who differ widely in ability, integrity and energy.'[57] No English judge (let alone barrister) would agree with this recommendation. Factors such as the lack of a common socializing process, alienation due to the size of the bench and the bar, and the advanced degree of specialization among the higher echelons of the American legal profession all contribute to make American judges much less willing to rely solely on the arguments of counsel. Thus the whole relationship between bench and bar is itself one of the institutional factors that tends to lead to different perceptions of the judicial role, and ultimately to different conceptions of the law itself. It is therefore necessary to understand something of this relationship, and in chapters 12 and 13 we shall look further at some of its aspects.

4. LAW CLERKS

As we have noted above, many American judges, especially appellate judges, are today provided with law clerks;[58] these are usually young graduates fresh from law school, who spend a year or two clerking before taking up more permanent appointments. There are at present about 1,500 of these law clerk positions in the United States. In the federal system and in most states the law clerk is a temporary (often a one-year) appointment, and the clerk is a personal appointee of the judge for whom he works (although the government pays his salary). But some state courts, such as the California Supreme Court, actually have a full-time professional research staff ('staff attorneys'), though they also make use of the more traditional one-year clerks. In 1978 the Supreme Court of California had thirty-three research attorneys of whom twenty-seven were permanent employees.[59] The way in which this court functions today begins to resemble a bureaucracy rather than a court as

---

[56] See Posner, *supra*, n. 1, at 109–10.

[57] Kagan, Cartwright, Friedman, and Wheeler, *supra*, n. 16, at 973.

[58] On law clerks, see generally J. Oakley and R. Thompson, *Law Clerks and the Judicial Process* (U. Cal. Press, Berkeley, 1980); Baier, 'The Law Clerks: Profile of an Institution', 26 *Vand. L. Rev.* 1125 (1973); Posner, *supra*, n. 1, at 102–19.

[59] Oakley and Thompson, *supra*, n. 58, at 30 n. 2. 77 and 77 n. 5. 79.

traditionally understood.[60] Clerks and research staff read the material pertaining to an appeal, discuss the issues with the judge, 'advise' him how the case should be disposed of, and draft opinions which he may use with or without alteration. This method of operation is close to that of an English government department with a ministerial head. It seems to be somewhat exceptional even in America, though there are growing anxieties about the 'bureaucratization' of the judiciary, with all that this entails in loss of a sense of individual responsibility for decisions.[61]

The law clerks may well influence the nature of the judicial function in another respect. In any court where the judges have three or more clerks each, the office of each judge becomes almost like a mini law firm. Debate and discussion takes place in each 'firm', but relations *between* the judges (and their 'firms') may change. The clerks may even negotiate with each other, and they answer each other's footnotes with rival drafts. Collective deliberation between the judges is lessened, and again the process becomes more bureaucratic.

The law clerks are, however, a most important bridge between the judges and the academic legal community in America, helping to make the judges better informed about the latest academic ideas and theories, and tending to make the judges themselves more interested in addressing the academic community.[62] The highly substantive orientation of American law schools (which we discuss in chapter 14) thus enters the judges' chambers in flesh and blood. Judges in the higher and more prestigious American courts tend to attract very able young graduates from the best law schools in the country. Most of these young clerks will have been editors of their law school law review and they will usually be interested in writing (or encouraging their judges to write) opinions that will raise interest in academic legal circles, opinions with some significant public impact. They are likely to be less interested in the more mundane aspects of judging, that is, of simply deciding disputes between parties in response to the arguments presented by their lawyers. It is hardly surprising if the presence of an able young law clerk at the judge's elbow brings the judge into closer contact with current academic writing and ideas—much of which is fertile and innovative. It is noteworthy, and partly due to the influence of law clerks, that American judges cite academic literature in their opinions quite frequently; a recent survey, for instance, found that in 11.9% of opinions in state supreme courts

---

[60] Stolz, *supra*, n. 29, at 346–60.

[61] See Fiss, 'The Bureaucratization of the Judiciary', 92 *Yale LJ* 1442 (1983); Wade McCree, 'Bureaucratic Justice: An Early Warning', 129 *U. Pa. L. Rev.* 777 (1981).

[62] See Oakley and Thompson, *supra*, n. 58.

there was some reference to law review articles.[63] In important opinions, such articles are nearly always cited.

As we shall suggest later, English judges do not see themselves as addressing their opinions to scholars to any significant degree, nor do they really pay a great deal of attention to academic literature. It is doubtful if 1% of English judicial opinions refer to academic literature on novel or difficult questions, though research and statistics do not exist. English judges tend to assume that, if something ought to be brought to their attention in a particular case, counsel will do it for them. But this assumption means that, if counsel are traditionally minded and conservative in their outlook, novel arguments and viewpoints may simply not be put before the judges. So also English opinions are written in the first instance for the counsel on the two sides, addressing and meeting (or accepting) the various arguments which they have advanced. But the American system of written briefs depersonalizes the exchange between bench and bar, and American appellate judges do not feel that they are particularly required to see an appeal within the confines of the brief or to write an opinion which addresses all the main points raised in the brief.

A further consequence of the availability of law clerks and even research attorneys, as well as of the system of written briefs, is that American judges are (or at least seem to be) less worried about the possible ramifications of highly innovative decisions. In England, the narrow focus of counsel and judges on the immediate points at issue tends to make judges anxious about the possible effects of the decision on surrounding areas of the law if they stray too far.[64] The anxiety is compounded by the fear of creating uncertainty, a special concern of English lawyers and judges. American judges are less worried by the spectre of uncertainty, and are more willing to leave new problems thrown up by the instant case to future cases. To some degree this may be influenced by the system of written briefs and the work of law clerks, for these may enable the judges to take greater account of the possible ramifications of a decision.

5. LEVELS OF DISSENT

In this section we propose to draw attention to the variations in the levels of dissent in the appellate courts in the two countries, and to suggest that these variations may tell us something about judicial views

[63] Friedman, Kagan, Cartwright, and Wheeler, 'State Supreme Courts: A Century of Style and Citation', 33 *Stan. L. Rev.* 773, 811 (1981).

[64] Lord Simon especially makes this point in the *Miliangos* case [1976] AC 443 at 479–82.

of the role of courts and of the theories of law to which judges may be implicitly adhering. We will suggest, in particular, that the higher levels of dissent in America (and above all, reiteration of dissent when the court later employs the new rule) tend to show that American judges are less inclined to see law as a system of formal rules.

There are unfortunately many difficulties in making meaningful comparisons of the prevalence of dissent in England and the United States. One problem is that most courts of last resort are larger in America, and it is obviously more difficult to secure unanimity among nine or even seven judges than it is among the five who customarily hear appeals in the House of Lords. Another problem for comparisons is that the House of Lords hears fewer cases than most courts of last resort in the United States—indeed it hears so few (in the past sometimes as few as 30 or 40 a year, but today more typically 80 or 90 a year[65]) that perhaps comparisons should be more meaningfully drawn between the English Court of Appeal and courts of last resort in America. A third difference is that (as we have seen[66]) the Supreme Court of the US and many state supreme courts have power to select their own cases for hearing and sometimes seek, in making these selections, to advance their own causes. Yet another problem about making comparisons is that some American states have no intermediate appellate court, and this naturally means that the final court in such a state will often be asked to hear appeals in very clear cases in which there is little to be said on one side; dissent in such circumstances would hardly be expected.[67] But apart from this factor, we would, other things being equal, expect higher dissent rates in the United States due to the structure of the courts and the system of case selection.

Nevertheless, it does appear possible to say that dissent plays a more important role in the American than in the English judicial scene. In the United States Supreme Court dissent has greatly increased over the years.[68] In the 1930s, for example, the number of non-unanimous decisions was often less that 20% each year, while in the 1970s it was

[65] See *Judicial Statistics 1982* (HMSO, 1983). The number of appeals seems to have increased quite significantly recently, though figures for earlier years were not published.

[66] See *supra*, at 271 ff.

[67] Empirical studies in America confirm that the existence of intermediate level appeal courts produces higher dissent rates in courts of last resort, presumably for this reason. H. R. Glick and K. N. Vines, *State Court Systems*, 79 (Prentice-Hall, Englewood Cliffs, NJ, 1973); Project, *supra*, n. 29; Canon and Jaros, 'External Variables, Institutional Structure and Dissent on State Supreme Courts', 3 *Polity* 175 (1970).

[68] See Fuld, 'The Voices of Dissent', 62 *Col. L. Rev.* 923, 928 (1962); Zobell, 'Division of Opinion in the Supreme Court: A History of Judicial Disintegration', 44 *Cornell LQ* 186 (1959).

common for more than 70% of full opinions to attract some dissent.[69] In the 1980 term, 68.8% of full opinions attracted dissent, and even 28.4% of memorandum orders did so.[70] Over one third (119 out of 338) of all full opinions was a dissent.[71]

As already noted, comparisons with the House of Lords are neither easy nor perhaps very meaningful, but for what they are worth, the figures in Table 1 are taken from Blom-Cooper and Drewry's study of the House of Lords[72] (with the addition of a figure for 1980 taken from the Appeal Cases volume of the Law Reports).[73]

TABLE 1

Year	Total number of HL appeals heard	Number and percentage of cases with dissents
1952	25	2 (8%)
1960	34	10 (29.4%)
1966	30	9 (30%)
1980	26	7 (26.9%)

Although the percentage rate is not low—indeed it is higher than that in many state supreme courts—the absolute number of dissenting opinions is very low indeed; this makes the figures even less reliable statistically, but in any event the very low number of dissents is itself significant.

Among state supreme courts, the percentage of cases in which there is some dissent varies widely. In 1966, Michigan had a dissenting opinion in 46.5% of its cases, while the judges on the court of last resort in Massachusetts dissented in only 1.2% of that court's cases.[74] A more recent study reveals similar variations.[75] Although the position of each state has varied over the years, the overall average has not changed much.[76] In some states, the supreme court is wracked by repeated dissents, and the judges fall into clearly identifiable 'blocs', often closely

---

[69] 'The Supreme Court, 1980 Term', 95 *Harv. L. Rev.* 339 (1981).

[70] *Ibid.*, at 441. A 'memorandum order' decides the case without assigning any reasons.

[71] *Ibid.*

[72] *Final Appeal, supra*, n. 31, Table 22, 186.

[73] As already noted, not all HL decisions are reported, but the number of dissents in unreported decisions is probably negligible.

[74] Glick and Vines, *supra*, n. 67, at 79. See also Karlen, *supra*, n. 49, at 39–40 (116 cases with dissent out of 390 in New York CA in 1958–9).

[75] Project, *supra*, n. 29.

[76] Glick and Vines, *supra*, n. 67, at 79.

correlated with their political affiliations. In other states a more socializing role seems to be played by the court as an institutional whole, and such factionalism is unknown.[77] Again, the differences between English and American practice must not be exaggerated; despite wide disparities, unanimity, not dissent, is still the rule in most state supreme courts. A random sampling of cases from 16 representative state courts of last resort between 1960 and 1970 revealed unanimity in 83.5% of the cases, concurrences in 3.7%, and dissents in 12.8%.[78]

However, even these dissent rates seem very high compared to those in the English Court of Appeal which is the court of last resort for the overwhelming majority of cases in England. Comparisons are again very difficult, partly because a much higher proportion of English decisions is unreported, but a crude comparison may be obtained by taking the cases reported in the English Law Reports and adding to them figures drawn from the unreported cases noted in the *Current Law Yearbook*. For example, if the figures of English Court of Appeal cases reported in the 1980 volumes of the Law Reports[79] are added to the unreported cases noted in the *Current Law Yearbook* for 1981 (which covers 1980), the result reveals 6 cases out of 539 in which there was dissent, that is, a dissent rate of just over 1% in (approximately) one year.

This does not mean that dissent in American state supreme courts is twelve times more common than in the English Court of Appeal, because the American figures exclude a small number of unpublished opinions, and also exclude very short opinions of under one page in length. There is no ready way of knowing to what extent these factors reduce the real disparity between the English and the American figures. On the other hand, it must be remembered that the American figures cited above are totals drawn from 16 states; as we have noted, some states have very low dissent rates, from which it follows, of course, that some must have dissent rates above the average. There can, we think, be no doubt that many American state supreme courts have dissent rates far higher than those which prevail in England; and although other states conform more to the English pattern, it is often the larger states with the more influential supreme courts which have the higher dissent rates.

Dissenting judges' behaviour in later cases demonstrates an even more striking contrast in the patterns of judicial conduct in the courts of the two countries. In England a dissenting judge in the House of Lords (or

---

[77] Adamany, 'The Party Variable in Judges' Voting: Conceptual Notes and a Case Study', 63 *Am. Pol. Sc. Rev.* 57 (1969); H. R. Glick, *Supreme Courts in State Politics*, 3 (Basic Books, NY, 1971).

[78] Friedman, Kagan, Cartwright, and Wheeler, *supra*, n. 63, at 787.

[79] These figures do not relate only to cases decided in 1980, but there is no reason to suppose that they vary much from one year to another.

even the Court of Appeal) regards the decision of the majority as creating 'binding' law—the decision settles the applicable rule and even the dissenter is bound by that rule in future cases, unless and until it is properly overruled by a court competent to do so, or by legislative enactment. All English judges (with the exception of Lord Denning who, especially in his later years, never really accepted the strict doctrine of *stare decisis* at all) observe this tradition.[80]

Although some American judges on some courts may follow the English practice in this respect, it is not unusual for judges in the United States to engage in the contrary practice. A judge may dissent from a majority opinion adopting a certain rule, and may adhere to and repeat that dissent in future cases in which the now established rule is applied. Holmes frequently did this when sitting on the United States Supreme Court. So did Justices Black and Douglas with respect to the interpretation of the First Amendment.[81] In modern times, perhaps the most notable example of this reiteration of dissents occurs in the Supreme Court death penalty cases. Although a majority of the court recognized the constitutionality of the death penalty in *Gregg* v. *Georgia*,[82] Justices Brennan and Marshall have repeatedly refused to accept this majority decision, and routinely dissent in all cases in which the Court affirms (or even refuses to review) a death penalty decision.[83]

What is the relevance to our theme of varying dissent rates? One possibility is that such practices simply reflect the homogeneity of English judges and English society and values, on the one hand, and the greater diversity of judges and values within the United States. Thus there may be more scope for reasonable disagreement about 'what the law is' in America, and this could explain greater dissent rates. This may well be part of the story (and we will return to it in chapter 12), but it is not the whole story.

Judges who are more concerned to impress the public with the idea that law in some sense represents neutral and eternal values of truth, and that the judges themselves have no political role in deciding the law, may be more inclined to present a united front and suppress any differences

---

[80] A particularly striking example of judicial adherence to this practice is to be found in the behaviour of Lord Reid in *Shaw v D.P.P.* [1962] AC 220 and *Reg.* v. *Knuller (Publishing) Ltd.* [1973] AC 435 (Lord Reid dissented in the first case but, though he still thought the decision wrong, adhered to it in the second, after the 1966 Practice Direction gave the HL power to overrule its own decisions.)

[81] They insisted that the First Amendment should be literally interpreted as a prohibition on *any* interference with free speech, but the majority of the court has never adopted this view. Many examples of this are to be found in Bernard Schwartz, *Super Chief, passim* (New York U. Press, NY, 1983).

[82] 428 US 153, 187, 226 (1976).

[83] See, e.g., *Lockett* v. *Ohio*, 438 US 586, 619 (1978); *Gardner* v. *Florida*, 430 US 349, 365–6 (1977).

of opinion. Hence, the infrequency of dissent in a particular jurisdiction may reflect 'acceptance of the notion that unanimity denotes precision and truth, and therefore is more convincing'.[84] We think that English judges are more influenced than most American judges by the desire to promote this goal, which is perhaps an example of the English judges pursuing a genuine 'policy' which they themselves might not recognize as such. As evidence for this, we would draw attention to our earlier discussion of the elitist traditions of the English judiciary, and the way in which these traditions have led them to prefer to maintain the formal integrity of a rule of law, leaving for extra-legal processes measures of equitable modification or dispensation.[85]

Moreover, judges who perceive the law as a system of rules binding on them, as on everyone else, are surely more likely to arrive at the same conclusion in a given case, especially where their values and training are so homogeneous as those of English judges. For, to say the least, such a view of the nature of law and the judicial role narrows the range of choice open to the judge, and therefore makes unanimity more likely. On the other hand, where many judges see their function as a quasi-legislative one, where such judges are ready to indulge in 'social engineering' on a massive scale and decide cases for broad social or political reasons, disagreement is likely to be more common.[86] Activism, after all, involves choosing in *what direction* to act, but there is in general only one way of holding onto the status quo!

Even in America, the desirability of presenting a united front in highly controversial cases does seem to weigh with the judges from time to time. We think it is no coincidence that in two of the most important political decisions of modern times, *Brown* v. *Board of Education*[87] and *United States* v. *Nixon*,[88] the Supreme Court delivered a unanimous opinion.

But if the purpose of striving after unanimity is similar in the two countries, though more rarely achieved in the United States, it also seems to us that the purpose of dissents themselves is seen differently. In lower appellate courts, dissent may quite legitimately be seen as a set of arguments presented for the consideration of the final court of appeals, and there seems no reason to doubt that in both countries this is largely the function of such dissents. But in courts of last resort, dissents in England represent no more than the fairly formal desire of a judge to dissociate himself from a decision which his 'legal conscience' prevents

---

[84] Glick, *supra*, n. 77, at 3.
[85] See *supra*, at 92–3, 181–2.
[86] Kagan, Cartwright, Friedman, and Wheeler, *supra*, n. 16, at 997.
[87] 347 US 483 (1954).
[88] 418 US 683 (1974).

him from accepting and, as a matter of courtesy to his colleagues and to counsel, explaining why he does so. In America, dissents often seem to serve a different purpose. Apart from the fact that a dissent may be an appeal to a later court to reconsider the present decision, as some American judges quite clearly recognise,[89] it has been suggested that many American judges see their dissents as a way of asserting 'a personal or individual responsibility... of a higher order than the institutional responsibility owed by each to the Court, or by the Court to the public'.[90] Sometimes it seems almost as though a dissent in such a case is an appeal to the people—perhaps yet one further indication of the greater weight attributed to reasons of substance in the United States.

In suggesting in this section that higher dissent rates in America are evidence of a greater disposition to follow reasons of substance and less inclination to adhere to formal reasons for decisions, we do not suggest that this evidence is conclusive, or that other factors may not be at work. Indeed, it seems indisputable from American research that dissent rates are significantly affected by a wide variety of factors, and possibly above all by the cultural norms of the court in question.[91] But here, as elsewhere, the contrast between England and America fits an overall pattern. *Most*, indeed, nearly all, English judges adopt the more traditional, conservative view of the judicial function in which dissent is unusual; *many* American judges adopt a more radical, broader view of the judicial function in which dissent inevitably becomes more common.

6. LOWER COURTS

We turn now to consider some of the more striking differences between the practices and functions of lower courts, focusing in particular on distinctions that cast light on the degree to which the courts of the two countries are more formal or more substantive in their approach. We need not repeat our discussion concerning the greater level of judicial activism in the United States; generally speaking, what has already been said of courts of last resort is also applicable, *mutatis mutandis*, to lower courts. But there are a number of additional factors bearing on the lower courts that also reveal major differences between the two countries.

In the first place, the English court structure is more centralized and more hierarchical than the American. In England, lower courts are expected to—and do—conform without question to the rulings of higher courts. We think an English lawyer would regard this as so much a

---

[89] See *supra*, at 130.

[90] Zobell, *supra*, n. 68, at 203. Compare Lord Diplock in *Carter* v. *Bradbeer* [1975] 1 WLR 1204, 1206–7, *supra*, 130–131 n. 63.

[91] Friedman, Kagan, Cartwright, and Wheeler, *supra*, n. 29, at 788–92.

matter of course that he would be surprised at any inquiry into it. No explanations would be called for; it is simply part of the system, accepted by all. If we are to venture any explanations, it seems to us clear that there are basically two reasons for the absence of any deviations from the accepted theory and practice. Judges and lawyers are socialized by their traditions to accept this aspect of the system (as, indeed, all other aspects). Furthermore, any sign of aberrant judicial behaviour by lower court judges is quickly stamped out by higher courts.

In a small centralized legal system like England's, it is not difficult for the higher courts to correct all instances of deviant behaviour brought to their attention; given a small (and also centralized) legal profession, it is highly likely that serious instances of deviant behaviour will be rapidly appealed and overturned. The fact that the publicity media are national in their coverage also contributes in some measure to strengthen these traditions. For example, when a judge took the very unusual course of putting a convicted rapist on probation in 1981, the case received widespread media coverage and was the subject of much comment. This kind of aberrant judicial behaviour is difficult to control directly because in England no appeal can be brought by a prosecutor on grounds of inadequacy of the sentence. Indirect means of control therefore have to be sought. In this instance, the Court of Appeal, hearing appeals in a number of other rape cases shortly after this event, seized the opportunity to make a public pronouncement about the sentences it regarded as appropriate for rape in differing circumstances.[92] Trial judges are expected to conform to this ruling.[93]

With minor judicial officers, such as magistrates, seriously aberrant judicial behaviour would almost certainly be widely reported in the media, and would in all probability lead rapidly to removal from office by the Lord Chancellor. So far as the higher judiciary are concerned, there are also other factors encouraging loyalty to the system, several of which were considered in the previous chapter.

We have said that 'all' English judges accept the traditions of loyalty to higher court rulings; but we must admit that Lord Denning was an exception to this generalization as he was to so many others about the English judiciary. He does, however, provide us with an excellent illustration of what happens in the rare case when an English judge throws over the traces, and behaves out of character. In *Cassell & Co. Ltd.* v. *Broome*,[94] Lord Denning succeeded in persuading his two

---

[92] *Reg.* v. *Roberts* 74 Cr. App. Rep. 242, 244 (1982).

[93] Indeed, there was nothing really new in the ruling in *Reg.* v. *Roberts*, which makes no explicit reference to the earlier case, but was clearly motivated by the need to allay public criticism of that case.

[94] [1972] AC 1027.

colleagues in the Court of Appeal that *Rookes* v. *Barnard*,[95] decided by the House of Lords a few years earlier (limiting the availability of punitive damages in tort), had been decided *per incuriam* and should not be followed; in addition the court instructed trial judges that in future they should not follow *Rookes*. In the English legal system this was little short of rank mutiny. Retribution followed swiftly and, one is tempted to add, inevitably. An unusually large panel of seven law lords was convened to hear the appeal in *Cassell & Co. Ltd.* v. *Broome* and a solemn magisterial rebuke was administered to Lord Denning for this conduct which was said to raise 'constitutional' issues.[96] Lord Denning himself was able to shrug off this rebuke without apparent discomfort—he was already the longest-serving judge in England—but it seems unlikely that many other English judges will wish to run the risk of this sort of treatment from a higher court.

The position in the United States differs from that in England in many ways, and for many reasons. The federal system means that there is no simple hierarchical pyramidical structure of courts with jurisdiction over the entire country. Rather, there are two separate levels of courts, state court systems and federal court systems. With the exception of United States Supreme Court decisions, which bind the state judges, the state and federal judicial systems are largely independent of each other. Both the state and the federal systems have trial and appellate court levels, but though these courts may have an internal hierarchical structure, they are much less centralized than those in England. For example, the federal appeals courts (with a fixed membership) are far more independent of each other than the different panels of the English Court of Appeal, whose members regularly interchange; and even though some appeals courts treat the first decision of a panel of their judges as creating a binding precedent, none of the appeals courts regard themselves as bound by decisions of the other appeals courts. Conflicting decisions on federal questions are therefore common, and may persist for years before the Supreme Court speaks.

But in addition to the normally hierarchical structure of federal and state courts, there are also many courts of special jurisdiction and other courts with limited jurisdictional powers. Even within a single state, the number and complexity of the relationships between the different courts is often such that 'the actual operation of most state judicial systems

---

[95] [1964] AC 1129.

[96] The rebuke was all the more striking for being concurred in by all seven law lords even though at least two of them in substance agreed with Lord Denning in thinking *Rookes* wrongly decided. (It will be appreciated that, in England, to refer to an issue as 'constitutional' merely means it is of high political importance.)

does not make state judges part of a well regulated, cohesive hierarchy'.[97] And when one adds on top of this the relationship between state and federal judicial systems, one can see that the result is a ramshackle structure only bearing a slight resemblance to the classical pyramidical structure of a centralized hierarchical judicial system such as that of England. Consider just one example of the sort of problems to which this can give rise: in general, state supreme court decisions are appealable only to the United States Supreme Court and then only when an issue of federal or constitutional law arises. But several of the federal courts of appeals may have made constitutional decisions on a point at issue. A state supreme court could decline to follow these decisions, claiming quite correctly that it is only bound by decisions of the Supreme Court. The issue might even be one which the Supreme Court just does not care to review at the present time, so the state decision will stand.

We do not deny, however, that many judges in the American legal system subscribe in theory, and often also in practice, to a position not essentially different from that prevailing in England. So, for example, we find an American scholar asserting of lower court attitudes that 'the duty of obedience to the views of the [United States Supreme] Court within the judicial system is taken for granted.'[98] But it must also be appreciated that, even if this is the norm in the American judicial system, as the comparable duty is in England, the norm in America is not so widely or universally observed. The sheer size of the country, and the quantity of litigation, and the number of lower courts in a particular state, make it impossible for higher courts adequately to control deviant lower court behaviour. For instance, in California alone in 1979 there were 65,000 contested dispositions in state superior courts, 5,750 in courts of appeal, and 123 in the Supreme Court.[99] One commentator has noted:

In theory, whenever a trial or intermediate appellate court departs from the law as announced by the highest court, the decision can and should be reversed through the process of appeal. In fact, appellate review is an inefficient system for correcting error. Misapplications of law can be shielded from review, deliberately or otherwise, in any number of ways, and the sheer volume of cases makes it unrealistic to suppose that a supreme court itself, even with the willing aid of the intermediate appellate courts, can reach any significant percentage of what litigants think are possible mistakes by the trial courts... The California Supreme Court is dependent on the willingness of the lower courts to follow the law as the court announces it; the court cannot compel obedience. An obvious prerequisite to compliance is a reasonably intelligent lower court bench capable of understanding and alert to follow the Supreme Court's opinions. With one

---

[97] Glick and Vines, *supra*, n. 67, at 33.
[98] Kelman, 'The Force of Precedent in the Lower Courts', 14 *Wayne L. Rev.* 3, 5 (1967).
[99] Stolz, *supra*, n. 29, at 408.

thousand two hundred overworked judges that is not easily come by. In addition, the lower courts must be possessed of an attitude of willing and ready compliance even with decisions that some judges consider wrong or repugnant.[100]

If this is the position even within a single state, the problems of federal control of aberrant judicial behaviour with respect to the Constitution may be even worse. The federal judicial system itself contains ample scope for diversity of approach among the circuits. As one author has noted, 'the potential for forum shopping, specialization and Balkanization of federal law can hardly require elaboration.'[101] Then again, the more political nature of the American judicial role means that judges—especially state judges—often have a political 'constituency' to consider,[102] and their loyalties to this political constituency sometimes outweigh their loyalties to the judicial hierarchy and even the constitutional supremacy of Supreme Court decisions.[103] And the problem may be aggravated by the parochialism of much of the media, which means that local court decisions may receive litle publicity outside the immediate locality.

In certain areas—notably the desegregation and religious establishment cases[104]—some state courts waged a long rearguard campaign against the decisions of the United States Supreme Court. Although very few state judges have ever openly declared their refusal to implement Supreme Court decisions,[105] or to abide by the terms of the Constitution,[106] there has been a long history of delay, evasion, and prevarica-

---

[100] *Ibid.*

[101] J. Woodford Howard, Jr., *supra*, n. 46, at 55. On the lower federal courts, see especially W. Kitchin, *Federal District Judges: An Analysis of Judicial Perceptions* (College Press, Baltimore, 1978).

[102] G. Alan Tarr, *Judicial Impact and State Supreme Courts*, esp. at 111–17 (1977); R. J. Richardson and K. N. Vines, *The Politics of Federal Courts: Lower Courts in the United States*, 131, 132, 145 (Little Brown, Boston, 1970).

[103] Indeed, part of the very *raison d'être* of lower federal courts, distinct from state courts, is distrust of the willingness or ability of state judges to be wholly faithful to the demands of federal law. Compare the Canadian and Australian constitutions, which vested all federal jurisdiction at the outset in the provincial or state courts, except for the Supreme Court of Canada and the High Court of Australia.

[104] It is less clear whether state court reactions to the reapportionment decisions differed from federal court reactions (and might therefore have been more non-compliant with US Supreme Court opinions). See Beiser, 'A Comparative Analysis of State and Federal Judicial Behavior: The Reapportionment Cases', 62 *Am. Pol. Sc. Rev.* 788 (1968).

[105] Though in 1957 an Alabama judge denounced the Fourteenth Amendment as unconstitutional: Murphy, 'Lower Court Checks on Supreme Court Power', 53 *Am. Pol. Sc. Rev.* 1017, 1020 (1959). (Of course, in one sense he was right since the necessary state ratifications of the Fourteenth Amendment were only secured by coercion.)

[106] However, the late Dan O'Connell, Chichele Professor of International Law at Oxford, used to recount an anecdote which deserves to be recorded. O'Connell related that he was once pulled over by a traffic policeman while driving in Virginia. The policeman

tion in some parts of the country. The line between evasion and outright defiance of Supreme Court rulings has undoubtedly been crossed in some cases despite judicial assertions to the contrary. One study of the impact of United States Supreme Court decisions on the religious establishment issue identifies 15 clear cases of state supreme court non-compliance with US Supreme Court rulings, out of a total of 97 cases decided by state supreme courts on this subject.[107] In several of these cases the state supreme court judges relied on dissenting rather than majority opinions, or on Supreme Court decisions which had been overruled.[108] Extreme and manifestly erroneous dicta abound in these state supreme court opinions, for example, the assertion in one that religious toleration 'was never thought to encompass the ungodly'.[109]

Another study[110] suggests that the Florida Supreme Court's initial reception of the *Gideon*,[111] *Escobeda*,[112] and *Miranda*[113] decisions was 'hesitant', 'narrow', and 'suspicious' and indeed in some cases seems to have gone well beyond a reluctant and 'begrudging acceptance' to downright evasion.[114] Even some lower federal courts have demonstrated, perhaps most notoriously in the segregation cases, less than total fidelity to Supreme Court precedents.[115]

The Supreme Court of the United States simply cannot exercise adequate and effective supervision over the judicial system of the entire

---

failed to recognize the Australian driving licence which O'Connell produced, and he was cited (*anglice*, summonsed) for driving without a licence. On appearing before a justice of the peace, O'Connell produced a copy of the UN Treaty on recognition of foreign visitors' driving licences, and a certified copy of the Senate ratification of this Treaty, by virtue of which, of course, the Treaty should have been recognized as law throughout the United States. After pondering these documents for a few minutes the justice of the peace declared that, although the United States might have entered into the Treaty, the 'Sovereign State of Virginia' had not; O'Connell was convicted and fined!

[107] Tarr, *supra*, n. 102.

[108] *Ibid.*, at 40ff.

[109] *Torcaso* v. *Watkins*, 162 A. 2d 438, 443, a decision summarily reversed by the US Supreme Court, 367 US 488 (1961).

[110] R. Bruce Carruthers, 'Gideon, Escobedo, Miranda: Begrudging Acceptance of the US Supreme Court's Mandates in Florida', 21 *U. Fla. L. Rev.* 346 (1969).

[111] 372 US 335 (1963).

[112] 378 US 478 (1964).

[113] 384 US 436 (1966).

[114] See, e.g., *Myrick* v. *State*, 177 So. 2d 845 (1965) and *Holston* v. *State*, 208 So. 2d 98 (1968).

[115] Note, 'Lower Court Disavowal of Supreme Court Precedent', 60 *Va. L. Rev.* 494 (1974). For other examples of state and federal rejection of Supreme Court precedents, see Vines, 'Southern State Supreme Courts and Race Relations', 18 *Western Political Q.* 5, 16 (1965); R. J. Richardson and K. N. Vines, *supra*, n. 102, at 145, 160, 168. See also *supra*, p. 191, n. 16.

nation, even with respect to federal questions.[116] When widespread evasion of Supreme Court rulings takes place at lower levels of the judicial system (though we do not suggest that this kind of thing is generally an everyday affair), there is absolutely no guarantee that a litigant—even if he has the time and the money—can ultimately obtain a decision in accordance with those rulings. Although such results are unthinkable to an English lawyer, the American judicial system does not fit a hierarchical model of the English kind.[117] The fact is that the Supreme Court has virtually ceased to be an ordinary appeal court whose functions are to correct the errors of lower courts; its role is a much grander one, and it cannot effectively combine its high political role with that of a court of error.[118]

A further dimension to this problem is that the Supreme Court rarely renders a final decision in cases which it does hear; its normal practice is to remand cases to the state supreme court for further action or consideration in accordance with its opinion.[119] Even after such a remand, state supreme courts have sometimes—to put it mildly—failed to show due loyalty to the US Supreme Court opinion. One study of 175 such cases remanded to state supreme courts between 1941 and 1951 found that the party successful in the US Supreme Court was unsuccessful following the remand in nearly half the cases.[120] The author of this study found that these results were often explicable on grounds other than deliberate non-compliance, but there was certainly evidence of cases in which state supreme courts simply flouted US Supreme Court opinions on remand, sometimes more than once.[121]

Only marginally less defiant of higher court decisions is the use of delaying tactics by trial court judges to frustrate litigants. Delays can

[116] See Jack Peltason, *Fifty-eight Lonely Men* (U. of Illinois Press, Urbana, revised edn., 1971); Richardson and Vines, *supra*, n. 102, at 157.

[117] Richardson and Vines, *supra*, n. 102, at 144, 160.

[118] See Hellman, 'Error Correction, Lawmaking, and the Supreme Court's Exercise of Discretionary Review', 44 *U. Pitt. L. Rev.* 795 (1983) (suggesting that there is a consensus among all concerned that review for error should play a minor part in the court's work).

[119] Circuit courts also follow this procedure in a significant proportion of cases, though it is unclear to what extent such remands are followed by recalcitrant judicial action in courts below: J. Woodford Howard, Jr., *supra*, n. 46, at 43.

[120] Note, 'Evasion of Supreme Court Mandates in Cases Remanded to State Courts since 1941', 67 *Harv. L. Rev.* 1251 (1954).

[121] See, e.g., *Chamberlin* v. *Dade County Bd. of Public Instruction*, 143 So. 2d 21 (Fla. 1962), remanded 374 US 487, affirmed on remand, 160 So. 2d 97 (Fla. 1964), and finally summarily reversed by the US Supreme Court, 377 US 402 (1964); see also *Naim* v. *Naim*, 350 US 891 (1955) where the Supreme Court remanded the case to the Virginia Supreme Court for return to the trial court on the ground that the record was inadequate to enable the constitutional question to be determined, but the Virginia court reaffirmed its previous decision on the ground that the record was perfectly adequate: 197 Va. 734, 90 SE 2d 849 (1956). The Supreme Court then threw in its hand, see Bernard Schwartz, *supra*, n. 81, at 158–62. See also cases cited by Murphy, *supra*, n. 105.

sometimes deprive a litigant of all effective redress when time is of the essence, and even where this is not the case, only the hardiest litigant can face the combined evasive tactics of his opponent and a biased trial judge. 'At pre-trial, trial, pre-verdict and post-appellate verdict stages, a district judge's considerable freedom to schedule and dispose of his calendar provides ample opportunity for subjecting plaintiffs to the passage of time.'[122]

One reason for this disregard of clearly binding decisions, particularly, but not exclusively, in the case of state courts, appears to be that, the further down the judicial ladder one goes, the less insulated the judge is from the local political constituency.[123] The only really effective way to control courts when the assumption of good faith compliance breaks down is to appoint judges who are more likely to comply with the spirit of the law. Yet political factors often prevent this. Even President Kennedy, for instance, had little choice but to appoint federal judges in Southern districts whose loyalty to the law and the Constitution left much to be desired in civil rights litigation.[124]

Another reason stems from the increasing tendency of appellate judges to regard their primary function as that of law making, rather than correcting lower court errors and ensuring that lower courts observe the established law. While this role has been increasingly thrust on the United States Supreme Court by the force of events and numbers, other appellate courts have often taken the Supreme Court as their model even where this is not so necessary. The result has been that trial court judges may feel that, if they are hearing cases unlikely to prove of interest to appeal courts, they are free to decide with little danger of reversal or even appellate scrutiny. Their own fidelity to law may in the result be weakened.[125] As Dean Paul Carrington has observed, the paradoxical result of the enhanced law-making role of the appellate courts may in the end become self-defeating:

A legal system that is not able to assure the accountability of officials for their fidelity to law is one that allows little opportunity for truly effective judicial law-making...At some point, which happily we have not reached, judicial law-making becomes a conceit or a self-indulgence. When every judge seeks in every case to emulate the creative career of Learned Hand there can be no Learned Hands, because little that any of them write can be expected to control the

---

[122] Note, 'Judicial Performance in the Fifth Circuit', 73 *Yale LJ* 90 (1963).

[123] *Ibid.*, at 95; see also Kenneth M. Dolbeare, *Trial Courts in Urban Politics* (Wiley & Sons, NY, 1967).

[124] See Note cited *supra*, n. 120. See also L. Jaffe, *English and American Judges as Lawmakers*, 63 (Clarendon Press, Oxford, 1969).

[125] There is evidence that supervision of federal district courts by appeals courts is patchy and varies from field to field and place to place: J. Woodford Howard, Jr., *supra*, n. 46, at 40–1.

behavior and decisions of other judges in the future who claim equal wisdom and equal right to the creative role.[126]

The problem of recalcitrant behaviour among lower court judges not surprisingly reflects back on superior courts and produces anti-evasion tactics. For instance, a number of the Draconian sanctions devised by the Supreme Court in regard to criminal procedure have clearly been a response to the 'passive resistance' of some state courts.[127] Similarly, some of these same Supreme Court decisions have clearly been designed to control illegal and extreme police interrogation methods in various states and locales.

We must again enter some caveats and reminders. We do not suggest that evasion and defiance of United States Supreme Court decisions is commonplace. Indeed, a large part of the credit for the ultimate success of the desegregation decisions is due to the work of many lower court federal judges, who, often at great personal cost, maintained unswerving loyalty to the Supreme Court's decisions. But we are engaged on a *comparative* work; and we must note that loyalty to higher court decisions cannot always be counted upon in America to the extent that it can be in England. Nor can we overlook those occasions and issues on which widespread evasion and even defiance have occurred in America in the past in ways which have no parallel in England.

By this stage it should scarcely be necessary for us to add much to show how the issues dealt with here relate to the main theme of this work. It is clear that a legal system in which formal reasons for decisions are to be overwhelmingly predominant must have a strict hierarchical structure; that it must be able to rely upon judges who willingly comply with the mandates of higher courts; and that higher courts, for their part, must regard it as one of the their chief functions to police the errors of lower courts. The English lawyer who thinks that 'the law is the law' is certainly wrong if he sees the American legal system as one of lawless chaos—the kind of behaviour we have discussed in this section is unusual even in America—but the fact that such behaviour occurs at all demonstrates that America has a legal system in which formal reasoning stands at a significant discount.

[126] See Paul D. Carrington, *supra*, n. 28, at 860, 862.
[127] These two phrases come from R. Neely, *supra*, n. 13, at 162–3.

11

The Makers and the Making of Statute Law

1. INTRODUCTION

In chapters 3 and 4 we identified, in connection with statute law, various respects in which English law is more formal than American. In particular, we suggested that the English political–legal system relies more heavily than the American on statute law and less on case-law, and that, because statute law is more formal than case-law, this is one factor which makes English law more formal. We also suggested that even English statutes dealing with the same subject matter as American statutes tend to be more formal in a number of respects, for example, they have higher content formality, higher mandatory formality, and higher interpretive formality than most comparable American statutes. In this chapter we shall try to offer some explanations for these differences by looking at the processes by which legislation is made, and at the bodies and people responsible for its production. What we offer is in the nature of reasoned speculation. The various factors to be explored are, we think, part effect and part cause; that is, the relations are often interactive and mutually reinforcing, rather than causal in a single linear direction.

Following our earlier analysis, our task here will be twofold. First, we shall offer some explanations for the fact that the American political–legal system relies so much less than the English on legislation for the implementation of legal change, so that courts loom so much larger as lawmakers in America than in England. And secondly, we shall offer some explanations for the fact that American statutes, even when enacted, tend to be less formal than comparable English legislation. For the most part, what we offer will take the form of an analysis of the institutional differences in the constitutional and political arrangements of the two countries, but we shall also say a little about the personnel involved in the production of legislation—legislators and legislative draftsmen. So far as institutional factors are concerned, our thesis, in brief, will be that the relationships between executive officials, legislatures, and courts in the two countries, and the relations between all these institutions with the political parties, tend to correlate closely with the formal-substantive divide.

2. THE RELATIONS BETWEEN EXECUTIVE AND LEGISLATURE: ENGLAND

Our first question concerns the relative importance of legislation and judge-made law in the two countries. Why does England rely on legislation so much more readily to resolve questions that in America are left to the courts? There are two fundamental—and indeed obvious— answers. First, England has strong centralized political institutions, while in America both federalism and the separation-of-powers doctrine fragment political power, and thus greatly weaken government. And secondly, for similar reasons, the English judiciary is a relatively weak body with a very minor political role, as compared with the forces of the centralized executive–legislative machinery, while in America, of course, the judiciary (and particularly the federal judiciary) is immensely powerful as a result of the extent of its constitutional control over the other branches of government. We have already dealt with the position of the judiciary in the previous chapter, so in this section we shall look at the relations between executive and legislative bodies.

The greater relative strength of British governments, as compared with American governments, is most obviously visible in the relations between executive officials and the legislatures. In England, the ministerial heads of the executive departments are all members of, and exercise a powerful control over, the legislature; the English parliamentary system to a large extent actually combines the executive and legislative powers, through the party system, in one central governing body, the Cabinet. Thus statute law making in England is subject to strong centralized control. In America, executive officials are barred from legislative membership, and statutory law-making power is fragmented between, or within, law-making bodies and is subject to external executive influence (including the formal veto power). Further, control over the legislators is not, to any significant degree, generally wielded by the political parties, who are relatively weak, and legislators are more often beholden to special interest groups, rather than to their parties.

Similar differences affect non-statutory legislation—what in England is called delegated legislation and in America administrative regulations. We shall not deal separately in detail with this kind of subordinate legislation. Most such legislation in England is made by ministers, that is, political heads of executive departments, while in America it emanates from executive agencies, who are much more independent of the executive (and legislature) than English executive departments. Again, therefore, the immediate and obvious contrast between the two countries is that such legislation is in England subject to the same sort of centralized control as other legislation, while in America it is the subject of diffused political power.

We will now enlarge on these basic differences, beginning with England. Statute-making in England is done by Parliament and (as to subordinate legislation) by ministers, but these legislative powers are in practice almost completely controlled by the executive. In the first place, the executive is almost entirely in control of what legislative proposals should be put before Parliament or made by ministers. The Cabinet (backed by the entire civil service machine, as well as the non-Cabinet ministers) constitutes a body of persons with a continuous responsibility for overseeing the management of the entire body politic. They are a kind of Board of Directors, in matters of legislation, of the whole country. It is their responsibility, among other things, to oversee the law, to study social problems, and to bring forward proposals for change where these are felt to be necessary.

In modern times, it is very uncommon for any legislative proposals approved by the Cabinet not to secure passage through Parliament. Legislation can be amended during its passage through Parliament, but the Cabinet, through the party system, exercises such control over the legislative machine that amendments can rarely be *forced* on a government by an adverse parliamentary vote.[1] The most that is likely to happen is that the pressure of speeches from government supporters may persuade the minister in charge of a bill that it is necessary or at least expedient to make concessions; if he really feels the concessions cannot be made without threatening the essence of the proposals, he will resist them, explaining probably in more detail why he does so in a private party meeting, and the government will ultimately impose a 'three-line whip' which requires all party members to support the government in the voting lobby, at grave risk to themselves if they fail.

In this system of government minor amendments to the law and the administrative machinery of the state are common and easily obtained. If the matter is small there will be little or no difficulty in having the necessary legislation prepared and introduced into Parliament, even if it may be controversial. There may be delay, of course, because Parliament is busy and has limited time for legislation. But every department has its

---

[1] On the extent to which bills are amended during their passage through Parliament, see J. A. G. Griffith, *Parliamentary Scrutiny of Government Bills* (Allen and Unwin, London, 1974). Since 1970 governments have been defeated in one or other House much more frequently than in earlier decades, see P. Norton, *Parliament in the 1980s* (Blackwells, Oxford, 1985). Most of these defeats were on relatively minor issues, but in 1986 a major government bill (to repeal the Sunday trading laws) was rejected by the House of Commons (see *Hansard*, Sixth Series, Commons, vol. 95, cols. 584–702). This seems the only example of such a defeat since World War II at a time when the government had a large overall majority.

annual opportunity to demand a place in the legislative timetable, though not all will succeed every year.

Furthermore, once this kind of routine legislation is introduced, there is little difficulty about securing its enactment, more or less in the form desired by the minister and his executive officials. Because the minister is both head of his executive department and a member of the legislature, he is responsible for getting these minor reforms carried through, for explaining to the legislature why they are required, and for persuading his colleagues that any necessary finance should be provided. When the bill is introduced, a minister will be in charge of it as it goes through the Houses of Parliament. The minister will always be fully briefed for this job by his civil servants, including the draftsman of the bill. These officials and, above all, the draftsman, know exactly why each provision is in the bill, what it is intended to do, and how it is is intended to dovetail with other bodies of law. Members of Parliament will not usually appreciate these niceties, but the minister will. Thus, in the English system, it is to some extent immaterial that many Members of Parliament do not understand the canons of statutory interpretation, or the legal technicalities governing the subject matter of the bill. These matters will always be fully comprehended by the draftsman and other officials who will do their best to explain them to the minister.

Of course, it is not always as easy as this. More complex legislative proposals may have to take their place in the queue for parliamentary time. The government's legislative timetable is invariably congested, and Parliament can only deal with so much at a time, even when (as is also the case in England) it is largely the government which determines how Parliament's time is to be allocated. So also with seriously controversial proposals, much political activity and discussion may be needed before the Cabinet is prepared to approve the legislation and allow it to be introduced in the government's name. And in the last decade or two, Members of Parliament have begun to show increasing signs of a willingness to vote against their party, thus forcing governments to make more concessions and compromises. But it is still rare for a government with an overall majority in the House of Commons to be forced to compromise on the essential structure of a legislative proposal.

The parliamentary and party system as it operates in England also operates *negatively*, in a very simple fashion. Very little private Members' legislation is ever passed in England, and when it is, it tends to be on non-political and non-party issues.[2] A private Member of

---

[2] That is not to say that private Members' legislation deals solely with uncontroversial issues. In recent years a convention has grown up of leaving sensitive 'liberal' or

Parliament can in England, as a Senator or Congressman can in America, introduce a bill as a gesture, as a symbolic act, to draw attention to some issue which he wishes to ventilate. But such bills cannot be passed, or usually even secure any significant debating time, if the government opposes them. So any proposal for legislation which emanates from a private Member of Parliament will be examined by the civil service, and it would be a rare civil servant who could not find plenty of good reasons for advising that the proposal is a bad one which should not be supported by the minister. Any proposal, for instance, which seems to emanate from some special interest group, and fails to take due account of other interests or of the public interest at large, would simply be scotched and killed in the civil service machine—unless that interest group is the majority parliamentary party or closely associated with it,[3] in which case the proposal will be taken over by the government itself. Any legislative proposal which is going to cost money is particularly subject to scrutiny because of the procedural rule of the House of Commons that a bill containing such proposals cannot be introduced without the support of a minister.[4] This rule is designed to ensure that those who are responsible for collecting taxes—or for putting forward proposals for the collecting of taxes—must approve a measure which is going to require additional taxes.

The control exercised by the British Cabinet over the legislature derives, of course, from the party system.[5] In modern times, it is very difficult indeed for anyone to be elected to the House of Commons without the support of one of the major political parties; and in return for party nomination, money, and support at election time, the party expects and exacts a high degree of loyalty from its members. A Member

---

'conscience' issues to be dealt with by private Members' bills. Thus the laws relating to obscenity, homosexual offences, capital punishment, and abortion were all liberalized as a result of private Members' bills.

[3] Of course some would say that the trade unions, on the one side, and City or commercial/industrial interests, on the other, are such minority groups whose interests are regularly preferred by one party or the other over those of the nation at large.

[4] Erskine May, *Treatise on the Law etc., of Parliament*, 760 ff. (20th edn., Butterworths, 1983).

[5] On the party system in England, see generally, S. E. Finer, *The Changing British Party System 1945–1979*, (American Enterprise Institute for Public Policy Research, Washington, DC, 1980); V. Bogdanor, *The People and the Party System* (Cambridge U. Press, Cambridge, 1981); A. H. Birch, 'The Theory and Practice of Modern British Democracy', in *The Changing Constitution* (J. Jowell and D. Oliver, edd., Clarendon Press, Oxford, 1985) (arguing that the British party system has become less strict recently); for comparative studies, see *Parties and Democracy in Britain and America* (V. Bogdanor, ed., Praeger, NY, 1984).

of Parliament, especially if he is a member on the government side, is expected to vote as his party requires him, though he may speak against his party (with moderation, and not too often) or at least ask the minister for concessions or variations to his policy. Thus it is common to see many government supporters speak against some proposal and then dutifully vote for the government. Of course, 'rebellions' do occur, government supporters are not sheep, and their views must be taken into consideration; but rebellions are usually settled behind closed doors at party meetings, and ultimately, most will toe the line, though concessions may have to be made. A few votes 'of conscience' against his government may be allowed the Member (and rather more freedom is usually allowed Opposition Members), but if the Member repeats the process too often he is likely to jeopardize any chance of being selected for office by the Prime Minister. 'Voting against one's party [in Britain] is like a Bostonian in the stands at Fenway Park rooting vociferously for the Yankees. One can do it, but it is dangerous.'[6] In the last resort a Member of Parliament may be expelled from his party, and recent experience has shown that the chances of his losing his seat at the next election are then high, even if he should stand as an independent without party support. The chief reasons for this are that the British electorate traditionally votes for a party rather than a person, that it is very difficult for a private Member to build up any sort of campaign organization, and that contributions to election funds have traditionally been funded through the parties and not to individual Members.

The discipline of the party system, as it operates in modern Britain, is perhaps a further illustration of a major theme of this book, namely that British political and legal institutions (which in the long run have an impact on the use of formality in law) rest on a high degree of trust between their component parts. The party system and the legislative system together constitute a highly integrated political system, based in major part on trust and loyalty. Members of Parliament do what their parties tell them—often without further or detailed examination of the substantive issues themselves, or of the reasons for voting in a particular way—because, by and large, they trust the party machines. Although there is much muttering about party discipline and the tyranny of the whips, the British political system just would not be the same without this degree of trust. The result is that all Members of Parliament do not need to study the substantive arguments for and against particular proposals or amendments to bills in the way that American legislators may feel obliged to do, though some must obviously do so if Parliament

---

[6] Anthony King, 'How to Strengthen Legislatures—Assuming That We Want To', 77, 88, in *The Role of the Legislature in Western Democracies* (N. J. Ornstein, ed., American Enterprise Institute for Public Policy Research, Washington, 1981).

is to perform effectively at all. This also goes far to explain why British Members of Parliament have so little in the way of research facilities and support:[7] this has traditionally been provided through the political parties.

But although the British party system thus exacts loyalty and imposes discipline on its political supporters, it also tends to insulate them from some of the extremes of populism. A very large proportion (probably four-fifths or more) of parliamentary constituencies are so dominated by one party that the party's nominee has little to fear from the electorate itself.[8] So long as he retains the support of the party itself (or at least of the local party officials), he can normally be confident of being continually re-elected. This helps to give Members of Parliament a degree of independence from the electorate which few elected American politicians enjoy. And this in turn means that the English political process does not conform to the American model of the democratic process as one in which elected representatives of various interest groups simply compete for power and distributions of goods. British Members of Parliament are often free to support and vote for proposals which the majority of their constituents would reject if they had the opportunity. It is for this reason that it was possible for Parliament to abolish capital punishment in 1965, and since then several times reject proposals for its reintroduction, even though opinion polls nearly always show a majority in favour of its use.

The party system, as it operates in modern Britain, also has another, more subtle, effect on political and legal debate, and ultimately on the formal nature of the legal system. It provides an important institutional unity to the non-government forces, personified by the official (and salaried) post of Leader of the Opposition, to which there is of course no parallel in America, either at the federal or at the state level. This unity helps to polarize opinion on a great many issues, a result rather well symbolized by the insistence of both Houses that the seating should be arranged in rows of opposing benches (with only a few 'cross benches'), as contrasted with the semi-circular arrangement favoured in America and also in most European legislative chambers. In Britain, the government broadly stands for one approach to most problems, and the chief opposition party for an opposing approach. Shades of opinion are, of course, to be found within the parties, and often also in minority

---

[7] See Ranney, 'The Working Conditions of Members of Parliament and Congress: Changing the Tools Changes the Job', in Ornstein, *supra*, n. 6 at 67.

[8] In British general elections, the number of members of the winning party who lose their seats is usually negligible; and the number of the losing party who lose their seats is rarely more than 50 or 60 (out of a total House of Commons membership of 650). See S. E. Finer, *supra*, n. 5, Table 4.

parties, but the two-party system has dominated British politics for well over a century, with only a few exceptional years.

Polarization also exists in another way in the British political system. In the absence of electoral primaries, the British voter is usually offered a choice between two or three candidates representing the main political parties, and he has to accept or reject the party packages *en masse*. He cannot indicate general support (for instance) for party X but policy Z—when party X does not support policy Z.

The polarization of opinion in Britain has two results which are important for our theme. First, it makes it easier for legislation to get passed, and secondly it tends to make that legislation crisper, more uncompromising. As to the first point, it may seem surprising that polarization of opinion makes it easier to pass legislation, but that is because the British tradition merely requires a bare majority for legislative change. As to the second, the polarization of opinion also tends to make British political debate highly adversarial—like common law litigation—so that political and moral questions tend to be converted into adversarial rather than pluralistic issues. Issues tend to be sharpened, and legislation can take a much more precise and consistent approach, once a majority exists for the principle.

For the same reasons, coalitions are largely unnecessary in modern British politics. For many years most British governments have had absolute majority control of the House of Commons, and the governments have been governments of a single party without the need for formal coalition support. This makes it possible for governments and ministers to formulate clear policies and to instruct their officials to produce bills which give effect to them. There is very rarely any need in the British political system for a government deliberately to choose a legislative provision which obfuscates a troublesome point, or fudges a confusing compromise, or ducks an issue altogether by passing the buck to the judiciary. Few incidents of this nature have occurred in recent decades in the British House of Commons, but two occurred during the very exceptional period 1974–5 when the Labour Party was in power but without an absolute majority over all other parties.[9]

From the point of view of the law and legal change, the features of the British parliamentary system referred to above tend to lead to a number

[9] The first was s. 5 of the Trade Union and Labour Relations Act 1974 which was amended as soon as Labour obtained an absolute majority in the election of October 1974, see s. 53 of the Employment Protection Act 1975. The second incident concerned the Labour government's attempt to pass legislation indemnifying some Labour local government councillors for illegalities committed while the Conservatives were in power, see s. 1 of the Housing Finance (Special Provisions) Act 1975. (In fact this latter Act was passed while Labour technically did have an overall majority, but the majority was so small that a few deserters on this occasion prevented the government getting their way.)

of important results, which are very different from those we find in the American legal system. First, hasty and ill-considered legislation is unlikely to be introduced, let alone passed. Similarly, legislation drawn up to further the wishes of one interest group cannot get passed unless (we have seen) that interest group happens to be the majority parliamentary party, or closely associated with it. On the other hand, necessary and well-supported legislation is very easy to pass, even if it is strongly opposed by minority interest groups. Although some degree of compromise necessarily occurs when party policy is being formulated, especially on marginal matters, legislative policy is usually clear and basic political compromises are not needed for the passage of legislation. If there is still obscurity in much modern English legislation, it results not so much from political compromises, nor from failure to face up to necessary decisions, as from drafting techniques and the inherent difficulties of language.

Some of what we have said so far may be an idealized rather than a realistic version of the British political system insofar as it affects the legislative process. In practice, things do not always work as well as we have implied. Needed and useful reforms are sometimes postponed for lack of ministerial interest or energy; the problem of not antagonizing an important section of party supporters may sometimes prevent legislation on this or that topic; the need to maintain party support, or to appear to comply with electoral promises, may occasionally require some fudging of legislative policy.[10] And it cannot be denied that one of the fundamental threats posed by the British system of government, which the American system was designed to avoid—the threat of a tyrannical majority party bulldozing through legislation in the sole interest of a small segment of the people who happen to be associated with the majority party—has reared its head from time to time in recent years. But our purpose is not so much to praise the British system, as to describe and compare it with the American.

3. THE RELATIONS BETWEEN EXECUTIVES AND LEGISLATURES: AMERICA

In all the respects we have discussed above, the institutional position in America differs fundamentally from that in Britain. Even at the federal level, there hardly exists in America a Cabinet in the British sense—that is, a body of political leaders with overall responsibility for the

---

[10] A good example is to be found in the Trade Union and Labour Relations Act 1974 which was passed to give effect to explicit Labour promises to repeal the hated Conservative Industrial Relations Act 1971, but which also retained parts of the 1971 Act which actually gave the workers enhanced rights.

management of the body politic and the legal system. Of course, a large part of the affairs of the body politic simply do not fall within any sphere of central federal responsibility. Rather, they fall to the state legislatures and are often dealt with by them in very different ways. Moreover, the separation of the executive from the legislature at both the federal and state levels means that neither the political parties nor individual leaders feel (or apparently feel, so far as observers can judge) the same sense of ultimate responsibility for initiating, planning, and implementing policy changes through law[11] as do members of the British Cabinet. In addition, the very different nature of the party system in America means that most political figures are not controllable by, nor answerable to, their parties to the same degree as in England.

The upshot is that no single institutional force controls the content of American federal statutes, and when such statutes are enacted they are often watered down or adopted in compromise form, not merely on marginal, but even on basic, issues. As a result they are liable to be less sharp and precise in their policy, and are less likely to contain hard and fast rules embodying clear-cut legislative policy decisions. Though they may include considerable detail, that detail will often incorporate open-ended concepts on which it was not possible to generate more detailed agreement. Thus, as Judge Posner has recently said, '[F]ederal statutes often emerge from the legislative process radically incomplete, and the courts are left to complete them by a process that is only formally interpretive.'[12]

We now proceed to look more closely at some of the specific differences between the institutional relations in the two countries which explain why so much American federal statute law differs fundamentally from English statute law. The legislative process in Congress differs in many vital respects from that in the British Parliament. Most obviously, the executive does not control the proceedings, and the legislature is not dominated by party lines. So, even where the legislation originates with

[11] See, e.g., Davidson, 'The Two Congresses and How they Are Changing', in Ornstein, ed., *supra*, n. 6, at 3, 10–11. Because everyone concerned can throw responsibility onto others for the failure to enact the necessary legislation, we thus have the spectacle, from time to time, of legislatures failing to pass budgets in time, with threats that government money will run out, and public officials will not be paid. This could not happen in Britain because the responsibility for such a failure would plainly lie on the government: indeed, a government which failed to secure passage of its budget would have to resign and be replaced by one which could. In the Australian parliamentary system (which is substantially the same as that of Britain) the failure of Mr Whitlam's government to have its budget passed by the Senate in 1975 ultimately led to his dismissal by the Governor-General. See Sir John Kerr, *Matters of Judgment* (Melbourne, 1978).

[12] Richard A. Posner, *The Federal Courts: Crisis and Reform*, 19 (Harvard U. Press, Cambridge, 1985). Needless to say Posner is here using the term 'formally interpretive' to mean 'nominally interpretive'.

the executive, the legislature may amend it in ways contrary to the wishes of the executive. The policy wishes of Congress may simply differ from those of the executive or the President. Sometimes, expert official advice within the executive is being disregarded when Congress amends a bill in ways contrary to its design. Thus from a technical legal point of view, bills often emerge flawed, lacking a coherent structure, or containing provisions which do not fit together well, so that, when they become Acts, they will not operate well until they have been filtered through the courts. Again, a bill may be sponsored by a Senator or Congressman who is not necessarily himself thoroughly conversant with the complexities of the subject. Further, whenever the bill emanates from a committee, amendments may also be made on the floor of the House or the Senate without the assistance of legislative draftsmen and, given the traditional differences in the relations between legislature and courts in the two countries, it is anyhow more likely that Congressional legislation will leave matters for judicial resolution which in England would be spelled out in detail in the Act itself.

The differing role of the political parties in America is also a significant factor in this overall picture. Not only are legislators free from direct political control by the executive (though, of course, much political arm-twisting may occur), but they are also often free from any significant degree of party control. The American party system has for some years been getting looser and weaker, as many political commentators have observed.[13] American Senators and Congressmen owe far less allegiance to their parties than do British Members of Parliament. Once elected, they have enormous advantages as incumbents, and can usually secure re-election with a minimum of party support. Conversely, however, they owe far more to interest groups of various kinds, for both political and financial support. At election time, campaign funds are derived largely from interest groups, and not from the parties. It is true that most American legislators still need a party label at election time, but that label can often be acquired by securing the party nomination at a primary, without having in any way to kowtow to a central party machine. Moreover, the voters' habits of 'ticket-splitting', for example,

---

[13] See Bogdanor, *supra*, n. 5; Martin P. Wattenberg, *The Decline of American Political Parties 1952–1980* (Harvard U. Press, Cambridge, 1984). For a discussion of voting patterns in Parliament and American legislatures, see William J. Keefe and Morris S. Ogul, *The American Legislative Process: Congress and the States*, 287–8 (5th edn., Prentice-Hall, Englewood Cliffs, NJ, 1981). Party strength varies a great deal between the states, but even in New York, generally reckoned a 'strong' party state, it was possible for Mayor Koch to secure the nomination of both major parties for the election of 1981: Smith, 'New York', in *The Political Life of the American States*, at 266 (A. Rosenthal and M. Moakley, edd., Praeger, NY, 1984). This was unusual even in New York but would be quite impossible in England.

voting into office a governor of one party and an assembly majority of the other party, is now very common, and also weakens the American party system.

Similarly, American legislators do not turn to their parties for research and support facilities: at the federal level they have their own research and support staff, financed by the taxpayers, on a scale which is mind-boggling in its lavishness by British standards, and far more extensive (though less centralized) than anything organized by British political parties. At the state level, the position is very variable—the legislators may have adequate support and research staff, or they may have little or none. But in either event, in the absence of a strong party system, American legislators are far more likely to have to, and to want to, make up their own minds on the need for legislation, and on the contents of that legislation.

These differences have a profound effect on policy formulation. Where British policy choices are often seen to be Yes/No choices, or choices between one or another method of introducing change, alternatives usually produced and worked out by the political parties, in America the formulation of policy is often conducted in a much looser, less structured sort of way. American legislators do not have governments in charge of them to formulate policies for them to adopt; nor does the executive act as an intermediary between the civil service and the legislators. American legislators thus need to obtain their own advice and information to help them formulate policy, but obtaining this advice and information is an individual, almost entrepreneurial responsibility. Some of it, especially on complex legal issues, comes directly from academics such as law professors who may draft bills, advise legislators, and give expert evidence to legislative committees. But advisers of this kind—unlike British civil servants—do not operate in a hierarchicial bureaucratic structure. So their opinions and advice do not lead to clear-cut solutions to problems; indeed, there may be as many opinions and different forms of advice as there are legislators. Only over a long period of time may a consensus slowly congeal, and even then, the only thing that may be generally agreed is that something ought to be done about a problem. Beyond that, there may be no agreement at all, thus once again making the production of legislation far more difficult in America than in Britain.

An additional difference between the American position and the English stems from the vast size of the United States and the basic structure of the federal system itself. Party divisions often give way to local allegiances. Especially at the federal level, all the members from a particular state may have more in common than those from other states, even across the party lines.[14] But this can also happen at the state level, especially in the larger states, and states where regional interests differ markedly.

Thus, where British political institutions help to polarise opinion on most issues, producing highly adversarial politics, and hence clear-cut policy decisions which translate into formal statutes, American politics is much less polarised. The American use of primaries also militates against polarization, because primaries enable the public to choose between political packages more selectively. And within the federal Congress itself there are many factors which tend to prevent polarization of opinion.[15] Many political issues in America tend to become 'polycentric'—multi-sided and interdependent—whereas in England they would become two-sided and adversarial. In the absence of powerful executives and party leaders in the legislative bodies themselves, there is a lack of 'organising issues in lines of battle...In place of identifiable, consistent voting blocks, there is a multitude of floating, ever-changing coalitions around specific issues.'[16]

On the other hand, where British Members of Parliament are subject to party control and discipline, they are also (as we have seen) relatively insulated by party support from the direct impact of electoral opinion, or of the power of interest groups. In American politics, the position is quite otherwise. American politicians are far more directly accountable to the electorate (and to interest groups) than English politicians, because the mediating effects of powerful political parties are absent, and also because of the role of primaries in the American electoral system. The result is that elected American Congressmen and Senators are under greater pressure to consider the possible impact of their actions on the voters at every turn. This tends to make them take more ambiguous and less clear-cut positions on many controversial issues. Politicians who take such ambiguous positions are less likely to be unseated at election time than those who take sharp and clear positions. Thus a statute that means all things to all people, or is at least susceptible of opposing interpretations, can readily serve the ends of those seeking re-election. The consequence is that legislation is often a product of vague and ill-defined compromises, and the fudging of issues which would be more likely to receive clear cut resolution in Britain.

Occasions for compromise and the fudging of issues, indeed, arise

---

[14] Rosenthal, 'Analyzing States', in *The Political Life of the American States, supra*, n. 13, at 3.

[15] See generally, Malcolm E. Jewell and Samuel C. Patterson, *The Legislative Process in the United States*, 9 (3rd edn., Random House, NY, 1977).

[16] Davidson, 'The Two Congresses and How they Are Changing', in Ornstein, ed., *supra*, n. 6, at 19.

constantly in the American legislative process; the American system of necessity requires compromise on a grand scale[17] because political power is so fragmented that in the absence of compromise it would often be difficult to achieve anything at all. Even within legislatures, power is diffused among various officers and groups, such as committees, chairmen of committees, seniority leaders, officers of the House, sectional spokesmen, and so on.[18] At the federal level, individual members have to compromise with each other, the House committees often have to compromise with each other, the House and the Senate may have to compromise with each other, and both Houses may have to compromise with the President. Similarly, pressure to compromise within and between the two Houses, and between the legislature and the governor often exists in the states. By contrast, as we have seen, the Cabinet in Britain usually controls, through the party system, the entire legislative process from top to bottom.

There is, indeed, a substantial American literature,[19] somewhat neglected by lawyers,[20] on the theory of legislation, which treats legislation as a product supplied to interest groups in a kind of political market-place. According to this theory, legislatures rarely act as lawyers tend to assume they act, that is, in a way which is vaguely in the 'public interest'; on the contrary, legislatures act to supply private interest groups with laws they want. The function of the legislature is thus not to ascertain what is the 'public interest' but to provide a meeting place in which coalitions, ever-shifting coalitions, can come together to obtain some particular piece of legislation. Most legislation on this view consists of political compromises. A statute itself is full of compromises; further, a vote for one statute may be exchanged for a vote for another statute, and so on. This theory of legislation is a product of American legislative processes. It bears no relationship whatever to the way in which the British Parliament behaves. And it may exaggerate one aspect of the American legislative process at the expense of others. But insofar as it does capture the reality of American legislative activity, it also helps to explain why statutes are so often enacted in a way which eschews clear cut solutions and solutions of high formality.

[17] 'Compromise...builds coalitions through negotiation over the *content* of legislation. Each side agrees to modify policy goals on a given bill in a way that is generally acceptable to the other.' W. Oleszek, *Congressional Procedures and Policy*, 16 (Congressional Quarterly Press, Washington, 1978). Or again: '[V]irtually all general legislation is vulnerable to skewing in the interest of local, narrow, or regional advantage.' W. Keefe, *Congress and the American People*, 12 (Prentice-Hall, Englewood Cliffs, NJ, 1980).

[18] See Keefe and Ogul, *supra*, n. 13, at 263–4.

[19] See, e.g., J. Berry, *The Interest Group Society* (Little Brown, Boston, 1984); George J. Stigler, *The Citizen and the State: Essays on Regulation* (U. of Chicago Press, Chicago, 1975).

[20] But see Posner, *supra*, n. 12, at 262–7.

The constitutional powers of the courts, which we referred to in the last chapter, must also be remembered in considering the way in which the American legislative process works. As we have already noted several times, the institutional features of the American political process which we are here discussing both influence and are influenced by each other. The very fact that the courts have the power to strike down legislation as unconstitutional may sometimes make legislatures less hesitant to pass laws which some members have qualms about. Why risk political unpopularity by standing up for minorities, or by espousing minority causes, when one can vote for a bill possibly contrary to those interests, knowing that if it is so found, the courts can strike it down? There is a strong temptation for American politicians to pass unpleasant political issues to the courts in this way.[21] Indeed, it is argued by some writers that the American political system encourages legislatures to refuse to face up to controversial issues which demand a clear answer;[22] that they pass the buck to the courts, that they fudge political compromises which will end up with the courts, designedly or undesignedly.[23] Some see the explosion of litigation as due in part to the failure of the legislatures to resolve fundamental value conflicts, and the resulting tendency to take these conflicts to the courts.[24] Thus American courts are frequently called upon to deal with deep moral issues of a novel kind which in England would be legislated upon, perhaps after some kind of inquiry had been established. Recent examples relate to experimental research on embryos, the problems of 'surrogate mothers', and so on.[25]

So far we have been talking mostly of the federal Congress, but at the state level some of these factors are further magnified. The fact that most high state executive officers are independently elected, and are not appointed by, or answerable to, the governor, means that there is nothing remotely resembling the British Cabinet in the state government

---

[21] Thayer long ago noted the tendency of judicial review to make legislators less responsible. 'The Origin and Scope of the American Doctrine of Constitutional Law', 7 *Harv. L. Rev.* 129 (1893); see also Bickel, *The Least Dangerous Branch*, at 21–3, 35–44 (Bobbs-Merrill, Indianapolis, 1962).

[22] Barton, 'Behind the Legal Explosion', 27 *Stan. L. Rev.* 567, at 576 (1975); Aldisert, 'An American View of the Judicial Function', 77, in *Legal Institutions Today: English and American Approaches Compared* (H. W. Jones, ed., ABA, 1977).

[23] Jaffe, 'An Essay on Delegation of Legislative Power: I', 47 *Col. L. Rev.* 359, 366–7 (1947).

[24] M. Rosenberg, 'Devising Procedures that are Civil to Promote Justice that is Civilized', 69 *Mich. L. Rev.* 797, 810 (1971).

[25] See the Surrogacy Arrangements Act 1985 which was enacted after (though it did not in all respects follow) the Report of the Warnock Committee of Inquiry into Human Fertilization and Embryology (Cmnd. 9314, 1984).

system.[26] Similarly, state legislators owe little to their parties[27] and much to various interest groups. They do not generally have powerful and efficient civil service machines to point out the deficiencies in legislative proposals, or to bring forward their own. Even those states which do have efficient executive departments with competent administrative officials and legal draftsmen do not have the same relationship between these public officials and the legislators that England does. State legislators are bombarded with legislative proposals from private interest groups and offered a variety of inducements to introduce them. These inducements are regarded in American political theory as the means by which interest groups make their views felt to elected politicians, but because politicans require financial support from interest groups at election times, there is a powerful coercive element to this relationship.[28]

Another peculiarity of the American legislative process is that most legislatures (including the Congress) have erected severe procedural impediments to the passage of legislation, impediments that often mean that no statute on the subject is ever passed, or that its enactment is delayed for very long periods. These delays are frequently due to a procedural feature of the American legislative process, namely the requirement that legislation must be favourably 'reported out of committee'.[29] The power of committee chairmen inside American legislative bodies continues despite efforts at reform. Today it still remains largely true in many American legislatures, especially at the state level, that if the chairman simply declines to put the bill on the agenda for hearings, it will never be reported out of the committee or subcommittee and never reach the floor of the House. It will therefore die without ever being voted down. And since many legislatures only have a two-year life anyhow, the procrastination does not have to be prolonged very long to achieve this result.

English lawyers and parliamentarians would be astonished by this technique which they would regard as designed to thwart the legislature's will, and thus the electorate's will. Sometimes this is no doubt the case,[30]

---

[26] As J. Bryce pointed out a century ago: *The American Commonwealth*, vol. 1, at 507, vol. 2, at 348 (2nd edn., Macmillan, NY, 1908).

[27] Jewell and Patterson, *supra*, n. 15, at 99.

[28] Bryce, *supra*, n. 26, vol. 1, 521. Things seem to have changed little since then, see Neely, *How Courts Govern America*, at 79–92 (Yale U. Press, New Haven, Conn., 1981).

[29] For a concise, yet thorough, account of a bill's progress toward enactment in the US, see K. Bradshaw and D. Pring, *Parliament and Congress*, 274–89 (U. of Texas Press, Austin, 1972); see also J. Harris, *Congress and the Legislative Process*, 126–56, (2nd edn., McGraw Hill, NY, 1972); W. Oleszek, *supra*, n. 17.

[30] As with many of the instances of state legislatures' refusal to enact comparative negligence bills. For an example of a state legislature being prevented from even

but it is by no means always the case. The passage of bills in a state legislature often says very little about the 'will' of the legislature, and still less about the will of the electorate. In the absence of an English-type party system, and of party manifestos and election programmes in the English style, an American state legislature is not elected to carry out a well-defined programme of highly specific policies. Nor indeed can it do so for the reasons already mentioned. There is thus much truth in the observation made by Bryce over a century ago,[31] and recently repeated by others,[32] that most Americans think that legislation is prima facie likely to do more harm than good, and that the main function of the legislative machine is therefore to prevent bad legislation from being passed. Such a machine requires elaborate brakes.

These procedural impediments to legislation in America appear to be the result of the lack of centralized control over the legislative process which would otherwise make it very easy for the legislature to be 'hijacked' into passing (or rejecting) legislation without a full appreciation of the implications. In particular, once a bill is through committee in an American legislature, especially a state legislature, its subsequent passage is often a mere formality.[33] So it is very important that bad bills should not emerge from committee.

The creation of an obstacle course[34] to the passage of bad legislation in American legislatures inevitably results in the failure of many legislatures to pass good legislation as well. This naturally throws a heavier burden on the courts to introduce desirable and necessary reforms themselves. The inability of American legislatures to introduce reforms also forces the courts to cope with problems arising from obsolete statutes which the legislatures just do not get around to repealing or modifying as new conditions demand.[35] Such indeed is the problem created by obsolete statutes that Calabresi has suggested that the courts should have power to declare them at some point to be spent, leaving it

---

considering the issue, see Harper, James, and Gray, *The Law of Torts*, vol. 4, p. 417 n. 1 (Maryland) (2nd edn., Little Brown, Boston, 1986).

[31] Bryce, *supra*, n. 26, vol. 1, at 527, 531.

[32] See, e.g., Neely, *supra*, n. 28, at 55, 56, 147–8.

[33] Keefe and Ogul, *supra*, n. 13, at 255.

[34] '[N]ormally legislation must pass successfully through multiple decision points. One Congressional report identified more than 100 specific steps...' W. Oleszek, *supra*, n. 17, at 14. In the 94th Congress (1975–6) 968 bills out of 16,982 introduced became law, an 8% success rate. W. Keefe, *supra*, n. 17, at 21.

[35] See Calabresi, *A Common Law for the Age of Statutes*, (Harvard U. Press, Cambridge, 1982).

to the legislature to re-enact them if it wishes.[36] Although obsolete statutes can occasionally cause problems in English law, this is, on the whole, a much less common phenomenon today (although it was more serious until about fifty years ago) for the reasons already given. Normal ministerial legislation will routinely update and repeal obsolete statutes as part of the regular work of the political machine.

Judge Posner has recently argued that many of the canons of statutory interpretation used by the courts display ignorance of the legislative process.[37] A realistic understanding of the legislative process is, he says, 'devastating to the canons of construction'.[38] Legislators, he urges, do not know anything about these canons of interpretation and it is farcical to attribute such knowledge to them. For example, the presumption that implied repeals are not intended is based on the wholly unreal implication that legislators comb the statute book before passing a bill to see what previous legislation may be inconsistent with it.[39] Much of this critique of methods of statutory interpretation may be valid in America, and indeed it is often assumed in America that the canons of interpretation do not mean very much anyhow. Low interpretive formality is thus one rational result of the American legislative process. But as we have already seen, this is not true in England. Although Members of Parliament may not know much about the rules of statutory interpretation, the draftsman of the bill does, and the minister who pilots the bill through Parliament will be taught as much as he needs to know about them by his draftsman and public officials. So these arguments about the relationship between methods of interpretation and the legislative process are inapplicable to England.

4. THE DRAFTING OF LEGISLATION

We now turn to another major institutional difference between the English and the American statute-making processes, which also helps account for the more formal character of English statute law. In summary terms, the drafting of legislation is much more professional-ized in England. All parliamentary legislation in England is drafted in the Office of Parliamentary Counsel, a very small office of highly skilled and dedicated professional draftsmen, of great technical proficiency and with strong traditions as to methodology and technique. The British

[36] *Ibid.*, ch. 4. But not everyone agrees with Calabresi that obsolete statutes are a major legal problem in the US. See, e.g., the review of Calabresi's book by Judge Frank M. Coffin, Chief Judge of the US Court of Appeals for the First Circuit, in 91 *Yale LJ* 827, 836 (1982).

[37] Posner, *supra*, n. 12, at 276ff.

[38] *Ibid.*, 276.

[39] Posner, 'Statutory Interpretation: In the Classroom and in the Courtroom', 50 *U. Ch. L. Rev.* 800, 812 (1983).

government's control over the legislative process is so great in modern times that it is almost impossible for any bill, or even an amendment to a bill, to be passed by Parliament, unless it has been drafted by (or in some rare cases, approved by) the Parliamentary Counsel[40]—and they (it should be stressed) are officials of the executive government, not of Parliament itself.

The Office of Parliamentary Counsel is a very powerful one in the British governmental machine because the draftsmen have secured a monopoly over the production of legislative bills. Thus their views as to the needs of their work are largely respected by successive governments. A draftsman who says he needs six months to prepare a major bill will not be pressed to produce it earlier in the absence of compelling reasons. Equally, departmental lawyers and policy makers have learnt that the draftsman needs and expects in general to be given very detailed instructions before he starts to draft. Thus the preparation of legislation is an exceptionally thorough exercise in modern Britain, both at the preliminary and at the drafting stages.

English Parliamentary Counsel are not simply skilled draftsmen in the abstract. They know and understand the way in which English judges interpret statutes, and they draft bills in the knowledge that they will be interpreted in the traditional literal manner. Because of the uniformity of approach of English judges this aspect of the work of Parliamentary Counsel is greatly simplified. There is also, of course, a corresponding reaction on the part of the judges, who interpret statutes in the way Parliamentary Counsel expect because the style of drafting is so uniform that this facilitates such an approach to the problems of interpretation. Interpretation and drafting are thus reciprocal and complementary functions, each of which is affected by the uniformity of technique of the other.

Thus there is nothing at all absurd in assuming that an English Act should be read in light of the canons of interpretation; Acts are *designed* to be interpreted in this way by the draftsman, and, although his views are not those of Parliament at large, his views are (where necessary) transmitted by the minister in charge of the bill to the relevant House. Consider, for instance, the presumption against implied repeals. One of the most important (and best-performed) functions of Parliamentary Counsel is to ensure that any bill drafted by him expressly amends or repeals any provisions of prior legislation which require such treatment as a result of the present bill. No such case is ever left to inference (and hence possible doubts) except unwittingly. Thus it makes perfectly good

---

[40] See generally Reed Dickerson, 'Legislative Drafting in London and Washington', [1959] *Camb. LJ* 49; Hutton, 'How the English Meet the Problem', in *Professionalizing Legislative Drafting*, 110, 113 (Reed Dickerson, ed., ABA, Chicago, 1973).

sense for an English judge to assume that an implied repeal was probably not intended by the draftsman.

Private Members' bills (that is, bills not introduced by or on behalf of the government) are occasionally passed, if they relate to non-political subjects (though usually not more than five or six a year), but no modern British government would permit even a bill of this kind to be passed unless they were satisfied that it had been properly drafted. This can be done either by making the facilities of the Parliamentary Counsel available to the private Member, if the government is basically sympathetic to the aims of the bill, or by simply inviting the Parliamentary Counsel to vet the bill if it has been drafted by someone else. Similarly, amendments to government bills are often made (though almost never if the government is seriously opposed to them), but here also the practice is to refer the amendments to Parliamentary Counsel for his views on their technical legal soundness. If they are found unsatisfactory from this point of view, the minister in charge of the bill will table his own amendment to give effect to the intention behind the other amendment. Indeed, the normal practice today, where the government is prepared to accept the substance of a proposed amendment, is for the minister to tell the House that he will table a government amendment at a later stage of the bill to meet the point being raised, and the Member who has moved the present amendment will then normally accept this assurance and withdraw his own amendment.

We do not mean, in the above account, to suggest that the British system of drafting is beyond criticism. Many lawyers today find the style of parliamentary drafting obscure and tortuous; it is often quite impossible to get a general idea of the intent of a statute from a casual reading; and of course, occasional mistakes, ambiguities, and inconsistencies inevitably occur. Moreover, within the English context, draftsmen may complain that bills (or more usually amendments) sometimes have to be drafted with inadequate time for preparation.[41] Our point is the relatively narrow one that inconsistencies and conflicting provisions are rarely to be found between one statute and another, still less within the same statute, and that the absence of such flaws is largely due to the ability of British governments to control the content of statutes which are passed by Parliament, and to ensure that they are drafted by lawyers of high professional competence.

[41] See Engle, 'Bills are Made to Pass as Razors are Made to Sell: Practical Constraints in the Preparation of Legislation', *Statute L. Rev.* 7, at 14, 15–20 (1983). But even so, there is no comparison between the position in England and that in many American states. One state legislative draftsman, for instance, has related how he is sometimes asked by a legislator to draft a major bill, without written instructions of any sort, in a matter of days. (Personal communication with the first named author).

The style and competence with which legislation is drafted is bound to have a considerable impact, not only on the detailed methods of interpretation adopted by the courts, but on the whole relationship between the legislature and the courts. If the legislature chooses to give its instructions in the form of exceptionally precise and detailed commands, drafted with great technical skill, those whose business it is to apply and interpret such commands may well find that the sensible course is to interpret them at face value, and not to look too deeply for underlying purposes or the spirit of the legislation. This tendency will be reinforced if, as is also the case in England, as we shall explain later, Parliament tends to update statutes with relative frequency, and to correct errors thrown up by legal cases reasonably promptly.

We have no reason to suppose that many of the legislative counsel who draft Congressional legislation are any less skilled or dedicated than their English counterparts. But there are institutional reasons why, in the result, much American legislation—even federal legislation—tends to be a less satisfactory source of clear rules than most English legislation; and hence is less easy to treat as a source of formal reasons.[42]

In the first place there is no single centralized office where all Congressional legislation is prepared, and where control of methodology, technique, and also training-on-the-job can be undertaken. Both the Senate and the House of Representatives have their own Offices of Legislative Counsel, and, in some respects, these Offices resemble the Office of Parliamentary Counsel in England. In the initial drafting of bills, the members of the Office of the Legislative Counsel exercise a high degree of independence, and left to themselves, they are probably capable of producing work as skilled and technically sound as their English counterparts.[43] But American Legislative Counsel have to contend with difficulties not faced by English Parliamentary Counsel. For example, American legislative draftsmen have to recognize that their bills will be interpreted by a judiciary which is far from being the compact, homogeneous English judiciary. As we shall see in more detail in the next chapter, even the federal judiciary is a relatively large and diversified body; and federal statutes will also often have to be interpreted and applied by state judges who may be still more diversified in their skills and experience. This is bound to make drafting more

---

[42] See generally, Reed Dickerson, *Professionalizing Legislative Drafting*, supra, n. 40. Recommendations of the ABA following this conference have had no result, see Reed Dickerson, *Materials on Legal Drafting*, 376–85 (West, St. Paul, 1981).

[43] Reed Dickerson, 'Legislative Drafting: American and British Practices Compared', 44 *ABAJ* 865, 868 (1958). On the Congressional draftsmen generally, see Kenneth Kofmehl, *Professional Staffs of Congress*, 117–26, 189–93 (3rd edn., 1977).

difficult, because the draftsman cannot assume that the judges will all understand the particular styles and methods which he uses.

In the second place, American Legislative Counsel's position differs from that of English Parliamentary Counsel because their instructions generally come, not from the government, as in England, but from the individual Members of the two Houses.[44] This means that they have, of course, a large number of taskmasters; and they may spend a great deal of time preparing bills which will never be passed. Enormous numbers of bills are introduced into all American legislatures, very few of which are ever enacted.[45] These bills all have to be drafted by someone, and if Legislative Counsel have to give time to preparing such large quantities of bills, their work is likely to suffer. This does not happen in England. Very few bills—almost no government bills—are introduced which are not passed; only rarely, indeed, are they not passed in the same session in which they are first introduced.

A third major difference between the role of American Legislative Counsel and English Parliamentary Counsel is that, even if Legislative Counsel's bill is well drafted initially, once the bill reaches the Committee Stage, significant changes are likely to be made by committee members themselves. The result is that the draftsman may lose control of the bill in a way that does not happen in England. Much of the initial draft may even be rewritten, usually under difficult conditions even for the most expert of draftsmen. There is a tendency to 'rush into "legal language" each tentative expression of uncrystallized policy'.[46] More-over, once the committee has finished its deliberations, the bill's sponsors frequently try to push it through the legislature as quickly as possible, preventing the Legislative Counsel from putting in the time necessary to produce a well-drafted statute that may capture the essence of the committee's agreement. Thus 'what started out as an adequately drafted bill may end up as crude patchwork'.[47]

These obstacles to the satisfactory drafting of statutes in America are encountered even when a bill has been initially drafted by the expert draftsmen of the Office of Legislative Counsel. But today less than half of all federal legislation originates in Congress.[48] A substantial amount of legislation derives initially from the executive, including all the various

---

[44] Reed Dickerson, *supra*, n. 43, at 865.

[45] See *supra*, n. 34.

[46] Reed Dickerson, 'The Federal Experience', at 77, in Reed Dickerson, *supra*, n. 43, at 867.

[47] Reed Dickerson, *supra*, n. 43, at 868 (1958).

[48] J. Kernochan, *The Legislative Process*, 8 (1981). A further difference between English and American institutional arrangements which probably contributes to the much greater power exercised by the English Parliamentary Counsel's Office arises from the American practice of treating senior public service appointments as political offices which change with each administration.

bureaux, departments, and other agencies of the national government. Proposed legislation from these sources is drafted by personnel within each particular agency, personnel who are sometimes inadequately trained and experienced in drafting legislation.[49] When these executive proposals reach Congress, there is no assurance that they will be further evaluated by professional draftsmen. The Legislative Counsel of the two Houses do not even see most of the proposals from these sources.[50] It is true that every bill from an executive agency must pass through a check by the Office of Management and Budget (and some also by the Department of Justice), but this check is primarily to ensure that the substance of the bill is consistent with presidential policy, not to review the bill for the quality of its draftsmanship.[51] Indeed, this check does not always ensure that bills emanating from the various executive departments are consistent with one another. Conflicting provisions in bills may thus be enacted even in a single session, though this may be due more to what happens to a bill after it leaves the OMB than to its original drafting.[52]

Still worse are legislative proposals which originate in the private sector—in labour or civic groups, in public interest associations, or in professional, business, or agricultural organizations. Here the proposals are often tendered in the form of bills prepared by lay draftsmen, and again, the Legislative Counsel cannot supervise or revise the drafting of all these bills.

This lack of centralization in the drafting of federal legislation in America is itself the cause of many problems arising from the use of legislation as a source of law. Indeed, it has been said by America's foremost authority on the subject that 'the most fertile single source of confused, difficult-to-read, overlapping and conflicting statutes is the lack of uniformity in approach, terminology and style'.[53]

There is, perhaps, some hope for at least a kind of retroactively imposed uniformity in the approach, terminology, and style of federal statute law in the process of codification begun by Congress in 1946.[54] Codification in American terminology is a restatement of existing substantive legislation, what in England would be called consolidation. But the process is likely to be long; thus far only a few titles have been completed and the work progresses slowly. Most of the codification projects have taken several years to complete,[55] and as a result, many

---

[49]   Report of ABA standing Committee on Legislative Drafting, in Reed Dickerson, *Professionalizing Legislative Drafting, supra*, n. 40, at 171.

[50]   *Ibid.*, at 172.

[51]   *Ibid.*

[52]   Reed Dickerson, ed., *supra*, n. 40 at 150–151.

[53]   Reed Dickerson, *supra*, n. 43, at 907.

[54]   1 USC [Preface] (1946).

[55]   *Ibid.*, at 65.

executive departments have been reluctant to embark on such long-term projects. Codification requires the skills of the department's best draftsmen, and departments are unwilling to spare these people because they need their services for current legislation.

So far we have been talking mainly in terms of federal legislation, but the differences between parliamentary and congressional legislation are probably much less than the differences between other sorts of legislation in the two countries. Though a few states (in particular, California and Wisconsin) do have efficient legislative drafting offices, this is very far from being the norm in the states. In general, state legislation is more likely to be drafted by lawyers of lesser technical proficiency, or even by state legislators who may have no drafting experience and are perhaps not even lawyers. A common problem (which again illustrates the immense institutional differences between England and America) arises from the fact that the state governor may not even be in control of the office and staff of the state's chief legal officer. In many states the Attorney-General is an independently elected official who is not accountable to the governor, and owes him no allegiance; the draftsman of a legislative proposal which emanates from a state executive department is therefore likely to be a lawyer in the department in question, rather than in the Attorney-General's department—hence the usual problem of lack of centralization in the drafting of bills.

It is not surprising if legislation drafted in such departments raises problems, not merely of constitutional validity (state and federal) but also of obscurity, ambiguity, and contradiction with other statutory provisions.[56] Of course not all these problems affect all state legislation. There are, for instance, a number of uniform laws which are free from many of these problems. Experienced, professional draftsmen from a variety of sources contribute to the drafting of these laws, and, so far as concerns technical proficiency and clarity of expression, it may fairly be said that these laws are as good as or better than the national statutes enacted by Congress. The most obvious example of such a law is the Uniform Commercial Code, at least one version of which has been adopted in all states save one. It may also be that things are slowly improving: certainly, state legislators today have larger staff, and more of them sit annually, and for longer periods, and more serious work may

---

[56] Hale, 'How the Problem Looks to the Legislative Audience', at 44–45, in Reed Dickerson, ed., *supra*, n. 40. For one hilarious example of what can happen when state legislatures try to reform law which they do not understand, see the account of the attempt to abolish the rule in *Shelley's case* by the legislature of New Mexico in Leach, 'Perpetuities: Staying the Slaughter of the Innocents', 68 *Law Q. Rev.* 35, 38, n. 5 (1952).

today be done in committees;[57] but it is unclear whether these changes have had much result. One knowledgeable commentator at least has been unable to discern any improvement in the quality of state legislation over the past thirty years.[58]

Similar considerations probably apply to much subordinate or delegated legislation, known in American practice as administrative regulations, which in both countries greatly exceeds statutory enactments in sheer bulk. For those who believe that enacted law should be a formal source of law, setting forth precise and detailed rules and regulations which can be observed by the people to whom they are addressed, it is perhaps even more important that regulations or delegated legislation should be well drafted than that the statutes themselves should be well drafted. Not only is there much more law in this form,[59] but such regulations (or delegated legislation) are often the law closest to the citizen. Statutes are 'merely the forerunners of the more detailed regulations . . . [It is the regulations] that really set forth the code of conduct for the people whom [the statutes] affect.'[60] Of course, such subordinate legislation can fill in the gaps in statutes, thereby setting out detailed guidelines for legislative policy,[61] and thus to some degree substituting hard and fast rules for more flexible statutory provisions, but many American statutes are enacted for which no administrative regulations are ever passed. Moreover, much uncertainty arises in America over the possibly *ultra vires* nature of such regulations, and this breeds litigation.

In England subordinate legislation of this character is usually drafted by departmental lawyers in the government machine and not by Parliamentary Counsel; and although the standards of technical proficiency may not be so high, there is all the same a fairly taut professional competence which goes far to ensure a high degree of uniformity of technique, and avoids most of the pitfalls of legislative drafting. In America, regulations are drafted by the various regulatory and administrative agencies themselves, and the standard is much lower than that pertaining to Congressional legislation.[62]

A number of factors peculiar to the process of drafting regulations may explain the failures of good draftsmanship here. First, unlike proposals

---

[57] See Rosenthal, 'The State of State Legislatures: An Overview', 11 *Hofstra L. Rev.* 1185 (1983).

[58] William J. Pierce, *Introduction* to the *Symposium* in 11 *Hofstra L. Rev.* 1119 (1983).

[59] Saperstein and Minor, 'Role of the Executive Agency', at 82, in Reed Dickerson, ed., *supra*, n. 40.

[60] *Ibid.*

[61] E. Gellhorn, *Administrative Law and Process*, 121 (West, St. Paul, 1972).

[62] For very critical comments on the drafting of American administrative regulations, see Saperstein and Minor, *supra*, n. 59, at 82 (citing James B. Minor).

for new legislation, there is not even the chance of some ultimate review of the regulations by legislative counsel or some other centralized drafting professionals. Nor have regulations ever been the focus of a serious effort at codification, nor have the agencies ever developed adequate drafting procedures. Some of the smaller agencies may not even have professional draftsmen on their own staff, and apparently there is no adequate pool of expert draftsmen in the OMB or the Department of Justice to assist such agencies.[63] Moreover, of the agencies which do have draftsmen, there are few with adequate training facilities.

One final point is worth making about this comparison of drafting techniques in England and America. England has a long tradition of narrow, detailed drafting; the English draftsman has always (or at any rate for at least two centuries) tried to produce language which is capable of neutral, non-purposive interpretation. An English statute has traditionally been drafted in such detail that it can be said to be a catalogue of rules. It is not really a set of *principles* which the judges can be left to apply to a variety of situations, not expressly governed by the wording, or which they can be encouraged to build on, as though they were common law principles. By contrast America has a tradition (which goes back to Jefferson[64]) of drafting in broader language, using legislation to state wide general principles, such as in the federal Constitution itself. To be sure, not all modern American legislation is drafted quite as tersely as the Constitution. The federal Internal Revenue Code, for instance, is scarcely less detailed than the corresponding English legislation. Nevertheless, the tradition of using broad statutory language is far from dead in America, as it is in England, and the Constitution is a permanent and living reminder that written law can be expressed in the language of principle, rather than detailed rule.

5. DIFFERENCES IN STATUTE-MAKING: SOME ILLUSTRATIONS

One result of the factors affecting the American legislative process which we have identified above is that Congress and state legislatures often legislate in outline only, enacting broad principles rather than detailed legislative codes. An early example of such a statute is the Sherman Antitrust Act of 1890 which in a single paragraph declares all restraints of trade to be illegal. This statute reflects the fact that American courts are already entrusted with great powers under the Constitution, and that legislators—although they may have some distrust of the courts—some-

---

[63] Martin, Mills and Littell, 'How the Problem Looks to the Legislative Branch', in R. Dickerson ed., *supra*, n. 40, at 17.
[64] See *The Writings of Thomas Jefferson*, 103–29, vol. 2 (P. Ford, ed., 1893).

times find it suits their purposes to hand over enormous new powers to them with very little guidance as to how those powers are to be exercised. To some degree, the Act also reflects the fact that American legislators openly recognise the law-making function of the courts, and regard the courts as partners in the general legislative enterprise. Thus Senator Sherman said, in introducing the 1890 Antitrust law:

I admit that it is difficult to determine in legal language the precise line between lawful and unlawful combinations. This must be left for the courts to determine in each particular case. All that we, as lawmakers, can do is to declare general principles, and we can be assured that the courts will apply them so as to carry out the meaning of the law . . .[65]

By contrast, this subject has been dealt with in England by many detailed statutes of great complexity. The first attempt to make restraints of trade illegal was made in the Restrictive Trade Practices Act 1956, a statute of 38 sections and almost 30 printed pages in length. The Act contained detailed provisions as to the grounds on which restraints of trade might be held justifiable or illegal, and even then the Act gave rise to much controversy on the ground that it delegated fundamental issues of policy to the courts.[66] Since that Act was passed, the special court established under it to hear cases concerning restrictive agreements has delivered a number of lengthy and complex judgments,[67] but the initiative in relation to the policy issues involved has remained firmly in the hands of Parliament, and much further legislation has been passed.[68] This legislation remains entirely in the British tradition: it is detailed, complex, and of high content and mandatory formality. The American law, by contrast, remains largely case-law, and although it too is now detailed and complex, it is law of much lower content and mandatory formality.

Our next example concerns a more modern Congressional statute. Now, many recent Congressional Acts create 'rights' in new areas, but in the process, it has been said, 'there has . . . been a clearly discernible trend toward glib generality'.[69] This is exactly the kind of result which tends to follow from the separation of legislative and executive authority

[65] 21 Cong. Rec. 2460 (1890).

[66] See R. B. Stevens and B. S. Yamey, *The Restrictive Practices Court*, esp. ch. 3 (Weidenfeld & Nicolson, London, 1965).

[67] Many of the early decisions of the court are reviewed in Stevens and Yamey, *supra*, n. 66, at ch. 9.

[68] See, e.g., Restrictive Trade Practices Act 1976; Resale Prices Act 1976; Fair Trading Act 1973; Competition Act 1980. However, in this particular instance, some parts of English law are gradually becoming less formal because the EEC Treaty (which is now part of English law) contains some very general provisions (articles 85 and 86) dealing with antitrust law, and these are subject to interpretation by the European Court. Thus English antitrust law is slowly becoming more of a case-law subject.

[69] See Horowitz, 'Decreeing Organizational Change: Judicial Supervision of Public Institutions', *Duke LJ* 1265, 1282 (1983).

in the American system of government. Legislators seek the support of certain segments of the electorate by passing legislation which creates rights, but they also try to avoid the difficulties of making the detailed policy and financial decisions which such right creation entails. Our illustration here is the Education for All Handicapped Children Act 1975,[70] which requires all states in receipt of federal funds under its provisions (which means all the states) to adopt a policy of assuring 'all handicapped children the right to a free appropriate public education'. Nowhere does the Act spell out precisely what this means, nor does the Act even explicitly delegate to the states the task of deciding what is a 'free appropriate public education' for handicapped children. It therefore becomes a matter for the courts to decide this question. But the question is fundamentally political, raising obvious financial implications, and no guidance is given to the courts as to how these issues are to be resolved. The courts will therefore have to feel their way, case by case,[71] and will draw their ideas, as they usually do, from a wide range of writing and commentary, particularly by law professors.[72] Because case law is a more substantive source of law than legislation, and because academic writing can only justify itself by the strength of its substantive reasoning, this process of law making is highly substantive in its nature.

In this instance we are able to point to a directly comparable statute in Britain, namely, the Education Act 1981. This Act appears, at first sight, to be somewhat similar to the Congressional Act of 1975. It deals with the 'special educational needs' of children who have a 'learning difficulty'. But the Act operates in a very different way from the Congressional statute. The broad effect of the Act is to confer discretion on local education authorities, and clearly one of the relevant factors to be taken into account in exercising that discretion will be the question of cost and the resources available. This does not mean that the Act is totally outside judicial control. A local education authority which actually breaches its legal duties under the Act may have its decisions reviewed and quashed by the courts,[73] and in performing this function the courts may be compelled to interpret particular statutory provisions, but the courts have no general power to decide the broad issue of what is 'special educational provision' or what kind of provision ought to be

---

[70] Pub. L. No. 94-142, 89 Stat. 773 (1975) codified as amended at 20 USC §§ 1401, 1412.

[71] The first Supreme Court decision offers little general guidance: *Board of Education* v. *Rowley* 458 US 176 (1982).

[72] For a specimen, see Bartlett, 'Educational Decisionmaking for the Handicapped Child', 48 *Law and Contemp. Prob.* 7 (1985) (suggesting that state spending on handicapped children should reflect state spending, relative to other states, on all children).

[73] See *Reg.* v. *Surrey County Council Education Committee, ex p. H.* (1984) 83 LGR 219; *Reg.* v. *Hereford and Worcester County Council, The Times Law Report*, 10 Nov. 1986. But cf. *Reg.* v. *Hampshire CC, The Times Law Report*, 5 Dec. 1985.

provided in particular cases. It is in fact inconceivable that a statute imposing such a responsibility on the courts would be passed in modern times in Britain. Nor would any British government allow legislation to pass through Parliament similar to the Congressional Act of 1975 which confers rights in such a casual way, with the predictable result that courts are left to work out the implications. The way in which resources are spent on such matters as special educational provision would always be regarded in Britain as a matter for elected or executive bodies to decide within discretionary power, and never for the courts.

The differences in drafting technique in the two countries can also be illustrated by many other examples. In an earlier chapter we saw a number of cases in which American courts have had to cope with gross legislative blunders,[74] thereby showing how highly substantive reasoning can and sometimes must be used in applying American statute law. Here we will content ourselves with one further example of differences in drafting techniques which affect the formality of legislation, though in this instance we find the American drafting technique preferable to the English. The Uniform Commercial Code has one short section (2-302), divided into two subsections, giving the courts power to strike down contractual clauses which are 'unconscionable'. The term 'unconsciona-ble' is not defined in the Code. Nor is the extent of the application of the section strictly controlled by the Code, because although the section appears in the Sales Article of the Code, the American courts have applied many of the provisions of the Code by analogy to other contracts, which is wholly in accord with their liberal treatment of statutes in modern times. Moreover, section 2-302 may well be largely superfluous anyhow, since many American state courts would probably hold unconscionable contracts void at common law. The result is that this section has low formality in all four ways, that is, low authoritative formality (its legislative source matters little), low content formality (it is not under-inclusive or over-inclusive), low mandatory formality (its application is discretionary, an unconsionable clause may be enforced in part, and so on), and low interpretive formality (its meaning is almost totally dependent on the open-ended word 'unconscionable').

By contrast, this subject is dealt with in England by the Unfair Contract Terms Act 1977, a statute with 31 sections and four schedules. Many of the sections are lengthy, complex, and difficult to understand, the drafting is highly technical in approach, and the interrelationship of the various provisions is extremely intricate. Although the court is given some open discretion to strike down certain 'unreasonable' exclusion clauses, and to that extent the Act includes a provision of low content

---

[74] *Supra*, at 63–66.

formality, this discretion is embedded within a very tight framework of fixed rules of high content and mandatory formality. Further, the whole statute is so technically drafted that it is bound to have high interpretive formality when applied. It also has high authoritative formality since there is no question of its provisions merely being declaratory of the common law: it was clearly passed (as a result of two Law Commission Reports[75]) precisely because the common law was thought to be very unsatisfactory. The different style of these two statutes is highly revealing, and confirms much of what we have said about the influence of institutional factors on the formality of legislation in the two countries.

Another illustration of differences affecting the legislative process concerns a matter of private law reform. The law of contributory negligence was reformed by the Law Reform (Contributory Negligence) Act 1945 in England: this statute introduced a system of comparative negligence which has worked well. But in many American states, it proved very difficult to secure this reform through legislative means. In *Maki* v. *Frelk*,[76] where it was sought to persuade the Illinois Supreme Court to introduce comparative negligence on its own authority, Ward J. asserted that there had been nine bills to achieve this result in Illinois since 1937, but that none of the bills had ever reached the floor of either House.[77] Eventually, the refusal of state legislatures to reform the law of contributory negligence led a number of state supreme courts to introduce the reform themselves,[78] including Illinois.[79] Of course, where reform of this kind comes through judicial decisions, the result is likely to be law of lower formality than where it comes through legislation, especially English-style legislation.

Our next illustration of the consequences of the special features of the American legislative process concerns the results of legislative compromises. The Newspaper Preservation Act 1970[80] was a highly controversial statute in which Congress attempted to balance the competing interests of threatened newspapers and the antitrust laws. Two versions of the bill were introduced in the two Houses, and the ultimate Act was the result of a legislative compromise: the effect of some of the House amendments which were agreed to by the Senate were left vague quite intentionally, or so it seems. The result was that the meaning of the Act was utterly ambiguous on one crucial and central

[75] See Law Commission Reports on Exemption Clauses in Contract, First Report (Law Com. No. 24, 1969) and Second Report (Law Com. No. 69, 1975).
[76] 40 Ill. 2d 193, 202, 239 NE 2d 445, 450 (1968).
[77] See also the case of Maryland referred to in n. 30.
[78] See V. Schwartz, *Comparative Negligence* §1.5 (2nd edn., A. Smith Co., Indianapolis, 1986).
[79] See *supra*, p. 136, n. 82.
[80] PL 91-353, 84 Stat. 466 (1970) (codified at 15 USC §§ 1801–4 (1982)).

element of the statute. And because Congress had here created such a legislative ambiguity, the courts were forced to treat the statute with low interpretive formality and delve with particular care into the Congressional purpose.[81]

We have previously pointed out that this sort of compromise legislation is very rare in England, and that amendments are hardly ever passed to bills in the House of Commons unless they are acceptable to the government and the draftsman. The only modern examples of such compromise legislation which fudges an issue are those referred to earlier,[82] where the government of 1974 exceptionally did not have an absolute majority in the House of Commons, and the result was indeed to produce confusing legislation of a kind which would doubtless have caused problems but for subsequent amendments.

Other examples come from state legislation, and illustrate the result of hasty and ill-considered action by legislators who sometimes do not think through the implications of the statutes which they pass. We have already given an illustration of this phenomenon in chapter 6, where we referred to a state narcotics law which judges and prosecutors simply refused to enforce literally because the results would have been so unjust.[83] Here, therefore, are further illustrations of the way in which the American legislative process may lead to the passing of statutes which have to be treated by the courts with low mandatory formality if utterly intolerable results are to be avoided.

We have not intended in this section to be critical of the American legislative process. Many people will think that there are grounds for criticism, and in particular, many think that the American political system tends to encourage legislatures to avoid making the kinds of policy decisions which in a democracy should be made by legislative bodies. We are not concerned to take a position on such questions here. Our purpose rather is to show how and why the features of the legislative process which we have identified in this chapter tend to result in legislation not being passed at all, or alternatively in legislation being enacted which is of low formality. We do not deny that some of these features often produce thoroughly bad legislation, but there can also be compensating advantages to the system. The variety of opinion among legislators, the lack of a strict party system as understood in England, and also the lack of the deadening inertia of a competent (but highly conservative) civil service to point out all the reasons for *not* legislating on a given topic, sometimes lead to desirable experimentation and

---

[81] See *Newspaper Guild* v. *Levi* 539 F. 2d 755, 761 (DC Cir. 1976), where these difficulties had to be resolved.

[82] *Supra*, p. 305, n. 9.

[83] *Supra*, pp. 184–5.

willingness to try novel solutions. In the nature of the case, these will often require some assistance from the courts to make them workable, but in the end something worthwhile may emerge. It does not, however, emerge in the English way, that is, by careful and detailed study of the problem, by deciding on a particular change, and then by implementing that change in such a way as to make it clear that it is intended to be a change. Further, when novel moral and deeply divisive questions arise in a society, it is not obvious that the British method of rapid legislative solution is necessarily better than a slow maturing of public opinion which judicial debate permits in America.

6. DIFFERENCES IN LEGISLATIVE PERSONNEL

There is some evidence that the more formal character of English statute law—particularly perhaps its embodiment in hard and fast rules—may in part be attributable to differences in the personnel who make up the legislative bodies in the two countries. Any such proposition would be extremely difficult to establish, if only because systematic comparative studies of the personnel elected to legislative bodies in the two countries simply do not exist. But there are at least two grounds for thinking that differences in personnel correlate with some of the factors which we have identified.

First, as we have seen, the party system is one of the major differences between the two countries. In England, differences of opinion are resolved, and coalitions form, under the wing of strong parties; so that in the result, two major parties present their rival views in Parliament, with smaller parties playing a very subsidiary role. In America, by contrast, the parties are weak, the coalitions shifting, and differences of view are rarely suppressed within a party in the interests of enabling a single party position to be presented in the legislature. Now it seems to us plausible to think that one major cause of these differences in the strength of the political parties is itself the diversity of views and the heterogeneity of the personnel involved in American political parties. Strong political parties are likely to exist only where the differences which divide the members are less important than the issues which unite them; and that, in turn, is likely to happen only where the diversity of opinion within the party is limited, and where party members constitute a fairly homogeneous group.

Secondly, a more direct impact on the formal quality of legislation may be produced by the relative professionalism of legislators. Legislators who treat their job—as Bentham would have wished them to—as a skilled scientific profession, requiring training and application, may at least be more likely to avoid the most egregious drafting errors, may be more willing to make clear-cut decisions, and may be less willing to leave to the courts more than is inherently required of them. For these reasons it seems to us plausible to suppose that a more professionally oriented legislature will tend to legislate—other things being equal—in a somewhat more formal way.

With these two suggestions in mind, we propose in this section to devote a little time to an analysis of some features of the personnel of the legislatures in Britain and the United States, though we must disclaim any pretence to a sociological analysis.

We will leave aside the House of Lords whose political influence in modern times is almost negligible, though it may sometimes be a fine sounding-board for high quality speeches. The House of Commons consists today of 650 members. At the general election of 1983 the Conservatives obtained 397 seats, the Labour Party, 209 seats, and the Liberal/SDP Alliance, 23 seats. The balance of the seats went to Irish Members (whose politics is peculiarly their own) and a small number of smaller parties. Despite the political differences between the Members, there is no doubt that socially speaking they are a remarkably homogeneous group. Of the 629 members of the three main parties, 320 had been to 'public schools' (in the peculiar English terminology, meaning, of course, private schools), 403 had received a university education, and no fewer than 228 had been to Oxford or Cambridge. Even on the Labour side, more than half the members (111 out of 209) were university graduates.[84]

Within the Conservative Party itself, the homogeneity of background is even more remarkable. Of the 397 members of that party elected in 1983, no fewer than 278 had been to public schools and 190 to Oxford or Cambridge, 92 of the others having been to other universities. The Labour Party, as is well enough known, tends to be less homogeneous. Only 30 of their members had been to public schools, only 31 to Oxford or Cambridge, and nearly half were not university graduates.[85] The impression given by these figures is also confirmed by the analysis of professional background of the Members. On the Conservative side 45% of the Members were accounted professionals, civil servants, teachers, and members of the armed forces, another 36% were (or had been) in industry as directors or executives, while a further 19% came from miscellaneous white-collar employment, such as journalism, publishing, and also farming. Only 4 members of the Conservative Party (1%) appeared to have a working-class background. Even on the Labour side, only a third of the Members had a working-class background, and 42%

---

[84] All these figures come from D. Butler and D. Kavanagh, *The British General Election 1983*, Table 10.3, at 235 (Macmillans, London, 1984).

[85] *Ibid.*

(almost as many as the Conservatives) were professionals, teachers or civil servants.[86]

Finally, there were only 23 women elected to the House of Commons in 1983, and not a single black (although there were 19 black candidates).[87] Thus the general picture is one of white, male, middle and upper middle-class membership, with a small leavening (about 15%) of members of working-class origin. It would certainly be wrong to portray the House of Commons as an institution dominated by a single homogeneous social group; it unquestionably is a group which represents many diverse types and views. But it is more homogeneous than the society which it represents, and that society is itself, of course, much more homogeneous than American society.

Although these social comparisons are very difficult to make with any confidence, American legislators seem to represent a broader spectrum of American society than English legislators do of English society; and, of course, American society is itself far more heterogeneous than English society. A higher proportion of American legislators are college graduates; almost all have college degrees,[88] but these are of the most varied kind, and they run the gamut of America's 3,000 institutions of higher education, situated all over the country.[89] These institutions, it must be stressed, are far more varied than English institutions of higher education—we shall see something of the variety of law schools in particular in chapter 14—varying from the excellence of world-renowned universities to institutions of marginal quality in the outer reaches. Within particular states, there is naturally more homogeneity of educational background, but many states have a wide diversity of educational institutions, and many legislators have been educated in other states. This contrasts with the English position where over a third of Members of Parliament have been to Oxford or Cambridge, and there is much less diversity even among other universities and institutions of higher education.

Ethnic variety among American legislators is also much more marked than in England—indeed (as noted above) there is at present not a single black Member of Parliament. For example, in 1979–80 blacks made up

---

[86] *Ibid.*, Table 10.4, at 236. The figures for professional background do not add up to 100% because information was lacking on some Members.

[87] *Ibid.*, 230, 231.

[88] Well over half of all state legislators attended college. G. Blair, *American Legislatures*, 120–2 (Harper & Row, NY, 1967); D. Lockard, 'The State Legislator', in *State Legislatures in American Politics*, 106 (A. Heard, ed., Prentice-Hall, Englewood Cliffs, NJ, 1966). Almost all federal legislators have college degrees. R. Davidson and W. Oleszek, *Congress and Its Members*, 112 (2d edn., 1985).

[89] For example, see Hacker, 'The Elected and the Annointed: Two American Elites', 55 *Am. Pol. Sc. Rev.* 539 (1961).

4% of American state legislators,[90] and in 1985 4% of the Members of the US Congress were black.[91] There are also members of other ethnic groups, including Hispanic and Oriental groups, in American legislatures.[92] There are also many more women state legislators (about 13%)[93] than English women Members of Parliament, though in the federal Congress the position is much closer to the English.[94]

The diversity of income levels and occupational groups among American legislators may also be wider than that represented in the British Parliament, though this too is very difficult to gauge in the absence of detailed statistical studies. American legislatures certainly have a wide range of members from middle and lower middle-class occupations, such as teachers, real estate brokers, labour leaders, and farmers,[95] but this is also true of the British Parliament. Lawyers remain particularly prominent in American state legislatures today (supplying about 20% of the members[96] in 1979), but these are themselves drawn from very diverse backgrounds; although in Britain, too, lawyers are always a prominent group in Parliament, English lawyers (as we shall see in chapter 13) are a far more homogeneous group than American lawyers. The recent growth of black representation in American legislatures does, however, suggest that it is somewhat easier in America for minority and disadvantaged groups to find their own representation in the state legislature in a way which is very difficult in Britain. The British parties, unlike the American, almost completely control the selection of candidates for elections, and the parties have a national and centralized outlook which militates against the representation of minority groups.

The second major difference between British and American legislators which may have some impact on the shape of statute law is the greater professionalism of the British Parliament. It seems reasonable to suppose that the more amateur the legislative process, the less likely that policy issues will be dealt with carefully and embodied in formal and relatively hard and fast rules. And the more amateur the process, the less likely that sound legislative priorities will be set so that needed legislation will be duly considered and enacted. This is particularly the case where the legislature is so divorced from the executive as in

---

[90] A. Rosenthal, *Legislative Life: People, Process and Performance in the States*, 30 (Harper & Row, NY, 1981).

[91] R. Davidson and W. Oleszek, *supra*, n. 88, at 113.

[92] *Ibid.*

[93] Rosenthal, 'The State of State Legislatures: An Overview', 11 *Hofstra L. Rev.* 1185, 1192–3 (1983).

[94] R. Davidson and W. Oleszek, *supra*, n. 88, at 113. (In 1985, two women in Senate and 22 in House).

[95] G. Berkley and D. Fox, *80,000 Governments: The Politics of Subnational America*, 82–3 (Allyn & Bacon, Boston, 1978).

[96] Rosenthal, *supra*, n. 57, at 1193.

America, and where therefore there is often a lack of strong leadership in the legislature, or anyhow a lack of leaders who are in day-to-day contact with the actual problems of government and administration.

In these respects the differences between the English and the American position are more easily detected. For instance, membership of the English House of Commons is regarded as a full-time occupation (though not so as to wholly rule out some continued professional work). The House sits every year, in almost continuous session, though of course with breaks. Furthermore, most persons elected to the House of Commons can expect a fairly lengthy spell of service. Although the available figures do not enable us to say what is the average length of tenure by a Member of Parliament, it is possible to say that of the 650 Members elected to the 1983 Parliament, some 376 had already served for more than 9 years and 172 for over 14 years.[97] The great majority of these Members will serve until the next election, and since elections are normally held only once every four to five years, even the 150 Members newly elected in 1983 will already be seasoned Members by the next election. Most of them, moreover, can confidently be expected to be re-elected.

The fact that the executive ministers sit in the legislature also makes a profound difference to the professionalism of Parliament. Every government has close to one hundred ministers, if all junior ministers are included, though some of these must, by convention, sit in the House of Lords; and each of them must learn to handle the work of his department sufficiently thoroughly to be able to represent it and defend it in the House of which he is a Member. Many of them will have been responsible for carrying legislation through Parliament, and in that capacity will have been obliged to study the text of a bill prepared by their officials with great care, ready to explain what each clause is intended to achieve, and why this or that amendment proposed by another Member will not work well. When a party is defeated at a general election, these ex-ministers will become part of the Opposition, and new ministers will be appointed from the other party. Thus at any given time there will often be as many as 150 Members of the House of Commons who are, or have been, ministers, and these will, naturally, include most of the abler and more influential Members of the House. These are true legislative professionals: although they are not themselves draftsmen, they understand a good deal about the technicalities of legislation, how it is drafted, how it is expected to work, how the different parts of a bill fit together, and so on.

---

[97] Figures drawn from, or calculated from, those in D. Butler and D. Kavanagh, *supra*, n. 84, at Table 10.2, at 233 (1984).

American legislatures are generally more amateurish than the British Parliament. The position here varies a good deal between the state legislatures, whose traditions are often quite different, and also the federal Congress, which is more professional, so generalizations are difficult. In the 1980s the average Congressman had served 10 years and the average Senator about 10.5 years,[98] figures which are probably not much less than those for an average British Member of Parliament. Furthermore, Members of Congress serve full time, like British Members, and have continuous annual sessions. They are also well served by massive support staffs. The less formal nature of federal statute law cannot therefore be explained by the lower degree of political professionalism of the American Congress. And the same may well be true of the position in a few of the states, for example, California.

But in most state legislatures, the position is very different. Here the terms of office are (at least in the lower House) usually only two years, the sessions are often very short (in a few states, only biennial),[99] and the turnover of members often very high.[100] Many state legislators serve only two or three two-year terms.[101] In the last thirty years, about a third of all state legislators in each session were serving their first term. Where legislative sessions are very short, members naturally tend to be part-time politicians only. Furthermore, because the executive is separated from the legislature, most American legislators do not have the opportunity to acquire the greater professional legislative skills which English ministers have to learn. In some of the larger states (for example, California) the legislature may have adequate drafting and other supporting services, but in many states such services are distinctly lacking.

As we have noted above, this lack of adequate support staff for many state legislators, together with other factors explained in chapter 14, often leads to the use of law professors as advisers and draftsmen to individual state legislators. Even federal legislation has sometimes been drafted or much influenced by individual law professors.[102] Given the

---

[98] R. Davidson and W. Oleszek, *supra*, n. 88, at 104.

[99] M. Jewell, *Representation in State Legislatures*, 7–8 (U. Press of Kentucky, Lexington, 1982).

[100] G. Blair, supra, n. 88, at 129–34; see also W. Crane Jr. and M. Watts, Jr., *State Legislative Systems*, 48–50 (Prentice Hall, 1968).

[101] But the trend is up. A. Rosenthal, *supra*, n. 90 at 136.

[102] For example, Professor Chafee drafted the Federal Interpleader Act. B. Kaplan, 'Zachariah Chafee, Jr.: Private-Law Writings', 70 *Harv. L. Rev.* 1345, 1347 (1957). Professor Stanley Surrey had a large hand in drafting various federal tax provisions. Andrews, 'A Source of Inspiration', 98 *Harv. L. Rev.* 332, 334 (1984). Many professors have also helped in the preparation of state legislation, e.g., Professor Chadbourn provided the groundwork for California's evidence codification. Weinstein, 'Writings of James H.

traditional American legal theories (which we have dealt with in chapters 8 and 9), which are particularly strong in law schools, it is not surprising if legislation emanating from such sources is strongly substantive in its leanings. In England, by comparison, law professors have a negligible influence on the direct legislative processes of Parliament, although they do sometimes have some influence in drawing attention to areas of law where reforms are needed, and they also are occasionally recruited to sit on commissions of inquiry into the reform of particular areas of law.

It might have been thought that the relatively large number of lawyers who serve in legislative assemblies would make a marked difference to the formality of legislation enacted. In fact this does not seem to be a factor of great significance. In England, the centralized party control and the highly professional nature of the whole legislative process already makes for formality; in the United States, lawyers are more diverse, have a more substantive vision of law, and are more willing to leave the courts to sort out problems—which itself leads to a more substantive approach.

Chadbourn', 96 *Harv. L. Rev.* 364, 367 (1982). The second-named author of this book drafted several pages of the Oregon Revised Statutes while a professor at the University of Oregon Law School.

12

The Judges

1. INTRODUCTION

The judges have the largest role in determining the extent to which a legal system is formal or substantive in character. They must not only apply standards for identifying valid law, but to some extent they must create those very standards. They may even be empowered to choose, within limits, whether these standards are to be embodied in hard and fast rules or in flexible and open-ended formulations more congenial to substantive analysis. So too, when standards of validity conflict, the judges may have freedom not only to apply formal hierarchical rules of priority, but also to invoke substantive reasons in thus determining the validity of laws.

Judges also have considerable power in the common law system to make the law, and here, too, they may choose to exercise this power by making case-law in the form of hard and fast rules, or of more flexible rules. Judges determine the nature of the system of precedent and thus exercise great power over the degree of mandatory formality to be accorded to prior cases. Similarly, the degree of interpretive formality of statute law depends on how far the judges are willing to go outside the formal language of legislation to take account of purposes and substantive analysis.

Statute law, we have suggested in chapter 4, is a more formal source of law than case-law, and the proportion of statute law within the system as a whole is of course ultimately a matter for the legislature; but the extent to which legislation is required to keep a legal system up to date is also partly a result of the way the judges work. For example, judges who seldom undertake to reform or modernize the existing law are necessarily throwing the responsibility on to the legislature, and in this respect also contribute to making the legal system more formal.

Furthermore, many of the most important disputes over the application of law to fact must be resolved largely in the courts in the Anglo-American legal systems. To the extent that judges refuse to allow extrinsic factors to influence the outcome of disputes over issues of fact, or over the application of law to fact, the judges foster a more formal system of law. It is therefore the judges who largely determine how far the formal law in books translates into law in action.

336

In all these, and other ways, therefore, the judges can have a decisive effect on the relative formality or lack of formality of a legal system. Whether the legal system is more, or less, formal will thus to a significant degree be affected by the sort of persons the judges are: their qualifications, backgrounds, and characteristics. How they make law, and how they identify, interpret, and apply the law is to some extent affected by the kind of people they are, the educational and other socializing experiences to which they are subject, and the conditions under which they hold office. Furthermore, the size, structure, and homogeneity of the judiciary are of special relevance, because (as we shall suggest) a formal legal system is much easier to operate with a small, centralized, and homogeneous judiciary. Of course this is not to say that there are no influences running the other way: the sort of people who become judges is in turn influenced *by* the kind of legal system which exists. As in social affairs generally, once a stable society and a stable legal system exist, there is mutual action and reaction between the system and the people who operate it. In this chapter we shall discuss some of the more obvious differences between the English and the American judiciary (we confine our remarks largely to the judiciary of the present day), and we shall suggest that there are today substantial differences in the character of the judiciary in the two countries which are both influenced by, and operate in their turn to produce an effect on, the degree to which the two systems pursue a more formal approach to law (in England) and a less formal one (in America).[1]

2. SIZE AND STRUCTURE OF THE JUDICIARY

Perhaps the most important difference between the judiciary of the two countries is one of the least observed, namely their relative size. By comparison with the American, the English judiciary is tiny, and exceptionally tightly organized. The higher judiciary, which in England consists of judges of the High Court and appellate courts, comprises the Lord Chancellor, the Lord Chief Justice, the Master of the Rolls (who is President of the Court of Appeal), 11 Lords of Appeal, 18 lords justices of appeal, the Vice-Chancellor (the senior judge of the Chancery Division of the High Court), the President of the Family Division of the High Court, and 80 other judges of the High Court, a total of 114. These are the only judges of general or appellate jurisdiction in the entire country. The next tier of the system comprises the Circuit judges who try criminal cases in the Crown Courts and civil cases in the County Courts,

[1] See generally L. Jaffe, *English and American Judges as Lawmakers* (Clarendon Press, Oxford, 1969); Henry Cecil, *The English Judge* (Hamlyn Lectures, Stevens, London, 1970); S. Shetreet, *Judges on Trial* (North Holland, Amsterdam, 1976).

but, in both cases, subject to jurisdictional limits. There are less than 400 Circuit judges. These are the only people who are properly called 'judges' in the English legal system.[2]

By contrast, the American judiciary is enormous. In 1984 the federal judiciary alone comprised over 700 Article III judges. There were the nine justices of the Supreme Court and 168 judges of the 13 courts of appeals (including the DC Court and the federal Court) whose work is almost entirely appellate. Then there were 545 District Judges,[3] who are trial judges, all of whom rank, in terms of jurisdiction and power, with English High Court judges, so far as federal jurisdiction extends. In the state court systems, the total number of judges today exceeds 7,500[4] though many of these may have limited jurisdiction and powers similar to (or less than those of) English Circuit judges. (Although it is difficult to be sure that we are always comparing like with like, these figures do not include minor magistrates, justices of the peace, and traffic court judges in America, or magistrates in England.[5]) The federal judiciary and over forty states have a three-tiered court system like England's, with intermediate and final appellate courts.[6] The number of judges in many of the larger states greatly outnumbers the entire judiciary of England. California alone, for instance, has 759 judges,[7] although the population of England is almost twice that of California.

In addition, American judges operate in a far less centralized system. Not only does each state have its own judicial system within its own borders, distinct from the federal system which covers the whole country, but even the federal system itself is decentralized to a significant degree. Federal appeals courts, for instance, which hear appeals from federal District Judges, are constituted in 12 distinct courts of appeals (and a further court for Washington DC), and these appeals courts, being themselves large collegiate bodies, geographically remote from each other, exercise a considerable degree of independence. The judges within each appeals court commonly sit in panels of three which in turn are not always in step with each other. Further, each appeals court as a whole does not regard itself as bound to follow decisions of other such courts and divergent views on constitutional and federal law are common.

---

[2] See Megarry, 'Barristers and Judges in England Today', 51 *Fordham L. Rev.* 387 (1982). In 1986 there were 391 Circuit judges: *The Independent*, 30 Dec. 1986.

[3] See R. Posner, *The Federal Courts: Crisis and Reform*, 357 and Preface, ix (Harvard U. Press, Cambridge, 1985).

[4] See *1986–87 Book of the States*, 155–8 (figures for state courts of last resort, intermediate appellate courts, and general trial courts).

[5] Including minor traffic court judges and magistrates, the total number of American judges is over 27,000: Posner, *supra*, n. 3, at 45–46.

[6] *1986–87 Book of the States*, 157–8 (Table 4.2).

[7] *Ibid.*, at 155–7.

Moreover, as we have already seen, the supervision exercised by the United States Supreme Court over the appeals courts is in practice far more limited than the corresponding control exercised by the House of Lords over the English Court of Appeal. The state court systems are in similar ways more decentralized than the English system.[8]

These differences of size and centralization are relevant to our thesis in a number of ways. In England, the court system has a much tighter 'command' structure, ranging over a limited number of subordinates. This enables the judges in the highest echelons to impose and enforce much more control over decision making. This is a necesssary condition for the existence of a highly formal system, because such a system at least presupposes close and precisely articulated agreement on the criteria for determining the validity of putative law. Such agreement is possible in the small, closely knit hierarchy of the English judiciary. In such a system, law can indeed be 'laid down from above', by legislature or by higher courts. It can be faithfully and uniformly followed by lower court judges. It can take the form of hard and fast rules, the uniform application of which can be closely policed through the tight command structure of the higher judiciary. *Stare decisis*, and a uniform general approach to statutory interpretation, can be taken very seriously. Given these conditions, which are very far removed from those prevailing in America, and given further differences now to be considered, it is hardly surprising that the English system is much more formal than the American.

2. QUALIFICATIONS, MODES OF APPOINTMENT, AND TENURE

There are many well-known differences between the laws and conventions governing the qualifications, modes of appointment, and tenure of the judiciary in the two countries. There is no need to rehearse these in great detail, and we content ourselves with a bare summary; we shall also confine our remarks to the higher judiciary in the two countries.

All the higher judges in England have to be qualified barristers of at least ten years' standing. This is a statutory requirement.[9] But it is today also a firm convention that nobody is appointed a judge who has not had many years of active professional practice at the bar. Thus the statutory requirement of ten years' standing would not in practice be regarded as satisfied by someone who had not been in active practice for at least that

---

[8] In 1979 state expenditure on judges and judicial support was over $1.8 billion, while local expenditure on similar items was little less, at $1.2 billion. Posner, *supra*, n. 3, at 46.

[9] Supreme Court Act 1981, section 10(3)(*c*).

length of time; in fact few judges are appointed who have not been active barristers for at least 20 to 25 years. Contrary to American practice, no law professor has, as such, ever been appointed to the English bench, although some very distinguished judges (for example, William Blackstone and, in modern times, Lord Goff) were at one time academics who subsequently became qualified for appointment to the bench through professional practice. Because of the orality of legal proceedings in England, and the consequent need to make many decisions on the spot without time for reflection, it is generally accepted that academics without adequate experience of actual trial practice would not be acceptable as trial judges, though it has occasionally been suggested that academics might be appointed to appellate courts. But as yet, there has been no indication that this move would be acceptable to the profession,[10] and it is symptomatic of the political power of the profession that it is hard to imagine that such an innovation could be introduced over their opposition.

Until comparatively recent times—perhaps the Second World War marks the turning point—previous political service was valuable in securing judicial appointment. Indeed, until the early years of this century it was rare for the highest posts—Lord Chief Justice and Master of the Rolls—to be offered to anyone who had not been active in politics on the side of the government making the appointment. It was also far from unknown for party hacks of low professional esteem to be appointed to the High Court bench, to the great disgust of the legal profession. But for the past 40 or even 50 years this has no longer been the case.[11] Fewer and fewer politicians now make the transition to the bench (except for the anomalous post of Lord Chancellor, which combines high political and high judicial office); and even those who do—it is now safe to say—are appointed on professional merit. Indeed, it is now clear that the Lord Chancellor expects aspirants for high judicial office to have served as part-time judges (in the post of 'Recorder') and to have demonstrated their competence in that capacity.[12]

Nominally, all judges are appointed by the Queen, but in practice, the

---

[10] One reason for this may be the belief that if academics are appointed, it would become very difficult to resist the appointment of solicitors—which is much more worrying to the bar as it would pose a greater threat to their monopoly of higher judicial appointments. The ineligibility of solicitors for such appointments is a permanently controversial issue between the two parts of the profession.

[11] See Megarry, *supra*, n. 2, at 395; J. A. G. Griffith, *The Politics of the Judiciary*, 17–25 (3rd edn., Fontana Press, Douglas, Isle of Man, 1985).

[12] See *Judicial Appointments* (Lord Chancellor's Department, London, 1986) a booklet setting out some of the practices and procedures followed by the Lord Chancellor in relation to appointments for which he is responsible.

power to recommend appointment of higher judges lies, by convention, in the hands of the Prime Minister (in the case of appellate judges) and the Lord Chancellor (in the case of trial judges).[13] It is today scarcely open to doubt, even in the case of appellate judges, that the Lord Chancellor's advice would normally be sought and accepted by the Prime Minister. Since personal and political patronage now scarcely plays a role in these matters, the professional advice of the professionals is likely to determine the appointments. The Lord Chancellor, in his turn, consults widely among other judges as well as senior barristers before an appointment is made.[14]

Although there is no statutory requirement that appellate judges should have some experience as trial judges, it is today quite exceptional for anyone to be appointed to an appellate court in England straight from the bar.[15] It is also very unusual for a trial judge to be appointed direct to the House of Lords unless he has served some years in the Court of Appeal.[16] There is absolutely no legal or constitutional control over these powers of appointment. We shall later comment on the implications of vesting such appointments in a single, centralized source.

Since the Act of Settlement 1701, all of the higher judges are irremovable except on an 'address' by both Houses of Parliament, though there is now a compulsory retirement age of 72. The age is unusually high, because the nature of the appointment is such that few people can expect to begin a judicial career before the age of 55, and a judge must serve 15 years in order to earn a full pension.

In all these respects, the position differs fundamentally in the United States. First, the formal qualifications needed for appointment to the bench—so far as professional or legal experience goes—are minimal. There are no constitutional or statutory requirements for federal judicial appointments, other than that a District Judge must be a United States citizen and a resident in the district to which he is appointed. Twenty-two of the states require some minimum number of years of legal practice before a person is qualified for appointment to the bench. The requirement ranges from 3 to 10 years.[17] Many states merely require

---

[13] Heuston, *Lives of the Lord Chancellors, 1870–1940* (1964) gives some entertaining examples of the consultations between Prime Ministers and Lord Chancellors over judicial appointments.

[14] See *Judicial Appointments, supra,* n. 12.

[15] The two last such cases were those of Lord Radcliffe (1949) and Lord Somervell (1946). The conventions governing the appointments of Scots law lords are somewhat different, direct appointment from the bar being more common, see L. Blom-Cooper and G. Drewry, *Final Appeal,* 156 (Clarendon Press, Oxford, 1972).

[16] Lord Wilberforce was the last person to be promoted over the Court of Appeal (in 1964) and he proved to be (in the opinion of some) one of the best appellate English judges of the century.

[17] *1986–87 Book of the States,* 159 (Table 4.4).

judges to be 'learned in the law', and even the ABA Model Judiciary Act of 1962 provides only that a judicial appointee must be 'licensed to practice law in the courts of the state'. Many states require no formal legal qualification at all, and though a person without any such qualifications would be unlikely to secure a judicial appointment, in states where judges are elected it is not impossible for a totally unqualified person to become a judge.

Most judicial appointments in America are treated as political, and public or political service in some shape or form is usually more important as a qualification for getting on the bench than the extent of professional experience or high standing in the profession.[18] Almost without exception, American judges, on appointment, are known to be adherents to, or at least supporters of, one of the major political parties. About a third of state supreme court judges have held elective political office before becoming judges,[19] probably more than half of state judges in all were politically active at the time of their appointment,[20] and, with very few exceptions, appointed judges in America come from the same party as the appointing official.[21] An examination of the judicial appointments of the American Presidents from Johnson to Carter vividly displays this trend. Presidents Johnson and Carter were Democrats. Ninety-five per cent of Johnson's Court of Appeals appointees and 94.8% of his district court appointees were Democrats. The figures for Carter were 89.3% and 94.1%. The Republican Presidents Nixon and Ford had similar biases. Of the judges that Nixon appointed to the Court of Appeals, 93.3% were Republicans; 92.2% of his District of Columbia appointees also belonged to that party. Similarly, Ford's Court of Appeals appointees were 91.7% Republican and district court

---

[18] To say that all judicial appointments in the US are 'political' may obscure two very different things. The appointment of a justice of the US Supreme Court is 'political' because the President and the Senate want to influence the future direction of Supreme Court decision making. The appointment of most other (federal and state) judges is 'political' because such appointments are regarded as political patronage available for distribution to party supporters. The degree to which federal appointments below the Supreme Court have been influenced by these two different 'political' factors has varied over the years. See Solomon, 'The Politics of Appointment and the Federal Courts' Role in Regulating America: US Courts of Appeals Judgeships from TR to FDR', *ABFRJ* 285 (1984). President Reagan appears to have been appointing judges who agree with his ideological leanings to an even greater degree than previous Presidents.

[19] Kagan, Infelise, and Detlefsen, 'American State Supreme Court Justices 1900–1970', *ABFRJ* 371, 388 (1984).

[20] J. Ryan, Ashman, Sales, and Shane-Dubow, *American Trial Judges*, 126–7 (Free Press, NY, 1980).

[21] Of the first hundred judges of the US Supreme Court, ninety came from the same political party as the President who appointed them, and nearly 90% of most federal judicial appointments go to members of the President's party. See generally Henry J. Abraham, *Justices and Presidents*, esp. at 67 (2nd edn., Oxford U. Press, NY, 1985).

appointees were 78.8% Republican.[22] Furthermore, in the case of state judges, requirements of electoral confirmation are by no means always a formality. Politics can enter significantly into this process. Although state supreme court judges, once appointed and (if necessary) confirmed, are usually safe from the electorate, in 1986 Chief Justice Rose Bird of the California Supreme Court (and two other justices of the same court) failed to obtain electoral confirmation after a campaign in which they were accused of being 'soft on crime'.[23] Recent attempts to depoliticize the appointing processes of state judges have perhaps been more successful in improving the quality of the judiciary than in depoliticizing it.[24]

Formally, methods of appointment vary widely. Federal judges are, of course, appointed by the President, subject to Senate confirmation. State judges are appointed in a variety of different ways that can be classified in five main groups: appointment by the governor (typically with confirmation by a legislative body); by the legislature; by non-partisan election; by partisan election; and by some variant of the so-called Missouri-plan.[25] The 'Missouri-plan' system of appointment also has many varieties, but it has certain essential features, such as the use of a non-partisan commission of lawyers and non-lawyers to recruit and assess candidates. The commission will select a small number of candidates, relying on professional and personal merit, not party affiliation, and submit the list to the governor (or the legislature, as with South Carolina), who makes the appointment from the list. The appointee frequently serves a short term and then runs unopposed for re-election.[26] But there are many variations within the five different classes; for example, in some states, judges are appointed in the first instance by the governor, but may have to seek re-election or electoral confirmation after a certain length of time. In addition, formal powers of appointment are significantly affected by political custom or convention. For instance, federal District Judges are usually appointed on the nomination of the

[22] See Goldman, 'Carter's Judicial Appointments: A Lasting Legacy', 64 *Judicature* 344, 346–48 (1981).

[23] For Bird's narrow confirmation in 1978, see Stolz, *Judging Judges*, 119 (Free Press, NY, 1981). Judges may also be responsive to electoral opinion even when they are not personally threatened. See Kuklinski and Stanga, 'Political Participation and Government Responsiveness: The Behavior of the California Superior Courts', 73 *Am. Pol. Sc. Rev.* 1090 (1979).

[24] Richard A. Watson, 'Missouri Lawyers Evaluate the Merit Plan for Selection and Tenure of Judges', in *Selected Readings: Judicial Selection and Tenure*, 116, 120–1 (rev. edn., Glenn R. Winters, ed., American Judicature Society, Chicago, 1973); R. Watson and R. Downing, *The Politics of the Bench and the Bar*, 319 (Wiley, NY, 1969).

[25] See *1986–87 Book of the States*, 161 (Table 4.4: Selection and Retention of Judges). See also Symposium on Judicial Selection and Tenure in 40 *Sw. L. J.* 1–117 (1986).

[26] See, e.g., Berkson, 'Judicial Selection in the United States: A Special Report', 64 *Judicature* 176, 177–8 (1980).

governing party's Senator, if any;[27] and many state judges who are in theory supposed to be elected are in the first instance appointed by the governor to a 'casual vacancy' (often in fact carefully engineered) and only subsequently required to submit themselves to electoral confirmation, with the considerable advantage then (as all American experience shows) of being already incumbents.[28]

The position as to tenure also varies widely. Federal judges enjoy the same life tenure as English judges (without the compulsory retirement age), but few state judges enjoy life tenure. Only three states (Massachusetts, New Hampshire, and Rhode Island) give state appellate judges tenure for life or until retirement age. The judges in the remaining 47 states must seek re-election or reappointment after terms that vary from 6 to 14 years for most supreme court judges,[29] but are as short as 4 years for some state trial judges.[30]

The conventions governing appointments differ from those followed in England almost as much as the strict legal position. For instance, American appellate judges frequently have no prior judicial experience at all,[31] and sometimes very little trial experience even as practising lawyers. Consider, for example, President Carter's and President Reagan's appointments to the District of Columbia Court of Appeals which, apart from the Supreme Court, may be the most influential federal court in the United States. The two Presidents placed 6 appointees on the 11-member court in a three-year span. Four of the appointees were law professors, one a former Congresswoman, and one a Justice Department lawyer. None of the six had any previous judicial experience.[32]

The same pattern generally holds of other federal appointments. Only 41 of the 100 justices who served on the United States Supreme Court until 1976 had prior judicial experience. Of the judges holding office in 1963, only 31% of federal district court judges and 38.7% of federal appellate judges had prior judicial experience.[33] One study indicates that approximately one third of the judges on state courts of last resort had not served as judges before their appointment.[34] Prior judicial experi-

[27] See Harold W. Chase, *Federal Judges: The Appointing Process* (U. of Minnesota Press, Minneapolis, 1972) for the conventions and practices governing the appointment of federal judges.

[28] See Glenn R. Winters, 'One-Man Judicial Selection', in Glenn R. Winters, ed., *supra*, n. 24, at 85.

[29] See *1986–87 Book of the States*, 155–6 (Table 4.1: State Courts of Last Resort).

[30] *Ibid.*, at 157–8 (Table 4.2: State Intermediate Appellate Courts and General Trial Courts: Number of Judges and Terms).

[31] Over half of all state supreme court judges have had no, or less than five years, experience as lower court judges. Kagan *et al.*, *supra*, n. 19, at 391.

[32] *National LJ*, 2 May 1983, p. 24, col. 2.

[33] Boroweic, 'Pathways to the Top', 7 *NC Central LJ* 280, 282 (1976).

[34] *Ibid.*

ence is not thought to be very important by many American lawyers,[35] although the ABA, which has now acquired some influence in federal judicial selection,[36] does regard prior trial experience as an important requirement at least for a trial judge.[37] Yet even trial judges are quite often appointed from those with no previous trial experience; according to one recent study, 58% of state trial judges were formerly lawyers in private legal practice, 24% were lower court judges, 10% came from the District Attorney's Office (where they would have had no experience of *civil* cases), and the remainder had little or no trial experience.[38] Academics are not infrequently appointed to federal and state judicial posts, even though they have had little or no experience as practising lawyers.[39] No doubt political considerations occasionally lead to the appointment of a judge of low competence whose legal knowledge and training are inadequate by any professional standard. Even in the case of federal appointments, where the standards are generally higher than in many states, some judges have been appointed over the protests of the ABA which has rated them 'not qualified' according to its own evaluation and criteria.[40]

As often before, we stress that discussion of these differences in convention are not designed as criticisms of one legal system or the other. American lawyers who are appointed as appellate judges without trial practice operate in a legal system which is very different from England's. Because of the system of written briefs, and the very much more 'office' like procedures of American appellate courts (of which more later), an American appellate judge does not *need* trial experience as much as an English appellate judge would. But in turn these differences in past experience lead to different orientations; the English appellate judge is more professionally oriented; the American, more politically and socially oriented. Again, the American judge *needs* to be more politically and socially oriented than his English colleague if he is to perform satisfactorily within the American system. However, this is not to say that American judges would not sometimes be better judges if

---

[35] A much quoted remark is that of Frankfurter J. that 'the correlation between prior judicial experience and fitness for the functions of the Supreme Court is zero.' 'The Supreme Court in the Mirror of Justice', 105 *U. Pa. L. Rev.* 781, 795 (1957).

[36] See Harold W. Chase, *supra*, n. 27, ch. IV, for the role of the ABA Special Committee on the Federal Judiciary.

[37] Joel B. Grossman, *Lawyers and Judges*, 111–13, 138–9 (Wiley, NY, 1965).

[38] Ryan, Ashman, Sales, and Shane-Dubow, *supra*, n. 20, at 125.

[39] Some of America's most distinguished judges have been former professors, both in federal courts (e.g. Felix Frankfurter in the US Supreme Court) and in state courts (e.g. Roger Traynor in the Supreme Court of California).

[40] For statistics on the ABA ratings of the judicial appointments of Presidents Carter, Ford, Nixon, and Johnson, see Goldman, 'Carter's Judicial Appointments: A Lasting Legacy', 64 *Judicature* 344 (1981).

they had greater professional experience and skill; nor that English judges would not sometimes be better if they were less intensely professional and technically 'legal' in their approach.

Other important differences exist between the conventions governing the judiciary in the two countries. In England, the position of High Court judge (or above) is regarded as the apex of a professional career, and as the end of any other career. Nobody with political ambitions would become a High Court judge in England; and almost nobody resigns from such a position in order to return to a political, or indeed any other, career. Instances of deviation from these traditions are rare indeed.[41] In the United States, of course, judges can and do move from the bench back to politics, and sometimes very aggressive and partisan politics. Even US Supreme Court justices have on rare occasions done this,[42] and many state court judges do not regard their positions as lifetime jobs—indeed, lack of tenure often precludes that view.

Another relevant factor in this picture is that English judges are well paid by English standards.[43] Doubtless some practising barristers earn more than judges, but any financial sacrifice involved in becoming a judge is significantly compensated for by the right to earn a judicial pension in only 15 years. At any rate, it is not usually difficult to fill higher judicial posts from among the leaders of the bar. Although American judges are well paid in relation to average incomes for all careers, their salaries are low compared to those available in private practice in America. Salaries of state trial judges in 1983 ranged from $42,735 per year in Michigan to over $77,000 per year in Alaska. Salaries of state supreme court judges in 1983 ranged from $50,452 per year in Montana to $94,147 per year in California.[44] These salaries may appear substantial at first sight, but they are put in perspective when one considers that *starting* salaries for attorneys in Wall Street firms in 1986 were $65,000 a year, and senior partners frequently receive earnings well into six figures; the *average* earnings of a partner in firms with more than

---

[41] There has only been one instance of an English judge resigning in recent history to take up another position—Sir Henry Fisher resigned in 1970, and subsequently became President of Wolfson College, Oxford. In 1921 Viscount Reading resigned as Lord Chief Justice to become Viceroy of India.

[42] For example, Charles Evans Hughes resigned from the Supreme Court in 1916 to run for President; Arthur Goldberg resigned from the Supreme Court in 1965 to take up the post of ambassador to the United Nations.

[43] The salaries of English High Court judges were raised in 1985 to £60,000 p.a., in a much publicized and highly controversial move which was only narrowly approved in the House of Commons.

[44] *1986–87 Book of the States*, 172 (Table 4.6: Compensation of Judges of Appellate Courts and General Trial Courts).

40 lawyers was estimated in 1980 to be $88,200.[45] A full professor in one of the top law schools in the United States can expect to earn more than most American appellate judges; in England a law professor's salary is about one third that of a High Court judge. The relevance of these figures to this work is that they help explain the kind of person who becomes a judge: in England judges are invariably drawn from the leaders of the practising profession, in America they are not.

4. THE PROFESSIONALIZATION OF THE JUDICIARY

The fact that all higher judges in England have spent 20 years or more as barristers—and as successful barristers—is itself important as a further indicator of the kind of person who becomes a judge in England, and therefore helps to explain, in the last analysis, the way courts behave. In England, as we have already seen, judges are today nearly always appointed from non-political sources. But the English conventions are today even stricter than this. It would probably be regarded as improper today for a judge to declare his political affiliations (for example in directories like *Who's Who*) and possibly even for a judge to be a subscribing member of a political party. In 1977 a minor Scots judge was actually removed from office for allowing himself to be photographed for a political campaign while wearing his judicial robes.[46]

An English judge writing an opinion is doing something very similar to what he was doing for perhaps 20 years as a barrister. At the bar, the judge will have written many 'counsel's opinions'. He will have become highly expert at this task, which is conceived to be almost exclusively a technical inquiry into what the law is, and not what it ought to be. This, together with other factors discussed above, helps to explain the more formal vision of law prevalent in England. Thus substantive policy and moral arguments are taken to be largely irrelevant to counsel seeking to determine what the law is, except insofar as he perceives that they may sway the judge in doubtful cases. Mostly, counsel concentrates on what he takes to be 'the law' as laid down. What can be more natural for the newly appointed judge who now finds himself writing judicial opinions than to carry on in the same style? This is not, by itself, a complete explanation of the judicial tendency to eschew political, moral, or other substantive considerations, because if judges habitually discussed such issues in their opinions, as they do in many American appellate courts, then counsel advising even on what the law 'is' would have to spend more time examining the substantive reasons which he thinks will

---

[45] Julie Taylor, 'Demographics of the American Legal Profession', in A. Kaufman, *Problems in Professional Responsibility*, 835, 859 (2nd edn., Little Brown, Boston 1984).
[46] See Griffith, *supra*, n. 11, at 19 for a brief account of this case.

influence the judges. But the perspective is obviously different: counsel is merely identifying and applying law to fact, and he does not feel a sense of responsibility with regard to the political, moral, or other substantive issues that may be involved. He does not, like the judge, have to *decide* about these political or moral considerations, and it is, therefore, to be expected that, if counsel addresses them at all, he will treat them in a more neutral sort of way. So it does not seem surprising if English judges, who have spent many years performing this sort of exercise as counsel, do not always appreciate that a totally neutral perspective may not be wholly appropriate for the judge himself, but may tend to carry on in the same way.

Consider next the position of an English barrister who aspires to become a judge. There is one person above all others whose eye he must catch—the Lord Chancellor's; there are two groups of persons whom he must impress with his professional skills—the existing judges and, to a lesser extent, his professional colleagues. The views of the political parties, the media, and the public are of almost no consequence at all; furthermore, anything in the nature of 'campaigning for office' would be utterly foreign to English custom today, although in former days it was not uncommon for aspirants to press their claims privately on the Lord Chancellor or the Prime Minister. Consider, next, the position of an English judge. He has 'arrived'; he holds office for life, or at least until retirement; he has social status and prestige. But most such judges would like to be promoted to an appellate court. The work tends to be more interesting, the pressure less, and there is no obligation to travel to other cities, because all appellate work is done in London. How does a judge get promoted? Again, largely by impressing his colleagues and senior judges with his professional skills.

Given this intense professionalization of the judicial role in England, and of the entire appointment process, it is not surprising that judges should adhere to a very formal vision of law, nor that they should be very rule-minded lawyers, wedded to *stare decisis* and strongly of the opinion that significant change in the law should be left to Parliament and the politicians. The fact that appellate judges have nearly all served a long apprenticeship as trial judges, and a still longer one as barristers appearing almost daily in court, may also play its part in tending to make English judges more practical or pragmatic in attitude and somewhat distrustful of theory. There is, indeed, a long tradition among English barristers and judges that 'practical experience' (especially, of course, practical experience at the bar) is far more valuable than any amount of theoretical learning or university-acquired knowledge. This distrust of theory may to some degree have been reinforced by the fact that (until very recently) many English judges had never been to law school at all, and many of those who had been to law school had received their legal education prior to World War II, when the standard of English legal education was admittedly low.

These attitudes of mind naturally encourage a 'law is law' formal approach to rules and principles, and discourage the activist judge who seeks to venture into the substantive waters of policy and instrumentalist law making.[47] Lower court judges are, likewise, unlikely to be candidates for promotion to appellate courts if they display deviant tendencies to reject or disregard appellate court precedents, just as barristers are unlikely to be candidates for appointment to judicial office if they have given any indication that they reject conventional ideas of *stare decisis* or embrace radical views of the judicial role. Appellate court judges—at least in the House of Lords—are, it is true, free from such constraints, but the conventional requirement for prior experience as a trial judge means that few judges reach the House of Lords under the age of 60.[48] By that time an English judge will have been exposed to upwards of 35 years of socializing pressure in the conventions of the judicial role. At such an age, any inclination for radical innovation is apt to wane. Over several centuries, only one judge—Lord Denning—can be said to have retained such tendencies.[49] This does not mean that English judges—especially in higher courts—believe that they have no proper role in developing or modifying the law. Most of them believe that there is such a role,[50] though many of them also believe, perhaps inconsistently, that judges should not meddle in 'policy'.[51]

Of course, within the parameters of the English judicial tradition, levels of activism vary with the individual judges (as no doubt they do in America) and also with the times. Robert Stevens, for instance, has argued with a good deal of supporting evidence[52] that the English law lords saw themselves as having a more policy, if not downright political, function in the late nineteenth and early twentieth centuries, that the period 1940–55 was a period of extreme abdication from policy, a period of high formalism, while in the years between 1956 and 1976, a move back towards a more policy-oriented approach can be discerned. Others may wish to qualify this picture in various ways, or may find the dating

[47] For a remarkable recent example, see Lord Lane CJ in *R.* v. *Howe* [1986] 1 All ER at 836–7 (asserting that judges should be careful in using academic writings not to pay attention to statements as to what the law ought to be, but only to statements of what the law is).

[48] L. Blom-Cooper and G. Drewry, *supra*, n. 15, Table 13 (only 16 out of 63 law lords appointed between 1876 and 1969 were under 60).

[49] See *Lord Denning: The Judge and the Law*, (J. Jowell and J. P. MacAuslan, edd., Sweet & Maxwell, London, 1984).

[50] See, e.g., Roskill, 'Law Lords, Reactionaries or Reformers', 37 *Cur. Leg. Prob.* 247 (1984).

[51] See Lord Scarman in *McLoughlin* v. *O'Brian* [1983] 1 AC at 430.

[52] See R. Stevens, *Law and Politics* (U. of N. Carolina Press, Chapel Hill, 1978).

of these periods open to question. But for present purposes, it is enough to say that these movements in the direction of a substantive approach in the House of Lords are minimal in comparison with the degree of policy orientation displayed by the more adventurous American judges. With very rare exceptions, English appellate judges for at least the past century[53] have been professional lawyers whose main loyalty has been to the profession and to the law as a non-political institution, as they thought it to be.

Compare now the position in the United States. In the first place, a person who wishes to become a judge may have to court (and join) a political party; he may, if he seeks elective state office, need to attract public attention; even an aspirant for a federal judgeship must normally 'make it clear that he wants the post'.[54] Furthermore, because judicial office is itself more political and is often a stepping stone to other political posts, more politically minded people are attracted to judicial office. One study suggests that in recent times one out of every two state judges was politically active before appointment.[55] On the other side of the coin, the leaders of the legal profession (for instance, senior partners in leading city firms) are often less attracted to judicial posts. By American standards, as we have already seen, judges are not particularly well paid, and in the case of the state judiciary, the lack of tenure may be a significant disincentive to more professional and non-political lawyers.[56]

Even after appointment to a judicial post, these factors may continue to influence behaviour. For a judge who sees the judicial post as a stepping stone to political office, a high public profile may be an asset. This may be achieved by doing (and saying) unusual things, rather than by being a 'safe', tradition-minded judge who adheres to *stare decisis* and settled doctrine. Nevertheless, we must beware of exaggerating the political nature of the judicial role in America. Judges do not like to be reversed by appeal courts in America, any more than in England, so there will always be some degree of professional orientation to their work. It also remains true there, as it is in England, that 'judges . . . have a tradition of reticence', and that it is generally thought 'unseemly for

[53] On the whole, the further one goes back, the more signs there are of occasional involvement of some of the judges in political controversy and political issues. The tradition of total political neutrality (which is of course seen anyhow as a myth by many of those on the left) is perhaps no older than the Second World War, and even today the office of Lord Chancellor is a permanent embodiment of the relationship between the political and the judicial function. For the earlier periods, see Brian Abel-Smith and Robert Stevens, *Lawyers and the Courts*, chs. 1–3 (Heinemann, London, 1967).

[54] Harold W. Chase, *supra*, n. 27, at 30.

[55] Ryan, Ashman, Sales, and Shane-Dubow, *supra*, n. 20, at 127 (admitting that this is a bit of a guess).

[56] As noted above, p. 344, only three states provide life tenure.

them to lobby, to seek more power, or to press for reforms that encourage the use of the courts'.[57] But the tradition of judicial reticence seems more widely observed in England than in America. In England, for example, under the so-called Kilmuir rules, judges do not give interviews to journalists, appear on radio or television, or write for the press. Needless to say, nothing comparable to these rules exists in America. Indeed, some American judges frequently make public pronouncements of relevance to their work, and some have even written books while still on the bench, discussing their own views and aspects of their work in some detail.[58]

Even for those who see a judicial post as a life career (and most federal judges certainly do), there are pressures that may lead an American judge to adopt a more adventurous role than his English counterpart. Some of these have already been discussed above, for example, the unresponsiveness of legislatures, the constitutional role of judges which accustoms them to making important political decisions, and so forth. Others have been touched upon, but remain to be developed further. For example, the relationship between bench and bar and the nature of the cases brought before the courts are themselves factors relevant to the levels of judicial activism to be expected, and hence to the theory of law likely to be adhered to. Where lawyers have incentives to bring unprecedented and extraordinary claims before the judges, for example, judges may respond in unprecedented and extraordinary ways. Where no such claims are ever brought, judges have no opportunity to respond in these ways. We discuss some of these matters again in chapter 13. Further, the American judge is sometimes less interested in impressing other judges or practising lawyers, and more interested in impressing scholars, law reviews, and the academic community generally.[59] Hence trial skills, fact finding, and adherence to rule are less highly regarded skills than law making in the grand manner. The fact that many appellate judges in America have been politically active lawyers or law professors also means that they have usually been more accustomed to thinking of the law in a broad and critical way, thinking of the law as it ought to be, and less preoccupied with identifying what the law is. It is not surprising that they, like English judges, continue to be influenced when on the bench by ways of thought to which they became accustomed in earlier years.

[57] Kagan, Cartwright, Friedman, and Wheeler, 'The Evolution of State Supreme Courts', 76 *Mich. L. Rev.* 961, 979 (1978).

[58] The 'Kilmuir rules' are a set of informal rules or understandings, agreed between the Lord Chancellor (at that time, Lord Kilmuir) and the judges in the late 1950s, governing media appearances, etc. Lord Devlin has recently written in justification of his own account of one of his cases—nearly 30 years earlier; see Patrick Devlin, *Easing the Passing, Postscript*, (Faber, London, 1986).

[59] *Cf.* R. Posner, *supra*, n. 3, at 44.

There are, of course, great differences in the degree of politicization of judicial posts in the United States. Some American judges have a perception of the judicial role which is probably not very different from that which prevails in England. But others have a very different view indeed. To some extent these differing perceptions of the nature of the judicial role may correlate with methods of appointment, though other variables are undoubtedly also involved. Contrary to earlier belief, it now seems that gubernatorially appointed judges are often less well trained than elected judges,[60] but it also seems to be widely accepted that the more professionalized modes of appointment such as are involved in variants of the merit-based, non-partisan 'Missouri-plan' produce more traditional or safer judges. For example, Watson and Downing quote an anonymous critic who says that the Missouri plan:

will not produce a maverick. On the other hand, if you select your judges under the elective system, you may get all kinds of whacky characters going on the bench, who will frequently dissent from the views of their colleagues, and who will air different view points and thus let a little ventilation into the process of justice.[61]

And another study has found that levels of dissent tend to be higher in state supreme courts where the judges do not all come from the same political party.[62]

But by comparison with the English position, these differences are minor matters of degree. Many American judges do not share the long years of professional experience that English judges do, and many American appellate judges have not experienced the years of sitting at first instance which nearly all English judges have. On the other hand, most American judges share a far more political background than English judges.

It is, of course, not obvious or simple to explain how political background translates into a particular set of attitudes or approaches on the judicial bench. It may be too facile to suggest that qualifications and methods of appointment correlate in a simple way with behaviour on the bench. For example, there is evidence in America that prior judicial experience does not correlate with a tendency to uphold *stare decisis*.[63] It also seems much more difficult than was once thought to demonstrate clear correlations between political party affiliation and the propensity to decide certain types of cases favourably to certain parties (for

[60] Jacob, 'The Effect of Institutional Differences in the Recruitment Process: The Case of State Judges', 13 *J. Pub. Law*, 104, 109 (1964).
[61] Watson and Downing, *supra*, n. 24, at 319.
[62] See Kagan *et al.*, *supra*, n. 19.
[63] Schmidhauser, '*Stare Decisis*, Dissent and the Background of the Justices of the Supreme Court of the United States', 14 *U. Tor. L. Rev.* 194, 205–07 (1962).

example, labour unions, worker's compensation—or industrial injury—claims, insurance claims), although *some* correlations have been repeatedly found between the political affiliation of American judges and their decisions on issues of this kind.[64] But we do believe that an intricate network of factors, many of which we have by now identified, interact to produce greater fidelity to the formal vision of law in England, and the more substantive vision in America.

5. DIVERSITY AND HOMOGENEITY IN THE JUDICIARY

A further distinction of considerable importance between the English and the American judiciaries is that the former are far more homogeneous than the latter. It is important not merely that the background, qualifications, and experience of American judges differ widely from those of English judges; it is also just as relevant that American judges vary widely among themselves with respect to these matters. By contrast, English judges are a homogeneous social group who also share exceptionally uniform social backgrounds and professional experience.

Nearly all English judges tend to have upper or upper middle class backgrounds.[65] Of English High Court judges appointed between 1951 and 1968, for instance, 10.5% came from the traditional landed upper class, over 74% from professional, commercial, and other middle class groups, while only 1.2% (representing in fact one judge) came from the working classes (the origins of 14% were not known).[66] Another survey in 1970 of 359 judges (including some lower court judges and magistrates) found that 81% had been to 'public schools' and 76% to Oxford or Cambridge Universities.[67] There has been little change in these figures in the past few decades.[68] One reason why English judges tend to come from such a small section of the social classes is simply that they all come

[64] For some samples of a large and controversial literature, see G. Schubert, *Quantitative Analysis of Judicial Behavior*, 129–42 (Free Press, Glencoe, Ill., 1959); G. Schubert, *The Judicial Mind* (Northwestern U. Press, Evanston, Ill., 1965); *The Judicial Mind Revisited* (Oxford U. Press, NY, 1974); Goldman, 'Voting Behavior on the United States Courts of Appeals, 1961–1964', 60 *Am. Pol. Sc. Rev.* 374 (1966); Goldman, 'Voting Behavior on the United States Court of Appeals Revisited', 69 *Am. Pol. Sc. Rev.* 491 (1975); Nagel, 'Political Party Affiliation and Judges' Decisions', 55 *Am. Pol. Sc. Rev.* 843 (1961); Ulmer, 'The Political Party Variable in the Michigan Supreme Court', 11 *J. Pub. Law* 352 (1962); Adamany, 'The Party Variable in Judges' Voting: Conceptual Notes and a Case Study', 63 *Am. Pol. Sc. Rev.* 57 (1969); Feely, 'Another Look at the "Party Variable" in Judicial Decision-Making: An Analysis of the Michigan Supreme Court', 4 *Polity* 91 (1971); Anthony Champagne and Stuart S. Nagel in *The Psychology of the Courtroom* (Norbert L. Kerr and Robert M. Bray, edd., Academic Press, NY, 1982).
[65] Griffith, *supra*, n. 11, at 25–31.
[66] *Ibid.*
[67] *Ibid.*
[68] *Ibid.*

from the bar, and, because all barristers have to be self-employed, the bar is not an easy profession in which to begin except for those with some private means. American judges come from much more diversified backgrounds.[69] In English terms, a few may come from the upper classes, but most of them are, as one would expect, of middle-class origins, many come from lower middle-class families, and some from the working classes.[70]

The ethnic backgrounds of English and American judges reveal a similar pattern. There are no members of the English High Court bench from ethnic minorities; there is one black Circuit judge and there are two black deputy Recorders (part time judges).[71] By contrast, there were in 1985 over 600 black judges in the American judiciary.[72] Of these some 500 served in state courts, ten blacks were serving on state supreme courts,[73] 95 in federal courts, and one in the United States Supreme Court.[74] There are also far more women serving as judges in America than in England. Although three English High Court judges and 16 Circuit judges are women, no woman has yet been appointed to the English Court of Appeal or House of Lords. But in America, in 1986 one Supreme Court justice and ten federal appeal judges are women.[75]

In educational background, the pattern is again one of striking homogeneity in England and radical diversity in America. For example, in 1975 the 16 members of the English Court of Appeal had all attended a 'public' (that is, private) school, and, with a single exception, all had been to Oxford or Cambridge.[76] A similar, though not quite so striking, pattern is to be found among the law lords who sit in the House of Lords, as well as among trial judges. For instance, of the 63 law lords appointed between 1876 and 1969, no fewer than 47 studied at Oxford or

---

[69] See *New York Times*, 1 Sept. 1985 at 32. But note that some of these 'judges' would be called 'magistrates' in England—and there certainly are some black magistrates in England.

[70] As to federal judges, see generally, J. W. Howard Jr., *Courts of Appeals in the Federal Judicial System*, at 87–124 (Princeton U. Press, Princeton, 1981); J. Schmidhauser, *Judges and Justices*, ch. 3 (Little Brown, Boston, 1979). As to state judges, see J. Ryan *et al.*, *supra*, n. 20, at 129–30.

[71] According to a *Sunday Times* report (20 July 1986) the Home Secretary would like to increase the numbers of black judges but the Lord Chancellor is resisting any interference with his control over judicial appointments.

[72] G. Crockett, Jr., R. DeBow, and L. Berkson, *National Roster of Black Judicial Officers*, 5 (American Judicature Society, 1980).

[73] See *New York Times* article, *supra*, n. 69.

[74] Thurgood Marshall, the only black to sit on the Supreme Court, is still serving at the time of writing; he was appointed by President Johnson in 1967.

[75] L. Berkson and D. Vandenberg, *National Roster of Women Judges* (American Judicature Society, 1980). A survey in 1980 revealed that over 600 women were serving as state court judges. *Ibid.*

[76] Meador, 'English Appellate Judges From an American Perspective', 66 *Geo. LJ* 1349, 1371 (1978).

Cambridge.[77] (Many of the older English judges did not study law at university, a point we return to again below.) We have already seen, also, how all English judges have served many years as barristers, while American judges come from a much wider variety of careers, often political, sometimes academic, and frequently with little actual practice of the law.[78]

Another striking difference between the English and the American judiciary is attributable to the fact that English judges serve within a much smaller country, and indeed most of them have worked in London for the greater part of their lives. Most English High Court judges sit most of the time in London, and appeal courts sit there exclusively. American judges, of course, come from all over a continent; few of them know judges from other states well, and there is no such thing as a single legal culture among the American judiciary. The traditions and culture of the American judiciary have been said to be 'doggedly local. A Tennessee judge does not transfer to Nevada. Judges of one state for the most part do not meet judges from other states socially or professionally.'[79]

The homogeneity of the English judiciary (and the senior bar) is of immense importance to the whole legal culture of England; it certainly plays a part in determining how questions of law are viewed and decided. And this leads to important conclusions, because to the extent that judges share the same 'inarticulate major premisses', traditional legal reasoning is not nearly so bogus as American realism has been credited with demonstrating.[80] When we bear in mind all the other institutional factors which we have discussed, it also seems to us manifest that the indeterminacy of rules in the English legal system is far less acute than it is in the United States. English judges believe in rules more than American judges, partly because rules do have a greater objective reality in the English legal system. There is wider agreement about the criteria for determining the validity of rules. Law is more often formulated in terms of rules to begin with, and rules are much more often applied strictly in accord with their terms, and thus remain of high mandatory formality. This belief in rules is, of course, one of the chief factors which makes the approach of English law more formal.

The fact that homogeneity enables English judges to reach opinions which the great majority of them are likely to share takes no account of the criticisms of those who attack this very homogeneity on the ground

---

[77] See Blom-Cooper and Drewry, *supra*, n. 15, at 160–3. Many of the other law lords came from Scotland and Ireland and naturally went to Scottish or Irish universities.

[78] See *supra*, at 350.

[79] Kagan, Cartwright, Friedman, and Wheeler, 'The Business of State Supreme Courts, 1870–1970', 30 *Stan. L. Rev.* 121, 124, n. 7 (1977).

[80] See R. Posner, *supra*, n. 3, at 201.

that it only goes to show that the judges are all of the same upper middle-class background, and are therefore not representative of the mass of the people. Naturally, it follows that their values are not necessarily the values of the community at large.[81] This is an important political criticism of the English legal system, but it does not affect the validity of the point we are making. Our point is simply that the formality of the English legal system is profoundly affected by the institutional and other factors that we have identified here.

Another facet of this distinction between the English and the American judiciary is that the latter appear to be much more influenced by their law school education than the former; indeed, some of England's most distinguished judges of recent years did not study law at universities at all. Lord Wilberforce 'read' (in the English terminology) classics,[82] and Lord Diplock, chemistry. But in America it would be rare indeed to find a judge who had not been to law school, and most of the higher federal judges attended the more elite law schools, though many other judges have attended a wide range of less distinguished law schools. Furthermore, a substantial number of former law professors are now serving on federal and state court benches, and many of the others will be influenced by their law clerks, recent graduates from the law schools, whose role we have discussed in an earlier chapter. The general approach of many American judges, and their legal culture as a whole, often appears to be substantially derived from the law schools;[83] moreover, many such judges see the law schools as one of the main groups addressed in their opinions.[84] They certainly cite more academic literature in their opinions,[85] and some of them at least seem generally more interested in theoretical and intellectual issues than their English counterparts. They often contribute thoughtful articles to the law reviews themselves and present papers at conferences and seminars in which they adopt the standards of the law schools, for example by showing their awareness of the existing academic literature and the intellectual issues currently regarded as important in academic circles. Many of them, too, seem more aware of the nature of the value judgments which they have to make in judicial decisions.

In England, by contrast, the professional legal culture of lawyers and judges appears to be centred in the Inns of Court, which are professional associations to which barristers must belong, and which are governed by

---

[81] See, e.g., Griffith, *supra*, n. 11.

[82] Is it yet another illustration of the compactness and homogeneity of outlook of English judges and positivist theorists that Lord Wilberforce was a student colleague of H. L. A. Hart, both of whom 'read' classics ('Greats') at New College, Oxford?

[83] J. W. Howard Jr., *supra*, n. 70, at 94, 111–17.

[84] *Ibid.*, at 152.

[85] See *supra*, p. 282.

'Benchers', most of whom are judges or senior counsel. It is very doubtful if many English judges see their opinions as addressed to university students or even professors.[86] With some distinguished exceptions, they rarely write scholarly works themselves,[87] often display a staggering ignorance of recent scholarly literature, and tend to be scornful of the value of theory. Some may feel this is an unfair portrait, and there are signs that things are changing as more judges reach the bench who received a rather better legal education than their predecessors and have apparently greater academic interests. But, as things stand at present, we regard this as an accurate picture, though we must point out that our criticisms of English judges for their lack of interest in theoretical analysis and intellectual issues is matched by our appreciation of their pragmatic strengths. It is not unlikely that many English judges would even regard it as complimentary to be told that they are suspected of having little interest in theory or an academic approach to legal issues. It seems clear to us that the varying styles of legal education in the two countries, and the very different roles of the law schools, contribute to the different judicial styles. We return to this theme when we look at the law schools in chapter 14.

Finally, we must add that there is a much greater range of competence among the American judiciary than among the English. While the best American judges stand comparison with the best English judges in regard to integrity, competence, fairness, and acumen (and outclass them in social and political awareness), we think it more than probable that the worst American judges are worse than the worst English judges, and it cannot be denied that there are relatively more of them.[88] A distinguished French professor has recently put this in rather unkind terms: 'As regards their judiciary, as on many scores, the motto of the United States could be borrowed from the commercial slogan of a French department store: "*On trouve toute à la Samaritaine*". Everything can be found in the United States: the best and the worst, among the judges as in any other matters. The average level, however, is

---

[86] See Alan Paterson, *The Law Lords*, 15 (Macmillan, London, 1982).

[87] It was at one time common in England for new editions of established legal textbooks to be prepared by senior barristers or judges, but the results were usually found unsatisfactory for expository purposes, and it has become increasingly the practice for this kind of work to be done by academics.

[88] A random survey of ABA members in 1980 revealed that by far the most important issue which concerned them professionally was the quality of the judiciary: 66 *ABAJ* 842 (1980). Criticisms of the judiciary tend understandably to be couched in general terms. For one recent example see Alan Dershowitz, *The Best Defence*, 111 (Random House, NY, 1982): 'It is amazing how many judges—especially, but not exclusively, state judges—lack the basic intelligence to understand a moderately complex legal argument. Some are just plain stupid; others lack the necessary legal education; still others are lazy or impatient.'

certainly much below that of the English judiciary.'[89] Competence enters into the total picture, alongside many other factors. For example, the more formal approach to law requires judges to take judicial opinions seriously, requires them loyally to search for the *ratio decidendi* of earlier cases, and requires them in general to treat legal rules as having some serious degree of content, interpretive, and mandatory formality. Less competent judges may find it easier to avoid such 'technicalities' and decide cases in accordance with what seem to them to be the obvious substantive merits of the case.

At this point we must draw attention to some of the earlier discussion in this book, especially our discussions of legislation in chapter 4, of case-law in chapter 5, and of the jury system in chapter 6. The various institutional factors we have been discussing must, as we have repeatedly stressed, be looked at as a whole because they clearly react on one another. It may well be, for instance, that some American judges have a perception of the judicial role which does not differ significantly from that of most English judges. But even the most tradition-minded or conservative American judge operates in a different milieu from English judges. The raw material he deals with, the sources of law, legislation and cases, differ from those with which the English judge works. Even a very tradition-minded American state supreme court judge may, for instance, have to ask himself whether he feels his court should stick rigidly to a prior decision, when most other state supreme courts have followed a different line. No English judge ever has to face such a question. Similarly, as we have seen, American judges have to deal with much statutory material that is very different from English statutory material.

---

[89] Tunc, 'The not so Common Law of England and the United States, Or, Precedent in England and In the United States, a Field Study by an Outsider', 47 *Mod. L. Rev.* 150, 169 (1984).

13

The Legal Professions

As with the judges, the nature of the legal profession, the sort of people who become lawyers, how they are organized, their manner of practice, and the traditions they observe have a profound effect on the legal systems of the two countries. But although many of these differences are well known, little attention has been paid to the relationship between these differences and the legal systems themselves. Yet the differences between the legal professions in the two countries are, we believe, closely associated with their tendency to be more or less formal, and with the legal theories they implicitly adhere to; conversely, the more or less formal nature of the legal systems and their theories of law may also have an effect on the legal professions.

We start with some general comments about the basic structure of the legal professions in the two countries. It is, of course, widely known that in England the legal profession is divided into two distinct branches, barristers and solicitors, whereas America only knows the one professional status of lawyer, attorney or counsel (or sometimes, counsellor). Americans often make the common mistake of assuming that English barristers are 'trial lawyers' who devote all their time to advocacy, while solicitors are office lawyers who do no advocacy. This is, in fact, only partially true. Nearly all barristers spend a great deal of time in 'office' work (or chambers work, as it would be known in England). They draw legal documents, they give many advisory opinions on the law, and they also draw pleadings and do other paper and advisory work in connection with possible or actual litigation. Conversely, many English solicitors do in fact a considerable amount of advocacy in lower courts. Only in the High Court and the appellate courts do solicitors have no (or very restricted) rights of audience; in magistrates' courts and County Courts solicitors do have the right to appear as advocates, and some of them specialize in this kind of work, just as much as barristers. Indeed, there must be some solicitors who do more trial work than some barristers.

The reality is that what distinguishes English barristers from solicitors is not primarily, and certainly not merely, that barristers do more advocacy and trial work than solicitors. As we shall see more fully in the next section, the distinguishing characteristics of the English bar are to be found in a number of other peculiarities, in particular, its very small size, its centralized structure and homogeneity, the special relations between barristers and judges, and the degree to which a barrister is truly an officer of the court, and thus a guardian of the judicial process and not merely a mouthpiece of his clients.

These peculiar features of the English bar are not to be found in any section of the American legal profession. So any apparent resemblance between American trial lawyers and English barristers is superficial and misleading. Of course it is true that the American legal profession includes highly specialized practitioners of trial and appellate work. But it is our view that the differences between these lawyers and English barristers are so great that it is more appropriate to compare even American trial and appellate lawyers with English solicitors. For most practical puposes America simply does not have lawyers like English barristers, and we therefore examine the English bar largely on its own in section 2 of this chapter, and then we go on, in the main, to compare the English solicitors' profession with the whole American legal profession in section 3.

2. THE ENGLISH BAR: A UNIQUE INSTITUTION

The distinctive features of the English bar which are not duplicated at all in America can be summed up under under four headings: first, their very small number, their centralized structure, and their homogeneity; secondly, their relationship to the bench; thirdly, the orality of appellate proceedings, with all that that entails; and fourthly, their traditions of competence and integrity and the degree to which they are expected to have regard to the public interest as well as their clients' interests.

The English bar is an exceedingly small profession—like the English judiciary which, indeed, it resembles in many other ways, as we shall see. There are today about 5,300 practising barristers in England and Wales, which is only about one tenth the number of practising solicitors.[1] The smallness of the size of the profession as a whole is still further accentuated by a subdivision existing within it. Barristers are divided into two classes—junior barristers, or at least those known as 'juniors' though in fact they may be barristers of many years standing, and 'Queen's Counsel' (or QCs), who are not appointed as such until they have become established barristers of at least ten, and often 15 or 20, years' standing. The title of QC is bestowed by the Lord Chancellor, after consultation with other judges and senior barristers, and is much sought after. Its significance is partly social (it carries some prestige because the

---

[1] See *Social Trends No. 17, 1987 edition*, Table 12.34 (HMSO, London), and the *Report of the Royal Commission on Legal Services*, Cmnd. 7648, ch. 3 (HMSO, London, 1979), for these and other details of the legal professions in England.

title is well known to the public) but mainly professional, in that it signifies both the kind of work which may be undertaken and the general level of fees that may be required. There are only about five hundred practising Queen's Counsel at the present time.[2]

QCs do less paperwork than juniors (for example, they do not draw pleadings), though they do a lot of advisory work. One important factor explaining why the title of QC is so valuable is that when a solicitor is faced with a difficult point of law on which he wishes to obtain a specialist or more advanced opinion, he will often like to take the opinion of a QC, especially if the solicitor practises outside London and does not have a great deal of contact with the bar. To him, the title of QC is some assurance of standing and competence in the profession, and that is important, because one of the main reasons that often moves a solicitor (or indeed, a lay institution) to take counsel's opinion is that it may serve to insulate the solicitor (or the institution) from liability for negligence. This insulation is not a matter of law, but a matter of what is reasonable: someone who relies on an opinion from a QC will normally be held to have acted reasonably, unless there are special circumstances suggesting for some reason that the opinion is unreliable.

An important factor which strengthens the cohesiveness of this tightly knit profession is that the great majority of barristers practise in London, and nearly all have chambers in a very limited number of areas. It is, indeed, a professional requirement that a barrister should have chambers in an 'approved' place ('approved' by his Inn of Court, that is), and nearly all barristers have their chambers in rooms owned and let by the Inns. These Inns of Court are the professional associations of the barristers; there are four of them, the Inner Temple, the Middle Temple, Lincoln's Inn, and Gray's Inn, and they are common law corporations of great age. They control entry into the barrister's side of the legal profession, though in practice they have for some years delegated the conduct of lecture and training courses and of examinations. They are also the ultimate authority for disciplinary proceedings (subject to appeal to the judges) since they alone can suspend or disbar a barrister.

Most barristers have their chambers in the Inns (which are in close proximity to the Law Courts in the Strand, the centre of legal London) and they naturally use the facilities of their Inns to a great extent. These facilities comprise in particular the Inn libraries (which are much larger than those which barristers' chambers themselves could carry) and also their lunching facilities. Use of these facilities among such a small profession means that many barristers come to know a high proportion

---

[2] In 1978 there were 404 (*ibid.*, at vol. 2, 479) but since then the profession has increased somewhat in size.

of other barristers; furthermore, the orality of proceedings in the appellate courts, and some degree of specialization by senior barristers, mean that there are many cases in which senior barristers will encounter familiar foes on the opposite side. There are, for instance, a relatively small number of senior barristers who handle much commercial work; there may be as few as 20 or 30 such senior barristers and, indeed, perhaps only 10 Queen's Counsel who can expect to be regularly called on for the highest class of appellate court, such as leading commercial cases in the House of Lords. Naturally, therefore, these barristers get to know each other well; furthermore, they do not have permanent retainers from particular clients, in the way that English firms of solicitors, like their American counterparts, may do, so one counsel may be representing one client in one case, and acting against them in another case a year later; the counsel on the other side may also be the same person in the two cases. These factors help to explain the camaraderie which grows up among barristers who are a very 'cliquey' group. It would not be at all unusual for one barrister to telephone the barrister appearing on the opposite side in a case to discuss some possible arrangement in advance—for example, to agree that they will confine their argument to such and such a point, or to warn the other side that they intend to make some late application to the judge which could delay matters if the other side was taken by surprise. It would be very unusual and regarded as unfriendly, if not downright unprofessional, to allow professional rivalry to interfere with good personal working relations which enure to the benefit of the clients on both sides in this sort of way.

We have already discussed in chapter 12 the exceptionally homogeneous nature of the higher English judiciary, and much of what we have said there is also applicable to the bar. Senior barristers, especially, have been moulded over many years of common socializing experience with their colleagues. The daily fraternizing over professional matters, the daily appearances in higher courts, and the strongly conformist pressures on a barrister who wishes to be successful all help this moulding process. In addition, the orality of English judicial and appellate proceedings, and the highly stylized type of language which barristers become accustomed to using, encourage a conformist and somewhat conservative (and also individualized) attitude of mind. For instance, barristers talk a great deal about what is 'proper' or 'improper', what is 'acceptable' or 'tolerable', and so on. Much of this kind of language is the language judges use in their judicial opinions, and suggests that both judges and barristers tend to think in the same sort of concepts and with the same sorts of values as those which figure in judicial opinions. Even the traditions of dress at the bar are exceptionally conformist.

One peculiar feature of the organization of the English bar is that every barrister has to be self-employed; no partnerships or salaried assistants are permitted by the rules of the profession. This seems to be one of the chief factors producing the paradoxical result of a strongly conformist profession based on individual values. Since barristers are self-employed, and since they are by and large people of some ability, used to looking after themselves, it is not surprising that they tend to become somewhat individualistic in their outlook. But their individualism must be limited because they need to attract work from solicitors, and in order to do this, they must demonstrate their ability to work successfully in court, and in accordance with the styles and traditions of the bar. Judges are likely to frown on barristers who do not accept these styles and traditions, and solicitors do not want to instruct or 'brief' barristers who are frowned upon by judges (and there are strict professional rules generally forbidding a barrister from taking instructions directly from a lay client without the intervention of a solicitor). So the result is that slightly curious mixture: a tendency to individualism, but a single conformist pattern of individualist behaviour and even of modes of speech and probably thought as well.

The homogeneity of outlook among barristers may to some degree be furthered by their class origins. Little is known in detail about the social origins of English barristers, though these days very few come to the bar who have not had a university education, and not very many come who have not been to Oxford or Cambridge. This by itself does not mean a great deal, since about half the students at these two universities have been to state-maintained schools and could be of working-class origin, given the English system of state aid for university education. However, there are other factors which probably discourage working-class aspirants for the bar. One (virtual) requirement of conformist behaviour at the bar is the ability to speak 'BBC' English; those who arrive at university with pronounced working-class accents may receive a good education but they will face severe handicaps at the bar. At the present time there are also other difficulties for those of lower social status.

First, the bar is very overcrowded, chambers are extremely full, and it is very difficult indeed to obtain a 'seat' in chambers (without which one cannot even practise the profession at all) except through some friendly or family contact with those already in chambers. And secondly, it may be difficult to make an adequate living for some years, so private means or family support may be necessary. Neither of these factors, however, is a permanent feature of life at the bar. The crowdedness of the profession tends to move in relatively short cycles of perhaps ten years, so that only a few years ago there was more work available than the bar could easily cope with, and young barristers were making good incomes almost from the start. Furthermore, the Inns have substantial scholarships available to young barristers which can help to tide them over a year or two while they get established. Also, the difficulty of obtaining seats in chambers has rarely been as severe as it is now.

There is also one totally new phenomenon which is beginning to affect the homogeneity of the bar, though its impact is still small: there is now a 'black' bar. There are today quite a significant number of black barristers, and also several of Indian and Asiatic origin. Some of these barristers show signs of resisting the conformist pressures and maintaining some of their own traditions. They are often sought after by black or coloured clients, whether solicitors or lay clients, and some of them have styles of address and speech which are more flamboyant and aggressive than the English bar has been accustomed to hear for many years (though such styles existed in former days). All the same, it must be admitted that the bar does still appear to be largely dominated by Oxbridge graduates of the middle or upper middle-classes, as it has been for a very long time.

The second distinctive feature of the English bar, which we mentioned above, is the relationship between bar and bench. All the higher judges are appointed from the ranks of the bar, and nearly all from the small pool of QCs. The bar and the judges, therefore, tend to share a very strong common culture. All higher judges have spent many years at the bar, and many senior barristers aspire to become judges. They have shared a common socializing experience over many years in a small, closely-knit, professional community. They have lunched together and joked together.[3] They are members of the same Inns and, indeed, in the case of the judges and the senior barristers, they are most likely to be members of the governing bodies of these Inns, 'Benchers'. Socially, many senior barristers and judges will be friends; they may mix in the same social milieu, and play golf together at the weekends.

Professionally, also, judges and barristers are really members of the same group. They speak a common language, and they address each other in court. Counsels' arguments are addressed to judges, and the judges' opinions are (mainly) addressed to the bar. The judge may occasionally, be aware that there is a public interest in some case he is deciding (though this happens far less frequently than in America), and this moves him to insert passages in his opinion which are addressed mainly to the public through the media. Usually these will consist of ritual incantations to the effect that the judges are only concerned with the law as it is, and not with the 'merits' of the case or substantive policy arguments as to what the law 'ought to be', which are matters for Parliament. But most of the legal argument in judicial opinions is

---

[3] For some details of these socializing factors, see Megarry, 'Barristers and Judges in England Today', 51 *Fordham L. Rev.* 387, 388–97 (1982).

addressed to barristers and a judge seeks to justify his opinion by arguments that barristers will recognize as justifications. The fact that all argument is oral strengthens these traditions. So does the custom (not now always observed) that judges usually read their opinions out in open court (or give extempore oral opinions) and that counsel are normally expected to be in their places to hear the opinions read or delivered.

There is a sense in which the English bar is almost an apprenticeship for becoming a judge. Senior barristers appearing almost daily in court become so well acquainted with the role of the judge that they can move from bar to bench overnight, doffing the role of advocate and adopting that of judge with (apparently) effortless ease. (Of course, there are exceptions, some do not make the transition so easily, and some can never forget the role of advocate.) Further (as we noted in chapter 12), they are used to writing opinions, as barristers, which are not very different in style from those written by judges. A counsel's opinion in England is a form of training, which every barrister learns from his earliest days, for the writing of judicial opinions. It is written in a similar style, with as much detachment from the client's problem and (as a rule) as much impartiality, as a judge's opinions. Further, counsel's opinion is apt (and with more justification) to be even more strongly concerned than judicial opinions with the law 'as it is' rather than as 'it ought to be'.

One other factor helps to establish the bar as the senior half of the legal profession. In addition to providing all the higher judicial posts, the bar also has a monopoly of three plum political appointments, those of Lord Chancellor, Attorney-General and Solicitor-General. The Lord Chancellor is an extraordinarily anomalous person, speaking institutionally. He is at one and the same time a leading political personage, and also head of the judiciary. He is a member of the Cabinet, and shares to the full the normal political role of a Cabinet minister. In addition he presides in the House of Lords in its legislative capacity and is the leading government spokesman in that House, playing a large part in debates on government bills. Then he is also the presiding judge in the House of Lords in its judicial capacity, and has vast powers of patronage over judicial appointments, senior and junior. The Attorney-General and the Solicitor-General (who is in effect the deputy Attorney-General) are the government's 'Law Officers', that is, the government's legal advisers, who appear in court on behalf of the government in many important appellate cases, and also are members of the House of Commons and play a prominent part in debates on legal points. All these three appointments must, by custom, be filled from senior members of the bar. The latter two were formerly stepping stones to high judicial office, but as this has largely ceased to be the case, they are offices which tend to lead to a blind alley, except for the possibility of later appointment as

Lord Chancellor. Otherwise the Law Officers must today look to political careers if they wish to advance.

The fact that three senior members of the profession are always to be found in, or as junior members of, the government, also naturally strengthens the hold which the traditional view of the legal profession has on the political scene. Thus governments in modern England have been trained by their legal advisers to accept the same fundamentally positivist approach to law and law making and law reform as the judges and the bar. The supremacy of Parliament is never forgotten, but governments and Parliaments do not today deny that the law *is* what the judges say it is; if the government dislikes a decision of the judicial House of Lords it can and will (as we have seen) introduce legislation to overrule it, and the legislation will be passed. But neither government nor Parliament would ever claim that the judges had actually *got the law wrong*; even if, as occasionally happens, the government feels compelled to overturn a judicial decision with retrospective effect, it still does not do so on the ground that the judges made a mistake, but merely on the ground that *the law* as correctly declared by the judges was unsatisfactory and that, for special reasons, a retrospective change was necessary. Indeed, we think that in modern times most English lawyers and parliamentarians would think it conceptually impossible to declare even the common law to be something different from what the judges say it is, although Parliament is a supreme and omnicompetent legislature which at one time claimed (and through the House of Lords still does claim) to be the ultimate determining body in saying what the common law actually is.[4] The purity of the line between the 'is' and the 'ought' of the law is thus maintained, and has indeed become a standard feature of the common political understanding in England.

The third distinctive feature of the bar which we mentioned earlier concerns the orality of proceedings in appellate courts. We need devote no extended treatment to this point separately because its importance will already be implicit in what we have said above. It is the orality of proceedings which is responsible for much of the nature of the relationship between bar and bench, and for the relationships between barristers. The disappearance of the civil jury also means that oral argument in English courts tends today to encourage skill in arguing strict points of law in a fairly narrow, technical way—with little stress on substantive reasons—which matches the approach of English judges. Flamboyance and stridency are not popular characteristics at the bar. Indeed, the professional prohibition on advertising is still interpreted in

---

[4] See Atiyah, 'Common Law and Statute Law', 48 *Mod. L. Rev.* 1, 19 (1985).

a very broad way to include many forms of conduct which invite attention to a barrister in his professional capacity.

Again, in the same way that the pressures of oral argument (and the desirability of speed in disposing of cases) tends to discourage judges from roving across the law in a broad way, the same factors operate on members of the bar. They are not interested, as a rule, in seeking 'social engineering' through the forensic process; they are not entrepreneurs in their approach to legal cases; they have a limited loyalty even to their clients, and while of course every barrister wants to put his client's case as strongly as he can, and every barrister wants to win his cases, still, there is an element of detachment about the traditional way in which a barrister approaches a case. The English barrister is a kind of embryonic judge, a point confirmed by the fact that senior barristers are now expected to serve as part-time judges ('Recorders') before they can hope for judicial appointments.[5] And if judges believe that 'the law is the law' and that they have no (or very little) power to do anything other than apply it, it is hardly surprising that barristers share these beliefs.

The fourth distinctive characteristic of the English bar concerns the role of the barrister as a genuine officer of the court and guardian of the judicial process. English barristers, by custom and to some degree by professional ethics, do not regard themselves as retainers hired purely to secure a result for their clients by any means. They retain a degree of detachment from the causes of their clients. For example, barristers in England are not usually willing to initiate proceedings on the simple instructions of a client; if they think the client has no case they will say so in no uncertain terms, and only an unusually stubborn (and wealthy) client will persist regardless of such advice; similarly, barristers are not expected to draw a notice of appeal unless they are satisfied that there is some properly arguable ground of appeal; they are not expected to argue every possible point in court, but only those which are properly arguable. In the conduct of litigation, barristers often assist the court, both on the facts (for example, waiving technical objections to the admissibility of written evidence) and with regard to the law (for example, drawing attention to precedents against their present argument), and thus do not always act in a purely adversarial way. Similarly, barristers are not expected to make serious allegations against other parties or against witnesses (for instance, of fraud or crime) unless they have some evidence to substantiate those assertions. And so on. Thus the English barrister acts to a substantial degree as a filter through whom assertions and arguments have to be made; in this respect he is not just a hired retainer, but almost a public official, with important responsibilities for

[5] See *Judicial Appointments*, 3 (Lord Chancellor's Department, HMSO, London, 1986).

the working of the legal system as a whole. Very large numbers of potential claims, defences, and arguments are simply filtered out by barristers and never presented to a court. It is impossible that England could manage with such a tiny judiciary if barristers did not behave like this.

In addition, the integrity of the bar means that counsel's word can be and is relied on in legal proceedings; for example, where matters of exceptional urgency are brought before a court, sometimes *ex parte* before there has even been time to issue a writ or file an affidavit, English judges commonly rely on the mere word of counsel that a writ will be issued and an affidavit filed.[6]

American lawyers do not seem to work in this way to anything like the same degree. Certainly to an English lawyer, it sometimes looks as though many American attorneys are prepared to argue almost *any* point, though this is doubtless partly due to the greater complexity of much American law. Although the Federal Rules of Civil Procedure[7] declare that counsel's signature on a pleading or motion attests his belief that it is well grounded in fact and is warranted by law (or by a good faith argument for the extension, modification, or reversal of existing law), there seems in practice to be very wide latitude as to such matters, and there is (as we also noted earlier) no comparable provision with respect to notices of appeal. Many American trial lawyers generally seem to take minor and technical points at almost every turn, such as challenges to the jurors, objections to the evidence, motions for a new trial on the ground of prejudice, and the like. An American observer who recently made a study of the English criminal trial summed up the different approaches of the English barrister in this context as follows:

Generally speaking, the barrister representing the accused in England ... does not proceed upon the notion that his function is to obtain an acquittal by enforcing each and every rule applicable to the trial in the hope that the prosecution will falter. Nor does the defense barrister consider it proper to interject irrelevant matters into the case to confuse the jury, to require witnesses testifying as to uncontested matters to appear in court, to object to break the flow of damaging testimony, to turn the trial into an accusation against the complainant or the police where not called for clearly by the evidence, or to ask the jury to try the prosecutor, the judge, or society rather than the accused.[8]

These traditions of self-restraint on the part of the English barrister also mean that he will not normally be a party to the launching of wild

---

[6] See P. S. Atiyah, *Pragmatism and Theory in English Law*, 57 (Hamlyn Lectures, Stevens, London, 1987).

[7] Rule 11.

[8] Michael H. Graham, *Tightening the Reins of Justice in America*, 236 (Greenwood Press, Westport, Conn., 1983).

and speculative claims, and that there are severe limits to the extent to which he will accept instructions to make hopeless or dilatory pleas by way of defence. We have commented earlier on the fact that such procedures are in any event severely discouraged by the English legal system, as a result of the sanctions of costs and pre-judgment interest, and also the efficient use of summary procedures for striking out claims or defences. Barristers, of course, advise their clients about these matters, and there are strong practical limits beyond which a barrister cannot be pushed in drafting wild and futile pleadings or hopeless grounds of appeal.

The result of these traditions can perhaps best be illustrated by reference to one of the more extreme arguments about uncertainty in the legal system which surfaced during the realist movement in America. In an article published in 1931,[9] Jerome Frank criticised the claim made by Roscoe Pound that, at least in commercial cases relating to promissory notes and bills of exchange, the law was usually precise and clear. It is, suggested Frank, 'always possible' even in such cases 'to introduce some question of fact relating to fraud, negligence, mistake or estoppel'. And if such a suggestion was made and the question of fact went to the jury, it was absurd to suppose that the law would be mechanically applied. In light of the above comments about English barristers, it will be seen that the answer to this remark would simply be that it is not true in England. It is *not* 'always possible' to raise factual allegations of this kind, unless there is some evidence to support them, and an English barrister would want to know what sort of evidence there is before he prepares a defence to such a claim, or asks a court for leave to defend such a claim in summary proceedings. Of course, we do not doubt that many American lawyers would disagree with Frank's remarks even in the American context.[10]

3. ATTORNEYS AND SOLICITORS

The American legal profession resembles the English solicitors' profession in many ways, though there are also great differences. In the first place, both professions are much larger and more decentralized than the English bar. There are in England about 50,000 practising solicitors, spread over the country. The American legal profession is, of course, far

---

[9] 'Are Judges Human?' 80 *U. Pa. L. Rev.* 17, 31–33, and 233, at 235–6 (1931).

[10] But there seem to be some members of the CLS movement who agree with him, even though it is not always easy to be sure precisely what they do believe in. At least many of them seem to doubt that legal rules produce definitive results, however certain the rules may appear to be. See, e.g., Unger, 'The Critical Legal Studies Movement', 96 *Harv. L. Rev.* 563 (1983); Singer, 'The Player and the Cards: Nihilism and Legal Theory', 94 *Yale LJ* 1 (1984).

larger, indeed, it is enormous. According to the American Bar Foundation Research Study released in 1985, there are about 675,000 lawyers in America.[11]

Like the English solicitors' profession, the American legal profession is also far less homogeneous than the English bar. There is greater diversity in terms of background, culture, values, and probably also of competence and integrity, among the American legal profession than among English barristers, or even among English solicitors. The latter are a much more diverse group than the members of the English bar, but most of them will today have been to similar law schools or polytechnics (though there are still many older members of the profession who did not go to law schools at all but qualified through the 'articles'—or apprenticeship—system), most of them will have a fair share of technical competence and professional skill (they would not have been able to pass the professional examinations without them), and most of them will be rather middle class in their values and outlook.

The nature of English legal practice varies widely, as it does in America. On the one hand, there are about a dozen large 'City' (of London) firms, which increasingly resemble the (New York) Wall Street firms in size, in the nature of their work, in their corporate clientele, and generally in their professional approach to matters of business. On the other hand, there are large numbers of small firms practising in provincial towns, doing mostly routine legal work such as conveyancing, minor criminal and divorce matters, and other similar work. There are probably not quite so many solo practitioners (proportionately) in England as there may be in America. Nor has England yet faced the situation in which large numbers of legally qualified attorneys simply cannot make a living as legal practitioners, and so combine the nominal practice of law with a number of other commercial activities.

But in America, the diversities in the profession are enormous, compared with those in England. It is not merely that the nature of legal practice may vary more broadly across the spectrum from Wall Street practitioner in New York City to country lawyer in Halfway, Oregon. The background, education, and cultural traditions of the American profession are also more diversified. In the first place, American lawyers come from a wide range of economic and social backgrounds, and probably include more members from the lowest rungs of the working-classes than do English lawyers, although of course the great majority in

---

[11] B. Curran, *The Lawyer Statistical Report: A Statistical Profile of the US Legal Profession in the 1980s* (ABF, Chicago, 1985). For earlier estimates, see Julie Taylor, 'Demographics of the American Legal Profession', in A. Kaufman, *Problems in Professional Responsibility* 835, 837 (2nd edn., 1984).

both countries come from upper and middle class backgrounds.[12] But certainly there are proportionately more American lawyers from different ethnic groups. For example, in 1980 there were some 15,600 black lawyers, 8,900 of Spanish origin, and even about 900 native American lawyers.[13] However, lawyers from minority groups remain under-represented in the profession, and (despite affirmative action programmes) minority law students are under-represented in law schools,[14] so this trend is likely to continue. Although there are today increasing numbers of Asian and black solicitors in England (precise figures are unavailable), there are very few in the law schools, so it will be many years before the number of solicitors from these groups matches their numbers in the population at large.

Legal education (as we shall see in more detail in the next chapter) is also more diversified in America than in England, and this naturally influences the diversity in the profession itself. Nearly all American practitioners have attended an American law school, and then passed a state bar examination, but there is an immense difference in the quality of the education of those who have attended the more respectable law schools and those who have not.[15] There are 174 accredited law schools in America, of which (in 1971) 53 had evening programmes.[16] In these night-schools, a sufficient legal training may be acquired while doing another job in the daytime, to make it possible for most of these students (many of whom are themselves well qualified academically) to pass the state bar examinations and so qualify to practise law.[17] Among the more respectable law schools, there is (as we shall discuss further in the next chapter) a far greater range of quality than among English university law faculties, though this range has narrowed in the last two decades. Until quite recently, Wall Street firms recruited very largely among graduates

[12] F. K. Zemans and V. G. Rosenblum, *The Making of a Public Profession*, 31–5, 39, 41 (ABF, Chicago, 1981); J. Heinz and Edward O. Laumann, *Chicago Lawyers* (Russell Sage Foundation and ABF, 1982). See also Schwartz, 'The Reach and Limits of Legal Education', 32 *J. Leg. Ed.* 543, 548–9 (1982).

[13] Bureau of Census data, as reported in Silas, 'Business Reasons to Hire Minorities', 70 *ABAJ* 52, 53 (April 1984). In England there are no proper statistics as to the number of solicitors from minority ethnic groups, see the Royal Commission Report, *supra*, n. 1, vol. 2, at 501.

[14] *A Review of Legal Education in the United States*, 67 (ABA, Fall 1984).

[15] This statement is made cautiously, but some empirical studies appear to support it. See Cramton, 'Rising Expectations in Law Practice and Legal Education', 7 *N. Ky. L. Rev.* 159, 171 n. 35 (1980).

[16] See Cramton, 'Comments on Professional Preparation in England and the United States', at 2 (unpublished paper presented to ABA meeting, London 1985); V. Countryman, T. Finman, and T. Schneyer, *The Lawyer in Modern Society*, 707 (2nd edn., 1976) (citing Kelso, *The AALS Study of Part-Time Legal Education* (AALS, Washington, 1972)); Taylor, *supra*, n. 11, at 841.

[17] See Robert Stevens, *Law School* (U. of North Carolina Press, Chapel Hill, 1983) for details of these night-schools.

of a handful of elite law schools.[18] Today they recruit from among
graduates of about 50 law schools.

Modes of practice are strikingly diverse in a number of ways, but these
diversities are also largely found in England. About two-thirds of all
American lawyers are in private practice,[19] with some ten per cent in
government service.[20] As in England, the profession is now dominated
by the large city firms. In 1983 there were 183 American firms with over
one hundred lawyers each; fourteen had over 300.[21] These large firms
tend to hire graduates from the more prestigious law schools, and they
now offer a range of specialized expertise in such fields as taxation,
securities, large-scale commercial litigation, and so on.[22] They are also
growing fast. But in all these respects the position of the London ('City')
firms is much the same, though there are not so many of them, nor are
they quite so large, nor are there any (as yet) outside London. On the
other hand, as many as 165,000 lawyers are estimated to be sole
practitioners in America,[23] so it can hardly be said that this style of
practice is dead, despite the growth of the huge city firms in modern
times.

Because so much appellate work is today done through written briefs,
the American profession has proportionately fewer well-qualified and
specialist oral advocates of the English type, able to argue points of law
before appellate courts. There are, of course, trial lawyers who specialize
in the conduct of litigation, especially before juries, and there are
criminal law specialists. There are also a number of American lawyers
who specialize in appellate advocacy, but of course in most American
courts the main burden of this kind of work consists of the writing of
appellate briefs, rather than of oral advocacy in court. This means that
such lawyers have no particular and regular contact with other specialists
in advocacy in the style of the English bar. It would also be exceedingly
rare for an American lawyer to represent alternately clients drawn from
fundamentally opposing interests, such as employers on one hand and
labour groups on the other, or personal injury plaintiffs and insurance
companies, or environmentalist groups and heavy industries alleged to
be responsible for pollution. On the contrary, American practitioners

---

[18] J. Auerbach, *Unequal Justice*, 23–8 (Oxford U. Press, NY, 1976).
[19] Taylor, *supra*, n. 11, at 843.
[20] *Ibid.*
[21] Kagan and Rosen, 'On the Social Significance of Large Law Firm Practice', 37 *Stan. L. Rev.* 399 (1985).
[22] *Ibid*; M. Galanter, 'Mega-Law and Mega-Lawyering in the Contemporary United States', in *The Sociology of the Professions*, 152 (R. Dingwall and P. Lewis, edd., St. Martin's Press, NY, 1983); Kagan and Rosen, *supra*, n. 21, at 408.
[23] Compare Curran's figures with Taylor, *supra*, n. 11, at 835, n. 1 and 843, n. 54 with accompanying text.

tend to become identified with one or other of the two sides in such conflicts, and thereafter appear only for that side.[24] The country's leading practising lawyers (though not those who are best known to the public) are corporate lawyers in the large city firms, not independent advocates available for hire to any client who can afford their services.

A major result of these differences between the structures of the English and the American legal professions is that the lawyers in America who work in the corporate law firms share less of their professional lives with the judges than do the English bar. In England, legal argument is an oral dialogue between the barrister and the judge, but American appellate work is much more depersonalized. Sometimes, the American lawyer may even write his brief with an eye to the highest courts, while the judge himself may feel under no pressure to answer all the points made in an attorney's brief.[25] Arguments and opinions are occasionally even addressed to the public, the media, and the law schools,[26] as well as to judges and other attorneys. Indeed, the sheer size of the profession, the quantity of litigation, and the number of reported (or reportable decisions) may themselves contribute to an alienation between judges and practising lawyers.[27] Increasing specialization also means that each lawyer tends more and more to read only opinions in his field. Unlike an English barrister who is a specialist in *advocacy* but (usually) a generalist in *law* (or anyhow large areas of law[28]) many American lawyers are likely to specialize in a narrow area, and may have little sense of the general values and ideas influencing judges in other areas.

The diversity of background and values among American lawyers matches that among the judges, so there is much less of a common legal culture in the United States, shared among lawyers and judges, than there is in England. Once again it is the English bar which makes the difference. Outside the bar, English lawyers, like American lawyers, tend to fall into the two major classes (corporate city firms and smaller country firms), each of which no doubt has a good deal of homogeneity of interest and culture. But, as we have seen, the English bar and the judges are far closer and more homogeneous than this, and they

[24] Galanter, *supra*, n. 22; Heinz and Laumann, 'The Legal Profession: Client Interests, Professional Roles and Social Hierarchies', 76 *Mich. L. Rev.* 1111, 1117 (1978).

[25] See Stolz, *Judging Judges*, 403-4 (Free Press, NY, 1981).

[26] See *supra*, p. 282, n. 63, citing the recent survey showing that nearly 12% of state supreme court opinions refer to academic literature.

[27] Stolz, *supra*, n. 25, at 406 (as to California, remarking that this has led to the disappearance of the role of the bar as a part of the 'organized constituency' of the courts and judges).

[28] English barristers do specialize to a limited extent—there are, for instance, commercial chambers, tax chambers, chancery chambers, and so on. But the specializations are generally broad and not very rigid.

dominate English legal culture. The American legal profession is too large, too diverse, and too scattered across an entire continent for this to be possible. Insofar as there is anything that can be called a national legal culture in America it may be found not in the practising profession, but in the law schools. This may be one reason why academic lawyers have so much more influence on the development of American law than they do in England. We shall return in chapter 14 to the importance of legal education and the academic profession. Here we note that practising lawyers often look to leading academics (and leading law reviews) for imaginative and innovative ideas, for new lines of argument, and sometimes for social scientific and statistical data that can buttress policy arguments. It is not uncommon for leading law firms even to consult academics on the legal theories which ought be pursued in complex cases.[29] And we have already noted that appellate briefs in important cases are occasionally written by law professors, and not by attorneys at all.[30]

There is one further difference between the two countries. The English legal profession is homogeneous in a very special way. It takes its cue, so to speak, from hierarchical elites. Thus the appellate judges set standards of formality which are followed by trial judges; trial judges set standards of formality which are followed by barristers; and solicitors necessarily follow along. But the American legal profession simply has no such closely knit judicial hierarchy from which to take its cue. Even the federal judiciary is not a hierarchy in this sense, though in a few of the smaller American states there may be a relatively closely knit hierarchy.[31] At the same time, most American lawyers (unlike English barristers) do not regularly appear before judges anyhow, and those who do, find themselves before a wide variety of judges, state and federal, trial and appellate.

Thus the total scene closely resembles that relating to the judges. Diversity in America, homogeneity in England, centralization (at least of the bar and major solicitors' firms) in England, decentralization in America. It is hardly surprising if factors which tend to encourage a more formal approach to law among the English judges find their echo in the English legal profession, while factors tending to a greater use of reasons

---

[29] It may not be irrelevant that English practising lawyers would not use the word 'theory' in this way at all; they would perhaps talk of 'lines of argument'.

[30] In 1982–3 it was widely reported in the Boston press that one Harvard Law School professor had a more extensive Supreme Court practice in constitutional matters than any practising attorney.

[31] Other factors tending to Balkanization of the American legal profession include the system of state-by-state admission to the bar, and also localized procedures for the disciplining of lawyers.

of substance in American judicial opinions also find their echo in the American legal profession.

4. QUALIFICATIONS OF LAWYERS AND THE FORM-SUBSTANCE DISTINCTION

We have no reason to believe that standards of competence and skill at the top of the two professions are not fully comparable, but it is very difficult to make comparisons concerning the rest of the professions. Despite the constant lamentations of some prominent American judges (former Burger CJ being prominent among them[32]) about the quality of the American bar, we are unable to offer any evidence to suggest that the English legal profession today is free from similar weaknesses. Even the English bar is widely thought to have increasing numbers of relatively less competent members in its lower echelons, and with many young practitioners, it certainly has a good number of inexperienced barristers.[33]

What does seem to be true, however, is that entry standards to the American legal profession are more variable than those operative in England today. To become a qualified lawyer in America, an applicant must complete an undergraduate college degree course in four years, then attend a law school for a further three years, and finally pass a state bar examination. While variations in law school standards may have lessened in recent decades (we discuss law schools in the next chapter), the state bar examinations vary greatly in their difficulty. These examinations are not under the control of the professions, but of the state judiciary, and hence are more local in their orientation. In some states virtually all candidates are passed, while in others (California, for instance) fewer than half succeed at any one sitting.

In England the entry to both sides of the profession is controlled by the professions themselves—another example of greater centralization. Both sides now demand (in most cases) a university degree in which six 'core' legal subjects are passed with at least second-class honours; both then

---

[32] See, e.g., the reports of Chief Justice Burger's addresses to the ABA at its meetings in February and August of 1978. 64 *ABAJ*. 313, 1329 (1978). For a slightly different view, see Cramton, 'Lawyer Competence and the Law Schools', 4 *U. Ark.-Little Rock LJ* 1, 4–5 (1981).

[33] There have been rumours in the English press to the effect that the present Lord Chancellor believes that much of the criminal legal aid work done by younger barristers is of relatively low quality, and that many of them lack adequate skills: this is thought to explain the Lord Chancellor's unwillingness to sanction increases in remuneration for legal aid work sufficient to satisfy the bar, which led to the remarkable legal proceedings in 1986 in which the Lord Chancellor's actions were challenged by way of judicial review. The proceedings were settled and remain unreported.

require twelve months' attendance at professional training schools, followed by the passing of the respective professional examination, and a further period of 'articles' (for a solicitor) or 'reading in chambers' (for a barrister). The solicitors' professional examination has generally been reputed to be difficult, and only about half the candidates pass at one sitting. The bar final examination has never been regarded as a serious entry test though it has recently been stiffened.

In the upshot, we can only say that the standards in the American legal profession appear to cover a wider range than in the English legal profession, and it seems probable (given the quality of some law schools and some state bar examinations) that there are proportionately more lawyers of lower technical proficiency in America than in England.

Whether or not we are right in our assertions about the present day, what we say is almost certainly true of the past. The reasons for this stem to some degree from ideological factors, and have a bearing on our thesis. In particular, there is an old American tradition which holds that almost anyone is *entitled* to practise law; the practice of law used to be seen as a democratic right, partly because of a kind of simplistic ideological belief that law should not be allowed to become an arcane mystery, the preserve of a limited number of qualified lawyers who monopolize legal practice and overcharge the public for their services;[34] and partly because the practice of law in America has been almost a prerequisite to the practice of politics, especially at the federal level. The political system is so legal in its basis and so interwoven with the legal system that a politician without a legal background is at something of a disadvantage in the United States. Thus to deny legal education and a legal qualification to anyone in America is to diminish the opportunity to embark on a political career; this has become particularly important in recent years in that the effective political representation of minority groups may well depend on the availability of many more minority lawyer-politicians than there are at present. As we noted earlier, these factors have been partially responsible for the continued existence of the 'night-schools' which help a small number of people of limited resources to qualify as lawyers, and also thereby open up possible opportunities in politics. It was only by a prolonged and unceasing battle that the American Bar Association gradually persuaded state legislatures that entry to the legal profession should be restricted to those with proven qualifications.[35]

The notion that the public needs to be protected from incompetent

---

[34] J. Auerbach, *supra*, n. 18, at 110–11.
[35] See Robert Stevens, *supra*, n. 17, ch. 6.

lawyers, while it is not wholly without force in modern America, is often looked at with the sort of suspicion with which Adam Smith regarded all professional claims to a monopoly. Many Americans would probably subscribe to the thesis that there is a demand for lawyers of all grades in the market, and that it is inefficient, wrong, and undemocratic to prevent the market supplying this demand.[36] Indeed, many economists would argue that if the qualifications required for becoming an attorney are raised, the very people who at present are served by lesser qualified lawyers will be the most hurt, because they will be left without any lawyers at all.

The English tradition, at any rate in recent times, has, by contrast, been more elitist and paternalist. The public, it is assumed, must be protected from incompetent lawyers, and the possession of a legal qualification is seen as some kind of a warranty of reasonable competence offered by the controlling authorities, which in the ultimate analysis includes the State itself. It is, of course, accepted that there will be some lawyers who are better than others, and that this will reflect itself in their earnings and status; but the necessary minimum threshold is regarded as an important public protection.

It will be noted how these factors relate to the thrust of our thesis. The American democratic ideal, with its assumption that law should not be an arcane mystery, controlled by a narrow class of lawyers, is surely not unrelated to the American vision of law as fundamentally about substantive justice, and not about formal and technical legal doctrines. On the other hand, the English tradition is just the opposite: law in English eyes *is* technical and rightly so; it *does* require years of study and effort to obtain the requisite skills; it is *not* something in which the public at large can be expected to be competent. As Coke CJ said on a famous occasion when James I claimed that law was merely the embodiment of reason, and that he, the King, had as much reason as any of his judges,

True it was, that God had endowed his Majesty with excellent Science, and great endowments of Nature; but his Majesty was not learned in the Laws of his Realm of England, and Causes which concern the Life, or Inheritance, or goods, or fortunes of his Subjects, are not to be decided by Natural Reason, but by the artificial reason and Judgment of Law, which Law is an Art which requires long Study and Experience, before that a Man can attain to the Cognizance of it.[37]

---

[36] It is widely thought that many state and local governments, compelled by the Supreme Court to provide legal counsel to indigenous criminal defendants, allocate meagre resources to this, and thus themselves constitute a large part of the demand for less qualified (and hence cheap) lawyers. The position in England may be similar. Of course in both countries many of the lawyers employed for this work are perfectly capable.

[37] *Prohibitions del Roy*, 12 Co. Rep. 63 (1608).

5. THE PUBLIC POLICY ROLE OF LAWYERS

Like judges, lawyers in America are often much more political than lawyers in England, and in a variety of ways they play a correspondingly larger role in the formulation of policy. Generally speaking it would be true to say today that the English legal profession, as such, tries to keep out of politics in much the same way as the English judiciary. This does not mean that English lawyers are never interested in matters of policy (especially policy which may affect their professional interests) but, as we have seen above, most English lawyers and judges try to distinguish between policy and politics. The distinction may, as we have already conceded, be theoretically indefensible, but there can be no doubt that it is very widely believed in, nor that it is one of the features of the English legal profession which seems closely related to the positivist tradition.

There are, of course, many individual lawyers who enter politics in England. Indeed, the lawyers often form one of the largest professional groups in the House of Commons, and, as we have already noted, there are always important legal spokesmen on the government side in both Houses of Parliament. But, in general, lawyers in Parliament do not have as such any distinctive roles, they tend to divide on most issues on normal party lines and their presence hardly signifies the kind of merger of law and politics one finds in America, where politics is often half-law.

Furthermore, since the disappearance of the tradition that senior judicial posts were the political 'pickings' of good party supporters, and especially of the Law Officers, it is unusual for senior lawyers to play a major role both in professional life and also in partisan politics, except perhaps for the occasional Lord Chancellor like Lord Hailsham. Indeed, even in former days, when politicians were regularly appointed to judicial posts, it was always part of political folklore in England that, though good lawyers might make competent administrators, they rarely made outstanding politicians. It is noteworthy how few of those who were trained as lawyers have risen really high in English political life. In over 150 years only two barristers (H. H. Asquith and Margaret Thatcher) and one solicitor (Lloyd George) have risen to become Prime Minister.

Things are, of course, very different indeed in the United States. Law and politics are there interwoven in a great many ways, and this necessarily has a bearing on the role of the practising lawyers and their relationship with political issues. In the first place, the notion that politics and policy are two different things is a pretty threadbare fiction in America, even if there are some who still try to sustain it. Generally, it is widely recognised that law—and especially constitutional law—is in its very essence and nature highly political. This is, of course, the main reason that the appointment of Supreme Court justices is such a political process, and why Presidents look for judges with whom they are in basic political agreement. But what influences judges also influences the entire legal profession. As we have previously observed, knowledge of law is particularly useful for politicians in America. It is more difficult to be an effective politician if one does not have at least a basic grasp of the limits on the powers of the federal and the state governments imposed by the courts, and of the nature of the relationship between the central and the state governments arising from the federal system of government. Furthermore, many of these important legal questions are replicated, to some degree, in state constitutions, so that a state politician must also have some grasp of the implications of the legal system even at lower levels of government.

Lawyers swarm all over the political scene in the United States. Twenty-three of America's thirty-nine Presidents have been lawyers or trained as lawyers.[38] For many decades, about half the Members of both Houses of the US Congress have been lawyers, and lawyers still hold about 40% of the seats in Congress. State legislatures have for long been dominated by lawyers, though this has been changing for some time. Similarly, lawyers are to be found all over the administration, not only in legal capacities, but also as heads and directors of government agencies and other similar bodies. Many of these persons move to, or from, the bench. For example, William O. Douglas was head of the Securities and Exchange Commission when he was appointed to the United States Supreme Court, Justice Hugo Black was a US Senator when he was appointed, Earl Warren was Governor of California when he was appointed Chief Justice; conversely Arthur Goldberg was a justice of the Supreme Court when he was appointed ambassador to the United Nations.

But it is not just a matter of personnel. The political involvement of lawyers in America leads to other, more subtle influences upon the law and the legal system. Some lawyers believe that, if they want things done, it may be easier to achieve them through the courts than through the political process. At the same time, some lawyers see a need to play a more active role in going out into the field, as it were, to see how and where the law needs to be supplemented, changed, and made more readily enforceable. The more passive English lawyer leaves these activities to agencies of the government.

This tendency of the law and lawyers in America to become associated with political causes of various kinds became particularly pronounced in the civil rights movement in the 1960s, itself drawing on an aggressive

---

[38] Henry J. Abraham, *Justices and Presidents*, 7 (2nd edn., Oxford U. Press, NY, 1985).

style of litigation developed much earlier in the century by the NAACP and the ACLU. The federal Office of Economic Opportunity also encouraged lawyers to adopt a more active style of litigation, to go out and look for violations of the law, to pursue more investigatory methods, rather than to wait for complaints to come in.[39] Since then, the same techniques have come to be used in a whole series of other causes, such as environmental protection causes and consumer protection issues.

But in these areas, unlike the civil rights movement, many of the proponents are private interest groups, not supported by government forces, indeed, often bitterly opposed by them, especially state and local ones. It has often been the judiciary, thus encouraged by lawyers, who were in the van of change and reform on these issues. These private interest groups are now becoming associated with an entrepreneurial kind of lawyer who is willing to invest enormous time and money in investigating the possibility of bringing, and then proceeding to launch, massive public litigation, usually by way of class action.[40] If successful in such litigation, many of the lawyers expect to be remunerated out of enormous damage awards before anything is made available for distribution to the class members on whose behalf the litigation is brought. This kind of litigation, therefore, combines the contingent fee arrangements of smaller scale litigation with a significant public interest issue. Lawyers may, of course, do this kind of work in a purely business way, as a kind of large-scale if somewhat speculative investment, but they are more likely to do it if they have some active personal involvement in the causes at stake.

Another manifestation of this more active role for lawyers is to be found in the creation of many public interest law firms in the 1960s and 1970s. These were financed by a variety of sources, in particular from foundations and charitable sources, but more recently statutes have enabled such firms to recover their costs or fees in a significant number of the cases they are engaged in.[41] Many of these firms take a vigorous part in the new public interest or public law litigation which has been touched upon in chapter 5. This kind of litigation, as we have noted, is usually designed to further the recognition and enforcement of rights, and is itself one of the symptoms of the more fluid and less formal American legal system. But the scope given for politically minded

[39] J. Auerbach, *supra*, n. 18, at 268 ff.

[40] See *supra*, ch. 5, section 5; see also R. Rabin, 'Lawyers for Social Change: Perspectives on Public Interest Law', 28 *Stan. L. Rev.* 207 (1976); Comment, 'The New Public Interest Lawyers', 79 *Yale LJ* 1069 (1970); M. Rosenberg, 'Contemporary Litigation in the United States', in *Legal Institutions Today: English and American Approaches Compared*, 152 (H. W. Jones, ed., ABA, 1977).

[41] See Horowitz, 'Decreeing Organizational Change: Judicial Supervision of Public Institutions', *Duke LJ* 1265, 1276–9 (1983).

lawyers to pursue political ideals through the legal system by these means has been greatly increased.

Manifestly, activities of this kind are nurtured and fed by the substantive traditions of the American legal profession and the legal system as a whole. Equally obviously, they feed back into the legal system, influencing in many obvious and more subtle ways the role of law and lawyers and the vision of law to which they and the public adhere. It is hardly necessary to suggest that activities of this kind, blending as they do the overtly political pursuit of 'causes' with the legal methodology, are unlikely to fit comfortably into a more traditional, formal vision of law and the legal system. Those who pursue this kind of litigation do so not primarily to ensure enforcement of formal rules of law, but to persuade the courts 'to recognize new rights, impose new duties and enunciate new legal doctrines'.[42] They do this in pursuit of substantive ideals, and perhaps principles, which are not always easy to identify precisely, but certainly do not derive from a belief in a formal legal system.

Further, there can be no doubt that some American lawyers are often willing to start legal proceedings on totally new and unprecedented grounds. A casual glance at the American press will usually reveal examples of several extraordinary claims being presented to the courts somewhere in the country in the course of a single week. Of course what looks extraordinary to an English lawyer may often seem less extravagant to an American. And so also, the fact that a claim is unprecedented is no guarantee that it will fail, especially in one of the more innovative jurisdictions in America. But some of these extraordinary claims look very unlikely to succeed, if indeed they are not doomed from the start,[43] and it may be asked why lawyers are willing to launch them at all. The answer seems to lie in two factors.

First, it may well be that the system of contingent fees gives attorneys an interest in 'trying on' novel claims, which encourages them to push forwards the frontiers of legal liability. Many American lawyers do not believe the contingent fee has this tendency, because a lawyer who takes a case on a contingent fee will earn nothing if he loses the case, and it is therefore widely thought that lawyers will be cautious (rather than the

[42] *Ibid.*
[43] For a random example, see *New York Times*, 3 Nov. 1982, reporting a suit in Washington brought against US Steel by a woman who claimed that her husband had divorced her after US Steel had relocated him. The suit was dismissed by Washington State Court of Appeals. Other extraordinary claims receiving widespread media coverage in 1983 involved an action against a man who had promised to pay $10,000 for a baby to be borne by a 'surrogate mother'; and an action by a woman against a man claiming breach of a promise to impregnate her.

reverse) in taking cases on this fee basis.[44] While there may be truth in this, it also seems the case that the very large sums which can be earned by American lawyers from a handful of personal injury cases taken on a contingent fee basis may encourage them to try out unusual and even unprecedented cases, where an English lawyer would be much more likely to advise his client that the prospects of success do not warrant litigation. For instance, an American lawyer may be much more willing to take on a case where he assesses the chances of a recovery at only one in three (assuming he is unable to work to capacity on more probable winners), because one in three such cases may well pay for the others with a handsome profit left over for the lawyer.[45] It has also been suggested that an American trial lawyer who handles a large number of claims has an interest in pursuing them beyond the point at which a client's interest would be served by settling the claim. A lawyer only has to win one huge verdict to cover his costs on a number of claims, and the more claims he pursues to the bitter end, the greater is the chance of hitting the jackpot once in a while.[46] Certainly it is hard to believe that the contingent fee system has nothing to do with the enormous efforts presently being put into attempts to hold liable cigarette and whiskey and handgun manufacturers for the harms attributable to these products.[47]

But secondly, these extraordinary claims do produce occasional successes. Sometimes success may be short lived, because appellate reversal follows, but a sufficient number to make them attractive to lawyers do eventually succeed.[48] These successes themselves of course

[44] Clermont and Currivan, 'Improving on the Contingent Fee', 63 *Cornell L. Rev.* 529, 571–2 (1978).

[45] It is also arguable that American civil procedure puts such a huge burden on a defendant that blackmailing suits are encouraged: plaintiff merely has to file suit and seek discovery to impose legal costs on a defendant out of all proportion to those incurred by the plaintiff. Naturally, an offer to settle can sometimes be extracted in such circumstances.

[46] See Reder, 'Contingent Fees in Litigation with Special Reference to Medical Malpractice', in *The Economics of Medical Malpractice*, 211, 224–9, 231 (Rottenberg, ed., 1978) (arguing that lawyers on contingent fees are able to refuse settlements more profitably than plaintiffs who may lose all, because the lawyer can offset some losses against a few big wins). But this is arguable: lawyers on contingent fees might find it more profitable to turn over cases more quickly and thus settle more readily.

[47] Whatever merits the contingent fee has as a method of giving poor people access to courts and justice, we do not doubt that it sometimes plays a role in encouraging lawyers to seek potential clients and to foment litigation. The antics of the infamous 'ambulance chasers' in personal injury litigation are too well known (if often exaggerated) to need documenting in any detail here. See, for example, J. O'Connell, *The Injury Industry and the Remedy of No-Fault Insurance*, ch. VI (U. Ill. Press, Urbana, 1971).

[48] Moreover, as Calabresi points out, jurors who have vague memories of newspaper reports of such extraordinary claims may believe that they succeeded and act accordingly, if only the judge leaves the case to them: *A Common Law for the Age of Statutes*, 168 (Harvard U. Press, Cambridge, 1982).

reflect the much more open and substantive character of the American legal system. As we have indicated above, given the returns that can be anticipated from a successful claim, it only needs a small success rate to make the process worthwhile. Furthermore, even if these cases never make it to court and verdict, they may become a sufficient threat to be worth a substantial sum in settlement from the other side which wishes to buy off the claims and so avert even a minor risk of losing what may be enormous sums, both in pre-trial costs and ultimately in damages or lost profits. Apart from the rare cases that actually do succeed, and then become pace-setters for other courts, such claims may also persuade courts that less extraordinary (but still innovative) claims are quite moderate extensions of legal doctrine. In this way, the nature and customs of the legal profession add their bit in making extraordinary legal innovations possible; and this in turn may help to add to the indeterminacy and uncertainty of American law, and hence to the less formal view of law.

Highly innovative claims of the kind discussed above do not themselves reflect any discredit on the American legal system. Indeed, many Americans (lawyers and others) would congratulate themselves on having a legal system which is so responsive to substantive reasoning that it can readily cope with new problems in this way. But this kind of innovation can, of course, lead to abuse, and to frivolous litigation. This aspect of the American legal system is highly visible, though doubtless of small dimensions in the total context, and naturally brings in its train much criticism, especially from foreign observers. Some of the criticism is justified, but it should not be exaggerated. Further, in recent times increasing efforts have been made to discipline American lawyers who assert frivolous claims and defences.[49] Indeed, such lawyers have even been sued, and held liable for fees (costs) and damages,[50] though it is hard to say whether this substantiates our point or requires it to be qualified!

---

[49] See Cann, 'Frivolous Lawsuits: The Lawyer's Duty to Say "No"', 52 *U. of Colorado L. Rev.* 367 (1981).

[50] *Ibid.*; see also C. W. Wolfram, *Modern Legal Ethics*, 594, section 11. 2 (West, St. Paul, 1984).

14

Law Schools, Legal Education, and Legal Literature

1. INTRODUCTION

In this chapter we conclude our survey of the institutional factors affecting the style of the English and the American legal systems with an examination of the role of law schools, legal education, and legal literature. Although English law schools may now be changing fast (on which, more later), it was certainly true as recently as twenty years ago that a formal (and in some respects even formalistic) vision of law dominated English law schools and legal education, and that vision continues to be significantly influential within many English law faculties today.[1] In America, on the other hand, a much more substantive vision of law has been and continues to be dominant in the law schools.[2]

It might seem that the law schools in both countries ought to be more strategically placed than other institutions, perhaps more even than the judiciaries, to shape and reinforce the respective styles of the two legal systems, formal in England, substantive in America. After all, in many fields those who teach commonly have direct and lasting influence on those who are taught, and in this case the taught are the very ones who run the legal system, especially the lawyers and the judges. We do think that this institutional factor has been powerful in the United States, where the ethos of the leading law schools has played a major role in shaping the substantive character of the modern American legal system. But (as we shall see) the same is not really true of English legal education. Indeed, until quite recently, English legal education seems to have been for the most part more a pale reflection of the legal system than itself an active force in shaping that system.

2. THE NATURE AND STATUS OF LAW SCHOOLS

There are great differences between the nature and the status of law

---

[1] For details of law teaching in England, see Wilson, 'A Survey of Legal Education in the United Kingdom', IX *Journal of the SPTL* 1 (1966), and Wilson and Marsh, 'A Second Survey of Legal Education in the United Kingdom', XIII *Journal of the SPTL* 239 (1975).

[2] See generally, Robert Stevens, *Law School* (U. of North Carolina Press, Chapel Hill, 1983).

schools in England and America, differences which are part cause and part result of the differing roles they play in their respective legal systems.

The leading American law schools are great centres of research and great sources of ideas about, and influence on, the law, and indeed on public policy. These law schools are themselves formidable institutions both within their own universities, and even nationally. They are graduate-level schools, and function quite autonomously within their own university frameworks, usually with their own buildings, their own budgets, and their own non-teaching personnel. They make their own teaching appointments (subject to approval by the university president or board of regents), determine their own curriculum, and set their own admission policies. They also have their own separate salary scale with a 'professional differential' that translates into salaries above those elsewhere in the university. This enables law schools to retain high quality faculty who have constant opportunities to earn more in practice. It also means that these schools can compete in a national market for established professors with a high reputation. The result is that some of the top law schools become genuine centres of excellence to which exceptional faculty gravitate.

On the national scene, too, the leading law schools stand out as powerful and influential institutions. Their alumni often occupy high places in the profession, in the judiciary, in industry, and in government, both federal and state. (For example, as we saw before, 40% of the members of Congress are lawyers.) Many of them also have massive endowments, and it is no rare thing for one of them to raise a multi-million dollar fund to construct a new building or library. These law schools are thus truly national institutions in a country which (outside the federal government and large industry) has few truly national institutions. And, as we shall see, it may even be said that these law schools dominate the country's legal system and its legal culture. The Harvard Law School, to name just the most famous of all, is thus a powerful national institution whose activities attract much media attention, and whose dean has a title which has in the past counted for more than that of any other lawyer except a justice of the US Supreme Court.[3]

The contrasts with the position of law schools in England are striking. English law schools do not have this great prestige within their own universities or as national institutions. They have, indeed, often been seen as mere 'trade schools' whose job is to contribute to the training of practising lawyers. They do not by any means have the same status as

---

[3] See generally Stevens, *supra*, n. 2.

great centres of research and writing on such an immense range of public policy issues. When governments in England require prestigious lawyers to head commissions of inquiry or the like, they nearly always turn to barristers and judges, and rarely to academics.

As compared with the American scene, a number of factors contribute to the relatively low standing of law schools in England. First, law teaching in England is an ordinary undergraduate subject, studied in most universities for three years of what would, in America, be called 'college'. While English university education is rather more advanced than American 'college' education, it is certainly not as advanced as that offered in the best American graduate schools. Also, because law is an undergraduate subject, English law teachers must assume that most students have very little (if any) knowledge of economics or philosophy or political theory when they start the study of law; the teaching of law insofar as it touches such cognate subjects must, therefore, aim at relatively modest standards.

Secondly, English law schools are not the quasi-independent bodies that many American law schools are. They are simply departments within the universities. They do have substantial academic autonomy so far as curriculum and examinations are concerned, but even as to these matters there are often limits. And as to many other important matters, English law schools are far less autonomous. They do not have complete control over the appointment of new members of the faculty, for example, since such appointments will normally reside in the hands of an electoral committee on which other university teachers will be found.

In other important respects, English law schools have virtually no autonomy. For example, they have little budgetary control. In particular there is no autonomy over salaries. University teachers are all paid on a scale fixed by the government (nominally after negotiations with the relevant trade union) and there is exceedingly little room for adjustment. While this may seem a relatively minor point, it is in fact a major explanation of the differences between English and American law schools. No English law school can go into the market and lure distinguished academics away from other law schools by offering them larger salaries and fringe benefits. A small amount of this kind of thing can happen at lower levels of the academic profession (a lecturer can be tempted by an offer of a senior lectureship, perhaps), but this system rules out 'shopping round' for senior and established scholars with national or international reputations. Among other results, this lack of competetive salary differentiation makes it very difficult for any one institution in England to establish the kind of academic prestige and pre-eminence that the handful of really top law schools have established in

America. On the other hand, it means that scholarly merit is more evenly distributed in England.

Some of these factors also go far to explain why, by comparison with America, English legal academics are still generally held in relatively little esteem among the practising profession, though there have always been exceptions to this generalization. The judges and the bar are socially and professionally so far above the academic lawyer that the opinions of a law professor count for little in English legal circles. Hence, academic writings are little cited and little read by practising lawyers and judges, and academics who do want to be accepted as part of the legal 'establishment' have to accept the conventions of the bar and the bench, for example, by writing works which are strongly black-letter in their orientation.

We now need to enter two caveats. First, the English academic legal profession is today changing fast. For some years there have been signs of vigorous growth of interest in theory, in interdisciplinary work, in critical analysis of how the law actually works (law in action, not just law in books), in law reform, and in law as an instrument of 'social engineering'. But at the same time, the black-letter tradition is still strong and has many adherents. Moreover, even among the younger and more critical elements in the academic profession, the positivist tradition survives, at least in the sense that law reformers and critics nearly all work with the Benthamite methodology; that is, they seek to distinguish sharply between what the law is and what it ought to be. They regard it as preferable first to analyse what the law is, and then to argue for change. In this way, they are of course implicitly adopting the positivist tradition and methodology, even if they are unaware of the fact, but they may only be doing so because they find it the most effective way of proceeding, given that the country's legal and political institutions are so wedded to this theory and methodology.

Academics are also playing a more significant role in policy formulation, for example on the Law Commission and other law reform agencies and committees of inquiry and the like. Many contemporary law teachers are highly contextual in their approach, stress the purposes of law, insist on the values implicit in law and in legal choices and decisions, and are often very critical of judicial decisions.[4] Judges too are beginning to pay more attention to academic legal writings, and more of those now on the bench have been to law schools. There has also been a significant increase in the number of English legal periodicals devoted to academic discussion of the law, and this has been matched by an

---

[4] John Bell, *Policy Arguments in Judicial Decisions* (Clarendon Press, Oxford, 1983) is a recent notable example.

improvement in the quality of much that is published. It is possible that England is slowly moving in the American direction, but it is still a long way from reaching the same position.[5]

Our second caveat concerns American law schools. We must stress that not all American law schools are like the ones we portray in this chapter. As with so much else in America, the best is as good as, (and in this instance many would say, much better than) anything comparable in England, or perhaps indeed the world. The top ten or twenty American law schools are institutions of real excellence in teaching and research. But not all law schools in America are like this. There is still a large number of law schools of lesser quality which have no pretensions as scholarly institutions.[6] In between these schools and the top ten or twenty, there are scores of middle-of-the-road law schools, which in many respects are likely to resemble English law schools. In these schools (many of which will be oriented towards the law of the state in which they are located, and will draw their students largely from the one state) law is likely to be taught in a more black-letter style, the academics will range from the competent to the dead-wood, the facilities and salaries will be much less dramatic than in the top schools, and the autonomy of the law school may be subject to severe constraints both from university authorities and from their alumni. The local judges and Bar Associations will often have their own ideas of what legal education ought to be about, and what a law school ought to be doing—and may try to impose their ideas on these local law schools as well.

These caveats need to be borne in mind throughout this chapter; but we shall all the same say little further about them. In both cases what dictates our approach is the desire to assess the general impact of law schools on the character of the legal system as a whole. It is the leading American law schools which are important for this purpose; and it is the traditional system of English legal education, even if now passing away, which is likewise important in understanding the contemporary English legal scene.

3. AMERICAN AND ENGLISH LEGAL EDUCATION

The leading American law schools have been highly influential institutions, setting the tone for other law schools (except for a few vocationally

---

[5] Perhaps nothing illustrates the gulf which still separates English and American law schools more than the way in which England's premier law journal, *The Law Quarterly Review*, has been taken over by the practising profession, being edited from 'chambers' in London by a Circuit judge. We doubt if anything short of a constitutional amendment could shift the control of the *Harvard Law Review* to a Wall Street firm of attorneys!

[6] See Stevens, *supra*, n. 2, at 243 estimating that there may have been as many as 20,000 students in 'unaccredited' schools in 1979.

oriented ones) and having also a major impact on the nation's entire legal (and hence also constitutional and political) system. These leading law schools are 'national' in the sense that they draw their students from all over the country and have faculties who teach a kind of national law and do much research with national implications. Among the best known are Berkeley, Chicago, Columbia, Cornell, Duke, Harvard, Michigan, New York University, Northwestern, Pennsylvania, Stanford, Virginia, and Yale.[7]

Students enter American law schools after four years of college, and attend for three more years. These are thus graduate-level institutions, unlike English law schools. Many of the courses studied by American law students bear the same titles as those taken by English law students. But here similarity ends, especially if we compare the leading American law schools of the past fifty years with English law schools up to about twenty years ago. Education in these American law schools differs dramatically in purpose, subject matter, teaching materials, and teaching methods. Here we will focus mainly on differences of relevance to our general theme—the relatively substantive nature of the American system as compared with the relatively formal character of the English.

The leading American law schools perceive and are generally thought to carry out their teaching objectives in remarkably similar fashion;[8] indeed, they have often been criticized for being too homogeneous.[9] The essence of these objectives is well captured in an essay, written in 1961, by Professor David F. Cavers, of Harvard, and we quote now a fairly lengthy extract from this essay:[10]

[T]he case method of law teaching [is] the distinctive feature of American legal education. The case method was first developed by a New York lawyer who was appointed Dean of the Harvard Law School in 1870 and who bore the improbable name of Christopher Columbus Langdell. Dean Langdell rebelled against the doctrinaire lecturing which was typical of the law schools of that day. He insisted that the decisions of the courts were the true materials of legal science in a common-law system. Accordingly, he decided to focus legal instruction upon judicial opinions. For his course in the law of contracts, he brought together in one volume a selection of leading opinions of English and American courts in contracts cases, presenting these in a logical sequence that was to be followed in the classroom. Thus was born the first casebook.

[7] Harvard has been the most influential of all. See Stevens, *supra*, n. 2, at chs. 3 and 4; see also A. E. Sutherland, *The Law at Harvard* (Belknap Press, Cambridge, 1967).

[8] We express this proposition cautiously because the extent to which a uniform style of teaching exists in American law schools today is not documented. We rely on personal impressions and experience of many law schools.

[9] See Stevens, *supra*, n. 2, at ch. 13.

[10] 'Legal Education in the United States', in *Talks on American Law*, 273–75 (rev. ed., H. Berman, ed., Vintage Books, NY, 1971).

By 1900, after years of steady growth, despite much debate, the tested merits of the case method had persuaded all the major schools in the United States to adopt it. Casebooks had been compiled in all the main fields of law study, even those in which statutory law predominated. Today the case method, enriched and diversified in many ways, is used in law schools throughout the country.

In case-method instruction, the law teacher seldom delivers formal lectures, even though he may have 150 or 200 students in his class. Instead, by asking probing questions and by posing a succession of problems, he directs his students in a close analysis of the judicial opinions assigned for the day's class. The teacher tries to stimulate a lively discussion among the students. The student taking part in this must have a firm grasp of each case and not only know the court's reasoning but be prepared to criticize it. He cannot accept the court's decision as necessarily authoritative, for the very next case he reads may be drawn from the law reports of another state which takes a squarely contrary position. Or the student may find himself comparing the different solutions which two state legislatures have found for the same problem. He must grow adept in analyzing, comparing, evaluating, and projecting the lines of judicial decisions and legislation which have been developed in those fifty social laboratories, the states.

Out of this study—which is essentially comparative in character—the student can scarcely gain a precise knowledge of a single body of legal doctrine, except perhaps in some fields of federal law. He does learn the main rules and principles that the courts have been developing, but more valuable than this knowledge is the insight he gains into the way legal problems arise and the processes by which lawyers and courts and legislatures have been seeking to solve them. As his study continues, he learns to think like a lawyer, as we law teachers like to say. He learns how to work with legal source materials, constantly to relate legal doctrines to concrete facts and facts in turn to doctrine, to look beneath the doctrines to underlying issues of social policy or practical administration. As each of his courses has progressed, he has had to review the cases analysed in class and his notes of each day's discussion. From these materials, he endeavors to construct, for his own guidance, an orderly statement of the legal rules and principles in the course's field. The result may not be a very learned summary of law, but it is his own, the product of hard, independent thought. From the experience of making it, he has learned more than his professor could have taught him.

The young men who emerge from this process are usually tough-minded, skeptical, pragmatic and resourceful. They have come, even as law students, to see law as an instrument which is constantly reshaping the American society and economy. Since American judges, in writing opinions, tend to discuss the political, economic and social policies that bear upon their decisions, students who have made these opinions a principal basis of their work for three years naturally tend to think of the significance of particular legal rules and decisions in terms of policies. Without often having become interested in the formal systems of legal philosophy, most law students have, consciously or unconsciously, absorbed the basic ideas of sociological jurisprudence championed throughout his long career by Dean Roscoe Pound, for many years head of the law faculty at Harvard.

Many of the central objectives of American legal education are explicit or implicit in this passage.[11] These objectives in turn are profoundly substantive in character. Thus the primary aim is not to teach formal black-letter rules, nor to teach *the law* of the land (which would be impossible in a national law school anyhow because the law varies from state to state). Rather the primary aim is to teach the student a methodology—how to construct, analyse, compare, evaluate, and criticize arguments and decisions (including rules), and to 'project' lines of judicial decisions and legislation. In this way the instructor implicitly inculcates faith in the power of substantive reasoning, in policy arguments, rather than in the mere arbitrium of formal rules. Law is not seen as a body of authoritative doctrine, so much as an 'instrument of political, economic and social policy'.

Thus the American system of instruction is designed to be normative as well as positive, to treat the law as it 'ought to be', as well as the law that 'is'—indeed, to avoid insisting on too sharp a line between them. So also, its purpose is to develop the evaluative and critical powers of students as well as their ability to grasp existing law. And in teaching students how to grasp existing law, American instructors (unlike many of their English counterparts until quite recently) stress the necessity of going behind black-letter rules to 'the underlying issues of social policy and practical administration'. The American approach stresses active 'problem-solving' rather than mere passive absorption of doctrine. In the course of this, insights into how problems arise and into the legal processes by which they are resolved receive as much emphasis as the content of particular solutions. It is also recognized that the 'is' of the law is not infrequently in the process of becoming something different from what it has been, even perhaps becoming what it 'ought to be'.[12] As a result it is important for students to learn, as they do in America, how to 'project' the 'lines of judicial decision and legislation which have been developed' up to now, as Professor Cavers puts it. Thus recent decisions are not necessarily mere pieces to be fitted into the existing system. They may also be events in a developing process.

The substantive orientation of the American law school is perhaps best conveyed by considering how the students are expected to prepare for class. The students know that they must come to class ready to state the

---

[11] For an extensive listing of objectives, at a lower level of detail, see Summers, 'The Future of Economics in Legal Education: Limits and Constraints', 33 *J. Leg. Ed.* 337, 355–8 (1983).

[12] For an influential statement, see Lon L. Fuller, *The Law in Quest of Itself* (Northwestern U. Press, 1940).

reasons given by a court for its decision. They must also have an opinion as to whether the decision is right, and be ready to offer some reasons with which to defend that view. The instructor will frequently challenge the student to weigh and balance conflicting reasons, and will seek to sharpen student sensitivity to the justificatory resources available in the facts of a case and the decisional context. This does not mean that all matters are open to question. It does mean that at least the intermediate premises of the question at hand are always on trial, as it were, open to challenge and demanding justification.

The subject matter of American legal education, especially after the great instrumentalist revolution in the first half of the twentieth century, also contrasts markedly with the relatively narrow and formal conception of that subject matter which has traditionally held sway in England.[13] For one thing, the diversity of American jurisdictions introduces the necessity for a comparative method in the study of law. Unlike members of English law faculties who operate within the confines of a unitary jurisdiction with a tight hierarchical command structure, in which the law is laid down from above, members of America's elite law schools operate in a system in which there may be many different rules dealing with the same problem—different solutions arrived at by different states, or different appeals courts in the federal system. Accordingly, American law professors often teach more than one 'solution' to a problem. As Professor Cavers noted, the student, in this system of legal education, 'cannot accept the court's decision as necessarily authoritative, for the very next case he reads may be drawn from the law reports of another state which takes a squarely contrary position'. In such an educational milieu, the justificatory force of supporting substantive reasoning, not the authoritativeness of formal reasoning, becomes the primary focus.

A second basic difference of subject matter relevant to our theme is partly traceable to another factor. Today, in the American law school classroom, students regularly study law, in Professor Cavers's phrase, as an instrument of 'political, economic and social policies'. This kind of multidisciplinary approach is still much less common in England, for the simple reason that law is an undergraduate subject in English universities. In America, many students at law school have already acquired some understanding of political theory, economics, and social and political philosophy.

---

[13] On this subject matter in America, see generally, Stevens, *supra*, n. 2, at chs. 3, 12, and 14. On the subject matter of English law degrees in 1966, see Wilson, *supra*, n. 1, at 41–7, and for the position in 1975, by which time there had been some introduction of new subjects, see Wilson and Marsh, *supra*, n. 1, at 278–84. The list of subjects at 280–1 still looks narrow compared with the offerings in leading American law schools.

In still another (also related) way, the subject matter of legal instruction in the leading American law schools is wider and less formal than most of the standard fare of English law courses. Law is not taught as an abstraction from the historical and social forces that shaped it. Legal doctrine is not presented as if it were a wholly autonomous body of knowledge, independent of its social, political, and economic background. In the above cited passage, Professor Cavers referred to ideas of 'sociological jurisprudence' widely accepted in America. These ideas are an important factor here, for they are not at all congenial to a view of law as a self-contained system divorced from the conflicting interests that shape it.

Professor Cavers also refers, in the passage quoted above, to the standard teaching materials as 'casebooks'. Actually, this is a misnomer. Teaching materials consist largely of appellate judicial opinions from different jurisdictions but since the 1930s they have also included other important materials.[14] These may consist of notes on political, social, and economic considerations relevant to the cases; notes providing historical background, commercial context, or the like; extracts from law review articles criticizing the cases or providing insights into the processes by which the cases arose; excerpts from briefs or oral argument or the trial record; hypothetical problems calling for the student to *use* statutes or cases already in the book for solutions; special sequences of cases revealing some trend in the law, and more. The instructor can utilize this sort of material to stimulate lively discussions on the substantive issues arising from the cases.

Further, as Professor Cavers also points out in the above passage, the judicial opinions which the American student is expected to read and discuss will themselves often include substantive reasoning. The casebook selections will usually include a high proportion of path-breaking decisions and borderline cases where nearly everything turns on the force of substantive reasons. Occasionally the focus may be on formal reasons—on the reasons that arise under a statute or a precedent, though it may well be that formal reasoning tends not to gets its due in American legal education. But that only confirms our thesis that legal education, like much else in the American legal scene, is highly substantive and sometimes even 'substantivistic'. Formal reasoning tends to get brushed aside, and instead the classroom focus tends to be redirected to the substantive reasons underlying the rules or principles from which the formal reason emerges, to whether those substantive reasons really apply to the case at hand, to whether they would apply to some hypothetical

---

[14] See generally, Currie, 'The Materials of Law Study, Parts I and II', 3 *J. Leg. Ed.* 331 (1951) and Part III, 8 *J. Leg. Ed.* 1 (1955).

variant of the facts of that case, and ultimately, to whether the rule or principle is itself substantively sound. At least this is often so in common law subjects.

By contrast with all this, the standard teaching tool in most English law school classrooms remains the textbook, which frequently consists largely of page after page of black-letter legal rules with examples usually based on the cases.[15] The pattern of the English student textbook is now well established though there is of course much variation in style and in emphasis, as well as in quality. In the standard textbook, the law is stated in a series of semi-authoritative pronouncements, for which some authoritative source is given. From time to time, the author may pause to criticise, analyse, explain more fully, or sketch out some problem relating to policies or values not fully discussed in the sources. But in most textbooks these discussions are relatively brief, and sometimes rather tendentious. Textbook writers' analysis of policy issues are often rather facile, amounting sometimes to little more than jejune statements about what seems 'fair' (often without the slightest hint of complicating factors such as, in some tort cases, the way in which insurance makes examination of 'fairness' very difficult, if not of doubtful relevance anyhow).

The tone of textbooks is often dogmatic, with decisions presented as if they were strict deductions from basic principles. The conceptual framework and classificatory apparatus of the law also tend to be taken for granted. In stating the law, every effort is made to keep the law that 'is' sharply differentiated from law that 'ought to be'. Concessions are rarely made to the possibility that the law might be in a continuous process of change, becoming different tomorrow from what it was yesterday, closer perhaps to what it 'ought to be'. The ultimate and all-pervasive aim is to lay out the law as it stood on the day the book went to press. Indeed, authors of such textbooks often seem oblivious to the value judgments they are themselves subscribing to when they demarcate an area and call it an existing 'subject', or the value judgments they subscribe to when they adopt one conceptual framework rather than another. For example, the modern English law of torts still suffers from the fact that early writers on torts thought that what was important about tort law was the kind of conduct which was alleged against the defendant, and that what was unimportant was the kind of injury or loss of which the plaintiff was complaining.[16] Thus early textbooks drew no distinctions between personal injury and property damage, for instance,

---

[15] For a critique of English textbooks, see Twining, 'Is Your Textbook Really Necessary?' XI *Journal of the SPTL* 81 (1970).

[16] See Atiyah, 'The Legacy of Holmes through English Eyes', 63 *BUL Rev.* 341 at 350 (1983).

in the context of negligence actions; and made no mention at all of the possibility of the plaintiff complaining of pure economic loss. One possible result of this was that the law relating to personal injury and the law relating to property damage developed along almost identical lines although there were arguably very important policy distinctions to be drawn between them. It matters not whether this suggestion is right or wrong. Our point is that the textbook genre of legal literature has a strong positivist tendency to treat law as something existing, as something *laid down* by authoritative sources, and to conceal the choices being made in the very process of selecting some parts of it as suitable for treatment together in a particular shape. This tendency is then reinforced by the whole style in which textbooks come to be written.

In fairness to English textbook writers, we must point out how the textbook is related to other aspects of the English legal scene which we have already discussed. Textbooks assume that the law is largely a matter of logical deduction from basic principles, because judges and barristers speak as though it is; and the tendency of judges and barristers to treat it as such is reinforced by the literature from which they were educated. Policy issues are rarely discussed at any depth in textbooks because they are rarely canvassed by counsel or referred to in judicial opinions; thus the textbook writers are mirroring the way in which the law appears to work in courts and elsewhere in England. In performing this exercise, many textbooks do a very good job, nonetheless valuable for being a very formal exercise. Indeed, American lawyers are mistaken if they think that such textbooks are necessarily a poor form of legal literature on the ground that they do not accurately reflect the way the law works. Of course they do not accurately reflect the very substantive way in which American law works, but the better English textbooks do reflect the formal way in which much English law works.

However, this does not affect the point we are making here—that English legal education is highly formal partly as a result of the style of English legal textbooks. The great majority of English law students are still expected to buy at least one standard textbook for each course, and to use that textbook as a constant aid and companion and reference book. They may (and the better students certainly will) read other source material—cases, articles, and statutory provisions—but the textbook is the staple diet for most students, supplemented of course by lecture notes. A three-year diet of legal textbooks is apt to confirm most students in their initial belief that law is fundamentally a system of rules, and that they have come to law school to learn as many of those rules as they can remember.

This is not to say that the casebook is unknown to English legal education, nor that the texbook is unknown in American legal education.

Some English law faculties are making increasing use of casebooks, and American students are sometimes assigned textbooks (called 'hornbooks' in America) as optional course reading, though this is rare at the leading law schools. But in any event (apart from the surprising fact that few students make much use of hornbooks) the hornbook differs in subtle ways from the English textbook. It tends to be more comparative in approach, less dogmatic in tone. For every major problem, a variety of solutions is often offered: some are in favour in one group of states, some in another; or some may have been followed at one period, while others have been more fashionable at a later time. These contrasting answers to a problem are weighed and evaluated in the best hornbooks to a much greater degree than is usually done by an English textbook. The contrast between American and English student books is also to be found with practitioners' works. The large scale treatises, like Corbin on Contract, Wigmore on Evidence, or Harper, James, and Gray on the Law of Torts, have no real parallel in England at all: they devote far more attention to discussion of theory, principles, and policies, and less to expounding the rules of law, than English practitioners' works.

Once again, it is important to keep things in perspective. We are here generalizing in rather sweeping fashion, and we are not citing evidence for our generalizations. To cite evidence would require a detailed and minute comparison of the styles of particular English textbooks and American hornbooks; for most readers this would be tedious and unprofitable. We are therefore relying on impressionistic evidence, and in any event we need to qualify the general picture we have painted. Obviously, the style and quality of textbooks vary a great deal in both countries; equally obviously neither country has a single monolithic type of legal textbook or hornbook. In recent years legal literature in England has diversified in several different directions (for example with the *Law in Context* series), and today there may well be a richer variety of legal texts, treatises, and the like available in England than in America (whose tradition is surprisingly poor in this regard).

The differences in legal literature are reflected in different teaching methods in the two systems of legal education. Though again things are changing in England, the dominant method of instruction in most law faculties is the didactic lecture,[17] supplemented by tutorials in which problems and questions are discussed in smaller groups.[18] Of course, lectures do not necessarily deal with the law in a formal or formalistic manner. They can be used to treat the law and its ingredients in a substantive and critical fashion, but the traditional English law school

---

[17] See Wilson and Marsh, *supra*, n. 1, at 284–5.
[18] *Ibid.*, at 285–6.

lecture has generally been devoted to black-letter doctrinal teaching of a kind likely to reinforce the formal vision of law in many if not all of its facets.

In American law schools, the point of view that an instructor posits in a Socratically run class is frequently that of a judge in a state without any authoritative decision on the point at issue. It has been suggested by former Dean Griswold that in the long run this may also play its part in the creation of an activist judiciary.[19] Similarly, the late Professor Goodhart suggested that the American student is taught to regard every judicial opinion 'with suspicion', and that this approach necessarily weakens his devotion to the doctrine of *stare decisis*, whereas the English law student is taught to accept the doctrine in a case as 'laying down the law'.[20] Once again, we must beware of overstating the case. There are no doubt many American law schools where law is taught in a much more mechanical way as something to be memorized in order to pass examinations. Conversely, many English law school teachers would today vigorously deny that English legal education consists of requiring students to memorize cases, or accept what they decide uncritically, as the law 'laid down'. Indeed, it may even be wondered if the critical approach to judicial decisions has not gone somewhat too far, in that it often seems to be thought adequate criticism of a case to say that the result 'seems unfair'. Perhaps the real difference today between much of the better quality legal education in both countries, and much of the less good, is not that criticism is not encouraged in the latter, but that too much slapdash criticism is encouraged, and that this often lacks any real intellectual rigour behind it. All the same, it remains, we think, true that the average English law student is expected to learn more *actual law*, and that he does approach it in a different spirit from his American counterpart; although he may be prepared to criticize *the law*, and indeed may do so too freely, he tends to accept the existing legal concepts as a pretty powerful and unyielding framework; and even when he criticizes the law, he follows the solid Benthamite tradition of distinguishing sharply between the law as it is, and the law as (he claims) it ought to be.

There is another respect in which American teaching fits more easily with a tradition in which judges play an activist role. Many casebooks today include chapters or sections which follow a chronological

---

[19] *Law and Lawyers in the United States*, at 62–3 (Hamlyn Lectures, Stevens, London, 1964).

[20] A. L. Goodhart, *Essays in Jurisprudence and the Common Law*, 70–1 (Cambridge U. Press, Cambridge, 1931); accord, Catlett, 'The Development of the Doctrine of Stare Decisis and the Extent to Which it Should be Applied', 21 *Wash. L. Rev.* 158, 169–70 (1946).

arrangement, treating the growth and development (and sometimes decline) of legal doctrines.[21] A sequence of such cases emphasizes law as a changing dynamic force, and the reader naturally sees the last case as a springboard for further development. The temptation to extrapolate from a line of cases is almost irresistible. But the ordinary text-book—certainly the modern English textbook—treats cases as atemporal phenomena for the most part. The cases form a pattern, a mosaic, and no sense is conveyed of law evolving as a dynamic institution, as a chronological line of cases extending into the future. The reader is invited to find the answer to a new case in the existing mosaic, rather than to think of pushing on from the last case. In this respect, English textbooks mirror the ostensible approach of English courts, but they may fail to reveal new trends.

In sum, the tradition in American legal education has been far more substantive in its orientation than in English legal education, and although there are signs of change in England, they have so far affected academic research and some (non-textbook) forms of writing more than they have affected legal education, still less the national legal culture.

4. THE POLICY ROLE OF LAW PROFESSORS

Research and writing are, of course, central activities in both English and American law schools. But the kind of research done by law professors in the two countries has for many years been somewhat different. In England the tradition, until quite recently, has been in the direction of doctrinal or black-letter research and writing—the analysis and restatement of 'existing' legal doctrine. Of course there has always been, in addition, a strong 'cultural' component to law school activities in England—the study of legal history, of Roman law, of legal theory, and so on. But insofar as actual English law was concerned, the emphasis has been on law 'as laid down', either in legislative or judicial form. Changes here, as elsewhere, are afoot today. For example, empirical research has become an important feature of the work of many English academics,[22] and there have been some major research projects in the field of accident

---

[21] In his review of Langdell's *Cases on the Law of Contract* in 5 *Am. L. Rev.* 539 (1871) Holmes commented on the chronological arrangement as 'most instructive and interesting'. Of course Langdell did not see his casebook as an exercise in realism, or as a handbook for the judicial activist (indeed, his title page refers to his book as 'Prepared for use as a text-book') but the very form of some casebooks seems to have forwarded understanding of the nature of the creative judicial role.

[22] For discussion of major changes of late, see Harris, 'The Development of Socio-Legal Studies in the United Kingdom', 3 *Legal Studies* 315 (1983).

compensation,[23] the criminal justice system,[24] and family law.[25] Many of these studies have been linked with a concern for the reform of the law, and, so far as concerns the criminal justice system, many of them have actually been funded by the central government. But here too the separation of law and policy has been generally kept firmly in view. The research projects are carefully structured to be as neutral as possible, and the results may be drawn on to support or refute the desirability for a proposed reform.

Legal research and writing in America have for many years reflected a broader vision of the academic lawyer's role and, in particular, of his role as something of a public policy expert. Of course a certain amount of traditional doctrinal writing takes place in America, though little of it is to be found in the leading American law schools. It is unlikely that there will be many examples of new multi-volume treatises (such as Williston and Corbin on Contract, or Scott on Trusts, or Wigmore on Evidence), even though these works remain of great value and continue to be edited. Significant empirical research has been and is now being done at a number of leading law schools.[26] The main object of most such research is some kind of reform, but this is not invariably so. Sometimes the main object is simply to deepen our understanding of the actual effects of a doctrine, or the roles of legal personnel, or the internal workings of a process, or the like. Some of this research is carried out today by interdisciplinary teams, in which sociologists, psychologists, and economists may join with law professors. This kind of research is sometimes even backed by huge financial resources of a kind which would make the English professor's mouth water. Its sponsors often include government agencies, federal and state, private foundations, the American Bar Asociation, and others, but most such research continues to be done at the leading law schools.

Even where American legal research lacks this empirical dimension, it is often far broader in its orientation than much English research. Because law is so central to the whole political system in America, and because courts are often engaged in policy analysis on a large-scale, many American law professors have become specialists in the policies of a given field, and do not confine themselves to law in any narrow or technical sense. For example, there are American law professors who are

[23] See the work of the Oxford Socio-Legal Centre published in Donald Harris and others, *Compensation and Support for Illness and Injury* (Clarendon Press, Oxford, 1984).

[24] See especially the work of M. Zander some of which is summarized in 'Promoting Change in the Legal System', 42 *Mod. L. Rev.* 489 (1979).

[25] See for a sample, J. Eekelaar and E. Clive, *Custody after Divorce* (SSRC Centre of Socio-Legal Studies, 1977).

[26] For a concise account of what has been done and a call for more, see Trubek, 'A Strategy for Legal Studies: Getting Bok to Work', 33 *J. Leg. Ed.* 586 (1983).

specialists in medical health care delivery policy, in nuclear energy policy, in environmental policy issues, and scores of other similar subjects, none of which would generally be regarded as appropriate subjects for specialization by English law professors. In England the division of labour between lawyers and policy makers (reflecting, of course, the formal vision of law itself) is much more clearly delineated and respected, not only as between courts and the executive and legislative branches of government, but also as between law professors and policy formulators in the government bureaucracy. Law in America thus becomes almost synonymous with public policy in general; or at least it embraces issues of economic and social policy, of public and social administration, and law professors play a significant role, in their research and writing, in helping to formulate policy. To some degree they simply duplicate work that may be done in public services, but offering alternative analyses and proposals to those which emanate from these bureaucracies. But to some extent the academics engage in public policy formulation in areas which are neglected by the public service bureaucracies, either because these are matters of state responsibility and are neglected by many state bureaucracies, or because they cut across traditional classifications and are just not well done by established bureaucracies.

The policy making role of law professors, as we have noted already, has to be more substantive in character than the policy making role of civil servants operating in a bureaucratic hierarchy. The policy formulations of a hierarchical body acquire a certain force from the authoritative position of the senior members of the hierarchy. But the policy formulations of law professors have to compete in the market-place of ideas and have no authoritative status or rank at all. Unless they are perceived to be substantively better than the formulations which emerge from bureaucratic hierarchies, they will not have any influence; and as between themselves, of course, they must also compete on their substantive merits. An additional relevant factor here, which is also part of the action and reaction process, is that the quality of the law professors in top American law schools is probably significantly better than the quality of American public officials, even at the federal level, and certainly at the state level. Thus few American executives or legislators would start from the basic assumption that policy formulated by their public officials is likely to be sounder than alternative formulations emanating from serious law professors. In England, the reverse is true. The quality of the public service is very high, and governments and Parliament are likely to assume that policy advice from civil servants is generally better thought out than similar ideas from academics. Thus the advice ministers receive from their civil servants has a quasi-authoritative status which is unlikely to be overturned, save in quite exceptional circumstances, as a result of the substantive policy arguments emanating from some law professor.

The policy activities of American law professors take many forms apart from the mere matter of research and writing. They are, for instance, often called on by eminent firms of lawyers to write (or review) briefs in important cases, and occasionally even to argue especially significant cases in the highest courts. For example, in the famous Pentagon papers case before the Supreme Court of the United States,[27] Professor Alexander Bickel of Yale was arrayed in oral argument against Professor Emeritus Erwin Griswold of Harvard. Law professors also frequently take leave to do government work. A large segment of the Harvard Law Faculty left Cambridge for several years to serve in the Kennedy administration.[28] (A similar exodus of academics from Oxford occurred in 1964 to serve Mr Wilson's new Labour government, but these were all economists and not lawyers.) Two high posts in the federal government, that of Solicitor-General and the headship of the Anti-trust division of the Department of Justice, regularly go to law professors. At least three of the last six in each office have been law professors.[29] At one point a few years ago, one fifth of the rather small Cornell Law School faculty held major federal government posts.[30]

American law professors also have much greater opportunities to influence the development of the law through institutions such as the American Law Institute which is responsible for the various Restatements. Similarly, many of the most striking legislative reforms and developments in private law in recent decades have largely been the responsibility of law professors, for example, the Uniform Commercial Code, statutory schemes of no-fault insurance, and the new federal Bankruptcy Code. It is only very recently that English law professors have been drawn into roles of this kind through the work of the Law Commission, and even then their role is far more limited.

As we have noted earlier, American law professors also contribute in major ways to the law laid down by courts, and to legislation. So far as the courts are concerned, this influence is partly indirect, stemming from the writings of law professors which influence judges, although it hardly captures the American position to call this an 'indirect' influence. A

---

[27] *New York Times Co.* v. *United States*, 403 US 713 (1971).

[28] Giving rise to Dean Griswold's remark: 'Old Deans never die, they just lose their faculties.'

[29] In fact four of the last six Solicitors-General have been former law professors.

[30] See Moffatt, 'Cornell Law Faculty in Washington', *Cornell Law Forum*, Feb. 1977, 26.

striking and far from isolated illustration of the extraordinary impact
which academic ideas have on the daily administration of the law can be
found in the way in which in the 1970s and 1980s American state courts
across the country accepted the arguments of a junior law professor (at a
lesser known law school) for allowing punitive damages more generously
in products liability cases.[31] Since then such damage awards (for good or
ill) have become almost routine, with very dramatic results. Indeed,
almost the whole of the modern law of strict products liability in tort has
originated with academic writings.[32]

American law professors also have an indirect influence on the courts
through their clerks but they have often a more direct influence simply
because nowadays so many law professors have been appointed to the
bench. Professors may also be called on to give seminars for judges in
continuing education programmes at annual judicial conferences and the
like. One of the present authors, for instance, has participated in more
than a dozen such programmes. As regards the research and writing
activities of professors, we have also seen how demonstrated expertise
often leads to professors being called upon for advice and assistance by
state legislators for the preparation of state legislation, or to give
evidence before legislative committees, and the like.

In addition, almost every law school has its own law journal. Students
staff these journals and decide and carry out major research projects,
often with advice from professors who may have a special reform
agenda.[33] Since it is the better students who obtain these coveted
positions on their journal's editorial boards, and it is often these very
same students who proceed to work as judges' clerks for a year or two
after leaving law school, this itself carries a virtually direct channel of
communication from the law schools into the judicial process—especially if it is true (as has been suggested[34]) that many judicial opinions in
appellate courts are now drafted in the first instance by law clerks, fresh
out of law school.

English legal academics have far fewer avenues through which they
can make their views felt, either in the bureaucracy, or in executive,

[31] See Owen, 'Punitive Damages in Products Liability Litigation', 74 *Mich. L. Rev.* 1257
(1976), an article said to have been cited within a few years in at least 20 jurisdictions:
Fischer v. *Johns-Manville Corp.* 193 NJ Super. 113, 121–2, 472 A. 2d 577, 582 (1984).
[32] See Priest, 'The Invention of Enterprise Liability: A Critical History of the Intellectual
Foundations of Modern Tort Law', XIV *J. Leg. St.* 461 (1985). Although the California
Supreme Court under Traynor CJ gave the lead here, their mentor was Professor W. L.
Prosser, and anyhow Traynor himself was a former law professor.
[33] See Cramton, 'The Most Remarkable Institution: The American Law Review', 36 *J.
Leg. Ed.* 1 (1986).
[34] R. Posner, *The Federal Courts: Crisis and Reform*, 104 ff. (Harvard U. Press,
Cambridge, 1985).

legislative, or judicial centres.[35] In the nature of the case, a more formal system of law seems to have less scope for the influence of the academic lawyer. Unless the law professor acquires a semi-authoritative status (as in Roman law, and modern civil law systems descended from Roman law) he cannot hope to make his voice heard very effectively. He lacks the authoritative status which in a formal system is required to give his voice any weight, and he can therefore only address himself to substantive arguments which are not very influential outside the legislative process. English academic writings are rarely cited to the courts, and carry little weight where they are cited. Not very long ago it was regarded as improper to cite the writings of living authors to the courts at all, and though that tradition has certainly been abandoned, it remains true that judges do not accord a great deal of weight to academic writings.[36] And the English law professor has little opportunity to influence the legislative process either: for (as we have seen) that process is dominated by the executive, and the executive gets its advice from the bureaucracy and not from academics. These considerations help to explain why English law professors do not indulge in public policy activities to the same extent that Americans do, and why their research has tended to be more formal and doctrinal in nature. But here again, changes do appear to be occurring. English legal academics are now playing a prominent role on the Law Commission, a statutory law reform agency which has had a fairly significant impact during the past twenty years,[37] and, as we have mentioned, the nature of legal research and writing in England has recently broadened out considerably.

5. THE OVERALL INFLUENCE OF LAW SCHOOLS

The leading American law schools have had a great influence on the American legal order, though no doubt the kind of institution the leading law school has become has itself been partly determined by the American legal order. By comparison, English law schools have a negligible

---

[35] Pollock seems to have been the first English academic to appreciate this, see 39 *Law Q. Rev.* 163, 164 (1923) (review of book by Pound). English academics have more access to policy making by the political parties, but the parties also maintain their own centralized research departments.

[36] But see the handsome compliments paid to the academic profession by Lord Goff (himself a former academic) in 'The Search for Principle', LXIX *Proc. Brit. Acad.* 169 (1983).

[37] For some account of this law reform work by two academics recently returned to the academy, see Cretney, 'The Politics of Law Reform: A View from the Inside', 48 *Mod. L. Rev.* 493 (1985), and North, 'Law Reform, Processes and Problems', 101 *Law Q. Rev.* 338 (1985). But Cretney argues for a limited role for lawyers in law reform, on the very ground that the ultimate issues are ones of policy on which politicians (and less justifiably, civil servants) are entitled to the last word.

influence on the English legal order, except in quite marginal and technical ways. In this section we shall concentrate on how the leading American law schools have been, and continue to be, major sources of basic ideas and bodies of knowledge that shape the legal system.[38]

First of all, as is indeed to be expected, American law schools have been the source of the dominant general theory of law in America. We discussed that theory in chapter 9, where we called it 'instrumentalism' because it conceives of law essentially as a pragmatic instrument of social improvement. Instrumentalism was born in the leading law schools (even if its birth was itself influenced by the conditions of American law), and the second named author has written elsewhere about the substantive influence of instrumentalist legal theory on American law.[39] There can be no doubt that this theory has had and continues to have profound influence. It was Holmes who pointed out that theory itself is the most important part of the law, and that powerful theoretical forces can be seen at work behind the most detailed legal rules.[40]

When we turn to England, the scene is very different. The dominant general theory of law in the last two centuries, Austinian analytical positivism, does not owe what influence it has had on bench and bar to the fact that it originated in a course of lectures first given at University College, London. Nor does it owe its influence on the bench and the profession to the fact that it has been taught in the twentieth century to students taking jurisprudence courses in the universities. Until quite recently, the majority of judges did not even study law at university, and many nineteenth and twentieth-century judges probably never read Austin's *Province of Jurisprudence Determined*. We believe that Austinian positivism owes its influence rather to the fact that it was itself an expression of ideas about law already highly congenial to the bench and the profession. The idea that valid law is something originally laid down by the legislature and the courts, that this law consists essentially of rules, that a sharp line can and should be drawn between the law as it is and the law as it ought to be, and that the courts have little or no power to alter the law (a view, incidentally that Austin did not fully subscribe to) are all ideas that were already highly congenial to English judges and lawyers in the nineteenth century, and they continue to be so to this day. Thus the Austinian theory of law is more in the nature of a reflection

---

[38] See, for example, W. Chase, *The American Law School and the Rise of Administrative Government* (U. of Wisconsin Press, Madison, 1982) (discussing such influence in one major context and offering critical reflections.)

[39] See Summers, *Instrumentalism and American Legal Theory* (Cornell U. Press, Ithaca, 1982), and see also *supra*, ch. 9.

[40] 'The Path of the Law', 10 *Harv. L. Rev.* 457 (1897).

than a shaping influence; though doubtless it has played some role in reinforcing ideas already held. So although we do not doubt that in both countries the dominant legal theories have been both a cause of, and a result of, conditions in the legal systems of those countries, we think that in England the primary causal influence was from the legal order to legal theory, whereas in America it was clearly the other way about.

The leading American law schools have also served as a major source—nay, *the* major source—of influential ideas about appropriate legal method. It was the instrumentalist legal theorists who led the way here too.[41] They overthrew a formalistic legal method, characterized by a drily logical mode of legal reasoning unduly concerned with the law's internal symmetry and largely indifferent to its social effects. By mid-century, the instrumentalists had virtually revolutionized the American approach to law. The leadership here came almost entirely from the universities, and the extent of their influence can hardly be denied. American bench and bar no longer believe that the only kind of reason or argument appropriate in a court of law is one that appeals to existing legal authority, that is, a purely formal reason. It is widely recognized that a variety of social forces exert pressure on American judges to be creative, and even to change existing case-law. In turn it is widely understood that substantive reasons are often relevant. Lawyers also know that to do their jobs well they cannot confine themselves in a formal fashion merely to the law in books. They must also be mindful of how the law in action may diverge from the law in books. Bench and bar alike are mistrustful of high level generality in the formulation of legal rules. They prefer narrow, fact-oriented categories which take account of substantively significant distinctions. They are also mindful not only of what judges say they are doing, but of what they actually decide. All these and other methodological changes have been so fully accepted by bench and bar in America that they are now commonplace. Yet it was not always so, and it seems virtually certain that the American legal scene would be very different from what it is today if the leading law schools had not revolutionized American ideas of appropriate legal method.

As part and parcel of the general methodological transformation in America, the leading law schools also generated a body of normative ideas about the appropriate collaborative roles of courts, legislatures, and administrative agencies in the making and administration of law.[42] This body of ideas has enormous importance, extending even to

---

[41] See Summers, *supra*, n. 39, at ch. 6.
[42] Particularly influential has been the looseleaf work of H. M. Hart and A. L. Sacks, *The Legal Process* (unpublished teaching materials 1958) (broadly arguing that the differing roles of different branches of the government are based on ideas of institutional competence derived from differing procedures and different forms of decision making).

providing some theoretical underpinning or justification for the basic American constitutional arrangements under which separation-of-powers doctrine continues to be entrenched. While these ideas thus are in a sense part of political theory, they are also highly pragmatic and instrumental, and have had considerable influence on the way in which courts and legislatures see their functions.

It is only necessary to add that the English judiciary and legal profession have not been similarly affected in matters of method by ideas emanating from the English law schools. These law schools have not generated a body of methodological ideas comparable to those developed in American law schools during the first half of this century. Perhaps there was less scope for such a development in the first place. But even had this occurred, we can be fairly confident that the ideas would have been influential only so far as congenial to the ethos already prevailing among English lawyers. Nor have English academic lawyers had much influence on political theory in recent years.

If we now try to summarise the role of law schools in America, it may help to see the law schools as one of the institutional forces which compete for influence on the legal order as a whole. These include, in particular, the judiciary, the legal profession, the legislative and executive branches of government, and the leading law schools. Now it seems that there is in America today a kind of positive interaction between the law schools and these other institutional forces, which produces a sort of multiplier effect, enhancing the influence of the law schools several times over. For example, when courts follow the views of leading academic writers, as they often do, this in turn elevates the role of the writer in question. In turn, his work is then taken even more seriously by the practising side of the profession, and is cited still more often in legal briefs, with the result that it is relied upon yet more often in appellate opinions. This kind of positive interaction operates too with other institutions in the legal order so that, for instance, a legislature in one state may enact legislation, borrowing from the ideas of a law professor, and this may encourage other legislatures to follow suit, which in turn may enhance the prestige of the professor and thus encourage judges to follow his views without waiting perhaps for legislative sanction. And so on. Then, too, as we have seen, the diversity and geographical spread of the American judiciary and profession means that there is no common legal culture across the country centred in these institutions. If there is such a common culture at all in America, it is centred in the leading law schools which are more homogeneous institutions, and peopled by more homogeneous members, than the judiciary or the practising profession.

In England, on the other hand, we perceive a relatively neutral, or perhaps even negative, interaction between the law schools on the one hand and the judiciary and legal profession on the other. For example, policy issues otherwise of interest to academics are rarely discussed in any depth in textbooks because they are rarely canvassed by counsel or referred to in judicial opinions. The refusal of English courts to take academic writings seriously has sometimes held up the development of a whole academic subject, as for instance happened with the law of restitution.[43] This seems to us to occur in part because there is in England a common legal culture which does not really include the law schools at all. That culture is, of course, centred in the Inns of Court and the Law Courts in London where the judiciary, the bar, and much of the rest of the profession are centred. It is easier for a culture that thus excludes academics to develop where most academics have not themselves practised law, and are viewed as outsiders, both geographically and intellectually. Furthermore, English academics to some degree acknowledge the superiority of the legal profession and the judges, and concede their right to be the central forces in shaping the legal culture. For example, English law schools do not pretend to train their students so as to fit them for practice, so that the professions are obliged to provide a year of post-university education. So also, English academics have abandoned certain subjects entirely to the professions. Thus there is very little (if any) law school teaching of such subjects as legal ethics and civil procedure, and not much more of tax law. American academics concede no exclusive turf to practitioners or to the judiciary, and such subjects as civil procedure and tax are law school courses which are not only taught, but are also the focus of academic writings. Thus English law schools are the least important of the major legal institutions competing to influence the legal order as a whole; whereas in America, the leading law schools are the most important.

---

[43] See Jackson, 'The Scope of the Term Contract', 53 *Law Q. Rev.* 525 (1937); P. S. Atiyah, *The Rise and Fall of Freedom of Contract*, 480–3 (Clarendon Press, Oxford, 1979).

15

Concluding Remarks

1. SUMMARY

Our primary thesis has been that the English and the American legal systems, for all their surface similarities, differ profoundly. The English system is highly formal, and the American highly substantive. In attempting to substantiate this primary thesis, we have offered an elaborate conceptual scheme which explains in detail what we mean by 'formal' and 'substantive'. Whatever validity our primary thesis may eventually be found to possess, we think that the conceptual apparatus we have introduced has independent value. Our differentiation of the basic types of formal attributes of legal reasoning should be of use in analysing the degree of formality of legal reasoning in particular instances, and in a legal system as a whole. The apparatus is sufficiently flexible to accommodate the very great complexity of legal reasoning. At the same time, we believe that the varied formal–substantive contrasts sharpen awareness of the diversity of substantive reasoning and the many ways in such reasoning can enter into, or affect, formal reasoning. Similarly, the concepts of truth formality, enforcement formality, and rule of law formality seem to us to have some value, independently of the primary thesis of this book. These too can be deployed, not only in the analysis of particular legal systems, but also in comparing such systems with one another.

We do not claim finality for the particular attributes or concepts we have introduced to characterize formality in legal reasoning, though we do think that the relative formality of legal systems is an important characteristic of such systems as a whole, and our scheme of analysis at least offers one way of treating that characteristic.

Earlier attempts to understand the formality of legal reasoning, though we have found them helpful and suggestive,[1] have tended to concentrate on only one aspect of legal formality—what we have called mandatory formality—and have also tended to see that attribute as an 'on–off' matter. That is, they have tended to see it as either applicable—thus excluding some substantive reasons from consideration altogether—or as inapplicable—thus leaving substantive reasons to have their full weight. We have characterized this feature of legal reasoning as merely

---

[1] See citations in n. 3 to ch. 1, *supra*, p. 2.

408

one of the four key formal attributes, rather than as a single dominant attribute. We have also sought to distinguish between prima-facie mandatory formality and ultimate mandatory formality. In these and other ways, we have thus presented it as a matter of degree, often reducing the weight of substantive reasons, rather than as excluding them altogether.

In demonstrating the validity of our main thesis, we have marshalled evidence in chapters 2 through 7 to show how legal reasoning in many different contexts—whether in dealing with rules generally, or with statutes or with case-law—tends to be more formal in England. We emphasize, once again, that the mere existence of greater formality in the English system does not, in our view, necessarily make that system better or worse as a legal system. It does make make that system significantly different from the American.

We have shown, in detail, how English legal reasoning generally displays much greater formality than American. The authoritativeness of law in English legal reasoning is more formal, for English law very largely derives its validity from merely source-oriented standards, rather than having also to satisfy content-oriented standards. So, too, in the English legal system conflicts between two species of otherwise valid law are generally resolved by formal rules of hierarchical priority, rather than by reference to substantive considerations arising at the point of conflict. At the same time, English legal reasoning generally exhibits higher levels of what we have called content formality than American legal reasoning. Thus the English system relies more heavily on genuine rules, particularly statutory rules, with consequent high levels of over- and under-inclusion. English case-law is likewise applied in light of strict notions of the *ratio decidendi*, whereas in America, it is commonly applied in the light of the substantive reasons on which the precedent is based. Similarly, statutes tend to be interpreted in England in accord with literal or plain meanings of the words used, whereas in America judges much more readily consider the purposes and rationales behind the words, and even consult their own political morality in the process. Thus English legal reasoning reflects higher levels of interpretive formality. The mandatory formality of most English legal reasoning is higher, too, for it more often overrides, excludes, or assigns lower weight to countervailing substantive reasons arising at the point of application. This goes in hand with a rather narrow law-making role for the courts in England, as compared with the much larger law-making role in America.

We have also identified a number of important ways in which the law in books more often translates into the law in action in England. In our view, this occurs mainly because English fact-finding processes are more truth-oriented (higher truth formality) and also because the law tends to be more strictly enforced, both in and out of court (higher enforcement formality). At the same time, we believe that generally the law is more certain, more predictable, and more even-handedly applied in England. Hence that system exhibits more 'rule of law' formality also.

Of course no legal system can be viable without incorporating or otherwise relying upon substantive reasoning, and England is no exception. At the same time, the American system must and does rely significantly on formal legal reasoning. But the mix of the formal and the substantive in the two systems is very different.

It has been a secondary thesis—a holistic corollary of the first thesis—that each of the two systems is strikingly coherent in its tendency to be more or less formal, more or less substantive. Although there are some counter-examples in some fields, by and large we are convinced that each of these two legal systems is all of a piece in a very large number of respects. First, English legal reasoning and the English legal system are relatively formal in all relevant dimensions. In America, although there is a greater diversity, legal reasoning is also *relatively* substantive in all dimensions. Beyond this, the relatively formal nature of legal reasoning in England correlates with a large number of institutional, historical, and cultural factors there, and the relatively substantive character of legal reasoning in America correlates with a similarly wide range of factors in that country. Moreover, as we have shown in detail in chapters 8 through 14, all these factors in each country tend to fit together with the dominant traditions in legal theory in each country. These traditions differ profoundly, England having been dominated by positivism, a theory that tends to be highly formal, and America having been much influenced by natural law and, latterly, by instrumentalist theories which are much more substantive.

Finally, we have introduced the idea of a relatively coherent general vision of law—a set of ideas about the nature of law and its place in society, as the public and perhaps also judges, lawyers, and politicians might visualize it. In our view, as we will explain in the next section, the English people incline to a more formal vision of law than the American people. In this basic respect, too, the systems are all of a piece.

We reiterate that we do not believe simple linear causal explanations exist between the styles of legal reasoning and the other factors we have identified as correlating with it. We do not think, for example, that such simple causal relationships exist between the levels of formality in each dimension of legal reasoning, nor between these levels of formality and institutional factors, nor between legal theory and institutional practice. Rather our secondary thesis is that the pieces in each system fit together, like the pieces of a mosaic, in determining the degree of formality of the English and American legal systems. How courts reason, how judges are appointed, their homogeneity, their degree of political involvement, their relationship to legislatures and the practising profession, the way legislatures and executives function, the way statutes are drafted, and so on—all these, and numerous other factors, tend to fit together. These factors mutually reinforce each other, so that, in the end, it becomes impossible to trace simple linear causal relationships. This does not mean, however, that such causal relationships do not exist.

2. TWO VISIONS OF LAW

In chapter 1 we introduced the concept of a 'vision' of law, and we have utilized this concept from time to time throughout, but we have yet to provide a more systematic account. This task has been postponed until now because the idea of a vision is synoptic in character, and is therefore best understood at the end, with the whole of our analysis and its subject matter in view.[2]

We define a vision of law as a set of inarticulate and perhaps even unconscious beliefs held by the general public at large and, to some extent, also by politicians, judges, and legal practitioners, as to the nature and functions of law—how and by whom it should be made, interpreted, applied, and enforced. Of course, insofar as we have thus defined a vision as a set of beliefs held by many professional lawyers as well as by the general public, it is clear that we are proceeding at a fairly high level of abstraction. Plainly, the views of professional lawyers and judges about the law are bound to be more soundly based and more sophisticated than the views of the general public. So there can never be a complete congruence between the two. But both such sets of views can be, we suggest, relatively formal or relatively substantive.

Some scepticism may be felt, especially in England, that the public at large hold any such beliefs.[3] In the American context, with its less technical and more substantive inclinations, the idea is certainly more credible. It is also somewhat easier in America to postulate a relatively close connection between the law and public visions of law. But even in England, we believe that the legal system as a whole, with its highly formal tendencies, does in fact correlate rather closely with general

---

[2] The concept of a general vision of law, formal or substantive, is little discused in legal literature. For a bare beginning, see R. Summers, 'Working Conceptions of the Law', in *Law, Morality and Rights*, 25–8 (M. Stewart, ed., D. Reidel Publishing, Dordrecht, 1983), and also in 1 *Law and Philosophy* 285–8 (1982).

[3] See C. K. Allen, *Law in the Making*, 93–111 (7th edn., Clarendon Press, Oxford, 1964). But these doubts may themselves reflect the more formal, positivist theories which have always been more prevalent in England, where (as we have seen) the idea that law is 'technical' and has no necessary connection with justice is very deep-rooted.

public perceptions of what law is about. This can be seen from casual commentary, the media, periodical writing and reporting, and the like.

In the daily life of a society, it is not possible to maintain a firm line between evidence of a 'vision' of law and evidence of an explicit theory of the nature or uses of law. Members of the public in England and America regularly express general views about law, views ranging from the highly formal to the highly substantive. No doubt people express such views even in societies in which legal theorists have never existed, or have had virtually no influence. But when elements of a general theory of law become firmly embedded in the legal culture and in the content and workings of the law in a particular society, so that they become part of the general stock of ideas, much political and legal discourse will be cast in the language of that theory. For example, anyone acquainted with the English legal system will know that English lawyers 'talk positivism' even when they are being at their most pragmatic and disclaiming all interest in legal theory. Much lay discourse is also of this genre, and can (we think) be taken as an expression of a formal vision of law, a vision which would very likely be held even if legal theorists had never existed in England. Conversely, American legal and political discourse tends to be cast in different terms—though less uniformly. Thus much of it is cast in terms of reason or rational goals or rights or the like. We think that this discourse also frequently expresses a substantive vision of law, a vision that might exist even if there had never been any legal theorists in America.

We shall now go on to set out, in rather schematic fashion, two *models* of the contrasting visions of law. We believe (although it is difficult to substantiate this belief) that at least the more articulate and legally conscious members of the public hold some version of one or other of these visions. We also think—as is indeed evident from our holistic thesis—that the legal theories which are dominant in England and America correlate with these contrasting visions of law, so that there is a fit between the views of the professionals and the lay public in both countries, even though the former obviously have a more sophisticated understanding than the general public of their own legal system.

(1) In a formal vision, virtually all standards for the identification of valid law are conceived of as source-oriented, so that the substantive content of the law is thought to be almost entirely irrelevant to its validity. This conception may come to be so strongly held that it dominates understanding of the very *nature* of law, an understanding in which law is the formal *act* (enactment) of an authority on high. In a substantive vision, on the other hand, people think of the legal system as recognizing, in addition to source-oriented standards of validity, many

content-oriented standards, requiring, in effect, that for law to be valid, it must also conform in some degree to common notions of what is substantively right, just, or good. Moreover, it is thought incumbent on the judges to recognize general moral principles that 'float' throughout the legal system, and which can be invoked as substantive reasons, along with standards of validity and the law so identified, to influence the outcome of many particular cases.

(2) In a formal vision, conflicts between otherwise valid laws are thought to be resolved by reference to rules of hierarchical priority that leave little scope for the play of substantive considerations. In a substantive vision, such conflicts are expected to be resolved by a process of analysis that takes account not only of rules of hierarchical priority, but, in addition, of moral, policy-oriented, and other substantive considerations—which may or may not be very closely implicated in the rules of priority themselves.

(3) In a formal vision, the forms of law are very largely conceived of as determinate hard and fast mandatory rules, with a consequent high order of over-inclusion and under-inclusion. In a more substantive vision, the forms of valid law are believed to consist primarily of flexible legal rules granting discretion or incorporating general clauses and the like, or as broad legal principles, and thus as forms of law inviting major infusions of moral, policy-oriented, or other substantive reasoning at the point of application.

(4) In a formal vision, legislatures are assumed to enact precise, clear, and comprehensive statutory rules, and it is believed that most law consists of statute law. In a more substantive vision, legislatures are thought to adopt very broad statutes which confer upon courts power to develop the law in particular cases, in light of the substantive considerations arising in the circumstances.

(5) In a formal vision, the function of the courts in dealing with statute law is seen as one of interpreting and applying statutory law relatively literally, and with little scope for expanding or developing principles of law out of the raw material supplied by the statutes. In a more substantive vision, courts are expected to interpret and apply all statutes, including narrowly and tightly drafted statutes, not literally, but in light of their actual or rationally attributable purposes—which implicate substantive considerations.

(6) In a formal vision courts are expected to interpret precedents strictly, and largely without reference to underlying moral, policy-oriented, or other substantive reasons. In a more substantive vision, courts are expected to interpret a precedent not strictly, but liberally, in light of the facts and the substantive reasons on which the precedent is based.

(7) In a formal vision, the precedents of higher courts are believed to create 'binding' law, binding even on those courts. In a more substantive vision, precedents of courts are understood merely as prima-facie guides to the law, and are expected to be disregarded or overruled if they seem wrong or unjust or bad or obsolete.

(8) In a formal vision, the almost exclusive task of the courts is conceived to be that of applying pre-existing statutory, judge-made, and other valid law to resolve particular disputes, a task which is to be carried out even in the face of competing substantive considerations arising in the circumstances, and which might otherwise outweigh the substantive considerations embodied in the formal law. The function of appeal courts is perceived as that of merely correcting errors in the rulings of lower courts. In a more substantive vision, the primary task of the highest courts, and a major task of other appellate courts, is to examine and improve upon the substantive quality of the law involved in the appeal.

(9) In a formal vision, it is expected that the courts will rarely make new law or reform old law, and thus seldom directly invoke substantive considerations; instead they will leave the making of new law to the legislature. In a more substantive vision, the courts make new law when needed, and readily reform existing law. They defer to the legislature only when the proposed reform is beyond the implementive powers of courts.

(10) In a formal vision, legislation and legislative rules are conceived of as the paradigmatic form of law. Hence most important law is thought to be legislative in form, and the legislature (or legislatures) is expected to reform existing law readily; in a more substantive vision, reasoned judicial decisions (relying on reasons of substance) are the paradigmatic form of law, and the legislature is expected to leave more to the courts, either by not legislating or by legislating in broad terms.

(11) In a formal vision, when factual disputes arise and the courts are called upon to resolve them, it is taken for granted that generally they will correctly ascertain the true facts and then apply the formal law, with the result that the law in books will translate into effective action. In a more substantive vision, it is assumed that the legal system allows courts in effect to evade the formal application of the law where it is believed that its application to the true facts would produce bad or unjust results, so that law in action frequently diverges from law in books.

(12) In a formal vision, it is believed that out-of-court uses of law, including private settlements, should and do approximate closely to the results which would be achieved if cases were fully tried to judgment. In a more substantive vision, out-of-court settlements are expected to diverge from the formal legal rules more widely, partly because the law

will often be less clear, and partly because such applications of law will reflect the input of non-rule justice into trials which occurs in a more substantive vision.

(13) In a formal vision, the law is thought of as imposing a relatively categorical duty on citizens to obey the criminal and other regulatory law, and levels of voluntary compliance tend to be high. Similarly high levels of compliance with duties imposed by the civil law (for example, the payment of debts) are expected, and citizens are generally expected also to comply voluntarily with legal requirements even where sanctions are not threatened. If levels of compliance are low in some areas of the legal system (which may happen) this is felt to be unsatisfactory, and it is expected that steps will be taken to ensure higher levels of compliance, either by stricter enforcement of the law or, sometimes, by moderating the law's demands so that compliance is more likely to be achieved. In a more substantive vision, the law is expected to allow a wide range of defences to criminal charges, including even collateral nullifying doctrines such as 'entrapment', 'discriminatory prosecution', perhaps even 'civil disobedience', and so on. Levels of voluntary compliance tend to be lower, and relatively lower levels of compliance are more likely to be tolerated and found acceptable. The same is true with regard to the civil law.

(14) In a formal vision, 'rule of law' values are stressed and highly respected, for example, the reduction of law to prospective general rules, clarity, certainty, predictability, equality before the law, and provision of a fair opportunity to obey. These values not only inform the content of many forms of law, but also generate 'floating' reasons of great weight which judges and officials invoke to justify their actions as necessary. In a more substantive vision, it is acknowledged that there will often have to be sacrifices of these 'rule of law' values in the pursuit of justice in the individual case.

The above contrasting models of differing visions of law may be viewed as polar opposites. As we have already said, it seems to us clear that the English vision of law tends to the formal side, while the American tends to the substantive, even though we do not here attempt to substantiate this with any specific evidence. We believe that this is, therefore, another major respect in which the two systems are all of a piece. Moreover, we can also see how the public vision in each system fits into that system's mosaic, though we would not claim that each public vision is in itself entirely coherent.

3. UNIVERSAL JURISPRUDENCE?

Most philosophers and legal theorists have assumed that there is one universal subject matter of legal theory, which is itself to be abstracted from the variant phenomena of law in all societies, past, present, and future. The English positivist John Austin, for instance, conceived of a science of 'General Jurisprudence' the object of which was to lay bare the essential nature of law in all societies.[4] And in our own day, the debates between positivists such as Hart and Raz, or 'natural law' theorists like John Finnis[5] and Charles Fried,[6] or (if he can be classed with them for this purpose) Ronald Dworkin,[7] have frequently proceeded as though it were possible to provide universal answers to fundamental questions about the 'true' nature of law, or the 'proper role' of the judges, or the 'correct' approach to statutory interpretation usually without due regard to the general contexts and problems of particular legal systems.[8]

It now seems to us that legal theorists would do well to approach many of the standard questions of jurisprudence at a lower level of abstraction, a level that at least takes account of *basic* variations in the phenomena of law from system to system—such as variations in the nature of valid law, in the role of judges, and in the methods of statutory interpretation (to cite just a few examples). We believe that the answers to most such questions will depend in major part upon the degree to which a given legal system is (appropriately) more formal or (appropriately) more substantive, matters that cannot be ascertained in the abstract. We do not deny that it may be possible, at some high level of generality, to identify a set of features that the phenomena of law in all societies have in common, features that may be said to be essential to the *very concept of law itself.* Nor do we deny that more specific types of legal phenomena, such as valid laws, legislatures, courts, precedents, and the like, may exist in all modern societies, and may thus be viewed as instantiations of very general concepts of such phenomena. It is plain that in both England and America people use the *concept* of law, the *concept* of legislation, the *concept* of a judge, and the *concept* of precedent. But—to borrow a distinction first used by W. B. Gallie,[9] and subsequently by John Rawls[10]

---

[4] See Austin, 'The Uses of the Study of Jurisprudence', in John Austin, *The Province of Jurisprudence Determined*, 365–93 (Library of Ideas, H. L. A. Hart, ed., Weidenfeld & Nicolson, 1955).

[5] See John Finnis, *Natural Law and Natural Rights* (Clarendon Press, Oxford, 1980).

[6] See, e.g., Charles Fried, *Right and Wrong* (Harvard U. Press, Cambridge, Mass. and London, 1978).

[7] See Ronald Dworkin, *Taking Rights Seriously* (revised impression, Harvard U. Press, Cambridge, and Duckworth, London, 1978); *Law's Empire* (Harvard U. Press, Cambridge, Mass. and London, and Fontana Press, 1986).

[8] Or even with sole regard to the English and American legal systems, as if generalities based on these two systems could be universally applied.

[9] See Gallie, 'Essentially Contested Concepts', 56 *Proc. of the Arist. Soc.* 167 (1955–6).

[10] *A Theory of Justice*, 5 (Belknap Press, Cambridge, Mass., 1971).

and Ronald Dworkin[11]—it seems to us evident (and we have surely demonstrated) that, at an intermediate and at a still lower level of generality, these phenomena do differ, even in basic ways. Accordingly, the appropriate *conceptions* of these phenomena also vary. And surely the primary task of the theorist here must be to devise conceptions and terminology which can be used to represent *these phenomena* faithfully.

Take, for a start, the very nature of law itself. Certainly England and America, and indeed all modern societies, recognise and use some *concept* of law. Yet the attributes of law in the English and American legal systems differ in basic respects, as we have tried to demonstrate, and these two legal systems therefore embrace very different *conceptions* of law. In the English conception, formal attributes, particularly the authoritative *source* of putative laws, are the dominant, indeed, the overwhelming, factor in identifying law, and hence in understanding what law (in this basic respect) actually *is*. But the America conception, as we have attempted to demonstrate, is different. Laws in America often have to satisfy content-oriented criteria of validity as well as source-oriented standards. For example (as we have demonstrated), both countries recognise the *concept* of binding precedent, but their *conceptions* of precedent are very different, and these differences are rooted in the phenomena. The English conception is more formal: precedents bind because of their source, because they are decisions of higher courts, irrespective of their content. In America the authority of precedents is less exclusively source-oriented. Precedents tend to bind because the principles they embody are widely thought to be right and good, and if they are not right and good, they are less likely to be treated as binding. Thus, in this basic respect, among others, the very nature of law in America is different from what it is in England.

As we have already said, we do not deny that it may be possible to devise theories at a sufficiently high level of abstraction to accommodate all the variations between the differing conceptions of law used in particular legal systems. But it seems to us much more promising for the theorist to work at the level of conceptions as well as the level of

---

[11] In *Law's Empire*, at 139 and elsewhere, Dworkin uses this distinction in a similar way, even though he uses the term 'a conception of law' in a much wider sense than we do here to mean 'a general, abstract interpretation of legal practice as whole'. In this sense Dworkin's use of the term 'conception' is closer to our idea of a 'vision' of law. Dworkin does here distinguish three different 'conceptions' of law, the conventional, the pragmatic, and the model of integrity, and the first two bear a passing resemblance to the English and the American visions of law, as we identify them. But he rejects both, to adopt the 'integrity' version, partly on the ground that it fits Anglo-American practice better than either of the others. He draws no distinction between the two countries, simply taking it for granted that they both have the same 'conception' of law.

concepts, and this requires a degree of understanding of the nature of valid law in a particular society or societies. Also, a comparative method, such as we have used, seems to us to have the great virtue of bringing out variations in the conceptions of law, so as to enhance understanding of the nature of law itself. The comparativist will argue, and we think rightly, that an observer cannot understand his own legal system sufficiently until he understands what his system is *not*. Without comparing it to a relevantly different system, he simply cannot adequately grasp what his own system is not. The relative formality of the English system is best grasped, not in isolation, but by way of contrast, in the relevant respects, with the much more substantive character of the American system, and of course vice versa.

In our view, then, the primary subject matter of jurisprudence is not a single universal subject matter, abstracted from the variant phenomena of law in all societies. It should, rather, consist of the relevant features of the phenomena of law in one or more particular societies.

But it is not only the very nature of law itself which differs in such fundamental ways in different societies. Many specific types of legal phenomena may differ in similarly fundamental ways. We have, for instance, already suggested that the conception of a rule is different in the two countries.[12] We believe most American lawyers tend to think of a case-law rule as in some sense and to some degree incorporating its underlying reasons, so that it tends to be a mere guide to decision making, a kind of approximation of the sum of the underlying reasons. In England, on the other hand, a much sharper line prevails between the reasons for a rule and the rule itself. A rule is thought to operate largely independently of the reasons for it, except in borderline cases where the rule may be ambiguous or unclear. The American conception is thus more substantive, the English more formal. Of course, as we have already demonstrated, neither country does or probably could adhere exclusively to one or other polarity here. Here again, therefore, although both legal systems recognise and make extensive use of the *concept* of a rule, their dominant *conceptions* differ. Any attempt to analyse *the concept* of a rule in abstract, without reference to the context of the legal system in question, necessarily neglects the possibility of such vital differences.

Precisely the same argument can be made with regard to statutes. Both countries recognise the *concept* of legislation, but their *conceptions* of this kind of law are very different. And surely this is entirely appropriate. Legislation drafted in the English style and passed by a British

---

[12] See *supra*, p. 88.

Parliament is very different from legislation drafted as many American statutes are drafted and enacted by procedures such as often prevail in American legislatures. The English conception also reflects the English belief that interpretation should follow traditional English literal methods. Given this basic conception of the nature and purposes of a statute, the very words of the legislation are all important to the draftsman, to Parliament, and to the interpreters. By contrast, much (we do not say all) American legislation is adopted in the form of general principles—general guidelines to the courts—in which the precise wording is less important to the draftsman, the legislature, and the interpreters. The substance, the underlying reasons, are more important. Hence the American conception of legislation is different, and appropriately so.

There is thus a sense in which this work may be seen as advocating a kind of 'jurisprudential relativism', an insistence that legal phenomena cannot be understood, and ought not to be studied, apart from the context in which they operate. Of course, to some, 'jurisprudential relativism' may seem like a first cousin of moral or ethical relativism of one sort or another. And for that reason, critics of moral relativism may feel inclined to dismiss the implications of our findings for the same reasons they reject moral relativism itself. After all, the mere fact that we have (perhaps) explained why legal positivism has flourished in English soil while natural law theory has found a more congenial home in America may be thought to say nothing about the *truth* of these theories. But in this respect we cannot accept the equation of legal theory and moral theory. If legal theory is to answer questions about the nature of law, and the role of judges, and methods of statutory interpretation or common law development, it must, at the end of the day (indeed, perhaps at the beginning of the day), keep its feet firmly planted on the ground. Law *is* inescapably a social artefact with immense practical importance and pervasive *factual* manifestations. Jurisprudential relativism cannot be refuted as some may feel that moral relativism can be refuted by claiming that moral codes and beliefs which actually exist among human beings are no evidence of their *truth*. Legal theories must take account of actual legal phenomena as we know them, if they are to have adequate descriptive power. If we find that some legal theories more accurately represent features of some legal systems, and other legal theories better fit other systems, then the prima-facie conclusion must surely be that the search for universal legal theories about the very *nature* of law and other legal phenomena is of rather limited utility.

We have so far said little of normative analysis in legal theory. The task of the theorist is not, of course, confined to devising concepts and terminology to clarify and advance our understanding. The theorist is also concerned with issues of evaluation and reform as well. But we suggest that universalism is hazardous here too. It is no doubt possible to confine one's attention to an idealized Utopia, and try to discuss what the role of law, judges, and legislators ought to be in such a state. But the moment any practical policy recommendations are to be drawn from such theorizing, it becomes imperative to recall that (short anyhow of total revolutions) such Utopias have to be created step by step; and that what may be an ideal role for law or judges or legislators in a Utopia where all the functions of all the other officials are likewise ideally defined, may be an utterly unacceptable role in a particular legal system whose other political institutions remain the result of history, tradition, or culture. So it is no use recommending that judges ought to behave in such-and-such a way because, ideally, this is how judges ought to behave, if those responsible for appointing judges habitually appoint people who do not want to behave in those ways, or if legislatures persist in behaving in ways which make it impossible for judges to behave as ideally they should. What is the practical utility of a theory which postulates how Hercules J. ought to behave on the bench, if appointing authorities insist on nominating judges who do not even want to emulate Hercules?

4. EVALUATION AND CRITICISM

For the most part in this book we have refrained from criticism and evaluation. The main burden of our book is to try to advance understanding, not to offer suggestions for improvement, nor even to evaluate particular features of the legal systems we have been studying. Yet we claim to have offered some clarification that may facilitate critical analysis. For instance, we have stressed that formal reasoning is not, *per se*, bad, and we have insisted on the importance of distinguishing beween the formal and the formalistic in legal reasoning. We have sought to provide an analysis of formalistic reasoning as consisting of various degenerate species of formal reasoning, and we have suggested that 'substantivistic' reasoning can be analysed in the same way. In these ways we hope we have clarified the general vocabulary for criticism of the law.

We now proceed to offer some tentative comments of an evaluative and critical nature on the English and the American systems. This is not the place for a comprehensive critique of either system, and we offer our criticisms largely to demonstrate the value of our conceptual apparatus in providing focal points for evaluation. We also add that some of our evaluations may not be of much use for practical reformers, because we appreciate that some of the features of these two systems which we think are open to criticism may not be readily reformable. They may simply reflect the price of the benefits which these two systems confer on their people, so they cannot be easily reformed without imperilling those very benefits. This does not mean that evaluation is pointless. We may be prepared to pay the price of the benefits which a system confers upon us, but it is desirable to know what the price is.

We begin with some criticism—perhaps 'anxieties' would better express our views—of the English formal vision of law. For two hundred years one of the most dominant tenets in English positivist thought about law has been the separation of law and morals, the insistence that actual, positive law is not necessarily morally good law, and this tenet seems to us to have become a firm feature of the English vision of law. From Bentham to Hart English positivists have argued that the mere fact that something is law does not say anything about its moral worth. Their position has been justified, not merely in terms of logical and descriptive accuracy, but also in terms of various tendencies which they have claimed for their theoretical positions. Thus positivists claim not only that they describe law more accurately in separating law and morals, but also that this leads to a healthier critical attitude towards the law. If it is thought that laws in some sense carry with them some moral justification of their own, just by virtue of being laws, then morally bad laws may come to have a degree of public support which they do not deserve. On the other hand, once it is conceded that laws are not necessarily morally good, the public can approach laws in a more critical frame of mind. Although both Bentham and Hart argued that laws should anyhow prima facie be obeyed except in extreme cases, they insisted that there is nothing sacred about law, and that all laws should be regarded as open to justified moral criticism. The motto ought to be, as Bentham declared, 'obey punctually' but 'censure freely'.[13]

Whatever the merits of English positivist theory may be as regards its logical soundness and descriptive accuracy, it seems to us that these arguments—about the probability of a healthy public attitude to law flowing from positivist ideas—are open to doubts on purely empirical grounds.[14] And given that leading positivists like Bentham and Hart have claimed that their theories are likely to have these beneficial tendencies, it is hardly open to positivists to object if their theories are criticised on the very ground that their effects may be harmful, rather than beneficial. For our part, although we would not attribute major causal importance to pure legal *theory*, we do think that constant

---

[13] Hart, 'Positivism and the Separation of Law and Morals', 71 *Harv. L. Rev.* 593, 597 (1958); compare Fuller, 'Positivism and Fidelity to Law: A Reply to Professor Hart', 71 *Harv L. Rev.* 630 (1958).

[14] See Deryck Beyleveld and Roger Brownsword, 'The Practical Difference between Natural-Law Theory and Legal Positivism', 5 *Ox. J. Leg. St.* 1 (1985).

reiteration of the simple and unqualified message—'What the law is, is one thing; what it ought to be, is quite another'—has helped to foster a general *vision* of law in England which is highly formal, as we argued in the last section. One consequence of this vision is that law comes to be seen essentially as a kind of formal husk, with only technical content.[15] Roscoe Pound (who certainly did not hold such a formal view himself) once described a formal conception of this kind in these terms:[16]

One need but look at a mass of legal precepts that make up the bulk of legal systems today in order to see that they are anything but authoritative promulgations of ethical custom. For the most part they represent juristic or judicial search for a rule that will follow logically from the traditional legal materials, or for a rule that may be said to have authority behind it. They are technical workings over of the traditional precepts, or technical adaptations of authoritative extra-legal propositions. They are the technical scientific custom of the courts and lawyers.

On such an extreme view, formal law and substantive reasons, which includes moral reasons, are simply considered to be more or less different things. Specific rules of law are essentially technical and amoral. In our terms, they have high content formality.

Now it seems to us to be essentially an empirical question whether the tendency of positivist theory in this respect is to encourage a healthy public attitude to law or, perhaps, the very reverse. And we believe there is some evidence that the consequences are far from always being beneficial, though we do not say that such results are inevitable. For instance, it is no uncommon thing in England, after a major legal case of high public importance has been decided, for the politicians, the public, and the media to approach the issue as though the substantive issues were to be decided completely anew. It is thus widely assumed that the decisions of the courts are almost entirely concerned with technical, formal law, and that substantive reasons play almost no part in such decisions.[17] Yet this is often a gross caricature of the legal process,

---

[15] It is true that many American legal theorists also espoused this positivist tenet, yet the American vision of law is highly substantive. See R. S. Summers, *Instrumentalism and American Legal Theory*, ch. 7 (Cornell U. Press, Ithaca, 1982). We have explained this apparent paradox, *supra*, p. 256.

[16] R. Pound, *Law and Morals*, 122–3 (U. North Carolina Press, Chapel Hill, 1924). See for a rather similar view, Simpson, 'The Common Law and Legal Theory', 77 in *Oxford Essays in Jurisprudence* (Second series, A. W. B. Simpson, ed., Clarendon Press, Oxford, 1973).

[17] This was very much the reaction of the public and the media to the House of Lords' decision in *Gillick* v. *West Norfolk etc. Area Health Authority* [1985] 3 WLR 830 (holding that doctors can lawfully prescribe contraceptives in certain circumstances to girls under 16 without parental consent).

because even in England, it is rare that cases before the House of Lords can be disposed of without reference to substantive reasons at all.

A related, though alternative, posture is to assume that, insofar as judicial decisions do involve reasons of substance, the views of the judges are entitled to no more weight than those of anyone else. For instance, decisions of the European Court of Human Rights under the Strasbourg Convention often lack moral support in England, because they are easily dismissed as merely the 'opinions' of judges (and foreign judges at that) which are assumed either to involve purely matters of technical, formal law, or alternatively to involve decisions of substance which are more appropriate for legislatures than courts. This is also a part of the English vision of law, as it seems to us, but this too fails to understand the appropriate place of substantive reasoning in the law. In particular, it fails to give adequate weight to the value of decisions reached after due process, in a calm adjudicative atmosphere in which judges at least try to set aside prejudice and passion and preconceived ideas. Thus when such cases reach the forum of public opinion it is often found that the substantive reasons canvassed before the courts—and sometimes convincingly relied upon, or refuted—surface again in far less sophisticated shape, and may even lead to legislation overturning the decisions of the courts.[18]

Another unhappy consequence of this high formal vision of law is that law may become less useful in guiding or reinforcing social morality in the first place. If (for instance) Parliament wishes to use legislation to eliminate all forms of racial and sexual discrimination at a time when public opinion does not wholly support such measures, it may become difficult to persuade the public that such anti-discrimination laws are based on any moral substantive reasons, rather than merely on their technical legal authoritativeness.

Of course, there is a self-fulfilling aspect to the teachings of positivism in these respects. If judges and legal practitioners adopt the legal positivist's sharp logical separation of law and morals, then they will naturally tend to think that the only job of the courts is to follow the technical, formal law, and to leave moral and other substantive issues entirely to the legislature. The more that they pursue this course, the more may the law they apply indeed become amoral, if not downright immoral. Thus even existing moral principles, already embedded in the law, may not be expanded or used to reform and improve the law,[19] but

---

[18] Of course Britain cannot reverse decisions of the European Court by legislation, but this process is not uncommon with national legislation. One example is provided by the Law Reform (Miscellaneous Provisions) Act 1971 which enacted that widows' damages under the Fatal Accidents Acts should not be reduced on account of remarriage.

[19] See Lon L. Fuller, *The Law in Quest of Itself* (Northwestern U. Press, 1940).

may wither, leaving judge-made law to become even more of a technical, legal husk. Perhaps the decline of English Equity in the nineteenth century is a major case in point.

A further danger of the high formal vision of law which seems to us to be held in England is that it may encourage a deeply sceptical attitude to *all* law, good and bad. This naturally contributes to weakening a general respect for law as such. If law is viewed as nothing more, or as little more, than a formal husk of technicality, it is certainly less likely to command respect than if it is viewed as embodying substantive moral reasons. We have no doubt that, in a tolerably well-ordered society, a weakening of general respect for the law is a bad thing for all sorts of reasons. Of course, brilliant social reformers such as Bentham and Hart can always readily differentiate truly evil laws from those worthy of moral respect. Within such elite circles, there is not likely to be any general weakening of respect for the law. But what of the man in the street, or the woman on the Clapham omnibus? The high formal vision of law (such as we think is widely held in England) may only be tolerable so long as it is confined to discriminating analysts such as Bentham and Hart, but not when held by the general public.

In these respects, it seems to us that a more substantive vision of law may have more desirable social results. To say the least, we think that a healthier public attitude to law is likely to exist in a society where it is believed that the law and judicial decisions are probably grounded in good substantive moral (and other) reasons. This in no way involves an abdication of the right to criticise; nor is it necessarily even inconsistent with many sophisticated theories of legal positivism. But it does seem to us that English positivism has played its part in creating a very strong formal vision of law in England which is by no means a sign of a healthy attitude to law.

On the other hand, we must also suggest that the American vision of law may well be too substantive in a variety of respects. For example, the degree to which American courts feel compelled to resort to substantive reasoning, often because the state (or even federal) legislatures are seemingly incapable of operating as efficient producers of well-drafted statutes, is an indictment of the legislative process in some American jurisdictions. If state legislatures are incapable of producing satisfactory law reform because of their organization, or because of political constraints, or because of their separation from executive branches, or because they are unwilling to devote funds to the necessary drafting, then courts may feel compelled to fill the void by themselves using substantive reasoning in a wide range of situations. This may explain what happens in the American legal system, but it does not necessarily justify it, nor does it immunize the system from reasoned criticism. It seems to us clear that American legislative processes are often too weak, and that courts are forced to resort to substantive reasoning to a degree which imperils many traditional values, such as democracy, the idea of an impartial judiciary, and the separation of adjudicative and legislative functions. However, this is a familiar theme, and we do not pursue it.

Similarly, the substantive vision in America may well be largely responsible for the extensive role of the jury in civil litigation, and whatever valuable role the jury may have in injecting substantive reasoning into the criminal law, we think the price paid for the use of the civil jury in America is heavy indeed, in terms of sacrifices of predictability and uniformity in law.

We turn now to some more detailed points of evaluation and criticism, not of the differing visions of law, as such, but rather of the actual use of formal and substantive reasoning in the two systems. On the English side, it seems to us that the mandatory formality of English legal reasoning is often excessive, and that this seriously imperils other values of high importance. We have already given examples[20] of the unwillingness of English courts to allow countervailing substantive considerations to be taken account of in the criminal law, and their frequent preference for dealing with such matters through mitigation of sentence, or even by executive clemency. But it must be appreciated that this means that people are in danger of being punished, and sometimes sent to jail, for doing things for which there were overwhelmingly strong substantive reasons. Citizens have even been punished, not because it is thought they have done anything substantively wrong, but because it is feared that others, in less justifiable circumstances, may be tempted to violate the law.[21] This seems to us to amount to a species of formalism, a failure to restrict the mandatory formality of criminal prohibitions where appropriate. America, on the whole, avoids this sort of excess because prosecutors, judges, and jury are more willing to take account of such substantive considerations in criminal cases. We think there is more room for English juries to introduce substantive reasoning in criminal cases, even at the expense of formal law.

So too, while American observers have, we think, exaggerated the grounds for criticism of English methods of interpretation, we do believe that instances of formalistic interpretation are still too numerous.[22]

On the American side, we now offer a few illustrative criticisms arising

[20] See examples cited in ch. 6, *supra*, pp. 179–180 and nn. 69–75.
[21] See the case cited in ch. 6, n. 80.
[22] See for one recent example, *Rogers* v. *Essex County Council* [1986] 3 All ER 321 (child held not entitled to free transport to school where shortest 'available' route was under three miles, even though route was dangerous for unaccompanied child). An amendment to a bill before Parliament has already (1986) been tabled by the government to reverse this decision.

from our study. We believe that American legal procedures are often far too lax in the control of abuse and harassing tactics, and this laxity very often stems from the unwillingness of the courts to use formal reasoning where it would be appropriate to do so. The unwillingness to accord adequate finality to a decision duly made by a court also appears to us to arise from a determination to pursue (first level) substantive reasons almost without regard to (second level) reasons which would dictate that formal reasons should be given greater weight. We also find it little short of astonishing that so many American jurisdictions are still reluctant to award pre-judgment interest to deserving plaintiffs, apparently on the (substantive, or perhaps substantivistic) ground that defendants should always be entitled to put their case. The second-level justification for formal reasoning is here so strong that it is hard to see what answer there can be to it: a plaintiff should be compensated for the defendant's failure to comply with his obligations before trial, irrespective of the reasons for that failure.

More broadly, it seems to us that a few American courts are now 'substantivistic' in the extreme. The California Supreme Court, in particular, has recently become perhaps the most 'substantivistic' common law court of all time. In a number of areas, it seems to have reduced the mandatory formality of its own doctrines to little short of zero, on one occasion (cited earlier[23]) actually *twice* changing its mind after making a final decision in the same piece of litigation. This court has in recent times frequently seemed willing to make new law with virtually no concern for the limitations of the judicial role, on the assumption that courts are just as able as legislatures to assess all relevant substantive reasons, and ought to do so in any case. We suggest that this court, and a number of others, have become unduly legislative, at the expense not only of democratic values, but also of the quality of the law itself. Judicial law making in large leaps in common law fields is fraught with dangers, a truth most judges feel in their bones.

5. PRACTICAL REFORM—ESPECIALLY 'TRANSPLANTS'

In the last section we offered a number of evaluative and critical comments without concerning ourselves with the praticalities of change and reform. But we do not see our book as irrelevant to the possibilities of practical reform. It is true that, in one respect, our overall thesis might be construed as inimical to proposals for reform. We have argued that the English and American legal systems are not only different, but are, in each case, part and parcel of larger and interrelated wholes. But this does

---

[23] See *supra*, p. 211, n. 99.

not mean that reform is impossible. It means only that, if a given change is introduced into one system, this may call for other changes if the desired reform is to be achieved. Because each system is a single whole consisting of interacting parts, any given proposal for reform by way of a 'legal transplant' from one system to another must take due account of this fact.

Our principal practical conclusions are modest. If we are correct in the way we have identified the extreme interlocking nature of the many facets of the two legal systems in question, it will be evident that transplants from the one system to the other will not work easily. It is, we think, clear that (for instance) the extreme activism of many American judges could not be recommended for exportation to England, because American judicial activism is closely tied to a whole range of institutional factors about courts, legislatures, and political and executive offices which are not replicated in England. Equally, Americans who look admiringly at the greater dignity of English courts and the smooth efficiency of English court procedures must realize that these desiderata cannot be transported to America without a vast amount of accompanying institutional and cultural baggage which could not easily be accommodated within the American tradition.

But we do not see our message as totally negative. We do not say that legal transplants will never strike root. What we say is that the environment must be carefully prepared for a transplant, and the ecological ramifications must be fully considered.

For example, English lawyers and politicians who advocate the introduction of a constitutional Bill of Rights in England, with some power of judicial review, must become more aware of the political ramifications and implications of such a move. These could, for instance, bear upon methods of judicial selection, the styles of legislative drafting, and a complete reappraisal of the relative values of certainty and justice in the individual case. It could even raise conflicts of ultimate values—such as are involved in the clash between utilitarian and rights-based theories—and, even more difficult perhaps for the English lawyer to swallow, it could leave the resolution of such ultimate conflicts to the judges from time to time, rather than to some legislative directive. All these possible changes could bring with them further significant changes whose outcome is likely to be unforeseeable at the outset. For instance, alterations in the mode of judicial selection may need to be quite dramatic to cope with a British Bill of Rights. It may be necessary to open the door to much more politically minded lawyers, and to break up the cosy homogeneity of the present English bench. This in turn may lead to fundamental alterations in the role of the bar, and its whole professional *raison d'être* as an independent profession may come under question as judges are drawn from the ranks of other lawyers. We neither advocate, nor are we frightened by, such changes. We are simply concerned to stress that legal transplants will require very careful study of their possible ramifications. Similarly, on the American side, those who believe that judicial activism has burst all reasonable bounds, and that courts are threatening the integrity of the democratic process, must ask themselves what is to happen if judges withdraw to a more traditional role of the English type. The lesson here must be that, unless fundamental changes take place in the political roles of executive and legislative officials, a judicial withdrawal will leave much legal territory quite unoccupied and unpoliced by officers of justice. And if that happens, enormous tensions will build up as a frustrated public finds it impossible to secure reforms whichever way it turns. Unless legislative and executive bodies can therefore be expected and encouraged to change *their* ways, any such large-scale change by the judges could prove disastrous. Of course we do not oppose reform. Our message is that there must be a greater attempt to study at least the next outer layer of probable consequences which may ensue from such changes here and now. Scholars, law reformers, and political reformers need to broaden their horizons to study at least the significant second-stage effects of the changes they wish to introduce. As we have tried to suggest in this work, we do not regard this as an impossible task.

Of course, the more diversity is to be found in a given legal system the more hospitable it may be to reform proposals and even to transplants from other systems. And the American legal system is highly diverse, so it may be quite receptive to transplants in some areas, while continuing its traditional ways in other areas.

6. FUTURE RESEARCH

The conceptual apparatus we have devised and deployed to explain and substantiate our primary thesis about the higher formality of the English legal system can itself be refined and developed further. Have we appropriately conceptualized each attribute of formal reasoning? Have we identified all the major attributes? Have we appropriately conceptualized the relations between these attributes, and generally between the formal and the substantive in legal reasoning? These and similar questions will undoubtedly require further consideration.

More work remains to be done with respect to our thesis that the English system is more formal, and that both systems are, in their own ways, all of a piece. No pair of scholars can hope to be fully conversant with the whole of one system of law, let alone two. We have identified some counter-examples to our theses, but we claim that our theses nonetheless hold overwhelmingly. Have we overlooked other counter-examples? If so, do they require that we qualify our theses?

How far have we identified all the major pieces that figure in the mosaic in each system, and all the major ways in which they so figure? For example, how far is the more formal nature of the English system related to a more paternalist or elitist tendency on the part of English judges? Does the more substantive nature of the American system reinforce the democratic tradition there by fostering a public feeling that the law has a close commitment to the sense of justice and is thus responsive to the public's vision of law? Questions of this kind are profound and difficult, and they call for more than we have been able to provide.

At the same time, we believe this book includes a number of more specific hypotheses that specialists may, by their own methods, confirm or qualify or refute. For example, social scientists may wish to study and compare what we have called the public's vision of law in the two countries, and seek to confirm or refute our hypothesis that the public in England inclines to a much more formal vision of law than the American public. Or they may wish to test our view that recent graduates of law schools as clerks to American judges strongly influence those judges in substantive directions. Some American judges do not have such clerks. How do their opinions compare with those who do? Likewise historians of ideas may be interested to test, for example, what we say about the influence of legal theories on a legal system, and about the factors that account for the reception of such theories in America and England over time.

Our study also opens up material for comparative research. We have revealed at least two major dimensions in which legal systems generally may be fruitfully compared and contrasted, dimensions so far largely neglected in the history of comparative studies. Legal systems may be compared in terms of their relative reliance on formal reasoning, on truth formality, on enforcement formality, and on rule of law formality. Such comparisons cannot of course be made in quantitative terms, but they can be made in qualitative terms along the lines we have ourselves followed with respect to England and America.

Further, two systems may be compared with respect to the extent to which they are, in formal or substantive terms, more or less coherent wholes. We have suggested that both the English and the American system are strikingly coherent in their formal or substantive orientation, going well beyond the kind of formal unity which positivist legal theory seeks to demonstrate, such as the claim that laws must all satisfy common criteria of validity. But we do not see this kind of coherence as inevitable, and other legal systems may be found to be more diverse in these respects.

Our study opens up the possibility of interesting comparative research especially, perhaps, into legal systems which have indulged in much borrowing, such as that of West Germany. Before World War II, Germany had a legal system in which legal reasoning of rather high formality was the norm. After the war, the country adopted a constitution that injected much substantive reasoning into the whole system.[24] How far do formal attributes of legal reasoning in that country today track each other? Has the overall level of formality in legal reasoning declined? Or consider another kind of example. Japan (as well as various other nations) has borrowed large segments of its legal system (including whole codes) from foreign countries. Compared with England and America, is there, in these borrowing countries, a relative lack of *fit* (or a significantly lower level of fit) between the degree of formality of legal reasoning, and other pieces that go into the mosaic? To cite but one more example, in what ways does the appropriate mix between the formal and the substantive vary from one legal system to another? As we have seen, the mix is certainly very different in England and America, two legal systems that on the surface seem very similar. How does the mix vary as between two systems much more diverse in character and traditions?

Our study may also have implications for some current fashions in legal research. We have argued that a legal system consists of so many interlocking parts—including not only the substantive law, but also the conventions and customs governing the personnel of the law—that changes in one part must be expected to have rippling ramifications elsewhere. But it will often take time for other parts of the legal system to realign themselves with changes of this character. In the American legal system, this is especially true of the substantive law itself, because (as we have seen) it is often difficult to secure change in the law by legislative means, and judicial change (even in America) must often wait the opportunity and the moment. This means that it is dangerous to take a corner of the substantive law—especially a striking and apparently anomalous corner—and then try to explain *why* the law is thus, on the assumption that there must be a rational explanation for such a law. This is a method which is today indulged in by American academics using techniques of positive economc analysis.[25] It seems to us a technique to be used with great care, because often the most obvious explanation for the continued retention of some apparently anomalous or odd piece of

---

[24] See R. Dreier, Zur Problematik und Situation der Verfassungsinterpretation', in R. Dreier, *Recht-Moral-Ideologie*, 106–45 (Suhrkamp, Frankfurt, 1981).

[25] See, e.g., R. Posner, *Economic Analysis of Law* (3rd edn., Little Brown, Boston, 1986).

substantive law is the sheer difficulty of securing legislative change in America.

We believe that our distinction between formal and legal reasoning may also help in understanding why there sometimes seems almost no common ground at all between most lawyers, who work within the traditional confines of the legal system, and some radical critics belonging to the so-called Critical Legal Studies movement. Many members of this movement seem unwilling to accept any (or virtually any) fixed data or starting-points when they examine legal disputes. If they are faced, for instance, with a legal dispute between an employee and an employer, they wish to introduce into the dispute fundamental arguments about the relative social and economic status of the parties; or if they are faced with a dispute between two landowners, they may wish to examine fundamental assumptions about the nature of property entitlements, and the allocation of such entitlements. This alone is not troublesome. It may even be salutary. But members of the CLS movement seem to want even *judges* to get into these global questions, too.[26] Now it seems fairly obvious to us that this is an attempt to introduce substantive arguments at a point and place at which more formal arguments would normally be more appropriate. Obviously, in a relatively stable political society like England or America, fundamental questions about the binding nature of the employment contract, or the allocation of property entitlements, raise enormously important substantive issues; but equally obviously, these issues are more appropriately debated in some fora than others. In particular, they are more appropriate debated in places more overtly devoted to broad political issues, such as in legislative assemblies, or even in the media and other organs of public opinion. Courts of law, as traditionally operated in England and America, have more narrow terms of reference—that is, they are usually constrained by all sorts of formal reasons from embarking on very broad political policies. And although these constraints are much looser in America than in England, even in America, fundamental political issues of this kind have to be addressed on relatively rare occasions, when the arguments and issues have been carefully set up, and relevant legislative or policy-fact inquiries have been made.

The very nature of formal reasoning helps to explain why and how it is usually so inappropriate to try to introduce global substantive arguments into, say, a simple employment dispute or a straightforward nuisance action between adjoining landowners. Formal reasoning, in this kind of context, operates as part of a simple division of labour. Some kinds of

[26] See, e.g., Kennedy, 'Distributive and Paternalistic Motives in Contract and Tort Law', 41 *Md. L. Rev.* 563 (1982).

issues need to be debated or argued over in one way; others in another way; some issues can be settled by an adjudicator, others must go before a different body altogether. In these respects, formal reasons are a very efficient means of planning and institutionalizing a general societal agenda for decision making. Planning such an agenda requires the setting aside of special times, places, and persons for the resolution of different classes of disputes; it requires a proper division of labour as to who is to make such decisions, and so on.

In suggesting that formal reasons assist in the efficient making of decisions, and therefore, in a broad sense, in being an efficient tool of government, law, and administration, we do not prejudge issues which in the ultimate analysis may be involved in the concept of efficiency. We do assert that the widespread use of formal reasoning in a legal system at least helps to make that system a less costly one. Although we have not specifically addressed issues of cost, our comparisons between the English and American legal system have been sufficient to show that the latter is more costly, and that one major reason for this is that it uses substantive reasons more extensively. But what is efficient in the long run depends largely upon what a society wants. If Americans are more wedded to substantive justice than the English, and if they are willing to pay the additional costs involved in a system of law and administration which is more inclined to use substantive reasons, then the American legal system is probably just as 'efficient' as the English legal system.

Index